"**Los Angeles** county and its cities

School Rankings (STAR test) for pub̲ ̲ ̲ ̲ ̲o̲o̲l̲s̲, college placements by high school, SAT scores by high school, a directory of private schools — they are all inside.

Community profiles. Home prices, rents. Descriptions of cities, towns and neighborhoods.

The perfect guide for new comers or parents or people shopping for homes or apartments or just interested in finding out more about Los Angeles County, its schools and its communities.

"**Los Angeles County 2001**" describes the local weather.

Hospital services and medical care. Directory of hospitals.

Vital statistics. Population, education by town. Republicans and Democrats. Grocery prices. Taxes, Crime. History, trivia and much more.

McCormack's Guides, edited by former newspaper reporters and editors, was established in 1984 and publishes the most popular general-interest guides to California counties.

Our other guides include, "Santa Barbara-Ventura 2001," "Riverside-San Bernardino 2001" and "Orange County 2001."

For a list of our other guides and an order form, see the last page.

Publisher and editor Don McCormack formed McCormack's Guides in 1984 to publish annual guides to California counties. A graduate of the University of California-Berkeley, McCormack joined the Contra Costa Times in 1969 and covered police, schools, politics, planning, courts and government. Later with the Richmond Independent and Berkeley Gazette, he worked as a reporter, then editor and columnist.

Assistant publisher Mary Jennings is a native Californian who holds a Diversified Liberal Arts degree from Saint Mary's College in Moraga. She has worked for many years to improve residential support services for adults with developmental disabilities. Mary now brings her data management and writing experience to publishing.

Maps illustrator Louis Liu has a B.A. in Teaching English as a Second Language. He loves art and enjoys drawing and painting. Louis attended Los Medanos College and the Academy of Art College in San Francisco, where he majored in illustration. He is now the art director of Tartan Sports in Hayward, a golf equipment manufacturer and wholesaler. To contact Louis, please call (925) 779-0206.

Ad graphics by T Graphics, Antioch, California

Many thanks to the people who write, edit, layout and help publish McCormack's Guides: Easter, John V., Krista, Louis, Mary, Jeremy, Rob, Theresa, Talita, Meghan, Tanya.

DISCLAIMER
Although facts and statements in this book have been checked and rechecked, mistakes — typographical and otherwise — may have occurred. Census data, test scores, and other information have been updated to the time of publication using cost-of-living figures, mathematical averaging, and other tools, which by their nature must be considered estimates. This book was written to entertain and inform. The authors, the editors and the publisher shall have no liability or responsibility for damages or alleged damages arising out of information contained in the "Los Angeles County 2001" edition of McCormack's Guides.

All rights reserved. No portion of this book may be copied, reproduced or used, except for brief quotations in a review, without the permission of the publisher.

Copyright ©1997, 1998, 1999, 2000, 2001 by McCormack's Guides, Inc.
Indexed   ISBN 1-929365-13-6

—BARRY BURNETT—

Your personal, full-service Realtor for the next 33 years...

After that, you're on your own!

Independent, discreet, superior, professional service, Barry Burnett has personally closed over 3,300 transactions in 28 years. Serving Southern California Commercial & Investment markets & Residences in the San Fernando Valley, West San Gabriel Valley, Cresenta Valley and Santa Clarita Valley. Centrally headquartered in Beautiful Downtown Burbank – the true Hollywood.

818-842-2611
818-843-2129 Fax
800-818-SOLD

barryburnett@hotmail.com

2620 W. Burbank Blvd. Burbank, Ca 91505

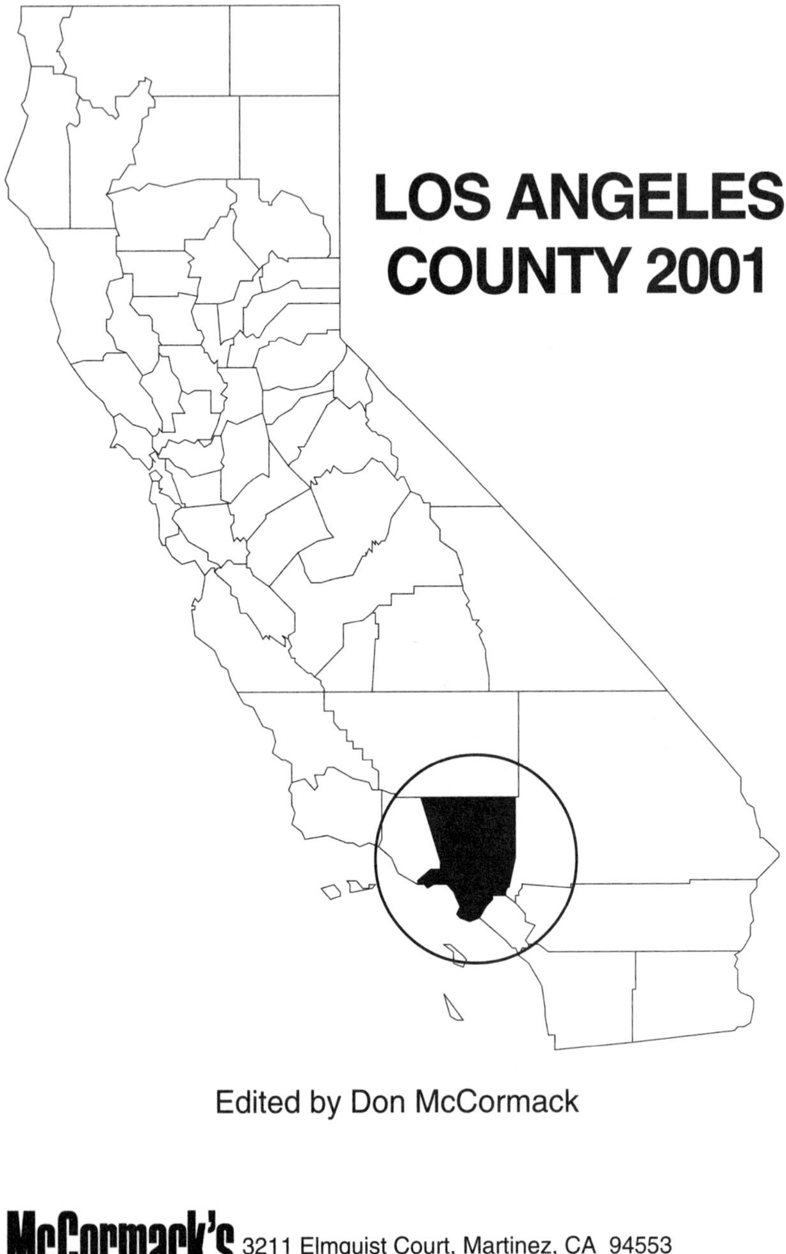

LOS ANGELES COUNTY 2001

Edited by Don McCormack

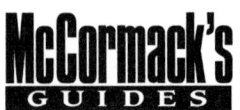

McCormack's GUIDES
3211 Elmquist Court, Martinez, CA 94553
Phone: (800) 222-3602 & Fax: (925) 228-7223
www.mccormacks.com • bookinfo@mccormacks.com

Contents

Chapter	1	**Los Angeles County at a Glance** Population, baby names, education by town, home prices, rents. Voter registration.	8
Chapter	2	**Public School Rankings-State Comparisons** How local public schools ranked against all other public schools in the state. Based on STAR test.	28
Chapter	3	**How Public Schools Work** SAT scores by high school, college attendance rates. California state universities and UCs chosen by local grads.	106
Chapter	4	**Private Schools** Directory. College attendance.	140
Chapter	5	**City Profiles** Descriptions of neighborhoods, cities and towns.	165
Chapter	6	**Newcomers Guide** How to get a driver's license. How to register to vote. Grocery prices. Taxes. Utilities.	294
Chapter	7	**New Housing** Developments in Los Angeles County.	304

| Chapter 8 | **Hospitals & Health Care** | 311 |

Overview of local medical care and insurance. Directory of hospitals.

| Chapter 9 | **Crime** | 322 |

Crime ratings for L.A. County and cities. A perspective on crime.

On the Cover
One of the happy enticements of Los Angeles life: its beaches.

COUNTY AT A GLANCE 7

LOS ANGELES COUNTY

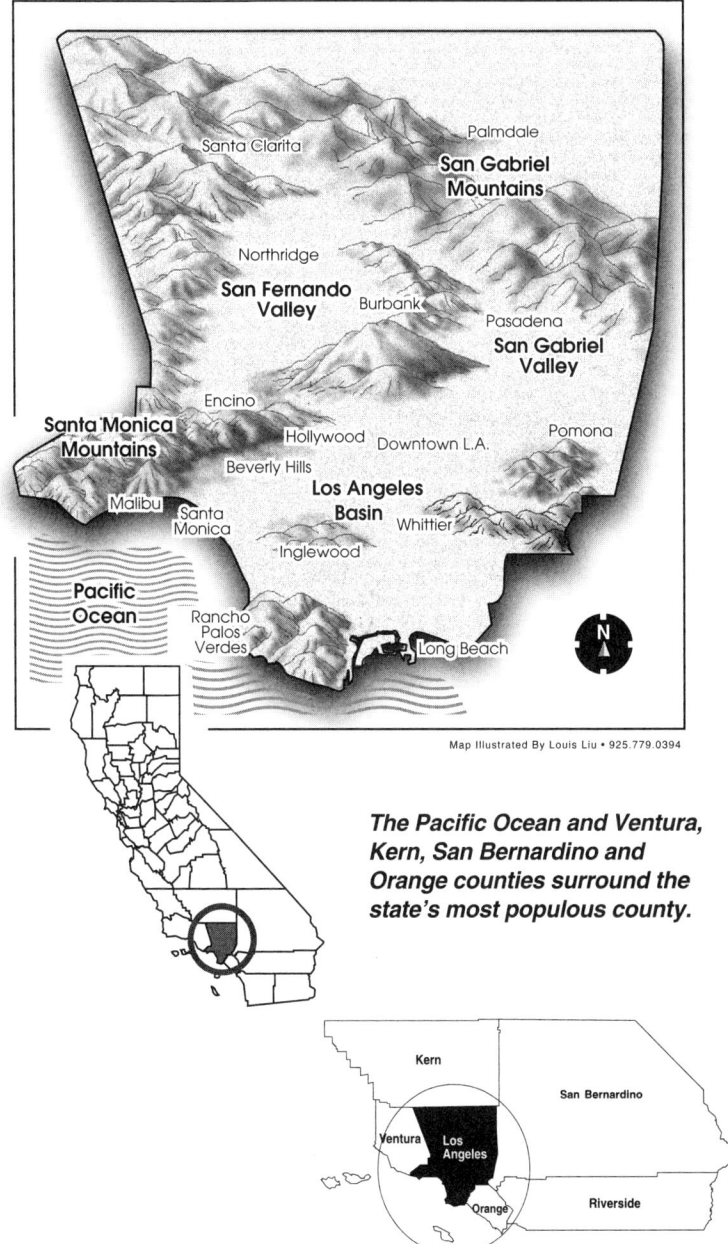

The Pacific Ocean and Ventura, Kern, San Bernardino and Orange counties surround the state's most populous county.

Chapter 1

LOS ANGELES COUNTY
at a Glance

A LAND OF MOUNTAINS AND SHORES, Los Angeles is a diverse and dynamic metropolis identified in two ways, by city and by county.

The City of Los Angeles is inhabited by 3,822,955 residents and is the largest city in Los Angeles County.

Los Angeles County has a population of 9,884,255 and includes about 125 other cities and towns, some world famous: Beverly Hills, Burbank, Long Beach, Malibu, Pasadena (See map on Page 6).

Often L.A. the City and L.A. the County are spoken of as one. "I'm going to L.A." could mean that I'm going to L.A. the City or the County (or one of the other cities in the county) and for most situations no harm is done. But if you are moving into L.A., it is important to distinguish between the two.

This guide covers all of Los Angeles County and pays special attention to its largest city. See maps on pages 10 and 11.

Dimensions

In land, Los Angeles County covers about 4,070 square miles, about half the size of Israel or Massachusetts. It is not the largest county in California. That honor goes to its neighbor, San Bernardino, about three times its size.

Los Angeles the City covers about 465 square miles. It is the largest and most populous city in California and in comparison to its reputed rival, San Francisco, a giant. San Francisco covers only 48 square miles.

If you drove a freeway east to west across L.A. County at about its middle, the distance covered would be about 55-65 miles. In the dead of night, L.A. County can be traversed in less than an hour. At peak commute hours, the story is much different.

Although the most populous county in the nation, Los Angeles in many places is sparsely inhabited. The San Gabriel Mountains, with their cliffs and steep ravines, run across the center of the county. Mt. San Antonio, also known as Mt. Baldy, is the highest peak, 10,064 feet.

In Los Angeles County, it is possible to hike a desert, ski a mountain and surf an ocean wave, all in the same day.

You can also sail off to an island. Santa Catalina, 21 miles into the Pacific, is part of L.A. County. So too is a section of Edwards Air Force Base, where the space shuttle occasionally lands.

Towns and Cities

If you don't understand the distinction between them — an easy job — little else will make sense.

In California, cities are legal entities with precise boundaries and specific political powers. Cities are run by city councils. A city may be large or small, it may have many or few people. Los Angeles, population 3.8 million, is a city. So is Monterey Park, population 67,409.

In power and influence, Los Angeles far exceeds Monterey Park but within its borders Monterey Park decides what will be built, how lots will be zoned, how much police protection will be provided, and more.

Many cities have their own police departments but some cities contract with the sheriff's office to provide police protection.

Los Angeles County has 88 legal cities. Among them are Beverly Hills, Santa Monica, West Hollywood, Long Beach, Claremont, Pomona, Pasadena, Lancaster, Redondo Beach and Malibu.

"Towns" of the City of L.A.

Want to start a fight? Just tell someone from Brentwood or Bel Air or Pacific Palisades or Northridge or Watts or Van Nuys that he or she is a Los Angeleno.

All these "towns" are part of the City of Los Angeles and legally all their residents are L.A. City residents. All are protected by the L.A. Police Department and governed by the L.A. City Council.

But all have strong local identities and go by their traditional names. The closest equivalent is probably the City of New York and its boroughs: Manhattan, Bronx, Brooklyn, Staten Island, Queens.

In its formative years, L.A. seized control of the water supply and told outlying communities that if they wanted water, they would have to annex to L.A. Many communities came in begrudgingly and retained their identities.

When their names come up on television or radio or in the newspaper, almost never are they identified as part of L.A. City. Instead, they are Reseda, Encino, San Pedro and so on. The same holds for private conversation.

The Getty Museum was erected in Brentwood but it's very much a part of the City of Los Angeles.

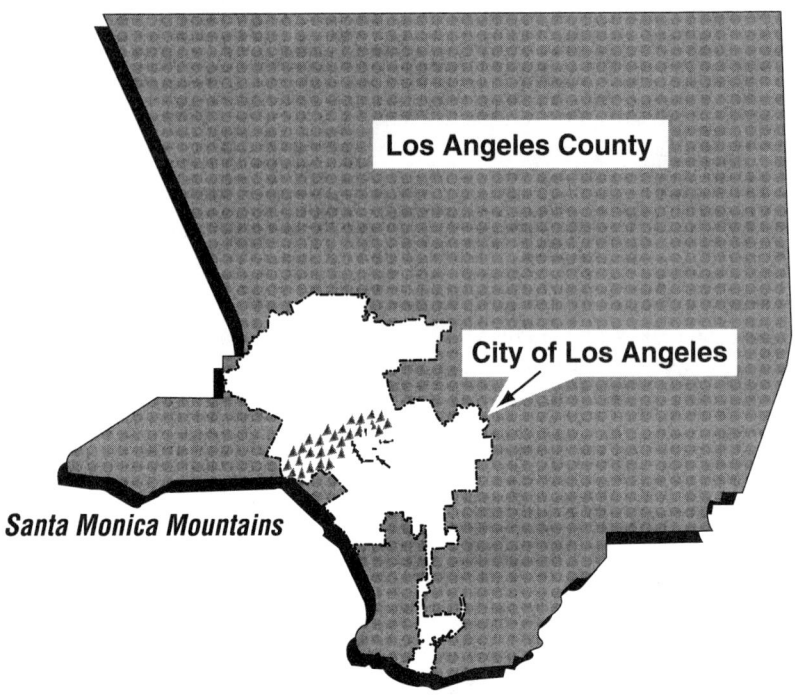

Although they lack formal powers, town and neighborhood groups exercise a lot of indirect power because the politicians listen to them and use them to sound out voter opinions.

Towns Unincorporated

Everything outside a city is considered unincorporated. Much of the unincorporated land is sparsely inhabited but where development takes place, often "town" names follow.

Unincorporated towns are governed by the County Board of Supervisors and patrolled by sheriff's deputies.

Altadena, Rowland Heights, Hacienda Heights and Baldwin Hills are unincorporated towns. About 10 percent of the county's residents, 1,036,277 people, live in unincorporated areas.

Regions

In everyday conversation and in the media, Los Angeles County is often divided into the San Fernando Valley (also known as The Valley), the Basin, and the San Gabriel Valley. See map on page 7.

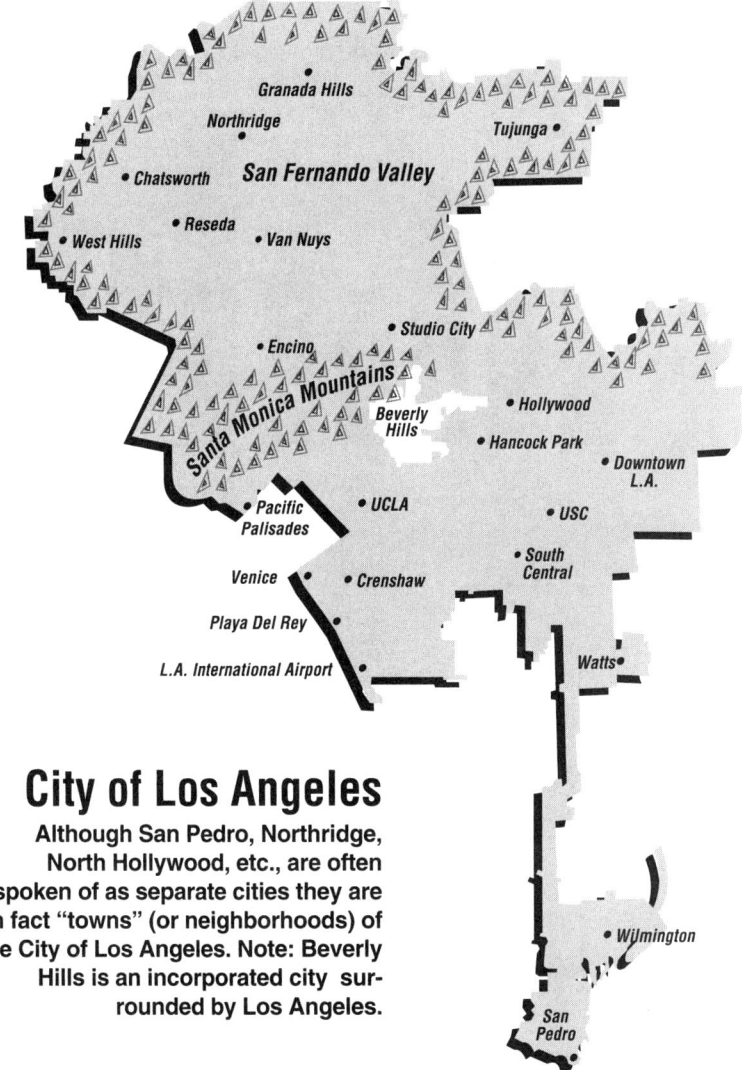

City of Los Angeles

Although San Pedro, Northridge, North Hollywood, etc., are often spoken of as separate cities they are in fact "towns" (or neighborhoods) of the City of Los Angeles. Note: Beverly Hills is an incorporated city surrounded by Los Angeles.

Weather

For most residents, predictable and balmy. L.A. averages about 15 inches of rain per year, almost all of it falling between October and May. January is usually the wettest month.

January is also the coolest month. Temperatures average 65 on the high side, 46 on the low.

In August, the hottest month, the highs average 82 degrees, the lows, 60.

As you move inland, behind the hills and mountains, temperatures

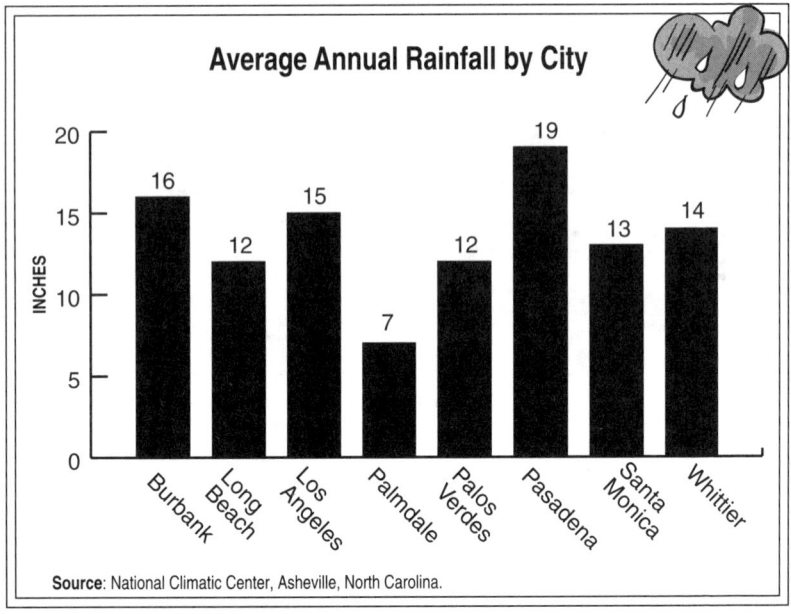

increase. On a typical summer day, L.A. International Airport (on the ocean) might register 75 degrees and L.A. downtown, 83. The San Fernando Valley, behind the Santa Monica Mountains, would heat up to 92 and Lancaster, behind the San Gabriel Mountains, to 100.

These temperatures may sound unbearable but they are made comfortable by a dearth of what bedevils the East Coast: high humidity. The dry air keeps the humidity low.

Los Angeles County has many mini-climates. Lancaster and Palmdale are in the high desert, elevations 2,000 to 4,000. The days are hot, the nights often cold. Drive a little farther inland, to the low desert, and days and nights will be hot. Sometimes a hill or ridge will keep out or capture smog.

Smog

Still a problem but the air is the cleanest it has been in over 50 years. In 1970, the Los Angeles Basin coughed and wheezed through 148 Stage One alerts. In 1997, Stage One alerts dropped to one and in 2000 they bottomed, zero. In 1999, Houston, not L.A., was tagged the smoggiest city in U.S.

Rarely praised for its physical beauty, the City of Los Angeles has a glorious backdrop, the San Gabriel Mountains, which in winter often don a mantle of snow. Smog frequently obscured the mountains; now on a greater number of days they show themselves in all their glory.

An inversion layer stops pollutants from moving up and out, the hills and

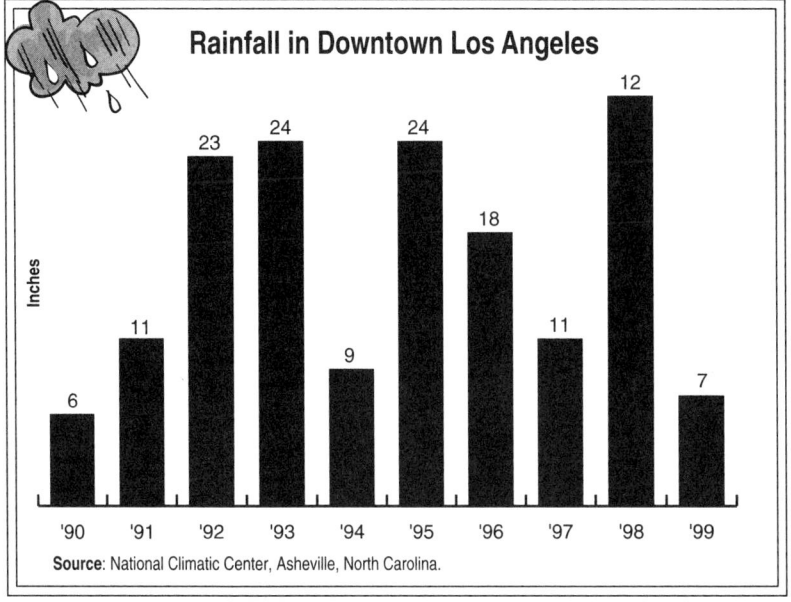

mountains trap them in basins or valleys, notably the L.A. Basin, the San Fernando Valley, and particularly the San Gabriel Valley (See map on Page 7).

This is a simplified explanation of the complex forces at work. Some pollutants are more troublesome in the winter months, some in the summer. Cities and towns on or near the coast suffer less smog than inland cities.

The desert cities — Lancaster, Palmdale, etc. — escape the smog. Or, like Santa Clarita, they get less of it.

Los Angeles and California have probably the toughest pollution laws on earth, aimed at motor vehicles and plants and factories. In 1999, agreement was reached on methods to cut even more pollution. Sometimes the government works the way it should.

Radio and TV stations broadcast smog alerts. Newspapers routinely carry air quality forecasts. For more information, call the South Coast Air Quality Management District at 909-396-2000.

Mother Nature's Goody Bag

It includes earthquakes and the Santa Ana winds. California straddles two tectonic plates that are grinding past each other. The plates hang up, pressures build, then, pow! a lurch, also known as a temblor or an earthquake.

The main fault, the San Andreas, runs up the east side of the San Gabriel Mountains but fault lines run throughout the region.

In the 20th century, major quakes have occurred in Long Beach and

Average Daily Temperatures

City	Ja	Fb	Mr	Ap	My	Ju	Jy	Au	Sp	Oc	No	De
Burbank	55	57	58	62	66	70	76	76	73	68	60	54
Canoga Park	54	56	57	61	67	71	76	77	73	67	59	54
Long Beach	56	57	59	62	65	69	73	74	72	78	71	56
Los Angeles	58	60	71	63	66	70	74	75	74	70	63	58
Palmdale	45	59	52	58	66	74	81	80	73	63	52	45
Pasadena	56	58	59	62	65	50	75	76	74	69	61	56
Pomona	54	56	57	60	64	69	75	75	73	67	60	55
Santa Monica	57	58	57	59	60	62	65	67	67	65	61	58
Torrance	56	57	58	60	63	66	70	71	70	67	61	56

Source: National Climatic Center, Asheville, North Carolina. Figures derived from 1961-1990 records.

Temperatures for Selected Cities
Number of Days Greater than 90 Degrees

City	Jy	Au	Sp	Oc	No	Dc	Ja	Fb	Mr	Ap	My	Ju
Burbank	12	22	3	2	0	0	0	0	0	4	0	1
Canoga Park	23	30	14	2	0	0	0	0	0	5	2	15
Long Beach	8	17	3	2	0	0	0	0	0	0	0	0
Los Angeles	7	17	3	1	0	0	0	0	0	0	0	0
Pasadena	21	28	5	2	0	0	0	0	0	4	0	6

Source: National Climatic Center, Asheville, N.C. July 1998-June 1999.

Temperatures for Selected Cities
Number of Days 32 Degrees or Less

City	Jy	Au	Sp	Oc	No	Dc	Ja	Fb	Mr	Ap	My	Ju
Burbank	0	0	0	0	0	4	0	0	0	0	0	4
Canoga Park	0	0	0	0	0	5	0	0	0	0	0	5
Long Beach	0	0	0	0	0	0	0	0	0	0	0	0
Los Angeles	0	0	0	0	0	0	0	0	0	0	0	0
Pasadena	0	0	0	0	0	1	0	0	0	0	0	1

Source: National Climatic Center, Asheville, N.C. July 1998-June 1999.

Northridge in the San Fernando Valley. What to do: read the beginning of your phone book for practical advice.

In fall, a dry wind called Santa Ana sweeps in from the interior, creating conditions ideal for fires. The prudent clear away the brush and use fire-retardant building materials.

Why People Come to L.A.

Fires, earthquakes, smog, occasional floods and landslides, fog — who needs this? L.A., however, continues to attract people. Jobs help a lot, beaches beguile but the single most popular attraction is probably the weather. If you dislike frigid temperatures, if humidity leaves you wilted, if snow and slush are not your thing, L.A. County, despite its drawbacks, is the place for you.

Schools

In raw numbers, L.A. County schools advance more students to the top public universities in the state than any other county.

Of the 22 California high schools that scored over 600 in math in the 1999 SAT, seven were located in L.A. County.

L.A. boasts some of the top universities in the nation, among them University of California at Los Angeles (UCLA), University of Southern California (USC), California Institute of Technology (Caltech) and Pepperdine.

Yet the county also has many of the lowest-scoring schools in the state. For decades, residents have been fighting over integration plans and what to do about the L.A. Unified School District, which enrolls about 696,000 students. Many parents want to break it up into smaller districts. L.A. County also boasts the highest number of private schools of any county in the state.

Diversity and Politics

Los Angeles has experienced heavy immigration from Mexico and Latin America and has its ethnic communities where this or that minority greatly outnumbers all others. In recent years many people of Asian descent have settled in the San Gabriel Valley.

But rare is the community where one group, even Caucasians, forms 100 percent of the population. School districts, even in the rich towns, often enroll a diverse group of students. Integration efforts through the schools help mix the kids.

The state estimates that by mid-2001 Los Angeles County will have 3,134,369 Caucasians, 4,579,089 Hispanics, 1,262,155 Asians, 921,740 African-Americans and 28,060 American Indians.

All this is not to say that L.A. is one big happy melting pot of ethnic groups. It has the same tensions, the same divisions found in urban America. In the past 40 years, racial tensions in South Central L.A. have sparked two riots that cost dozens of lives and did severe property damage.

Neither is it to say that everyone is at each other's throat. Many people get along and go along and try to resolve conflicts amicably.

In the last presidential election, Los Angeles County favored Al Gore, 1,710,505, over George Bush, 871,930.

Housing

In 2000, the state estimated that L.A. County had 3,272,169 residential units, of which 1,588,957 were single-detached homes and 211,948 were single attached homes. Single homes, in one form or another, make up 55 percent of the housing.

Population, Education

City or Town	Population	Bachelor's Degree
Agoura Hills	22,143	17%
Alhambra	92,809	10%
Altadena	*44,728	13%
Arcadia	54,013	17%
Artesia	17,132	6%
Avalon	3,608	6%
Azusa	46,261	5%
Baldwin Hills/West Adams/Leimert Park	77,356	NA
Baldwin Park	77,124	4%
Bel Air/Beverly Crest	20,951	22%
Bell	38,044	1%
Bellflower	68,345	6%
Bell Gardens	45,733	0%
Beverly Hills	35,096	19%
Boyle Heights	100,716	1%
Bradbury	965	13%
Brentwood/Pacific Palisades**	57,772	NA
Burbank	106,480	12%
Calabasas	20,455	21%
Canoga Park/West Hills/Woodland Hills	164,972	13%
Carson	93,196	8%
Cerritos	58,063	16%
Chatsworth/Porter Ranch**	90,747	na
Claremont	35,968	15%
Commerce, City of	13,370	2%
Compton	97,966	2%
Covina	47,988	7%
Cudahy	25,857	1%
Culver City	42,776	15%
Diamond Bar	59,101	16%
Downey	102,103	7%
Downtown L.A.	26,815	6%
Downtown L.A., North	22,052	4%
Duarte	23,000	10%
East Los Angeles	*131,647	1%
Echo Park/Silverlake	82,469	10%
El Monte	119,992	2%
El Segundo	16,864	16%
Encino/Tarzana	74,496	18%
Florence	*59,545	1%
Gardena	59,557	9%
Glendale	203,734	13%
Glendora	53,761	10%
Granada Hills/Knollwood	58,755	13%
Hacienda Heights	*62,928	12%
Harbor Gateway	37,310	NA
Hawaiian Gardens	15,205	3%
Hawthorne	80,459	7%
Hermosa Beach	19,631	30%

Copyright © 2001 McCormack's Guides. No reproduction without permission.

Population, Education

City or Town	Population	Bachelor's Degree
Huntington Park	63,626	2%
Industry, City of	689	3%
Inglewood	121,035	6%
Irwindale	1,202	2%
La Cañada Flintridge	21,103	20%
La Crescenta	*17,621	14%
La Habra Heights	6,896	18%
Lakewood	80,952	9%
La Mirada	49,918	8%
Lancaster	132,402	6%
La Puente	42,189	3%
La Verne	34,802	12%
Lawndale	30,862	6%
Lomita	20,951	10%
Long Beach	457,608	10%
Los Angeles	3,822,955	9%
Lynwood	69,328	1%
Malibu	13,324	18%
Manhattan Beach	36,124	26%
Marina Del Rey	*7,715	30%
Mar Vista/Palms	111,707	16%
Maywood	30,408	0%
Mission Hills/Panorama City/North Hills	114,979	8%
Monrovia	41,037	9%
Montebello	64,952	6%
Monterey Park	67,409	10%
Northeast L.A.	256,870	6%
North Hollywood	135,530	10%
Northridge	65,629	15%
Norwalk	104,473	4%
Pacoima/Arleta	96,722	2%
Palmdale	122,392	5%
Palos Verdes Estates	14,742	26%
Paramount	56,596	2%
Pasadena	143,874	14%
Pico Rivera	65,202	3%
Pomona	147,656	5%
Rancho Palos Verdes	44,933	21%
Redondo Beach	67,638	20%
Reseda/West Van Nuys	95,166	9%
Rolling Hills	2,066	21%
Rolling Hills Estates	8,787	22%
Rosemead	57,328	4%
Rowland Heights	*46,276	12%
San Dimas	37,357	12%
San Fernando	24,722	2%
San Gabriel	41,604	10%
San Marino	14,006	21%
San Pedro	83,433	9%
Santa Clarita	151,260	11%

Copyright © 2001 McCormack's Guides. No reproduction without permission.

Population, Education

City or Town	Population	Bachelor's Degree
Hidden Hills	2,052	16%
Hollywood	225,681	12%
Santa Fe Springs	16,463	3%
Santa Monica	96,528	20%
Sherman Oaks/Studio City/Toluca Lake	77,205	NA
Sierra Madre	11,719	17%
Signal Hill	9,247	10%
Silver Lake	*44,433	10%
South Central Los Angeles	269,203	2%
South El Monte	22,717	1%
South Gate	95,326	2%
South Pasadena	25,997	21%
Southeast Los Angeles	257,055	1%
Sun Valley	81,568	5%
Sunland/Tujunga	57,513	4%
Sylmar	63,797	5%
Temple City	34,731	10%
Torrance	147,414	15%
Van Nuys/North Sherman Oaks	145,235	11%
Venice	44,729	18%
Vernon	85	0%
View Park/Windsor Hills	*12,218	15%
Walnut	33,203	14%
Westchester/Playa Del Rey	53,027	NA
West Covina	107,631	9%
West Hollywood	38,913	22%
Westlake	107,195	NA
Westlake Village	8,593	20%
West Los Angeles/Century City/Rancho Park	73,856	NA
Westwood	43,436	17%
Whittier	86,152	9%
Wilmington/Harbor City	78,077	1%
Wilshire District	290,752	11%
County Total:	9,884.255	NA

Source: Bachelor degrees, 1990 census. All populations are educated guesses made after the 1990 census. Town populations, marked with *, were made in 1997. All others in 2000. Los Angeles Planning Dept., Southern California Association of Governments, California Dept. of Industrial Relations. Grouped towns are identifed by double asterisks (**). Some populations of unincorporated towns or L.A. neighborhoods will differ elsewhere in guide. These sections have vague boundaries and are subject to different interpretations by different groups. One group, for example, might go by tradition, another by zip code.

Apartment complexes with two to four units numbered 286,883 or about 9 percent of the housing stock, and complexes with five or more units number 1,128,591 or 34 percent of the stock. Mobile homes, 55,790, bring up the rear, about 2 percent of all residential units.

For housing styles, 1945 is a good dividing line. Following World War II, L.A. roared into a construction boom. Census figures tell the story: 2.8 million residents in 1940, to 4.2 million by 1950, to 6 million by 1960, to 7 million by

1970, then 7.5 million by 1980, and in the 1990 census, 8.9 million. Since then, the county has added slightly more than 1 million residents.

The closer the community to downtown L.A., generally the older the housing. As you move out, the housing becomes newer. Many homes in west L.A. favor a Spanish-moorish motif, the style popular before the war.

The San Fernando Valley, developed after the war, runs to what might be called modern American tract. Some communities got almost all their postwar development in a rush and one look dominates the town. After World War II, L.A. and much of America, afraid the Depression might return, tiptoed into the two-bedroom, one bathroom, one-car garage home. Then as prosperity caught on, another bathroom and bedroom were added and the garage expanded.

In the 1970s, four-bedroom homes became more popular and the great speculative boom in the 1980s fueled a market for bigger homes, with smaller lots. These are generalizations with many exceptions but for home and apartment hunters possibly helpful generalizations.

If you want to move into a high-income community (usually high academic scores), you might be able to find older, smaller homes in your price range. Same for beach towns. Yes, the closer you get to the Pacific, the higher usually the price but many beach towns have small homes that predate the war.

Some older towns that you might expect to fade into problems just haven't. Residents have kept handy with the mower and the paint brush and supported property values. Other cities, built in the same era, have lost some of their luster. But in overall appearance, L.A. comes off well. Even in the so-called worst of neighborhoods, you will find on weekend mornings someone swinging a hammer or trimming the hedges. For new homes at low or moderate prices, look to Santa Clarita, Palmdale and Lancaster and the communities near these cities.

School Districts

In California, schools and city and county governments are separate entities, although they often cooperate on recreational activities. School district boundaries often differ from municipal boundaries. Some school districts serve several towns and cities.

Renting a home or apartment

In the accompanying chart, rents are averages at large complexes. In each location, you can find rents higher and lower than the ranges listed.

- Apartment sharing is common near universities. Information, posting boards can be found at housing offices. With the sharp rise in rents and home prices in the 1990s, statistics suggest that more people are taking roommates or squeezing in with relatives or friends.

- Many single homes are rented out. If an apartment is not for you, see the classifieds. Often these rentals are handled by property management firms.

Average Rents by City

City	Studio	1BR,1BA	2BR, 2BA
Agoura	NA	$1,278	$1,480
Artesia	$558	$750	$885
Azusa	$521	$786	$936
Bellflower	$460	$698	$916
Brentwood	NA	$2,300	$3,267
Burbank	$821	$1,090	$1,370
Calabasas	NA	$1,177	$1,494
Canoga Park	$675	$807	$1,029
Canyon Country (Santa Clarita)	NA	$855	$1,038
Cerritos	$810	$892	$1,525
Chatsworth	$713	$1026	$1,215
Claremont	NA	$815	$1,030
Compton	NA	NA	NA
Covina	NA	$837	$1,029
Culver City	$883	$1,194	$1,378
Diamond Bar	NA	$1,067	$1,522
Downey	NA	$786	$1,029
Duarte	$805	$953	$1,171
El Monte	$450	$550	NA
Encino	$819	$988	$1,340
Gardena	$465	$565	$745
Glendale	NA	$1,070	$1,274
Hacienda Heights	$767	$889	$1,108
Harbor City	NA	$1,050	NA
Hawaiian Gardens	NA	$840	$1,100
Hawthorne	$512	$616	$815
Hermosa Beach	$1,020	$1,363	$1,693
Hollywood	NA	$841	$1,250
La Puente	NA	$688	$823
Lakeview Terrace	$450	$710	$863
Lakewood	$575	$770	$953
Lancaster	$410	$532	$638
La Verne	NA	$891	$1,188
Long Beach	$728	$942	$1,381
Los Angeles (Downtown)	$824	$1,020	$1,504
Marina Del Rey	$1,079	$1,571	$2,327
Montebello	NA	$800	$1,000
Monterey Park	$725	$850	NA
Newhall (Santa Clarita)	NA	$815	$1,071
North Hollywood	$588	$769	$1,103
Northridge	$714	$908	$1,194
Norwalk	$640	$778	$1,053
Pacoima	NA	$625	$795
Palmdale	NA	$513	$615
Palms	$740	$1,040	$1,280
Panorama City	$458	$620	$850
Paramount	NA	$758	$1,051
Pasadena	NA	$1,295	$1,779
Pico Rivera	NA	$760	$975

Copyright © 2001 McCormack's Guides. No reproduction without permission.

Average Rents By City

City	Studio	1 br. 1 ba.	2br. 2 ba.
Playa Del Rey	$1,000	$1,387	$1,723
Pomona	$630	$825	$1,015
Rancho Palos Verdes	$800	$1,335	$1,793
Redondo Beach	$1,191	$1,292	$2,043
Reseda	$698	$786	$1,058
Rowland Heights	NA	$901	$1,063
San Dimas	$675	$778	$1,019
San Pedro	$975	$1,049	$1,513
Santa Clarita	NA	$863	$1,021
Santa Monica	$1,531	$3,806	$6,933
Saugus (Santa Clarita)	NA	$723	$955
Sherman Oaks	$864	$1,205	$1,589
Studio City	$1,056	$1,162	$1,547
Sylmar	NA	$600	$700
Tarzana	$613	$801	$1,045
Toluca Lake	$1,037	$1,397	$1,777
Torrance	$842	$1,011	$1,298
Valencia (Santa Clarita)	NA	$1,138	$1,382
Van Nuys	$661	$813	$1,044
Walnut	NA	$708	NA
West Covina	$638	$790	$968
West Hollywood	$1,000	$1,162	$1,629
West Los Angeles	$976	$1,401	$1,891
Westchester	NA	$1,232	$1,552
Westlake Village	$925	$1,168	$1,458
Westwood	$1,003	$1,052	$1,467
Whittier	NA	$872	$1,223
Woodland Hills	$899	$1,064	$1,378
Countywide	$799	$1,033	$1,348

Source: Realfacts of Novato, CA, December, 2000. NA Not Available.

- Many apartment complexes advertise. Call "For Rent" at (800) 882-2830 or "Apartment Magazine" at (310) 479-5541. Pomona, Claremont and the east county cities are sometimes classified under the Inland Empire.

- Many apartments ask for a security deposit and first month's rent. State law limits deposits to a maximum two months rent for an unfurnished apartment and three months for a furnished (this includes the last month's rent.) You will probably be asked to fill out a credit report and list references. If you sign a lease, you may get a month's free rent.

- Fair Housing laws apply: no discrimination based on sex, family status and so on. But some complexes will be designed to welcome certain renters and discourage others. A "family" complex might have a tot lot, a "singles" complex, a workout room. Some apartments forbid pets. Some accept only cats or cats and small dogs. Many ask for a pet deposit.

(Continued on Page 27)

Voter Registration

City	Democrat	Republican	*NP	Total
Agoura Hills	4,961	4,875	1,765	12,162
Alhambra	17,419	9,026	6,945	34,787
Altadena**	16,417	6,462	2,282	25,882
Arcadia	8,009	13,719	5,181	27,805
Artesia	3,206	1,852	929	6,237
Avalon	693	827	214	1,818
Azusa	7,875	5,363	2,481	16,518
Baldwin Park	13,843	4,059	3,595	22,429
Bell	5,177	1,272	1,209	7,998
Bellflower	16,767	8,184	3,506	29,793
Bell Gardens	6,064	1,019	1,277	8,841
Beverly Hills	11,365	5,503	3,512	21,102
Bradbury	131	361	68	581
Burbank	24,711	19,674	8,070	54,944
Calabasas	5,734	4,609	1,714	12,563
Carson	27,256	7,341	5,799	42,314
Cerritos	11,823	10,281	5,048	28,017
Claremont	9,030	7,892	3,209	21,398
Commerce	3,623	493	532	4,815
Compton	27,213	2,070	2,720	34,781
Covina	9,986	9,156	3,149	23,268
Cudahy	2,865	595	592	4,240
Culver City	13,739	5,097	3,303	23,206
Diamond Bar	10,393	11,706	2,217	28,301
Downey	23,151	15,848	4,837	45,496
Duarte	4,851	3,564	1,510	10,355
East Los Angeles**	16,276	1,943	1,612	20,309
El Monte	16,276	5,815	4,713	28,164
El Segundo	10,798	4,933	1,721	10,798
Florence**	10,340	777	891	12,394
Gardena	14,548	4,640	3,233	23,490
Glendale	34,611	36,625	14,054	89,186
Glendora	8,786	14,462	3,522	27,922
Hacienda Heights**	10,551	10,477	3,156	24,894
Hawaiian Gardens	2,482	706	574	3,981
Hawthorne	17,795	5,464	3,929	28,925
Hermosa Beach	4,957	5,937	2,717	14,413
Hidden Hills	489	608	125	1,258
Huntington Park	8,504	1,835	1,651	12,620
Industry	44	57	21	129
Inglewood	34,714	3,796	4,503	45,424
Irwindale	482	109	78	701
La Cañada Flintridge	3,602	8,064	1,589	13,613
La Crescenta**	2,487	4,210	735	7,671
Ladera Heights**	4,025	901	351	5,369
La Habra Heights	759	2,084	384	3,350
Lakewood	21,327	15,783	5,319	44,151
La Mirada	10,030	11,394	2,920	25,326
Lancaster	18,455	23,449	6,569	51,032
La Puente	8,406	2,050	1,742	12,741
La Verne	6,774	8,911	2,393	18,829
Lawndale	5,620	2,714	1,734	10,728

Voter Registration

City	Democrat	Republican	*NP	Total
Lomita	4,318	4,010	1,560	10,417
Long Beach	111,078	59,746	28,420	210,765
Los Angeles	879,989	324,093	214,386	1,496,025
Lynwood	12,523	1,639	2,052	17,186
Malibu	3,783	3,269	1,399	9,003
Manhattan Beach	8,718	11,534	3,618	24,912
Marina Del Rey**	2,586	1,864	854	5,538
Maywood	3,832	738	932	5,801
Monrovia	7,935	7,479	2,671	18,981
Montebello	16,361	4,910	3,136	25,271
Monterey Park	13,063	6,213	5,518	25,727
Norwalk	22,707	8,891	4,621	37,798
Palmdale	19,179	18,360	6,015	45,745
Palos Verdes Estates	2,431	5,980	1,260	9,983
Paramount	9,862	2,440	1,967	15,015
Pasadena	40,139	23,654	10,374	77,407
Pico Rivera	18,969	3,805	2,701	26,366
Pomona	26,294	11,330	6,693	46,507
Rancho Palos Verdes	8,509	14,344	3,588	27,326
Redondo Beach	14,624	15,601	6,528	38,719
Rolling Hills	269	970	143	1,415
Rolling Hills Estates	1,433	3,289	605	5,489
Rosemead	8,964	3,878	3,421	7,031
Rowland Heights**	7,481	6,662	2,507	17,299
San Dimas	7,038	9,294	2,704	19,840
San Fernando	4,796	1,157	921	7,163
San Gabriel	6,829	4,640	2,944	14,957
San Marino	1,647	4,832	1,597	8,274
Santa Clarita	25,279	38,042	10,479	77,253
Santa Fe Springs	5,057	1,511	862	7,686
Santa Monica	32,323	12,820	10,378	59,305
Sierra Madre	2,753	3,625	1,080	7,838
Signal Hill	2,403	1,347	725	4,730
South El Monte	3,881	811	762	5,689
South Gate	16,808	4,033	3,237	25,239
South Pasadena	6,578	5,318	2,703	15,242
South Whittier**	12,846	8,780	2,380	24,836
Stevenson Ranch**	731	1,266	309	2,377
Temple City	6,409	6,453	2,831	16,378
Torrance	29,002	32,861	11,743	76,776
Vernon	33	18	10	61
View Park**	6,444	566	467	8,090
Walnut	5,328	5,229	3,291	14,376
West Covina	23,379	15,153	6,749	47,197
West Hollywood	15,652	3,337	4,774	25,114
Westlake Village	1,728	2,948	780	5,674
Whittier	18,268	16,032	4,764	40,720
Unincorporated	225,865	112,924	53,707	412,076
Countywide	2,168,085	1,132,380	578,522	4,075,037

Source: County registrar of voters, 2000. *Non-partisan (Declined to state any political party preference.) Total includes those who registered for other political parties. **Unincorporated towns, data from 1996.

Los Angeles County Single-Family Home Prices

Place	Sales	Lowest	Highest	Median	Average
Acton	38	$63,000	$540,000	$244,000	$253,077
Agoura Hills	126	$135,000	$1,395,000	$382,500	$462,619
Alhambra	510	$25,000	$711,818	$180,000	$191,817
Altadena	158	$75,000	$1,195,000	$225,000	$272,970
Arcadia	215	$30,000	$1,950,000	$390,000	$453,704
Artesia	49	$70,000	$350,000	$177,750	$177,716
Avalon	11	$66,000	$500,000	$87,000	$226,364
Azusa	97	$55,000	$750,000	$150,381	$168,687
Baldwin Park	142	$36,000	$881,300	$143,000	$149,046
Bel Air	37	$215,000	$12,650,000	$757,500	$1,320,056
Bell/Compton	971	$27,000	$550,227	$123,000	$124,857
Beverly Hills	147	$25,000	$4,000,000	$895,000	$1,146,379
Brentwood	59	$510,000	$2,210,000	$875,000	$990,000
Burbank	253	$30,000	$1,300,000	$265,000	$288,136
Calabasas	104	$51,500	$3,350,000	$625,000	$753,883
Canoga Park	428	$72,000	$1,349,090	$223,500	$249,135
Carson	147	$51,500	$290,000	$185,500	$188,259
Castaic	75	$40,000	$370,000	$190,000	$193,813
Cerritos	164	$34,545	$690,000	$283,000	$303,006
Chatsworth	117	$83,000	$1,700,000	$276,250	$326,881
Claremont	134	$60,000	$1,210,000	$243,500	$274,823
Commerce	109	$40,000	$200,000	$136,000	$130,250
Covina	223	$50,500	$760,000	$185,000	$207,913
Culver City	69	$150,000	$655,000	$338,500	$349,290
Cypress	3	$288,000	$365,000	$289,000	$314,000
Diamond Bar	190	$30,000	$2,450,000	$274,000	$338,755
Downey	283	$77,272	$750,000	$220,000	$231,587
Duarte	92	$100,000	$1,480,000	$165,000	$218,379
El Monte	172	$71,000	$1,200,000	$156,500	$174,408
El Segundo	34	$125,000	$739,000	$405,000	$419,258
Encino	149	$38,000	$1,950,000	$410,000	$481,648
Gardena	140	$92,000	$482,181	$185,000	$187,188
Glendale	441	$65,000	$1,550,000	$339,500	$373,029
Glendora	176	$70,000	$830,000	$228,000	$267,049
Harbor City	35	$166,000	$791,590	$250,000	$263,645
Hawaiian Gardens	24	$35,000	$200,909	$121,500	$120,600
Hawthorne	124	$39,500	$921,000	$190,000	$201,041
Hermosa Beach	45	$275,000	$2,380,000	$460,000	$632,567
Hollywood	752	$60,000	$5,350,000	$425,000	$485,158
Huntington Park	98	$42,000	$230,000	$154,500	$152,517
Inglewood	188	$42,500	$442,000	$150,000	$161,861
La Canada Flintridge	123	$116,000	$2,110,000	$585,000	$689,029
La Habra	36	$130,000	$885,000	$365,000	$394,208
La Mirada	168	$94,000	$550,000	$222,000	$238,269
La Puente	620	$44,772	$854,000	$172,000	$213,888
La Verne	113	$46,500	$590,000	$237,500	$263,105
Lake Hughes	13	$26,000	$1,036,000	$124,000	$193,346
Lakewood	322	$54,000	$540,000	$209,000	$210,822
Lancaster	784	$25,000	$618,000	$90,000	$99,993
Lawndale	42	$70,000	$325,000	$183,000	$183,520

Copyright © 2001 McCormack's Guides. No reproduction without permission.

Los Angeles County Single-Family Home Prices

City	Sales	Lowest	Highest	Median	Average
Littlerock	55	$25,000	$202,000	$87,500	$86,871
Llano	6	$33,500	$160,000	$139,500	$125,833
Lomita	32	$152,727	$460,000	$295,000	$290,214
Long Beach	1,037	$26,500	$4,200,000	$210,000	$245,012
Los Angeles	380	$42,500	$1,600,000	$310,000	$344,779
Lynwood	138	$32,000	$470,000	$134,500	$130,005
Malibu	82	$145,500	$4,790,000	$975,000	$1,319,000
Manhattan Beach	189	$111,500	$3,900,000	$659,500	$804,094
Marina Del Rey	8	$275,000	$1,225,000	$705,000	$720,375
Maywood	27	$89,000	$195,500	$151,000	$145,926
Monrovia	118	$45,000	$750,000	$245,000	$279,640
Montebello	86	$67,000	$340,000	$193,500	$204,118
Monterey Park	112	$35,000	$540,000	$223,000	$232,710
Montrose	9	$193,000	$315,000	$260,000	$257,889
North Hollywood	310	$25,500	$2,225,000	$204,500	$276,038
Northridge	261	$45,454	$900,000	$317,500	$318,417
Norwalk	300	$43,000	$249,000	$162,000	$157,596
Pacific Palisades	82	$300,000	$4,402,000	$885,000	$1,057,019
Pacoima	200	$45,000	$649,227	$155,000	$156,891
Palmdale	801	$33,000	$387,500	$101,750	$112,898
Palos Verdes Penin.	151	$108,000	$2,900,000	$820,000	$933,541
Paramount	56	$84,000	$224,500	$139,000	$147,553
Pasadena	457	$40,000	$2,900,000	$299,000	$368,536
Pearblossom	7	$32,000	$110,000	$80,000	$77,667
Pico Rivera	132	$28,000	$280,000	$156,000	$158,457
Playa Del Rey	18	$355,000	$1,325,000	$659,500	$677,518
Pomona	484	$54,000	$815,000	$128,000	$148,794
Ran. Palos Verdes	198	$81,863	$3,517,000	$592,500	$661,180
Redondo Beach	174	$50,000	$2,225,000	$382,000	$448,061
Reseda	217	$40,000	$777,272	$180,000	$195,153
Rosemead	103	$82,500	$328,200	$170,000	$180,415
San Dimas	132	$86,000	$1,465,000	$217,000	$248,681
San Fernando	639	$70,000	$625,000	$200,000	$213,362
San Gabriel	165	$30,600	$590,000	$253,000	$273,525
San Marino	82	$127,000	$3,188,000	$662,500	$740,140
San Pedro	149	$86,000	$554,000	$260,000	$269,573
Santa Clarita	553	$30,000	$1,480,000	$230,000	$260,389
Santa Fe Springs	35	$78,000	$235,000	$164,000	$165,414
Santa Monica	261	$53,100	$5,450,000	$445,000	$604,139
Sherman Oaks	204	$53,000	$1,650,000	$417,500	$471,264
Sierra Madre	40	$150,000	$1,260,000	$376,000	$460,388
South Gate	197	$25,000	$396,500	$152,000	$150,733
South Pasadena	55	$220,000	$750,000	$411,250	$431,657
South-Central LA	1,010	$30,500	$580,000	$130,000	$140,169
Stevenson Ranch	38	$160,090	$564,000	$327,500	$328,331
Studio City	98	$58,500	$2,675,000	$455,000	$522,047
Sun Valley	109	$59,000	$625,000	$166,500	$196,973
Sunland	78	$28,000	$879,000	$205,000	$237,130
Tarzana	104	$40,000	$3,767,272	$490,000	$558,646

Copyright © 2001 McCormack's Guides. No reproduction without permission.

Los Angeles County Single-Family Home Prices

City	Sales	Lowest	Highest	Median	Average
Temple City	99	$30,000	$530,000	$242,000	$254,308
Topanga	38	$100,000	$1,885,000	$498,750	$535,039
Torrance	397	$50,000	$740,000	$320,000	$321,013
Tujunga	94	$35,000	$370,000	$184,000	$191,850
Valencia	92	$95,454	$512,000	$272,500	$289,433
Van Nuys	475	$45,000	$855,000	$188,654	$211,477
Venice	73	$125,000	$2,350,000	$385,000	$454,342
Walnut	180	$94,500	$1,260,000	$272,000	$307,007
West Covina	298	$32,500	$655,000	$190,000	$208,413
Westchester	135	$180,000	$1,500,000	$379,000	$411,445
Whittier	532	$65,000	$1,075,000	$183,500	$210,946
Wilmington	50	$76,000	$215,000	$150,000	$153,493
Woodland Hills	288	$120,500	$2,273,090	$336,000	$384,319

Source: DataQuick Information Systems Inc., La Jolla, CA. Key: Resale single-family detached housing sales from May 1, 2000 to July 31, 2000.

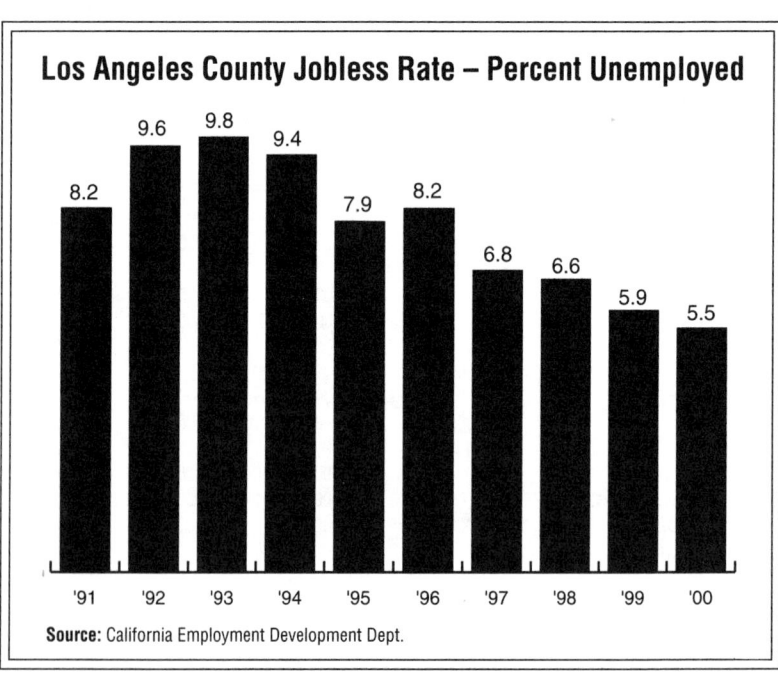

Los Angeles County Jobless Rate – Percent Unemployed

'91	'92	'93	'94	'95	'96	'97	'98	'99	'00
8.2	9.6	9.8	9.4	7.9	8.2	6.8	6.6	5.9	5.5

Source: California Employment Development Dept.

Top 25 Baby Names

Los Angeles County

Boys	Girls
Daniel (1,557)	Ashley (1,078)
Jose (1,438)	Jennifer (1,014)
Anthony (1,409)	Samantha (936)
David (1,212)	Emily (732)
Andrew (1,176)	Jessica (709)
Jonathan (1,119)	Stephanie (709)
Michael (1,106)	Kimberly (654)
Christopher (1,098)	Natalie (600)
Matthew (998)	Vanessa (596)
Kevin (955)	Elizabeth (564)
Joshua (926)	Jasmine (555)
Luis (894)	Alexis (534)
Angel (863)	Leslie (526)
Juan (829)	Maria (526)
Joseph (818)	Alyssa (499)
Carlos (749)	Michelle (499)
Christian (745)	Melissa (488)
Brandon (734)	Sarah (487)
Justin (711)	Andrea (458)
Jacob (710)	Brianna (446)
Jesus (682)	Diana (440)
Alexander (640)	Destiny (421)
Brian (611)	Victoria (407)
Adrian (610)	Jacqueline (379)
Ryan (610)	Jocelyn (369)

California

Boys	Girls
Daniel (4,321)	Emily (2,799)
Jose (3,831)	Samantha (2,776)
Anthony (3,783)	Jennifer (2,660)
Michael (3,719)	Ashley (2,590)
Andrew (3,574)	Jessica (2,486)
David (3,450)	Alyssa (2,066)
Jacob (3,436)	Alexis (1,964)
Matthew (3,285)	Sarah (1,962)
Christopher (3,231)	Elizabeth (1,841)
Joshua (3,106)	Vanessa (1,766)
Jonathan (3,004)	Stephanie (1,747)
Joseph (2,781)	Hannah (1,675)
Nicholas (2,513)	Jasmine (1,650)
Ryan (2,497)	Natalie (1,642)
Brandon (2,473)	Maria (1,569)
Juan (2,324)	Victoria (1,455)
Christian (2,311)	Lauren (1,383)
Kevin (2,300)	Madison (1,370)
Luis (2,261)	Kimberly (1,347)
Alexander (2,218)	Brianna (1,341)
Justin (2,218)	Andrea (1,301)
Angel (2,034)	Michelle (1,263)
Jesus (1,990)	Melissa (1,246)
Carlos (1,956)	Taylor (1,204)
John (1,736)	Nicole (1,202)

Source: Calif. Dept. of Health Services, 1999 records. In parentheses is number of children with given name. Some names would move higher on list if the state grouped essentially same names with slightly different spellings — Sarah and Sara. But state computer goes by exact spellings.

(Continued from Page 21)

- Apartments pay for garbage pickup. You pay for phone, TV cable and usually gas and electric.

- If you can't afford furniture, rent it. Check in the phone book under Furniture Renting. Almost every Saturday morning, L.A. County (even the upscale towns), cuts loose with garage sales. Many items go cheap.

- For parents, your address will usually determine what public school your child will attend. See chapter on how public schools work. Check to see that day care is available nearby.

- If you're renting while scouting for a home, check out residency hotels. They often add touches — laundry, maid service, equipped kitchens — not found in regular hotels.

- Many apartment complexes offer gates, guards, extra lighting.

Chapter 2

State School Rankings

- **What do these numbers mean?**

These percentile rankings, drawn from the scores on the 2000 STAR test, compare California schools and grades, one against the other.

If a school scores in the 91st percentile, it has done better than 91 percent of the other public schools in the state. If it scores in the 51st percentile, it has done better than 51 percent of the others; the 40th rank, better than 40 percent of the others. If a school scores in the first percentile, 99 percent of the other schools have scored higher.

- **Do the numbers in this chapter tell whether California education is improving?**

No. Ranking systems don't recognize overall gains or losses. If every school in California raised raw scores 20 percent, some schools would still be ranked at the bottom, a few at the top. The same if every raw score dropped. A ranking system shows how one school did against all other schools.

Schools and school districts have more information on scores. For more information, please call them. For phone numbers of school districts, see Chapter 3.

Bird Lorraine & Associates
CRP, CRS, ABR, GRI

Professional Services with a Personal Touch

Providing Realtor Services Since 1978

- Top Producing Agent
- Committed to client's and family's needs
- Finely tuned negotiating skills to benefit you
- Attention to every detail of the transaction
- Exhibits unusual patience and initiative
- FREE comparable market analysis, buyers' and sellers' counseling sessions.
- FREE One Year Home Protection Plan

Service areas: **Hermosa, Manhattan, Redondo Beach Areas, Palos Verdes Peninsula Areas, Torrance, El Segundo, Hawthorne, Lawndale, Gardena, San Pedro & Carson**

Memberships include: Re/Max Hall of Fame, Top 10 Agents, 100% Club, Certified Relocation Professional, Accredited Buyer Representative, Certified Residential Specialist

RE/MAX Execs	Direct & Voice Mail
1720 So. Elena Avenue	(310) 318-9294
Redondo Beach, CA	(888) 279-8288
90277	(310) 318-3103 Fax

E-mail: lorraine@southbayhomesla.com
Web Site: www.southbayhomesla.com

30 STATE SCHOOL RANKINGS

Scores range from 1-99. A school scoring 75 has done better than 75 percent of other public schools in California.
Key: Rd (Reading), Ma (Math), Lg (Language), Sp (Spelling), Sci (Science) and SS (Social Science).

Grade	Rd	Ma	Lg	Sp	Sci	SS	Grade	Rd	Ma	Lg	Sp	Sci	SS
ABC Unified School Dist.							**Furgeson Elem., Hawaiian Gardens**						
ABC Secondary Alt.							2	10	20	26	13		
9	49	13	38		20	15	3	6	5	6	5		
10	31	14	13		18	29	4	3	3	17	4		
11	36	36	30		30	32	5	1	1	1	1		
Aloha Elem., Lakewood							6	3	12	17	3		
2	36	49	35	40			**Gahr High, Cerritos**						
3	51	45	50	72			9	58	70	66		63	60
4	39	42	36	50			10	58	72	62		52	56
5	33	22	15	43			11	59	77	65		62	65
6	23	21	25	30			**Gonsalves Elem., Cerritos**						
Artesia High, Lakewood							2	94	98	91	98		
9	31	44	38		38	42	3	93	99	98	99		
10	38	56	41		51	29	4	93	99	99	98		
11	44	61	43		50	45	5	93	96	92	97		
Bragg Elem., Cerritos							6	92	98	97	98		
2	85	76	82	94			**Haskell Middle, Cerritos**						
3	81	70	84	94			7	38	40	49	49		
4	89	95	96	95			8	47	41	55	67		
5	84	88	83	92			**Hawaiian Elem., Hawaiian Gardens**						
6	82	86	88	89			2	5	5	6	6		
Burbank Elem., Artesia							3	13	4	15	7		
2	23	19	24	26			4	11	5	9	10		
3	30	32	33	37			5	8	3	10	6		
4	39	42	41	40			6	1	2	1	1		
5	37	50	38	31			**Juarez Elem., Cerritos**						
6	40	31	47	50			2	31	23	30	46		
Carmenita Middle, Cerritos							3	37	42	50	53		
7	88	94	92	95			4	27	34	27	37		
8	84	94	90	97			5	23	38	28	19		
Carver Elem., Cerritos							6	34	30	36	40		
2	62	73	73	78			**Kennedy Elem., Artesia**						
3	65	81	77	92			2	85	84	94	97		
4	63	70	60	79			3	85	87	94	95		
5	70	89	83	90			4	91	90	95	97		
6	84	85	84	93			5	53	51	54	57		
Cerritos Elem., Cerritos							6	68	71	72	67		
2	95	96	97	99			**Leal Elem., Cerritos**						
3	85	94	94	98			2	93	98	96	99		
4	87	98	94	97			3	89	99	99	99		
5	90	96	94	99			4	80	92	87	95		
6	89	96	96	98			5	90	98	97	98		
Cerritos High, Cerritos							6	95	97	98	98		
9	88	96	97		92	94	**Melbourne Elem., Lakewood**						
10	82	96	94		82	79	2	26	19	34	20		
11	93	98	97		91	94	3	21	17	17	16		
Elliott Elem., Artesia							4	31	29	36	26		
2	59	52	68	48			5	33	32	40	37		
3	52	61	59	43			6	34	27	46	44		
4	41	40	62	57			**Niemes Elem., Artesia**						
5	50	55	61	55			2	60	85	56	58		
6	58	60	75	80			3	34	52	44	32		
Fedde Middle, Hawaiian Gardens							4	36	45	40	35		
7	15	20	21	13			5	34	55	35	31		
8	12	14	16	11			6	30	47	50	46		

Scores range from 1-99. A school scoring 75 has done better than 75 percent of other public schools in California.
Key: Rd (Reading), Ma (Math), Lg (Language), Sp (Spelling), Sci (Science) and SS (Social Science).

Grade	Rd	Ma	Lg	Sp	Sci	SS
Nixon Elem., Cerritos						
2	83	89	88	94		
3	86	90	93	95		
4	74	84	88	93		
5	79	77	78	91		
6	82	82	88	88		
Palms Elem., Lakewood						
2	46	68	53	42		
3	51	82	62	89		
4	43	62	51	50		
5	39	38	44	45		
6	54	60	64	62		
Ross Middle, Artesia						
7	40	42	30	45		
8	39	39	27	38		
Stowers Elem., Cerritos						
2	93	97	88	99		
3	77	96	86	96		
4	81	96	94	95		
5	86	96	94	95		
6	91	96	98	98		
Tetzlaff Middle, Cerritos						
7	58	79	64	74		
8	45	70	55	71		
Tracy High (Cont.), Cerritos						
10	21	17	16		15	13
11	11	4	5		10	20
Whitney High, Cerritos						
7	99	99	99	99		
8	99	99	99	99		
9	99	99	99		99	99
10	99	99	99		99	99
11	99	99	99		99	99
Willow Elem., Lakewood						
2	16	16	20	15		
3	25	40	25	13		
4	19	26	15	13		
5	16	17	10	12		
6	17	26	18	18		
Wittmann Elem., Cerritos						
2	94	93	91	98		
3	91	96	96	98		
4	93	98	98	98		
5	84	95	92	97		
6	97	98	98	99		

Acton-Agua Dulce Unified School Dist.

Grade	Rd	Ma	Lg	Sp	Sci	SS
Acton Elem., Acton						
3	64	63	71	70		
4	69	70	69	57		
5	62	62	60	60		
6	76	71	70	74		
Agua Dulce Elem., Agua Dulce						
2	67	52	61	34		
3	71	44	56	41		
4	72	67	56	62		
5	67	72	74	69		
6	76	71	64	62		
High Desert, Acton						
7	71	63	76	58		
8	66	58	70	59		
Meadowlark Elem., Acton						
2	59	46	45	60		
Vasquez High, Acton						
9	75	56	74		73	72
10	64	56	67		67	73
11	75	55	78		76	67

Alhambra City Elem. School Dist.

Grade	Rd	Ma	Lg	Sp	Sci	SS
Baldwin Elem., Alhambra						
2	45	70	50	67		
3	39	61	60	73		
4	50	50	62	87		
5	33	44	42	57		
6	42	63	47	64		
7	41	60	53	60		
8	43	73	53	59		
Brightwood Elem., Monterey Park						
2	53	68	65	78		
3	70	79	81	95		
4	68	67	65	86		
5	68	77	81	85		
6	75	79	80	85		
7	80	90	88	93		
8	76	92	85	91		
Emery Park Elem., Alhambra						
2	43	60	49	58		
3	37	23	35	53		
4	43	44	33	44		
5	45	41	58	51		
6	53	30	47	48		
7	25	35	30	28		
8	29	26	33	43		
Fremont Elem., Alhambra						
2	55	55	63	65		
3	42	32	38	62		
4	47	48	53	60		
5	46	39	47	57		
6	42	24	34	34		
7	48	53	47	74		
8	56	54	42	74		
Garfield Elem., Alhambra						
2	52	62	63	73		
3	42	28	48	59		
4	53	50	60	62		
5	61	64	69	70		
6	54	45	46	66		
7	50	67	58	62		
8	42	58	50	67		
Granada Elem., Alhambra						
2	38	38	55	60		
3	34	42	38	50		
4	37	44	31	35		
5	36	51	47	49		
6	32	22	33	40		
7	44	60	38	52		
8	43	33	44	31		

STATE SCHOOL RANKINGS

Scores range from 1-99. A school scoring 75 has done better than 75 percent of other public schools in California.
Key: Rd (Reading), Ma (Math), Lg (Language), Sp (Spelling), Sci (Science) and SS (Social Science).

Marguerita Elem., Alhambra

Grade	Rd	Ma	Lg	Sp	Sci	SS
2	40	62	43	54		
3	47	50	57	70		
4	45	48	43	59		
5	55	67	56	61		
6	56	45	47	48		
7	57	55	71	86		
8	49	68	67	71		

Monterey Highlands Elem., Monterey Park

Grade	Rd	Ma	Lg	Sp	Sci	SS
2	67	82	78	94		
3	45	58	63	82		
4	50	65	67	74		
5	64	78	75	89		
6	65	76	60	81		
7	64	86	73	62		
8	55	83	74	89		

Northrup Elem., Alhambra

Grade	Rd	Ma	Lg	Sp	Sci	SS
2	35	38	37	56		
3	47	85	72	78		
4	33	31	41	38		
5	39	38	51	51		
6	26	14	20	32		
7	34	42	33	43		
8	24	51	27	31		

Park Elem., Alhambra

Grade	Rd	Ma	Lg	Sp	Sci	SS
2	32	55	30	42		
3	32	50	36	57		
4	52	57	67	65		
5	48	53	58	70		
6	42	38	34	52		
7	41	63	37	54		
8	33	47	39	61		

Ramona Elem., Alhambra

Grade	Rd	Ma	Lg	Sp	Sci	SS
2	35	40	41	64		
3	39	47	50	62		
4	44	53	47	60		
5	33	56	51	65		
6	44	60	56	66		
7	50	57	54	68		
8	43	62	70	53		

Repetto Elem., Monterey Park

Grade	Rd	Ma	Lg	Sp	Sci	SS
2	46	43	60	75		
3	47	49	48	68		
4	59	68	60	74		
5	50	46	51	67		
6	61	67	60	76		
7	57	69	52	76		
8	64	81	57	79		

Ynez Elem., Monterey Park

Grade	Rd	Ma	Lg	Sp	Sci	SS
2	65	79	76	91		
3	39	63	52	75		
4	50	68	64	77		
5	45	68	64	70		
6	54	68	60	78		
7	55	81	66	78		
8	60	88	73	89		

Alhambra City High School Dist.

Alhambra High, Alhambra

Grade	Rd	Ma	Lg	Sp	Sci	SS
9	55	85	76		60	62
10	51	90	65		66	68
11	51	90	63		69	67

Century High (Cont.), Alhambra

Grade	Rd	Ma	Lg	Sp	Sci	SS
10	5	14	2		1	1
11	30	24	31		22	27

Independence High (Alt.) Alhambra

Grade	Rd	Ma	Lg	Sp	Sci	SS
9	25	32	27		10	5
10	11	29	13		10	4
11	17	22	31		12	12

Mark Keppel High, Alhambra

Grade	Rd	Ma	Lg	Sp	Sci	SS
9	60	81	76		58	60
10	62	90	75		70	71
11	55	89	65		58	53

San Gabriel High, San Gabriel

Grade	Rd	Ma	Lg	Sp	Sci	SS
9	36	52	50		40	42
10	41	69	54		49	51
11	37	65	49		42	45

Antelope Valley High School Dist.

Antelope Valley High, Palmdale

Grade	Rd	Ma	Lg	Sp	Sci	SS
9	47	37	46		47	34
10	54	48	50		53	49
11	53	46	51		53	44

Desert Winds Cont. High, Lancaster

Grade	Rd	Ma	Lg	Sp	Sci	SS
9	17	11	8		12	34
10	18	14	10		18	23
11	24	16	19		24	23

Highland High, Lancaster

Grade	Rd	Ma	Lg	Sp	Sci	SS
9	63	56	66		60	55
10	70	59	69		68	66
11	69	68	74		72	67

Lancaster High, Lancaster

Grade	Rd	Ma	Lg	Sp	Sci	SS
9	60	50	62		58	50
10	65	57	72		67	59
11	71	62	69		69	58

Littlerock High, Littlerock

Grade	Rd	Ma	Lg	Sp	Sci	SS
9	51	52	59		50	47
10	52	52	57		53	51
11	55	52	57		52	47

Palmdale High, Palmdale

Grade	Rd	Ma	Lg	Sp	Sci	SS
9	49	44	49		47	37
10	54	49	53		53	47
11	53	50	57		53	47

Phoenix High Comm. Day, Lancaster

Grade	Rd	Ma	Lg	Sp	Sci	SS
9	14	3	5		12	3
10	7	14	8		6	6
11	24	30	17		28	18

Quartz Hill High, Quartz Hill

Grade	Rd	Ma	Lg	Sp	Sci	SS
9	81	81	78		82	66
10	82	76	75		79	73
11	77	75	74		79	69

STATE SCHOOL RANKINGS

Scores range from 1-99. A school scoring 75 has done better than 75 percent of other public schools in California.
Key: Rd (Reading), Ma (Math), Lg (Language), Sp (Spelling), Sci (Science) and SS (Social Science).

Arcadia Unified School Dist.

Arcadia High, Arcadia

Grade	Rd	Ma	Lg	Sp	Sci	SS
9	88	97	96		89	96
10	92	98	97		94	93
11	89	98	96		92	89

Baldwin Stocker Elem., Arcadia

Grade	Rd	Ma	Lg	Sp
2	82	85	90	98
3	86	87	92	98
4	92	94	97	98
5	84	93	94	98

Camino Grove Elem., Arcadia

Grade	Rd	Ma	Lg	Sp
2	86	81	80	95
3	76	65	75	86
4	93	97	99	98
5	90	92	96	97

Dana Middle, Arcadia

Grade	Rd	Ma	Lg	Sp
6	81	89	91	93
7	91	97	92	97
8	87	96	90	92

First Ave. Middle, Arcadia

Grade	Rd	Ma	Lg	Sp
6	79	90	88	92
7	86	96	86	89
8	69	94	78	81

Foothills Middle, Arcadia

Grade	Rd	Ma	Lg	Sp
6	95	98	98	98
7	94	99	97	98
8	90	98	94	96

Highland Oaks Elem., Arcadia

Grade	Rd	Ma	Lg	Sp
2	98	97	95	99
3	94	93	97	98
4	97	94	95	98
5	95	96	98	98

Holly Ave. Elem., Arcadia

Grade	Rd	Ma	Lg	Sp
2	86	92	80	94
3	70	76	81	94
4	85	80	92	92
5	80	84	88	89

Hugo Reid Elem., Arcadia

Grade	Rd	Ma	Lg	Sp
2	89	81	82	93
3	71	81	79	79
4	85	92	96	96
5	81	84	87	92

Longley Way Elem., Arcadia

Grade	Rd	Ma	Lg	Sp
2	73	74	78	88
3	83	95	94	99
4	77	85	91	92
5	88	94	94	98

Rancho Learning Ctr. (Alt.), Arcadia

Grade	Rd	Ma	Lg	Sp	Sci	SS
10	25	24	38		8	31
11	28	28	23		39	61

Azusa Unified School Dist.

Azusa High, Azusa

Grade	Rd	Ma	Lg	Sp	Sci	SS
9	28	37	27		36	21
10	36	42	32		40	26
11	33	46	28		35	28

Center Middle, Azusa

Grade	Rd	Ma	Lg	Sp
6	17	16	14	30
7	22	36	20	19
8	13	26	11	13

Dalton Elem., Azusa

Grade	Rd	Ma	Lg	Sp
2	8	27	17	5
3	21	42	26	20
4	17	36	18	11
5	23	48	25	19

Ellington Elem., Azusa

Grade	Rd	Ma	Lg	Sp
2	28	30	40	29
3	49	44	38	28
4	33	31	36	40
5	26	48	40	39

Foothill Middle, Azusa

Grade	Rd	Ma	Lg	Sp
6	21	22	11	20
7	20	35	17	22
8	20	28	14	20

Gladstone High, Covina

Grade	Rd	Ma	Lg	Sp	Sci	SS
9	33	37	36		36	34
10	29	36	36		35	26
11	39	40	45		37	45

Gladstone St. Elem., Azusa

Grade	Rd	Ma	Lg	Sp
2	40	44	30	33
3	15	30	13	13
4	16	36	20	22
5	21	50	30	19

Hodge Elem., Azusa

Grade	Rd	Ma	Lg	Sp
2	25	38	43	14
3	27	17	26	12
4	17	24	13	8
5	31	41	28	21

Lee Elem., Azusa

Grade	Rd	Ma	Lg	Sp
2	23	32	30	4
3	11	47	17	12
4	9	16	9	4
5	10	29	13	14

Magnolia Elem., Azusa

Grade	Rd	Ma	Lg	Sp
2	35	66	61	38
3	55	73	65	41
4	36	57	43	29
5	25	44	44	25

Mountain View Elem., Azusa

Grade	Rd	Ma	Lg	Sp
2	16	40	16	17
3	9	16	4	9
4	20	22	27	22
5	39	56	23	39

Murray Elem., Azusa

Grade	Rd	Ma	Lg	Sp
2	7	12	7	11
3	27	22	17	18
4	2	21	3	1
5	8	29	15	5

Paramount Elem., Azusa

Grade	Rd	Ma	Lg	Sp
2	4	3	9	3
3	29	20	33	25
4	20	16	15	17
5	10	21	11	12

STATE SCHOOL RANKINGS

Scores range from 1-99. A school scoring 75 has done better than 75 percent of other public schools in California.
Key: Rd (Reading), Ma (Math), Lg (Language), Sp (Spelling), Sci (Science) and SS (Social Science).

Grade	Rd	Ma	Lg	Sp	Sci	SS
Powell Elem., Azusa						
2	30	32	23	26		
3	17	16	9	18		
4	34	46	31	37		
5	39	62	44	49		
Sierra High (Cont.), Glendora						
10	2	2	1		4	8
11	2	3	1		4	7
Slauson Int., Azusa						
6	23	22	17	30		
7	20	20	10	17		
8	22	37	26	24		
Valleydale Elem., Azusa						
2	6	10	8	6		
3	19	25	21	10		
4	27	31	26	24		
5	14	32	10	18		

Baldwin Park Unified School Dist.

Grade	Rd	Ma	Lg	Sp	Sci	SS
Baldwin Park (Alt.), Baldwin Park						
9	37	11	34		36	17
10	15	24	16		20	18
11	13	12	13		12	16
Baldwin Park High, Baldwin Park						
9	24	27	30		23	27
10	29	36	35		24	21
11	30	34	31		24	22
Bursch Elem., Baldwin Park						
2	23	17	20	22		
3	30	35	38	32		
4	24	34	24	35		
5	7	19	7	19		
6	38	31	38	44		
Central Elem., Baldwin Park						
2	13	7	18	15		
3	25	28	40	30		
4	14	17	20	15		
5	16	17	20	18		
6	21	35	33	22		
DeAnza Elem., Baldwin Park						
2	26	23	31	27		
3	19	28	25	25		
4	22	15	24	40		
5	10	17	10	14		
6	15	35	13	20		
Elwin Elem., Baldwin Park						
2	16	10	21	15		
3	21	28	20	13		
4	8	17	12	15		
5	10	10	8	7		
6	12	22	22	18		
Foster Elem., Baldwin Park						
2	40	30	43	48		
3	30	35	47	43		
4	20	19	27	33		
5	23	40	40	21		
6	27	55	52	48		
Geddes Elem., Baldwin Park						
2	26	9	25	42		
3	26	35	38	53		
4	5	10	10	10		
5	10	9	6	6		
Heath Elem., Baldwin Park						
2	21	25	17	15		
3	15	30	18	20		
4	30	38	37	24		
5	10	28	11	9		
6	26	24	29	36		
Holland Middle, Baldwin Park						
6	21	30	20	18		
7	22	22	19	22		
8	24	26	24	18		
Jones Jr. High, Baldwin Park						
7	15	20	16	15		
8	16	23	18	18		
Kenmore Elem., Baldwin Park						
2	33	19	35	33		
3	21	28	33	16		
4	22	21	24	29		
5	19	31	51	23		
6	6	24	17	14		
North Park Cont. High, Baldwin Park						
9	11	11	9		10	17
10	9	17	8		7	13
11	11	9	13		19	9
Olive Middle, Baldwin Park						
6	17	7	8	14		
7	26	22	25	24		
8	22	29	24	22		
Pleasant View Elem., Baldwin Park						
2	28	20	21	22		
3	15	51	18	13		
4	17	17	15	13		
5	16	4	11	21		
6	9	7	5	11		
Santa Fe Elem., Baldwin Park						
3	41	42	54	68		
4	24	19	31	20		
5	46	61	53	49		
6	48	42	50	69		
7	65	50	66	65		
8	60	51	70	61		
Sierra Vista High, Baldwin Park						
9	31	37	41		28	29
10	38	52	41		40	35
11	37	52	43		37	38
Sierra Vista Jr. High, Baldwin Park						
7	18	19	31	28		
8	27	33	39	36		
Tracy Elem., Baldwin Park						
2	28	37	41	31		
3	13	19	15	15		
4	14	24	15	19		
5	14	13	15	25		
6	13	6	20	22		

Copyright © 2001 McCormack's Guides. No reproduction without permission.

STATE SCHOOL RANKINGS

Scores range from 1-99. A school scoring 75 has done better than 75 percent of other public schools in California.
Key: Rd (Reading), Ma (Math), Lg (Language), Sp (Spelling), Sci (Science) and SS (Social Science).

Vineland Elem., Baldwin Park

Grade	Rd	Ma	Lg	Sp	Sci	SS
2	28	35	44	24		
3	17	35	20	30		
4	19	33	26	31		
5	19	31	18	27		
6	32	47	36	28		

Walnut Elem., Baldwin Park

Grade	Rd	Ma	Lg	Sp	Sci	SS
2	32	60	41	27		
3	22	47	28	13		
4	20	35	22	19		
5	12	19	16	18		

Bassett Unified School Dist.

Bassett Sr. High, La Puente

Grade	Rd	Ma	Lg	Sp	Sci	SS
9	18	32	27		23	31
10	21	38	27		24	26
11	24	40	30		19	37

Edgewood Acad. Elem., La Puente

Grade	Rd	Ma	Lg	Sp	Sci	SS
2	38	7	34	54		
3	19	20	18	32		
4	20	19	18	15		
5	26	31	21	31		
6	34	40	42	50		
7	34	60	28	30		
8	36	83	34	51		

Erwin Elem., La Puente

Grade	Rd	Ma	Lg	Sp	Sci	SS
2	35	38	43	40		
3	29	32	26	37		
4	22	24	10	24		
5	21	14	16	25		
6	26	35	44	55		
7	15	38	19	16		
8	34	56	44	36		

Julian Elem., La Puente

Grade	Rd	Ma	Lg	Sp	Sci	SS
2	41	42	56	46		
3	27	30	36	28		
4	28	44	27	26		
5	17	28	20	6		
6	26	60	40	25		
7	29	55	25	15		

Nueva Vista Cont. High, La Puente

Grade	Rd	Ma	Lg	Sp	Sci	SS
10	1	4	2		3	1
11	4	12	2		10	7

Sunkist Elem., La Puente

Grade	Rd	Ma	Lg	Sp	Sci	SS
2	18	11	11	14		
3	21	42	30	37		
4	19	27	33	13		
5	3	2	7	1		
6	9	9	16	11		
7	22	35	33	41		
8	33	58	34	46		

Torch Middle, City of Industry

Grade	Rd	Ma	Lg	Sp	Sci	SS
6	9	14	8	6		
7	11	17	16	8		
8	7	17	9	6		

Vanwig Elem., La Puente

Grade	Rd	Ma	Lg	Sp	Sci	SS
2	36	11	31	56		
3	26	27	36	41		
4	25	40	12	22		
5	25	53	36	29		
6	48	76	64	55		
7	22	60	24	24		
8	27	41	28	24		

Bellflower Unified School Dist.

Baxter Elem., Bellflower

Grade	Rd	Ma	Lg	Sp	Sci	SS
2	16	30	9	22		
3	22	28	15	32		
4	22	27	22	26		
5	45	64	71	47		
6	27	27	42	25		

Bellflower High, Bellflower

Grade	Rd	Ma	Lg	Sp	Sci	SS
7	24	19	31	28		
8	18	14	18	22		
9	31	37	41		36	42
10	38	40	47		45	43
11	42	43	51		38	54

Bellflower Intensive Lrng Ctr. Elem., Lakewood

Grade	Rd	Ma	Lg	Sp	Sci	SS
2	87	92	86	93		
3	80	87	81	92		
4	80	89	80	95		
5	66	82	72	84		
6	72	85	75	86		

Foster Elem., Lakewood

Grade	Rd	Ma	Lg	Sp	Sci	SS
2	85	89	79	78		
3	84	82	77	79		
4	81	88	72	74		
5	73	72	72	65		
6	68	79	68	67		

Jefferson Elem., Bellflower

Grade	Rd	Ma	Lg	Sp	Sci	SS
2	28	45	30	20		
3	34	40	25	41		
4	19	19	13	22		
5	31	26	21	18		
6	29	40	20	42		

Las Flores Elem., Bellflower

Grade	Rd	Ma	Lg	Sp	Sci	SS
2	9	50	8	9		
3	6	32	8	18		
4	36	53	27	35		
5	16	34	18	12		
6	12	19	8	3		

Lindstrom Elem., Lakewood

Grade	Rd	Ma	Lg	Sp	Sci	SS
2	71	78	79	67		
3	67	74	65	77		
4	63	74	69	73		
5	66	68	58	61		
6	67	68	72	69		

Mayfair High, Lakewood

Grade	Rd	Ma	Lg	Sp	Sci	SS
7	48	55	45	65		
8	47	47	36	56		
9	51	48	56		56	64
10	64	57	62		69	66
11	59	58	57		56	75

36 STATE SCHOOL RANKINGS

Scores range from 1-99. A school scoring 75 has done better than 75 percent of other public schools in California.
Key: Rd (Reading), Ma (Math), Lg (Language), Sp (Spelling), Sci (Science) and SS (Social Science).

Grade	Rd	Ma	Lg	Sp	Sci	SS
Pyle Elem., Bellflower						
2	26	33	24	33		
3	21	28	15	30		
4	37	46	27	44		
5	28	16	33	27		
6	26	25	40	34		
Ramona Elem., Bellflower						
2	16	16	11	19		
3	22	25	21	22		
4	37	44	29	35		
5	26	31	30	25		
6	26	22	27	32		
Somerset Cont. High, Bellflower						
9	9	9	6		7	17
10	15	20	20		27	21
11	19	6	23		12	13
Washington Elem., Bellflower						
2	30	28	13	24		
3	39	58	49	59		
4	20	29	27	20		
5	25	32	18	27		
6	26	36	23	30		
Williams Elem., Lakewood						
2	23	35	30	26		
3	29	28	20	16		
4	22	33	22	28		
5	16	12	23	12		
6	26	24	29	34		
Woodruff Elem., Bellflower						
2	14	12	14	17		
3	13	14	12	15		
4	20	17	24	22		
5	12	14	33	18		
6	13	14	25	22		
Beverly Hills Unified School Dist.						
Beverly Hills High, Beverly Hills						
9	95	98	98		89	97
10	94	97	98		94	92
11	97	98	98		95	96
Beverly Vista Elem., Beverly Hills						
2	93	94	94	96		
3	87	84	87	83		
4	92	89	90	91		
5	92	85	88	89		
6	85	90	83	93		
7	96	94	95	96		
8	99	98	99	99		
El Rodeo Elem., Beverly Hills						
2	94	96	91	93		
3	90	95	91	95		
4	94	97	90	88		
5	93	94	93	93		
6	91	94	94	95		
7	98	97	97	94		
8	96	97	96	97		

Grade	Rd	Ma	Lg	Sp	Sci	SS
Hawthorne Elem., Beverly Hills						
2	90	89	94	95		
3	90	90	93	91		
4	94	94	97	95		
5	89	92	92	89		
6	82	88	82	85		
7	95	95	98	94		
8	91	92	89	85		
Horace Mann Elem., Beverly Hillls						
2	96	90	91	98		
3	95	98	96	97		
4	89	93	90	95		
5	90	94	89	93		
6	89	91	92	94		
7	94	96	94	92		
8	93	92	87	88		
Moreno High (Cont.), Beverly Hillls						
10	56	74	82		61	55
Bonita Unified School Dist.						
Allen Ave. Elem., San Dimas						
2	71	81	73	73		
3	71	73	85	68		
4	70	73	72	65		
5	76	74	64	70		
Bonita High, La Verne						
9	77	75	81		77	82
10	79	84	82		82	80
11	79	83	77		73	73
Chaparral High (Cont.), San Dimas						
10	25	26	21		27	26
11	19	22	10		28	20
Ekstrand Elem., San Dimas						
2	50	63	49	60		
3	55	56	60	57		
4	53	40	37	54		
5	40	40	32	41		
Gladstone Elem., San Dimas						
2	60	89	78	64		
3	71	81	74	62		
4	69	75	58	59		
5	59	69	56	59		
J. Marion Roynon Elem., La Verne						
2	60	62	68	69		
3	58	44	57	48		
4	62	52	56	62		
5	61	48	49	53		
La Verne Heights Elem., La Verne						
2	77	73	83	85		
3	85	81	82	75		
4	84	92	88	81		
5	80	86	82	89		
Lone Hill Middle, San Dimas						
6	60	64	46	64		
7	57	60	58	68		
8	64	62	60	61		

STATE SCHOOL RANKINGS

Scores range from 1-99. A school scoring 75 has done better than 75 percent of other public schools in California.
Key: Rd (Reading), Ma (Math), Lg (Language), Sp (Spelling), Sci (Science) and SS (Social Science).

Grade	Rd	Ma	Lg	Sp	Sci	SS	Grade	Rd	Ma	Lg	Sp	Sci	SS
Miller Elem., La Verne							**Harte Elem., Burbank**						
2	79	81	73	83			2	48	40	60	48		
3	79	71	66	73			3	58	68	68	48		
4	63	58	62	57			4	69	76	71	67		
5	74	65	58	63			5	66	65	66	77		
Oak Mesa Elem., La Verne							**Jefferson Elem., Burbank**						
2	86	92	90	85			2	67	70	72	72		
3	83	91	91	86			3	72	63	74	72		
4	87	92	87	89			4	77	80	78	77		
5	79	86	77	81			5	76	82	78	75		
Ramona Middle, La Verne							**Jordan Middle, Burbank**						
6	67	82	58	67			6	54	45	52	58		
7	75	76	73	71			7	58	58	63	62		
8	73	76	78	64			8	58	56	60	61		
San Dimas High, San Dimas							**McKinley Elem., Burbank**						
9	72	71	74		71	72	2	41	40	47	42		
10	80	74	75		79	76	3	37	35	40	43		
11	76	70	74		69	77	4	44	53	41	54		
Shull Elem., San Dimas							5	46	53	53	43		
2	83	73	88	73			**Miller Elem., Burbank**						
3	77	91	79	79			2	50	45	50	52		
4	63	65	62	70			3	49	60	55	55		
5	83	78	81	82			4	55	70	64	55		
Vista Alt., San Dimas							5	46	53	61	53		
7	27	29	24	17			**Monterey High (Cont.), Burbank**						
8	20	14	19	11			10	23	29	29		30	29
9	49	32	38		24	17	11	15	36	21		29	28
10	43	40	43		35	31	**Muir Middle, Burbank**						
11	42	39	34		52	31	6	54	58	56	55		
							7	60	69	64	65		
Burbank Unified School Dist.							8	56	66	57	56		
Burbank High, Burbank							**Options for Youth-Burbank Charter, Burbank**						
9	58	67	72		56	55	7	11	3	4	10		
10	67	79	79		67	64	8	22	5	6	15		
11	67	79	77		71	75	9	37	26	28		31	42
Burbank Middle, Burbank							10	49	31	38		35	43
6	44	43	56	56			11	51	38	43		42	40
7	57	55	69	65			**Providencia Elem., Burbank**						
8	60	64	62	64			2	46	62	67	52		
Burroughs High, Burbank							3	47	40	60	46		
9	66	64	66		63	57	4	47	60	64	60		
10	79	78	79		79	66	5	40	36	53	49		
11	75	73	74		67	61	**Roosevelt Elem., Burbank**						
Disney Elem., Burbank							2	57	42	63	48		
2	55	62	65	64			3	77	70	77	64		
3	51	61	65	70			4	75	57	77	74		
4	56	63	60	60			5	84	78	83	72		
5	42	48	42	45			**Stevenson Elem., Burbank**						
Edison Elem., Burbank							2	82	65	76	78		
2	67	52	73	56			3	64	68	65	48		
3	77	74	79	73			4	65	62	64	76		
4	66	58	65	59			5	80	62	74	53		
5	64	52	58	51			**Washington Elem., Burbank**						
Emerson Elem., Burbank							2	45	47	46	48		
2	60	63	68	58			3	51	71	69	59		
3	65	58	71	64			4	60	68	65	55		
4	70	77	75	63			5	64	73	72	63		
5	59	44	64	55									

Copyright © 2001 McCormack's Guides. No reproduction without permission.

STATE SCHOOL RANKINGS

Scores range from 1-99. A school scoring 75 has done better than 75 percent of other public schools in California.
Key: Rd (Reading), Ma (Math), Lg (Language), Sp (Spelling), Sci (Science) and SS (Social Science).

Castaic Union Elem. School Dist.

Castaic Elem., Castaic
Grade	Rd	Ma	Lg	Sp	Sci	SS
2	65	66	80	65		
3	77	88	85	73		

Castaic Middle, Castaic
Grade	Rd	Ma	Lg	Sp	Sci	SS
4	70	73	75	67		
5	64	69	61	61		
6	67	58	64	58		
7	62	65	58	68		
8	68	66	67	71		

Live Oak Elem., Castaic
Grade	Rd	Ma	Lg	Sp	Sci	SS
2	60	70	71	52		
3	55	54	62	50		

Centinela Valley High School Dist.

Hawthorne High, Hawthorne
Grade	Rd	Ma	Lg	Sp	Sci	SS
9	24	29	32		24	29
10	29	34	35		29	23
11	33	36	33		33	31

Lawndale High, Lawndale
Grade	Rd	Ma	Lg	Sp	Sci	SS
9	31	34	38		38	47
10	36	36	41		33	40
11	44	35	46		33	44

Leuzinger High, Lawndale
Grade	Rd	Ma	Lg	Sp	Sci	SS
9	14	22	19		18	19
10	11	26	23		20	21
11	19	30	21		22	28

Lloyde High (Cont.), Lawndale
Grade	Rd	Ma	Lg	Sp	Sci	SS
9	19	5	19		10	15
10	18	8	23		12	8
11	21	3	15		8	23

Charter Oak Unified School Dist.

Arrow High (Cont.), Glendora
Grade	Rd	Ma	Lg	Sp	Sci	SS
10	11	24	10		12	19
11	2	3	5		13	7

Badillo Elem., Covina
Grade	Rd	Ma	Lg	Sp	Sci	SS
2	48	58	61	56		
3	41	37	49	41		
4	49	53	49	59		
5	46	32	51	45		

Cedargrove Elem., Covina
Grade	Rd	Ma	Lg	Sp	Sci	SS
2	69	58	58	65		
3	67	71	66	62		
4	69	73	65	63		
5	64	55	61	53		

Charter Oak High, Covina
Grade	Rd	Ma	Lg	Sp	Sci	SS
9	69	68	64		69	62
10	77	65	73		69	66
11	77	73	74		65	69

Glen Oak Elem., Covina
Grade	Rd	Ma	Lg	Sp	Sci	SS
2	62	58	63	60		
3	55	25	40	57		
4	58	63	58	65		
5	53	46	54	53		

Oak Knoll (Alt.), Covina
Grade	Rd	Ma	Lg	Sp	Sci	SS
3	44	52	30	35		
6	50	31	52	20		
7	48	43	45	50		
9	47	19	27		21	27
10	38	26	23		54	47
11	21	19	11		40	10

Royal Oak Int., Covina
Grade	Rd	Ma	Lg	Sp	Sci	SS
6	50	47	40	52		
7	53	58	49	56		
8	60	64	55	64		

Washington Elem., Glendora
Grade	Rd	Ma	Lg	Sp	Sci	SS
2	69	70	64	56		
3	70	73	71	64		
4	70	73	75	74		
5	61	46	61	53		

Willow Elem., Glendora
Grade	Rd	Ma	Lg	Sp	Sci	SS
2	71	50	71	73		
3	80	82	77	79		
4	49	55	45	59		
5	53	36	40	55		

Claremont Unified School Dist.

Chaparral Elem., Claremont
Grade	Rd	Ma	Lg	Sp	Sci	SS
2	62	63	80	72		
3	85	82	86	75		
4	83	81	74	89		
5	89	91	88	93		
6	85	78	87	88		

Claremont High, Claremont
Grade	Rd	Ma	Lg	Sp	Sci	SS
9	89	89	88		93	88
10	94	89	94		91	90
11	96	94	95		93	91

Community Day
Grade	Rd	Ma	Lg	Sp	Sci	SS
7	24	29	12	39		
9	34	22	21		38	29

Condit Elem., Claremont
Grade	Rd	Ma	Lg	Sp	Sci	SS
2	85	85	87	87		
3	80	67	78	68		
4	87	75	80	75		
5	88	86	87	85		
6	89	85	88	86		

El Roble Int., Claremont
Grade	Rd	Ma	Lg	Sp	Sci	SS
7	82	72	79	76		
8	84	79	91	86		

Mountain View Elem., Claremont
Grade	Rd	Ma	Lg	Sp	Sci	SS
2	41	38	41	54		
3	60	65	66	64		
4	59	71	74	63		
5	53	32	64	47		
6	65	66	80	76		

Oakmont Elem., Claremont
Grade	Rd	Ma	Lg	Sp	Sci	SS
2	52	39	55	56		
3	52	40	57	59		
4	50	31	53	57		
5	53	38	56	61		
6	81	76	83	81		

STATE SCHOOL RANKINGS

Scores range from 1-99. A school scoring 75 has done better than 75 percent of other public schools in California.
Key: Rd (Reading), Ma (Math), Lg (Language), Sp (Spelling), Sci (Science) and SS (Social Science).

San Antonio High (Cont.), Claremont

Grade	Rd	Ma	Lg	Sp	Sci	SS
10	5	17	4		3	4
11	26	26	25	26		18

Sumner Elem., Claremont

Grade	Rd	Ma	Lg	Sp
2	77	70	69	69
3	72	70	68	64
4	78	68	78	70
5	77	67	77	73
6	79	76	67	73

Sycamore Elem., Claremont

Grade	Rd	Ma	Lg	Sp
2	69	55	64	54
3	85	52	65	53
4	92	63	84	81
5	86	58	78	65
6	92	64	80	81

Vista del Valle Elem., Claremont

Grade	Rd	Ma	Lg	Sp
2	26	17	13	46
3	27	12	40	25
4	30	26	40	22
5	48	48	66	53
6	60	50	69	62

Compton Unified School Dist.

Anderson Elem., Compton

Grade	Rd	Ma	Lg	Sp
2	11	3	6	8
3	1	1	1	3
4	2	1	1	7
5	1	1	1	1

Bunche Elem., Carson

Grade	Rd	Ma	Lg	Sp
2	25	42	17	47
3	11	7	5	26
4	13	6	11	44
5	21	30	8	38

Bunche Middle, Compton

Grade	Rd	Ma	Lg	Sp
5	1	1	1	1
6	2	3	1	5
7	6	10	5	12
8	8	15	9	13

Bursch Elem., Compton

Grade	Rd	Ma	Lg	Sp
2	22	24	11	28
3	19	8	17	19
4	28	31	38	30
5	30	30	29	36

Caldwell St. Elem., Compton

Grade	Rd	Ma	Lg	Sp
2	45	24	20	62
3	36	29	35	20
4	35	21	17	23
5	48	48	40	39

Carver Elem., Los Angeles

Grade	Rd	Ma	Lg	Sp
2	28	7	11	52
3	9	2	11	26
4	8	5	7	24
5	7	3	6	20

Centennial High, Compton

Grade	Rd	Ma	Lg	Sp	Sci	SS
9	9	16	20		9	6
10	16	18	31		18	9
11	46	33	30		23	10

Chavez Cont. High, Compton

Grade	Rd	Ma	Lg	Sp	Sci	SS
11	2	6	3		1	10

Compton Community Day Middle

Grade	Rd	Ma	Lg	Sp
8	1	1		2

Compton High, Compton

Grade	Rd	Ma	Lg	Sp	Sci	SS
9	9	21	20		7	8
10	12	25	25		13	6
11	19	34	24		17	16

Davis Middle, Compton

Grade	Rd	Ma	Lg	Sp
5	1	1	1	1
6	1	3	3	4
7	3	5	4	5
8	3	6	5	9

Dickison Elem., Compton

Grade	Rd	Ma	Lg	Sp
2	27	37	17	34
3	5	7	8	14
4	10	8	8	14
5	18	20	10	16

Dominguez High, Compton

Grade	Rd	Ma	Lg	Sp	Sci	SS
9	11	24	23		18	9
10	9	22	21		16	9
11	17	27	29		20	13

Emerson Elem., Compton

Grade	Rd	Ma	Lg	Sp
2	3	4	1	2
3	9	15	12	6
4	2	1	1	8
5	3	3	1	5

Enterprise Middle, Compton

Grade	Rd	Ma	Lg	Sp
5	2	1	1	1
6	8	12	12	14
7	9	8	16	19
8	17	17	24	34

Foster Elem., Compton

Grade	Rd	Ma	Lg	Sp
2	25	13	16	24
3	21	3	20	20
4	11	10	16	30
5	7	16	10	31

Jefferson Elem., Compton

Grade	Rd	Ma	Lg	Sp
2	13	21	10	32
3	12	16	20	15
4	4	10	7	8
5	31	50	35	54

Kelly Elem., Compton

Grade	Rd	Ma	Lg	Sp
2	27	28	17	22
3	5	7	7	14
4	11	12	9	17
5	9	11	12	18

Kennedy Elem., Compton

Grade	Rd	Ma	Lg	Sp
2	59	65	54	70
3	24	42	44	72
4	3	4	5	10
5	7	20	20	22

King Elem., Compton

Grade	Rd	Ma	Lg	Sp
2	19	7	14	11
3	4	3	4	14
4	2	2	4	11

STATE SCHOOL RANKINGS

Scores range from 1-99. A school scoring 75 has done better than 75 percent of other public schools in California.
Key: Rd (Reading), Ma (Math), Lg (Language), Sp (Spelling), Sci (Science) and SS (Social Science).

Laurel St. Elem., Compton

Grade	Rd	Ma	Lg	Sp	Sci	SS
2	43	55	64	56		
3	23	32	33	44		
4	11	26	24	21		

Lincoln Elem., Los Angeles

Grade	Rd	Ma	Lg	Sp
2	4	2	4	5
3	3	2	5	8
4	3	1	3	8
5	1	1	1	2

Longfellow Elem., Compton

Grade	Rd	Ma	Lg	Sp
2	8	3	7	11
3	9	4	18	26
4	3	1	6	11
5	3	1	9	14

Marshall, Compton

Grade	Rd	Ma	Lg	Sp	Sci	SS
9	15	10	10			
10	16	8	31			
11	15	10	15		1	8

Mayo Elem., Compton

Grade	Rd	Ma	Lg	Sp
2	30	19	11	48
3	21	48	24	24

McKinley Elem., Compton

Grade	Rd	Ma	Lg	Sp
2	6	6	1	16
3	7	16	8	10

McNair Elem., Compton

Grade	Rd	Ma	Lg	Sp
2	28	42	23	50
3	24	31	35	53
4	10	18	8	14
5	13	12	10	27

Roosevelt Elem., Compton

Grade	Rd	Ma	Lg	Sp
2	15	14	3	14
3	8	12	16	19
4	8	18	8	23
5	14	11	6	14

Roosevelt Middle, Compton

Grade	Rd	Ma	Lg	Sp
5	1	1	1	1
6	5	4	5	9
7	3	7	9	9
8	6	8	11	10

Rosecrans Elem., Compton

Grade	Rd	Ma	Lg	Sp
2	6	4	2	9
3	14	21	12	17
4	6	18	16	14
5	13	12	10	6

Tibby Elem., Compton

Grade	Rd	Ma	Lg	Sp
2	19	5	8	24
3	11	4	14	14
4	10	8	12	11
5	16	7	10	13

Tubman Cont. High, Compton

Grade	Rd	Ma	Lg	Sp	Sci	SS
10	48	75	6		1	1
11	17	3	11			1

Vanguard Learning Ctr, Los Angeles

Grade	Rd	Ma	Lg	Sp
4	28	25	26	62
5	13	15	20	20
6	29	40	27	53
7	14	16	22	16
8	38	9	23	42

Walton Middle, Compton

Grade	Rd	Ma	Lg	Sp
5	1	1	1	1
6	6	7	7	9
7	7	7	9	6
8	14	17	10	12

Washington Elem., Compton

Grade	Rd	Ma	Lg	Sp
2	7	2	3	12
3	12	8	12	17
4	8	4	11	8
5	9	12	10	11

Whaley Middle, Compton

Grade	Rd	Ma	Lg	Sp
5	1	1	1	1
6	3	2	2	4
7	5	5	7	8
8	4	9	6	9

Willard Elem., Compton

Grade	Rd	Ma	Lg	Sp
4	8	6	8	11
5	3	7	5	9

Willowbrook Middle, Compton

Grade	Rd	Ma	Lg	Sp
5	1	1	1	1
6	3	2	2	17
7	6	6	4	9
8	3	6	7	10

Covina Valley Unified School Dist.

Barranca Elem., Covina

Grade	Rd	Ma	Lg	Sp
2	55	52	47	54
3	65	60	65	59
4	65	73	62	57
5	76	85	75	87

Ben Lomond Elem., Covina

Grade	Rd	Ma	Lg	Sp
2	38	45	55	31
3	56	65	65	55
4	62	62	56	57
5	52	46	58	59

Covina Elem., Covina

Grade	Rd	Ma	Lg	Sp
2	43	45	49	44
3	32	45	36	32
4	25	16	36	29
5	25	13	18	16

Covina High, Covina

Grade	Rd	Ma	Lg	Sp	Sci	SS
9	62	64	66		50	57
10	60	56	62		54	59
11	67	58	77		60	65

Cypress Elem., Covina

Grade	Rd	Ma	Lg	Sp
2	43	50	53	35
3	30	17	25	18
4	41	21	33	20
5	45	38	44	39

Fair Valley High (Cont.), Covina

Grade	Rd	Ma	Lg	Sp	Sci	SS
9	14	20	6		9	29
10	9	5	10		12	6
11	21	9	23		22	20

Grovecenter Elem., West Covina

Grade	Rd	Ma	Lg	Sp
2	64	71	58	56
3	71	79	82	80
4	72	67	75	700
5	77	82	69	89

Copyright © 2001 McCormack's Guides. No reproduction without permission.

STATE SCHOOL RANKINGS

Scores range from 1-99. A school scoring 75 has done better than 75 percent of other public schools in California.
Key: Rd (Reading), Ma (Math), Lg (Language), Sp (Spelling), Sci (Science) and SS (Social Science).

Lark Ellen Elem., Covina

Grade	Rd	Ma	Lg	Sp	Sci	SS
2	30	28	55	42		
3	45	60	55	55		
4	34	42	27	26		
5	53	46	51	49		

Las Palmas Int., Covina

Grade	Rd	Ma	Lg	Sp	Sci	SS
6	37	31	25	36		
7	41	52	35	39		
8	34	39	33	38		

Manzanita Elem., Covina

Grade	Rd	Ma	Lg	Sp	Sci	SS
2	26	20	38	31		
3	30	37	25	28		
4	22	29	31	33		
5	26	29	30	21		

Merwin Elem., Irwindale

Grade	Rd	Ma	Lg	Sp	Sci	SS
2	32	33	31	42		
3	32	27	38	41		
4	43	63	56	52		
5	40	44	49	55		

Mesa Elem., West Covina

Grade	Rd	Ma	Lg	Sp	Sci	SS
2	71	75	81	78		
3	74	79	80	85		
4	70	78	80	73		
5	81	92	88	94		

Northview High, Covina

Grade	Rd	Ma	Lg	Sp	Sci	SS
9	41	48	44		38	52
10	50	62	54		53	55
11	49	63	56		48	57

Ranger High (Alt.), Covina

Grade	Rd	Ma	Lg	Sp	Sci	SS
9	39	26	21		28	37
10	60	22	37		49	31
11	61	30	27		30	

Rowland Ave. Elem., West Covina

Grade	Rd	Ma	Lg	Sp	Sci	SS
2	32	42	28	28		
3	52	68	60	55		
4	60	67	71	55		
5	52	69	62	57		

Sierra Vista Int., Covina

Grade	Rd	Ma	Lg	Sp	Sci	SS
6	61	65	60	74		
7	58	74	58	60		
8	56	64	59	56		

South Hills High, West Covina

Grade	Rd	Ma	Lg	Sp	Sci	SS
9	69	75	66		58	70
10	76	79	79		75	73
11	81	82	82		73	79

Traweek Int., West Covina

Grade	Rd	Ma	Lg	Sp	Sci	SS
6	38	45	47	48		
7	35	44	33	35		
8	45	49	46	57		

Valencia Elem., Covina

Grade	Rd	Ma	Lg	Sp	Sci	SS
2	38	45	55	58		
3	30	67	55	51		
4	28	42	29	38		
5	40	46	49	33		

Workman Ave. Elem., West Covina

Grade	Rd	Ma	Lg	Sp	Sci	SS
2	43	40	46	54		
3	30	47	33	25		
4	53	57	41	48		
5	40	44	35	39		

Culver City Unified School Dist.

Culver City Middle, Culver City

Grade	Rd	Ma	Lg	Sp	Sci	SS
6	53	38	44	60		
7	50	42	54	56		
8	60	51	59	57		

Culver City Sr. High, Culver City

Grade	Rd	Ma	Lg	Sp	Sci	SS
9	70	69	74		56	77
10	74	78	78		60	78
11	76	77	75		62	81

Culver Park Cont. High, Culver City

Grade	Rd	Ma	Lg	Sp	Sci	SS
9	39	18	28		14	37
10	31	31	23		29	32
11	24	6	31		17	28

El Marino Elem., Culver City

Grade	Rd	Ma	Lg	Sp	Sci	SS
2	86	87	87	85		
3	93	91	88	64		
4	94	94	92	86		
5	92	84	93	84		

El Rincon Elem., Culver City

Grade	Rd	Ma	Lg	Sp	Sci	SS
2	67	30	56	78		
3	77	54	77	84		
4	45	38	41	44		
5	46	38	53	57		

Farragut Elem., Culver City

Grade	Rd	Ma	Lg	Sp	Sci	SS
2	65	44	56	69		
3	71	47	54	73		
4	72	45	64	57		
5	68	65	78	70		

Howe Elem., Culver City

Grade	Rd	Ma	Lg	Sp	Sci	SS
2	50	50	46	64		
3	51	60	40	57		
4	59	63	51	59		
5	58	59	47	59		

La Ballona Elem., Culver City

Grade	Rd	Ma	Lg	Sp	Sci	SS
2	46	35	32	54		
3	45	22	35	59		
4	53	36	51	47		
5	50	55	56	57		

Downey Unified School Dist.

Alameda Elem., Downey

Grade	Rd	Ma	Lg	Sp	Sci	SS
2	71	85	88	75		
3	47	70	65	57		

Carpenter Elem., Downey

Grade	Rd	Ma	Lg	Sp	Sci	SS
4	27	36	37	33		
5	29	48	44	37		

Columbus (Cont.), Downey

Grade	Rd	Ma	Lg	Sp	Sci	SS
9	3	5	5		6	8
10	18	20	13		12	13
11	7	12	11		6	9

Downey High, Downey

Grade	Rd	Ma	Lg	Sp	Sci	SS
9	54	56	66		45	52
10	62	67	69		58	61
11	62	63	63		48	57

East Middle, Downey

Grade	Rd	Ma	Lg	Sp	Sci	SS
6	42	56	67	58		
7	48	44	66	60		
8	49	41	61	53		

STATE SCHOOL RANKINGS

Scores range from 1-99. A school scoring 75 has done better than 75 percent of other public schools in California.
Key: Rd (Reading), Ma (Math), Lg (Language), Sp (Spelling), Sci (Science) and SS (Social Science).

Gallatin Elem., Downey

Grade	Rd	Ma	Lg	Sp	Sci	SS
2	65	79	76	78		
3	55	49	59	62		
4	49	60	58	69		
5	64	78	77	70		

Gauldin Elem., Downey

Grade	Rd	Ma	Lg	Sp	Sci	SS
2	50	62	71	62		
3	37	40	38	53		
4	17	19	26	29		
5	28	31	54	37		

Griffiths Middle, Downey

Grade	Rd	Ma	Lg	Sp	Sci	SS
6	38	52	60	50		
7	55	58	63	63		
8	53	54	62	71		

Imperial Elem., Downey

Grade	Rd	Ma	Lg	Sp	Sci	SS
2	60	78	71	69		
3	42	42	52	46		

Lewis Elem., Downey

Grade	Rd	Ma	Lg	Sp	Sci	SS
2	35	63	56	46		
3	44	56	49	43		
4	36	46	49	47		
5	52	62	61	63		

Old River Elem., Downey

Grade	Rd	Ma	Lg	Sp	Sci	SS
4	50	53	54	55		
5	36	43	44	43		

Pace Elem., Downey

Grade	Rd	Ma	Lg	Sp	Sci	SS
2	32	66	50	29		
3	55	70	55	41		

Price Elem., Downey

Grade	Rd	Ma	Lg	Sp	Sci	SS
2	45	65	68	52		
3	60	77	69	79		
4	44	52	45	45		
5	43	24	49	43		

Rio Hondo Elem., Downey

Grade	Rd	Ma	Lg	Sp	Sci	SS
2	55	53	72	54		
3	36	42	49	51		
4	43	45	56	50		
5	65	81	87	68		

Rio San Gabriel Elem., Downey

Grade	Rd	Ma	Lg	Sp	Sci	SS
2	62	85	88	65		
3	58	79	68	62		
4	55	71	81	60		
5	61	82	75	73		

South Middle, Downey

Grade	Rd	Ma	Lg	Sp	Sci	SS
6	29	40	34	38		
7	38	46	40	41		
8	36	39	42	43		

Unsworth Elem., Downey

Grade	Rd	Ma	Lg	Sp	Sci	SS
2	50	71	73	60		
3	37	38	44	41		
4	41	46	54	52		
5	39	53	64	51		

Ward Elem., Downey

Grade	Rd	Ma	Lg	Sp	Sci	SS
2	40	79	67	48		
3	41	35	36	41		

Warren High, Downey

Grade	Rd	Ma	Lg	Sp	Sci	SS
9	55	54	67		47	52
10	64	72	70		55	64
11	63	63	63		50	55

West Middle, Downey

Grade	Rd	Ma	Lg	Sp	Sci	SS
6	40	33	52	46		
7	48	37	56	47		
8	46	45	50	48		

Williams Elem., Downey

Grade	Rd	Ma	Lg	Sp	Sci	SS
2	43	58	56	52		
3	51	61	49	64		

Duarte Unified School Dist.

Andres Duarte Elem., Duarte

Grade	Rd	Ma	Lg	Sp	Sci	SS
2	23	28	17	42		
3	9	16	8	12		
4	17	19	10	26		
5	12	13	16	19		
6	17	27	25	40		

Beardslee Elem., Duarte

Grade	Rd	Ma	Lg	Sp	Sci	SS
2	25	35	35	31		
3	32	71	38	53		
4	41	65	56	76		
5	18	50	29	22		
6	34	55	44	44		

Duarte High, Duarte

Grade	Rd	Ma	Lg	Sp	Sci	SS
9	44	53	46		40	37
10	41	46	41		33	43
11	39	40	34		39	38

Maxwell Elem., Duarte

Grade	Rd	Ma	Lg	Sp	Sci	SS
2	9	27	13	2		
3	3	32	5	9		
4	11	27	27	8		
5	4	5	4	2		
6	8	13	9	9		

Mt. Olive Alt. Ed., Duarte

Grade	Rd	Ma	Lg	Sp	Sci	SS
9	24	28	25		40	40
10	45	49	31		47	82
11	5	22	17		38	31

Northview Int., Duarte

Grade	Rd	Ma	Lg	Sp	Sci	SS
7	36	32	42	33		
8	38	35	39	33		

Royal Oaks Elem., Duarte

Grade	Rd	Ma	Lg	Sp	Sci	SS
2	80	73	68	73		
3	55	71	69	80		
4	56	60	62	67		
5	45	50	45	39		
6	48	60	47	48		

Valley View Elem., Duarte

Grade	Rd	Ma	Lg	Sp	Sci	SS
2	33	39	32	35		
3	30	52	25	30		
4	45	71	64	48		
5	42	71	53	47		
6	46	60	50	74		

East Whittier City Elem. School Dist.

Ceres Elem., Whittier

Grade	Rd	Ma	Lg	Sp	Sci	SS
2	9	11	18	15		
3	19	4	12	6		
4	16	22	18	15		
5	12	16	14	10		

STATE SCHOOL RANKINGS

Scores range from 1-99. A school scoring 75 has done better than 75 percent of other public schools in California.
Key: Rd (Reading), Ma (Math), Lg (Language), Sp (Spelling), Sci (Science) and SS (Social Science).

East Whittier Middle, Whittier

Grade	Rd	Ma	Lg	Sp	Sci	SS
6	34	25	22	22		
7	35	35	26	31		
8	42	39	36	33		

Evergreen Elem., Whittier

Grade	Rd	Ma	Lg	Sp
2	6	20	9	5
3	13	27	9	10
4	20	45	22	26
5	28	33	37	18

Granada Middle, Whittier

Grade	Rd	Ma	Lg	Sp
6	53	30	44	51
7	62	54	60	74
8	56	62	53	67

Hillview Middle, Whittier

Grade	Rd	Ma	Lg	Sp
6	24	16	25	26
7	38	31	40	39
8	42	37	44	43

La Colima Elem., Whittier

Grade	Rd	Ma	Lg	Sp
2	33	52	43	33
3	47	56	44	35
4	37	27	22	35
5	42	19	25	35

Laurel Elem., Whittier

Grade	Rd	Ma	Lg	Sp
2	25	55	31	28
3	41	34	38	37
4	47	53	56	47
5	43	50	47	41

Leffingwell Elem., Whittier

Grade	Rd	Ma	Lg	Sp
2	52	49	73	44
3	72	68	69	73
4	75	76	80	77
5	55	53	64	57

Mulberry Elem., Whittier

Grade	Rd	Ma	Lg	Sp
2	30	32	38	29
3	41	49	42	41
4	37	29	40	29
5	42	36	37	41

Murphy Ranch Elem., Whittier

Grade	Rd	Ma	Lg	Sp
2	79	93	91	69
3	85	85	82	64
4	86	94	88	84
5	83	88	82	82

Ocean View Elem., Whittier

Grade	Rd	Ma	Lg	Sp
2	66	79	84	69
3	81	79	81	73
4	73	80	78	63
5	73	72	74	69

Orchard Dale Elem., Whittier

Grade	Rd	Ma	Lg	Sp
2	59	79	72	56
3	51	65	55	57
4	49	38	56	45
5	58	64	74	70

Scott Ave. Elem., Whittier

Grade	Rd	Ma	Lg	Sp
2	59	50	47	60
3	58	61	54	57
4	60	63	53	65
5	55	65	60	63

Eastside Union Elem. School Dist.

Cole Middle, Lancaster

Grade	Rd	Ma	Lg	Sp
6	21	15	20	15
7	29	16	28	30
8	47	39	53	54

Eastside Elem., Lancaster

Grade	Rd	Ma	Lg	Sp
2	25	27	25	14
3	19	16	15	10
4	28	16	22	13
5	19	19	22	22

Tierra Bonita North Elem., Lancaster

Grade	Rd	Ma	Lg	Sp
2	26	19	35	22
3	36	30	35	28

Tierra Bonita South Elem., Lancaster

Grade	Rd	Ma	Lg	Sp
3	39	22	38	28
4	36	24	27	29
5	31	19	23	27

El Monte City Elem. School Dist.

Cherrylee Elem., El Monte

Grade	Rd	Ma	Lg	Sp
2	38	16	37	33
3	31	28	35	28
4	47	38	53	55
5	52	61	56	43
6	35	53	50	32

Cleminson Elem., Temple City

Grade	Rd	Ma	Lg	Sp
2	60	68	67	64
3	54	65	66	62
4	52	45	56	47
5	43	50	51	49
6	37	47	50	55

Columbia Elem., El Monte

Grade	Rd	Ma	Lg	Sp
2	3	1	5	7
3	10	14	20	10
4	11	6	9	8
5	5	12	6	7
6	11	24	33	12
7	30	54	47	33
8	13	21	33	22

Cortada Elem., El Monte

Grade	Rd	Ma	Lg	Sp
2	30	45	32	44
3	15	30	17	35
4	11	26	17	22
5	28	53	40	52
6	18	36	25	32

Durfee Elem., El Monte

Grade	Rd	Ma	Lg	Sp
4	21	22	26	28
5	18	21	14	14
6	30	33	25	27
7	41	60	54	54
8	29	39	46	43

Gidley Elem., El Monte

Grade	Rd	Ma	Lg	Sp
2	40	66	65	64
3	51	35	52	55
4	33	27	24	49
5	62	80	82	87
6	17	22	20	15
7	20	28	31	21
8	30	37	44	41

STATE SCHOOL RANKINGS

Scores range from 1-99. A school scoring 75 has done better than 75 percent of other public schools in California.
Key: Rd (Reading), Ma (Math), Lg (Language), Sp (Spelling), Sci (Science) and SS (Social Science).

Grade	Rd	Ma	Lg	Sp	Sci	SS
Legore Elem., El Monte						
2	20	20	20	17		
3	6	8	11	7		
4	21	42	30	13		
5	23	33	40	19		
6	53	71	80	71		
Loma Elem., South El Monte						
2	4	7	7	1		
3	1	1	1	1		
4	1	4	3	1		
5	16	29	13	6		
6	1	9	2	1		
Mulhall Elem., El Monte						
2	23	6	12	29		
3	7	4	6	7		
4	6	17	12	10		
5	33	58	38	22		
6	26	36	27	12		
New Lexington Elem., El Monte						
2	13	6	9	13		
3	10	12	12	28		
4	16	26	13	10		
5	23	36	29	29		
6	20	38	38	29		
Norwood Elem., El Monte						
2	30	16	40	33		
3	27	19	26	51		
4	21	24	30	22		
5	34	33	40	45		
6	38	40	52	44		
Potrero Elem., El Monte						
2	4	23	4	3		
3	3	16	12	6		
4	8	35	17	8		
5	5	48	23	16		
6	6	24	14	15		
7	11	19	10	15		
8	22	37	31	18		
Rio Hondo Elem., Arcadia						
2	41	45	52	42		
3	26	19	20	32		
4	36	27	37	47		
5	37	38	45	53		
6	23	24	30	36		
7	36	47	52	54		
8	36	45	59	62		
Rio Vista Elem., El Monte						
2	53	58	61	73		
3	45	58	44	68		
4	47	65	56	47		
5	25	40	38	52		
6	53	47	64	55		
Shirpser Elem., El Monte						
2	16	13	9	10		
3	5	20	12	5		
4	8	13	6	4		
5	12	22	20	7		

Grade	Rd	Ma	Lg	Sp	Sci	SS
Thompson-Durfee Elem., El Monte						
2	18	22	21	24		
3	32	30	36	37		
Wilkerson Elem., El Monte						
2	25	39	23	20		
3	21	40	26	39		
4	30	46	41	31		
5	29	65	47	47		
6	26	53	34	42		
Wright Elem., El Monte						
2	57	42	49	58		
3	12	9	15	15		
4	17	17	13	10		
5	29	29	33	18		
6	17	31	27	22		
7	30	42	34	29		
8	31	37	39	39		

El Monte Union High School Dist.

Grade	Rd	Ma	Lg	Sp	Sci	SS
Arroyo High, El Monte						
9	37	44	47		38	37
10	53	59	60		43	53
11	55	63	57		55	65
El Monte High, El Monte						
9	21	32	28		26	29
10	38	50	41		36	43
11	45	47	45		35	49
Mountain View High, El Monte						
9	28	40	30		36	29
10	41	52	40		43	37
11	49	54	48		42	40
Rosemead High, Rosemead						
9	52	64	57		50	57
10	54	76	59		55	56
11	63	85	75		64	61
South El Monte High, South El Monte						
9	19	37	25		31	23
10	36	57	41		43	43
11	51	60	54		46	54
Valle Lindo Cont.High, El Monte						
9	7	9	10		12	15
10	15	8	8		10	13
11	19	22	15		24	18

El Rancho Unified School Dist.

Grade	Rd	Ma	Lg	Sp	Sci	SS
Birney Elem., Pico Rivera						
2	43	28	41	56		
3	32	32	23	30		
4	41	42	37	33		
5	40	41	42	35		
Burke Middle, Pico Rivera						
6	24	19	27	27		
7	32	35	34	30		
8	27	32	33	39		
Durfee Elem., Pico Rivera						
2	35	25	44	33		
3	19	8	15	18		
4	41	18	20	35		
5	50	31	54	47		

STATE SCHOOL RANKINGS

Scores range from 1-99. A school scoring 75 has done better than 75 percent of other public schools in California.
Key: Rd (Reading), Ma (Math), Lg (Language), Sp (Spelling), Sci (Science) and SS (Social Science).

El Rancho High, Pico Rivera

Grade	Rd	Ma	Lg	Sp	Sci	SS
9	24	40	36		34	40
10	32	48	48		37	35
11	39	50	53		39	47

Magee Elem., Pico Rivera

Grade	Rd	Ma	Lg	Sp
2	30	20	25	35
3	26	38	30	30
4	21	26	20	20
5	33	44	37	33

Meller Elem., Pico Rivera

Grade	Rd	Ma	Lg	Sp
2	26	22	25	33
3	41	47	40	43
4	28	11	31	31
5	26	17	27	33

North Park Middle, Pico Rivera

Grade	Rd	Ma	Lg	Sp
6	12	10	8	11
7	18	7	15	15
8	18	12	19	17

North Ranchito Elem., Pico Rivera

Grade	Rd	Ma	Lg	Sp
2	26	17	21	15
3	39	52	59	64
4	30	33	30	29
5	7	13	20	9

Obregon Elem., Pico Rivera

Grade	Rd	Ma	Lg	Sp
2	17	5	18	15
3	17	23	20	37
4	52	42	40	24

Pio Pico Elem., Pico Rivera

Grade	Rd	Ma	Lg	Sp
2	6	1	5	14
3	21	17	18	16
4	14	9	5	8
5	26	33	33	25

Rio Vista Elem., Pico Rivera

Grade	Rd	Ma	Lg	Sp
2	43	40	38	33
3	39	38	42	48
4	43	35	43	42
5	37	21	42	31

Rivera Elem., Pico Rivera

Grade	Rd	Ma	Lg	Sp
2	16	15	14	26
3	27	25	33	41
4	34	35	37	42
5	23	12	29	29

Rivera Middle, Pico Rivera

Grade	Rd	Ma	Lg	Sp
6	18	19	23	18
7	27	26	32	26
8	34	28	43	33

Salazar Cont., Pico Rivera

Grade	Rd	Ma	Lg	Sp	Sci	SS
11	2	4	5		10	7

Selby Grove Elem., Pico Rivera

Grade	Rd	Ma	Lg	Sp
2	38	30	32	42
3	29	28	31	41
4	12	5	7	8
5	25	17	18	19

South Ranchito Elem., Pico Rivera

Grade	Rd	Ma	Lg	Sp
2	50	73	72	62
3	41	34	45	53
4	21	18	24	22
5	19	24	25	22

Valencia Elem., Pico Rivera

Grade	Rd	Ma	Lg	Sp
2	25	27	24	32
3	36	19	35	22
4	27	23	33	28
5	34	19	25	33

El Segundo Unified School Dist.

Arena High (Cont.), El Segundo

Grade	Rd	Ma	Lg	Sp	Sci	SS
10	36	44	43		41	41
11	42	12	34		29	10

Center St. Elem., El Segundo

Grade	Rd	Ma	Lg	Sp
2	89	89	86	88
3	90	85	88	85
4	86	90	88	86
5	85	89	87	87

El Segundo High, El Segundo

Grade	Rd	Ma	Lg	Sp	Sci	SS
9	92	89	92		92	89
10	92	96	94		91	90
11	95	94	95		94	95

El Segundo Middle, El Segundo

Grade	Rd	Ma	Lg	Sp
6	81	89	78	88
7	86	93	82	85
8	84	92	85	83

Garvey Elem. School Dist.

Bitely Elem., Rosemead

Grade	Rd	Ma	Lg	Sp
2	11	13	6	17
3	17	25	26	46
4	25	44	45	35
5	19	33	22	18
6	35	56	46	34

Dewey Ave. Elem., San Gabriel

Grade	Rd	Ma	Lg	Sp
2	36	27	25	69
3	36	63	40	75
4	36	42	40	55
5	48	62	66	81
6	48	66	67	52

Duff Elem., Rosemead

Grade	Rd	Ma	Lg	Sp
2	22	7	20	44
3	17	20	15	55
4	33	18	37	40
5	21	8	8	35
6	32	38	23	30

Emerson Elem., Rosemead

Grade	Rd	Ma	Lg	Sp
2	43	55	45	62
3	42	47	52	79
4	44	70	58	70
5	52	67	58	74
6	56	73	60	69

Garvey Int., Rosemead

Grade	Rd	Ma	Lg	Sp
7	37	52	40	54
8	36	54	48	59

Hillcrest Elem., Monterey Park

Grade	Rd	Ma	Lg	Sp
2	57	57	60	62
3	55	58	66	70
4	59	81	77	86
5	53	68	61	72
6	70	85	82	83

STATE SCHOOL RANKINGS

Scores range from 1-99. A school scoring 75 has done better than 75 percent of other public schools in California.
Key: Rd (Reading), Ma (Math), Lg (Language), Sp (Spelling), Sci (Science) and SS (Social Science).

Marshall Elem., San Gabriel

Grade	Rd	Ma	Lg	Sp	Sci	SS
2	9	10	7	17		
3	19	49	42	59		
4	47	63	54	60		
5	31	28	32	49		
6	48	68	56	66		

Monterey Vista Elem., Monterey Park

Grade	Rd	Ma	Lg	Sp	Sci	SS
2	41	62	51	69		
3	34	61	49	68		
4	37	52	40	65		
5	65	72	60	86		
6	42	63	58	80		

Rice Elem., Rosemead

Grade	Rd	Ma	Lg	Sp	Sci	SS
2	32	20	28	48		
3	29	38	35	51		
4	34	36	53	44		
5	18	40	40	39		
6	29	43	44	36		

Sanchez Elem., Rosemead

Grade	Rd	Ma	Lg	Sp	Sci	SS
2	41	60	49	60		
3	55	79	70	89		
4	36	53	51	54		
5	19	33	40	41		
6	35	55	34	40		

Temple Int., Rosemead

Grade	Rd	Ma	Lg	Sp	Sci	SS
7	26	32	34	39		
8	20	33	28	31		

Willard Elem., Rosemead

Grade	Rd	Ma	Lg	Sp	Sci	SS
2	21	35	26	38		
3	21	76	42	55		
4	41	67	56	55		
5	31	53	44	41		
6	24	42	30	30		

Williams Elem., Rosemead

Grade	Rd	Ma	Lg	Sp	Sci	SS
2	71	93	75	83		
3	22	42	26	48		
4	49	53	60	54		
5	26	52	38	57		
6	23	55	30	58		

Glendale Unified School Dist.

Balboa Elem., Glendale

Grade	Rd	Ma	Lg	Sp	Sci	SS
2	55	63	60	64		
3	37	42	44	39		
4	50	71	60	62		
5	46	74	68	47		
6	61	79	74	48		

Cerritos Elem., Glendale

Grade	Rd	Ma	Lg	Sp	Sci	SS
2	20	25	31	33		
3	27	34	42	24		
4	19	33	30	31		
5	21	44	47	29		
6	37	50	42	34		

Clark Magnet High, La Crescenta

Grade	Rd	Ma	Lg	Sp	Sci	SS
9	92	96	97		91	92
10	93	97	97		89	88
11	88	97	95		82	88

Columbus Elem., Glendale

Grade	Rd	Ma	Lg	Sp	Sci	SS
2	30	39	45	33		
3	47	45	52	53		
4	45	58	54	62		
5	28	44	37	25		
6	44	56	54	40		

Crescenta Valley Sr. High, La Crescenta

Grade	Rd	Ma	Lg	Sp	Sci	SS
9	87	91	93		85	86
10	91	95	96		89	88
11	88	95	91		88	88

Daily High (Cont.), Glendale

Grade	Rd	Ma	Lg	Sp	Sci	SS
10	9	14	16		7	19
11	11	16	14		6	12

Dunsmore Elem., La Crescenta

Grade	Rd	Ma	Lg	Sp	Sci	SS
2	89	90	91	92		
3	92	97	85	95		
4	91	82	83	92		
5	90	86	89	85		
6	95	93	93	93		

Edison Elem., Glendale

Grade	Rd	Ma	Lg	Sp	Sci	SS
2	35	71	45	44		
3	29	47	33	43		
4	24	45	30	29		
5	19	28	23	23		
6	26	38	36	38		

Franklin Elem., Glendale

Grade	Rd	Ma	Lg	Sp	Sci	SS
2	40	47	60	62		
3	44	70	60	57		
4	60	71	69	76		
5	33	34	38	33		
6	38	60	50	22		

Fremont Elem., Glendale

Grade	Rd	Ma	Lg	Sp	Sci	SS
2	67	65	78	78		
3	73	70	72	70		
4	81	86	93	91		
5	86	85	90	86		
6	82	88	84	85		

Glendale Alt. High, Glendale

Grade	Rd	Ma	Lg	Sp	Sci	SS
11	1	4	1		4	1

Glendale Sr. High, Glendale

Grade	Rd	Ma	Lg	Sp	Sci	SS
9	43	58	74		43	45
10	50	63	65		43	45
11	55	74	79		52	62

Glenoaks Elem., Glendale

Grade	Rd	Ma	Lg	Sp	Sci	SS
2	81	84	81	90		
3	83	82	85	82		
4	83	84	84	89		
5	74	91	86	79		
6	84	88	90	93		

Hoover Sr. High, Glendale

Grade	Rd	Ma	Lg	Sp	Sci	SS
9	52	69	68		47	45
10	56	70	65		61	53
11	57	77	65		53	58

Jefferson Elem., Glendale

Grade	Rd	Ma	Lg	Sp	Sci	SS
2	28	44	37	29		
3	29	47	44	53		
4	28	42	47	29		
5	26	50	54	29		
6	50	45	58	38		

STATE SCHOOL RANKINGS

Scores range from 1-99. A school scoring 75 has done better than 75 percent of other public schools in California.
Key: Rd (Reading), Ma (Math), Lg (Language), Sp (Spelling), Sci (Science) and SS (Social Science).

Keppel Elem., Glendale

Grade	Rd	Ma	Lg	Sp	Sci	SS
2	53	63	63	65		
3	76	79	82	82		
4	65	80	71	69		
5	73	85	82	81		
6	72	85	80	86		

La Crescenta Elem., La Crescenta

Grade	Rd	Ma	Lg	Sp	Sci	SS
2	81	82	90	90		
3	71	76	75	84		
4	78	86	91	84		
5	70	80	72	77		
6	67	85	82	85		

Lincoln Elem., La Crescenta

Grade	Rd	Ma	Lg	Sp	Sci	SS
2	74	76	79	73		
3	73	82	84	86		
4	75	81	78	86		
5	70	77	84	78		
6	82	85	91	94		

Mann Elem., Glendale

Grade	Rd	Ma	Lg	Sp	Sci	SS
2	30	53	41	29		
3	22	27	30	32		
4	31	48	43	35		
5	25	26	35	25		
6	27	38	44	36		

Marshall Elem., Glendale

Grade	Rd	Ma	Lg	Sp	Sci	SS
2	33	44	37	46		
3	32	38	44	53		
4	30	42	31	40		
5	31	50	53	39		
6	40	53	60	56		

Monte Vista Elem., La Crescenta

Grade	Rd	Ma	Lg	Sp	Sci	SS
2	90	89	88	90		
3	93	91	90	95		
4	85	93	95	87		
5	83	85	90	87		
6	96	96	97	97		

Mountain Ave. Elem., La Crescenta

Grade	Rd	Ma	Lg	Sp	Sci	SS
2	86	90	90	88		
3	88	91	92	92		
4	91	94	96	94		
5	84	96	90	87		
6	93	96	98	95		

Muir Elem., Glendale

Grade	Rd	Ma	Lg	Sp	Sci	SS
2	25	47	41	26		
3	36	44	51	53		
4	33	42	45	38		
5	31	40	47	33		
6	29	50	47	25		

Roosevelt Middle, Glendale

Grade	Rd	Ma	Lg	Sp	Sci	SS
7	20	44	32	26		
8	26	45	34	24		

Rosemont Middle, La Crescenta

Grade	Rd	Ma	Lg	Sp	Sci	SS
7	87	89	90	90		
8	84	87	89	81		

Toll Middle Jr. High, Glendale

Grade	Rd	Ma	Lg	Sp	Sci	SS
7	46	76	68	65		
8	47	70	64	57		

Valley View Elem., La Crescenta

Grade	Rd	Ma	Lg	Sp	Sci	SS
2	89	94	91	98		
3	80	94	86	89		
4	87	97	94	94		
5	81	88	83	85		
6	89	97	95	96		

Verdugo Woodlands Elem., Glendale

Grade	Rd	Ma	Lg	Sp	Sci	SS
2	71	70	71	83		
3	76	84	77	84		
4	77	88	89	77		
5	76	88	87	82		
6	88	94	90	93		

White Elem., Glendale

Grade	Rd	Ma	Lg	Sp	Sci	SS
2	53	63	63	54		
3	45	51	57	59		
4	55	60	67	50		
5	46	62	68	43		
6	46	56	64	53		

Wilson Middle, Glendale

Grade	Rd	Ma	Lg	Sp	Sci	SS
7	57	81	68	65		
8	55	70	71	62		

Glendora Unified School Dist.

Cullen Elem., Glendora

Grade	Rd	Ma	Lg	Sp	Sci	SS
2	71	73	86	72		
3	84	71	81	73		
4	81	63	75	71		
5	88	88	79	85		

Glendora High, Glendora

Grade	Rd	Ma	Lg	Sp	Sci	SS
9	85	91	85		87	89
10	90	91	85		90	90
11	90	89	87		89	84

Goddard Middle, Glendora

Grade	Rd	Ma	Lg	Sp	Sci	SS
6	78	86	75	81		
7	80	82	79	86		
8	84	85	82	85		

La Fetra Elem., Glendora

Grade	Rd	Ma	Lg	Sp	Sci	SS
2	50	58	61	54		
3	60	54	68	64		
4	66	55	53	54		
5	71	86	82	78		

Sandburg Middle, Glendora

Grade	Rd	Ma	Lg	Sp	Sci	SS
6	69	65	69	64		
7	77	76	82	83		
8	68	64	67	71		

Sellers Elem., Glendora

Grade	Rd	Ma	Lg	Sp	Sci	SS
2	81	73	69	83		
3	90	77	88	86		
4	86	80	75	82		
5	84	73	78	91		

Stanton Elem., Glendora

Grade	Rd	Ma	Lg	Sp	Sci	SS
2	62	68	72	62		
3	70	70	85	66		
4	60	46	67	57		
5	68	61	68	65		

48 STATE SCHOOL RANKINGS

Scores range from 1-99. A school scoring 75 has done better than 75 percent of other public schools in California.
Key: Rd (Reading), Ma (Math), Lg (Language), Sp (Spelling), Sci (Science) and SS (Social Science).

Sutherland Elem., Glendora

Grade	Rd	Ma	Lg	Sp	Sci	SS
2	83	87	89	78		
3	74	81	71	64		
4	74	81	74	67		
5	86	78	81	79		

Whitcomb Cont. High, Glendora

Grade	Rd	Ma	Lg	Sp	Sci	SS
9	19	13	5		20	3
10	11	2	16		29	1
11	15	4	14		17	18

Williams Elem., Glendora

Grade	Rd	Ma	Lg	Sp
2	64	57	75	65
3	64	58	65	84
4	63	52	54	54
5	66	67	63	70

Gorman Elem. School Dist.

Gorman Elem., Gorman

Grade	Rd	Ma	Lg	Sp
3	32	19	23	20
4	27	21	31	38

Gorman Learning Ctr, Glendora

Grade	Rd	Ma	Lg	Sp	Sci	SS
2	74	55	55	52		
3	73	40	55	59		
4	78	55	54	73		
5	77	58	61	82		
6	79	57	52	60		
7	77	67	63	71		
8	46	23	21	34		
9	83	64	57		73	77
10	70	50	53		59	67
11	90	60	71		89	85

Hacienda La Puente Unified School Dist.

Baldwin Acad. Elem., La Puente

Grade	Rd	Ma	Lg	Sp
2	28	18	24	36
3	19	22	22	24
4	15	20	22	13
5	14	30	24	16

Bixby Elem., Hacienda Heights

Grade	Rd	Ma	Lg	Sp
2	38	40	40	47
3	41	32	42	62
4	41	57	49	52
5	37	36	58	49

California Elem., La Puente

Grade	Rd	Ma	Lg	Sp
2	28	15	16	34
3	26	23	25	35
4	32	38	38	47
5	33	23	25	31

Cedarlane Middle, Hacienda Heights

Grade	Rd	Ma	Lg	Sp
6	46	60	44	64
7	42	52	45	48
8	57	62	53	79

Del Valle Elem., La Puente

Grade	Rd	Ma	Lg	Sp
2	12	19	11	21
3	14	18	20	17
4	11	6	11	10
5	7	23	16	9

Fairgrove Acad., Hacienda Heights

Grade	Rd	Ma	Lg	Sp
2	48	67	58	60
3	41	51	44	60
4	58	38	40	45
5	48	35	29	49
6	25	18	17	17
7	50	44	45	60
8	44	43	34	42

Glenelder Elem., Hacienda Heights

Grade	Rd	Ma	Lg	Sp
2	8	13	12	12
3	9	1	4	5
4	24	21	38	39
5	31	18	35	39

Grandview Elem., Valinda

Grade	Rd	Ma	Lg	Sp
2	18	30	28	24
3	23	51	25	33
4	21	44	21	19
5	11	6	3	6
6	25	21	15	17
7	19	15	21	24
8	24	18	28	29

Grazide Elem., Hacienda Heights

Grade	Rd	Ma	Lg	Sp
2	86	95	90	99
3	87	99	90	99
4	77	95	80	92
5	91	98	95	98

Kwis Elem., Hacienda Heights

Grade	Rd	Ma	Lg	Sp
2	37	52	42	26
3	31	11	18	15
4	38	52	38	40
5	33	31	29	44

La Puente High, La Puente

Grade	Rd	Ma	Lg	Sp	Sci	SS
9	39	34	26		29	35
10	30	41	33		29	35
11	45	43	31		27	37

Lassalette Elem., La Puente

Grade	Rd	Ma	Lg	Sp
2	20	54	19	28
3	19	25	9	22
4	15	28	11	13
5	14	26	13	8
6	20	28	16	10
7	30	69	42	29

Los Altos Elem., Hacienda Heights

Grade	Rd	Ma	Lg	Sp
2	72	89	82	97
3	80	90	93	95
4	68	79	84	90
5	80	95	93	97

Los Altos High, Hacienda Heights

Grade	Rd	Ma	Lg	Sp	Sci	SS
9	70	81	76		69	74
10	69	83	70		65	71
11	75	88	74		72	71

Los Molinos Elem., Hacienda Heights

Grade	Rd	Ma	Lg	Sp
2	90	92	86	98
3	80	91	91	98
4	77	83	87	90
5	80	82	79	92

STATE SCHOOL RANKINGS

Scores range from 1-99. A school scoring 75 has done better than 75 percent of other public schools in California.
Key: Rd (Reading), Ma (Math), Lg (Language), Sp (Spelling), Sci (Science) and SS (Social Science).

Los Robles Acad., Hacienda Heights

Grade	Rd	Ma	Lg	Sp	Sci	SS
2	56	55	34	52		
3	47	39	49	53		
4	52	59	60	62		
5	70	68	79	74		

Mesa Robles Elem., Hacienda Heights

Grade	Rd	Ma	Lg	Sp	Sci	SS
2	77	76	81	92		
3	61	68	78	82		
4	77	86	81	86		
5	91	98	91	96		
6	85	95	86	93		
7	82	96	90	91		
8	85	96	91	97		

Nelson Elem., La Puente

Grade	Rd	Ma	Lg	Sp	Sci	SS
2	19	29	20	22		
3	29	31	37	31		
4	32	45	40	26		
5	25	35	31	27		

Newton Middle, Hacienda Heights

Grade	Rd	Ma	Lg	Sp	Sci	SS
6	62	69	76	71		
7	68	75	63	80		
8	70	88	71	92		

Opport. for Learning-Hacienda La Puente

Grade	Rd	Ma	Lg	Sp	Sci	SS
2	37	10	15	32		
3	44	5	16	19		
4	54	31	30	44		
5	67	31	49	46		
6	55	46	27	55		
7	43	11	27	35		
8	34	16	30	27		
9	34	21	27		29	30
10	39	27	33		36	38
11	46	30	38		41	31

Orange Grove Middle, Hacienda Heights

Grade	Rd	Ma	Lg	Sp	Sci	SS
6	55	48	52	62		
7	65	63	63	60		
8	70	64	63	76		

Palm Elem., Hacienda Heights

Grade	Rd	Ma	Lg	Sp	Sci	SS
2	24	32	39	38		
3	28	27	38	46		
4	35	33	51	44		
5	39	33	37	49		

Puente Hills High (Alt.), La Puente

Grade	Rd	Ma	Lg	Sp	Sci	SS
9	39	13	20		27	19
10	30	25	29		25	35
11	37	35	29		29	22

Shadybend Elem., Hacienda Heights

Grade	Rd	Ma	Lg	Sp	Sci	SS
2	35	21	19	34		
3	31	34	29	38		
4	33	33	42	23		
5	48	40	55	36		

Sierra Vista Middle, La Puente

Grade	Rd	Ma	Lg	Sp	Sci	SS
6	11	3	9	9		
7	26	10	15	20		
8	21	13	16	15		

Sparks Elem., La Puente

Grade	Rd	Ma	Lg	Sp	Sci	SS
2	12	11	17	8		
3	9	8	5	6		
4	8	9	6	5		
5	27	33	32	22		

Sparks Middle, La Puente

Grade	Rd	Ma	Lg	Sp	Sci	SS
6	8	7	6	7		
7	14	8	15	14		
8	18	10	21	19		

Sunset Elem., La Puente

Grade	Rd	Ma	Lg	Sp	Sci	SS
2	45	52	49	40		
3	26	16	37	24		
4	26	20	19	24		
5	23	23	13	18		

Temple Acad., La Puente

Grade	Rd	Ma	Lg	Sp	Sci	SS
2	32	16	33	38		
3	16	23	20	33		
4	18	23	19	30		
5	18	18	22	25		

Valinda Sch. of Academics, Valinda

Grade	Rd	Ma	Lg	Sp	Sci	SS
2	28	24	40	42		
3	38	34	35	46		
4	28	23	24	24		
5	57	71	58	60		
6	34	43	40	36		

Valley Alt. High, La Puente

Grade	Rd	Ma	Lg	Sp	Sci	SS
10	5	5	4		6	2
11	14	2	6		4	4

Wedgeworth Elem., Hacienda Heights

Grade	Rd	Ma	Lg	Sp	Sci	SS
2	72	87	65	89		
3	61	65	70	93		
4	66	84	78	85		
5	67	77	74	90		

Wilson High, Hacienda Heights

Grade	Rd	Ma	Lg	Sp	Sci	SS
9	79	90	88		83	79
10	81	96	88		91	80
11	78	92	83		77	73

Wing Lane Elem., Valinda

Grade	Rd	Ma	Lg	Sp	Sci	SS
2	8	2	6	9		
3	11	3	5	24		
4	16	8	12	11		
5	13	12	13	16		

Workman Elem., La Puente

Grade	Rd	Ma	Lg	Sp	Sci	SS
2	33	33	32	30		
3	23	23	29	26		
4	38	57	38	33		
5	13	26	27	22		

Workman High, City of Industry

Grade	Rd	Ma	Lg	Sp	Sci	SS
9	29	34	37		34	29
10	21	36	33		25	21
11	31	40	39		27	33

Hawthorne Elem. School Dist.

Eucalyptus Elem., Hawthorne

Grade	Rd	Ma	Lg	Sp	Sci	SS
2	16	27	28	24		
3	19	37	30	30		
4	13	18	9	10		
5	18	26	20	16		

Hawthorne Middle, Hawthorne

Grade	Rd	Ma	Lg	Sp	Sci	SS
6	23	22	17	18		
7	24	29	19	31		
8	29	32	21	24		

50 STATE SCHOOL RANKINGS

Scores range from 1-99. A school scoring 75 has done better than 75 percent of other public schools in California.
Key: Rd (Reading), Ma (Math), Lg (Language), Sp (Spelling), Sci (Science) and SS (Social Science).

Grade	Rd	Ma	Lg	Sp	Sci	SS
Jefferson Elem., Hawthorne						
2	23	22	40	42		
3	15	14	13	30		
4	34	35	37	47		
5	29	29	30	39		
Prairie Vista Middle, Hawthorne						
6	15	16	12	20		
7	19	17	19	22		
8	12	16	16	22		
Ramona Elem., Hawthorne						
2	25	9	21	29		
3	42	44	55	48		
4	33	44	30	45		
5	34	21	37	35		
Washington Elem., Hawthorne						
2	10	16	9	13		
3	24	20	25	25		
4	13	13	7	17		
5	12	10	11	16		
Williams Elem., Hawthorne						
4	22	27	26	38		
5	14	24	16	29		
York Elem., Hawthorne						
2	17	23	24	19		
3	21	11	15	22		
4	24	21	20	20		
5	21	36	25	31		
Yukon Middle, Hawthorne						
6	18	15	18	18		
7	18	11	20	17		
8	13	14	16	19		
Zela Davis Elem., Hawthorne						
2	20	12	21	35		
3	19	17	25	37		

Hermosa Beach City Elem. School Dist.

Grade	Rd	Ma	Lg	Sp	Sci	SS
Hermosa Valley Elem., Hermosa Beach						
3	92	82	90	82		
4	87	85	94	89		
5	93	88	92	92		
6	91	90	87	93		
7	88	92	88	85		
8	93	90	91	92		
Hermosa View Elem., Hermosa Beach						
2	90	75	96	80		

Hughes-Elizabeth Lakes School Dist.

Grade	Rd	Ma	Lg	Sp	Sci	SS
Hughes-Elizabeth Lakes Elem., Lake Hughes						
2	66	53	79	64		
3	45	28	42	30		
4	70	68	56	52		
5	76	69	72	74		
6	65	76	60	67		
7	45	56	56	52		
8	66	56	66	67		

Inglewood Unified School Dist.

Grade	Rd	Ma	Lg	Sp	Sci	SS
Bennett/Kew Elem., Inglewood						
2	81	84	71	88		
3	59	90	78	94		
4	55	71	72	77		
5	56	61	72	72		
Centinela Elem., Inglewood						
2	55	71	53	50		
3	45	54	68	68		
4	34	38	47	49		
5	34	31	38	49		
6	29	25	29	29		
Crozier Jr. High, Inglewood						
6	18	22	19	22		
7	22	22	16	22		
8	24	29	22	22		
Freeman Elem., Inglewood						
2	59	63	73	88		
3	59	47	74	92		
4	56	52	49	67		
5	37	48	38	61		
6	76	68	74	74		
Highland Elem., Inglewood						
2	86	82	83	87		
3	68	61	57	94		
4	55	70	53	79		
5	37	77	45	59		
Hillcrest High (Cont.), Inglewood						
10	2	1			3	4
11	8	6		9	3	10
Hudnall Elem., Inglewood						
2	81	89	81	93		
3	60	81	81	85		
4	53	58	53	63		
5	53	71	58	75		
Inglewood High, Inglewood						
9	21	26	27		21	21
10	21	24	29		20	19
11	26	28	30		22	23
Kelso Elem., Inglewood						
2	72	86	76	87		
3	70	88	90	95		
4	58	77	75	77		
5	62	81	78	78		
La Tijera Elem., Inglewood						
2	86	78	68	95		
3	54	25	66	92		
4	52	52	69	88		
5	28	21	40	52		
6	29	14	19	38		
7	28	17	24	35		
8	22	13	16	27		
Lane Elem., Inglewood						
2	46	58	43	64		
3	49	61	55	96		
4	24	21	31	42		
5	16	18	22	18		
6	44	21	38	53		
7	19	14	18	40		
8	32	14	31	41		

Copyright © 2001 McCormack's Guides. No reproduction without permission.

STATE SCHOOL RANKINGS

Scores range from 1-99. A school scoring 75 has done better than 75 percent of other public schools in California.
Key: Rd (Reading), Ma (Math), Lg (Language), Sp (Spelling), Sci (Science) and SS (Social Science).

Monroe Jr. High, Inglewood

Grade	Rd	Ma	Lg	Sp	Sci	SS
6	20	17	23	25		
7	22	19	34	35		
8	22	21	28	36		

Morningside High, Inglewood

Grade	Rd	Ma	Lg	Sp	Sci	SS
9	28	26	32		24	31
10	25	24	37		22	26
11	26	22	31		22	22

Oak St. Elem., Inglewood

Grade	Rd	Ma	Lg	Sp
2	52	62	38	58
3	37	58	38	59
4	34	48	47	60
5	26	58	56	43

Parent Elem., Inglewood

Grade	Rd	Ma	Lg	Sp
2	77	68	86	95
3	62	61	70	84
4	69	72	77	79
5	53	56	69	72
6	44	33	47	58
7	28	9	25	54
8	39	34	67	51

Payne Elem., Inglewood

Grade	Rd	Ma	Lg	Sp
2	77	79	94	91
3	41	79	70	68
4	45	75	71	63
5	37	59	60	67

Woodworth Elem., Inglewood

Grade	Rd	Ma	Lg	Sp
2	60	40	37	56
3	36	45	47	75
4	30	16	21	19
5	19	19	32	47

Worthington Elem., Inglewood

Grade	Rd	Ma	Lg	Sp
2	23	45	30	44
3	26	37	36	48
4	22	31	26	35
5	8	18	22	25

Keppel Union Elem. School Dist.

Almondale Middle, Littlerock

Grade	Rd	Ma	Lg	Sp
6	82	47	86	89
7	37	32	37	43
8	34	30	39	43

Alpine Elem., Littlerock

Grade	Rd	Ma	Lg	Sp
2	46	49	51	40
3	44	19	40	37
4	28	23	24	29
5	29	21	30	23
6	40	26	44	42

Antelope Elem., Littlerock

Grade	Rd	Ma	Lg	Sp
2	20	12	16	13
3	13	7	6	22
4	27	18	34	29
5	29	6	20	29
6	18	12	3	27

Gibson Elem., Palmdale

Grade	Rd	Ma	Lg	Sp
2	41	23	35	42
3	32	28	30	32
4	27	16	27	26
5	31	21	37	33
6	34	40	40	32

Lake Los Angeles Elem., Palmdale

Grade	Rd	Ma	Lg	Sp
2	40	28	37	48
3	21	12	23	25
4	22	13	17	19
5	23	14	16	23
6	46	38	42	36
7	30	37	35	22
8	36	52	43	51

Pearblossom Elem., Pearblossom

Grade	Rd	Ma	Lg	Sp
2	46	30	58	52
3	45	38	40	39
4	63	50	62	52
5	59	41	68	69
6	60	26	58	70

La Cañada Unified School Dist.

La Cañada Elem., La Cañada

Grade	Rd	Ma	Lg	Sp
2	98	98	97	94
3	97	95	95	88
4	98	97	96	95
5	97	97	97	97
6	94	97	96	96

La Cañada High, La Cañada

Grade	Rd	Ma	Lg	Sp	Sci	SS
7	96	97	95	98		
8	96	97	96	97		
9	98	98	98		98	97
10	98	98	99		98	99
11	99	99	99		98	98

Palm Crest Elem., La Cañada

Grade	Rd	Ma	Lg	Sp
2	95	94	94	93
3	96	85	93	86
4	95	95	97	96
5	95	96	98	96
6	98	98	96	98

Paradise Canyon Elem., La Cañada

Grade	Rd	Ma	Lg	Sp
2	96	90	95	96
3	97	97	97	96
4	95	91	92	93
5	94	94	95	96
6	98	97	92	97

Lancaster Elem. School Dist.

Cory Elem., Lancaster

Grade	Rd	Ma	Lg	Sp
2	33	45	40	26
3	49	47	45	41
4	45	38	45	44
5	47	34	35	45
6	64	53	58	56

Desert View Elem., Lancaster

Grade	Rd	Ma	Lg	Sp
2	13	15	13	13
3	29	17	20	13
4	24	15	10	20
5	31	29	30	33
6	44	53	38	44

El Dorado Elem., Lancaster

Grade	Rd	Ma	Lg	Sp
2	35	50	46	28
3	44	54	40	53
4	49	52	58	59
5	46	46	40	42

Copyright © 2001 McCormack's Guides. No reproduction without permission.

STATE SCHOOL RANKINGS

Scores range from 1-99. A school scoring 75 has done better than 75 percent of other public schools in California.
Key: Rd (Reading), Ma (Math), Lg (Language), Sp (Spelling), Sci (Science) and SS (Social Science).

Joshua Elem., Lancaster

Grade	Rd	Ma	Lg	Sp	Sci	SS
2	32	20	23	42		
3	36	25	25	37		
4	22	10	15	22		
5	31	22	25	37		

Lancaster Discovery & Achievement Ctr. (Alt.)

Grade	Rd	Ma	Lg	Sp	Sci	SS
4	36	13	36	35		
6	21	11	11	18		
7	75	54	82	84		
8	36	34	51	57		

Lancaster Elem., Lancaster

Grade	Rd	Ma	Lg	Sp	Sci	SS
2	50	50	38	46		
3	42	30	35	28		
4	52	44	45	47		
5	29	28	29	37		
6	61	50	62	48		

Lancaster Community Day, Lancaster

Grade	Rd	Ma	Lg	Sp	Sci	SS
7	10	2	2	6		
8	12	4	3	17		

Lincoln Elem., Lancaster

Grade	Rd	Ma	Lg	Sp	Sci	SS
2	43	40	41	40		
3	54	44	54	41		
4	44	36	36	49		
5	42	33	33	39		

Linda Verde Elem., Lancaster

Grade	Rd	Ma	Lg	Sp	Sci	SS
2	8	6	11	8		
3	15	10	20	5		
4	9	11	13	10		
5	16	18	16	14		

Mariposa Elem., Lancaster

Grade	Rd	Ma	Lg	Sp	Sci	SS
2	25	25	23	19		
3	26	37	23	15		
4	27	16	17	15		
5	25	28	25	18		

Monte Vista Elem., Lancaster

Grade	Rd	Ma	Lg	Sp	Sci	SS
2	45	22	47	46		
3	47	30	40	39		
4	55	46	43	47		
5	56	56	44	53		
6	57	50	47	55		

New Vista Middle, Lancaster

Grade	Rd	Ma	Lg	Sp	Sci	SS
6	53	30	42	56		
7	58	32	50	60		
8	57	32	46	59		

Northrop Elem., Lancaster

Grade	Rd	Ma	Lg	Sp	Sci	SS
2	35	57	41	35		
3	58	67	52	43		
4	58	58	49	54		
5	29	31	27	25		

Park View Int., Lancaster

Grade	Rd	Ma	Lg	Sp	Sci	SS
7	40	24	30	45		
8	42	32	36	48		

Piute Int., Lancaster

Grade	Rd	Ma	Lg	Sp	Sci	SS
6	18	11	8	15		
7	22	19	19	24		
8	27	16	24	24		

Sierra Elem., Lancaster

Grade	Rd	Ma	Lg	Sp	Sci	SS
2	23	15	21	20		
3	32	22	31	28		
4	31	35	17	20		
5	40	43	35	39		
6	38	30	29	42		

Sunnydale Elem., Lancaster

Grade	Rd	Ma	Lg	Sp	Sci	SS
2	22	18	21	22		
3	47	40	47	24		
4	41	35	40	38		
5	47	58	44	43		
6	23	21	9	25		

Las Virgenes Unified School Dist.

Agoura High, Agoura Hills

Grade	Rd	Ma	Lg	Sp	Sci	SS
9	97	98	98		97	97
10	97	97	98		97	97
11	98	97	99		97	98

Bay Laurel Elem., Calabasas

Grade	Rd	Ma	Lg	Sp	Sci	SS
2	87	90	86	90		
3	94	96	91	88		
4	91	93	93	95		
5	90	91	94	90		

Calabasas High, Calabasas

Grade	Rd	Ma	Lg	Sp	Sci	SS
9	97	97	97		93	97
10	98	97	98		96	97
11	97	97	98		95	97

Chaparral Elem., Calabasas

Grade	Rd	Ma	Lg	Sp	Sci	SS
2	85	84	90	91		
3	87	82	82	73		
4	92	93	96	93		
5	93	80	90	92		

Indian Hills Cont. High, Calabasas

Grade	Rd	Ma	Lg	Sp	Sci	SS
9	47	29	62		50	40
10	50	50	53		80	55
11	11	28	30		29	35

Lindero Canyon Middle, Agoura Hills

Grade	Rd	Ma	Lg	Sp	Sci	SS
6	95	91	91	93		
7	96	96	95	96		
8	95	96	97	95		

Lupin Hill Elem., Calabasas

Grade	Rd	Ma	Lg	Sp	Sci	SS
2	74	62	82	81		
3	85	77	86	86		
4	84	84	80	86		
5	88	85	86	87		

Round Meadow Elem., Calabasas

Grade	Rd	Ma	Lg	Sp	Sci	SS
2	95	98	98	97		
3	88	88	88	85		
4	89	86	86	92		
5	95	89	93	97		

Sumac Elem., Agoura Hills

Grade	Rd	Ma	Lg	Sp	Sci	SS
2	69	63	86	73		
3	85	76	80	66		
4	87	86	86	79		
5	92	81	90	85		

STATE SCHOOL RANKINGS

Scores range from 1-99. A school scoring 75 has done better than 75 percent of other public schools in California.
Key: Rd (Reading), Ma (Math), Lg (Language), Sp (Spelling), Sci (Science) and SS (Social Science).

Grade	Rd	Ma	Lg	Sp	Sci	SS
White Oak Elem., Westlake Village						
2	91	89	89	93		
3	98	99	98	91		
4	95	93	95	89		
5	96	95	94	95		
Willow Elem., Agoura Hills						
2	86	86	91	78		
3	87	87	85	80		
4	89	76	87	93		
5	94	95	94	92		
Wright Middle, Calabasas						
6	86	88	82	88		
7	93	92	93	94		
8	91	94	96	92		
Yerba Buena Elem., Agoura Hills						
2	85	75	91	91		
3	96	98	93	92		
4	92	90	91	84		
5	89	82	90	86		

Lawndale Elem. School Dist.

Grade	Rd	Ma	Lg	Sp	Sci	SS
Addams Elem., Lawndale						
2	30	44	41	38		
3	17	32	28	18		
4	25	45	37	33		
5	16	18	30	14		
6	19	12	17	16		
Anderson Elem., Lawndale						
2	26	22	31	22		
3	19	27	30	44		
4	27	27	34	24		
5	28	28	29	29		
6	26	18	36	23		
Green Elem., Lawndale						
2	22	44	43	32		
3	12	9	20	24		
4	21	35	12	22		
5	19	19	30	27		
6	21	24	23	29		
Mitchell Elem., Lawndale						
2	40	30	43	35		
3	26	25	30	30		
4	22	23	17	28		
5	26	13	22	33		
6	21	24	36	18		
Rogers Middle, Lawndale						
6	1	1	1	1		
7	16	16	18	22		
8	24	30	25	27		
Roosevelt Elem., Lawndale						
2	8	11	13	20		
3	9	12	13	18		
4	9	13	9	11		
5	8	14	11	5		
6	12	9	6	20		
Twain Elem., Lawndale						
2	30	42	28	29		
3	42	35	44	24		
4	62	62	58	50		
5	58	62	69	55		
6	58	78	78	62		

Lennox Elem. School Dist.

Grade	Rd	Ma	Lg	Sp	Sci	SS
Buford Elem., Lennox						
2	6	18	9	11		
3	6	9	6	4		
4	3	5	7	10		
5	7	10	16	9		
Felton Elem., Lennox						
2	4	11	8	7		
3	7	7	3	9		
4	1	1	1	1		
5	5	4	5	6		
Jefferson Elem., Lennox						
2	7	12	14	19		
3	5	6	8	6		
4	13	11	12	8		
5	4	7	5	3		
Lennox Middle, Lennox						
6	8	13	13	6		
7	15	19	16	11		
8	18	30	22	15		
Moffett Elem., Lennox						
2	4	6	7	11		
3	3	2	3	4		
4	5	3	9	7		
5	8	3	7	7		
Whelan Elem., Lennox						
2	2	11	6	14		
3	10	14	6	13		
4	6	19	7	11		
5	14	21	22	12		

Little Lake City Elem. School Dist.

Grade	Rd	Ma	Lg	Sp	Sci	SS
Cresson Elem., Norwalk						
2	38	25	32	42		
3	29	20	28	35		
4	36	38	45	40		
5	40	52	47	47		
Jersey Avenue Elem., Santa Fe Springs						
2	20	22	26	18		
3	26	25	31	30		
4	33	21	28	26		
5	37	29	51	35		
Lake Center Elem., Santa Fe Springs						
6	17	19	19	17		
7	28	24	30	29		
8	36	28	28	34		
Lakeland Elem., Norwalk						
2	30	45	49	33		
3	31	44	40	25		
4	14	16	12	22		
5	33	38	49	43		

54 STATE SCHOOL RANKINGS

Scores range from 1-99. A school scoring 75 has done better than 75 percent of other public schools in California.
Key: Rd (Reading), Ma (Math), Lg (Language), Sp (Spelling), Sci (Science) and SS (Social Science).

Lakeside Elem., Norwalk

Grade	Rd	Ma	Lg	Sp	Sci	SS
6	21	15	17	17		
7	41	26	30	41		
8	32	23	29	44		

Lakeview Elem., Santa Fe Springs

Grade	Rd	Ma	Lg	Sp	Sci	SS
2	59	42	60	60		
3	49	60	54	51		
4	41	47	40	38		
5	34	28	30	23		

Orr Elem., Norwalk

Grade	Rd	Ma	Lg	Sp	Sci	SS
2	23	11	41	35		
3	36	25	22	37		
4	31	27	30	33		
5	33	36	42	43		

Paddison Elem., Norwalk

Grade	Rd	Ma	Lg	Sp	Sci	SS
2	23	9	11	19		
3	29	30	36	30		
4	34	29	43	35		
5	37	38	44	45		

Studebaker Elem., Norwalk

Grade	Rd	Ma	Lg	Sp	Sci	SS
2	28	18	37	32		
3	47	23	52	53		
4	39	42	58	44		
5	34	36	44	45		

Long Beach Unified School Dist.

Addams Elem., Long Beach

Grade	Rd	Ma	Lg	Sp	Sci	SS
2	41	51	31	50		
3	30	53	38	50		
4	29	55	41	45		
5	15	39	27	41		

Alvarado Elem., Signal Hill

Grade	Rd	Ma	Lg	Sp	Sci	SS
2	52	68	38	67		
3	47	71	55	85		
4	48	39	50	79		
5	46	44	71	61		

Avalon, Avalon

Grade	Rd	Ma	Lg	Sp	Sci	SS
2	24	38	25	20		
3	45	64	34	14		
4	47	63	50	45		
5	37	37	43	31		
6	30	58	32	31		
7	49	43	45	34		
8	67	59	71	41		
9	51	76	54		62	67
10	45	54	51		39	42
11	67	61	69		65	60

Bancroft Middle, Long Beach

Grade	Rd	Ma	Lg	Sp	Sci	SS
6	59	66	71	76		
7	62	55	68	75		
8	65	64	67	82		

Barton Elem., Long Beach

Grade	Rd	Ma	Lg	Sp	Sci	SS
2	33	28	24	50		
3	28	30	32	52		
4	14	15	23	34		
5	21	24	27	31		

Birney Elem., Long Beach

Grade	Rd	Ma	Lg	Sp	Sci	SS
2	67	77	67	79		
3	63	74	66	78		
4	37	51	48	58		
5	36	34	52	55		

Bixby Elem., Long Beach

Grade	Rd	Ma	Lg	Sp	Sci	SS
2	55	65	62	59		
3	72	63	64	69		
4	37	53	61	52		
5	32	27	38	37		

Bryant Elem., Long Beach

Grade	Rd	Ma	Lg	Sp	Sci	SS
2	41	39	26	51		
3	50	69	55	59		
4	44	39	39	50		
5	37	32	27	33		

Buffum Elem., Long Beach

Grade	Rd	Ma	Lg	Sp	Sci	SS
2	52	59	54	53		
3	69	83	78	83		
4	52	50	50	62		
5	43	36	42	51		

Burbank Elem., Long Beach

Grade	Rd	Ma	Lg	Sp	Sci	SS
2	24	25	18	31		
3	34	40	36	27		
4	25	30	26	36		
5	28	36	49	31		

Burcham Elem., Long Beach

Grade	Rd	Ma	Lg	Sp	Sci	SS
2	46	61	52	55		
3	37	38	45	21		
4	36	43	37	34		
5	24	29	27	23		

Burnett Elem., Long Beach

Grade	Rd	Ma	Lg	Sp	Sci	SS
2	28	28	22	37		
3	19	40	23	32		
4	14	17	26	18		
5	17	39	23	23		

Burroughs Elem., Long Beach

Grade	Rd	Ma	Lg	Sp	Sci	SS
2	58	58	56	69		
3	63	74	68	55		
4	47	39	70	65		
5	74	73	78	63		

Butler Elem., Long Beach

Grade	Rd	Ma	Lg	Sp	Sci	SS
2	11	5	11	27		
3	22	14	14	47		
4	11	29	20	31		
5	8	22	17	26		
6	7	12	8	18		
7	7	13	9	21		
8	11	19	17	28		

Cabrillo High, Long Beach

Grade	Rd	Ma	Lg	Sp	Sci	SS
9	10	25	18		14	16
10	20	40	27		22	17
11	28	39	32		21	28

California Acad. of Math & Science, Carson

Grade	Rd	Ma	Lg	Sp	Sci	SS
9	99	99	99		99	98
10	99	99	99		99	99
11	99	99	99		99	99

STATE SCHOOL RANKINGS 55

Scores range from 1-99. A school scoring 75 has done better than 75 percent of other public schools in California.
Key: Rd (Reading), Ma (Math), Lg (Language), Sp (Spelling), Sci (Science) and SS (Social Science).

Carver Elem., Long Beach

Grade	Rd	Ma	Lg	Sp	Sci	SS
2	46	48	46	58		
3	57	52	50	61		
4	45	58	52	57		
5	39	34	43	65		

Cleveland Elem., Lakewood

Grade	Rd	Ma	Lg	Sp	Sci	SS
2	46	45	46	59		
3	59	64	66	71		
4	45	42	43	40		
5	29	16	28	29		

Constellation Comm. Middle, Long Beach

Grade	Rd	Ma	Lg	Sp	Sci	SS
6	4	5	3	8		
7	20	17	17	19		
8	23	10	19	16		

Cubberley Elem., Long Beach

Grade	Rd	Ma	Lg	Sp	Sci	SS
2	88	93	83	90		
3	78	83	85	80		
4	57	55	67	67		
5	62	62	67	71		
6	63	56	71	77		
7	69	86	75	75		
8	67	77	65	73		

DeMille Middle, Long Beach

Grade	Rd	Ma	Lg	Sp	Sci	SS
6	13	23	20	18		
7	14	16	21	16		
8	27	24	23	19		

Edison Elem., Long Beach

Grade	Rd	Ma	Lg	Sp	Sci	SS
2	28	52	18	43		
3	13	16	15	23		

Ed. Partnership High, Long Beach

Grade	Rd	Ma	Lg	Sp	Sci	SS
9	23	25	16		23	26
10	17	16	12		24	20
11	17	14	17		19	21

Emerson Elem., Long Beach

Grade	Rd	Ma	Lg	Sp	Sci	SS
2	48	39	36	59		
3	42	59	50	55		
4	42	48	50	54		
5	28	31	40	26		

Franklin Middle, Long Beach

Grade	Rd	Ma	Lg	Sp	Sci	SS
6	4	8	6	8		
7	6	17	8	12		
8	5	19	7	8		

Fremont Elem., Long Beach

Grade	Rd	Ma	Lg	Sp	Sci	SS
2	79	82	72	74		
3	89	96	95	92		
4	91	94	94	96		
5	55	47	50	57		

Gant Elem., Long Beach

Grade	Rd	Ma	Lg	Sp	Sci	SS
2	89	97	91	88		
3	93	98	97	92		
4	82	85	82	88		
5	96	98	97	93		

Garfield Elem., Long Beach

Grade	Rd	Ma	Lg	Sp	Sci	SS
2	17	29	7	27		
3	16	33	18	18		
4	7	15	7	14		
5	14	20	21	27		

Gompers Elem., Lakewood

Grade	Rd	Ma	Lg	Sp	Sci	SS
2	46	33	43	61		
3	63	83	68	68		
4	25	44	33	29		
5	21	24	30	29		

Grant Elem., Long Beach

Grade	Rd	Ma	Lg	Sp	Sci	SS
2	39	34	32	46		
3	27	13	15	25		
4	25	38	23	27		
5	26	36	27	31		

Hamilton Middle, Long Beach

Grade	Rd	Ma	Lg	Sp	Sci	SS
6	10	16	7	15		
7	9	13	6	15		
8	16	21	12	18		

Harte Elem., Long Beach

Grade	Rd	Ma	Lg	Sp	Sci	SS
2	43	45	38	58		
3	32	43	34	45		
4	36	22	27	36		
5	34	24	24	41		

Henry Elem., Long Beach

Grade	Rd	Ma	Lg	Sp	Sci	SS
2	46	52	36	39		
3	52	69	62	32		
4	22	29	31	25		
5	36	37	43	27		

Hill Middle, Long Beach

Grade	Rd	Ma	Lg	Sp	Sci	SS
6	16	11	14	20		
7	24	22	29	28		
8	22	15	22	20		

Holmes Elem., Lakewood

Grade	Rd	Ma	Lg	Sp	Sci	SS
2	55	61	52	58		
3	49	57	58	61		
4	29	32	43	41		
5	37	36	43	51		

Hoover Middle, Lakewood

Grade	Rd	Ma	Lg	Sp	Sci	SS
6	37	55	28	47		
7	38	39	28	41		
8	39	41	31	48		

Hudson Elem., Long Beach

Grade	Rd	Ma	Lg	Sp	Sci	SS
2	39	45	47	58		
3	34	45	47	59		
4	34	24	47	60		
5	45	59	65	75		
6	40	67	40	60		
7	27	38	28	37		
8	41	56	45	51		

Hughes Middle, Long Beach

Grade	Rd	Ma	Lg	Sp	Sci	SS
6	56	58	66	69		
7	76	81	79	83		
8	72	82	77	84		

International Elem., Long Beach

Grade	Rd	Ma	Lg	Sp	Sci	SS
2	33	41	21	35		
3	17	26	24	32		
4	25	29	31	27		
5	15	16	15	27		

Jefferson Leadership Acad., Long Beach

Grade	Rd	Ma	Lg	Sp	Sci	SS
6	10	13	15	20		
7	11	18	18	17		
8	16	21	17	18		

Copyright © 2001 McCormack's Guides. No reproduction without permission.

56 STATE SCHOOL RANKINGS

Scores range from 1-99. A school scoring 75 has done better than 75 percent of other public schools in California.
Key: Rd (Reading), Ma (Math), Lg (Language), Sp (Spelling), Sci (Science) and SS (Social Science).

Jordan High, Long Beach

Grade	Rd	Ma	Lg	Sp	Sci	SS
9	23	40	26		28	26
10	25	45	34		28	26
11	35	48	37		37	36

Keller Elem., Long Beach

Grade	Rd	Ma	Lg	Sp
2	15	25	21	25
3	20	28	21	13
4	6	17	10	9
5	3	5	9	7

Kettering Elem., Long Beach

Grade	Rd	Ma	Lg	Sp
2	69	77	68	53
3	68	74	77	61
4	56	39	54	46
5	59	42	67	73

King Elem., Long Beach

Grade	Rd	Ma	Lg	Sp
2	33	41	15	39
3	22	32	15	34
4	12	22	20	29
5	8	14	7	19

Lafayette Elem., Long Beach

Grade	Rd	Ma	Lg	Sp
2	40	80	35	65
3	24	47	21	36
4	19	39	29	20
5	21	27	27	31

Lakewood High, Lakewood

Grade	Rd	Ma	Lg	Sp	Sci	SS
9	48	67	60		54	46
10	57	73	60		61	54
11	50	66	55		60	57

Lee Elem., Long Beach

Grade	Rd	Ma	Lg	Sp
2	34	52	17	39
3	15	26	10	20

Lincoln Elem., Long Beach

Grade	Rd	Ma	Lg	Sp
2	25	16	21	41
3	11	8	18	34
4	23	32	33	27
5	24	31	45	33

Lindbergh Middle, Long Beach

Grade	Rd	Ma	Lg	Sp
6	5	8	10	8
7	12	11	14	15
8	11	12	14	14

Long Beach Prep. Acad. (Alt.), Signal Hill

Grade	Rd	Ma	Lg	Sp
8	7	7	4	5

Longfellow Elem., Long Beach

Grade	Rd	Ma	Lg	Sp
2	77	77	82	81
3	84	76	82	80
4	73	71	78	76
5	81	73	78	87

Los Cerritos Elem., Long Beach

Grade	Rd	Ma	Lg	Sp
2	63	90	59	69
3	66	77	68	65
4	59	74	61	48
5	50	68	61	51

Lowell Elem., Long Beach

Grade	Rd	Ma	Lg	Sp
2	88	90	92	92
3	88	80	92	85
4	80	80	86	80
5	90	94	96	96

MacArthur Elem., Lakewood

Grade	Rd	Ma	Lg	Sp
2	52	34	38	50
3	43	53	45	36
4	22	19	23	18
5	31	31	32	27

Madison Elem., Lakewood

Grade	Rd	Ma	Lg	Sp
2	60	65	61	63
3	77	82	82	73
4	72	61	74	77
5	48	50	62	68

Mann Elem., Long Beach

Grade	Rd	Ma	Lg	Sp
2	70	66	59	74
3	36	38	38	50
4	31	24	33	52
5	29	25	40	35

Marshall Middle, Long Beach

Grade	Rd	Ma	Lg	Sp
6	25	22	30	34
7	31	26	38	32
8	35	33	42	46

McKinley Elem., Long Beach

Grade	Rd	Ma	Lg	Sp
2	6	8	11	11
3	8	8	9	9
4	15	21	23	14
5	10	13	30	27

Millikan Sr. High, Long Beach

Grade	Rd	Ma	Lg	Sp	Sci	SS
9	46	61	50		49	49
10	55	73	60		61	58
11	60	68	61		61	66

Monroe Elem., Lakewood

Grade	Rd	Ma	Lg	Sp
2	43	58	38	35
3	15	16	21	16
4	24	22	23	33
5	37	46	54	33

Muir Elem., Long Beach

Grade	Rd	Ma	Lg	Sp
2	34	22	26	52
3	27	35	31	43
4	22	15	26	36
5	26	17	27	33

Naples Elem., Long Beach

Grade	Rd	Ma	Lg	Sp
2	95	95	98	94
3	83	85	83	88
4	81	90	81	83
5	65	88	74	70

Newcomb Elem., Long Beach

Grade	Rd	Ma	Lg	Sp
2	88	94	88	92
3	96	98	95	92
4	82	80	82	81
5	79	77	87	85
6	79	84	84	81
7	73	79	75	70
8	78	73	80	89

Polytechnic High, Long Beach

Grade	Rd	Ma	Lg	Sp	Sci	SS
9	74	81	77		70	87
10	73	81	80		73	76
11	69	78	75		70	80

Scores range from 1-99. A school scoring 75 has done better than 75 percent of other public schools in California.
Key: Rd (Reading), Ma (Math), Lg (Language), Sp (Spelling), Sci (Science) and SS (Social Science).

Grade	Rd	Ma	Lg	Sp	Sci	SS
Powell Acad. for Success, Long Beach						
2	23	12	13	29		
3	15	7	8	21		
4	7	7	7	18		
5	26	20	25	29		
6	12	4	13	9		
7	8	8	8	11		
8	19	21	13	14		
Prisk Elem., Long Beach						
2	86	90	90	81		
3	65	74	73	73		
4	74	69	78	76		
5	84	80	84	89		
Reid Sr. High (Cont.), Long Beach						
5	1	1	1	1		
7	2	1	1	1		
8	1	3	2	1		
9	10	12	15		10	9
10	8	13	20		8	17
11	10	23	19		12	9
Riley Elem., Lakewood						
2	55	77	56	63		
3	25	41	34	39		
4	15	22	11	20		
5	37	46	38	41		
Robinson Elem., Long Beach						
2	57	53	44	65		
3	60	79	57	75		
4	29	34	23	33		
5	32	31	35	31		
6	40	51	36	44		
7	38	60	31	37		
8	30	36	31	36		
Rogers Middle, Long Beach						
6	74	69	77	79		
7	76	82	82	78		
8	63	66	71	56		
Roosevelt Elem., Long Beach						
2	29	47	19	50		
3	19	24	15	25		
Savannah Acad., Long Beach						
9	28	52	35		23	39
Signal Hill Elem., Long Beach						
2	41	55	44	50		
3	54	69	58	77		
4	37	53	45	57		
5	39	56	47	55		
Stanford Middle, Long Beach						
6	73	81	71	80		
7	67	80	68	71		
8	71	83	69	75		
Stephens Middle, Long Beach						
6	19	23	27	28		
7	22	18	28	34		
8	24	29	25	38		

Grade	Rd	Ma	Lg	Sp	Sci	SS
Stevenson Elem., Long Beach						
2	41	48	41	61		
3	27	41	26	32		
4	25	38	29	33		
5	23	31	25	25		
Sutter Elem., Long Beach						
2	38	34	34	48		
3	32	38	41	28		
4	24	33	37	24		
5	29	27	40	41		
Tincher Elem., Long Beach						
2	58	82	58	67		
3	56	61	60	62		
4	28	34	37	43		
5	29	22	43	39		
6	35	40	44	60		
Tucker Elem., Long Beach						
2	9	2	1	15		
3	7	13	18	18		
4	15	27	26	27		
5	15	5	21	21		
Twain Elem., Long Beach						
2	88	90	84	85		
3	89	92	91	78		
4	78	81	75	83		
5	84	88	86	87		
Washington Middle, Long Beach						
4	22	30	33	33		
5	12	25	12	19		
6	2	12	3	6		
7	7	24	10	8		
8	8	24	10	13		
Webster Elem., Long Beach						
2	9	20	9	10		
3	19	22	18	10		
4	20	24	16	24		
5	23	25	28	39		
Whittier Elem., Long Beach						
2	34	65	18	39		
3	15	47	21	34		
4	11	42	22	17		
5	4	20	14	15		
Willard Elem., Long Beach						
2	40	34	26	53		
3	28	37	28	52		
4	24	44	29	41		
5	31	42	33	47		
Wilson High, Long Beach						
9	58	68	65		62	59
10	63	65	68		63	67
11	71	75	71		72	74

Los Angeles Co. Off. Ed.
Alternative/Opportunity

Grade	Rd	Ma	Lg	Sp	Sci	SS
7	6	3	3	7		
8	5	4	3	5		
9	14	15	14		14	17
10	20	22	13		12	16
11	17	15	13		10	8

58 STATE SCHOOL RANKINGS

Scores range from 1-99. A school scoring 75 has done better than 75 percent of other public schools in California.
Key: Rd (Reading), Ma (Math), Lg (Language), Sp (Spelling), Sci (Science) and SS (Social Science).

Grade	Rd	Ma	Lg	Sp	Sci	SS
Antelope Val. Co. Comm. Day, Lancaster						
7	7	2	3	10		
8	5	4	3	8		
9	21	20	17		23	50
East L. A. Comm. Day, Monterey Park						
7	1	2	2	2		
8	11	2	3	10		
9	8	4	10		16	23
10	5	22	13		8	10
11	5	3	5		6	6
Eastern Community Day						
7	2	3	3	2		
8	6	3	1	15		
9	16	20	19		63	99
10	9	36	22		6	4
Int'l Polytechnic High, Pomona						
9	89	76	94		69	82
10	87	75	87		73	78
11	84	60	83		75	71
Juvenile Hall/Community, Downey						
7	1	1	2	2		
8	1	1	1	1		
9	3	7	3		2	8
10	4	8	4		4	6
11	3	4	1		4	3
L.A. County High School for the Arts						
9	99	83	98		91	96
10	98	90	99		94	94
11	96	85	97		90	95
Northwest Community Day						
10	2	5	13		2	23
Odyssey Charter						
2	65	63	71	73		
3	65	50	65	73		
4	42	29	20	44		
5	70	55	49	47		
6	50	33	29	32		
7	55	27	24	45		
8	69	49	76	76		
Soledad Enrichment Action						
8	1	2	2	2		
9	2	4	3		3	3
10	1	4	2		4	4
11	2	4	4		4	4
Southern Community Day						
9	21	27	20		16	19
10	7	17	7		22	10
11	5	16	10		8	3
Southwest Comm. Day, Lawndale						
7	1	1	1	5		
8	2	3	2	1		
9	2	4	6		18	4
10	23	14	36		22	29
11	13	28	15		14	6

Grade	Rd	Ma	Lg	Sp	Sci	SS
Special Education						
2	11	1	4	5		
3	1	1	1	1		
4	7	1	1	4		
5	1	1	1	1		
6	1	1	1	1		
7	2	2	2	3		
8	2	2	2	7		
9	2	3	3		2	11
10	4	14	4		6	13
11	1	2	1		3	2
Tri-C Community Day						
9	1	5	1		4	1
10	3	22	4		8	13
11	3	9	2		14	3

Los Angeles Unified School Dist.

Grade	Rd	Ma	Lg	Sp	Sci	SS
Accelerated Sch., Near Coliseum						
2	38	50	28	54		
3	49	65	54	55		
4	28	26	32	21		
5	50	88	64	52		
6	50	48	44	40		
7	68	52	52	62		
Adams Middle, Near USC						
6	3	2	5	4		
7	4	6	6	6		
8	6	7	8	6		
Addams (Cont.), Granada Hills						
10	41	51	35		51	37
11	37	12	25		8	25
Albion St. Elem., Near El Sereno						
2	16	18	27	44		
3	3	4	3	22		
4	13	24	17	20		
5	26	33	25	23		
Aldama Elem., Mt. Washington						
2	13	35	24	18		
3	17	14	17	33		
4	9	27	18	33		
5	12	18	27	22		
Alexandria Ave. Elem., Near Hollywood						
2	13	23	23	19		
3	26	23	35	28		
4	16	11	9	15		
5	19	22	22	25		
Aliso High (Cont.), Reseda						
10	26	33	23		30	37
11	30	19	30		22	34
Allesandro Elem., Cypress Park, L.A.						
2	40	53	56	48		
3	21	35	33	25		
4	31	38	28	35		
5	23	19	29	23		
6	72	82	62	74		

STATE SCHOOL RANKINGS

Scores range from 1-99. A school scoring 75 has done better than 75 percent of other public schools in California.
Key: Rd (Reading), Ma (Math), Lg (Language), Sp (Spelling), Sci (Science) and SS (Social Science).

Grade	Rd	Ma	Lg	Sp	Sci	SS
Alta Loma Elem., Near Mid City						
2	7	7	16	13		
3	13	20	25	15		
4	8	6	6	5		
5	18	12	10	19		
Ambler Ave. Elem., Carson						
2	48	49	64	72		
3	59	51	77	80		
4	39	45	51	38		
5	56	41	49	61		
Amestoy Elem., Gardena						
2	17	15	23	33		
3	15	22	28	30		
4	11	10	9	14		
5	16	18	20	12		
Anatola Ave. Elem., Van Nuys						
2	18	15	19	35		
3	55	65	66	68		
4	34	36	34	38		
5	39	48	38	52		
Andasol Ave. Elem., Northridge						
2	77	78	89	88		
3	83	77	88	91		
4	74	78	86	86		
5	58	44	56	59		
Angel's Gate (Cont.), San Pedro						
10	29	29	32		36	53
Angeles Mesa Elem., West L.A.						
2	17	13	23	26		
3	10	5	15	22		
4	11	3	4	10		
5	7	3	3	9		
Ann St. Elem., Chinatown						
2	2	2	7	7		
3	4	10	6	15		
4	9	13	10	7		
5	21	13	6	17		
Annalee Ave. Elem., Carson						
2	52	22	37	78		
3	42	35	54	73		
4	31	18	28	40		
5	34	13	18	22		
Annandale Elem., Highland Park, L.A.						
2	48	35	46	69		
3	49	56	66	75		
4	31	44	43	44		
5	39	43	49	45		
Apperson St. Elem., Sunland						
2	46	37	55	58		
3	65	56	59	46		
4	60	47	56	50		
5	61	50	40	39		
Aragon Ave. Elem., Cypress Park						
2	3	4	4	7		
3	9	10	9	15		
4	24	26	21	31		
5	19	22	27	19		

Grade	Rd	Ma	Lg	Sp	Sci	SS
Arco Iris Primary Ctr, Los Angeles						
2	2	8	4	4		
Arlington Heights Elem., Country Club Park						
2	6	13	11	20		
3	7	9	15	13		
4	13	13	6	15		
5	14	4	5	10		
Arminta St. Elem., North Hollywood						
2	17	35	30	26		
3	4	3	4	4		
4	8	9	5	3		
5	8	9	8	4		
Arroyo Seco,						
2	28	18	18	22		
3	21	22	26	24		
4	34	31	40	47		
5	31	40	25	12		
6	26	14	20	29		
7	28	21	25	26		
8	44	26	32	34		
Ascot Ave. Elem., L.A. Near Vernon						
2	8	20	11	9		
3	3	5	2	2		
4	2	11	3	2		
5	4	7	7	3		
Atwater Ave. Elem., Silver Lake						
2	26	53	43	32		
3	27	35	31	24		
4	31	44	40	35		
5	34	43	47	27		
Audubon Middle, Leimert Park						
6	12	7	7	12		
7	11	10	11	24		
8	12	8	13	22		
Avalon (Cont.), Wilmington						
9	14	11	24		5	3
10	12	4	5		7	4
Avalon Gardens Elem., Near Compton						
2	17	3	13	24		
3	22	5	26	53		
4	24	5	13	22		
5	7	1	1	2		
Balboa Gifted Magnet Elem., Northridge						
2	99	99	99	99		
3	99	99	99	99		
4	99	99	99	99		
5	99	99	99	99		
Baldwin Hills Elem., Baldwin						
2	50	35	53	87		
3	45	34	45	64		
4	56	35	60	64		
5	52	29	53	46		
Bancroft Middle, Hollywood						
6	21	21	20	29		
7	30	28	37	38		
8	29	21	40	34		

STATE SCHOOL RANKINGS

Scores range from 1-99. A school scoring 75 has done better than 75 percent of other public schools in California.
Key: Rd (Reading), Ma (Math), Lg (Language), Sp (Spelling), Sci (Science) and SS (Social Science).

Bandini St. Elem., San Pedro

Grade	Rd	Ma	Lg	Sp	Sci	SS
2	22	4	11	14		
3	31	13	35	25		
4	26	18	17	22		
5	19	14	14	14		

Banning Sr. High, Wilmington

Grade	Rd	Ma	Lg	Sp	Sci	SS
9	22	29	28		20	23
10	29	38	41		25	26
11	33	46	46		29	37

Barrett Elem., Los Angeles

Grade	Rd	Ma	Lg	Sp	Sci	SS
2	28	37	41	32		
3	10	13	23	22		
4	16	15	14	24		
5	3	8	4	5		

Barton Hill Elem., San Pedro

Grade	Rd	Ma	Lg	Sp	Sci	SS
2	14	6	16	14		
3	4	4	5	6		
4	4	2	4	5		
5	7	3	4	6		

Bassett St. Elem., Van Nuys

Grade	Rd	Ma	Lg	Sp	Sci	SS
2	15	16	20	20		
3	7	11	11	9		
4	6	6	5	5		
5	12	16	11	11		

Beachy Ave. Elem., Pacoima

Grade	Rd	Ma	Lg	Sp	Sci	SS
2	7	15	16	11		
3	15	14	18	13		
4	16	5	10	17		
5	18	5	6	10		

Beckford Ave. Elem., Northridge

Grade	Rd	Ma	Lg	Sp	Sci	SS
2	75	79	78	91		
3	67	71	72	89		
4	77	78	83	88		
5	76	80	75	86		

Beethoven St. Elem., Near Mar Vista

Grade	Rd	Ma	Lg	Sp	Sci	SS
2	75	58	71	81		
3	47	52	63	66		
4	55	52	51	62		
5	68	67	74	72		

Bell Sr. High, Bell

Grade	Rd	Ma	Lg	Sp	Sci	SS
9	17	37	24		21	21
10	29	56	35		33	21
11	36	51	36		30	39

Bellevue Ave. Primary Ctr., Los Angeles

Grade	Rd	Ma	Lg	Sp	Sci	SS
2	13	24	21	24		

Belmont Sr. High, Westlake

Grade	Rd	Ma	Lg	Sp	Sci	SS
9	19	26	34		20	29
10	32	38	41		33	32
11	30	40	41		31	35

Belvedere Elem., East L.A.

Grade	Rd	Ma	Lg	Sp	Sci	SS
2	18	25	20	33		
3	13	25	25	13		
4	11	24	22	15		
5	5	22	22	9		

Belvedere Middle, East L.A.

Grade	Rd	Ma	Lg	Sp	Sci	SS
6	8	12	8	7		
7	11	17	9	7		
8	12	26	19	12		

Berendo Middle, Westlake

Grade	Rd	Ma	Lg	Sp	Sci	SS
6	3	7	5	5		
7	8	12	7	8		
8	10	17	12	7		

Bertrand Ave. Elem., Reseda

Grade	Rd	Ma	Lg	Sp	Sci	SS
2	7	18	8	6		
3	15	20	23	9		
4	6	3	3	8		
5	25	33	14	27		

Bethune Middle, South Central L.A.

Grade	Rd	Ma	Lg	Sp	Sci	SS
6	3	2	4	3		
7	2	3	5	2		
8	4	4	6	5		

Birmingham Sr. High, Van Nuys

Grade	Rd	Ma	Lg	Sp	Sci	SS
9	36	42	42		40	42
10	47	50	51		51	47
11	49	55	54		52	62

Blythe St. Elem., Reseda

Grade	Rd	Ma	Lg	Sp	Sci	SS
2	6	9	20	14		
3	5	4	3	13		
4	14	23	21	19		
5	19	7	10	7		

Bonita St. Elem., Carson

Grade	Rd	Ma	Lg	Sp	Sci	SS
2	38	30	51	67		
3	38	40	49	51		
4	34	36	30	45		
5	45	48	54	65		

Boyle Heights (Cont.), Boyle Hts.

Grade	Rd	Ma	Lg	Sp	Sci	SS
9	5	16	8		4	23

Braddock Dr. Elem., Culver City

Grade	Rd	Ma	Lg	Sp	Sci	SS
2	23	21	33	29		
3	26	32	37	30		
4	39	42	45	42		
5	26	33	23	19		

Bradley Env. Sci. and Hum., Leimark Pk

Grade	Rd	Ma	Lg	Sp	Sci	SS
2	40	23	58	60		
3	12	6	13	26		
4	21	6	10	28		
5	34	29	22	39		

Brainard Ave. Elem., Lake View Terrace

Grade	Rd	Ma	Lg	Sp	Sci	SS
2	17	10	28	28		
3	49	22	52	57		
4	53	40	51	40		
5	31	21	29	29		

Bravo Medical Magnet High, Boyle Heights

Grade	Rd	Ma	Lg	Sp	Sci	SS
9	75	88	87		79	76
10	86	91	87		85	79
11	88	94	89		86	84

Breed St. Elem., Boyle Heights

Grade	Rd	Ma	Lg	Sp	Sci	SS
2	27	37	33	26		
3	21	47	38	41		
4	13	15	28	19		
5	25	22	16	4		

Brentwood Science, Brentwood

Grade	Rd	Ma	Lg	Sp	Sci	SS
2	75	71	76	90		
3	74	77	85	92		
4	74	77	89	86		
5	80	80	84	79		

STATE SCHOOL RANKINGS

Scores range from 1-99. A school scoring 75 has done better than 75 percent of other public schools in California.
Key: Rd (Reading), Ma (Math), Lg (Language), Sp (Spelling), Sci (Science) and SS (Social Science).

Grade	Rd	Ma	Lg	Sp	Sci	SS
Bridge St. Elem., Boyle Heights						
2	16	11	17	26		
3	7	5	6	15		
4	8	23	7	8		
5	12	4	7	4		
Bright Elem., Los Angeles						
2	37	42	45	68		
3	27	17	42	41		
4	38	59	54	47		
5	39	44	54	35		
Broad Ave. Elem., Wilmington						
2	53	40	53	62		
3	38	22	49	48		
4	36	42	51	37		
5	39	44	45	39		
Broadacres Ave. Elem., Carson						
2	57	37	55	88		
3	51	60	52	79		
4	53	48	62	70		
5	56	46	45	67		
Broadous Elem., Pacoima						
2	1	1	1	1		
3	3	1	2	2		
4	8	2	4	2		
5	3	2	2	1		
Broadway Elem., Venice						
2	27	40	33	44		
3	31	63	59	53		
4	19	36	31	17		
5	19	14	22	27		
Brockton Ave. Elem., Near Santa Monica						
2	19	11	16	32		
3	29	13	30	44		
4	22	27	34	31		
5	40	22	38	29		
Brooklyn Ave. Elem., East L.A.						
2	6	7	11	4		
3	7	30	15	10		
4	4	13	7	5		
5	8	13	13	5		
Bryson Ave. Elem., South Gate						
2	13	9	14	22		
3	21	25	31	22		
4	24	31	30	28		
5	26	33	38	22		
Buchanan St. Elem., Highland Park						
2	25	39	38	38		
3	32	25	37	30		
4	37	36	43	37		
5	36	26	47	42		
Budlong Ave. Elem., Southeast L.A.						
2	6	3	7	7		
3	4	11	8	10		
4	6	4	7	14		
5	7	3	3	3		

Grade	Rd	Ma	Lg	Sp	Sci	SS
Burbank Blvd. Elem., North Hollywood						
2	36	27	46	38		
3	39	34	45	57		
4	37	26	34	38		
5	26	22	20	19		
Burbank Middle, Highland Park						
6	13	13	17	14		
7	12	14	9	10		
8	15	11	16	13		
Burroughs Middle, Hancock Park						
6	60	65	67	68		
7	54	54	66	65		
8	53	56	59	69		
Burton St. Elem., Panorama City						
2	10	12	13	10		
3	3	4	3	3		
4	3	2	4	4		
5	8	6	13	11		
Bushnell Way Elem., Highland Park						
2	10	7	11	10		
3	19	27	22	16		
4	17	18	13	11		
5	10	19	11	11		
Byrd Middle, Sun Valley						
6	11	8	11	9		
7	14	16	22	11		
8	15	17	21	13		
Cabrillo Ave. Elem., San Pedro						
2	25	21	31	38		
3	29	11	23	37		
4	16	11	15	13		
5	16	7	13	25		
Cahuenga Elem., Hancock Park						
2	33	68	47	69		
3	26	44	42	66		
4	28	42	30	50		
5	34	22	44	43		
Calabash St. Elem., Woodland Hills						
2	83	81	83	86		
3	70	70	85	79		
4	81	82	72	81		
5	65	68	71	67		
Calahan St. Elem., Northridge						
2	43	55	49	62		
3	70	71	82	80		
4	52	73	51	64		
5	58	69	60	49		
Calvert St. Elem., Woodland Hills						
2	66	45	60	81		
3	58	54	68	73		
4	65	45	69	70		
5	71	58	63	69		
Camellia Ave. Elem., North Hollywood						
2	12	11	19	18		
3	10	7	13	16		
4	3	4	7	3		
5	2	3	7	2		

STATE SCHOOL RANKINGS

Scores range from 1-99. A school scoring 75 has done better than 75 percent of other public schools in California.
Key: Rd (Reading), Ma (Math), Lg (Language), Sp (Spelling), Sci (Science) and SS (Social Science).

Grade	Rd	Ma	Lg	Sp	Sci	SS
Canfield Ave. Elem., Los Angeles						
2	45	47	63	52		
3	60	38	66	59		
4	60	65	69	65		
5	64	52	75	74		
Canoga Park Elem., Canoga Park						
2	16	9	12	18		
3	10	3	13	6		
4	14	16	10	15		
5	10	8	4	6		
Canoga Park Sr. High, Canoga Park						
9	29	40	30		31	27
10	41	54	45		48	47
11	51	65	53		48	58
Cantara St. Elem., Reseda						
2	30	32	23	32		
3	29	37	37	46		
4	26	47	34	37		
5	31	50	42	25		
Canterbury Ave. Elem., Pacoima						
2	45	53	60	69		
3	45	49	65	59		
4	44	47	45	49		
5	48	38	49	49		
Canyon Elem., Palisades						
2	93	94	94	92		
3	97	82	94	95		
4	95	77	94	93		
5	92	84	84	84		
Capistrano Ave. Elem., Canoga Park						
2	64	52	55	76		
3	32	20	26	37		
4	43	29	28	31		
5	50	36	32	35		
Carnegie Middle, Carson						
6	27	25	31	36		
7	34	26	30	35		
8	30	23	33	41		
Caroldale Ave. Elem., Carson						
2	48	35	60	76		
3	47	35	49	68		
4	43	42	54	59		
5	45	36	45	52		
6	34	24	42	51		
7	54	74	71	72		
8	44	41	39	48		
Carpenter Ave. Elem., Studio City						
2	94	92	98	94		
3	94	90	92	86		
4	89	85	92	85		
5	97	91	97	88		
Carson Sr. High, Carson						
9	41	37	46		40	37
10	47	46	53		43	41
11	46	44	48		42	46
Carson St. Elem., Carson						
2	15	10	20	29		
3	31	30	44	51		
4	33	24	40	45		
5	29	33	33	43		

Grade	Rd	Ma	Lg	Sp	Sci	SS
Carthay Ctr. Elem., Near Beverly Hills						
2	30	12	39	50		
3	36	19	40	48		
4	34	26	40	37		
5	47	36	49	57		
Carver Middle, Southeast L.A.						
6	2	3	2	2		
7	2	4	4	2		
8	5	7	6	4		
Castelar St. Elem., Chinatown						
2	36	55	46	65		
3	33	65	47	84		
4	56	82	69	80		
5	48	77	51	69		
Castle Heights Elem., Cheviot Hills						
2	43	42	47	64		
3	67	65	68	73		
4	66	52	75	71		
5	74	61	71	74		
Castlebay Ln. Elem., Northridge						
2	82	87	89	91		
3	80	85	82	91		
4	80	91	84	88		
5	86	90	87	90		
Catskill Ave. Elem., Carson						
2	57	45	58	73		
3	27	42	35	51		
4	31	40	34	45		
5	28	34	27	35		
Central (Cont.), Downtown						
9	19	19	18		28	21
10	23	22	23		22	19
11	30	9	23		6	23
Century Park Elem., Inglewood						
2	43	30	40	65		
3	19	4	15	35		
4	24	16	30	42		
5	23	14	16	37		
Chandler Elem., Van Nuys						
2	46	60	63	65		
3	39	27	45	57		
4	38	31	42	33		
5	50	50	58	47		
Chapman Elem., Gardena						
2	38	32	41	44		
3	41	35	51	57		
4	58	65	75	60		
5	58	44	56	46		
Charnock Rd. Elem., Palms						
2	30	18	37	56		
3	21	10	22	44		
4	49	47	58	44		
5	26	19	30	22		
Chase St. Elem., Panorama City						
2	16	15	20	38		
3	15	13	22	18		
4	24	29	21	20		
5	25	9	22	19		

Copyright © 2001 McCormack's Guides. No reproduction without permission.

STATE SCHOOL RANKINGS

Scores range from 1-99. A school scoring 75 has done better than 75 percent of other public schools in California.
Key: Rd (Reading), Ma (Math), Lg (Language), Sp (Spelling), Sci (Science) and SS (Social Science).

Grade	Rd	Ma	Lg	Sp	Sci	SS
Chatsworth Park Elem., Chatsworth						
2	50	35	53	67		
3	68	61	74	80		
4	56	50	60	75		
5	62	62	56	65		
Chatsworth Sr. High, Chatsworth						
9	55	58	59		58	50
10	65	67	67		65	57
11	71	75	77		73	69
Cheremoya Ave. Elem., Hollywood						
2	23	21	14	32		
3	13	14	12	26		
4	9	15	12	15		
5	19	33	32	18		
Cheviot Hills (Cont.), Cheviot Hills						
10	43	33	35		29	27
11	22	1	41		2	18
Cienega Elem., Crenshaw						
2	16	21	12	14		
3	13	14	17	13		
4	11	18	15	13		
5	16	7	18	20		
Cimarron Ave. Elem., Hawthorne						
2	30	22	41	54		
3	36	30	42	64		
4	27	6	18	35		
5	28	13	18	25		
City of Angels (Ind. Study), Los Angeles						
2	87	55	78	96		
3	64	28	56	57		
4	65	35	51	70		
5	83	55	58	77		
6	54	22	30	42		
7	66	40	52	71		
8	44	23	32	29		
9	37	24	32		31	29
10	41	27	33		31	38
11	36	26	36		24	29
City Terrace Elem., East L.A.						
2	15	11	9	15		
3	5	3	13	9		
4	9	11	13	20		
5	18	18	29	12		
Clay Middle, Near Hawthorne						
6	6	3	8	6		
7	4	3	7	6		
8	6	5	11	9		
Cleveland High, Reseda						
9	52	58	49		45	57
10	56	70	57		60	55
11	67	77	63		58	75
Clifford St. Elem., Silver Lake						
2	10	4	14	24		
3	27	40	28	24		
4	44	57	58	35		
5	34	81	64	47		

Grade	Rd	Ma	Lg	Sp	Sci	SS
Clover Ave. Elem., Palms						
2	93	87	97	97		
3	96	94	99	98		
4	91	92	95	93		
5	81	85	86	88		
Coeur D'Alene Ave. Elem., Venice						
2	69	75	81	83		
3	74	56	78	62		
4	69	45	72	64		
5	74	72	69	67		
Cohasset St. Elem., Van Nuys						
2	5	4	11	9		
3	21	16	23	26		
4	13	13	21	20		
5	5	8	13	9		
Coldwater Canyon Ave. Elem., N. Hollywood						
2	7	4	9	16		
3	15	19	20	35		
4	13	10	10	15		
5	7	10	5	6		
Colfax Ave. Elem., North Hollywood						
2	38	30	58	42		
3	51	35	57	46		
4	39	35	36	28		
5	70	68	75	55		
Coliseum St. Elem., Crenshaw						
2	20	11	37	44		
3	17	4	20	35		
4	34	9	26	31		
5	16	5	10	23		
Columbus Middle, Canoga Park						
6	29	26	31	32		
7	22	22	22	23		
8	24	21	25	22		
Commonwealth Ave. Elem., Westlake						
2	36	66	58	64		
3	19	45	46	44		
4	27	36	49	33		
5	43	71	77	59		
Community Charter Middle, ne Bev. Hils						
6	20	12	12	19		
Community Elem., Near Culver City						
2	85	87	90	97		
3	81	85	85	94		
4	91	91	93	90		
5	77	82	83	84		
Compton Ave. Elem., Los Angeles						
2	35	55	41	40		
3	13	25	23	44		
4	16	7	17	11		
5	12	19	18	25		
Cooper Opportunity High, San Pedro						
8	2	13	3	1		
9	7	5	12		14	13
Corona Ave. Elem., Bell						
2	9	13	9	13		
3	6	12	8	9		
4	16	16	12	13		
5	18	22	16	14		

Copyright © 2001 McCormack's Guides. No reproduction without permission.

STATE SCHOOL RANKINGS

Scores range from 1-99. A school scoring 75 has done better than 75 percent of other public schools in California.
Key: Rd (Reading), Ma (Math), Lg (Language), Sp (Spelling), Sci (Science) and SS (Social Science).

Cowan Ave. Elem., Westchester

Grade	Rd	Ma	Lg	Sp	Sci	SS
2	79	79	79	84		
3	76	70	80	84		
4	60	58	56	71		
5	74	59	60	70		

Crenshaw Sr. High, Leimert Park

Grade	Rd	Ma	Lg	Sp	Sci	SS
9	19	22	21		24	17
10	30	31	32		31	21
11	28	32	30		26	29

Crescent Hts. Blvd. Elem., Near Beverly Hills

Grade	Rd	Ma	Lg	Sp	Sci	SS
2	32	33	46	54		
3	44	34	59	46		
4	43	29	40	49		
5	31	24	35	25		

Crestwood St. Elem., San Pedro

Grade	Rd	Ma	Lg	Sp	Sci	SS
2	75	82	82	69		
3	65	60	65	48		
4	68	73	60	70		
5	74	73	61	70		

Curtiss Middle, Carson

Grade	Rd	Ma	Lg	Sp	Sci	SS
6	27	13	19	29		
7	30	19	26	35		
8	26	18	21	34		

Dahlia Heights Elem., Eagle Rock

Grade	Rd	Ma	Lg	Sp	Sci	SS
2	74	89	97	81		
3	58	54	62	48		
4	68	50	72	67		
5	68	26	53	42		
6	61	48	52	68		

Dana Middle, San Pedro

Grade	Rd	Ma	Lg	Sp	Sci	SS
6	23	18	19	22		
7	30	22	22	31		
8	30	25	28	29		

Danube Ave. Elem., Granada Hills

Grade	Rd	Ma	Lg	Sp	Sci	SS
2	50	27	41	68		
3	59	51	74	73		
4	49	44	56	71		
5	55	62	72	65		

Darby Ave. Elem., Northridge

Grade	Rd	Ma	Lg	Sp	Sci	SS
2	64	76	75	68		
3	39	45	44	68		
4	59	58	62	67		
5	36	38	35	37		

Dayton Heights Elem., Near Hollywood

Grade	Rd	Ma	Lg	Sp	Sci	SS
2	4	9	16	9		
3	5	7	6	16		
4	14	12	9	14		
5	8	5	10	11		
6	11	12	7	14		

De Portola Middle, Los Angeles

Grade	Rd	Ma	Lg	Sp	Sci	SS
6	64	55	70	70		
7	71	76	79	72		
8	84	76	82	85		

Dearborn St. Elem., Northridge

Grade	Rd	Ma	Lg	Sp	Sci	SS
2	53	52	65	62		
3	62	71	60	66		
4	55	44	49	50		
5	53	31	42	54		

Del Amo Elem., Carson

Grade	Rd	Ma	Lg	Sp	Sci	SS
2	38	9	30	56		
3	47	44	47	70		
4	33	36	28	47		
5	29	21	20	37		

Del Rey (Cont.), Westcheser

Grade	Rd	Ma	Lg	Sp	Sci	SS
10	38	17	16		31	53

Delevan Dr. Elem., Near Eagle Rock

Grade	Rd	Ma	Lg	Sp	Sci	SS
2	64	76	71	76		
3	51	47	59	75		
4	60	57	66	75		
5	56	55	45	61		
6	60	83	72	86		

Dena Elem., Boyle Heights

Grade	Rd	Ma	Lg	Sp	Sci	SS
2	2	3	3	3		
3	2	8	3	5		
4	2	9	4	2		
5	5	8	10	7		

Denker Ave. Elem., Gardena

Grade	Rd	Ma	Lg	Sp	Sci	SS
2	43	45	52	44		
3	39	44	44	48		
4	32	31	31	38		
5	29	36	25	31		

Dixie Canyon Ave. Elem., Sherman Oaks

Grade	Rd	Ma	Lg	Sp	Sci	SS
2	55	33	60	73		
3	65	32	60	48		
4	74	47	71	73		
5	80	64	74	79		

Dodson Middle, San Pedro

Grade	Rd	Ma	Lg	Sp	Sci	SS
6	54	42	44	55		
7	62	67	60	65		
8	64	70	64	74		

Dolores St. Elem., Carson

Grade	Rd	Ma	Lg	Sp	Sci	SS
2	36	30	39	65		
3	47	30	46	66		
4	38	26	36	47		
5	40	44	49	55		

Dominguez Elem., Carson

Grade	Rd	Ma	Lg	Sp	Sci	SS
2	28	25	33	46		
3	26	20	28	46		
4	24	19	21	28		
5	23	26	25	37		

Dorris Place Elem., Cypress Park

Grade	Rd	Ma	Lg	Sp	Sci	SS
2	33	42	53	60		
3	19	22	33	55		
4	28	27	34	35		
5	25	28	30	27		

Dorsey Sr. High, Crenshaw

Grade	Rd	Ma	Lg	Sp	Sci	SS
9	17	20	23		15	13
10	26	22	31		22	19
11	28	30	37		19	27

Downtown Business High, Los Angeles

Grade	Rd	Ma	Lg	Sp	Sci	SS
9	55	56	62		45	47
10	58	59	60		53	53
11	65	62	65		46	54

Drew Middle, Florence

Grade	Rd	Ma	Lg	Sp	Sci	SS
6	1	2	2	1		
7	2	3	3	3		
8	5	6	6	7		

Scores range from 1-99. A school scoring 75 has done better than 75 percent of other public schools in California.
Key: Rd (Reading), Ma (Math), Lg (Language), Sp (Spelling), Sci (Science) and SS (Social Science).

Grade	Rd	Ma	Lg	Sp	Sci	SS	Grade	Rd	Ma	Lg	Sp	Sci	SS
Dyer St. Elem., Sylmar							**Elizabeth Learning Center, Cudahy**						
2	7	6	13	6			2	3	4	5	6		
3	13	13	18	9			3	1	1	3	3		
4	14	15	9	8			4	2	1	3	2		
5	16	11	6	7			5	4	4	10	5		
Eagle Rock Elem., Eagle Rock							6	7	4	7	4		
2	66	62	72	75			7	12	11	12	6		
3	60	56	59	66			8	9	13	11	7		
4	69	65	64	70			9	37	38	38		47	57
5	66	65	63	61			10	26	29	33		25	24
6	72	60	64	74			11	42	35	43		36	35
Eagle Rock Jr-Sr High, Eagle Rock							**Ellington High (Cont.)**						
7	65	54	60	70			9	5	5	1		9	6
8	59	39	52	59			10	3	2	1		15	4
9	52	54	57		47	50	11	5	1	6		26	15
10	64	63	62		61	64	**Elysian Heights Elem., Echo Park**						
11	69	67	63		62	75	2	9	7	17	19		
Eagle Tree (Cont.), Carson							3	10	17	22	10		
9	11	7	3		11	3	4	24	33	43	37		
10	15	20	13		18	1	5	21	33	18	22		
Earhart (Cont.), N. Hollywood							**Emelita St. Elem., Encino**						
10	21	33	32		25	13	2	46	40	55	60		
Eastman Ave. Elem., East L.A.							3	36	42	51	44		
2	27	18	34	42			4	56	57	66	55		
3	19	28	23	10			5	50	46	61	52		
4	17	29	24	15			**Emerson Middle, Rancho Park**						
5	16	34	27	9			6	30	21	22	30		
Edison Middle, Florence							7	32	23	35	30		
6	1	2	4	2			8	32	28	29	34		
7	3	5	7	4			**Encino Elem., Encino**						
8	4	8	7	4			2	69	60	82	80		
Einstein (Cont.), Sepulveda							3	44	40	46	59		
9	22	7	21		34	19	4	55	55	67	67		
10	7	14	10		10	29	5	52	55	44	42		
11	13	6	17		8	25	**Erwin St. Elem., Van Nuys**						
El Camino Real Sr. High, Woodland Hills							2	28	23	45	48		
9	81	81	86		79	80	3	29	28	40	41		
10	90	90	90		88	88	4	27	16	31	29		
11	95	95	95		94	94	5	23	18	29	23		
El Dorado Ave. Elem., Sylmar							**Eshelman Ave. Elem., Lomita**						
2	23	55	37	19			2	28	32	25	35		
3	23	16	18	15			3	54	54	62	80		
4	30	36	37	33			4	34	47	47	42		
5	26	24	35	14			5	52	44	47	81		
El Oro Way Elem., Granada Hills							**Esperanza Elem., Westlake**						
2	64	84	75	80			2	1	5	2	1		
3	55	61	59	68			3	1	5	3	1		
4	41	31	30	37			4	1	7	5	1		
5	64	46	37	49			5	3	18	2	2		
El Sereno Elem., El Sereno							**Euclid Ave. Elem., Boyle Heights**						
2	33	53	27	46			2	12	22	23	16		
3	17	34	17	7			3	19	16	30	13		
4	11	27	18	11			4	16	19	24	13		
5	18	40	16	11			5	16	9	22	16		
El Sereno Middle, El Sereno							**Evergreen Ave. Elem., Boyle Heights**						
6	11	19	17	14			2	5	8	6	14		
7	14	28	20	18			3	10	9	11	12		
8	13	27	21	19			4	22	24	34	22		
							5	10	14	3	9		

STATE SCHOOL RANKINGS

Scores range from 1-99. A school scoring 75 has done better than 75 percent of other public schools in California.
Key: Rd (Reading), Ma (Math), Lg (Language), Sp (Spelling), Sci (Science) and SS (Social Science).

Evergreen (Cont.), Sylmar

Grade	Rd	Ma	Lg	Sp	Sci	SS
9	12	2	12		18	9
10	15	14	25		16	10

Fair Ave. Elem., North Hollywood

Grade	Rd	Ma	Lg	Sp
2	17	18	24	29
3	17	32	31	26
4	19	24	24	17
5	16	14	16	7

Fairburn Ave. Elem., Westwood

Grade	Rd	Ma	Lg	Sp
2	89	92	94	98
3	97	95	98	97
4	93	96	98	94
5	95	93	97	93

Fairfax Sr. High, North Hollywood

Grade	Rd	Ma	Lg	Sp	Sci	SS
9	39	45	50		40	31
10	38	54	51		41	35
11	42	65	59		42	47

Farmdale Elem., El Sereno

Grade	Rd	Ma	Lg	Sp
2	30	37	43	48
3	27	16	22	22
4	27	18	26	26
5	21	24	16	14

Fenton Ave. Elem., Pacoima

Grade	Rd	Ma	Lg	Sp
2	12	21	17	12
3	12	14	18	10
4	9	13	18	5
5	18	28	32	25

Fernangeles Elem., Sun Valley

Grade	Rd	Ma	Lg	Sp
2	15	7	11	8
3	7	6	6	3
4	9	12	6	2
5	7	6	3	4

Fifteenth St. Elem., San Pedro

Grade	Rd	Ma	Lg	Sp
2	5	9	9	8
3	15	12	18	18
4	17	9	6	8
5	14	9	11	12

Fifty-Fourth St. Elem., Windsor Hills

Grade	Rd	Ma	Lg	Sp
2	74	76	76	84
3	56	58	63	72
4	45	31	53	52
5	16	4	4	35

Fifty-Ninth St. Elem., Near Inglewood

Grade	Rd	Ma	Lg	Sp
2	17	12	31	29
3	9	10	23	16
4	19	12	17	28
5	19	9	16	23

Fifty-Second St. Elem., South Central L.A.

Grade	Rd	Ma	Lg	Sp
2	4	2	4	4
3	5	4	9	9
4	4	2	3	7
5	3	2	2	5

Figueroa St. Elem., South Central L.A.

Grade	Rd	Ma	Lg	Sp
2	3	3	8	3
3	7	5	9	13
4	2	2	2	2
5	3	2	5	2

First St. Elem., Boyle Heights

Grade	Rd	Ma	Lg	Sp
2	8	11	12	16
3	6	25	12	16
4	14	13	12	15
5	10	16	16	6

Fishburn Ave. Elem., Maywood

Grade	Rd	Ma	Lg	Sp
2	12	15	24	16
3	10	8	18	24
4	6	11	15	5
5	11	5	7	13

Fleming Middle, Lomita

Grade	Rd	Ma	Lg	Sp
6	27	21	23	30
7	26	16	25	24
8	26	21	29	29

Fletcher Dr. Elem., Glassell Park

Grade	Rd	Ma	Lg	Sp
2	3	1	5	4
3	4	8	7	12
4	4	4	7	5
5	3	5	4	3

Florence Avenue Elem., Florence

Grade	Rd	Ma	Lg	Sp
2	1	4	2	3
3	4	4	3	5
4	2	4	3	4
5	1	3	5	4

Flournoy Elem., Watts

Grade	Rd	Ma	Lg	Sp
2	16	11	17	28
3	8	10	18	26
4	13	6	22	17
5	16	24	25	31

Ford Blvd. Elem., East Los Angeles

Grade	Rd	Ma	Lg	Sp
2	12	10	25	4
3	5	7	15	4
4	6	7	6	2
5	5	4	4	2

Forty-Ninth St. Elem., SE Los Angeles

Grade	Rd	Ma	Lg	Sp
2	1	2	1	2
3	1	6	2	5
4	1	2	2	1
5	1	1	1	1

Forty-Second St. Elem., Leimert Park

Grade	Rd	Ma	Lg	Sp
2	22	19	35	56
3	31	23	35	48
4	19	9	17	20
5	25	11	18	39

Foshay Learning Ctr, Near Leimert Park

Grade	Rd	Ma	Lg	Sp	Sci	SS
2	12	7	17	24		
3	26	21	27	30		
4	43	55	45	42		
5	40	38	40	35		
6	10	6	11	11		
7	15	10	18	14		
8	16	11	18	13		
9	47	47	50		47	47
10	62	54	62		45	59
11	62	51	63		48	77

STATE SCHOOL RANKINGS

Scores range from 1-99. A school scoring 75 has done better than 75 percent of other public schools in California.
Key: Rd (Reading), Ma (Math), Lg (Language), Sp (Spelling), Sci (Science) and SS (Social Science).

Fourth St. Elem., East Los Angeles

Grade	Rd	Ma	Lg	Sp	Sci	SS
2	17	9	19	22		
3	12	17	17	9		
4	13	13	18	16		
5	19	21	33	20		

Francis Polytechnic, Sun Valley

Grade	Rd	Ma	Lg	Sp	Sci	SS
9	21	34	28		33	28
10	28	37	32		35	28
11	32	39	34		38	33

Franklin Ave. Elem., Near Hollywood

Grade	Rd	Ma	Lg	Sp	Sci	SS
2	67	30	58	78		
3	56	61	70	88		
4	49	48	53	71		
5	59	58	58	70		

Franklin Sr. High, Highland Park

Grade	Rd	Ma	Lg	Sp	Sci	SS
9	25	32	37		26	34
10	34	44	43		33	32
11	46	51	54		38	47

Fremont Sr. High, Southeast L.A.

Grade	Rd	Ma	Lg	Sp	Sci	SS
9	9	15	17		9	15
10	12	20	23		12	13
11	22	30	27		17	25

Fries Ave. Elem., Wilmington

Grade	Rd	Ma	Lg	Sp	Sci	SS
2	3	5	5	5		
3	7	8	7	9		
4	13	15	10	11		
5	7	7	6	6		

Frost Middle, Granada Hills

Grade	Rd	Ma	Lg	Sp	Sci	SS
6	53	45	58	56		
7	59	48	65	63		
8	62	51	64	64		

Fullbright Ave. Elem., Canoga Park

Grade	Rd	Ma	Lg	Sp	Sci	SS
2	30	22	30	46		
3	19	11	20	33		
4	27	31	28	29		
5	25	18	18	16		

Fulton Middle, Van Nuys

Grade	Rd	Ma	Lg	Sp	Sci	SS
6	6	3	6	4		
7	11	8	10	10		
8	13	8	12	8		

Gage Middle, Huntington Park

Grade	Rd	Ma	Lg	Sp	Sci	SS
6	4	4	5	3		
7	8	12	15	6		
8	8	11	13	9		

Garden Grove Elem., Reseda

Grade	Rd	Ma	Lg	Sp	Sci	SS
2	28	25	31	26		
3	19	30	26	35		
4	17	23	26	14		
5	36	33	27	49		

Gardena Elem., Gardena

Grade	Rd	Ma	Lg	Sp	Sci	SS
2	6	16	6	10		
3	9	19	15	13		
4	16	26	17	16		
5	19	21	20	20		

Gardena Sr. High, Gardena

Grade	Rd	Ma	Lg	Sp	Sci	SS
9	26	32	28		24	24
10	36	38	40		36	27
11	37	46	41		36	34

Gardner St. Elem., Hollywood

Grade	Rd	Ma	Lg	Sp	Sci	SS
2	52	53	53	58		
3	51	68	71	57		
4	55	70	71	60		
5	64	73	75	55		

Garfield Sr. High, East Los Angeles

Grade	Rd	Ma	Lg	Sp	Sci	SS
9	17	30	24		20	29
10	26	40	32		33	29
11	33	41	36		33	42

Garvanza Elem., Highland Park

Grade	Rd	Ma	Lg	Sp	Sci	SS
2	15	27	27	29		
3	21	8	23	20		
4	27	18	22	28		
5	25	14	23	27		

Gates St. Elem., Boyle Heights

Grade	Rd	Ma	Lg	Sp	Sci	SS
2	12	9	20	24		
3	9	11	8	26		
4	11	8	12	20		
5	9	8	6	11		

Gault Street Elem., Van Nuys

Grade	Rd	Ma	Lg	Sp	Sci	SS
2	30	45	37	35		
3	23	17	26	12		
4	32	31	24	26		
5	23	19	27	22		

Germain St. Elem., Chatsworth

Grade	Rd	Ma	Lg	Sp	Sci	SS
2	75	57	76	80		
3	73	81	81	73		
4	78	76	84	77		
5	83	81	82	78		

Glassell Park Elem., Glassell Park

Grade	Rd	Ma	Lg	Sp	Sci	SS
2	16	21	28	29		
3	17	17	20	18		
4	14	15	10	14		
5	23	22	20	27		

Gledhill St. Elem., North Hills

Grade	Rd	Ma	Lg	Sp	Sci	SS
2	38	37	53	56		
3	33	54	42	46		
4	33	38	42	44		
5	45	55	47	55		

Glen Alta Elem., Montecito Heights

Grade	Rd	Ma	Lg	Sp	Sci	SS
2	7	5	13	13		
3	23	23	26	30		
4	16	23	31	19		
5	31	31	42	25		
6	13	22	19	11		

Glenfeliz Blvd. Elem., Northeast Los Angeles

Grade	Rd	Ma	Lg	Sp	Sci	SS
2	25	39	40	26		
3	17	35	51	28		
4	39	58	43	45		
5	33	41	44	31		

Glenwood Elem., Sun Valley

Grade	Rd	Ma	Lg	Sp	Sci	SS
2	17	21	27	20		
3	17	29	22	22		
4	19	23	21	19		
5	12	4	3	9		

Gompers Middle, Southeast L.A.

Grade	Rd	Ma	Lg	Sp	Sci	SS
6	2	1	1	2		
7	2	4	3	3		
8	3	5	5	5		

Copyright © 2001 McCormack's Guides. No reproduction without permission.

68 STATE SCHOOL RANKINGS

Scores range from 1-99. A school scoring 75 has done better than 75 percent of other public schools in California.
Key: Rd (Reading), Ma (Math), Lg (Language), Sp (Spelling), Sci (Science) and SS (Social Science).

Grade	Rd	Ma	Lg	Sp	Sci	SS
Graham Elem., Watts						
2	3	1	3	3		
3	3	3	5	3		
4	2	1	2	2		
5	5	1	2	3		
Granada Elem., Granada Hills						
2	48	50	52	50		
3	47	54	56	62		
4	45	38	42	44		
5	40	36	35	43		
Granada Hills Sr. High, Granada Hills						
9	74	82	83		71	76
10	88	91	90		88	84
11	90	93	91		87	92
Grand View Blvd. Elem., Near Mar Vista						
2	37	37	39	38		
3	17	20	23	13		
4	24	24	30	17		
5	37	40	37	22		
Grant Elem., Hollywood						
2	22	28	25	29		
3	17	25	33	41		
4	24	29	18	22		
5	16	24	18	14		
Grant Sr. High, Van Nuys						
9	31	39	38		34	38
10	47	53	53		49	43
11	53	60	60		50	57
Grape St. Elem., Watts						
2	8	6	4	13		
3	1	1	2	7		
4	1	1	1	3		
5	2	8	5	6		
Gratts Elem., Los Angeles						
2	1	1	1	2		
3	1	3	2	3		
4	1	2	3	4		
5	2	2	5	2		
Grey (Cont.), Reseda						
9	34	16	24		1	9
10	56	38	59		57	47
Gridley St. Elem., San Fernando						
2	12	6	9	12		
3	4	5	3	5		
4	13	12	15	11		
5	9	9	6	3		
Griffin Ave. Elem., Northeast Los Angeles						
2	20	49	41	38		
3	6	25	18	18		
4	21	35	31	29		
5	12	40	25	14		
Griffith Middle, East Los Angeles						
6	5	5	7	4		
7	9	9	10	8		
8	10	10	12	8		
Griffith Joyner Elem., Watts						
2	16	5	12	19		
3	5	11	9	18		
4	11	7	8	11		
5	3	14	4	9		
Gulf Ave. Elem., Wilmington						
2	8	10	16	14		
3	10	16	23	15		
4	11	18	15	7		
5	10	14	23	9		
Haddon Ave. Elem., Pacoima						
2	4	5	6	2		
3	9	15	13	4		
4	9	9	9	3		
5	7	4	6	4		
Hale Middle, Woodland Hills						
6	72	68	72	76		
7	75	75	76	72		
8	75	75	75	78		
Halldale Elem., Torrance						
2	48	53	65	73		
3	41	51	60	70		
4	24	33	42	42		
5	34	41	44	29		
Hamasaki Elem., East Los Angeles						
2	8	15	9	13		
3	3	5	5	6		
4	6	8	4	4		
5	9	8	6	5		
Hamilton Sr. High, Near Culver City						
9	55	47	52		45	57
10	58	51	60		49	51
11	69	57	69		54	71
Hamlin St. Elem., Canoga Park						
2	25	16	27	38		
3	41	44	60	72		
4	47	48	53	44		
5	40	46	40	22		
Hammel St. Elem., East Los Angeles						
2	6	16	11	7		
3	4	12	7	6		
4	9	13	9	8		
5	10	24	20	7		
Hancock Park Elem., Hancock Park						
2	90	89	87	99		
3	88	96	97	99		
4	89	92	95	97		
5	81	90	84	89		
Harbor City Elem., Near Wilmington						
2	7	12	13	16		
3	19	16	26	24		
4	8	5	5	5		
5	16	7	20	16		
Harding St. Elem., Sylmar						
2	57	60	47	75		
3	51	60	51	46		
4	33	19	31	31		
5	42	41	37	29		

Copyright © 2001 McCormack's Guides. No reproduction without permission.

STATE SCHOOL RANKINGS 69

Scores range from 1-99. A school scoring 75 has done better than 75 percent of other public schools in California.
Key: Rd (Reading), Ma (Math), Lg (Language), Sp (Spelling), Sci (Science) and SS (Social Science).

Harrison St. Elem., East Los Angeles

Grade	Rd	Ma	Lg	Sp	Sci	SS
2	10	10	5	5		
3	5	13	7	4		
4	8	24	7	4		
5	7	26	14	6		
6	10	10	17	5		
7	10	13	15	6		
8	7	6	7	6		

Hart St. Elem., Canoga Park

Grade	Rd	Ma	Lg	Sp
2	7	13	11	9
3	12	16	12	13
4	5	4	7	7
5	6	14	8	7

Harte Prep. Int., South Central L.A.

Grade	Rd	Ma	Lg	Sp
6	3	1	3	2
7	5	4	9	5
8	9	7	12	12

Haskell Elem., Granada Hills

Grade	Rd	Ma	Lg	Sp
2	38	42	41	42
3	59	65	70	72
4	53	42	56	55
5	52	48	45	46

Hawaiian Ave. Elem., Wilmington

Grade	Rd	Ma	Lg	Sp
2	7	11	12	12
3	5	7	7	10
4	5	7	9	8
5	6	5	8	11

Haynes Elem., West Hills

Grade	Rd	Ma	Lg	Sp
2	52	75	60	73
3	64	51	57	66
4	63	54	54	62
5	62	65	60	43

Hazeltine Ave. Elem., Van Nuys

Grade	Rd	Ma	Lg	Sp
2	16	22	21	26
3	12	21	9	15
4	9	10	8	5
5	12	9	16	14

Heliotrope Ave. Elem., Maywood

Grade	Rd	Ma	Lg	Sp
2	12	22	14	13
3	7	17	9	10
4	9	13	13	4
5	9	8	14	7

Henry Middle, Granada Hills

Grade	Rd	Ma	Lg	Sp
6	44	38	36	46
7	48	48	42	43
8	46	49	43	41

Herrick Ave. Elem., Sylmar

Grade	Rd	Ma	Lg	Sp
2	40	47	49	30
3	27	15	26	18
4	26	23	34	19
5	34	33	38	23

Highland Park (Cont.), Highland Park

Grade	Rd	Ma	Lg	Sp	Sci	SS
9	28	5	7		14	23
10	34	14	31		8	56
11	42	38	34		29	50

Hillcrest Dr. Elem., Crenshaw

Grade	Rd	Ma	Lg	Sp
2	3	1	3	13
3	6	3	8	15
4	8	3	3	10
5	12	6	3	16

Hillside Elem., Montecito Heights

Grade	Rd	Ma	Lg	Sp
2	19	7	9	13
3	6	4	8	15
4	4	2	3	5
5	6	3	2	11

Hobart Blvd. Elem., Near Downtown L.A.

Grade	Rd	Ma	Lg	Sp
2	28	63	39	54
3	31	67	47	80
4	34	55	51	52
5	29	52	32	48

Hollenbeck Middle, Boyle Heights

Grade	Rd	Ma	Lg	Sp
6	6	6	3	5
7	5	8	6	5
8	8	8	7	5

Hollywood Sr. High, Hollywood

Grade	Rd	Ma	Lg	Sp	Sci	SS
9	29	28	38		20	31
10	38	38	48		33	29
11	47	43	51		40	42

Holmes Ave. Elem., Near Vernon

Grade	Rd	Ma	Lg	Sp
2	9	22	6	10
3	1	1	1	1
4	1	1	1	2
5	3	5	3	4

Holmes Middle, Northridge

Grade	Rd	Ma	Lg	Sp
6	35	24	36	40
7	46	29	42	45
8	46	37	46	48

Hooper Ave. Elem., Near Vernon

Grade	Rd	Ma	Lg	Sp
2	1	4	6	1
3	1	2	2	1
4	1	1	2	1
5	1	1	3	1

Hoover St. Elem., Westlake

Grade	Rd	Ma	Lg	Sp
2	3	6	5	8
3	3	4	4	5
4	5	3	5	5
5	10	9	6	3

Hope (Cont.), Downtown LA

Grade	Rd	Ma	Lg	Sp	Sci	SS
10	23	22	16		18	1

Hubbard St. Elem., Sylmar

Grade	Rd	Ma	Lg	Sp
2	33	50	58	38
3	33	29	33	37
4	28	18	24	26
5	23	28	20	25

Hughes Elem., Cudahy

Grade	Rd	Ma	Lg	Sp
2	6	3	13	10
3	14	22	33	17
4	13	21	22	14
5	18	24	35	25
6	10	19	20	14

Humphreys Ave. Elem., East Los Angeles

Grade	Rd	Ma	Lg	Sp
2	7	25	11	9
3	4	7	9	2
4	24	33	31	16
5	21	31	22	12

Huntington Dr. Elem., Montecito Heights

Grade	Rd	Ma	Lg	Sp
2	7	19	12	10
3	5	16	13	5
4	4	15	12	4
5	12	13	13	11

Copyright © 2001 McCormack's Guides. No reproduction without permission.

STATE SCHOOL RANKINGS

Scores range from 1-99. A school scoring 75 has done better than 75 percent of other public schools in California.
Key: Rd (Reading), Ma (Math), Lg (Language), Sp (Spelling), Sci (Science) and SS (Social Science).

Grade	Rd	Ma	Lg	Sp	Sci	SS
Huntington Park Sr. High, Huntington Park						
9	14	24	21		18	24
10	26	36	29		27	21
11	36	40	36		22	35
Hyde Park Blvd. Elem., Near Inglewood						
2	2	1	6	4		
3	3	2	4	9		
4	2	1	1	2		
5	7	1	1	2		
Independence (Cont.)						
9	64	30	38		47	37
10	45	33	25		31	24
11	47	30	51		64	54
Independence Elem., South Gate						
2	12	6	17	14		
3	5	10	8	8		
4	11	12	15	8		
5	16	15	16	8		
Indian Springs (Cont.), Sawtelle						
9	17	7	28		50	6
10	12	4	29		25	26
Irving Middle, Glassell Park						
6	20	17	20	19		
7	24	28	26	26		
8	24	21	24	20		
Ivanhoe Elem., Silver Park						
2	85	76	79	90		
3	83	63	75	57		
4	89	83	90	86		
5	90	81	89	92		
Jefferson New Middle, Los Angeles						
6	1	2	2	1		
7	2	4	3	1		
8	3	5	4			
Jefferson Sr. High, Near Vernon						
9	7	18	14		12	11
10	12	29	21		20	13
11	24	35	29		24	27
Johnson Opportunity High, E. 54th St.						
8	1	1	1	1		
9	9	7	7		15	8
10	7	2	10		4	9
11	4	16	7		15	12
Jordan Sr. High, Watts						
9	9	19	17		16	17
10	15	24	23		22	13
11	26	32	25		22	31
Justice St. Elem., Canoga Park						
2	91	84	90	93		
3	76	63	75	79		
4	69	60	69	71		
5	71	64	66	55		
Kennedy High, Granada Hills						
9	37	44	46		38	42
10	51	57	59		50	45
11	62	65	71		54	63

Grade	Rd	Ma	Lg	Sp	Sci	SS
Kennedy Elem., East Los Angeles						
2	9	21	17	10		
3	9	9	9	10		
4	11	6	6	3		
5	21	20	16	8		
Kenter Canyon Elem., Brentwood						
2	94	90	98	95		
3	95	85	93	85		
4	95	95	98	93		
5	85	82	83	69		
Kentwood Elem., Westchester						
2	74	45	71	76		
3	62	32	71	80		
4	73	52	75	80		
5	85	76	87	95		
Kester Ave. Elem., Van Nuys						
2	43	45	63	64		
3	49	44	68	59		
4	68	58	67	71		
5	73	67	66	70		
King Elem., Leimert Park						
2	25	47	39	26		
3	26	17	27	30		
4	21	26	32	17		
5	20	18	18	18		
King Middle, Silver Lake						
6	19	17	25	15		
7	18	19	22	16		
8	24	18	26	20		
King/Drew Medical Magnet High, Watts						
9	59	50	67		41	50
10	70	62	73		57	51
11	69	64	75		46	61
Kittridge St. Elem., Van Nuys						
2	15	15	23	20		
3	10	16	18	22		
4	13	19	15	16		
5	6	14	30	14		
Knollwood Elem., Granada Hills						
2	40	45	47	64		
3	65	68	77	68		
4	43	40	40	28		
5	36	26	25	29		
La Salle Ave. Elem., Near Inglewood						
2	16	8	12	35		
3	17	8	26	37		
4	6	3	12	17		
5	6	2	5	11		
Lanai Rd. Elem., Encino						
2	38	28	31	33		
3	13	10	22	30		
4	22	21	26	28		
5	36	26	25	42		
Lane Elem., Monterey Park						
2	64	59	63	58		
3	59	73	81	81		
4	50	70	64	59		
5	66	73	71	67		

STATE SCHOOL RANKINGS

Scores range from 1-99. A school scoring 75 has done better than 75 percent of other public schools in California.
Key: Rd (Reading), Ma (Math), Lg (Language), Sp (Spelling), Sci (Science) and SS (Social Science).

Langdon Ave. Elem., North Hills

Grade	Rd	Ma	Lg	Sp	Sci	SS
2	3	10	2	2		
3	2	17	2	3		
4	3	13	6	3		
5	2	7	2	1		

Lankershim Elem., North Hollywood

Grade	Rd	Ma	Lg	Sp	Sci	SS
2	15	6	21	24		
3	9	15	11	16		
4	16	18	21	22		
5	9	19	23	9		

Lassen Elem., North Hills

Grade	Rd	Ma	Lg	Sp	Sci	SS
2	38	39	28	40		
3	60	67	63	55		
4	36	38	31	55		
5	29	28	25	46		

Latona Ave. Elem., Montecito Heights

Grade	Rd	Ma	Lg	Sp	Sci	SS
2	16	13	17	22		
3	19	21	22	26		
4	17	24	24	24		
5	26	16	6	25		

Laurel Elem., West Hollywood

Grade	Rd	Ma	Lg	Sp	Sci	SS
2	32	47	64	60		
3	29	29	49	39		
4	36	54	38	31		
5	50	62	56	46		

Lawrence Middle, Chatsworth

Grade	Rd	Ma	Lg	Sp	Sci	SS
6	53	53	42	60		
7	46	46	44	54		
8	51	52	45	51		

Le Conte Middle, Hollywood

Grade	Rd	Ma	Lg	Sp	Sci	SS
6	12	8	14	14		
7	15	14	16	12		
8	16	18	21	19		

Leapwood Ave. Elem., Carson

Grade	Rd	Ma	Lg	Sp	Sci	SS
2	40	7	46	69		
3	39	25	60	72		
4	26	6	30	33		
5	25	9	25	42		

Leland St. Elem., San Pedro

Grade	Rd	Ma	Lg	Sp	Sci	SS
2	32	65	46	44		
3	44	56	52	51		
4	55	54	47	59		
5	50	40	40	29		

Lemay St. Elem., Van Nuys

Grade	Rd	Ma	Lg	Sp	Sci	SS
2	20	45	41	33		
3	33	37	28	35		
4	26	36	22	29		
5	53	59	49	37		

Leonis (Cont.), Woodland Hills

Grade	Rd	Ma	Lg	Sp	Sci	SS
9	19	7	9		11	3
10	32	11	47		36	45
11	7	6	15		39	15

Lewis (Cont.), Sun Valley

Grade	Rd	Ma	Lg	Sp	Sci	SS
9	14	16	12		7	29
10	26	5	29		18	32
11	39	29	25		44	47

Liberty Blvd. Elem., South Gate

Grade	Rd	Ma	Lg	Sp	Sci	SS
2	10	12	17	16		
3	10	25	26	16		
4	9	10	15	13		
5	9	9	16	16		

Liggett St. Elem., Panorama City

Grade	Rd	Ma	Lg	Sp	Sci	SS
2	12	12	11	16		
3	15	29	17	16		
4	16	27	24	20		
5	6	9	5	5		

Lillian St. Elem., Florence

Grade	Rd	Ma	Lg	Sp	Sci	SS
2	8	16	12	12		
3	7	17	13	16		
4	6	13	8	8		
5	4	5	7	4		

Limerick Ave. Elem., Canoga Park

Grade	Rd	Ma	Lg	Sp	Sci	SS
2	30	21	27	38		
3	26	35	35	35		
4	30	19	18	24		
5	40	34	40	29		

Lincoln Sr. High, Montecito Heights

Grade	Rd	Ma	Lg	Sp	Sci	SS
9	14	26	24		22	24
10	30	38	33		33	27
11	42	51	43		39	42

Locke Sr. High, Southeast L.A.

Grade	Rd	Ma	Lg	Sp	Sci	SS
9	5	9	8		9	8
10	9	11	13		12	9
11	15	24	11		15	13

Lockhurst Dr. Elem., Woodland Hills

Grade	Rd	Ma	Lg	Sp	Sci	SS
2	74	78	83	91		
3	65	67	75	88		
4	59	58	58	62		
5	70	73	69	77		

Lockwood Ave. Elem., Silver Lake

Grade	Rd	Ma	Lg	Sp	Sci	SS
2	3	3	5	7		
3	4	5	7	9		
4	6	6	9	14		
5	3	5	4	5		

Logan St. Elem., Echo Park

Grade	Rd	Ma	Lg	Sp	Sci	SS
2	25	39	34	30		
3	17	34	23	18		
4	22	26	28	19		
5	18	22	23	25		

Loma Vista Ave. Elem., Maywood

Grade	Rd	Ma	Lg	Sp	Sci	SS
2	6	4	8	12		
3	6	16	12	13		
4	9	12	13	8		
5	9	9	14	9		

Lomita Fund. Ctr Elem., Lomita

Grade	Rd	Ma	Lg	Sp	Sci	SS
2	69	60	77	80		
3	70	63	75	77		
4	56	50	62	66		
5	61	46	64	65		

London (Cont.), Van Nuys

Grade	Rd	Ma	Lg	Sp	Sci	SS
10	12	11	16		15	19
11	42	22	29		36	50

STATE SCHOOL RANKINGS

Scores range from 1-99. A school scoring 75 has done better than 75 percent of other public schools in California.
Key: Rd (Reading), Ma (Math), Lg (Language), Sp (Spelling), Sci (Science) and SS (Social Science).

Grade	Rd	Ma	Lg	Sp	Sci	SS
Lorena St. Elem., Near Boyle Heights						
2	3	11	7	3		
3	5	23	8	6		
4	9	13	8	5		
5	7	11	10	9		
Loreto St. Elem., Montecito Heights						
2	7	9	4	14		
3	9	9	7	4		
4	17	12	10	4		
5	10	13	11	5		
Lorne St. Elem., Northridge						
2	62	70	72	72		
3	68	79	72	75		
4	70	73	75	76		
5	65	62	74	71		
LA Center for Enriched Studies, Near Mid City						
6	81	71	80	74		
7	88	86	90	93		
8	94	85	93	95		
9	94	93	95		86	88
10	96	89	97		93	96
11	98	94	97		94	97
Los Angeles Elem., Los Angeles						
2	3	4	5	6		
3	5	3	4	3		
4	10	9	8	4		
5	12	7	3	4		
Los Angeles Sr. High, Country Club Park						
9	26	30	30		34	35
10	30	36	33		36	27
11	33	41	36		33	39
Los Angeles Unified Alt. Ed.						
9	17	13	19		15	21
10	23	14	19		20	24
11	26	12	24		10	25
Los Feliz Elem., Los Feliz						
2	15	37	27	22		
3	29	51	49	73		
4	26	47	24	37		
5	23	28	22	43		
Loyola Village Elem., Westchester						
2	69	35	63	75		
3	74	58	66	79		
4	72	70	72	77		
5	73	62	72	72		
Maclay Middle, Pacoima						
6	2	2	1	1		
7	6	8	5	4		
8	6	16	6	6		
Maclay Primary Center, Pacoima						
2	4	5	4	7		
Madison Middle, North Hollywood						
6	12	11	9	12		
7	19	21	20	19		
8	22	20	24	25		

Grade	Rd	Ma	Lg	Sp	Sci	SS
Magnolia Ave. Elem., Westlake						
2	4	28	9	12		
3	2	3	2	3		
4	2	4	2	2		
5	6	6	5	4		
Main St. Elem., Los Angeles						
2	3	8	5	4		
3	3	7	5	3		
4	1	2	1	1		
5	3	5	3	6		
Malabar St. Elem., Boyle Heights						
2	6	8	5	4		
3	6	11	9	7		
4	9	12	8	3		
5	10	12	11	4		
Manchester Ave. Elem., South Central L.A.						
2	4	3	7	4		
3	1	1	1	2		
4	2	2	1	2		
5	3	3	1	1		
Manhattan Place Elem., Near Inglewood						
2	37	25	34	42		
3	17	9	26	44		
4	13	6	10	20		
5	16	12	13	12		
Mann Jr. High, Near Inglewood						
6	7	2	3	10		
7	6	3	6	10		
8	5	4	6	12		
Manual Arts Sr. High, Near USC						
9	14	20	18		20	21
10	18	25	25		20	16
11	24	29	29		22	29
Mar Vista Elem., Mar Vista						
2	66	75	78	68		
3	67	61	72	53		
4	63	58	77	69		
5	64	68	82	63		
Marianna Ave. Elem., East Los Angeles						
2	8	9	12	9		
3	15	12	22	10		
4	8	10	21	5		
5	27	35	51	11		
6	27	36	36	27		
Marina del Rey Middle, Marina del Rey						
6	23	24	22	29		
7	19	24	20	24		
8	18	21	21	27		
Mark Twain Middle, Venice/Mar Vista						
6	21	18	40	25		
7	18	17	35	26		
8	22	18	36	25		
Markham Middle, Watts						
6	4	3	2	3		
7	3	4	4	4		
8	6	6	6	7		

STATE SCHOOL RANKINGS

Scores range from 1-99. A school scoring 75 has done better than 75 percent of other public schools in California.
Key: Rd (Reading), Ma (Math), Lg (Language), Sp (Spelling), Sci (Science) and SS (Social Science).

Grade	Rd	Ma	Lg	Sp	Sci	SS
Marlton, Crenshaw						
2	43	44	28	86		
3	41	63	74	64		
4	34	26	15	50		
5	14	6	12	20		
Marquez Ave. Elem., Pacific Palisades						
2	99	98	98	98		
3	99	97	99	97		
4	98	94	97	97		
5	98	89	96	94		
Marshall Sr. High, Silver Lake						
9	44	56	49		47	52
10	43	53	43		43	45
11	47	57	51		46	50
Marvin Elem., Near Culver City						
2	9	9	13	16		
3	13	25	25	20		
4	16	12	12	13		
5	12	12	7	12		
Mayall St. Elem., North Hills						
2	40	47	55	69		
3	54	58	71	73		
4	47	57	54	57		
5	45	35	45	46		
Mayberry St. Elem., Echo Park						
2	23	30	23	38		
3	21	25	28	16		
4	38	55	43	40		
5	27	40	23	20		
McAlister High, Los Angeles						
9	5	1	11		4	8
10	18	20	21		20	9
11	26	4	27		29	22
McKinley Ave. Elem., Southeast L.A.						
2	16	32	33	18		
3	9	25	20	13		
4	8	9	17	13		
5	16	16	27	27		
Melrose Ave. Elem., Hollywood						
2	16	22	35	18		
3	26	40	52	64		
4	30	27	34	35		
5	40	26	37	49		
Melvin Ave. Elem., Reseda						
2	20	35	30	35		
3	52	49	59	72		
4	36	31	45	31		
5	42	50	54	63		
Menlo Ave. Elem., Southeast L.A.						
2	15	27	13	16		
3	2	3	4	6		
4	1	1	1	1		
5	1	1	1	1		
Metropolitan (Cont.), Downtown						
9	12	13	18		7	17
10	21	24	25		18	23
11	17	4	29		8	18

Grade	Rd	Ma	Lg	Sp	Sci	SS
Meyler St. Elem., Near Torrance						
2	20	23	21	24		
3	12	13	22	18		
4	22	35	30	21		
5	25	56	29	20		
Micheltorena St. Elem., Silver Lake						
2	5	3	11	13		
3	3	2	3	5		
4	6	6	9	13		
5	4	4	7	7		
Mid City Magnet, Mid City						
2	28	60	64	50		
3	29	25	37	59		
4	16	9	30	38		
5	21	12	22	23		
6	21	11	13	20		
7	5	4	9	2		
8	19	6	16	20		
9	39	15	35		18	37
10	15	26	38		25	16
11	33	60	19		19	40
Middle College High (Alt.), Los Angeles						
9	66	50	68		56	62
10	53	40	53		55	38
11	57	35	55		33	48
Middleton St. Elem., Huntington Park						
2	2	4	2	2		
3	1	8	2	2		
4	1	3	3	2		
5	4	19	10	3		
Miles Ave. Elem., Huntington Park						
2	19	25	20	20		
3	23	38	30	26		
4	16	20	21	16		
5	16	19	23	16		
Miller Elem., South Central L.A.						
2	2	10	5	3		
3	1	2	2	3		
4	5	9	3	5		
5	9	4	3	11		
Millikan Middle, Sherman Oaks						
6	37	38	36	32		
7	38	35	45	40		
8	53	58	59	57		
Miramonte Elem., Florence						
2	2	7	2	3		
3	1	4	2	2		
4	1	1	1	1		
5	1	2	1	1		
Mission (Cont.), San Fernando						
9	7					23
10	15	5	16		9	24
11	19	22	25		22	24
Moneta (Cont.), Gardena						
9	11	9	20		31	23
10	12	10	27		15	16

STATE SCHOOL RANKINGS

Scores range from 1-99. A school scoring 75 has done better than 75 percent of other public schools in California.
Key: Rd (Reading), Ma (Math), Lg (Language), Sp (Spelling), Sci (Science) and SS (Social Science).

Grade	Rd	Ma	Lg	Sp	Sci	SS	Grade	Rd	Ma	Lg	Sp	Sci	SS
Monlux Elem., North Hollywood							**Mulholland Middle, Van Nuys**						
2	47	44	39	54			6	15	9	12	12		
3	31	34	35	53			7	12	17	9	11		
4	41	35	51	52			8	12	14	10	10		
5	36	41	40	29			**Multnomah St. Elem., Northeast Los Angeles**						
Monroe High, North Hills							2	35	45	41	40		
9	26	32	30		29	24	3	34	37	42	35		
10	38	44	41		38	37	4	49	54	45	38		
11	49	50	52		42	50	5	55	58	56	54		
Montague St. Elem., Pacoima							**Murchison St. Elem., Boyle Heights**						
2	15	18	9	16			2	5	13	20	9		
3	13	32	17	22			3	17	15	27	18		
4	11	21	14	10			4	5	10	12	7		
5	11	18	8	7			5	11	8	10	2		
Montara Ave. Elem., South Gate							**Napa St. Elem., Northridge**						
2	13	9	24	24			2	1	3	2	5		
3	15	15	23	41			3	6	8	7	12		
4	21	13	15	17			4	4	4	4	2		
5	11	11	18	11			5	3	4	2	1		
Monte Vista St. Elem., Highland Park							**Narbonne Sr. High, Harbor City**						
2	23	21	33	36			9	49	56	57		50	47
3	24	30	37	37			10	56	65	67		57	59
4	24	33	30	24			11	73	77	80		62	75
5	20	18	35	39			**Nestle Ave. Elem., Tarzana**						
Monterey (Cont.), East LA							2	67	68	79	87		
10	3	20	16		2	16	3	68	74	74	82		
Morningside Elem., San Fernando							4	60	76	78	50		
2	22	23	25	20			5	70	67	77	75		
3	21	22	28	30			**Nevada Ave. Elem., Canoga Park**						
4	6	10	8	5			2	32	25	45	50		
5	7	13	6	2			3	33	15	30	44		
Mountain View Elem., Tujunga							4	34	27	34	37		
2	45	37	52	56			5	31	22	30	23		
3	38	51	40	35			**Nevin Ave. Elem., Southeast L.A.**						
4	45	44	43	42			2	3	9	11	5		
5	48	55	49	43			3	3	4	7	7		
Mt. Gleason Middle, Sunland							4	1	3	3	2		
6	21	11	17	14			5	2	3	7	3		
7	32	25	32	29			**Newcastle Elem.**						
8	32	25	34	29			2	20	5	21	18		
Mt. Lukens (Cont.), Tujunga							3	19	4	20	26		
9	34	16	14		2	19	4	27	42	38	31		
10	29	31	19		36	49	5	11	12	20	9		
11	28	24	11		38	9	**Newmark (Cont.), Echo Park**						
Mt. Vernon Middle, Near Country Club Park							10	15	26	21		20	8
6	5	2	2	6			11	19	3	23		15	16
7	9	6	8	9			**Nightingale Middle, Cypress Park**						
8	16	9	11	13			6	8	11	17	10		
Mt. Washington Elem., Highland Park							7	6	9	11	11		
2	81	82	75	87			8	9	14	14	12		
3	92	73	90	84			**Nimitz Middle, Huntington Park**						
4	80	73	81	75			6	4	6	11	3		
5	96	84	87	90			7	6	6	12	5		
6	89	83	92	90			8	9	8	16	6		
Muir Middle, South Central L.A.							**98th St. Elem., Near LAX**						
6	2	1	2	5			2	17	21	17	24		
7	6	4	6	8			3	23	12	27	18		
8	6	5	6	9			4	14	4	9	21		
							5	23	9	14	29		

STATE SCHOOL RANKINGS

Scores range from 1-99. A school scoring 75 has done better than 75 percent of other public schools in California.
Key: Rd (Reading), Ma (Math), Lg (Language), Sp (Spelling), Sci (Science) and SS (Social Science).

Grade	Rd	Ma	Lg	Sp	Sci	SS
95th St. Elem., South Central L.A.						
2	5	13	7	9		
3	5	5	11	13		
4	3	5	2	11		
5	4	5	3	11		
99th St. Elem., Southeast L.A.						
2	16	3	24	24		
3	9	9	18	24		
4	6	4	4	13		
5	9	5	10	11		
92nd St. Elem., Watts						
2	1	2	3	1		
3	1	4	2	2		
4	4	4	4	2		
5	6	5	6	6		
96th St. Elem., Watts						
2	17	28	24	24		
3	6	10	12	12		
4	5	10	8	13		
5	3	6	6	3		
93rd St. Elem., Southeast L.A.						
2	30	32	27	36		
3	19	45	38	30		
4	13	16	17	21		
5	18	43	25	11		
9th St. Elem., Downtown Los Angeles						
2	8	6	20	10		
3	15	17	20	7		
4	22	40	28	5		
5	14	36	14	5		
Nobel Middle, Northridge						
6	61	68	60	76		
7	71	74	76	82		
8	70	75	71	79		
Noble Ave. Elem., Mission Hills						
2	8	9	8	5		
3	4	5	3	4		
4	5	6	3	3		
5	3	5	3	1		
Normandie Ave. Elem., Near USC						
2	1	1	3	2		
3	6	5	8	10		
4	2	2	3	3		
5	4	2	3	4		
Normont Elem., Harbor City						
2	30	32	30	30		
3	31	31	49	48		
4	16	13	21	19		
5	25	24	25	16		
N. Hollywood Sr. High, N. Hollywood						
9	39	48	46		43	52
10	53	62	60		55	61
11	59	65	63		62	62
Northridge Middle, Northridge						
6	8	6	4	10		
7	11	10	8	11		
8	11	14	9	10		
Norwood St. Elem., Downtown Los Angeles						
2	2	3	7	7		
3	5	11	9	7		
4	6	10	14	8		
5	9	8	10	5		
Nueva Vista Elem., Bell						
2	19	21	23	24		
3	17	37	27	22		
4	6	9	6	8		
5	21	20	23	16		
O'Melveny Elem., San Fernando						
2	19	15	23	18		
3	15	9	11	12		
4	22	16	12	13		
5	21	21	20	20		
Odyssey (Cont.), South Gate						
10	21	14	19		18	24
11	19	19	21		15	10
Olive Vista Middle, Sylmar						
6	10	6	8	6		
7	12	12	9	9		
8	12	11	13	9		
186th St. Elem., Southeast L.A.						
2	25	50	30	33		
3	29	49	42	39		
4	24	21	31	31		
5	16	11	13	9		
118th St. Elem., Los Angeles						
2	6	4	9	18		
3	1	2	8	4		
4	3	2	4	2		
5	2	1	2	2		
156th St. Elem., Gardena						
2	59	75	73	78		
3	73	61	70	79		
4	63	70	69	79		
5	50	46	63	67		
153rd St. Elem., Gardena						
2	13	23	19	26		
3	8	21	17	22		
4	19	24	26	29		
5	27	21	29	38		
109th St. Elem., Los Angeles						
2	10	12	9	19		
3	10	29	15	18		
4	8	6	9	7		
5	3	4	2	3		
107th St. Elem., Southeast L.A.						
2	1	1	1	3		
3	2	2	3	6		
4	3	1	1	2		
5	3	2	1	5		
116th Street Elem., Southeast L.A.						
2	17	27	12	26		
3	10	6	13	18		
4	9	13	12	10		
5	2	3	1	2		

Copyright © 2001 McCormack's Guides. No reproduction without permission.

76 STATE SCHOOL RANKINGS

Scores range from 1-99. A school scoring 75 has done better than 75 percent of other public schools in California.
Key: Rd (Reading), Ma (Math), Lg (Language), Sp (Spelling), Sci (Science) and SS (Social Science).

135th Street Elem., Gardena

Grade	Rd	Ma	Lg	Sp	Sci	SS
2	5	8	4	6		
3	12	12	15	20		
4	9	9	3	5		
5	14	14	8	20		

112th Street Elem., Watts

Grade	Rd	Ma	Lg	Sp	Sci	SS
2	10	10	8	16		
3	33	63	49	66		
4	2	6	5	7		
5	2	7	10	5		

122nd Street Elem., Southeast L.A.

Grade	Rd	Ma	Lg	Sp	Sci	SS
2	10	24	16	14		
3	4	10	7	7		
4	9	20	5	8		
5	6	7	3	2		

Open Magnet: Ctr. for Indiv., Near Culver City

Grade	Rd	Ma	Lg	Sp	Sci	SS
2	82	76	84	80		
3	95	93	95	92		
4	81	80	84	92		
5	95	88	94	94		

Osceola St. Elem., Sylmar

Grade	Rd	Ma	Lg	Sp	Sci	SS
2	20	21	31	24		
3	17	27	33	24		
4	17	12	21	21		
5	20	16	22	18		

Overland Ave. Elem., Cheviot Hills

Grade	Rd	Ma	Lg	Sp	Sci	SS
2	71	73	77	88		
3	95	88	96	91		
4	89	91	91	95		
5	84	81	87	84		

Owens Opportunity Center

Grade	Rd	Ma	Lg	Sp	Sci	SS
8	8	2	3	12		

Owensmouth (Cont.), Canton Park

Grade	Rd	Ma	Lg	Sp	Sci	SS
9	49	13			22	45
10	29	20	23		20	2
11	53	41		69		

Oxnard St. Elem., North Hollywood

Grade	Rd	Ma	Lg	Sp	Sci	SS
2	16	22	37	28		
3	12	19	22	35		
4	22	21	30	21		
5	20	23	25	14		

Pacific Palisades Elem., Pacific Palisades

Grade	Rd	Ma	Lg	Sp	Sci	SS
2	83	81	94	90		
3	97	94	97	96		
4	97	84	90	89		
5	84	68	75	85		

Pacoima Elem., Pacoima

Grade	Rd	Ma	Lg	Sp	Sci	SS
2	1	4	3	3		
3	2	5	1	2		
4	1	2	1	1		
5	1	2	1	1		

Pacoima Middle, Pacoima

Grade	Rd	Ma	Lg	Sp	Sci	SS
6	12	11	14	5		
7	15	17	15	10		
8	19	22	21	12		

Palisades Charter High, Pacific Palisades

Grade	Rd	Ma	Lg	Sp	Sci	SS
9	81	86	87		79	82
10	83	86	85		84	84
11	84	85	80		82	88

Palms Elem., Near Mar Vista

Grade	Rd	Ma	Lg	Sp	Sci	SS
2	43	40	43	56		
3	33	25	44	48		
4	34	33	42	52		
5	47	40	54	46		

Palms Middle, Near Mar Vista

Grade	Rd	Ma	Lg	Sp	Sci	SS
6	72	65	69	71		
7	69	63	73	74		
8	71	64	70	76		

Park Ave. Elem., Cudahy

Grade	Rd	Ma	Lg	Sp	Sci	SS
2	30	28	11	34		
3	17	27	23	7		
4	16	18	9	10		
5	9	12	8	7		
6	11	17	14	10		

Park Western Pl. Elem., San Pedro

Grade	Rd	Ma	Lg	Sp	Sci	SS
2	81	65	72	80		
3	90	94	95	95		
4	86	88	89	91		
5	88	92	88	88		

Parkman Middle, Woodland Hills

Grade	Rd	Ma	Lg	Sp	Sci	SS
6	44	36	36	38		
7	41	37	39	45		
8	42	42	34	39		

Parmelee Ave. Elem., Florence

Grade	Rd	Ma	Lg	Sp	Sci	SS
2	3	1	3	4		
3	1	4	3	1		
4	1	2	2	1		
5	1	3	2	1		

Parthenia St. Elem., Near Van Nuys Airport

Grade	Rd	Ma	Lg	Sp	Sci	SS
2	7	7	11	8		
3	10	12	17	20		
4	13	20	18	19		
5	14	7	14	6		

Paseo del Rey Fundamental, Playa Del Rey

Grade	Rd	Ma	Lg	Sp	Sci	SS
2	69	60	73	90		
3	71	72	78	80		
4	73	62	77	81		
5	56	40	56	59		

Patton (Cont.), Harbor City

Grade	Rd	Ma	Lg	Sp	Sci	SS
9	12	7	12		7	11
10	12	29		2		

Peary Middle, Gardena

Grade	Rd	Ma	Lg	Sp	Sci	SS
6	15	9	16	19		
7	20	14	24	23		
8	24	18	26	29		

Phoenix (Cont.), Mar Vista

Grade	Rd	Ma	Lg	Sp	Sci	SS
11	53	32			29	52

Pinewood Ave. Elem., Tujunga

Grade	Rd	Ma	Lg	Sp	Sci	SS
2	10	15	23	22		
3	12	16	17	18		
4	22	23	22	33		
5	25	15	22	13		

Copyright © 2001 McCormack's Guides. No reproduction without permission.

Scores range from 1-99. A school scoring 75 has done better than 75 percent of other public schools in California.
Key: Rd (Reading), Ma (Math), Lg (Language), Sp (Spelling), Sci (Science) and SS (Social Science).

Grade	Rd	Ma	Lg	Sp	Sci	SS
Pio Pico Elem., Near Country Club Park						
2	11	16	16	19		
3	12	7	12	17		
4	22	18	19	33		
5	25	15	20	22		
6	10	6	11	14		
7	12	13	11	12		
8	18	16	19	17		
Plainview Ave. Elem., Tujunga						
2	33	40	45	46		
3	24	19	20	26		
4	44	33	47	35		
5	50	43	49	43		
Plasencia Elem., Echo Park						
2	5	8	9	16		
3	13	22	18	26		
4	13	21	15	17		
5	7	19	13	11		
6	10	24	12	25		
Playa Del Rey Elem., Culver City						
2	62	50	79	87		
3	42	38	47	59		
4	56	54	49	47		
5	42	38	48	55		
Plummer Elem., North Hills						
2	2	3	4	5		
3	3	6	7	4		
4	4	4	6	5		
5	3	2	5	2		
Point Fermin Elem., Point Fermin						
2	59	58	73	68		
3	47	37	51	35		
4	78	70	69	66		
5	55	19	29	42		
Politi Elem., West of Downtown Los Angeles						
2	11	11	10	10		
3	3	4	4	7		
4	4	6	3	10		
5	14	8	8	6		
Pomelo Dr. Elem., Canoga Park						
2	95	96	94	99		
3	97	98	99	99		
4	93	83	96	95		
5	88	86	90	89		
Porter Middle, Granada Hills						
6	60	60	60	64		
7	77	81	76	78		
8	83	79	83	89		
President Ave. Elem., Harbor City						
2	69	62	78	75		
3	56	54	63	68		
4	39	38	32	44		
5	42	31	45	52		
Pueblo de Los Angeles Continua, Lincoln Hts.						
10	25	11	25		43	37
11	36	28	33		22	28

Grade	Rd	Ma	Lg	Sp	Sci	SS
Purche Ave. Elem., Gardena						
2	43	44	52	54		
3	24	12	27	55		
4	19	15	17	37		
5	20	16	16	31		
Queen Anne Elem., Near Country Club Park						
2	7	7	12	16		
3	12	21	20	37		
4	9	8	5	10		
5	18	19	20	33		
Ramona Elem., Hollywood						
2	33	52	51	54		
3	33	58	54	64		
4	27	33	43	52		
5	33	29	39	54		
Ramona Opportunity High, City Terrace						
9	13	15	11		11	13
10	5	8	10		5	6
11	15	4	25		8	18
Ranchito Ave. Elem., Panorama City						
2	13	12	16	13		
3	21	12	23	22		
4	19	10	15	16		
5	18	28	27	11		
Raymond Ave. Elem., South Central L.A.						
2	4	2	3	4		
3	10	2	3	16		
4	3	1	2	5		
5	3	2	2	9		
Reed Middle, North Hollywood						
6	48	40	50	51		
7	55	47	58	52		
8	50	47	52	48		
Reseda Elem., Reseda						
2	22	12	35	30		
3	15	17	23	33		
4	13	18	24	24		
5	27	36	40	39		
Reseda Sr. High, Reseda						
9	39	48	44		41	38
10	53	57	56		49	47
11	57	67	57		54	58
Revere Middle, Brentwood						
6	78	76	78	79		
7	73	75	75	76		
8	70	68	78	81		
Richland Ave. Elem., Near Cheviot Hills						
2	13	5	19	36		
3	23	16	25	35		
4	24	20	30	49		
5	42	40	40	42		
Riley High (Alt.), Watts						
9	5	9	12		12	6
10	29	14	25		22	6
11	19	10	19		6	20

78 STATE SCHOOL RANKINGS

Scores range from 1-99. A school scoring 75 has done better than 75 percent of other public schools in California.
Key: Rd (Reading), Ma (Math), Lg (Language), Sp (Spelling), Sci (Science) and SS (Social Science).

Rio Vista Elem., North Hollywood

Grade	Rd	Ma	Lg	Sp	Sci	SS
2	27	21	28	28		
3	47	46	51	39		
4	36	18	32	29		
5	35	31	30	35		

Ritter Elem., Watts

Grade	Rd	Ma	Lg	Sp	Sci	SS
2	3	2	7	10		
3	4	2	5	10		
4	9	9	3	5		
5	1	1	1	1		

Riverside Dr. Elem., Sherman Oaks

Grade	Rd	Ma	Lg	Sp	Sci	SS
2	71	65	64	73		
3	65	51	68	72		
4	62	47	66	67		
5	68	69	78	65		

Rockdale Elem., Eagle Rock

Grade	Rd	Ma	Lg	Sp	Sci	SS
2	22	12	20	32		
3	34	34	37	48		
4	41	36	45	31		
5	33	31	35	27		
6	48	50	40	40		

Rodia (Cont.), Watts

Grade	Rd	Ma	Lg	Sp	Sci	SS
9	9	18			26	47
10	26	50	23		53	32
11	24	51	24		31	28

Rogers (Cont.), Van Nuys

Grade	Rd	Ma	Lg	Sp	Sci	SS
9		22			29	15
10	9	8	2		3	2

Roosevelt Sr. High, Boyle Heights

Grade	Rd	Ma	Lg	Sp	Sci	SS
9	17	30	25		20	21
10	26	42	33		22	21
11	33	44	36		26	37

Roscoe Elem., Sun Valley

Grade	Rd	Ma	Lg	Sp	Sci	SS
2	9	6	8	6		
3	10	7	15	10		
4	5	7	17	4		
5	16	18	27	14		

Roscomare Rd. Elem., Bel Air

Grade	Rd	Ma	Lg	Sp	Sci	SS
2	99	98	99	99		
3	98	98	98	97		
4	94	92	94	97		
5	89	92	75	90		

Rosemont Ave. Elem., Echo Park

Grade	Rd	Ma	Lg	Sp	Sci	SS
2	13	22	16	24		
3	12	27	25	33		
4	14	20	18	19		
5	12	20	14	20		

Rosewood Ave. Elem., West Hollywood

Grade	Rd	Ma	Lg	Sp	Sci	SS
2	74	63	82	88		
3	39	35	47	57		
4	39	29	40	50		
5	52	56	60	65		

Rowan Ave. Elem., East Los Angeles

Grade	Rd	Ma	Lg	Sp	Sci	SS
2	5	6	5	6		
3	3	7	4	6		
4	6	10	10	8		
5	11	18	18	7		

Russell Elem., Florence

Grade	Rd	Ma	Lg	Sp	Sci	SS
2	1	4	3	5		
3	8	7	15	18		
4	17	15	12	10		
5	4	13	10	5		

San Antonio (Cont.), Huntington Park

Grade	Rd	Ma	Lg	Sp	Sci	SS
9	5	9	7		4	2

San Antonio Elem., Huntington Park

Grade	Rd	Ma	Lg	Sp	Sci	SS
2	6	5	11	9		
3	12	8	17	12		
4	23	23	30	17		
5	4	5	18	3		

San Fernando Elem., San Fernando

Grade	Rd	Ma	Lg	Sp	Sci	SS
2	7	11	7	6		
3	17	25	22	15		
4	16	20	21	10		
5	16	23	22	9		

San Fernando Middle, San Fernando

Grade	Rd	Ma	Lg	Sp	Sci	SS
6	6	9	4	7		
7	10	17	7	11		
8	12	22	12	15		

San Fernando Sr. High, San Fernando

Grade	Rd	Ma	Lg	Sp	Sci	SS
9	19	28	24		22	24
10	32	34	37		25	27
11	40	43	41		31	44

San Gabriel Ave. Elem., South Gate

Grade	Rd	Ma	Lg	Sp	Sci	SS
2	19	15	23	20		
3	10	6	15	12		
4	13	8	14	10		
5	14	13	16	13		

San Jose St. Elem., Mission Hills

Grade	Rd	Ma	Lg	Sp	Sci	SS
2	41	33	46	42		
3	55	42	59	59		
4	66	68	69	73		
5	67	58	58	57		

San Miguel Elem., South Gate

Grade	Rd	Ma	Lg	Sp	Sci	SS
2	19	15	15	16		
3	19	17	22	19		
4	17	20	12	19		
5	21	20	20	20		

San Pascual Ave. Elem., Highland Park

Grade	Rd	Ma	Lg	Sp	Sci	SS
2	41	55	43	38		
3	23	25	27	33		
4	32	26	28	33		
5	29	24	30	14		

San Pedro Sr. High, San Pedro

Grade	Rd	Ma	Lg	Sp	Sci	SS
9	56	54	52		50	60
10	69	62	65		67	71
11	78	68	78		72	84

San Pedro St. Elem., Downtown Los Angeles

Grade	Rd	Ma	Lg	Sp	Sci	SS
2	25	32	23	28		
3	21	44	28	26		
4	14	24	17	10		
5	6	26	18	18		

Santa Monica Blvd. Elem., Hollywood

Grade	Rd	Ma	Lg	Sp	Sci	SS
2	5	16	10	7		
3	9	13	15	15		
4	13	15	19	11		
5	14	7	16	9		

STATE SCHOOL RANKINGS

Scores range from 1-99. A school scoring 75 has done better than 75 percent of other public schools in California.
Key: Rd (Reading), Ma (Math), Lg (Language), Sp (Spelling), Sci (Science) and SS (Social Science).

Saticoy Elem., North Hollywood

Grade	Rd	Ma	Lg	Sp	Sci	SS
2	35	39	41	54		
3	26	47	40	33		
4	32	40	53	38		
5	16	36	49	20		

Saturn St. Elem., West Los Angeles

Grade	Rd	Ma	Lg	Sp	Sci	SS
2	9	18	20	13		
3	24	17	31	17		
4	22	23	36	21		
5	20	26	22	25		

2nd St. Elem., Boyle Heights

Grade	Rd	Ma	Lg	Sp	Sci	SS
2	5	12	11	4		
3	6	31	15	13		
4	16	16	12	8		
5	6	8	5	2		

Selma Ave. Elem., Hollywood

Grade	Rd	Ma	Lg	Sp	Sci	SS
2	28	32	40	40		
3	26	37	37	39		
4	28	35	32	22		
5	28	28	30	31		

Sepulveda Middle, North Hills

Grade	Rd	Ma	Lg	Sp	Sci	SS
6	12	11	9	11		
7	16	31	19	19		
8	24	35	22	25		

Serrania Ave. Elem., Woodland Hills

Grade	Rd	Ma	Lg	Sp	Sci	SS
2	66	65	75	65		
3	70	60	70	68		
4	74	64	67	67		
5	74	58	60	67		

7th St. Elem., San Pedro

Grade	Rd	Ma	Lg	Sp	Sci	SS
2	50	35	65	64		
3	68	48	75	66		
4	53	50	49	59		
5	58	48	60	49		

75th St. Elem., South Central L.A.

Grade	Rd	Ma	Lg	Sp	Sci	SS
2	3	5	5	6		
3	2	2	11	6		
4	6	1	4	2		
5	2	2	2	2		

74th St. Elem., Near Inglewood

Grade	Rd	Ma	Lg	Sp	Sci	SS
2	27	22	37	46		
3	15	5	22	24		
4	21	4	19	21		
5	28	9	20	20		

Sharp Ave. Elem., Pacoima

Grade	Rd	Ma	Lg	Sp	Sci	SS
2	2	5	4	2		
3	2	4	8	1		
4	5	10	6	2		
5	4	3	5	1		

Shenandoah St. Elem., Near Culver City

Grade	Rd	Ma	Lg	Sp	Sci	SS
2	4	1	6	9		
3	15	8	13	26		
4	17	7	12	14		
5	20	7	10	22		

Sheridan St. Elem., Boyle Heights

Grade	Rd	Ma	Lg	Sp	Sci	SS
2	7	15	21	8		
3	9	12	9	20		
4	6	12	17	8		
5	11	13	20	9		

Sherman Oaks Center (Alt.), Reseda

Grade	Rd	Ma	Lg	Sp	Sci	SS
4	81	75	83	86		
5	81	68	87	87		
6	78	74	82	85		
7	86	84	90	92		
8	83	82	85	87		
9	83	92	92		85	84
10	92	90	90		90	88
11	94	96	93		95	97

Sherman Oaks Elem., Sherman Oaks

Grade	Rd	Ma	Lg	Sp	Sci	SS
2	74	64	83	75		
3	64	54	65	59		
4	60	47	56	57		
5	61	62	61	54		

Shirley Ave. Elem., Reseda

Grade	Rd	Ma	Lg	Sp	Sci	SS
2	27	19	40	34		
3	29	13	33	22		
4	56	76	51	50		
5	39	46	37	33		

Short Ave. Elem., Near Marina del Rey

Grade	Rd	Ma	Lg	Sp	Sci	SS
2	38	33	43	70		
3	34	21	46	66		
4	36	33	43	52		
5	40	40	8	42		

Sierra Park Elem., El Sereno

Grade	Rd	Ma	Lg	Sp	Sci	SS
2	12	13	19	21		
3	6	15	9	10		
4	14	18	14	14		
5	12	21	10	13		

Sierra Vista Elem., Near Alhambra

Grade	Rd	Ma	Lg	Sp	Sci	SS
2	15	40	16	18		
3	8	17	4	10		
4	22	31	21	31		
5	20	38	20	20		

6th Ave. Elem., West Los Angeles

Grade	Rd	Ma	Lg	Sp	Sci	SS
2	10	2	16	13		
3	3	2	4	4		
4	5	3	3	3		
5	11	3	6	7		

68th St. Elem., South Central L.A.

Grade	Rd	Ma	Lg	Sp	Sci	SS
2	7	4	5	3		
3	13	31	33	33		
4	11	13	9	8		
5	11	8	12	7		

61st St. Elem., South Central L.A.

Grade	Rd	Ma	Lg	Sp	Sci	SS
2	4	8	3	4		
3	2	11	9	10		
4	5	5	8	5		
5	4	5	7	5		

66th St. Elem., Southeast L.A.

Grade	Rd	Ma	Lg	Sp	Sci	SS
2	3	7	6	4		
3	5	13	5	7		
4	3	6	3	2		
5	6	8	4	7		

Solano Ave. Elem., Near Echo Park

Grade	Rd	Ma	Lg	Sp	Sci	SS
2	50	65	46	92		
3	77	95	92	99		
4	43	62	62	70		
5	45	55	61	77		
6	50	50	62	79		

80 STATE SCHOOL RANKINGS

Scores range from 1-99. A school scoring 75 has done better than 75 percent of other public schools in California.
Key: Rd (Reading), Ma (Math), Lg (Language), Sp (Spelling), Sci (Science) and SS (Social Science).

Grade	Rd	Ma	Lg	Sp	Sci	SS
Soto St. Elem., Boyle Heights						
2	20	22	30	21		
3	4	7	8	7		
4	9	11	19	19		
5	6	18	10	5		
South Gate Middle, South Gate						
6	12	10	16	9		
7	15	11	16	11		
8	15	14	16	10		
South Gate Sr. High, South Gate						
9	29	30	32		24	35
10	34	38	38		27	29
11	42	41	39		33	46
South Park Elem., Southeast L.A.						
2	10	10	17	16		
3	4	4	11	12		
4	8	6	9	8		
5	2	3	6	5		
South Shores Visual & Per. Arts, San Pedro						
2	77	84	84	76		
3	73	54	77	68		
4	85	77	84	75		
5	86	44	81	82		
Stagg St. Elem., Van Nuys						
2		22	33	44		
3	33	29	44	33		
4	41	40	42	37		
5	25	21	13	16		
Stanford Ave. Elem., South Gate						
2	3	1	5	5		
3	6	10	18	9		
4	9	12	6	4		
5	3	7	3	2		
State St. Elem., South Gate						
2	16	7	14	22		
3	9	10	13	16		
4	9	7	5	13		
5	11	6	14	11		
Sterry Elem., Near Santa Monica						
2	25	25	39	32		
3	24	38	42	26		
4	16	31	30	22		
5	33	26	30	29		
Stevenson Middle, East Los Angeles						
6	6	8	8	5		
7	10	18	11	8		
8	15	22	16	9		
Stonehurst Ave. Elem., Sun Valley						
2	38	25	41	36		
3	26	22	22	20		
4	32	36	24	17		
5	16	9	6	7		
Stoner Ave. Elem., Culver City						
2	20	16	13	30		
3	19	15	22	12		
4	17	24	19	19		
5	16	21	23	11		

Grade	Rd	Ma	Lg	Sp	Sci	SS
Stoney Point (Cont.)						
10	73	42	32		73	55
11	64	52	47		86	55
Strathern St. Elem., North Hollywood						
2	13	28	13	18		
3	10	25	15	15		
4	17	31	19	21		
5	12	16	20	14		
Sun Valley Middle, Sun Valley						
6	7	5	3	5		
7	9	9	4	5		
8	11	10	8	7		
Sunland Elem., Sunland						
2	27	45	49	36		
3	39	32	52	46		
4	45	38	49	47		
5	39	23	27	43		
Sunny Brae Ave. Elem., Canoga Park						
2	9	30	13	13		
3	9	15	15	20		
4	11	21	12	6		
5	11	12	7	9		
Sunrise Elem., Boyle Heights						
2	2	15	5	2		
3	5	19	8	6		
4	13	26	22	14		
5	18	23	20	13		
Superior St. Elem., Chatsworth						
2	41	37	63	56		
3	55	61	52	57		
4	55	60	56	59		
5	53	46	51	61		
Sutter Middle, Canoga Park						
6	13	11	6	11		
7	19	21	16	18		
8	20	26	18	17		
Sylmar Elem., Sylmar						
2	1	3	3	2		
3	6	6	7	3		
4	6	4	4	3		
5	6	6	2	4		
Sylmar Sr. High, Sylmar						
9	26	29	30		22	24
10	36	42	40		36	32
11	46	52	47		42	47
Sylvan Park Elem., Van Nuys						
2	9	10	20	16		
3	10	5	12	13		
4	11	5	8	5		
5	11	9	7	4		
Taft Sr. High, Woodland Hills						
9	64	64	67		56	57
10	78	83	80		76	68
11	78	79	80		69	77
Taper Ave. Elem., San Pedro						
2	60	59	75	64		
3	62	60	70	68		
4	56	45	62	49		
5	65	52	64	52		

STATE SCHOOL RANKINGS

Scores range from 1-99. A school scoring 75 has done better than 75 percent of other public schools in California.
Key: Rd (Reading), Ma (Math), Lg (Language), Sp (Spelling), Sci (Science) and SS (Social Science).

Tarzana Elem., Tarzana

Grade	Rd	Ma	Lg	Sp	Sci	SS
2	40	62	52	56		
3	45	23	42	46		
4	45	47	43	49		
5	35	36	51	43		

Telfair Ave. Elem., Pacoima

Grade	Rd	Ma	Lg	Sp	Sci	SS
2	4	9	8	6		
3	6	7	11	5		
4	6	6	8	4		
5	7	5	3	4		

Temescal Canyon (Cont.), Pacific Pallisides

Grade	Rd	Ma	Lg	Sp	Sci	SS
11	51	39	41		50	49

10th St. Elem., Downtown Los Angeles

Grade	Rd	Ma	Lg	Sp	Sci	SS
2	2	5	5	5		
3	3	7	7	8		
4	1	4	2	3		
5	4	8	5	3		

3rd St. Elem., Hancock Park

Grade	Rd	Ma	Lg	Sp	Sci	SS
2	94	94	94	99		
3	80	85	89	99		
4	81	85	83	95		
5	81	89	84	96		

32nd St. USC Performing Arts, Near USC

Grade	Rd	Ma	Lg	Sp	Sci	SS
2	38	22	47	46		
3	49	48	56	66		
4	56	58	56	60		
5	58	57	51	64		
6	37	38	33	32		
7	54	29	52	47		
8	34	17	28	31		
9	69	50	70		45	53
10	60	53	58		52	57
11	73	67	80		65	82

Thoreau (Cont.), Wood Hills

Grade	Rd	Ma	Lg	Sp	Sci	SS
10	67	44	57		71	55
11	13	29	14		39	39

Toland Way Elem., Eagle Rock

Grade	Rd	Ma	Lg	Sp	Sci	SS
2	27	30	41	38		
3	42	42	42	37		
4	28	38	17	33		
5	33	41	20	48		

Toluca Lake Elem., North Hollywood

Grade	Rd	Ma	Lg	Sp	Sci	SS
2	30	25	33	36		
3	36	35	44	48		
4	21	16	24	22		
5	23	23	33	25		

Topanga Elem., Topanga

Grade	Rd	Ma	Lg	Sp	Sci	SS
2	95	86	97	91		
3	99	93	97	86		
4	95	83	84	91		
5	90	82	86	79		

Topeka Dr. Elem., Northridge

Grade	Rd	Ma	Lg	Sp	Sci	SS
2	87	93	97	97		
3	83	77	89	91		
4	78	80	80	81		
5	83	80	75	81		

Towne Ave. Elem., Carson

Grade	Rd	Ma	Lg	Sp	Sci	SS
2	45	49	35	62		
3	39	38	42	53		
4	36	54	43	44		
5	55	65	64	59		

Tri-C Community Day, Los Angeles

Grade	Rd	Ma	Lg	Sp	Sci	SS
6	6	1	1	6		
7	5	4	3	3		
8	8	7	6	7		
9	14	15	14		24	15
10	32	31	28		33	35
11	33	19	41		22	40

Trinity St. Elem., Southeast L.A.

Grade	Rd	Ma	Lg	Sp	Sci	SS
2	7	30	17	16		
3	3	4	7	6		
4	2	4	3	3		
5	3	6	2	4		

Truth (Cont.), South Central

Grade	Rd	Ma	Lg	Sp	Sci	SS
10	18	11	23		12	32
11	7	1			2	5

Tulsa St. Elem., Granada Hills

Grade	Rd	Ma	Lg	Sp	Sci	SS
2	54	50	67	64		
3	58	68	66	68		
4	52	60	66	64		
5	37	61	37	33		

Tweedy Elem., South Gate

Grade	Rd	Ma	Lg	Sp	Sci	SS
2	8	10	10	14		
3	10	6	12	12		
4	19	13	19	14		
5	12	12	13	14		

20th St. Elem., Near Vernon

Grade	Rd	Ma	Lg	Sp	Sci	SS
2	2	5	2	7		
3	3	5	4	3		
4	1	2	1	1		
5	1	2	1	1		

28th St. Elem., Jefferson Park

Grade	Rd	Ma	Lg	Sp	Sci	SS
2	2	2	3	4		
3	3	5	3	9		
4	1	2	1	2		
5	2	3	2	2		

24th St. Elem., West of Downtown L.A.

Grade	Rd	Ma	Lg	Sp	Sci	SS
2	13	25	24	22		
3	8	9	11	9		
4	4	4	4	7		
5	6	5	4	3		

232nd Pl. Elem., Carson

Grade	Rd	Ma	Lg	Sp	Sci	SS
2	52	47	58	65		
3	51	42	63	75		
4	58	59	66	57		
5	44	50	45	38		

Union Ave. Elem., Westlake

Grade	Rd	Ma	Lg	Sp	Sci	SS
2	3	7	2	9		
3	5	11	4	9		
4	2	4	4	3		
5	3	4	4	4		

University Sr. High, Near Santa Monica

Grade	Rd	Ma	Lg	Sp	Sci	SS
9	44	47	52		43	53
10	60	67	73		61	59
11	62	71	69		64	65

STATE SCHOOL RANKINGS

Scores range from 1-99. A school scoring 75 has done better than 75 percent of other public schools in California.
Key: Rd (Reading), Ma (Math), Lg (Language), Sp (Spelling), Sci (Science) and SS (Social Science).

Utah St. Elem., Boyle Heights

Grade	Rd	Ma	Lg	Sp	Sci	SS
2	1	2	4	2		
3	1	5	3	4		
4	5	12	5	5		
5	11	12	10	9		

Valerio St. Elem., Van Nuys

Grade	Rd	Ma	Lg	Sp	Sci	SS
2	5	6	10	9		
3	10	9	15	18		
4	6	8	3	5		
5	7	9	6	7		

Valley Magnet, Van Nuys

Grade	Rd	Ma	Lg	Sp	Sci	SS
2	69	50	72	80		
3	42	54	62	41		
4	60	53	71	42		
5	68	56	54	55		
6	42	47	29	24		
7	59	56	53	45		
8	58	35	53	57		
9	59	48	57		58	55
10	68	72	80		69	59
11	71	74	71		48	73

Valley View Elem., Hollywood Hills

Grade	Rd	Ma	Lg	Sp	Sci	SS
2	55	27	61	68		
3	39	49	65	72		
4	32	24	24	52		
5	35	24	30	31		
6	64	58	62	79		

Van Deene Ave. Elem., Torrance

Grade	Rd	Ma	Lg	Sp	Sci	SS
2	28	32	28	48		
3	33	46	38	39		
4	28	44	26	31		
5	37	65	45	46		

Van Gogh St. Elem., Granada Hills

Grade	Rd	Ma	Lg	Sp	Sci	SS
2	87	82	92	95		
3	70	74	89	88		
4	83	85	89	92		
5	81	84	94	82		

Van Ness Ave. Elem., Hollywood

Grade	Rd	Ma	Lg	Sp	Sci	SS
2	19	25	25	44		
3	17	31	33	44		
4	32	38	34	40		
5	27	29	25	38		

Van Nuys Elem., Van Nuys

Grade	Rd	Ma	Lg	Sp	Sci	SS
2	37	32	41	40		
3	14	13	28	28		
4	17	6	21	21		
5	9	2	4	8		

Van Nuys Middle, Van Nuys

Grade	Rd	Ma	Lg	Sp	Sci	SS
6	15	9	13	14		
7	20	29	26	19		
8	21	25	28	27		

Van Nuys Sr. High, Van Nuys

Grade	Rd	Ma	Lg	Sp	Sci	SS
9	52	62	62		56	66
10	65	77	73		76	69
11	69	75	75		73	75

Vanalden Ave. Elem., Reseda

Grade	Rd	Ma	Lg	Sp	Sci	SS
2	67	52	68	81		
3	55	70	70	77		
4	44	54	45	40		
5	56	41	53	71		

Vaughn St. Elem., San Fernando

Grade	Rd	Ma	Lg	Sp	Sci	SS
2	7	21	10	9		
3	9	21	15	7		
4	17	31	24	8		
5	11	8	12	11		

Vena Ave. Elem., Arleta

Grade	Rd	Ma	Lg	Sp	Sci	SS
2	54	53	55	62		
3	33	34	30	35		
4	53	62	55	55		
5	53	58	60	46		

Venice Sr. High, Venice

Grade	Rd	Ma	Lg	Sp	Sci	SS
9	43	47	42		50	45
10	53	59	51		60	55
11	59	68	54		67	62

Verdugo Hills Sr. High, Tujunga

Grade	Rd	Ma	Lg	Sp	Sci	SS
9	37	40	47		29	42
10	45	53	55		41	53
11	55	57	60		50	65

Vermont Ave. Elem., Near USC

Grade	Rd	Ma	Lg	Sp	Sci	SS
2	7	7	10	18		
3	5	3	13	10		
4	3	3	3	8		
5	14	15	6	9		

Vernon City Elem., Los Angeles

Grade	Rd	Ma	Lg	Sp	Sci	SS
2	12	37	6	26		
3	4	4	5	7		
4	5	21	17	11		
5	20	44	44	9		
6	21	50	34	20		

Victoria Ave. Elem., South Gate

Grade	Rd	Ma	Lg	Sp	Sci	SS
2	13	15	25	22		
3	10	13	25	24		
4	13	12	21	17		
5	12	15	18	11		

Victory Blvd. Elem., North Hollywood

Grade	Rd	Ma	Lg	Sp	Sci	SS
2	19	7	23	22		
3	15	10	20	26		
4	17	15	15	13		
5	16	21	18	11		

View Park (Cont.), Crenshaw

Grade	Rd	Ma	Lg	Sp	Sci	SS
9	2	3	1		4	5
10	5	4	4		3	8
11	5	12	1			16

View Park Prep. Accelerated, W. 54th St.

Grade	Rd	Ma	Lg	Sp	Sci	SS
2	64	60	49	86		
3	31	37	42	75		
4	77	81	86	93		
5	83	84	84	94		

Vine St. Elem., Hollywood

Grade	Rd	Ma	Lg	Sp	Sci	SS
2	33	22	47	38		
3	29	29	44	57		
4	28	18	30	33		
5	31	28	45	25		

Vinedale Elem., Sun Valley

Grade	Rd	Ma	Lg	Sp	Sci	SS
2	12	9	14	10		
3	12	7	22	22		
4	10	5	9	7		
5	23	13	25	31		

Scores range from 1-99. A school scoring 75 has done better than 75 percent of other public schools in California.
Key: Rd (Reading), Ma (Math), Lg (Language), Sp (Spelling), Sci (Science) and SS (Social Science).

Vintage St. Fundamental, North Hills

Grade	Rd	Ma	Lg	Sp	Sci	SS
2	71	68	78	78		
3	70	68	77	81		
4	69	77	71	78		
5	76	73	69	74		

Virgil Middle, Westlake

Grade	Rd	Ma	Lg	Sp	Sci	SS
6	6	7	9	5		
7	10	12	13	10		
8	10	11	12	10		

Virginia Rd. Elem., Jefferson Park

Grade	Rd	Ma	Lg	Sp	Sci	SS
2	13	3	16	14		
3	17	12	33	37		
4	21	18	24	21		
5	35	21	32	35		

Wadsworth Ave. Elem., South L.A.

Grade	Rd	Ma	Lg	Sp	Sci	SS
2	1	5	2	4		
3	2	8	4	4		
4	3	4	1	4		
5	2	4	2	4		

Walgrove Ave. Elem., Mar Vista

Grade	Rd	Ma	Lg	Sp	Sci	SS
2	25	24	30	28		
3	42	31	37	35		
4	34	27	22	55		
5	7	7	7	20		

Walnut Park Elem., Near Huntington Park

Grade	Rd	Ma	Lg	Sp	Sci	SS
2	11	11	23	16		
3	9	9	17	9		
4	10	8	14	6		
5	9	7	13	4		

Warner Ave. Elem., Westwood

Grade	Rd	Ma	Lg	Sp	Sci	SS
2	98	94	97	98		
3	96	93	98	98		
4	97	96	98	97		
5	99	98	99	99		

Washington Prep. High, Near Inglewood

Grade	Rd	Ma	Lg	Sp	Sci	SS
9	13	22	17		16	19
10	26	33	29		27	16
11	30	35	30		19	29

Watts Learning Center, Watts

Grade	Rd	Ma	Lg	Sp	Sci	SS
2	30	15	20	62		

Webster Middle, Near Santa Monica

Grade	Rd	Ma	Lg	Sp	Sci	SS
6	17	15	8	15		
7	16	14	11	13		
8	22	18	14	20		

Weemes Elem., Near USC

Grade	Rd	Ma	Lg	Sp	Sci	SS
2	22	15	20	34		
3	19	11	38	30		
4	14	8	17	16		
5	20	9	10	14		

Weigand Ave. Elem., Watts

Grade	Rd	Ma	Lg	Sp	Sci	SS
2	1	1	1	2		
3	1	11	3	1		
4	1	5	1	1		
5	1	2	2	1		

Welby Way Elem., Canoga Park

Grade	Rd	Ma	Lg	Sp	Sci	SS
2	96	94	97	97		
3	92	91	97	97		
4	97	96	98	97		
5	96	96	97	96		

West Athens Elem., Near Inglewood

Grade	Rd	Ma	Lg	Sp	Sci	SS
2	10	6	13	30		
3	14	8	12	19		
4	10	5	15	13		
5	3	3	7	6		

West Granada (Cont.), Northridge

Grade	Rd	Ma	Lg	Sp	Sci	SS
10	47	17	27		37	45
11	30	24	21		48	7

West Hollywood Elem., West Hollywood

Grade	Rd	Ma	Lg	Sp	Sci	SS
2	13	12	24	26		
3	8	10	9	22		
4	22	28	15	22		
5	18	24	18	14		

West Hollywood Opportunity, W. Hollywood

Grade	Rd	Ma	Lg	Sp	Sci	SS
8	8	2	8	3		
9	19	11	23		18	29
10	32	24	28		27	35
11	4	1	7		1	18

West Vernon Ave. Elem., Near USC

Grade	Rd	Ma	Lg	Sp	Sci	SS
2	1	2	1	1		
3	1	1	3	7		
4	1	1	1	1		
5	2	1	1	2		

Westchester Sr. High, Westchester

Grade	Rd	Ma	Lg	Sp	Sci	SS
9	52	42	57		41	55
10	54	46	57		43	53
11	55	50	59		48	49

Western Ave. Elem., South Central L.A.

Grade	Rd	Ma	Lg	Sp	Sci	SS
2	16	7	12	16		
3	12	4	7	10		
4	11	7	15	10		
5	7	4	6	11		

Westminster Ave. Elem., Venice

Grade	Rd	Ma	Lg	Sp	Sci	SS
2	27	37	33	42		
3	29	19	27	26		
4	30	20	24	21		
5	36	43	42	31		

Westport Heights Elem., Westchester

Grade	Rd	Ma	Lg	Sp	Sci	SS
2	60	45	51	81		
3	46	51	46	68		
4	49	44	49	75		
5	45	40	45	57		

Westside Leadership Magnet, Marina Del Rey

Grade	Rd	Ma	Lg	Sp	Sci	SS
2	62	35	47	78		
3	62	17	44	73		
4	31	43	43	28		
5	61	33	42	39		
6	27	50	29	30		
7	24	29	28	33		
8	32	28	39	36		
9	58	53	59		43	55
10	80	50	67		55	68
11	22	19	28		35	42

Westwood Elem., Los Angeles

Grade	Rd	Ma	Lg	Sp	Sci	SS
2	90	90	97	89		
3	92	81	95	88		
4	95	94	93	93		
5	97	88	96	88		

STATE SCHOOL RANKINGS

Scores range from 1-99. A school scoring 75 has done better than 75 percent of other public schools in California.
Key: Rd (Reading), Ma (Math), Lg (Language), Sp (Spelling), Sci (Science) and SS (Social Science).

Grade	Rd	Ma	Lg	Sp	Sci	SS
White House Prim. Center, Los Angeles							
2	13	6	13	19		
White Point Elem., San Pedro							
2	83	81	90	89		
3	85	81	90	72		
4	77	80	83	75		
5	65	73	72	65		
White Middle, Carson							
6	30	27	25	34		
7	27	23	22	35		
8	34	30	29	41		
Whitman (Cont.), Nr W. Hollywood							
10	21	18	32		25	16
11	26	12	36		26	16
Wilbur Ave. Elem., Tarzana							
2	93	86	91	93		
3	79	77	84	86		
4	78	76	83	76		
5	62	58	64	64		
Wilmington Middle, Wilmington							
6	8	7	8	6		
7	10	9	9	11		
8	16	13	16	15		
Wilmington Park Elem., Wilmington							
2	15	19	21	22		
3	6	13	14	10		
4	13	16	24	10		
5	21	18	30	20		
Wilshire Crest Elem., Near Hancock Park							
2	33	27	28	52		
3	36	34	38	62		
4	24	13	19	26		
5	18	16	10	24		
Wilson Sr. High, El Sereno							
9	26	39	34		29	29
10	36	51	41		38	32
11	42	53	43		36	48
Wilton Place Elem., Hancock Park							
2	38	50	53	70		
3	29	51	54	70		
4	39	59	55	62		
5	35	58	51	54		
Windsor Hills Math/Sci. Elem., Windsor Hills							
2	55	44	67	82		
3	55	40	67	66		
4	53	38	45	56		
5	58	58	49	64		
Winnetka Ave. Elem., Canoga Park							
2	32	49	40	40		
3	17	15	18	39		
4	22	26	26	31		
5	30	21	25	33		
Wonderland Ave. Elem., Hollywood Hills							
2	86	71	90	92		
3	98	99	98	98		
4	97	97	98	99		
5	96	97	97	97		

Grade	Rd	Ma	Lg	Sp	Sci	SS
Woodcrest Elem., South Central L.A.							
2	2	1	2	4		
3	10	12	18	19		
4	8	4	5	7		
5	6	2	3	8		
Woodlake Ave. Elem., Woodland Hills							
2	67	66	69	75		
3	68	58	71	64		
4	71	62	75	80		
5	77	81	77	86		
Woodland Hills Elem., Woodland Hills							
2	98	96	99	98		
3	95	93	96	95		
4	86	86	89	84		
5	86	96	93	89		
Woodlawn Ave. Elem., Bell							
2	5	6	10	4		
3	9	8	9	5		
4	17	16	21	10		
5	16	12	18	5		
Wright Middle, Westchester							
6	50	28	46	51		
7	55	42	58	56		
8	59	41	62	71		
Yorkdale Elem., Highland Park							
2	23	35	37	28		
3	27	21	30	22		
4	19	35	22	26		
5	28	29	25	29		
Young (Cont.), West LA							
11	9	4	1		1	10
Youth Opportunities Unlimited, Los Angeles							
9	2	2	5		7	9
10	9	4	5		3	2
11	4	2	2		2	2

Los Nietos Elem. School Dist.

Grade	Rd	Ma	Lg	Sp	Sci	SS
Aeolian Elem., Whittier							
2	20	44	34	16		
3	21	34	27	22		
4	23	8	24	17		
5	23	24	29	24		
Los Nietos Middle, Near Santa Fe Springs							
6	21	19	17	27		
7	27	26	25	29		
8	27	23	26	25		
Nelson Elem., Whittier							
2	19	19	20	10		
3	12	11	14	15		
4	26	28	26	29		
5	18	16	23	27		
Rancho Santa Gertrudes Elem., Santa Fe Springs							
2	45	35	39	40		
3	15	16	18	19		
4	17	16	19	16		
5	4	7	12	13		

STATE SCHOOL RANKINGS 85

Scores range from 1-99. A school scoring 75 has done better than 75 percent of other public schools in California.
Key: Rd (Reading), Ma (Math), Lg (Language), Sp (Spelling), Sci (Science) and SS (Social Science).

Grade	Rd	Ma	Lg	Sp	Sci	SS
Lowell Jt. Elem. School Dist.						
El Portal Elem., La Habra						
2	72	72	87	64		
3	81	91	94	82		
4	85	86	92	82		
5	70	82	86	82		
6	88	91	91	86		
Jordan Elem., Whittier						
2	75	86	92	82		
3	77	88	87	75		
4	66	77	87	78		
5	68	80	82	85		
6	81	85	93	92		
Macy Elem., La Habra						
2	95	98	97	80		
3	88	97	95	91		
4	89	91	95	82		
5	91	92	98	96		
6	94	89	96	88		
Meadow Green Elem., Whittier						
2	82	81	90	78		
3	62	87	71	53		
4	66	75	80	60		
5	73	72	85	74		
6	81	85	93	86		
Olita Elem., La Habra						
2	95	99	98	90		
3	88	98	93	85		
4	83	92	93	91		
5	68	86	93	77		
6	93	97	98	97		
Rancho-Starbuck Int., Whittier						
7	78	86	90	85		
8	79	83	91	83		
Lynwood Unified School Dist.						
Abbott Elem., Lynwood						
2	20	22	23	40		
3	12	5	12	41		
4	13	6	14	45		
5	12	8	16	27		
Agnes Elem., Lynwood						
2	12	12	6	10		
3	2	7	4	5		
4	10	12	10	13		
5	5	11	5	2		
Hosler Middle, Lynwood						
6	5	5	7	11		
7	10	14	9	13		
8	12	13	16	17		
Lincoln Elem., Lynwood						
2	17	19	22	28		
3	29	49	37	66		
4	17	28	14	22		
5	18	41	29	33		
Lindbergh Elem., Lynwood						
2	13	35	13	24		
3	10	9	8	10		
4	1	16	4	7		
5	6	16	10	20		
Lugo Elem., Lynwood						
2	32	25	33	34		
3	33	38	27	59		
4	30	35	36	37		
5	58	40	35	39		
Lynwood High, Lynwood						
9	24	28	28		29	19
10	26	31	33		29	24
11	31	35	33		26	29
Lynwood Middle, Lynwood						
6	5	4	5	9		
7	4	5	5	6		
8	8	9	8	10		
Rogers Elem., Lynwood						
2	15	15	17	13		
3	14	15	23	26		
4	6	4	5	10		
5	28	29	33	39		
Roosevelt Elem., Lynwood						
2	17	18	16	18		
3	17	16	20	44		
4	10	9	21	16		
5	5	5	8	11		
Twain Elem., Lynwood						
2	9	16	5	12		
3	9	12	11	13		
4	3	5	6	7		
5	9	9	12	18		
Vista High (Cont.), Lynwood						
7	1	1	33	1		
8	7	4	5	6		
9	9	13	9		7	11
10	12	11	10		12	6
11	9	6	11		8	10
Washington Elem., Lynwood						
2	59	55	47	54		
3	27	23	35	37		
4	47	24	24	56		
5	50	40	42	39		
Wilson Elem., Lynwood						
2	11	22	15	13		
3	12	16	22	13		
4	11	26	9	17		
5	12	11	8	20		
Manhattan Beach Unified School Dist.						
Grand View Elem., Manhattan Beach						
2	98	90	97	94		
3	94	93	98	88		
4	96	95	96	94		
5	98	97	98	94		

Copyright © 2001 McCormack's Guides. No reproduction without permission.

STATE SCHOOL RANKINGS

Scores range from 1-99. A school scoring 75 has done better than 75 percent of other public schools in California.
Key: Rd (Reading), Ma (Math), Lg (Language), Sp (Spelling), Sci (Science) and SS (Social Science).

Grade	Rd	Ma	Lg	Sp	Sci	SS	Grade	Rd	Ma	Lg	Sp	Sci	SS
Manhattan Beach Middle, Manhattan Beach							**Plymouth Elem., Monrovia**						
6	97	95	93	95			2	23	35	28	14		
7	97	93	96	93			3	42	36	40	39		
8	98	95	98	96			4	34	31	38	31		
Meadows Ave. Elem., Manhattan Beach							5	23	8	14	20		
2	95	92	95	89			**Santa Fe Middle, Monrovia**						
3	93	93	94	77			6	35	30	36	40		
4	89	90	95	89			7	57	46	50	47		
5	91	95	93	93			8	51	42	53	42		
Mira Costa High, Manhattan Beach							**Wild Rose Elem., Monrovia**						
9	96	92	96		94	96	2	28	42	30	28		
10	96	93	94		93	93	3	36	21	28	24		
11	94	93	90		91	90	4	53	42	47	50		
Pacific Elem., Manhattan Beach							5	35	35	39	31		

Montebello Unified School Dist.

Grade	Rd	Ma	Lg	Sp	Sci	SS	Grade	Rd	Ma	Lg	Sp	Sci	SS
Pacific Elem., Manhattan Beach							**Bandini Elem., City of Commerce**						
2	99	99	99	97			2	23	44	43	30		
3	97	95	97	82			3	26	51	30	19		
4	97	97	97	95			4	16	33	21	22		
5	97	98	97	95			**Bell Gardens Elem., Bell Gardens**						
Pennekamp Elem., Manhattan Beach							2	2	4	2	3		
2	98	95	98	94			3	1	2	1	1		
3	98	95	97	85			4	1	4	3	1		
4	96	90	91	92			**Bell Gardens High, Bell Gardens**						
5	98	98	98	96			9	19	30	25		18	24
Robinson Elem., Manhattan Beach							10	21	42	31		23	21
2	99	99	97	95			11	28	40	34		20	29
3	99	99	99	95			**Bell Gardens Int., Bell Gardens**						
4	97	94	97	95			5	5	9	8	3		
5	97	97	98	94			6	3	10	4	3		

Monrovia Unified School Dist.

Grade	Rd	Ma	Lg	Sp	Sci	SS	Grade	Rd	Ma	Lg	Sp	Sci	SS
Bradoaks Elem., Monrovia							7	4	11	5	5		
2	40	50	37	36			8	7	10	10	7		
3	39	34	44	39			**Bella Vista Elem., Monterey Park**						
4	27	21	32	21			2	28	30	37	30		
5	31	28	37	35			3	36	36	38	37		
Canyon High (Cont.), Monrovia							4	33	40	38	35		
9	9	22	18		6	24	**Chavez Elem., Bell Gardens**						
10	15	20	23		12	13	2	3	5	4	4		
11	7	10	21		4	1	3	2	3	1	1		
Clifton Middle, Monrovia							4	3	4	3	2		
6	48	35	50	56			**Eastmont Int. Montebello**						
7	51	44	50	41			5	9	9	8	9		
8	64	66	61	64			6	10	11	13	10		
Mayflower Elem., Monrovia							7	14	13	12	12		
2	40	44	46	38			8	17	25	19	13		
3	70	63	72	66			**Fremont Elem., Montebello**						
4	57	48	62	62			2	52	53	52	62		
5	73	81	87	64			3	52	25	54	53		
Monroe Elem., Monrovia							4	24	23	22	21		
2	42	44	45	36			**Garfield Elem., Bell Gardens**						
3	34	27	33	30			2	33	37	23	30		
4	44	28	36	37			3	24	22	9	10		
5	37	24	44	35			4	21	23	15	8		
Monrovia High, Monrovia							**Gascon Elem., Los Angeles**						
9	59	54	61		56	66	2	3	10	11	4		
10	67	62	70		67	64	3	5	10	4	2		
11	53	53	56		52	58	4	10	10	5	7		

Copyright © 2001 McCormack's Guides. No reproduction without permission.

STATE SCHOOL RANKINGS

Scores range from 1-99. A school scoring 75 has done better than 75 percent of other public schools in California.
Key: Rd (Reading), Ma (Math), Lg (Language), Sp (Spelling), Sci (Science) and SS (Social Science).

Grade	Rd	Ma	Lg	Sp	Sci	SS
Greenwood Elem., Montebello						
2	22	12	24	36		
3	24	23	27	22		
4	39	42	45	29		
La Merced Elem., Montebello						
2	30	24	34	34		
3	36	42	37	33		
4	23	18	16	17		
La Merced Int., Montebello						
5	23	9	20	25		
6	17	9	19	17		
7	22	14	30	23		
8	24	14	26	25		
Laguna Nueva Elem., Commerce						
2	8	2	5	4		
3	3	18	2	1		
4	5	8	3	1		
5	7	11	4	5		
6	10	6	10	9		
7	26	31	20	8		
Macy Int., Monterey Park						
5	42	41	42	48		
6	38	40	39	51		
7	43	54	44	56		
8	48	56	52	49		
Montebello Gardens Elem., Pico Rivera						
2	5	1	2	7		
3	34	60	28	51		
4	26	42	24	23		
Montebello High, Montebello						
9	26	34	35		24	29
10	30	46	37		34	29
11	37	54	39		41	42
Montebello Int., Montebello						
5	14	13	18	14		
6	13	18	17	12		
7	14	14	18	13		
8	19	22	20	22		
Montebello Park Elem., Los Angeles						
2	12	9	5	18		
3	9	1	4	4		
4	17	11	16	23		
Potrero Heights Elem., S. San Gabriel						
2	52	73	58	70		
3	52	58	56	59		
4	59	40	42	52		
Rosewood Park Elem., Commerce						
2	8	9	17	6		
3	14	22	11	10		
4	17	42	19	23		
Schurr High, Monebello						
9	37	45	38		31	38
10	47	57	48		43	51
11	42	55	39		46	40
Suva Elem., Bell Gardens						
2	1	1	1	1		
3	1	1	1	1		
4	3	8	2	1		
Suva Int., Bell Gardens						
5	5	8	5	4		
6	4	4	4	3		
7	6	6	6	4		
8	15	13	14	9		
Vail High Cont., Montebello						
9	9	5	13		4	3
10	9	11	16		6	11
11	9	4	11		3	9
Washington Elem., Montebello						
2	38	47	51	40		
3	31	22	27	28		
4	36	44	38	33		
Wilcox Elem., Montebello						
2	15	10	19	16		
3	27	18	15	10		
4	10	18	16	13		
Winter Gardens Elem., Los Angeles						
2	19	15	23	38		
3	27	32	30	19		
4	23	21	22	17		

Mountain View Elem. School Dist.

Grade	Rd	Ma	Lg	Sp	Sci	SS
Baker Elem., El Monte						
2	11	19	15	14		
3	6	21	4	12		
4	10	28	12	17		
5	7	15	12	9		
Cogswell Elem., El Monte						
2	12	16	11	13		
3	19	56	31	28		
4	3	8	10	4		
5	3	15	18	6		
6	3	15	12	10		
Kranz Int., El Monte						
7	16	21	26	15		
8	12	22	21	12		
La Primaria Elem., El Monte						
2	45	60	58	52		
3	23	58	20	28		
Madrid Middle, El Monte						
6	7	13	20	11		
7	17	21	26	19		
8	19	23	29	19		
Maxson Elem., El Monte						
2	16	25	16	14		
3	12	44	17	17		
4	19	48	22	21		
5	12	29	13	16		
6	8	17	7	12		
Miramonte Elem., El Monte						
2	7	12	11	10		
3	14	42	17	8		
4	8	21	16	11		
5	12	35	30	25		
6	11	22	17	17		

STATE SCHOOL RANKINGS

Scores range from 1-99. A school scoring 75 has done better than 75 percent of other public schools in California.
Key: Rd (Reading), Ma (Math), Lg (Language), Sp (Spelling), Sci (Science) and SS (Social Science).

Monte Vista Elem., El Monte

Grade	Rd	Ma	Lg	Sp	Sci	SS
2	20	52	23	28		
3	15	22	11	19		
4	13	28	14	21		
5	13	12	14	18		
6	20	18	19	20		

Parkview Elem., El Monte

Grade	Rd	Ma	Lg	Sp	Sci	SS
2	13	28	22	16		
3	10	27	17	22		
4	13	15	16	8		
5	13	13	16	16		
6	10	15	16	27		

Payne Elem., El Monte

Grade	Rd	Ma	Lg	Sp	Sci	SS
2	5	39	15	7		
3	10	34	12	10		
4	11	33	12	14		
5	2	11	16	9		
6	15	15	17	20		

Twin Lakes Elem., El Monte

Grade	Rd	Ma	Lg	Sp	Sci	SS
2	15	28	17	14		
3	24	32	28	30		
4	19	28	19	23		
5	18	26	29	22		

Voorhis Elem., El Monte.

Grade	Rd	Ma	Lg	Sp	Sci	SS
2	13	37	24	26		
3	14	44	20	19		
4	11	26	12	10		
5	11	24	20	11		

Newhall Elem. School Dist.

Meadows Elem., Santa Clarita

Grade	Rd	Ma	Lg	Sp	Sci	SS
2	87	82	89	84		
3	96	96	94	93		
4	90	94	93	89		
5	93	95	95	94		
6	95	91	92	90		

Newhall Elem., Santa Clarita

Grade	Rd	Ma	Lg	Sp	Sci	SS
2	40	37	39	42		
3	44	37	44	28		
4	43	48	56	50		
5	47	59	49	48		
6	54	57	52	64		

Old Orchard Elem., Santa Clarita

Grade	Rd	Ma	Lg	Sp	Sci	SS
2	67	62	72	78		
3	67	72	60	62		
4	72	75	78	75		
5	89	84	87	91		
6	78	83	82	74		

Peachland Ave. Elem., Santa Clarita

Grade	Rd	Ma	Lg	Sp	Sci	SS
2	62	57	60	62		
3	73	68	81	66		
4	68	62	64	56		
5	77	73	72	79		
6	76	85	77	79		

Stevenson Ranch Elem., Santa Clarita

Grade	Rd	Ma	Lg	Sp	Sci	SS
2	81	79	84	80		
3	88	82	92	79		
4	95	92	94	91		
5	91	90	93	93		
6	92	89	94	92		

Valencia Valley Elem., Santa Clarita

Grade	Rd	Ma	Lg	Sp	Sci	SS
2	83	70	90	84		
3	86	85	87	73		
4	80	77	74	71		
5	89	84	81	82		
6	88	88	90	88		

Wiley Canyon Elem., Santa Clarita

Grade	Rd	Ma	Lg	Sp	Sci	SS
2	85	82	82	75		
3	74	82	81	84		
4	73	80	84	76		
5	64	77	69	71		
6	75	90	83	78		

Norwalk-La Mirada Unified School Dist.

Benton Middle, La Mirada

Grade	Rd	Ma	Lg	Sp	Sci	SS
6	37	28	46	46		
7	59	65	65	62		
8	55	53	59	54		

Chavez Elem., Norwalk

Grade	Rd	Ma	Lg	Sp	Sci	SS
2	18	5	12	21		
3	26	13	15	22		
4	21	35	30	21		
5	25	23	22	22		

Corvallis Middle, Norwalk

Grade	Rd	Ma	Lg	Sp	Sci	SS
6	12	7	12	19		
7	11	14	13	18		
8	21	14	20	20		

Dolland Elem., Norwalk

Grade	Rd	Ma	Lg	Sp	Sci	SS
2	33	39	28	22		
3	26	32	23	19		
4	30	24	24	35		
5	33	41	32	31		

Dulles Elem., La Mirada

Grade	Rd	Ma	Lg	Sp	Sci	SS
2	47	18	46	38		
3	55	27	35	53		
4	74	56	71	57		
5	50	53	48	61		

Eastwood Elem., La Mirada

Grade	Rd	Ma	Lg	Sp	Sci	SS
2	67	60	74	70		
3	62	65	71	81		
4	59	50	66	64		
5	60	72	68	75		

Edmondson Elem., Norwalk

Grade	Rd	Ma	Lg	Sp	Sci	SS
2	27	42	43	40		
3	19	21	27	48		
4	28	18	36	24		
5	14	24	35	29		

El Camino High (Cont.), La Mirada

Grade	Rd	Ma	Lg	Sp	Sci	SS
9	17	10	15		11	8
10	5	8	4		6	4
11	9	4	11		5	5

Escalona Elem., La Mirada

Grade	Rd	Ma	Lg	Sp	Sci	SS
2	62	73	81	58		
3	73	73	77	77		
4	72	78	78	66		
5	55	58	68	57		

STATE SCHOOL RANKINGS

Scores range from 1-99. A school scoring 75 has done better than 75 percent of other public schools in California.
Key: Rd (Reading), Ma (Math), Lg (Language), Sp (Spelling), Sci (Science) and SS (Social Science).

Grade	Rd	Ma	Lg	Sp	Sci	SS	Grade	Rd	Ma	Lg	Sp	Sci	SS
	Foster Rd. Elem., La Mirada							**Moffitt Elem., Norwalk**					
2	25	13	15	21			2	20	30	28	19		
3	9	3	9	17			3	17	13	17	28		
4	30	23	12	19			4	17	15	30	16		
5	16	10	16	16			5	21	30	32	33		
	Gardenhill Elem., La Mirada							**Morrison Elem., Norwalk**					
2	60	52	61	58			2	28	42	45	36		
3	74	60	72	60			3	33	36	33	30		
4	62	55	69	62			4	26	31	34	21		
5	53	43	63	59			5	14	21	22	20		
	Glazier Elem., Norwalk							**New River Elem., Norwalk**					
2	30	33	27	36			2	43	28	45	44		
3	29	42	28	39			3	41	49	61	35		
4	38	47	43	38			4	36	29	43	37		
5	48	33	49	48			5	30	12	40	42		
	Glenn High, Norwalk							**Norwalk High, Norwalk**					
9	29	34	38		26	38	9	29	34	37		36	31
10	30	34	33		29	35	10	36	36	41		45	32
11	40	39	39		36	37	11	36	35	39		44	31
	Hargitt Middle, Norwalk							**Nuffer Elem., Norwalk**					
6	17	12	17	22			2	19	24	17	24		
7	24	33	20	26			3	19	37	11	22		
8	19	22	23	17			4	23	33	22	31		
	Huerta Elem., Norwalk						5	30	31	40	42		
2	11	28	16	12				**Sanchez Elem., Norwalk**					
3	15	16	15	10			2	23	21	14	26		
4	13	18	17	16			3	9	19	5	9		
5	21	15	30	22			4	14	18	14	16		
	Hutchinson Middle, La Mirada						5	16	16	30	14		
6	58	48	52	56				**Waite Middle, Norwalk**					
7	54	44	50	56			6	13	18	23	19		
8	50	30	50	44			7	26	21	32	30		
	Johnston Elem., Norwalk						8	23	11	23	22		
2	28	30	43	30									
3	34	44	49	33				**Palmdale Elem. School Dist.**					
4	38	35	47	54				**Barrel Springs Elem., Palmdale**					
5	33	36	39	39			2	64	54	75	62		
	La Mirada High, La Mirada						3	62	51	67	60		
9	54	48	59		52	40	4	52	42	51	57		
10	76	69	81		75	63	5	48	40	42	49		
11	69	64	75		67	59	6	44	35	39	53		
	La Pluma Elem., La Mirada							**Buena Vista Elem., Palmdale**					
2	28	21	31	26			2	48	42	41	46		
3	47	19	35	39			3	31	23	31	26		
4	62	56	71	67			4	49	65	56	42		
5	56	59	75	61			5	45	31	44	46		
	Lampton Elem., Norwalk						6	32	26	33	27		
2	52	68	64	62			7	39	35	42	35		
3	38	40	49	46			8	73	45	39	81		
4	44	60	62	60				**Cactus Elem., Palmdale**					
5	44	50	58	49			2	57	55	56	44		
	Los Alisos Middle, Norwalks						3	39	46	40	53		
6	21	17	33	32			4	36	33	43	42		
7	23	23	28	24			5	39	33	33	33		
8	32	27	39	34			6	44	46	56	60		
	Los Coyotes Middle						7	46	38	47	48		
6	58	38	52	60			8	44	30	33	46		
7	66	65	68	76									
8	39	28	43	51									

STATE SCHOOL RANKINGS

Scores range from 1-99. A school scoring 75 has done better than 75 percent of other public schools in California.
Key: Rd (Reading), Ma (Math), Lg (Language), Sp (Spelling), Sci (Science) and SS (Social Science).

Grade	Rd	Ma	Lg	Sp	Sci	SS
Chaparral Elem., Palmdale						
2	48	39	63	56		
3	41	46	37	44		
4	45	42	46	44		
5	37	20	39	49		
6	37	33	35	46		
Cimarron Elem., Palmdale						
2	37	47	56	50		
3	46	46	40	46		
4	44	28	34	45		
5	54	53	56	60		
6	64	50	52	53		
Desert Rose Elem., Palmdale						
2	48	37	49	48		
3	46	40	47	44		
4	47	52	56	56		
5	37	31	39	35		
6	36	22	31	53		
Joshua Hills Elem., Palmdale						
2	57	81	68	56		
3	58	67	67	57		
4	52	47	56	60		
5	55	48	63	59		
6	53	57	69	71		
Juniper Int., Palmdale						
7	28	21	24	30		
8	32	22	29	34		
Manzanita Elem., Palmdale						
2	20	33	37	22		
3	29	34	27	26		
4	28	48	38	29		
5	25	21	22	27		
6	46	52	36	34		
Mesa Int., Palmdale						
7	45	37	37	47		
8	46	43	33	51		
Mesquite Elem., Palmdale						
2	47	35	54	58		
3	44	42	44	39		
4	38	35	40	33		
5	50	65	64	55		
6	54	58	69	66		
Oak Tree Learning Ctr., Palmdale						
7	23	5	3	23		
8	32	12	25	36		
Ocotillo Elem., Palmdale						
2	43	67	58	40		
3	49	62	57	55		
4	54	64	62	49		
5	67	58	68	78		
6	50	52	52	55		
Palm Tree Hill Elem., Palmdale						
2	20	21	28	18		
3	44	44	47	48		
4	43	50	32	38		
5	39	50	37	42		
Palmdale Learning Plaza Elem., Palmdale						
2	90	73	78	78		
3	73	67	74	57		
4	60	24	40	47		
5	65	28	63	59		
6	42	38	42	42		
7	65	38	52	74		
8	66	51	67	67		
Quail Valley Elem., Palmdale						
2	50	55	51	60		
3	41	29	35	41		
4	41	29	38	47		
5	45	35	49	54		
6	36	28	36	36		
Shadow Hills Int., Palmdale						
7	37	25	37	45		
8	39	25	36	49		
Summerwind Elem., Palmdale						
2	50	45	47	54		
3	52	58	67	57		
4	58	64	71	54		
5	44	48	45	49		
6	44	50	50	44		
Tamarisk Elem., Palmdale						
2	22	30	24	26		
3	11	11	8	12		
4	26	20	30	24		
5	14	6	16	14		
6	19	6	8	19		
Tumbleweed Elem., Palmdale						
2	25	11	24	24		
3	19	7	12	24		
4	33	20	30	31		
5	18	3	9	11		
6	37	22	33	36		
Wildflower Elem., Palmdale						
2	48	50	58	54		
3	38	42	44	44		
4	41	31	40	42		
5	52	43	49	52		
6	30	24	35	38		
7	37	21	28	31		
8	24	18	18	20		
Yucca Elem., Palmdale						
2	5	7	12	3		
3	12	5	11	8		
4	10	18	19	13		
5	3	2	3	2		
6	8	8	7	3		

Palos Verdes Penin. Unified School Dist.

Grade	Rd	Ma	Lg	Sp	Sci	SS
Cornerstone, Rancho Palos Verdes						
2	98	99	97	98		
3	95	91	92	87		
4	99	99	98	99		
5	99	99	99	99		

STATE SCHOOL RANKINGS

Scores range from 1-99. A school scoring 75 has done better than 75 percent of other public schools in California.
Key: Rd (Reading), Ma (Math), Lg (Language), Sp (Spelling), Sci (Science) and SS (Social Science).

Dapplegray Elem.,

Grade	Rd	Ma	Lg	Sp	Sci	SS
2	90	86	92	94		
3	87	85	89	79		
4	96	97	95	90		
5	90	96	92	94		

Lunada Bay Elem., Rancho Palos Verdes

Grade	Rd	Ma	Lg	Sp	Sci	SS
2	94	95	91	93		
3	95	98	93	97		
4	94	97	94	95		
5	97	97	94	98		

Mira Catalina Elem., Rancho Palos Verdes

Grade	Rd	Ma	Lg	Sp	Sci	SS
2	97	97	95	95		
3	95	94	92	94		
4	87	92	81	87		
5	89	85	94	94		

Miraleste Int., Rancho Palos Verdes

Grade	Rd	Ma	Lg	Sp	Sci	SS
6	89	89	87	93		
7	93	95	88	93		
8	87	93	86	91		

Miraleste Kindergarten, Rancho Palos Verdes

Grade	Rd	Ma	Lg	Sp	Sci	SS
3	98	99	99	92		

Montemalaga Elem., Rancho Palos Verdes

Grade	Rd	Ma	Lg	Sp	Sci	SS
2	87	96	91	97		
3	98	99	98	98		
4	96	99	98	97		
5	93	97	98	99		

Palos Verdes Int., Rancho Palos Verdes

Grade	Rd	Ma	Lg	Sp	Sci	SS
6	95	97	95	97		
7	98	98	99	99		
8	98	99	98	98		

Palos Verdes Penin. High, Rolling Hills Est.

Grade	Rd	Ma	Lg	Sp	Sci	SS
9	98	99	98		98	97
10	96	98	98		97	97
11	98	98	99		98	98

Point Vicente Elem., Rancho Palos Verdes

Grade	Rd	Ma	Lg	Sp	Sci	SS
2	83	92	81	93		
3	90	97	95	97		
4	90	98	95	93		
5	92	96	95	97		

Rancho del Mar High (Cont.), Rolling Hills

Grade	Rd	Ma	Lg	Sp	Sci	SS
10	12	31	33		16	35
11	65	65	72		90	67

Rancho Vista Elem., Rolling Hills Est.

Grade	Rd	Ma	Lg	Sp	Sci	SS
2	91	95	89	92		
3	88	94	90	94		
4	90	95	86	94		
5	92	92	86	92		

Silver Spur Elem., Rancho Palos Verdes

Grade	Rd	Ma	Lg	Sp	Sci	SS
2	98	97	98	96		
3	96	98	97	98		
4	98	99	97	99		
5	94	98	95	97		

Soleado Elem., Rancho Palos Verdes

Grade	Rd	Ma	Lg	Sp	Sci	SS
2	94	99	92	94		
3	99	99	97	96		
4	98	99	90	97		
5	96	98	94	97		

Vista Grande Elem., Rancho Palos Verdes

Grade	Rd	Ma	Lg	Sp	Sci	SS
2	98	96	97	99		
3	91	98	95	99		
4	96	99	98	99		
5	91	98	90	98		

Paramount Unified School Dist.

Alondra Elem., Paramount

Grade	Rd	Ma	Lg	Sp	Sci	SS
2	30	33	41	47		
3	17	16	18	33		
4	16	20	21	23		
5	18	16	25	24		
6	3	2	3	6		
7	11	9	15	14		
8	21	20	20	22		

Collins Elem., Long Beach

Grade	Rd	Ma	Lg	Sp	Sci	SS
2	23	16	22	36		
3	44	37	46	39		
4	26	23	36	29		
5	20	10	12	13		
6	20	10	16	15		
7	18	14	16	18		
8	34	25	28	42		

Gaines Elem., Paramount

Grade	Rd	Ma	Lg	Sp	Sci	SS
2	11	10	15	16		
3	4	1	8	6		
4	8	6	10	13		
5	9	11	10	9		
6	3	2	4	6		
7	9	5	12	9		
8	7	6	8	6		

Hollydale Elem., South Gate

Grade	Rd	Ma	Lg	Sp	Sci	SS
2	22	13	27	28		
3	29	32	35	46		
4	19	16	36	24		
5	16	11	14	11		
6	11	4	17	9		
7	19	8	22	13		
8	21	10	26	15		

Keppel Elem., Paramount

Grade	Rd	Ma	Lg	Sp	Sci	SS
2	18	18	15	26		
3	12	19	23	20		
4	8	21	24	14		
5	6	21	25	11		
6	2	4	4	2		
7	3	6	5	2		
8	10	13	13	9		

Lakewood Elem., Lakewood

Grade	Rd	Ma	Lg	Sp	Sci	SS
2	30	35	31	40		
3	15	2	9	30		
4	27	16	28	38		
5	23	15	16	25		
6	23	4	19	32		
7	18	8	22	27		
8	18	13	18	22		

92 STATE SCHOOL RANKINGS

Scores range from 1-99. A school scoring 75 has done better than 75 percent of other public schools in California.
Key: Rd (Reading), Ma (Math), Lg (Language), Sp (Spelling), Sci (Science) and SS (Social Science).

Lincoln Elem., Paramount

Grade	Rd	Ma	Lg	Sp	Sci	SS
2	54	65	61	62		
3	36	46	44	37		
4	14	12	21	24		
5	13	7	20	11		
6	5	3	13	10		
7	15	7	21	13		
8	13	9	23	17		

Los Cerritos Elem., Paramount

Grade	Rd	Ma	Lg	Sp	Sci	SS
2	13	14	17	16		
3	8	21	9	10		
4	3	18	7	7		
5	3	3	5	4		
6	1	1	1	1		
7	3	3	5	3		
8	5	6	7	3		

Michelson Cont., Lakewood

Grade	Rd	Ma	Lg	Sp	Sci	SS
10	5	20	5		1	4
11	2	4	6		3	5

Mokler Elem., Paramount

Grade	Rd	Ma	Lg	Sp	Sci	SS
2	19	15	23	24		
3	12	16	14	22		
4	16	13	19	17		
5	14	7	13	22		
6	13	5	17	15		
7	18	9	21	18		
8	10	7	8	9		

Orange Ave. Elem., Paramount

Grade	Rd	Ma	Lg	Sp	Sci	SS
2	20	42	25	22		
3	12	19	11	22		
4	8	10	9	11		
5	14	26	22	14		
6	2	3	7	4		
7	12	9	12	13		
8	14	12	16	15		

Paramount High, Paramount

Grade	Rd	Ma	Lg	Sp	Sci	SS
9	17	27	29		20	21
10	23	39	29		27	21
11	24	38	29		24	29

Paramount Park Elem., Paramount

Grade	Rd	Ma	Lg	Sp	Sci	SS
2	24	27	30	34		
3	16	18	23	30		
4	8	4	10	13		
5	5	6	13	6		
6	3	1	6	5		
7	4	5	7	5		
8	6	6	9	5		

Roosevelt Elem., Paramount

Grade	Rd	Ma	Lg	Sp	Sci	SS
2	19	9	22	30		
3	12	12	14	15		
4	6	4	10	13		
5	11	8	12	16		
6	12	3	13	14		
7	8	3	9	12		
8	14	5	15	15		

Wirtz Elem., Paramount

Grade	Rd	Ma	Lg	Sp	Sci	SS
2	8	5	17	16		
3	12	8	15	9		
4	10	11	12	11		
5	16	18	23	13		
6	11	6	16	14		
7	3	2	4	6		
8	8	4	7	19		

Pasadena Unified School Dist.

Allendale Elem., Pasadena

Grade	Rd	Ma	Lg	Sp	Sci	SS
2	50	47	63	58		
3	81	79	78	93		
4	57	67	62	50		
5	28	46	32	25		
6	61	76	67	42		

Altadena Elem., Altadena

Grade	Rd	Ma	Lg	Sp	Sci	SS
2	6	3	3	7		
3	17	27	22	33		
4	36	28	28	37		
5	27	15	6	24		
6	29	21	14	15		

Blair High, Pasadena

Grade	Rd	Ma	Lg	Sp	Sci	SS
9	45	38	38		53	53
10	51	57	51		65	57
11	55	53	56		72	65

Burbank Elem., Altadena

Grade	Rd	Ma	Lg	Sp	Sci	SS
2	48	54	58	48		
3	29	32	28	33		
4	33	44	40	33		
5	35	46	37	44		
6	30	42	17	51		

Cleveland Elem., Pasadena

Grade	Rd	Ma	Lg	Sp	Sci	SS
2	59	78	46	54		
3	12	18	14	28		
4	10	23	8	11		
5	11	28	18	6		
6	32	48	35	20		

Coombs Alt., Pasadena

Grade	Rd	Ma	Lg	Sp	Sci	SS
2	55	49	80	47		
3	79	51	67	66		
4	60	20	53	38		
5	65	24	48	46		
6	97	63	86	93		
7	59	57	50	43		
8	42	54	43	49		

Don Benito Fund., Pasadena

Grade	Rd	Ma	Lg	Sp	Sci	SS
2	91	94	90	94		
3	85	91	84	89		
4	93	95	94	94		
5	88	93	89	94		

Edison Elem., Altadena

Grade	Rd	Ma	Lg	Sp	Sci	SS
2	20	47	27	36		
3	35	48	23	44		
4	38	42	28	47		
5	28	28	16	22		
6	17	7	39	20		

STATE SCHOOL RANKINGS

Scores range from 1-99. A school scoring 75 has done better than 75 percent of other public schools in California.
Key: Rd (Reading), Ma (Math), Lg (Language), Sp (Spelling), Sci (Science) and SS (Social Science).

Grade	Rd	Ma	Lg	Sp	Sci	SS
Eliot Middle, Altadena						
6	20	21	12	13		
7	35	33	32	43		
8	34	53	32	36		
Field Elem., Pasadena						
2	30	39	24	32		
3	39	63	33	28		
4	43	42	43	47		
5	35	41	51	29		
6	24	19	29	20		
Franklin Elem., Altadena						
2	62	86	69	80		
3	39	63	57	70		
4	19	33	19	31		
5	18	38	18	14		
6	15	11	14	12		
Hamilton Elem., Pasadena						
2	62	81	82	78		
3	44	63	56	62		
4	57	89	66	79		
5	35	24	40	39		
6	36	36	33	44		
Jackson Elem., Altadena						
2	45	68	40	48		
3	21	49	24	28		
4	15	28	14	13		
5	20	48	23	27		
6	34	90	47	11		
Jefferson Elem., Pasadena						
2	32	52	33	47		
3	38	58	38	41		
4	30	38	28	45		
5	31	26	23	27		
Linda Vista Elem., Pasadena						
2	38	42	44	50		
3	67	68	62	77		
4	47	47	55	64		
5	48	59	54	69		
6	7	13	14	10		
Loma Alta Elem., Altadena						
2	10	7	16	12		
3	24	22	22	40		
4	18	10	12	13		
5	16	6	14	13		
6	26	21	31	32		
Longfellow Elem., Pasadena						
2	27	55	27	32		
3	33	56	37	44		
4	34	52	40	37		
5	27	30	23	25		
6	10	22	11	13		
Madison Elem., Pasadena						
2	8	16	11	8		
3	23	44	15	33		
4	24	35	16	21		
5	18	36	18	18		
Marshall Fund., Pasadena						
6	34	40	39	34		
7	28	29	32	27		
8	32	34	36	31		
9	49	49	49		36	50
10	50	54	58		48	53
11	68	58	59		55	54
Muir High, Pasadena						
9	45	45	37		32	47
10	41	39	38		29	32
11	55	47	48		33	42
Noyes Elem., Altadena						
2	55	55	44	70		
3	64	63	62	66		
4	50	47	43	40		
5	58	61	44	54		
6	48	65	35	40		
Pasadena High, Pasadena						
9	43	51	42		45	50
10	51	54	53		50	49
11	61	67	61		48	54
Roosevelt Elem., Pasadena						
2	38	50	28	62		
3	33	46	33	79		
4	30	59	36	57		
5	23	46	22	38		
6	23	25	20	34		
Rose City High (Cont.), Pasadena						
9	5	11	11		11	9
10	15	11	10		29	6
11	11	16	17		5	4
San Rafael Elem., Pasadena						
2	22	13	17	24		
3	24	7	12	24		
4	33	35	43	35		
5	28	30	31	31		
6	24	35	20	30		
Sierra Madre Elem., Sierra Madre						
2	48	49	37	38		
3	59	68	56	57		
4	44	28	28	28		
5	37	48	29	36		
6	62	57	54	64		
Washington Middle, Pasadena						
2	11	7	8	13		
3	9	19	14	15		
4	10	8	7	7		
5	16	20	14	9		
6	11	9	6	11		
7	9	14	12	12		
8	12	13	12	9		
Webster Elem., Pasadena						
2	35	68	40	40		
3	38	48	40	35		
4	43	42	46	35		
5	25	40	32	27		
6	24	36	31	27		

STATE SCHOOL RANKINGS

Scores range from 1-99. A school scoring 75 has done better than 75 percent of other public schools in California.
Key: Rd (Reading), Ma (Math), Lg (Language), Sp (Spelling), Sci (Science) and SS (Social Science).

Willard Elem., Pasadena

Grade	Rd	Ma	Lg	Sp	Sci	SS
2	59	65	69	73		
3	67	84	74	89		
4	46	70	36	38		
5	37	64	40	44		

Wilson Middle, Pasadena

Grade	Rd	Ma	Lg	Sp	Sci	SS
6	32	40	33	40		
7	30	38	36	33		
8	32	35	36	37		

Pomona Unified School Dist.

Alcott Elem., Pomona

Grade	Rd	Ma	Lg	Sp	Sci	SS
2	16	30	22	16		
3	6	15	4	4		
4	11	28	19	8		
5	9	20	12	13		

Allison Elem., Pomona

Grade	Rd	Ma	Lg	Sp	Sci	SS
2	45	49	54	62		
3	56	54	47	77		
4	43	47	43	44		
5	37	35	25	44		

Armstrong Elem., Diamond Bar

Grade	Rd	Ma	Lg	Sp	Sci	SS
2	98	97	99	98		
3	73	76	80	89		
4	72	68	71	71		
5	80	88	85	91		
6	75	81	88	96		

Arroyo Elem., Pomona

Grade	Rd	Ma	Lg	Sp	Sci	SS
2	19	15	28	22		
3	17	12	15	22		
4	21	11	21	19		
5	13	16	23	16		

Barfield Elem., Pomona

Grade	Rd	Ma	Lg	Sp	Sci	SS
2	37	33	35	48		
3	27	7	24	28		
4	24	31	26	29		
5	14	24	29	20		
6	15	35	37	19		

Decker Elem., Pomona

Grade	Rd	Ma	Lg	Sp	Sci	SS
2	82	93	81	90		
3	77	90	82	98		
4	78	89	84	87		
5	81	80	82	89		
6	81	81	80	86		

Diamond Point Elem., Diamond Bar

Grade	Rd	Ma	Lg	Sp	Sci	SS
2	81	87	92	96		
3	77	73	75	87		
4	72	73	77	82		
5	79	78	77	85		
6	89	90	90	88		

Diamond Ranch High, Diamond Bar

Grade	Rd	Ma	Lg	Sp	Sci	SS
9	69	66	74		65	64
10	74	74	83		65	78
11	73	74	74		60	73

Emerson Middle, Pomona

Grade	Rd	Ma	Lg	Sp	Sci	SS
6	10	9	12	13		
7	17	21	16	21		
8	17	18	18	20		

Fremont Middle, Pomona

Grade	Rd	Ma	Lg	Sp	Sci	SS
6	6	7	8	7		
7	6	10	7	8		
8	12	14	18	19		

Ganesha Sr.High, Pomona

Grade	Rd	Ma	Lg	Sp	Sci	SS
9	17	33	32		24	24
10	23	34	37		38	27
11	31	36	37		33	34

Garey Sr.High, Pomona

Grade	Rd	Ma	Lg	Sp	Sci	SS
9	19	29	34		29	24
10	30	36	41		27	29
11	33	41	39		31	27

Golden Springs Elem., Diamond Bar

Grade	Rd	Ma	Lg	Sp	Sci	SS
2	94	97	92	96		
3	81	94	84	97		
4	94	99	95	97		
5	96	96	96	96		
6	94	97	99	97		

Harrison Elem., Pomona

Grade	Rd	Ma	Lg	Sp	Sci	SS
2	40	49	41	54		
3	38	34	28	37		
4	27	52	34	23		
5	23	18	20	18		

Kellogg Polytechnic Elem., Pomona

Grade	Rd	Ma	Lg	Sp	Sci	SS
2	50	62	65	62		
3	14	4	12	17		
4	13	4	11	3		
5	18	8	16	14		
6	24	10	13	20		

Kingsley Elem., Pomona

Grade	Rd	Ma	Lg	Sp	Sci	SS
2	37	26	40	68		
3	19	5	17	22		
4	30	21	24	31		
5	27	11	32	27		

Lexington Elem., Pomona

Grade	Rd	Ma	Lg	Sp	Sci	SS
2	33	33	34	21		
3	21	34	24	30		
4	8	26	28	17		
5	23	16	14	22		
6	29	31	31	14		

Lincoln Elem., Pomona

Grade	Rd	Ma	Lg	Sp	Sci	SS
2	7	5	6	5		
3	12	6	8	9		
4	6	3	2	2		
5	14	3	12	13		

Lorbeer Middle, Diamond Bar

Grade	Rd	Ma	Lg	Sp	Sci	SS
7	82	86	79	91		
8	79	84	80	92		

Madison Elem., Pomona

Grade	Rd	Ma	Lg	Sp	Sci	SS
2	18	28	12	18		
3	17	15	14	13		
4	13	18	17	7		
5	13	24	23	14		

Marshall Middle, Pomona

Grade	Rd	Ma	Lg	Sp	Sci	SS
6	5	6	8	5		
7	10	14	9	9		
8	12	18	20	17		

STATE SCHOOL RANKINGS

Scores range from 1-99. A school scoring 75 has done better than 75 percent of other public schools in California.
Key: Rd (Reading), Ma (Math), Lg (Language), Sp (Spelling), Sci (Science) and SS (Social Science).

Mendoza Elem., Pomona

Grade	Rd	Ma	Lg	Sp	Sci	SS
2	18	32	20	24		
3	5	2	7	15		
4	3	2	4	3		
5	3	1	4	3		

Montvue Elem., Pomona

Grade	Rd	Ma	Lg	Sp	Sci	SS
2	8	8	12	7		
3	17	2	14	14		
4	28	24	32	33		
5	30	21	29	58		
6	34	42	31	17		

Palomares Middle, Pomona

Grade	Rd	Ma	Lg	Sp	Sci	SS
6	13	12	12	17		
7	20	23	24	27		
8	18	15	20	20		

Park West High Cont., Pomona

Grade	Rd	Ma	Lg	Sp	Sci	SS
9	13	19	18		27	17
10	15	8	19		5	19
11	7	6	7		8	7

Philadelphia Elem., Pomona

Grade	Rd	Ma	Lg	Sp	Sci	SS
2	33	37	39	34		
3	33	12	24	51		
4	24	18	22	23		
5	23	16	27	27		
6	17	5	16	17		

Pomona Alt., Pomona

Grade	Rd	Ma	Lg	Sp	Sci	SS
7	4	2	3	10		
8	6	4	4	4		
9	14	13	16		18	13
10	16	18	16		27	24
11	13	19	14		22	16

Pomona Sr.High, Pomona

Grade	Rd	Ma	Lg	Sp	Sci	SS
9	31	31	32		29	24
10	39	54	38		48	41
11	28	41	38		29	48

Pueblo Elem., Pomona

Grade	Rd	Ma	Lg	Sp	Sci	SS
2	19	11	16	18		
3	26	6	12	14		
4	23	6	9	7		
5	7	3	10	11		
6	4	2	11	9		

Ranch Hills Elem., Pomona

Grade	Rd	Ma	Lg	Sp	Sci	SS
2	83	82	89	91		
3	88	88	90	94		
4	86	83	84	92		
5	80	78	81	85		
6	89	83	86	90		

Roosevelt Elem., Pomona

Grade	Rd	Ma	Lg	Sp	Sci	SS
2	13	7	14	16		
3	17	12	22	31		
4	5	2	4	6		
5	6	5	8	5		

San Antonio Elem., Pomona

Grade	Rd	Ma	Lg	Sp	Sci	SS
2	42	27	20	21		
3	35	21	20	31		
4	36	44	43	30		
5	18	15	29	33		

San Jose Elem., Pomona

Grade	Rd	Ma	Lg	Sp	Sci	SS
2	19	26	27	38		
3	46	37	56	51		
4	49	45	46	37		
5	31	36	40	44		

Simons Middle, Pomona

Grade	Rd	Ma	Lg	Sp	Sci	SS
6	2	10	11	4		
7	9	11	12	15		
8	11	12	15	9		

Vejar Elem., Pomona

Grade	Rd	Ma	Lg	Sp	Sci	SS
2	16	14	20	16		
3	7	3	7	14		
4	8	6	5	6		
5	11	5	18	9		
6	14	11	12	7		

Washington Elem., Pomona

Grade	Rd	Ma	Lg	Sp	Sci	SS
2	11	22	20	22		
3	11	7	14	15		
4	3	5	7	7		
5	2	1	5	2		

Westmont Elem., Pomona

Grade	Rd	Ma	Lg	Sp	Sci	SS
2	35	16	33	38		
3	24	9	17	20		
4	24	35	24	35		
5	44	59	64	42		
6	42	69	40	42		

Yorba Elem., Pomona

Grade	Rd	Ma	Lg	Sp	Sci	SS
2	40	18	40	44		
3	29	19	33	37		
4	43	26	51	38		
5	42	33	31	36		
6	29	18	25	22		

Redondo Beach Unified School Dist.

Adams Middle, Redondo Beach

Grade	Rd	Ma	Lg	Sp	Sci	SS
6	41	69	50	46		
7	55	69	55	63		
8	48	67	53	52		

Alta Vista Elem., Redondo Beach

Grade	Rd	Ma	Lg	Sp	Sci	SS
2	91	89	96	86		
3	90	82	92	81		
4	90	91	92	94		
5	88	93	87	82		

Beryl Heights Elem., Redondo Beach

Grade	Rd	Ma	Lg	Sp	Sci	SS
2	85	87	89	86		
3	82	76	76	87		
4	80	77	77	79		
5	77	88	78	77		

Birney Elem., Redondo Beach

Grade	Rd	Ma	Lg	Sp	Sci	SS
2	77	82	77	65		
3	61	75	83	46		
4	69	65	80	78		
5	85	87	89	78		
6	51	60	54	57		

Jefferson Elem., Redondo Beach

Grade	Rd	Ma	Lg	Sp	Sci	SS
2	95	97	93	92		
3	90	78	84	79		
4	91	94	90	85		
5	83	82	86	84		
6	89	94	90	98		

STATE SCHOOL RANKINGS

Scores range from 1-99. A school scoring 75 has done better than 75 percent of other public schools in California.
Key: Rd (Reading), Ma (Math), Lg (Language), Sp (Spelling), Sci (Science) and SS (Social Science).

Grade	Rd	Ma	Lg	Sp	Sci	SS
Lincoln Elem., Redondo Beach						
2	90	81	90	90		
3	73	70	73	66		
4	75	75	83	70		
5	73	68	71	78		
6	82	73	78	74		
Madison Elem., Redondo Beach						
2	60	65	66	72		
3	70	81	78	77		
4	75	83	76	70		
5	83	82	78	75		
Parras Middle, Redondo Beach						
6	70	78	56	58		
7	87	87	78	80		
8	83	83	80	79		
Redondo High, Redondo Beach						
9	77	82	79		83	74
10	83	87	83		84	81
11	73	75	76		76	71
Redondo Shores High (Cont.), Redondo Bh						
11	20	27	24		10	20
Tulita Elem., Redondo Beach						
2	91	97	93	89		
3	87	90	83	66		
4	83	81	81	75		
5	84	89	89	79		
6	73	63	62	53		
Washington Elem., Redondo Beach						
2	71	86	74	72		
3	62	65	59	46		
4	49	54	53	52		
5	68	83	71	61		

Rosemead Elem. School Dist.

Grade	Rd	Ma	Lg	Sp	Sci	SS
Encinita Elem., Rosemead						
2	30	57	47	48		
3	59	79	70	84		
4	50	60	64	50		
5	54	62	60	71		
6	36	73	62	53		
Janson Elem., Rosemead						
2	28	45	41	50		
3	42	63	51	66		
4	27	40	30	35		
5	52	65	63	74		
6	42	57	62	68		
Muscatel Middle, Rosemead						
7	48	69	47	52		
8	44	62	43	54		
Savannah Elem., Rosemead						
2	22	16	17	34		
3	23	27	29	31		
4	36	44	49	57		
5	50	48	55	67		
6	42	55	56	62		
Shuey Elem., Rosemead						
2	25	55	35	42		
3	65	76	75	87		
4	65	84	78	84		
5	61	81	71	77		
6	60	76	72	80		

Rowland Unified School Dist.

Grade	Rd	Ma	Lg	Sp	Sci	SS
Alvarado Int., Rowland Heights						
7	57	80	66	70		
8	59	76	71	74		
Blandford Elem., Rowland Heights						
2	64	70	68	84		
3	74	90	83	92		
4	73	84	89	90		
5	70	86	72	75		
6	67	82	77	71		
Farjardo Elem., Rowland Heights						
2	33	52	44	42		
3	39	65	47	55		
4	36	47	42	50		
5	41	57	42	48		
6	37	60	50	46		
Giano Int., La Puente						
7	19	38	36	21		
8	29	49	41	29		
Hollingworth Elem., West Covina						
2	57	59	63	64		
3	47	73	65	64		
4	52	65	74	54		
5	44	58	58	58		
6	36	68	46	42		
Hurley Elem., La Puente						
2	7	18	10	2		
3	5	12	12	7		
4	10	20	9	6		
5	14	33	20	8		
6	15	21	19	10		
Jellick Elem., Rowland Heights						
2	64	67	55	75		
3	47	81	63	81		
4	41	64	55	67		
5	47	72	72	58		
6	41	73	58	71		
Killian Elem., Rowland Heights						
2	82	94	86	93		
3	52	70	63	75		
4	69	92	86	86		
5	62	76	75	77		
6	73	92	84	86		
La Seda Elem., La Puente						
2	24	37	30	26		
3	24	39	31	26		
4	28	42	22	21		
5	18	24	22	16		
6	21	33	29	22		

Copyright © 2001 McCormack's Guides. No reproduction without permission.

STATE SCHOOL RANKINGS

Scores range from 1-99. A school scoring 75 has done better than 75 percent of other public schools in California.
Key: Rd (Reading), Ma (Math), Lg (Language), Sp (Spelling), Sci (Science) and SS (Social Science).

Grade	Rd	Ma	Lg	Sp	Sci	SS
Nogales High, La Puente						
9	43	51	54		39	48
10	48	64	54		45	45
11	51	57	56		48	48
Northam Elem., La Puente						
2	3	18	3	2		
3	16	73	25	12		
4	4	15	5	1		
5	7	13	6	5		
6	19	28	15	10		
Oswalt Elem., Walnut						
2	85	87	90	94		
3	83	96	92	95		
4	80	92	90	86		
5	75	88	85	88		
6	79	93	86	86		
Rincon Int., West Covina						
7	45	61	56	48		
8	55	70	61	64		
Rorimer Elem., La Puente						
2	35	64	52	26		
3	31	67	41	15		
4	52	73	47	39		
5	23	44	35	18		
6	39	66	52	27		
Rowland Elem., Rowland Heights						
2	50	60	55	64		
3	28	46	35	51		
4	30	47	43	35		
5	35	55	42	49		
6	58	78	76	79		
Rowland High, Rowland Heights						
9	70	86	79		79	79
10	73	93	81		78	71
11	79	93	87		81	71
Rowland Community Day, Rowland Heights						
11	57	62	52		50	59
Santana High Cont., Rowland Heights						
9	26	21	18		27	30
10	26	31	28		25	27
11	27	27	27		27	39
Shelyn Elem., Rowland Heights						
2	64	73	67	80		
3	78	87	84	92		
4	66	79	76	82		
5	76	84	83	89		
6	73	88	76	71		
Villacorta Elem., La Puente						
2	12	21	20	12		
3	17	31	22	20		
4	15	31	22	14		
5	23	43	27	34		
6	23	28	37	11		
Ybarra Elem., Walnut						
2	89	87	94	92		
3	76	84	73	93		
4	65	76	69	83		
5	76	93	77	85		
6	73	76	87	79		

Grade	Rd	Ma	Lg	Sp	Sci	SS
Yorbita Elem., La Puente						
2	12	29	16	12		
3	21	32	22	12		
4	32	47	40	24		
5	21	40	25	13		
6	12	22	20	13		

San Gabriel Unified School Dist.

Grade	Rd	Ma	Lg	Sp	Sci	SS
Community Ed. Ctr. (Cont.), San Gabriel						
11	17	24	27		17	26
Coolidge Elem., San Gabriel						
2	74	79	58	58		
3	62	76	80	66		
4	80	84	87	76		
5	67	73	77	67		
Gabrielino High, San Gabriel						
9	60	75	74		59	62
10	58	74	69		65	59
11	59	79	70		60	67
Jefferson Int., San Gabriel						
6	51	58	44	62		
7	55	69	65	65		
8	44	62	57	54		
McKinley Elem., San Gabriel						
2	48	68	52	70		
3	44	65	52	84		
4	49	64	64	70		
5	48	69	60	74		
Roosevelt Elem., San Gabriel						
2	19	5	17	18		
3	12	23	17	40		
4	35	38	26	37		
5	30	31	31	40		
Voyager Charter #117, San Gabriel						
2		27	42	38		
5	58	40	33	46		
6	62	36	58	48		
7	65	33	32	48		
8	34	7	11	17		
9	52	33	41		34	50
10	65	39	55		53	68
11	72	55	70		64	65
Washington Elem., San Gabriel						
2	56	35	46	47		
3	55	51	57	53		
4	52	56	62	49		
5	57	69	72	79		
Wilson Elem., San Gabriel						
2	62	64	65	64		
3	62	78	71	79		
4	62	86	67	75		
5	68	50	68	77		

San Marino Unified School Dist.

Grade	Rd	Ma	Lg	Sp	Sci	SS
Carver Elem., San Marino						
2	93	93	95	99		
3	94	97	97	98		
4	95	92	97	99		
5	92	95	96	98		

Copyright © 2001 McCormack's Guides. No reproduction without permission.

STATE SCHOOL RANKINGS

Scores range from 1-99. A school scoring 75 has done better than 75 percent of other public schools in California.
Key: Rd (Reading), Ma (Math), Lg (Language), Sp (Spelling), Sci (Science) and SS (Social Science).

Grade	Rd	Ma	Lg	Sp	Sci	SS
Huntington Int., San Marino						
6	96	97	95	98		
7	96	98	96	97		
8	96	99	98	98		
San Marino High, San Marino						
9	98	99	99		98	97
10	98	99	99		98	98
11	98	99	99		98	98
Valentine Elem., San Marino						
2	87	87	91	91		
3	97	98	99	98		
4	98	97	98	99		
5	94	96	97	97		

Santa Monica-Malibu School Dist.

Grade	Rd	Ma	Lg	Sp	Sci	SS
Adams Middle, Santa Monica						
6	67	58	62	62		
7	60	54	69	62		
8	60	45	64	52		
Cabrillo Elem., Malibu						
2	93	89	92	84		
3	90	70	74	66		
4	89	76	80	82		
5	89	85	87	94		
Edison Elem., Santa Monica						
3	39	36	33	8		
4	62	65	60	38		
5	55	61	53	39		
Franklin Elem., Santa Monica						
2	98	93	92	96		
3	96	98	93	93		
4	96	96	95	95		
5	96	94	92	96		
Grant Elem., Santa Monica						
2	71	72	75	62		
3	77	77	85	77		
4	81	78	77	82		
5	80	91	83	81		
Lincoln Middle, Santa Monica						
6	93	85	88	87		
7	96	94	94	91		
8	92	92	92	89		
Malibu High, Malibu						
6	91	78	80	83		
7	95	92	92	89		
8	97	87	92	89		
9	92	85	87		88	89
10	94	89	91		89	88
11	93	91	87		86	82
McKinley Elem., Santa Monica						
2	91	98	93	95		
3	80	84	81	79		
4	80	88	81	71		
5	58	64	60	67		
Muir Elem., Santa Monica						
2	56	62	47	54		
3	65	76	61	40		
4	49	35	46	40		
5	62	46	45	77		

Grade	Rd	Ma	Lg	Sp	Sci	SS
Olympic High (Cont.), Santa Monica						
11	5		9		20	20
Point Dume Elem., Malibu						
2	98	98	98	91		
3	95	72	94	84		
4	96	98	96	98		
5	95	94	92	88		
Rogers Elem., Santa Monica						
2	54	62	52	42		
3	73	65	65	51		
4	66	62	60	56		
5	77	80	83	72		
Roosevelt Elem., Santa Monica						
2	83	75	78	76		
3	92	82	89	81		
4	84	81	80	89		
5	95	98	94	94		
Santa Monica Alt., Santa Monica						
2	38	14	28	34		
3	90	29	74	26		
4	91	47	72	81		
5	89	52	68	55		
6	50	21	31	46		
7	60	46	66	70		
8	81	79	85	90		
Santa Monica High, Santa Monica						
9	89	92	87		83	88
10	82	86	82		78	80
11	90	90	86		80	87
Webster Elem., Malibu						
2	95	94	91	94		
3	96	90	97	91		
4	92	92	94	95		
5	93	84	91	89		

Saugus Union Elem. School Dist.

Grade	Rd	Ma	Lg	Sp	Sci	SS
Bouquet Canyon Elem., Santa Clarita						
2	88	82	90	92		
3	92	93	95	93		
4	89	93	90	94		
5	88	95	92	90		
6	88	96	91	92		
Cedarcreek Elem., Santa Clarita						
2	60	78	65	72		
3	58	58	52	51		
4	62	70	67	62		
5	48	57	55	55		
6	37	55	39	51		
Emblem Elem., Santa Clarita						
2	79	79	84	83		
3	87	93	92	88		
4	83	85	83	85		
5	73	85	74	67		
6	78	91	90	81		
Foster Elem., Santa Clarita						
2	79	79	82	89		
3	90	93	92	93		
4	83	89	89	80		
5	85	90	86	85		
6	84	94	92	88		

STATE SCHOOL RANKINGS

Scores range from 1-99. A school scoring 75 has done better than 75 percent of other public schools in California.
Key: Rd (Reading), Ma (Math), Lg (Language), Sp (Spelling), Sci (Science) and SS (Social Science).

Helmers Elem., Santa Clarita

Grade	Rd	Ma	Lg	Sp	Sci	SS
2	91	92	95	94		
3	96	91	97	92		
4	90	92	91	87		
5	85	90	91	88		
6	94	98	95	94		

Highlands Elem., Santa Clarita

Grade	Rd	Ma	Lg	Sp	Sci	SS
2	90	95	94	95		
3	85	81	87	84		
4	86	95	91	94		
5	84	97	89	82		
6	88	94	86	83		

Mountainview Elem., Santa Clarita

Grade	Rd	Ma	Lg	Sp	Sci	SS
2	85	92	90	90		
3	85	87	93	87		
4	85	86	90	84		
5	90	95	89	91		
6	93	93	90	92		

North Park Elem., Santa Clarita

Grade	Rd	Ma	Lg	Sp	Sci	SS
2	81	82	93	90		
3	82	85	83	79		
4	81	89	89	86		
5	84	88	94	77		
6	82	88	84	79		

Plum Canyon Elem., Santa Clarita

Grade	Rd	Ma	Lg	Sp	Sci	SS
2	74	75	80	72		
3	82	77	81	84		
4	85	84	81	84		
5	80	86	78	84		
6	76	81	75	73		

Rio Vista Elem., Santa Clarita

Grade	Rd	Ma	Lg	Sp	Sci	SS
2	69	70	77	80		
3	73	62	72	75		
4	68	72	71	73		
5	79	82	81	84		
6	69	78	78	74		

Rosedell Elem., Santa Clarita

Grade	Rd	Ma	Lg	Sp	Sci	SS
2	91	97	95	86		
3	87	95	91	88		
4	87	93	83	71		
5	85	89	85	84		
6	86	93	89	89		

Santa Clarita Elem., Santa Clarita

Grade	Rd	Ma	Lg	Sp	Sci	SS
2	88	92	90	87		
3	88	87	91	93		
4	66	73	67	64		
5	73	82	79	77		
6	82	88	80	82		

Skyblue Mesa Elem., Santa Clarita

Grade	Rd	Ma	Lg	Sp	Sci	SS
2	72	81	82	86		
3	65	63	65	72		
4	75	83	81	78		
5	81	82	88	91		
6	81	92	86	92		

South Pasadena Unified School Dist.

Arroyo Vista Elem., S. Pasadena

Grade	Rd	Ma	Lg	Sp	Sci	SS
2	69	65	78	87		
3	90	79	89	95		
4	85	81	84	86		
5	92	91	88	91		

Marengo Elem., S. Pasadena

Grade	Rd	Ma	Lg	Sp	Sci	SS
2	83	84	83	87		
3	89	91	92	84		
4	94	91	87	94		
5	93	93	93	90		

Monterey Hills Elem., S. Pasadena

Grade	Rd	Ma	Lg	Sp	Sci	SS
2	98	87	99	94		
3	87	81	91	95		
4	90	95	91	94		
5	91	91	95	97		

South Pasadena Middle, S. Pasadena

Grade	Rd	Ma	Lg	Sp	Sci	SS
6	84	86	77	87		
7	91	96	91	93		
8	87	94	92	91		

South Pasadena Sr.High, S. Pasadena

Grade	Rd	Ma	Lg	Sp	Sci	SS
9	92	94	94		91	95
10	94	98	94		94	96
11	94	95	91		92	88

South Whittier Elem. School Dist.

Carmela Elem., Whittier

Grade	Rd	Ma	Lg	Sp	Sci	SS
2	12	3	8	12		
3	8	16	16	15		
4	4	5	4	11		
5	3	5	6	5		
6	11	30	22	15		

Lake Marie Elem., Whittier

Grade	Rd	Ma	Lg	Sp	Sci	SS
2	45	57	49	36		
3	31	22	38	44		
4	19	40	32	28		
5	14	11	13	18		
6	32	36	42	30		

Loma Vista Elem., Whittier

Grade	Rd	Ma	Lg	Sp	Sci	SS
2	40	26	52	44		
3	27	34	41	62		
4	35	35	40	47		
5	27	40	48	54		
6	42	83	78	55		

Los Altos Elem., Whittier

Grade	Rd	Ma	Lg	Sp	Sci	SS
2	30	14	32	32		
3	52	60	71	70		

McKibben Elem., Whittier

Grade	Rd	Ma	Lg	Sp	Sci	SS
2	35	40	48	38		
3	42	68	47	60		
4	28	24	26	30		
5	33	36	35	29		
6	55	63	47	60		

Monte Vista Middle, Whittier

Grade	Rd	Ma	Lg	Sp	Sci	SS
3	28	42	49	55		
4	18	26	19	35		
5	52	61	61	65		
6	17	21	15	25		

100 STATE SCHOOL RANKINGS

Scores range from 1-99. A school scoring 75 has done better than 75 percent of other public schools in California.
Key: Rd (Reading), Ma (Math), Lg (Language), Sp (Spelling), Sci (Science) and SS (Social Science).

Grade	Rd	Ma	Lg	Sp	Sci	SS	Grade	Rd	Ma	Lg	Sp	Sci	SS
\multicolumn{7}{c}{South Whittier Int., Whittier}							\multicolumn{7}{c}{Emperor Elem., San Gabriel}						
7	24	31	22	24			2	90	94	90	98		
8	29	39	28	29			3	82	91	94	98		

South Whittier Int., Whittier
Grade	Rd	Ma	Lg	Sp
7	24	31	22	24
8	29	39	28	29

Telechron Elem., Whittier
Grade	Rd	Ma	Lg	Sp
2	66	54	67	76
3	17	52	37	37
4	32	54	30	49
5	35	41	72	52
6	41	60	60	48

Sulphur Springs Elem. Dist.

Canyon Springs Elem., Santa Clarita
Grade	Rd	Ma	Lg	Sp
2	67	70	78	78
3	58	65	68	73
4	50	52	58	67
5	56	64	61	69
6	32	40	37	44

Cox Elem., Santa Clarita
Grade	Rd	Ma	Lg	Sp
2	82	82	83	70
3	68	81	75	48
4	73	60	77	86
5	62	71	74	85
6	79	81	92	86

Mint Canyon Elem., Santa Clarita
Grade	Rd	Ma	Lg	Sp
2	62	54	65	58
3	47	67	61	60
4	38	47	49	57
5	57	73	72	79
6	46	66	64	58

Mitchell Elem., Santa Clarita
Grade	Rd	Ma	Lg	Sp
2	77	78	84	83
3	73	81	73	68
4	84	84	84	86
5	73	72	68	72
6	75	68	78	71

Pinetree Elem., Santa Clarita
Grade	Rd	Ma	Lg	Sp
2	75	82	80	72
3	82	79	81	84
4	84	84	80	81
5	74	73	77	72
6	78	78	86	79

Sulphur Springs Elem., Santa Clarita
Grade	Rd	Ma	Lg	Sp
2	81	82	83	84
3	83	91	89	92
4	83	81	87	90
5	77	82	85	82
6	86	88	86	87

Valley View Elem., Santa Clarita
Grade	Rd	Ma	Lg	Sp
2	67	81	71	68
3	70	84	78	81
4	63	72	67	73
5	76	71	77	74
6	65	68	75	68

Temple City Unified School Dist.

Cloverly Elem., Temple City
Grade	Rd	Ma	Lg	Sp
4	73	85	83	87
5	68	73	75	84
6	69	82	74	82

Emperor Elem., San Gabriel
Grade	Rd	Ma	Lg	Sp
2	90	94	90	98
3	82	91	94	98
4	80	91	90	95
5	74	82	87	88
6	94	97	94	98

La Rosa Elem., Temple City
Grade	Rd	Ma	Lg	Sp
2	79	70	69	93
3	76	91	81	92

Longden Elem., Temple City
Grade	Rd	Ma	Lg	Sp
2	74	65	61	92
3	78	88	86	97
4	75	90	94	92
5	70	88	89	91
6	82	90	90	90

Oak Avenue Int., Temple City
Grade	Rd	Ma	Lg	Sp
7	83	89	84	87
8	81	86	85	87

Temple City Alt., Temple City
Grade	Rd	Ma	Lg	Sp	Sci	SS
11	62	46	59		67	55

Temple City. Learning Ctr., Temple City
Grade	Rd	Ma	Lg	Sp	Sci	SS
11	5	4	2		2	1

Temple City High, Temple City
Grade	Rd	Ma	Lg	Sp	Sci	SS
9	80	91	90		77	84
10	78	92	87		82	79
11	81	95	90		78	81

Torrance Unified School Dist.

Adams Elem., Torrance
Grade	Rd	Ma	Lg	Sp
2	74	72	81	82
3	68	76	75	68
4	87	89	81	90
5	86	89	94	98

Anza Elem., Torrance
Grade	Rd	Ma	Lg	Sp
2	79	84	83	83
3	91	93	92	93
4	93	84	91	96
5	85	84	85	92

Arlington Elem., Torrance
Grade	Rd	Ma	Lg	Sp
2	75	72	78	78
3	87	90	86	91
4	81	90	90	89
5	80	78	86	86

Arnold Elem., Torrance
Grade	Rd	Ma	Lg	Sp
2	69	67	74	82
3	79	84	87	95
4	84	81	83	91
5	81	90	87	96

Calle Mayor Middle, Torrance
Grade	Rd	Ma	Lg	Sp
6	79	78	76	80
7	85	83	86	93
8	84	91	85	93

Carr Elem, Torrance.
Grade	Rd	Ma	Lg	Sp
2	56	54	60	68
3	62	52	67	73
4	60	57	69	81
5	65	81	74	75

Copyright © 2001 McCormack's Guides. No reproduction without permission.

Scores range from 1-99. A school scoring 75 has done better than 75 percent of other public schools in California.
Key: Rd (Reading), Ma (Math), Lg (Language), Sp (Spelling), Sci (Science) and SS (Social Science).

Casimir Middle, Torrance

Grade	Rd	Ma	Lg	Sp	Sci	SS
6	64	76	69	85		
7	75	84	79	89		
8	81	87	89	94		

Edison Elem., Torrance

Grade	Rd	Ma	Lg	Sp	Sci	SS
2	66	65	75	73		
3	67	63	73	73		
4	69	78	78	78		
5	87	85	86	84		

Fern Elem., Torrance

Grade	Rd	Ma	Lg	Sp	Sci	SS
2	57	54	52	72		
3	78	74	81	81		
4	68	77	77	80		
5	76	78	77	77		

Hickory Elem., Torrance

Grade	Rd	Ma	Lg	Sp	Sci	SS
2	77	82	87	89		
3	79	85	83	87		
4	77	81	80	88		
5	76	85	77	92		

Hull Middle, Torrance

Grade	Rd	Ma	Lg	Sp	Sci	SS
6	58	68	52	66		
7	62	67	60	68		
8	68	67	67	69		

Jefferson Middle, Torrance

Grade	Rd	Ma	Lg	Sp	Sci	SS
6	69	85	60	74		
7	71	78	66	78		
8	83	82	76	85		

Lincoln Elem., Torrance

Grade	Rd	Ma	Lg	Sp	Sci	SS
2	62	52	58	72		
3	64	67	71	89		
4	57	72	71	73		
5	74	84	78	90		

Lynn Middle, Torrance

Grade	Rd	Ma	Lg	Sp	Sci	SS
6	76	81	82	89		
7	89	90	88	93		
8	87	91	91	90		

Madrona Middle, Torrance

Grade	Rd	Ma	Lg	Sp	Sci	SS
6	69	71	62	71		
7	82	83	75	87		
8	75	82	76	83		

Magruder Middle, Torrance

Grade	Rd	Ma	Lg	Sp	Sci	SS
6	57	50	50	51		
7	59	57	63	72		
8	70	60	61	71		

North High, Torrance

Grade	Rd	Ma	Lg	Sp	Sci	SS
9	70	86	76		85	70
10	76	84	78		82	76
11	69	79	76		73	71

Richardson Middle, Torrance

Grade	Rd	Ma	Lg	Sp	Sci	SS
6	82	83	77	87		
7	80	86	73	82		
8	86	91	92	95		

Riviera Elem., Torrance

Grade	Rd	Ma	Lg	Sp	Sci	SS
2	91	92	95	93		
3	96	88	94	93		
4	86	86	86	89		
5	92	93	93	88		

Seaside Elem., Torrance

Grade	Rd	Ma	Lg	Sp	Sci	SS
2	90	93	93	93		
3	80	85	81	75		
4	75	90	86	78		
5	73	76	74	74		

Shery High (Cont.), Torrance

Grade	Rd	Ma	Lg	Sp	Sci	SS
10	45	29	42		73	51
11	28	16	27		33	32

South High, Torrance

Grade	Rd	Ma	Lg	Sp	Sci	SS
9	89	91	89		93	84
10	82	88	84		88	82
11	91	97	93		92	91

Torrance Elem., Torrance

Grade	Rd	Ma	Lg	Sp	Sci	SS
2	52	46	56	72		
3	51	51	57	60		
4	60	84	62	62		
5	50	68	55	49		

Torrance High, Torrance

Grade	Rd	Ma	Lg	Sp	Sci	SS
9	75	82	79		75	74
10	80	83	79		79	79
11	81	79	79		71	75

Towers Elem., Torrance

Grade	Rd	Ma	Lg	Sp	Sci	SS
2	91	86	96	93		
3	87	88	90	91		
4	81	86	83	92		
5	77	88	82	85		

Victor Elem., Torrance

Grade	Rd	Ma	Lg	Sp	Sci	SS
2	66	75	75	82		
3	76	84	87	93		
4	71	77	77	82		
5	73	80	83	85		

Walteria Elem., Torrance

Grade	Rd	Ma	Lg	Sp	Sci	SS
2	90	86	85	86		
3	79	81	87	84		
4	84	88	91	87		
5	76	73	78	82		

West High, Torrance

Grade	Rd	Ma	Lg	Sp	Sci	SS
9	85	94	93		91	86
10	88	96	94		93	88
11	87	96	90		89	84

Wood Elem., Torrance

Grade	Rd	Ma	Lg	Sp	Sci	SS
2	77	86	89	75		
3	76	73	75	72		
4	69	80	78	82		
5	68	85	82	81		

Yukon Elem., Torrance

Grade	Rd	Ma	Lg	Sp	Sci	SS
2	81	49	78	82		
3	67	52	65	72		
4	62	67	67	69		
5	74	77	75	74		

Valle Lindo Elem. School Dist.

New Temple Elem., El Monte

Grade	Rd	Ma	Lg	Sp	Sci	SS
2	24	28	28	36		
3	31	40	37	48		

STATE SCHOOL RANKINGS

Scores range from 1-99. A school scoring 75 has done better than 75 percent of other public schools in California.
Key: Rd (Reading), Ma (Math), Lg (Language), Sp (Spelling), Sci (Science) and SS (Social Science).

Shively Elem., El Monte

Grade	Rd	Ma	Lg	Sp	Sci	SS
4	28	25	36	49		
5	21	18	31	31		
6	32	30	47	44		
7	32	35	42	43		
8	36	34	53	44		

Walnut Valley Unified School Dist.

Castle Rock Elem., Diamond Bar

Grade	Rd	Ma	Lg	Sp	Sci	SS
2	75	75	72	86		
3	64	72	71	91		
4	71	79	77	90		
5	87	82	78	95		

Chaparral Middle, Diamond Bar

Grade	Rd	Ma	Lg	Sp	Sci	SS
6	78	90	87	92		
7	80	92	87	91		
8	83	93	87	94		

Collegewood Elem., Walnut

Grade	Rd	Ma	Lg	Sp	Sci	SS
2	82	93	80	92		
3	62	79	75	82		
4	68	80	84	78		
5	70	87	89	88		

Cyrus J. Morris Elem., Walnut

Grade	Rd	Ma	Lg	Sp	Sci	SS
2	82	87	81	87		
3	31	44	44	46		
4	50	62	47	59		
5	52	65	46	72		

Del Paso High (Cont.), Walnut

Grade	Rd	Ma	Lg	Sp	Sci	SS
10	39	41	48		45	38
11	28	16	34		31	26

Diamond Bar High, Diamond Bar

Grade	Rd	Ma	Lg	Sp	Sci	SS
9	85	91	92		82	93
10	88	96	92		93	91
11	87	97	94		92	87

Evergreen Elem., Diamond Bar

Grade	Rd	Ma	Lg	Sp	Sci	SS
2	86	92	81	90		
3	80	82	80	87		
4	90	97	90	95		
5	88	88	91	94		

Maple Hill Elem., Diamond Bar

Grade	Rd	Ma	Lg	Sp	Sci	SS
2	75	84	72	86		
3	61	74	67	82		
4	80	88	81	94		
5	68	78	78	94		

Quail Summit Elem., Diamond Bar

Grade	Rd	Ma	Lg	Sp	Sci	SS
2	83	87	93	89		
3	78	85	84	92		
4	72	85	84	82		
5	81	84	82	89		

South Pointe Middle, Walnut

Grade	Rd	Ma	Lg	Sp	Sci	SS
6	65	83	74	87		
7	83	90	87	89		
8	79	88	82	91		

Suzanne Middle, Walnut

Grade	Rd	Ma	Lg	Sp	Sci	SS
6	79	92	92	92		
7	83	98	91	95		
8	75	95	86	94		

Vejar Elem., Walnut

Grade	Rd	Ma	Lg	Sp	Sci	SS
2	64	84	74	82		
3	64	87	78	82		
4	72	80	78	85		
5	73	68	72	85		

Walnut Elem., Walnut

Grade	Rd	Ma	Lg	Sp	Sci	SS
2	58	54	64	65		
3	65	70	76	77		
4	62	76	74	78		
5	55	67	63	75		

Walnut High, Walnut

Grade	Rd	Ma	Lg	Sp	Sci	SS
9	87	95	92		89	94
10	87	95	90		85	86
11	91	97	94		92	94

Westhoff Elem., Walnut

Grade	Rd	Ma	Lg	Sp	Sci	SS
2	75	87	81	95		
3	74	90	87	95		
4	84	95	92	97		
5	75	92	87	92		

West Covina Unified School Dist.

California Elem., W Covina

Grade	Rd	Ma	Lg	Sp	Sci	SS
2	47	92	52	65		
3	46	60	57	68		
4	41	56	49	50		
5	44	61	37	49		

Cameron Elem., W Covina

Grade	Rd	Ma	Lg	Sp	Sci	SS
2	48	50	60	60		
3	47	48	65	77		
4	57	78	74	72		
5	62	65	68	74		

Coronado Cont. High, W Covina

Grade	Rd	Ma	Lg	Sp	Sci	SS
10	18	11	13		13	21
11	11	10	15		15	9

Edgewood Middle, W Covina

Grade	Rd	Ma	Lg	Sp	Sci	SS
6	25	17	25	38		
7	30	28	32	45		
8	42	39	45	47		

Hollencrest Middle, W Covina

Grade	Rd	Ma	Lg	Sp	Sci	SS
6	30	48	29	58		
7	37	44	36	42		
8	51	45	43	64		

Merced Elem., W Covina

Grade	Rd	Ma	Lg	Sp	Sci	SS
2	50	60	48	70		
3	44	67	52	44		
4	47	38	42	45		
5	54	50	60	65		

Merlinda Elem., W Covina

Grade	Rd	Ma	Lg	Sp	Sci	SS
2	62	65	75	52		
3	41	38	49	44		
4	28	31	38	44		
5	41	52	45	36		

Monte Vista Elem., W Covina

Grade	Rd	Ma	Lg	Sp	Sci	SS
2	28	14	22	32		
3	36	18	30	33		
4	30	25	28	61		
5	35	30	32	39		

Scores range from 1-99. A school scoring 75 has done better than 75 percent of other public schools in California.
Key: Rd (Reading), Ma (Math), Lg (Language), Sp (Spelling), Sci (Science) and SS (Social Science).

Orangewood Elem., W Covina

Grade	Rd	Ma	Lg	Sp	Sci	SS
2	54	57	49	47		
3	36	44	44	37		
4	41	36	19	31		
5	44	58	35	60		

San Jose-Edison Charter, W Covina

Grade	Rd	Ma	Lg	Sp	Sci	SS
2	67	78	80	70		
3	65	78	73	77		
4	47	44	53	57		
5	61	59	68	72		
6	62	58	56	62		

Vine Elem., W Covina

Grade	Rd	Ma	Lg	Sp	Sci	SS
2	59	62	65	76		
3	59	65	71	60		
4	58	79	69	62		
5	64	74	66	71		

Wescove Elem., W Covina

Grade	Rd	Ma	Lg	Sp	Sci	SS
2	47	35	41	48		
3	51	42	42	70		
4	38	52	40	56		
5	28	30	24	46		

West Covina High, W Covina

Grade	Rd	Ma	Lg	Sp	Sci	SS
9	49	54	54		45	55
10	54	49	56		52	59
11	65	57	70		57	71

Westside Union Elem. School Dist.

Cottonwood Elem., Palmdale

Grade	Rd	Ma	Lg	Sp	Sci	SS
2	60	67	68	62		
3	70	56	78	66		
4	72	57	74	61		
5	74	78	75	75		

Del Sur Sr. Elem., Lancaster

Grade	Rd	Ma	Lg	Sp	Sci	SS
2	64	40	55	42		
3	67	49	73	57		
4	44	37	46	37		
5	42	21	29	18		
6	55	31	37	57		
7	48	29	32	43		
8	75	54	59	99		

Hillview Middle, Palmdale

Grade	Rd	Ma	Lg	Sp	Sci	SS
6	72	57	56	62		
7	75	57	68	68		
8	70	67	62	64		

Leona Valley Elem., Leona Valley

Grade	Rd	Ma	Lg	Sp	Sci	SS
3	79	65	67	46		
4	84	81	71	67		
5	90	92	98	74		

Neenach Elem., Lancaster

Grade	Rd	Ma	Lg	Sp	Sci	SS
5	57	62	79	25		

Quartz Hill Elem., Quartz Hill

Grade	Rd	Ma	Lg	Sp	Sci	SS
2	52	32	64	44		
3	76	72	77	55		
4	65	60	69	62		
5	68	65	71	60		

Rancho Vista Elem., Palmdale

Grade	Rd	Ma	Lg	Sp	Sci	SS
2	75	64	75	70		
3	73	65	73	73		
4	72	68	72	76		
5	76	78	79	74		

Sundown Elem., Lancaster

Grade	Rd	Ma	Lg	Sp	Sci	SS
2	54	47	60	60		
3	80	78	84	84		
4	74	68	76	75		
5	73	68	71	74		

Valley View Elem., Lancaster

Grade	Rd	Ma	Lg	Sp	Sci	SS
2	62	64	68	62		
3	64	54	71	51		
4	66	48	55	52		
5	71	68	71	52		

Walker Middle, Quartz Hill

Grade	Rd	Ma	Lg	Sp	Sci	SS
6	60	46	54	55		
7	65	52	63	54		
8	70	62	75	74		

Whittier City Elem. School Dist.

Andrews N.W. Elem., Whittier

Grade	Rd	Ma	Lg	Sp	Sci	SS
2	48	47	54	54		
3	47	65	59	44		
4	38	23	38	33		
5	50	40	45	52		
6	51	40	54	36		

Dexter Middle, Whittier

Grade	Rd	Ma	Lg	Sp	Sci	SS
6	30	26	27	32		
7	37	25	30	35		
8	42	20	40	37		

Edwards Middle, Whittier

Grade	Rd	Ma	Lg	Sp	Sci	SS
6	12	18	16	13		
7	19	19	24	31		
8	23	20	24	22		

Hoover Elem., Whittier

Grade	Rd	Ma	Lg	Sp	Sci	SS
2	35	21	27	26		
3	31	18	24	17		
4	39	40	46	33		
5	50	20	40	36		

Jackson Elem., Whittier

Grade	Rd	Ma	Lg	Sp	Sci	SS
2	3	3	1	5		
3	4	3	4	2		
4	16	8	11	13		
5	27	11	20	16		

Lincoln Elem., Whittier

Grade	Rd	Ma	Lg	Sp	Sci	SS
2	27	30	42	12		
3	35	42	37	40		
4	32	23	17	21		
5	11	3	14	11		

Longfellow Elem., Whittier

Grade	Rd	Ma	Lg	Sp	Sci	SS
2	20	14	15	16		
3	26	11	20	17		
4	26	16	21	16		
5	25	10	32	16		

STATE SCHOOL RANKINGS

Scores range from 1-99. A school scoring 75 has done better than 75 percent of other public schools in California.
Key: Rd (Reading), Ma (Math), Lg (Language), Sp (Spelling), Sci (Science) and SS (Social Science).

Grade	Rd	Ma	Lg	Sp	Sci	SS
Mill Elem., Whittier						
2	19	6	7	14		
3	26	18	18	22		
4	32	28	19	26		
5	31	33	25	27		
Orange Grove Elem., Whittier						
2	19	30	30	24		
3	19	18	9	19		
4	38	42	40	39		
5	21	10	18	22		
Phelan Elem., Whittier						
2	18	14	20	18		
3	23	29	17	19		
Sorensen Elem., Whittier						
2	20	11	19	10		
3	23	32	30	22		
4	43	48	38	49		
5	20	28	20	24		
Washington Elem., Whittier						
3	17	13	9	7		
4	23	12	30	7		
5	33	40	40	24		
West Whittier Elem., Whittier						
2	7	18	10	6		
3	11	11	4	9		
4	10	4	7	4		
5	14	5	16	11		

Whittier Union High District

Grade	Rd	Ma	Lg	Sp	Sci	SS
California High, Whittier						
9	56	69	54		54	62
10	56	75	53		48	53
11	62	74	56		60	61
Frontier High (Cont.), Whittier						
10	12	11	13		10	11
11	9	19	7		10	12
La Serna High, Whittier						
9	72	83	76		65	68
10	74	88	73		71	77
11	64	74	59		55	52
Pioneer High, Whittier						
9	39	51	46		36	48
10	39	56	38		34	43
11	49	62	43		44	55
Santa Fe High, Santa Fe Springs						
9	41	45	46		39	42
10	53	60	52		43	51
11	55	57	48		48	52
Sierra Vista High (Alt.), Whittier						
9	26	15	24		15	21
10	34	25	28		20	32
11	31	19	24		27	33
Whittier High, Whittier						
9	49	51	46		39	45
10	47	56	45		41	41
11	45	47	41		36	39

William S. Hart High School Dist.

Grade	Rd	Ma	Lg	Sp	Sci	SS
Arroyo Seco Jr. High, Santa Clarita						
7	89	93	88	91		
8	83	91	85	87		
Bowman High (Cont.), Santa Clarita						
10	32	27	19		38	32
11	26	24	14		17	20
Canyon High, Santa Clarita						
9	72	79	74		73	72
10	76	79	75		82	80
11	81	80	80		81	85
Hart Sr. High, Santa Clarita						
9	83	88	81		88	84
10	82	84	77		88	85
11	82	85	84		83	89
La Mesa Jr. High, Santa Clarita						
7	78	74	90	84		
8	81	75	91	85		
Learning Post High (Alt.), Santa Clarita						
9	68	40	67		32	70
10	81	60	81		75	64
11	85	55	89		67	82
Opportunities for Learning, Santa Clarita						
7	73	46	69	58		
8	42	37	36	59		
9	34	24	24		27	42
10	41	29	35		41	27
11	42	30	38		42	35
Passport Acad., Santa Clarita						
9	34	27	23		27	21
Placerita Jr. High, Santa Clarita						
7	78	79	78	78		
8	70	75	71	76		
Saugus High, Santa Clarita						
9	89	97	94		91	89
10	90	92	92		90	89
11	87	90	86		82	91
Sierra Vista Jr. High, Santa Clarita						
7	62	69	68	78		
8	59	62	52	64		
Valencia High, Santa Clarita						
9	84	88	86		88	82
10	82	84	84		84	85
11	79	83	82		82	87

Wilsona Elem. School Dist.

Grade	Rd	Ma	Lg	Sp	Sci	SS
Challenger Middle, Lancaster						
6	27	33	25	32		
7	24	21	23	23		
8	34	45	30	29		
Vista San Gabriel Elem., Palmdale						
2	52	40	33	50		
3	35	31	35	33		
4	24	28	32	33		
5	33	26	39	20		

Scores range from 1-99. A school scoring 75 has done better than 75 percent of other public schools in California.
Key: Rd (Reading), Ma (Math), Lg (Language), Sp (Spelling), Sci (Science) and SS (Social Science).

Grade	Rd	Ma	Lg	Sp	Sci	SS
Wilsona Elem., Lancaster						
2	71	78	80	75		
3	36	62	57	51		
4	49	56	34	45		
5	41	31	32	33		
Wiseburn Elem. School Dist.						
Anza Elem., Hawthorne						
2	60	44	72	82		
3	65	56	74	64		
4	63	70	53	56		
5	68	76	63	74		
Burnett Elem., Hawthorne						
3	64	65	78	69		
4	62	57	58	72		
5	58	61	60	58		
Cabrillo Elem., Hawthorne						
2	71	62	67	70		
Dana Elem., Hawthorne						
6	64	65	67	71		
7	60	54	63	80		
8	62	53	63	64		

Chapter 3

LOS ANGELES COUNTY
How Public Schools Work

SCORES MEASURE ACADEMIC success but they have their shortcomings. Some students know the material but are not adept at taking tests and some tests are so poorly designed that they fail to assess what has been taught. The rankings in the previous chapter do not break out students as individuals. A basic exam tests the least the children should know, not the most. Scores cannot assess goodness, kindness or wisdom or predict how helpful students will be to society.

There are other legitimate criticisms of probably every test given to California school children. Nonetheless, the tests have their value and except for a few cases probably give an accurate picture of how the schools are doing academically. Students who do well in elementary school generally do well in high school and score high on the SAT and go on to succeed in college. With rare exceptions, the scores correlate with teacher assessments, and so on. The exceptions cannot be ignored. A student who does poorly in one educational arrangement may thrive in another.

When your children attend a school with high test scores, they are not assured of success. These schools have their failures. Neither can you be certain that your children will get the best teachers or the right programs. Other schools with lower scores might do better on these points. What you can be certain of is that your children are entering a setting that has proven successful for many students.

The main problem with making sense out of scores concerns what is called socioeconomics, a theory educators love, hate and widely believe.

Socioeconomics — The Bottom Line

In its crudest form, socioeconomics means rich kids score high, middle-class kids score about the middle and poor kids score low. Not all the time, not predictably by individual. Many children from poor and middle-class homes succeed in school and attend the best colleges.

But as a general rule socioeconomics enjoys much statistical support.

Compare the rankings in the preceding chapter with income by cities or
(Continued on Page 110)

High School Scholastic Aptitude Test (SAT) Scores

High School	Sr. Class	% Tested	Verbal	Math
Agoura	385	66	551	568
Alhambra	634	50	464	539
Antelope Valley	410	23	500	479
Arcadia	776	73	536	628
Arroyo	350	31	446	501
Artesia	341	27	430	497
Avalon	39	46	477	471
Azusa	206	18	470	469
Baldwin Park	377	26	449	455
Banning	470	42	393	393
Bassett	306	30	394	398
Bell	557	37	387	408
Bellflower	301	21	462	485
Bell Gardens	520	30	393	403
Belmont	541	29	386	399
Beverly Hills	466	80	548	591
Birmingham	551	38	445	458
Blair	179	25	465	437
Bonita	303	48	490	506
Bravo Medical	349	84	463	480
Burbank	376	37	485	520
Burroughs	389	45	497	497
Cabrillo	NA	42	373	384
Calabasas	346	78	554	578
California	402	40	463	482
California Academy	112	99	582	600
Canoga Park	331	39	447	464
Canyon	428	32	507	539
Carson	534	47	413	420
Centennial	205	30	354	344
Cerritos	494	70	531	608
Charter Oak	355	44	495	507
Chatsworth	536	45	480	507
Claremont	491	69	526	550
Cleveland	348	55	498	498
Compton	321	31	354	370
Covina	258	42	480	491
Crenshaw	307	57	392	370
Crescenta Valley	529	57	539	589
Culver City	337	48	508	521
Diamond Bar	699	72	508	573
Dominguez	271	33	352	352
Dorsey	204	39	392	381
Downey	573	31	500	532
Downtown Business	205	55	433	453
Duarte	206	24	473	484
Eagle Rock	375	45	446	447
El Camino Real	539	56	509	548
El Monte	283	21	438	469
El Rancho	567	38	404	415

Copyright © 2001 McCormack's Guides. No reproduction without permission.

High School Scholastic Aptitude Test (SAT) Scores

High School	Sr. Class	% Tested	Verbal	Math
El Segundo	175	51	512	521
Fairfax	377	47	428	448
Foshay	71	70	408	416
Francis Polytechnic	527	31	405	425
Franklin	570	58	394	394
Fremont	420	39	334	352
Gabrielino	289	46	476	546
Gahr	358	47	475	516
Ganesha	237	30	401	399
Gardena	427	37	401	410
Garey	386	26	416	433
Garfield	632	50	389	392
Gladstone	261	22	458	460
Glendale	645	33	471	527
Glendora	386	48	509	530
Glenn	253	23	405	416
Granada Hills	607	67	493	524
Grant	521	36	453	486
Hamilton	762	50	496	483
Hart	444	53	543	564
Hawthorne	517	19	417	426
Highland	453	52	470	478
Hollywood	371	28	379	422
Hoover	576	41	466	532
Huntington Park	535	39	392	393
Inglewood	334	38	394	377
Jefferson	376	43	349	365
Jordan (Long Beach)	534	29	391	421
Jordan (Los Angeles)	188	56	339	352
Kennedy	417	25	436	455
King/Drew Medical	60	91	435	427
La Cañada	305	80	558	612
Lakewood	718	28	465	500
La Mirada	399	34	473	496
La Puente	286	28	401	425
La Serna	388	47	483	508
Lancaster	5	44	489	482
Leuzinger	318	20	379	410
Lincoln	374	53	387	442
Littlerock	406	41	457	452
Locke	163	24	344	383
Los Altos	359	53	489	551
Los Angeles Co./Arts	180	88	540	496
Los Angeles Center	180	95	520	507
Los Angeles	506	44	374	396
Lynwood	619	37	394	388
Malibu	126	75	559	577
Manual Arts	432	43	351	349
Mark Keppel	446	54	478	573
Marshall Fund. (Pasadena)	175	52	468	461

High School Scholastic Aptitude Test (SAT) Scores

High School	Sr. Class	% Tested	Verbal	Math
Marshall (Los Angeles)	733	37	425	438
Mayfair	309	32	464	476
Millikan	772	33	438	447
Mira Costa	437	63	550	561
Monroe	584	30	444	452
Monrovia	316	30	490	487
Montebello	454	23	411	441
Morningside	185	31	382	362
Mountain View	278	25	431	453
Muir	237	34	445	450
Narbonne	372	35	461	484
Nogales	450	35	440	476
North	493	58	458	499
North Hollywood	547	58	466	478
Northview	239	34	480	504
Norwalk	325	28	420	425
Palisades	494	67	507	523
Palmdale	495	36	468	468
Palos Verdes Peninsula	696	89	567	614
Paramount	489	17	421	444
Pasadena	377	43	436	450
Pioneer	269	45	431	463
Polytechnic	923	56	488	510
Pomona	266	25	427	424
Quartz Hill	536	43	497	511
Redondo	288	51	507	256
Reseda	342	42	441	483
Roosevelt	604	41	388	413
Rosemead	341	35	457	512
Rowland	585	41	487	569
San Dimas	280	46	496	515
San Fernando	869	33	410	429
San Gabriel	384	41	434	504
San Marino	244	92	547	650
San Pedro	486	37	477	483
Santa Fe	399	26	435	454
Santa Monica	556	55	510	538
Saugus	433	40	544	569
Schurr	548	39	491	523
Sherman Oaks Center	153	66	521	524
Sierra Vista	284	28	438	477
South	398	61	506	573
South El Monte	180	15	404	449
South Gate	726	47	401	407
South Hills	281	52	504	517
South Pasadena	272	69	553	602
Sylmar	403	40	403	419
Taft	560	58	484	505
Temple City	388	58	496	561
Torrance	386	47	506	541

High School Scholastic Aptitude Test (SAT) Scores

High School	Sr. Class	% Tested	Verbal	Math
University	533	55	489	522
Valencia	414	42	509	539
Van Nuys	609	52	537	568
Vasquez	91	31	483	462
Venice	329	39	484	481
Verdugo Hills	283	38	433	448
Walnut	549	63	505	566
Warren	496	32	408	513
Washington Prep.	378	47	375	367
West	475	63	501	559
Westchester	370	68	433	432
West Covina	464	34	436	463
Whitney	167	99	660	682
Whittier	304	44	449	466
Wilson, Woodrow (Los Angeles)	438	48	314	407
Wilson, Glen (Hacienda Hts.)	346	50	512	588
Wilson (Long Beach)	619	31	481	492
Workman	219	31	438	425

Source: California Department of Education, 1999. NA -Not available.

(Continued from Page 106)

neighborhoods. Rancho Palos Verdes, rich or well-to-do, high scores; the City of Alhambra, middle class, middling plus scores; South Central L.A., low income, low scores. The same pattern shows up throughout California and indeed in other countries. The federal study, "Japanese Education Today," notes a "solid correlation between poverty and poor school performance ...."

Always there are exceptions, always it must be remembered that we are talking about broad patterns.

Family and Culture

In its refined form, socioeconomics moves away from the buck and toward culture and family influence.

Note the chart on pages 16-19 in Chapter 1 and the chart on pages 111-114. The towns or neighborhoods with the highest number of college educated parents are generally also the towns highest number of students moving up to college (But see insert on L.A. district scores.)

If your mom or dad attended college, chances are you will attend college or do well at school because in a thousand ways while you were growing up they and their milieu pushed you in this direction. Emphasis on "chances are." Nothing is certain when dealing with human beings.

What if mom and dad never got beyond the third grade? Or can't even speak English?

(Continued on Page 114)

California College Admissions of Public School Graduates

High School	City or Town	UC	CSU	Com
Agoura	Agoura Hills	57	30	89
Alhambra	Alhambra	96	86	253
Antelope Valley	Lancaster	5	10	89
Arcadia	Arcadia	245	94	246
Arroyo	El Monte	30	66	122
Artesia	Lakewood	15	22	87
Avalon	Avalon	1	8	6
Azusa	Azusa	4	18	49
Baldwin Park	Baldwin Park	23	31	29
Banning	Wilmington	11	51	166
Bassett	La Puente	10	26	42
Bell	Bell	35	58	151
Bellflower	Bellflower	14	23	112
Bell Gardens	Bell Gardens	7	34	159
Belmont	Westlake	13	43	238
Beverly Hills	Beverly Hills	71	31	214
Birmingham	Van Nuys	20	47	224
Blair	Pasadena	13	19	56
Bonita	La Verne	26	49	73
Bravo Med Mag	Boyle Hts.	66	7	1
Burbank	Burbank	27	40	163
Burroughs	Burbank	28	33	102
Calabasas	Calabasas	62	43	83
California	Whittier	18	35	139
California Acad.	Carson	34	20	2
Canoga Park	Canoga Park	13	23	97
Canyon	Santa Clarita	15	29	179
Carson	Carson	47	60	180
Centennial	Compton	1	9	42
Cerritos	Cerritos	126	79	125
Charter Oak	Covina	19	38	70
Chatsworth	Chatsworth	33	73	208
Claremont	Claremont	82	54	59
Cleveland	Reseda	65	45	140
Compton	Compton	4	23	44
Covina	Covina	13	43	34
Crenshaw	Leimart Park	26	62	167
Crescenta Valley	La Crescenta	75	48	214
Culver City	Culver City	34	25	137
Diamond Bar	Diamond Bar	158	132	38
Dominguez	Compton	1	28	34
Dorsey	Crenshaw	11	28	77
Downey	Downey	32	50	201
Downtown Business	L.A.	16	18	30
Duarte	Duarte	7	15	49
Eagle Rock	Eagle Rock	17	55	176
El Camino Real	Woodland Hills	66	71	262
El Monte	El Monte	24	29	100
El Rancho	Pico Rivera	17	62	135

Copyright © 2001 McCormack's Guides. No reproduction without permission.

California College Admissions of Public School Graduates

High School	City or Town	UC	CSU	Com
El Segundo	El Segundo	16	26	87
Fairfax	Hollywood	25	36	192
Francis Polytech	Sun Valley	23	81	141
Franklin	Highland Park	42	85	138
Fremont	Southeast L.A.	5	39	101
Gabrielino (new school)	San Gabriel	0	30	100
Gahr High	Cerritos	46	50	155
Ganesha	Pomona	7	16	3
Gardena	Gardena	8	36	185
Garey	Pomona	12	46	8
Garfield	East Los Angeles	40	52	227
Gladstone	Covina	6	14	70
Glendale	Glendale	63	39	281
Glendora	Glendora	38	78	158
Glenn	Norwalk	12	16	86
Granada Hills	Granada Hills	118	121	261
Grant	Van Nuys	30	48	176
Hamilton	Near Culver City	69	57	175
Hart	Santa Clarita	58	46	130
Hawthorne	Hawthorne	14	24	251
Highland	Palmdale	19	29	104
Hollywood	Hollywood	6	49	155
Hoover	Glendale	52	79	190
Huntington Park	Huntington Park	14	92	203
Inglewood	Inglewood	13	34	113
Jefferson	Near Vernon	11	33	109
Jordan	Long Beach	21	57	147
Jordan (David Starr)	Watts	11	32	51
Kennedy	Granada Hills	11	32	133
King/Drew Medical	Watts	14	13	2
La Cañada	La Cañada Flintridge	63	37	78
La Mirada	La Mirada	9	50	165
La Puente	La Puente	6	29	30
La Serna	Whittier	29	52	95
Lakewood	Lakewood	24	58	271
Leuzinger	Lawndale	11	20	131
Lincoln	Montecito Heights	27	88	107
Littlerock	Lancaster	15	22	106
Locke	Southeast L. A.	0	27	61
Los Altos	Hacienda Heights	52	42	36
Los Angeles	Country Club Park	13	75	397
Los Angeles Ctr.	W. Los Angeles	31	18	33
Los Angeles HS/Arts	Near Alhambra	20	9	0
Lynwood	Lynwood	16	58	140
Manual Arts	Near USC	13	35	167
Mark Keppel	Alhambra	75	91	139
Marshall Fund.	Pasadena	26	25	52
Marshall, John	Silver Lake	43	86	282
Mayfair	Lakewood	9	29	66

Copyright © 2001 McCormack's Guides. No reproduction without permission.

California College Admissions of Public School Graduates

High School	City or Town	UC	CSU	Com
Millikan	Long Beach	19	98	210
Mira Costa	Manhattan Beach	66	43	168
Monroe	North Hills	34	57	150
Monrovia	Monrovia	15	32	114
Montebello	Montebello	7	40	155
Morningside	Inglewood	6	19	53
Mountain View	El Monte	26	21	75
Muir	Pasadena	20	20	78
Narbonne	Harbor City	19	27	184
Nogales	La Puente	18	78	20
North	Torrance	70	34	105
North Hollywood	North Hollywood	56	62	170
Northview	Covina	9	23	40
Norwalk	Norwalk	6	16	116
Palisades	Pacific Palisades	68	35	192
Palmdale	Palmdale	12	40	178
Palos Verdes Peninsula	Rolling Hills Estates	161	65	56
Paramount	Paramount	14	23	126
Pasadena	Pasadena	19	46	157
Pioneer	Whittier	15	26	53
Polytechnic	Long Beach	107	149	194
Pomona	Pomona	13	30	12
Quartz Hill	Quartz Hill	16	17	114
Redondo	Redondo Beach	30	39	99
Reseda	Reseda	25	37	125
Roosevelt	Boyle Heights	35	83	217
Rosemead	Rosemead	43	30	111
Rowland	Rowland Heights	70	82	52
San Dimas	San Dimas	31	37	58
San Fernando	San Fernando	25	46	217
San Gabriel	San Gabriel	52	75	164
San Marino	San Marino	98	20	55
San Pedro	San Pedro	20	28	198
Santa Fe	Santa Fe Springs	15	54	90
Santa Monica	Santa Monica	99	46	262
Saugus	Santa Clarita	20	35	122
Schurr	Montebello	55	63	183
Sherman Oaks Center	Reseda	20	19	37
Sierra Vista	Baldwin Park	15	30	30
South	Torrance	55	35	112
South El Monte	So. El Monte	10	0	43
South Gate	South Gate	31	110	234
South Hills	Covina	41	44	43
South Pasadena	South Pasadena	57	28	105
Sylmar	Sylmar	11	45	148
Taft	Woodland Hills	51	60	240
Temple City	Temple City	47	57	128
Torrance	Torrance	47	75	186
University	Near Santa Monica	51	31	197

Copyright © 2001 McCormack's Guides. No reproduction without permission.

California College Admissions of Public School Graduates

High School	City or Town	UC	CSU	Com
Valencia High	Santa Clarita	37	21	140
Van Nuys	Van Nuys	130	88	180
Vasquez High	Acton	4	4	13
Venice	Venice	35	35	187
Verdugo Hills	Tujunga	15	49	83
Walnut	Walnut	110	76	15
Warren	Downey	27	59	187
Washington Prep.	Near Inglewood	13	59	130
West	Torrance	87	43	170
Westchester	Westchester	35	68	168
West Covina	West Covina	31	46	66
Whitney	Cerritos	71	7	16
Whittier	Whittier	19	19	81
Wilson	Long Beach	25	70	215
Wilson (Glen A.)	Hacienda Heights	66	42	25
Wilson (Woodrow)	El Sereno	23	58	141
Workman	City of Industry	13	27	7

Source: Postsecondary Education Commission. The chart lists the local public high schools and shows how many students they advanced in 1999 into California public colleges and universities. The state does not track graduates enrolling in private or out-of-state colleges. Continuation schools not included in list. **Key**: UC (University of California system); CSU (Cal State system); Com (Community Colleges). N.A. (not available).

(Continued from Page 110)

Historically, many poor and immigrant children have succeeded at school because their parents badgered, bullied and encouraged them every step of the way and made sacrifices so they would succeed. Asian kids are the latest example of poor kids succeeding but we can also point to the children of peasant Europeans and Africans bought to this country as slaves.

Does it make a difference if the child is English proficient? Of course! Immigrant children unfamiliar with English will have difficulty mastering subjects taught in English. They will need extra or special help. How much help, how should it be given — these are big-time arguments in L.A. County.

Nonetheless, the home-school correlation retains much validity: the stronger the educational support the child receives at home, the better he or she will do at school.

So thoroughly does the California Department of Education believe in socioeconomics that it worked the theory into a mathematical model.

Teachers collected data on almost all students: were they on welfare, did they have language problems (immigrants), how educated were their parents? The information was fed to computers and used to predict how students would score on tests.

The Socioeconomic flaw

If you carry the logic of socioeconomics too far, you may conclude that

(Continued on Page 118)

UCs Chosen by Public School Graduates

School	Berk	Davis	Irv	UCLA	Riv	SD	SB	SC	Total
Agoura	1	6	2	13	3	14	16	2	57
Alhambra	11	1	17	12	28	13	12	2	96
Antelope Valley	0	1	1	1	1	0	1	0	5
Arcadia	32	6	71	48	29	48	10	1	245
Arroyo	2	0	9	3	10	5	1	0	30
Artesia	0	1	4	2	7	0	1	0	15
Avalon	0	0	0	0	0	0	1	0	1
Azusa	0	0	1	0	2	0	1	0	4
Baldwin Park	4	1	5	2	7	2	0	2	23
Banning	3	0	3	3	1	0	0	1	11
Bassett	0	1	1	2	5	0	0	1	10
Bell	6	0	4	3	6	0	8	8	35
Bellflower	2	0	7	4	0	0	1	0	14
Bell Gardens	1	1	0	3	0	1	0	1	7
Belmont	0	0	3	4	2	1	2	1	13
Beverly Hills	18	1	8	20	3	6	12	3	71
Birmingham	2	2	2	6	2	0	6	0	20
Blair	1	0	2	3	2	0	5	0	13
Bonita	0	2	4	6	5	5	2	2	26
Bravo Medical	2	0	16	29	8	4	6	1	66
Burbank	1	2	7	5	6	4	2	0	27
Burroughs	4	2	3	3	5	5	3	3	28
Calabasas	9	7	5	14	1	5	19	2	62
California	0	0	6	3	3	0	3	3	18
California Acad.	11	1	5	5	5	2	3	2	34
Canoga Park	0	1	1	7	2	1	1	0	13
Canyon	2	1	2	2	1	4	3	0	15
Carson	0	0	8	25	8	1	5	0	47
Centennial	1	0	0	0	0	0	0	0	1
Cerritos	17	1	39	18	25	15	8	3	126
Charter Oak	0	1	9	2	3	2	2	0	19
Chatsworth	6	2	6	5	1	2	9	2	33
Claremont	9	4	15	8	17	9	5	5	82
Cleveland	13	1	6	16	2	4	18	5	65
Compton	0	0	1	0	2	0	1	0	4
Covina	1	1	3	4	2	2	0	0	13
Crenshaw	3	4	1	3	6	0	4	5	26
Crescenta Valley	13	4	11	16	8	13	7	3	75
Culver City	9	1	1	6	1	3	8	5	34
Diamond Bar	20	0	49	28	31	23	4	3	158
Dominguez	0	0	0	0	1	0	0	0	1
Dorsey	1	1	2	1	0	0	5	1	11
Downey	4	0	10	5	2	7	3	1	32
Downtown Business	0	0	4	6	6	0	0	0	16
Duarte	0	1	3	1	2	0	0	0	7
Eagle Rock	2	2	2	2	1	3	4	1	17
El Camino Real	12	4	11	16	4	6	12	1	66
El Monte	0	0	2	9	8	2	0	3	24
El Rancho	1	2	5	5	0	0	1	3	17

Copyright © 2001 McCormack's Guides. No reproduction without permission.

UCs Chosen by Public School Graduates

School	Berk	Davis	Irv	UCLA	Riv	SD	SB	SC	Total
El Segundo	0	0	6	1	1	1	5	2	16
Fairfax	6	2	5	4	5	3	0	0	25
Francis Polytech	1	2	2	14	3	0	1	0	23
Franklin	0	2	7	13	6	0	9	5	42
Fremont	1	0	0	4	0	0	0	0	5
Gahr	5	1	10	10	10	8	2	0	46
Ganesha	2	0	2	0	3	0	0	0	7
Gardena	1	1	2	3	1	0	0	0	8
Garey	1	0	2	4	5	0	0	0	12
Garfield	4	1	9	5	5	4	5	7	40
Gladstone	0	0	1	5	0	0	0	0	6
Glendale	3	0	7	13	9	17	9	5	63
Glendora	2	1	3	11	6	4	9	2	38
Glenn	0	0	2	6	2	1	1	0	12
Granada Hills	5	5	26	27	14	17	20	4	118
Grant	4	0	4	5	1	5	9	2	30
Hamilton	9	7	4	20	4	5	14	6	69
Hart	8	3	8	14	0	5	11	6	58
Hawthorne	3	1	5	2	2	0	1	0	14
Highland	2	0	5	2	3	3	3	1	19
Hollywood	1	1	0	1	0	0	1	2	6
Hoover	12	2	6	10	4	9	6	3	52
Huntington Park	1	1	0	3	4	3	1	1	14
Inglewood	0	1	0	6	1	0	3	2	13
Jefferson	0	5	0	2	0	1	1	2	11
Jordan	2	1	7	5	2	3	1	0	21
Jordan (Starr)	1	1	0	2	2	0	1	4	11
Kennedy	0	0	2	4	1	4	0	0	11
King/Drew Med.	3	1	0	5	4	0	1	0	14
La Cañada	4	7	10	6	7	12	13	4	63
La Mirada	0	0	5	0	2	0	1	1	9
La Puente	0	1	1	0	2	1	0	1	6
La Serna	2	4	7	3	4	5	4	0	29
Lakewood	1	2	6	7	3	2	2	1	24
Leuzinger	0	0	3	4	2	1	1	0	11
Lincoln	0	0	8	9	4	0	6	0	27
Littlerock	0	2	0	3	1	3	6	0	15
Locke	0	0	0	0	0	0	0	0	0
Los Altos	10	0	12	10	7	9	2	2	52
Los Angeles	0	1	3	5	0	1	1	2	13
Los Angeles Center	6	3	6	3	5	0	4	4	31
Los Angeles HS/Arts	2	0	2	11	0	0	1	4	20
Lynwood	3	0	5	5	0	0	3	0	16
Manual Arts	3	0	0	3	4	0	1	2	13
Mark Keppel	6	3	16	11	11	21	16	1	75
Marshall	5	4	7	11	8	4	4	0	43
Marshall Fundamental	2	2	3	9	4	3	2	1	26
Mayfair	1	0	2	2	2	0	2	0	9
Millikan	1	0	4	7	2	0	5	0	19a

Copyright © 2001 McCormack's Guides. No reproduction without permission.

UCs Chosen by Public School Graduates

School	Berk	Davis	Irv	UCLA	Riv	SD	SB	SC	Total
Mira Costa	9	4	7	7	1	6	2	10	66
Monroe	8	0	6	9	1	1	6	3	34
Monrovia	0	0	4	5	2	3	1	0	15
Montebello	0	0	1	3	2	1	0	0	7
Morningside	1	0	0	3	0	0	2	0	6
Mountain View	1	1	6	5	7	2	4	0	26
Muir	2	0	2	6	4	0	3	3	20
Narbonne	2	0	10	1	3	2	1	0	19
Nogales	1	0	3	6	6	0	1	1	18
North	2	3	20	13	14	11	6	1	70
North Hollywood	10	10	4	10	5	6	7	4	56
Northview	0	0	2	5	1	1	0	0	9
Norwalk	0	0	2	2	2	0	0	0	6
Palisades	7	2	10	11	5	12	11	10	68
Palmdale	0	0	1	3	1	4	3	0	12
Palos Verdes Pen.	32	4	25	25	16	28	21	10	161
Paramount	1	0	9	0	0	0	3	1	14
Pasadena	0	0	2	8	3	5	0	1	19
Pioneer	2	2	1	5	1	0	3	1	15
Polytechnic	18	2	20	27	5	11	18	6	107
Pomona	0	0	1	3	8	0	1	0	13
Quartz Hill	0	1	1	5	3	0	4	2	16
Redondo	3	1	7	9	1	2	6	1	30
Reseda	0	2	7	6	6	0	3	1	25
Roosevelt	1	5	3	12	5	1	5	3	35
Rosemead	2	2	12	8	9	9	0	1	43
Rowland	2	1	29	16	13	8	1	0	70
San Dimas	1	1	10	2	9	3	5	0	31
San Fernando	7	1	2	8	3	2	2	0	25
San Gabriel	2	0	13	6	18	11	1	1	52
San Marino	13	6	24	17	11	19	5	3	98
San Pedro	0	0	7	2	2	0	8	1	20
Santa Fe	0	0	3	8	1	2	1	0	15
Santa Monica	22	5	13	20	6	3	15	15	99
Saugus	4	0	3	2	3	3	4	1	20
Schurr	11	7	20	6	6	2	2	1	55
Sherman Oaks Center	2	0	5	3	0	1	7	2	20
Sierra Vista	1	1	4	4	4	1	1	0	15
South	4	3	20	15	1	7	4	1	55
South El Monte	1	3	0	4	1	1	0	0	10
South Gate	1	1	3	11	4	6	4	1	31
South Hills	5	4	11	4	6	6	2	3	41
South Pasadena	10	2	9	10	6	8	6	6	57
Sylmar	0	0	1	6	0	0	4	0	11
Taft	6	0	7	8	3	9	16	2	51
Temple City	6	0	11	9	12	4	4	1	47
Torrance	6	1	15	11	6	3	2	3	47
University	7	3	19	17	3	6	5	1	51
Valencia	1	3	8	3	6	5	9	2	37

Copyright © 2001 McCormack's Guides. No reproduction without permission.

UCs Chosen by Public School Graduates

School	Berk	Davis	Irv	UCLA	Riv	SD	SB	SC	Total
Van Nuys	16	2	27	32	16	15	21	1	130
Vasquez	0	0	1	0	1	1	1	0	4
Venice	5	2	5	7	6	3	3	4	35
Verdugo Hills	1	1	2	5	3	1	1	1	15
Walnut	14	1	29	18	28	17	3	0	110
Warren	0	0	10	5	6	4	1	1	27
Washington	4	3	0	4	1	0	1	0	13
West	5	2	28	18	14	11	6	3	87
Westchester	7	1	3	16	0	4	4	0	35
West Covina	1	0	14	1	7	2	6	0	31
Whitney	16	0	22	6	8	13	3	3	71
Whittier	0	0	10	2	1	1	2	3	19
Wilson (Long Beach)	2	2	7	3	4	1	6	0	25
Wilson, W. (El Sereno)	1	2	1	5	5	1	3	5	23
Wilson, G. (Hac. Hts.)	5	2	31	12	10	5	0	1	66
Workman	2	1	1	2	6	1	0	0	13

Source: California Postsecondary Education Commission. The chart shows the University of California choices of 1999 local public high school graduates. The state does not track graduates enrolling in private or out-of-state colleges. Continuation schools not included in list. Key: Berk (Berkeley), Irv (Irvine), Riv (Riverside), SD (San Diego), SB (Santa Barbara), SC (Santa Cruz). NA Not Available.

(Continued from Page 114)

schools and teachers and teaching methods don't matter: Students succeed or fail according to their family or societal backgrounds. Just not the case! No matter how dedicated or well-intentioned the parent, if the teacher is grossly inept the child probably will learn little. If material or textbooks are out-of-date or inaccurate, what the student learns will be useless or damaging.

Conversely, if the teacher is dedicated and knowledgeable, if the material is well-presented and appropriate, what the child comes away with will be helpful and, to society, more likely to be beneficial.

The late Albert Shanker, president of the American Federation of Teachers, argued that U.S. students would improve remarkably if schools refused to tolerate disruptive behavior, if national or state academic standards were adopted, if external agencies (not the schools themselves) tested students and if colleges and employers, in admissions and hiring, rewarded academic achievement and penalized failure.

These four reforms do little or nothing to address socioeconomics but many educators believe they have merit. Admittedly, however, academic achievement is a contentious matter, full of theories, never short of opinions.

Where the Confusion Enters

It's very difficult, if not impossible, to separate the influence of home and schools. When scores go up, often principals or superintendents credit this or

(Continued on Page 122)

Cal State Universities Chosen by Public School Graduates

School	SLO	Pom	Full	Dom	LB	LA	NR	SD	Hum	SJ
Agoura	4	2	0	0	5	0	10	2	1	0
Alhambra	1	31	3	0	6	33	1	1	0	1
Antelope Val.	0	1	0	0	0	0	4	0	2	1
Arcadia	7	55	3	0	12	4	6	2	1	1
Arroyo	0	37	13	0	5	8	1	0	0	2
Artesia	0	1	9	1	10	0	0	1	0	0
Avalon	1	0	2	0	4	0	0	0	1	0
Azusa	0	12	0	0	4	2	0	0	0	0
Baldwin Park	0	9	13	0	2	6	1	0	0	0
Banning	0	0	0	16	24	3	2	3	1	1
Bassett	0	13	10	0	0	2	1	0	0	0
Bell	0	6	5	6	18	18	1	1	0	0
Bellflower	0	1	4	2	14	1	0	0	0	0
Bell Gardens	0	4	2	2	9	11	2	1	3	0
Belmont	0	10	5	1	1	13	12	0	0	0
Beverly Hills	0	7	2	0	0	2	8	6	0	0
Birmingham	0	0	0	0	1	3	38	1	0	0
Blair	2	19	16	0	6	0	1	1	1	0
Bonita	0	13	8	0	1	0	1	1	1	0
Bravo Medical	0	1	0	0	4	0	0	0	0	1
Burbank	1	4	0	0	3	6	23	2	0	0
Burroughs	0	1	0	1	4	7	16	0	0	0
Calabasas	1	1	0	0	0	0	23	9	0	0
California	1	3	20	1	5	2	1	1	0	0
California Acad.	0	3	2	1	12	0	0	1	0	0
Canoga Park	1	2	0	0	0	0	18	0	1	0
Canyon	1	1	0	0	1	0	15	7	1	0
Carson	0	4	3	16	32	1	1	1	1	0
Centennial	0	0	0	3	0	1	4	0	0	0
Cerritos	1	22	13	2	20	0	0	1	0	0
Charter Oak	0	26	6	0	3	0	0	0	0	0
Chatsworth	1	6	1	2	2	1	50	4	2	1
Claremont	1	25	9	0	8	1	2	5	0	0
Cleveland	0	1	0	0	1	0	37	2	0	0
Compton	0	0	0	12	4	1	3	0	0	0
Covina	1	20	7	0	7	4	1	2	0	0
Crenshaw	1	0	1	17	3	4	14	3	3	1
Crescenta Val.	2	7	0	0	13	3	13	9	0	0
Culver City	1	4	0	1	6	2	6	3	0	0
Diamond Bar	0	67	54	0	9	1	3	4	1	0
Dominguez	0	0	0	13	5	2	2	2	0	1
Dorsey	1	1	2	6	2	6	9	0	0	0
Downey	2	10	9	3	20	1	0	3	2	0
Downtown Bus.	0	4	0	2	1	4	7	0	0	0
Duarte	0	8	2	0	0	3	0	0	0	0
Eagle Rock	0	6	0	0	2	28	15	0	1	1
El Camino Real	2	4	0	3	1	1	47	12	0	0
El Monte	1	13	2	0	7	5	1	0	0	0
El Rancho	0	6	20	5	13	11	1	4	0	1
El Segundo	2	1	0	0	0	0	2	4	0	0

Cal State Universities Chosen by Public School Graduates

School	SLO	Pom	Full	Dom	LB	LA	NR	SD	Hum	SJ
Fairfax	0	1	0	1	1	11	18	1	0	0
Francis Poly.	0	1	0	0	0	1	78	1	0	0
Franklin	2	5	1	2	2	52	20	0	0	0
Fremont	0	3	0	12	5	12	6	1	0	1
Gahr	0	9	13	2	20	1	2	1	0	1
Ganesha	0	6	4	0	2	1	0	1	0	1
Gardena	0	0	2	11	14	1	5	2	0	1
Garey	0	29	9	1	2	2	0	1	0	0
Garfield	0	3	9	0	5	21	7	5	0	0
Gladstone	0	8	4	0	1	0	0	0	0	0
Glendale	0	4	1	0	4	6	22	0	0	0
Glendora	2	35	11	0	11	11	1	4	0	0
Glenn	0	0	2	0	13	0	0	0	0	0
Granada Hills	6	6	0	0	3	6	87	7	0	1
Grant	0	2	0	0	3	4	33	4	1	0
Hamilton	0	1	0	6	1	5	29	3	1	1
Hart	8	2	0	0	4	0	21	3	1	0
Hawthorne	0	2	0	10	4	2	4	0	0	0
Highland	3	4	1	0	3	0	3	4	4	1
Hollywood	0	4	0	0	3	18	21	1	0	0
Hoover	1	13	2	0	5	5	48	4	0	0
Huntington Pk.	0	11	8	12	32	24	4	0	0	0
Inglewood	1	1	1	10	2	14	3	0	1	0
Jefferson	0	0	2	8	1	14	5	0	0	0
Jordan	0	2	0	8	44	1	1	1	0	0
Jordan (Starr)	0	0	0	11	0	8	11	0	0	0
Kennedy	0	0	1	3	0	0	28	0	0	0
King/Drew Med.	0	1	0	2	1	3	4	0	1	0
La Cañada	3	10	0	0	3	1	8	6	0	0
Lakewood	0	3	9	1	50	0	3	1	0	0
La Mirada	2	11	25	2	10	0	0	0	0	0
La Puente	0	12	7	0	2	2	2	0	1	0
Lancaster	2	3	0	1	5	0	3	3	0	0
La Serna	4	8	24	0	9	0	0	5	0	0
Leuzinger	0	6	1	5	4	0	1	2	0	1
Lincoln	0	14	0	1	3	55	15	0	0	0
Littlerock	3	2	0	0	1	1	1	3	1	0
Locke	2	0	1	6	8	8	1	1	0	0
Los Altos	0	16	18	0	4	1	1	0	0	0
Los Angeles	0	2	1	2	2	9	55	1	0	0
Los Angeles Ctr.	0	0	1	3	1	8	0	1	0	1
Los Angeles/Arts	0	0	0	0	3	3	0	1	0	0
Lynwood	0	0	2	27	21	4	1	1	0	0
Malibu	0	2	0	0	1	0	0	4	1	0
Manual Arts	0	0	3	5	4	10	5	2	3	0
Mark Keppel	0	0	0	0	0	0	0	1	0	0
Marshall	1	8	0	1	4	36	35	0	0	0
Marshall Fund.	1	5	0	0	0	16	2	1	0	0
Mayfair	1	3	3	0	19	0	0	1	0	0
Metropolitan	0	7	2	0	1	5	0	0	0	0

Cal State Universities Chosen by Public School Graduates

School	SLO	Pom	Full	Dom	LB	LA	NR	SD	Hum	SJ
Millikan	1	1	3	3	82	0	4	2	0	0
Mira Costa	5	6	0	1	13	1	9	0	0	1
Monroe	0	1	0	0	2	2	51	1	0	0
Monrovia	1	19	1	1	3	2	0	3	1	1
Montebello	1	5	4	0	8	21	0	1	0	0
Morningside	0	0	0	4	4	0	2	1	1	0
Mountain View	0	1	9	0	3	6	1	1	0	0
Muir	1	3	2	0	3	2	5	3	0	0
Narbonne	0	2	2	4	12	0	3	1	0	1
Nogales	0	39	14	1	3	1	14	3	0	0
North	1	1	3	3	17	3	1	2	0	0
No. Hollywood	1	1	0	0	4	1	52	1	0	0
Northview	0	9	8	0	1	1	0	0	0	0
Norwalk	0	2	5	0	8	0	0	1	0	0
Palisades	0	2	0	3	1	1	21	1	0	1
Palmdale	1	1	0	2	3	0	30	1	1	0
Palos Verdes	1	0	2	1	4	0	2	0	0	0
Pal. Ver. Penin.	12	8	0	0	24	0	0	7	3	1
Paramount	0	1	6	3	9	0	2	0	0	0
Pasadena	1	4	0	1	8	10	5	4	0	1
Pioneer	0	5	12	0	5	2	0	1	0	0
Polytechnic	0	8	8	10	99	2	1	12	2	1
Pomona	0	13	7	0	0	0	2	1	0	0
Quartz Hill	0	0	1	0	1	0	11	0	0	0
Redondo	2	5	0	1	13	0	2	10	0	0
Reseda	0	0	0	2	0	0	35	0	0	0
Roosevelt	0	6	3	1	9	45	12	2	0	1
Rosemead	1	16	2	0	2	8	1	0	0	0
Rowland	1	34	32	0	10	1	0	2	0	0
San Dimas	0	16	9	1	2	2	2	2	1	0
San Fernando	1	0	0	2	3	2	37	0	0	1
San Gabriel	2	35	8	0	8	13	3	1	0	0
San Marino	1	15	1	0	0	1	1	1	0	0
San Pedro	0	0	1	10	13	0	0	2	0	0
Santa Fe	0	8	14	1	24	4	0	2	0	0
Santa Monica	2	3	0	3	16	2	10	4	0	1
Saugus	2	1	0	0	0	0	18	9	0	1
Schurr	0	14	13	2	14	19	0	0	0	1
Sherman Oaks	0	0	0	0	1	2	8	5	0	0
Sierra Vista	0	16	6	0	4	1	0	0	0	0
South	3	2	2	1	16	1	1	4	0	0
South Gate	2	6	5	9	59	17	6	1	0	0
South Hills	0	11	18	1	4	1	1	5	0	0
So. Pasadena	1	4	0	0	7	5	5	2	0	0
Sylmar	0	1	2	0	0	4	34	0	0	2
Taft	0	1	0	0	0	3	47	6	0	1
Temple City	1	21	5	0	12	7	2	6	0	0
Torrance	1	6	6	3	36	1	6	10	1	0
University	0	0	1	2	2	1	21	2	0	0

Copyright © 2001 McCormack's Guides. No reproduction without permission.

Cal State Universities Chosen by Public School Graduates

School	SLO	Pom	Full	Dom	LB	LA	NR	SD	Hum	SJ
Valencia	0	3	1	0	3	0	7	6	0	0
Van Nuys	0	3	1	0	0	1	82	0	0	0
Venice	1	9	0	3	3	0	15	0	0	1
Verdugo Hills	0	0	0	0	0	10	35	1	2	0
Walnut	0	41	27	0	1	2	3	2	0	0
Warren	0	4	12	2	30	6	2	2	0	0
Washington	0	1	1	11	7	14	5	9	2	3
West	2	3	1	2	25	1	4	3	1	0
Westchester	0	1	2	9	6	4	25	11	2	1
West Covina	0	27	10	1	4	1	1	0	0	0
Whitney	0	1	0	0	5	0	0	0	0	0
Whittier	0	7	8	0	1	0	0	3	0	0
Wilson (El Ser.)	0	3	2	0	6	43	1	3	0	0
Wilson, (H. Hts.)	0	17	20	0	4	1	0	0	0	0
Wilson, (L.Beach)	2	4	3	2	51	0	0	3	3	0
Workman	0	10	9	0	1	5	0	0	0	0

Source: California Secondary Education Commission, fall, 1998. **Key**: SLO (San Luis Obispo), Pom (Pomona), Full (Fullerton), Dom (Dominguez Hills), LB (Long Beach), LA (Los Angeles), NR (Northridge), SD (San Diego), Hum (Humboldt), SJ (San Jose). The chart shows the most popular choices of 1998 local public high school graduates, not all Cal State universities. The state does not track graduates enrolling in private or out-of-state colleges. Continuation schools not included in list.

(Continued from Page 118)

that instructional program, or extra efforts by teachers.

But the scores may have risen because mom and dad cracked down on excessive TV. Or a city with old and faded low-income housing (low scores) approves a high-end development. The new residents are more middle class, more demographically inclined to push their kids academically.

One last joker-in-the deck, mobility. Johnny is doing great at his school, which has low to middling scores but programs that seem to be working. And his family is doing better. Mom has a job, Dad a promotion.

What does the family do? It moves. Happens all the time in the U.S.A. and this also makes precise interpretation of scores difficult.

Back to Scores

If a school's scores are middling, it may still be capable of doing an excellent job, if it has dedicated teachers and sound programs. The middling scores may reflect socioeconomics, not instructional quality.

Don't judge us by our overall scores, many schools say. Judge us by our ability to deliver for your son or daughter.

This gets tricky because the children do influence one another and high-income parents often interact differently with schools than low-income parents. To some extent, the school must structure its programs to ability of the students. But schools with middling and middling-plus grades can point to many successes.

How Average Schools Succeed

So many students attend the University of California and California State Universities that public and private high schools must of necessity teach classes demanded by these institutions.

Almost all high schools will also offer general education classes in math and English but these will not be as tough as the prep courses and will not be recognized by the state universities. And usually the school will teach some trades so those inclined can secure jobs upon graduation.

Can a school with mediocre or even low basic scores field a successful college prep program? With comprehensive programs, the answer is yes.

College Track

Freshmen attending a California State University, a public community college or a University of California (Berkeley, Los Angeles, San Diego, Davis, Riverside, etc.) are asked to identify their high schools. In this way and others, the state finds out how many students the individual high schools are advancing to college.

The chart on pages 111-114 breaks out the local high schools (data collected fall 1999) and shows how many students from each school went on to the public colleges.

The UCs generally restrict themselves to the top 13 percent in the state. The Cal States take the top third.

Every school on the chart is graduating kids into college but obviously some are more successful at it than others. Does this mean that the "lesser" schools have awful teachers or misguided programs? We have no idea. It simply may be socioeconomics at work.

Parents with college ambitions for their children should find out as much as possible about prospective schools and their programs and make sure that their kids get into the college-track classes.

Where does the chart mislead?

For starters, the Cal States and UCs run on academics, the community colleges run on academics and vocational classes. Just because a student attends a community college does not mean he or she is pursuing a bachelor's degree.

Secondly, students who qualify for a Cal State or even a UC often take their freshman and sophomore years at a community college. It's cheaper and closer to home. The chart suggests that middle- and low-income communities send more kids proportionally to community colleges than high-income towns.

Scores in the L.A. District

Students in the L.A. Unified School District, second largest in the nation (about 696,000 enrollment), generally attend neighborhood schools but the district encourages transfers to improve integration.

Also to promote integration and meet the special needs of students, the district has created magnet schools and other speciality schools.

Finally, short of space in some schools, the district buses some students out of their neighborhoods to schools with empty seats.

As a consequence, the correlation between scores and neighborhood or town quality is, in many situations, weak. Some of the richest towns in the county have schools that post scores well below what is demographically expected.

Magnet schools-programs for high-achieving children illustrate part of the pattern. L.A. Unified District runs about 135 of these schools-programs.

Say the school is located in a low-middle income neighborhood where the children are scoring in the 40th percentile. The magnet school gathers in high-scoring children from around the district and posts scores in the 90th percentile. This is all well and good but it can't be said that the school reflects the neighborhood.

Conversely, say 50 of the brightest students in a high-income neighborhood transfer to a magnet school some distance away. Scores may drop at the neighborhood school but this has nothing to do with neighborhood quality.

Similarly, if many children in a certain neighborhood attend private schools, this might lower scores at the neighborhood public school but it reflects little on neighborhood quality.

Perhaps the most important reason for the muddied scores is the nature of Los Angeles itself. In many places high- and low-income neighborhoods live side by side. The neighborhoods or towns are distinct; they have a sense of local identity and sometimes recognized borders.

But the school district, in drawing up its attendance zones, is not obliged to follow "town" or neighborhood boundaries. As a result, many L.A. schools mix children not only of diverse ethnic backgrounds but diverse social and economic backgrounds.

L.A. district is not alone. The same situation holds in many other districts around the county.

To attract minority students, the universities modified their admission policies, a practice that has critics and supporters. This policy, because of a recently passed state initiative, has been changed to admit the top students at each high school. In this manner, disputes over ethnicity are blunted and the results may be the same, a more diverse student body.

The chart does not track private colleges. It doesn't tell us how many local students went to the University of San Diego or Pepperdine or the University of Southern California or Stanford or Harvard. Or public colleges out of the state. Many college students drop out. These numbers are not included.

The chart does confirm the influence of socioeconomics: the rich towns, the educated towns or neighborhoods, send more kids to the UCs than the poorer ones.

But socioeconomics does not sweep the field. Not every student from a high-scoring school goes on to college. Many students from low- and middle-income towns come through.

Tips, Comments, Miscellaneous Info.

- Registering For School. To get into kindergarten, your child must turn five before Dec. 3 of the year he or she enters the grade. For first grade, your child must be six before Dec. 3. If he is six on Dec. 4, if she is a mature Jan. 6 birthday girl, speak to the school. There may be some wiggle room. In 2000, the state changed the law to allow schools to admit children who turn five or six before Sept. 2. But to take advantage of this law, a school must offer pre-kindergarten instruction. Many don't. The law also gives schools some say over whether the child is mature enough for school. Talk to the school.

  For registration, you are required to show proof of immunization for polio, diphtheria, tetanus, pertussis (whooping cough), hepatitis B, measles, rubella and mumps. If the kid is seven or older, you can skip mumps and whooping cough. New law: continuing students entering the seventh grade must show proof of being immunized against hepatitis B.

- Almost all public schools have attendance zones, usually the immediate neighborhood. The school comes with the neighborhood; often you have no choice.

  Always call the school district to find out what school your children will be attending. Sometimes school districts change attendance boundaries and do not inform local Realtors. It's always good to go to the first source.

  Just say something like, "I'm Mrs. Jones and we're thinking about moving into 1234 Main Street. What school will my six-year-old attend?"

Ask what elementary school your child will attend and what middle school and high school.

- Several school districts may serve one town or one district may serve a few or many towns. The L.A. Unified School District serves the City of L.A., and the cities of Bell, Carson, Cudahy, Gardena, Huntington Park, Lomita, Maywood, San Fernando, South Gate, Vernon, West Hollywood, and portions of 18 other cities.

  See following for list of school districts and phone numbers.

- Many schools in L.A. County run year-round. Schedules, called "tracks," vary district to district but all students attend a full academic year (175-180 teaching days or equivalent hours). Traditional holidays are observed. One group may start in summer, one in late summer and so on. Typical pattern is 12 weeks on, four weeks off. One track is always off, allowing another track to use its class space. Word of caution: The term "year-round" is used loosely by California districts. It may mean nothing more than an August start and a long winter break. Parents sometimes maneuver to get their kids on tracks convenient to family schedules.

- In the L.A. Unified School District, which has decentralized many operations, the start and the length of school year varies from school to school. Where the school year is shorter, the school day is longer. For enrollment information, call (213) 625-5437 or within the county (800) 933-8133.

- Register your child for school as soon as possible. Even if the school doesn't have a first-come, first-served policy, a problem may arise — an unexpected influx of students — and early registration might give you a leg up in any negotiations.

- If you're in need of day care, many elementary schools offer before- and after-school programs. Ask.

- Some school districts are simple and offer few choices. Others are loaded with choices. L.A. Unified offers about 135 magnet programs or schools. Admission procedures to magnet programs or schools can often be demanding and time consuming. In the 1997 school year, about 70,000 applications were filed for 13,000 magnet slots in the L.A. district.

- Ask about the school's advancement or grouping policy or gifted classes. Some California schools, responding to parents wishes, start "tracking" students in the first years of school by grouping them for part of the day in gifted classes (the college track).

Community College Transfers

ALTHOUGH PRIMARILY trade schools, community colleges are a major source of students for the University of California and for the California State universities.

The students usually take their freshman and sophomore classes at a community college, then transfer into a university.

Community colleges are cheap ($36 for average class) and, often, conveniently located.

The data below shows how many students each sector advances.

Tracking All L.A. Students to UCs & CSUs

Student Sector	Graduates	To UC	To CSU
Public High Schools	75,185	5,420	6,639
Private High Schools	N.A.	1,196	1,482
L.A. Community Colleges		2,480	10,275

UC, CSU Transfers by Community College Campus

Community College	To UC	To CSU
Antelope Valley CC	64	290
Cerritos CC	73	592
Citrus CC	32	426
College of Canyons	66	336
Compton CC	1	85
East L.A. College	97	552
El Camino CC	210	797
Glendale CC	167	482
L.A. City College	58	369
L.A. Harbor CC	34	274
L.A. Mission CC	15	108
L.A. Pierce CC	183	615
L.A. Southwest CC	10	121
L.A. Trade Tech CC	11	206
L.A. Valley CC	146	652
Long Beach CC	69	596
Mt. San Antonio CC	214	1,014
Pasadena CC	253	951
Rio Hondo	53	402
Santa Monica CC	632	802
West L.A. CC	30	215
Statewide	10,161	44,989

Source: California Postsecondary Education Commission. **Note**: Enrolling students counted in fall 1999 by UCs and Cal States.

At the middle schools, advanced students might be tracked into algebra, other students into everyday math. At high school, this type of dividing becomes more prevalent.

Without getting into the pros and cons of these practices, schools often tiptoe around them because they upset some parents. Sometimes the schools do not promote options, for instance, private tutoring.

- Common at many private schools, uniforms are showing up at public schools. The state legislature in 1994 passed a law allowing public schools, at their discretion, to require uniforms (usually toned-down clothes).

- In 1998, voters passed a state bond to spend $9.2 billion on school construction and renovation. Los Angeles County is expected to win millions from this bond for school construction and renovation. Locally, many school districts have passed renovation-construction bonds. L.A. District passed the biggest of them all, $2.4 billion.

- Private vs. public. A complex battle, it boils down to one side saying public schools are the best and fairest way to educate all children versus the other side saying public education is inefficient and will never reform until it has meaningful competition. The state is allowing up to 350 schools to restructure their programs according to local needs — an effort at eliminating unnecessary rules. These institutions are called charter schools. So far, they have been warily embraced by a few school districts. Typically, the schools trying the charter concept are low scoring and willing to try the new.

- Buoyed by a booming economy, California in recent years has funded the lowering of class sizes, to 20 students per teacher, in grades kindergarten through three. On the down side, because of a teacher shortage, some school districts have hired teachers without credentials.

- Many school districts profess policies that seem to give parents great flexibility in choosing schools. The law allows parents to claim job hardship and have the child placed in a school close to mom or dad's job. "Open enrollment" allows parents to pick any school within the home school district.

The two kickers: Space must be available in the chosen school and ethnicity guidelines must not be compromised. Often the highest-scoring schools have waiting lists and the ethnic makeup will be compromised. The result: The child winds up in the neighborhood school. Nonetheless, it pays to ask. School officials often try to work out arrangements to keep parents happy.

- Educational methods. Arguments rage over what will work. In a recent lurch, California schools went back to phonics to teach reading.

- Courts and school districts have sorted out Proposition 227, which curtailed non-English instruction in public schools. Parents can request a waiver, which under certain conditions allows instruction in the native language. Several ways to approach language instruction. Talk to the school. How limited-English kids are instructed remains a contentious topic in Los Angeles County.

- Closed campus vs. open campus. The former stops the students from leaving at lunch or at any time during the school day. The latter allows the kids to leave. Kids love open, parents love closed.

- The number of teaching days has been increased from about 172 to 180 but some of these days have come at the expense of prep time for teachers.

- For much of the 1990s, California, in a tough economy, pulled the purse strings tight against school spending. Teacher salaries fell behind what was paid in other states. Programs were cut. Quality, many believe, suffered. In the late 1990s, the economy came roaring back and pushed billions of extra dollars into the state treasury.

  The state put a lot of this money back into the public schools. Salaries were raised, class sizes lowered, programs restored. California is tiptoeing into incentive pay for schools that raise scores. The state is also giving extra money to the lowest-scoring schools and threatening to close them or take them over if they don't raise scores. So far the public — or much of it — has supported these moves. In November 2000, for the second time in about 10 years, California voters were asked to approve vouchers. The result, a resounding no. But many people are skeptical that the state will close schools.

  In 2000, voters approved lowering the "pass" rate for school construction bonds from almost 67 percent to 55 percent. This will make it easier to pass these bonds. In a variety of ways, the state is pumping money into programs and incentives for schools and teachers, with the goal of increasing scores and advancing more students to college.

- Over the past several years, the state Dept. of Education has adopted standards for science, history, math and reading. These standards define what the students are supposed to master at every grade level. Next to come are textbooks that reflect the new standards and after that tests based on the new standards. If students don't pass the tests, they may not be promoted. How much of this will be implemented remains to be seen. Testing is a touchy topic in California.

- Special education. Sore point in California education. When the feds and the state passed laws requiring schools to meet the special needs of students, they promised funding that never materialized. This forced school districts to take money from their regular programs to fund the

- special programs. Arguments and lawsuits followed accusing school districts of shorting special ed kids. In 2000, the state agreed to increase funding for these programs.

- More kids are being pushed into algebra, not only in high school but in the seventh and eighth grades. New law requires all students to take algebra before graduating from high school. First under the gun: the class of 2004. At the start of 2001, Governor Gray Davis said the state would provide more money to train teachers in algebra and math.

- In well-to-do neighborhoods and rich towns, parents are "taxing" themselves informally to raise money for schools. If you are new to one of these districts, you might be approached by the parents' group — never the school — and asked to contribute $100, $200 or $300 per child to the parents' group. Often the money is used to hire aides to help the teachers in the classroom.

- What if you or your neighborhood can't afford voluntary fees? Shop for bargains. Community colleges, in the summer, often run academic programs for children. Local tutors might work with small groups. Specific tutoring, say just in math, might be used to get the student over the rough spots. For information on tutors, look in the Yellow Pages under "Tutoring."

- Grad night. Not too many years ago, graduating seniors would whoop it up on grad night and some would drink and then drive and get injured or killed. At many high schools now, parents stage a grad night party at the school, load it with games, raffles and prizes, and lock the kids in until dawn. A lot of work but it keeps the darlings healthy.

- T-P. California tradition. Your son or daughter joins a school team and it wins a few games or the cheerleaders win some prize — any excuse will do — and some parent will drive the kids around and they will fling toilet paper over your house, car, trees and shrubs. Damn nuisance but the kids love it.

Does a Different School Make a Difference?

This may sound like a dumb question but it pays to understand some of the thinking behind choosing one school or school district over another. Two stories:

Researching past editions, we contacted a school district that refused to give us test results. This stuff is public information. By law, we (and you) should be able to obtain it routinely.

In so many words, the school administrator said, look, our scores are lousy because our demographics are awful: low income, parents poorly educated, etc. But our programs and staff are great. I'm not giving out the scores because parents will get the wrong idea about our district and keep their kids out of our schools (He later changed his mind and gave us the scores).

Second story, while working as a reporter, one of our editors covered a large urban school district and heard about a principal who was considered top notch. An interview was set up and the fellow seemed as good as his reputation: friendly, hardworking, supportive of his staff, a great role model for his students, many of whom he knew by their first names. But scores at the school were running in the 10th to 20th percentiles, very low.

The reason: the old failing of demographics, crime high, family structures weak, and so on.

Although neither person said this, the clear implication was that if the demographics were different, scores would be much higher. And they're probably right. If these schools got an influx of middle- and upper middle-class children, their scores would dramatically increase.

Why don't schools tell this to the public, to parents? Probably because socioeconomics is difficult to explain. Teachers want to work with parents, not alienate them with accusations of neglect. Some educators argue that even with poor socioeconomics, teachers should be able to do an effective job — controversy. Socioeconomics focuses attention on the problems of home and society to the possible detriment of schools (which also need help and funds). School, after all, is a limited activity: about six hours a day, about 180 teaching days a year.

When you strip away the fluff, schools seem to be saying that they are in the business of schools, not in reforming the larger society, and that they should be held accountable only for what they can influence: the children during the school day, on school grounds.

For these reasons — this is our opinion — many teachers and school administrators think that scores mislead and that parents often pay too much attention to scores and not enough to programs and the background and training of personnel. This is not to say that teachers ignore scores and measurements of accomplishment. They would love to see their students succeed. And schools find tests useful to determine whether their programs need changes.

No matter how low the scores, if you, as a parent, go into any school and ask — can my child get a good education here — you will be told, probably invariably, often enthusiastically, yes. First, there's the obvious reason: if the principal said no, his or her staff and bosses would be upset and angry. Second, by the reasoning common to public schools, "yes" means that the principal believes that the school and its teachers have the knowledge, training and dedication to turn out accomplished students. And the programs. Schools stress programs.

Is all this valid? Yes. Programs and training are important. Many schools with middling scores do turn out students that attend the best universities.

(Continued on Page 136)

National Scholastic Aptitude Test (SAT) Scores

State	*Tested (%)	Verbal	Math
Alabama	9	561	555
Alaska	50	516	514
Arizona	34	524	525
Arkansas	6	563	556
California	**49**	**497**	**514**
Colorado	32	536	540
Connecticut	80	510	509
Delaware	67	503	497
Dist. of Columbia	77	494	478
Florida	53	499	498
Georgia	63	487	482
Hawaii	52	482	513
Idaho	16	542	540
Illinois	12	569	585
Indiana	60	496	498
Iowa	5	594	598
Kansas	9	578	576
Kentucky	12	547	547
Louisiana	8	561	558
Maine	68	507	503
Maryland	65	507	507
Massachusetts	78	511	511
Michigan	11	557	565
Minnesota	9	586	598
Mississippi	4	563	548
Missouri	8	572	572
Montana	21	545	546
Nebraska	8	568	571
Nevada	34	512	517
New Hampshire	72	520	518
New Jersey	80	498	510
New Mexico	12	549	542
New York	76	495	502
North Carolina	61	493	493
North Dakota	5	594	605
Ohio	25	534	538
Oklahoma	8	567	560
Oregon	53	525	525
Pennsylvania	70	498	495
Rhode Island	70	504	499
South Carolina	61	479	475
South Dakota	4	585	588
Tennessee	13	559	553
Texas	50	494	499
Utah	5	570	568
Vermont	70	514	506
Virginia	65	508	499
Washington	52	525	526
West Virginia	18	527	512
Wisconsin	7	584	595
Wyoming	10	546	551
Nationwide	**43**	**505**	**511**

Source: California Dept. of Education, 1999 tests. *Percentage of class taking the test.

School Accountability Report Card

Want more information about a particular school or school district?

Every public school and district in the state is required by law to issue an annual School Accountability Report Card. The everyday name is the SARC report or the SARC card. SARCs are supposed to include:

- The ethnic makeup of the school and school district.
- Test results. The results may be presented in several ways but almost without exception the formats follow the presentation methods of the California Dept. of Education.
- Dropout rates for high schools.
- A description of facilities, the curriculum and the programs.
- Description of the teaching staff. How many have teaching credentials. Class sizes, teacher-pupil ratios.

To obtain a SARC, call the school and if the person answering the phone can't help you, ask for the superintendent's secretary or the curriculum department. Some schools want you to pick up the report in person; others will mail it to you. School Wise Press, a private firm, puts out, over the internet, detailed reports on the individual schools. Fee. See www.schoolwisepress.com. If you don't know the name of the neighborhood school, start with the school district. Here are the phone numbers of the districts and the towns they serve.

Los Angeles County Office of Education, (562) 922-6111.
ABC Unified Sch. Dist., (562) 926-5566.
Acton/Agua Dulce Unified Sch. Dist., (805) 269-5999.
Alhambra City Elem., (626) 308-2200.
Alhambra City High, (626) 308-2200.
Antelope Valley Union High, (661) 948-7655.
Arcadia Unified Sch. Dist., (626) 821-8300.
Azusa Unified Sch. Dist., (626) 967-6211.
Baldwin Park Unified Sch. Dist., (626) 962-3311.
Bassett Unified Sch. Dist., (626) 931-3000.
Bellflower Unified Sch. Dist., (562) 866-9011.
Beverly Hills Unified Sch. Dist., (310) 551-5100.
Bonita Unified Sch. Dist., (909) 599-6787.
Burbank Unified Sch. Dist., (818) 558-4600.
Castaic Sch. Dist., (661) 257-4500.
Centinela Valley Union High Dist., (310) 263-3200.
Charter Oak Unified Sch. Dist., (626) 966-8331.
Claremont Unified Sch. Dist., (909) 398-0600.
Compton Unified Sch. Dist., (310) 639-4321.
Covina-Valley Unified Sch. Dist., (626) 974-7000.

Culver City Unified Sch. Dist., (310) 842-4200.
Downey Unified Sch. Dist., (562) 904-3500.
Duarte Unified Sch. Dist., (626) 358-1191.
East Whittier City Elem., (562) 698-0351.
Eastside Union Sch. Dist., (661) 946-2813.
El Monte City Elem., (626) 453-3700.
El Monte Union High Sch. Dist., (626) 444-9005.
El Rancho Unified Sch. Dist., (562) 942-1500.
El Segundo Unified Sch. Dist., (310) 615-2650.
Garvey Elem., (626) 307-3400.
Glendale Unified Sch. Dist., (818) 241-3111.
Glendora Unified Sch. Dist., (626) 963-1611.
Gorman Elem., (661) 248-6441.
Hacienda La Puente Unified Sch. Dist., (626) 933-1000.
Hawthorne Dist., (310) 676-2276.
Hermosa Beach Dist., (310) 937-5877.
Hughes-Elizabeth Lakes Union Elem., (661) 724-1231.
Inglewood Unified Sch. Dist., (310) 419-2700
Keppel Union Elem., (661) 944-2155.
La Cañada Unified Sch. Dist., (818) 952-8300.
Lancaster Elem., (661) 948-4661.
Las Virgenes Unified Sch. Dist., (818) 880-4000.
Lawndale Elem., (310) 973-1300.
Lennox Elem., (310) 330-4950.
Little Lake City Elem., (562) 868-8241.
Long Beach Unified Sch. Dist., (562) 997-8000.
Los Angeles Unified Sch. Dist., (213) 625-6251
Los Nietos Elem., (562) 692-0271.
Lowell Joint Elem., (562) 943-0211.
Lynwood Unified Sch. Dist., (310) 886-1600.
Manhattan Beach Unified Sch. Dist., (310) 725-9050
Monrovia Unified Sch. Dist., (626) 471-2000
Montebello Unified Sch. Dist., (323) 887-7900.
Mountain View Elem., (626) 575-2151.
Newhall Elem., (661) 286-2200.
Norwalk-LaMirada Unified Sch. Dist., (562) 868-0431.
Palmdale Elem., (661) 947-7191.
Palos Verdes Peninsula Unified Sch. Dist., (310) 378-9966.
Paramount Unified Sch. Dist., (562) 602-6000.
Pasadena Unified Sch. Dist., (626) 795-6981.
Pomona Unified Sch. Dist., (909) 397-4800.
Redondo Beach Unified Sch. Dist., (310) 379-5449.
Rosemead Elem., (626) 312-2900.
Rowland Unified Sch. Dist., (626) 965-2541.
San Gabriel Unified Sch. Dist., (626) 285-3111.
San Marino Unified Sch. Dist., (626) 299-7000.
Santa Monica-Malibu Unified Sch. Dist., (310) 450-8338.
Saugus Union Elem., (661) 294-7500.
South Pasadena Unified Sch. Dist., (626) 441-5703.
South Whittier Elem., (562) 944-6231.
Sulphur Springs Union Elem., (661) 252-5131.
Temple City Unified Sch. Dist., (626) 285-2111.
Torrance Unified Sch. Dist., (310) 533-4200.
Valle Lindo Elem., (626) 580-0622.
Walnut Valley Unified Sch. Dist., (909) 595-1261.
West Covina Unified Sch. Dist., (626) 939-4600.
Westside Union Elem., (661) 948-2669.
Whittier City Sch. Dist., (562) 789-3000
Whittier Union High Sch. Dist., (562) 698-8121.
Wm. Hart Union High, (661) 259-0033.
Wilsona Sch. Dist., (661) 264-1111.
Wiseburn Elem., (310) 643-3025.

SAT Test Scores By County-1999

County	Enroll.	No. Tested	Verbal	Math
Alameda	11,809	5,518	492	523
Amador	443	122	527	513
Butte	2,222	696	507	521
Calaveras	459	113	507	522
Colusa	345	103	444	443
Contra Costa	9,204	4,335	521	538
Del Norte	346	93	502	516
El Dorado	2,026	699	538	562
Fresno	9,137	3,030	470	484
Glenn	402	136	478	478
Humboldt	1,615	491	542	546
Imperial	2,054	509	441	450
Inyo	248	91	511	509
Kern	7,651	2,006	490	500
Kings	1,476	330	470	454
Lake	613	130	497	499
Lassen	373	128	493	505
Los Angeles	85,175	32,808	467	494
Madera	1,489	312	496	498
Marin	1,965	1,086	550	554
Mariposa	180	53	529	561
Mendocino	1,063	359	535	537
Merced	3,197	668	469	477
Modoc	125	63	485	477
Mono	149	54	511	470
Monterey	3,319	1,134	478	482
Napa	1,268	471	525	532
Nevada	1,012	450	535	539
Orange	27,308	11,457	518	554
Placer	3,627	1,348	510	516
Plumas	269	96	509	503
Riverside	16,724	5,233	470	477
Sacramento	12,749	4,038	494	512
San Benito	588	235	442	483
San Bernardino	21,079	5,732	477	487
San Diego	25,998	11,320	501	515
San Francisco	3,719	2,383	463	518
San Joaquin	7,217	1,752	477	497
San Luis Obispo	2,498	916	530	538
San Mateo	5,777	2,406	505	535
Santa Barbara	3,641	1,219	524	539
Santa Clara	15,479	7,026	516	552
Santa Cruz	2,559	845	512	520
Shasta	2,032	494	522	518
Sierra	143	33	458	460
Siskiyou	588	170	519	515
Solano	4,340	1,409	495	508
Sonoma	4,427	1,518	529	537

SAT Test Scores By County-1999

County	Enroll.	No. Tested	Verbal	Math
Stanislaus	5,849	1,297	496	502
Sutter	1,077	264	483	502
Tehema	735	159	494	502
Trinity	176	55	524	512
Tulare	5,317	1,251	478	501
Tuolumne	560	198	524	519
Ventura	8,333	2,730	527	539
Yolo	1,798	642	523	549
Yuba	879	145	439	469
Statewide Totals	334,852	122,359	492	513

Source: California Dept. of Education, 1999 school year.

(Continued from Page 131)

But this approach has its skeptics. Many parents and educators believe that schools must be judged by their scores, that scores are the true test of quality.

Some parents fear that if their child or children are placed in classes with low-achieving or even middle-achieving children they will not try as hard as they would if their friends or classmates were more academic, or that in some situations their children will be enticed into mischief.

Some parents do not believe that a school with many low-scoring students can do justice to its few middle- and high-scoring students. To meet the needs of the majority, instruction might have to be slowed for everyone. Discipline is another problem. Teachers in low-scoring schools might have to spend more time on problem kids than teachers in high-scoring schools. There's much more but basically it comes down to the belief that schools do not stand alone, that they and their students are influenced by the values of parents, of classmates and of the immediate neighborhood.

To continue this logic, schools and school districts are different from one another and for this reason it pays to move into a neighborhood with high-scoring schools or one with at least middling-plus scores. Or to somehow secure a transfer to one of the schools in these neighborhoods. To an unknown extent, the marketplace has reinforced this belief. It rewards neighborhoods and towns with high-scoring schools by increasing the value (price) of their homes.

Woven into all this is the suspicion, held by many in California, that public schools have failed to dismiss incompetent teachers and have become inflexible and unable to address problems.

The parents who seem to do best at this business find out as much as possible about the schools, make decisions or compromises based on good information and work with the teachers and the schools to advance their children's interests.

High School Graduates College Choice By County

County	No. of Grads	UC	CSU	CC	Total
Alameda	11,779	12%	13%	33%	58%
Amador	341	5	8	27	41
Butte	1,814	3	14	41	58
Calaveras	444	4	8	28	40
Colusa	313	3	8	14	24
Contra Costa	9,073	11	10	35	55
Del Norte	267	5	6	26	37
El Dorado	1,740	5	8	38	50
Fresno	8,642	4	12	6	22
Glenn	325	1	13	30	43
Humboldt	1,364	5	14	33	51
Imperial	1,634	3	5	33	41
Inyo	244	3	5	21	30
Kern	7,496	3	8	27	39
Kings	1,131	4	7	42	53
Lake	524	3	8	24	35
Lassen	291	2	4	31	36
Los Angeles	82,810	8	10	31	49
Madera	1,136	3	9	11	22
Marin	2,015	18	10	17	45
Mariposa	165	2	6	31	39
Mendocino	983	7	6	31	43
Merced	2,651	4	8	32	44
Modoc	154	3	8	14	24
Mono	88	9	6	16	31
Monterey	3,585	6	9	33	48
Napa	1,295	7	10	19	35
Nevada	958	6	10	35	51
Orange	26,321	10	10	40	59
Placer	2,930	7	10	33	49
Plumas	234	2	9	31	43
Riverside	14,673	5	7	18	30
Sacramento	10,997	7	10	38	55
San Benito	578	4	11	36	50
San Bernardino	17,385	4	8	23	36
San Diego	24,739	8	11	35	54
San Francisco	5,192	15	17	24	57
San Joaquin	5,768	4	7	35	46
San Luis Obispo	2,221	5	10	44	59
San Mateo	5,478	12	12	35	58
Santa Barbara	3,378	7	6	41	53
Santa Clara	14,453	12	12	41	65
Santa Cruz	2,383	10	8	42	60
Shasta	1,890	3	5	37	44
Sierra	77	3	13	12	27
Siskiyou	499	2	6	18	26
Solano	3,909	5	10	26	41
Sonoma	3,971	7	8	46	61

Copyright © 2001 McCormack's Guides. No reproduction without permission.

High School Graduates Choice of School By County

County	No. of Grads	UC	CSU	CC	Total
Stanislaus	5,218	4%	9%	39%	52%
Sutter	880	3	7	18	27
Tehama	619	2	12	33	46
Trinity	161	1	8	27	37
Tulare	4,158	3	6	41	50
Tuolumne	513	3	10	41	54
Ventura	7,796	7	6	45	57
Yolo	1,516	13	9	27	49
Yuba	534	2	7	18	28
Total	311,730	8	10	30	47

Source: California Dept. of Education, students graduated in 1998. The chart shows the most popular choices of 1998 local public high school graduates. UC University of California, CSU California State University, CC Community College.

Top SAT Math Scores-1999

Public high schools in California scoring over 600 in math

High School	County	City	Math
Mission San Jose	Alameda	Fremont	619
Piedmont	Alameda	Piedmont	638
Campolindo	Contra Costa	Moraga	602
Miramonte	Contra Costa	Orinda	615
Cerritos	Los Angeles	Cerritos	608
Whitney	Los Angeles	Cerritos	682
Arcadia	Los Angeles	Arcadia	628
La Cañada	Los Angeles	La Cañada	612
Palos Verdes	Los Angeles	Rolling Hills Est.	614
San Marino	Los Angeles	San Marino	650
South Pasadena	Los Angeles	South Pasadena	602
Temescal	Napa	Napa	610
Sunny Hills	Orange	Fullerton	627
Troy	Orange	Fullerton	607
University	Orange	Irvine	640
Dos Pueblos	Santa Barbara	Goleta	608
Lynbrook	Santa Clara	San Jose	638
Monta Vista	Santa Clara	Cupertino	646
Saratoga	Santa Clara	Saratoga	634
Gunn	Santa Clara	Palo Alto	627
Palo Alto	Santa Clara	Palo Alto	617
Lowell	San Francisco	San Francisco	627

Source: Calif. Dept. of Education, 1999 tests.

How **much** is your **house worth?**

Go to www.dataquick.com to find the latest sale prices in your neighborhood. DataQuick products provide sale price and trend information, comparable sales and local crime reports in minutes from your computer.

Instant Access to **Property Information**

Complete property ownership information on every parcel in California and most properties across the U.S.

Perfect for lenders, appraisers, insurance providers, Realtors®, investors and investigators.

Available via the Internet, CD-ROM, list and dial-up network.

DataQuick is the nation's leading provider of real estate information products combining timely, in-depth real estate, consumer and business information with over 20 years of experience in product and technological innovation.

Call us today at 888.604.DATA
3 2 8 2
or visit www.dataquick.com

DataQuick®
a MacDonald Dettwiler Company

Chapter 4

LOS ANGELES COUNTY
Private Schools

ALTHOUGH PRIVATE SCHOOLS often enjoy a better reputation than public, they are not without problems. The typical private or parochial school is funded way below its public school counterpart.

In size, facilities and playing fields, and in programs, public schools usually far outstrip private schools. Private school teachers earn less than public school teachers.

"Typical" has to be emphasized. Some private schools are well-equipped, offer exceptional programs, pay their teachers competitively and limit class sizes to fewer than 15 students. Private schools vary widely in funding. But even when "typical," private schools enjoy certain advantages over public schools.

The Advantages

Public schools must accept all students, have almost no power to dismiss incompetent teachers and are at the mercy of their neighborhoods for the quality of students — the socioeconomic correlation. The unruly often cannot be expelled or effectively disciplined.

Much has been said about the ability of private schools to rid themselves of problem children and screen them out in the first place. But tuition, even when modest, probably does more than anything else to assure private schools quality students.

Parents who pay extra for their child's education and often agree to work closely with the school are, usually, demanding parents. The result: fewer discipline problems, fewer distractions in the class, more of a willingness to learn.

When you place your child in a good private school, you are, to a large extent, buying him or her scholastic classmates. They may not be the smartest children — many private schools accept children of varying ability — but generally they will have someone at home breathing down their necks to succeed in academics. The same attitude, a reflection of family values, is found in the high-achieving public schools.

When a child in one of these schools or a private school turns to his left and right, he will see and later talk to children who read books and newspapers. A child in a low-achieving school, public or private, will talk to classmates who watch a lot of television and rarely read.

(These are, necessarily, broad generalizations. Much depends on whom the children pick for friends. High-achieving students certainly watch television but, studies show, much less than low-achieving students. Critics contend that even high-scoring schools are graduating students poorly prepared for college.)

The Quality of Teaching

Do private schools have better teachers than public schools? Impossible to tell. Both sing the praises of their teachers. Private schools, compared to public, have more freedom to dismiss teachers but this can be abused. Private schools themselves advise parents to avoid schools with excessive teacher turnover. Although most can't pay as much as public schools, private institutions claim to attract people fed up with the limitations of public schools, particularly restrictions on disciplining and ejecting unruly children. Some proponents argue that private schools attract teachers "who really want to teach."

Religion and Private Schools

Some private schools are as secular as any public institution. But many are religious-oriented and talk in depth about religion or ethics, or teach a specific creed. Or possibly they teach values within a framework of western civilization or some other philosophy.

Until recently, public schools almost never talked about religion or religious figures. They now teach the history of major religions and the basic tenets of each, and they try to inculcate in children a respect for all religions. It's hard, if not impossible, however, for public schools to talk about values within a framework of religion or a system of ethics. Often, it's difficult for them to talk about values. Some people argue that this is major failing. Many religious schools accept students of different religions or no religion. Some schools offer these students broad courses in religion — less dogma.

Bishop Montgomery High School

5430 Torrance Boulevard, Torrance, CA 90503
(310) 540-2021

Speak Truth • Seek Justice • Serve With Honor

We produce intellectually mature persons who have learned to integrate world knowledge with Catholic beliefs and values

Money and Class Size

Private-school parents pay taxes for public schools and they pay tuition. Public-school parents pay taxes but not tuition. Big difference.

A few regular private schools have low teacher-pupil ratios, fewer than 15 students per teacher, occasionally around 10 to 1. Many parochial schools, however, run classes as least as large as public schools and in many cases larger. In recent years, public schools have gotten money to lower class sizes in grades kindergarten through three.

Ethnic Diversity

Many private schools are integrated and the great majority of private-school principals — the editor knows no exceptions — welcome minorities. Some principals fret over tuition, believing that it keeps many poor students out of private schools. Money, lack of it, weighs heavily on private schools. Scholarships, however, are awarded, adjustments made, family rates offered. Ask.

Choosing a Private School

1. Inspect the grounds, the school's buildings, ask plenty of questions. "I would make myself a real pest," advised one private school official. The good schools welcome this kind of attention.

2. Choose a school with a philosophy congenial to your own, and your child's. Carden schools emphasize structure. Montessori schools, while structured, encourage individual initiative and independence. Ask whether the school is accredited. Private schools are free to run almost any program they like, to set any standards they like, which may sound enticing but in some aspects might hurt the schools. A few bad ones spoil the reputation of the good.

To remedy this, many private schools sign up for inspections by independent agencies, such as the Western Association of Schools and Colleges and the California Association of Independent Schools. These agencies try to make sure that schools meet their own goals. Some good schools do not seek accreditation.

3. Get all details about tuition carefully explained. How is it to be paid? Are there extra fees? Book costs? Is there a refund if the student is withdrawn or dropped from the school?

4. Progress reports. Parent conferences. How often are they scheduled?

5. What are the entrance requirements? When must they be met? Although many schools use entrance tests, often they are employed to place the child in an academic program, not exclude him from the school.

6. For prep schools, what percentage of the students go on to college and to what colleges?

(Continued on Page 145)

UCs Chosen by Private School Graduates

High School	Berk	Dav	Irv	LA	Riv	SD	SB	SC	Total
Agbu Manoogian	0	0	7	2	0	0	0	0	9
Alemany	0	0	2	4	1	4	5	1	17
Alex Pilibos Armen.	0	0	1	1	0	0	1	0	3
Alverno	0	0	1	1	2	2	0	0	6
Armenian Mesrobian	1	0	3	0	1	0	0	0	5
Bellarmine-Jefferson	0	0	1	4	0	1	0	0	6
Bethel Christian Acad.	0	0	0	0	0	0	0	0	0
Bishop Amat	1	1	10	7	10	1	4	2	36
Bishop Conaty	1	0	1	0	0	0	0	0	2
Bishop Montgomery	0	5	17	8	11	4	2	3	50
Bishop Mora	0	0	1	0	0	0	2	2	5
Brentwood	5	0	0	6	0	4	0	4	19
Brethren	0	0	3	0	1	1	0	0	5
Buckley	1	1	1	5	0	0	1	0	9
Calvary Chapel	0	0	2	1	0	0	0	0	3
Campbell Hall	2	1	2	8	0	2	5	0	20
Cantwell	1	0	2	3	1	0	0	3	10
Cathedral	2	2	2	4	0	0	1	0	11
Chadwick	2	0	0	4	0	0	1	0	7
Chaminade	2	4	9	11	6	7	19	8	66
Concord	1	0	0	1	0	0	1	1	4
Crespi Carmelite	0	0	2	5	0	1	2	1	11
Crossroads	3	0	0	4	0	2	4	1	14
Damien	3	3	8	8	12	2	8	5	49
Daniel Murphy	0	0	2	2	1	2	3	0	10
Desert Christians	0	0	0	0	0	0	0	0	0
Faith Baptist	3	0	3	0	0	0	1	0	7
Flintridge Prep.	3	0	3	4	0	4	8	2	24
Flintridge Sacred Heart	1	1	1	3	1	5	3	1	16
Harvard-Westlake	5	2	0	7	0	7	7	1	29
Highland Hall	0	0	0	0	0	0	0	1	1
Holy Family Girls	1	0	1	0	1	0	0	0	3
Holy Martyrs Ferr.	0	0	2	3	1	0	1	0	7
Immaculate Heart	2	0	8	6	0	3	0	2	21
Junipero Serra	0	0	2	2	4	0	1	1	10
L.A. Baptist	0	1	1	2	1	2	0	0	7
L.A. Lutheran	0	1	0	0	0	0	1	0	2
Langston Hughes Acad.	0	1	0	0	0	0	0	0	1
La Salle	0	0	8	5	4	5	5	4	31
Le Lycee Francais	2	1	1	1	1	0	1	1	8
Louisville	4	1	4	8	0	1	2	2	22
Loyola	24	2	10	22	4	3	11	6	82
Lutheran	0	0	1	0	0	0	0	0	1
Maranatha	0	0	4	3	5	1	0	0	13
Marlborough	1	0	0	3	0	3	4	0	11
Mary Star of the Sea	1	0	1	8	1	0	2	0	13
Marymount	6	0	4	4	2	3	3	3	25
Mayfield	2	0	1	1	1	2	0	1	8
Montclair Prep.	0	0	0	1	0	1	0	0	2

UCs Chosen by Private School Graduates

High School	Berk	Dav	Irv	LA	Riv	SD	SB	SC	Total
New Jewish	5	2	0	6	1	3	10	0	27
Notre Dame Acad.	5	4	7	3	0	5	7	2	33
Notre Dame High	3	2	2	11	2	5	9	3	37
Oakwood	3	0	1	4	0	1	0	2	11
Pacific Hills	1	0	0	3	1	0	7	2	14
Paraclete	0	1	1	2	0	0	3	2	9
Pilgrim	3	0	1	1	1	0	0	0	6
Pius X	0	0	0	0	0	0	0	0	0
Polytechnic	5	0	1	2	0	4	1	0	13
Pomona Catholic	0	0	2	0	4	0	0	0	6
Princeton College Prep.	0	0	0	0	0	0	0	0	0
Providence	0	1	12	7	4	4	1	2	31
Ramona Convent	3	1	8	4	6	1	1	1	25
Ribet Acad.	0	0	0	0	0	1	1	0	2
Rio Hondo Prep.	0	0	1	0	0	0	0	0	1
Rolling Hills	0	1	2	1	0	0	0	0	4
Sacred Heart	2	1	1	0	2	0	1	0	7
San Gabriel Acad.	0	0	1	1	0	0	0	0	2
San Gabriel Mission	0	1	1	9	0	0	1	0	12
St. Anthony	0	0	3	0	0	0	1	0	4
St. Bernard	2	1	1	3	1	0	3	0	11
St. Francis	0	2	4	4	4	2	2	0	18
St. Genevieve	0	0	2	3	1	0	0	1	7
St. John Bosco	0	1	6	2	10	0	1	0	20
St. Joseph	0	1	11	3	3	0	2	2	22
St. Lucy's Priory	0	2	9	3	11	4	5	0	34
St. Mary's Acad.	2	0	1	3	3	0	1	0	10
St. Matthias	0	0	0	2	2	0	1	0	5
St. Monica	0	1	5	6	2	1	2	2	19
St. Paul	1	0	1	6	3	0	3	0	14
Valley Christian	2	0	2	1	1	0	0	0	6
Valley Torah	0	0	0	3	0	0	1	0	4
Verbum Dei	0	0	1	0	1	0	0	0	2
Viewpoint	1	0	1	4	1	1	1	0	9
Village Christian	0	0	5	5	1	2	0	0	13
Webb	1	1	1	0	1	0	0	0	4
West L.A. Baptist	0	0	1	0	0	0	0	0	1
Western Christian	0	0	0	0	3	1	1	0	5
Westridge	4	0	0	2	0	5	0	0	11
Windward	4	3	0	2	0	1	2	3	15
Yeshiva Gedolah	0	0	1	0	0	0	0	0	1
Yeshiva University	0	0	2	4	1	1	1	0	9

Source: California Postsecondary Education Commission. The chart shows the University of California choices of 1999 local private high school graduates. The state does not track graduates enrolling in private or out-of-state colleges. Key: Berk (Berkeley), Irv (Irvine), Dav (Davis), LA (UCLA), Riv (Riverside), SD (San Diego), SB (Santa Barbara), SC (Santa Cruz).

(Continued from Page 142)

7. How are discipline problems handled?

8. What are the teacher qualifications? What is the teacher turnover rate?

9. How sound financially is the school? How long has it been in existence? There is nothing wrong per se with new schools. But you want a school that has the wherewithal to do the job.

10. Do parents have to work at school functions? Are they required to "volunteer"?

11. Don't choose in haste but don't wait until the last minute. Some schools fill quickly, some fill certain classes quickly. Many schools decide on applications in January, and some high schools, in the year preceding the start of instruction.

12. Don't assume that because your child attends a private school you can expect everything will go all right, that neither the school nor the student needs your attention. The quality of private schools in California varies widely.

CSUs Chosen by Private School Graduates

High School	DH	Full	LB	LA	NR	Pom	SD	SLO	Son
Alemany	0	0	1	1	39	2	4	0	0
Alex Pilibos Armenian	0	0	0	0	2	0	0	0	0
Alverno	1	0	3	1	1	8	0	0	1
Armenian Mesrobian	0	3	2	0	1	1	0	0	0
Bellarmine-Jefferson	0	0	1	1	9	0	0	0	0
Bishop Amat	2	36	16	6	3	54	6	0	0
Bishop Conaty	0	0	1	11	6	0	1	0	0
Bishop Montgomery	4	3	39	3	1	2	3	8	0
Bishop Mora Salesian	0	1	3	8	4	0	2	0	0
Brentwood	0	0	0	0	0	0	0	0	0
Brethren	0	0	5	0	0	0	0	0	0
Buckley	0	0	0	0	1	0	0	0	0
California State Prep.	0	0	0	2	1	0	0	0	0
Campbell Hall	0	0	0	0	1	0	1	0	0
Cantwell Sacred Heart	1	2	1	8	1	4	1	0	0
Cathedral	1	1	2	17	5	1	1	0	0
Chaminade	0	1	5	0	14	2	4	7	0
Concord High	0	0	0	0	2	0	0	0	1
Crespi Carmelite	0	0	1	0	13	2	6	3	1
Crossroads	0	0	0	1	0	0	0	0	0
Damien	0	24	5	2	0	23	3	1	0
Daniel Murphy	0	2	0	3	9	2	0	0	0
Faith Baptist	0	0	0	0	0	0	1	1	0
Flintridge Prep.	0	0	0	1	0	3	1	1	0
Flintridge Sacred	0	0	3	0	1	0	1	0	0
Harvard-Westlake	0	0	0	0	1	0	0	0	0
Highland Hall	0	0	0	0	14	0	0	0	0
Holy Family Girls	0	0	2	2	2	2	0	0	0
Holy Martyrs Ferrahian	0	0	0	0	12	0	0	0	0
Immaculate Heart	0	0	4	3	4	5	2	1	2
Junipero Serra	13	2	6	0	4	4	0	0	3
L.A. Baptist	0	0	0	0	17	0	1	0	0
L.A. Lutheran	0	0	0	0	4	0	0	1	0
La Salle	0	3	6	0	1	12	9	11	0
Louisville	0	0	1	0	21	0	2	5	0
Loyola	1	2	3	2	10	6	0	3	1
Lutheran	0	0	0	0	1	2	0	0	0
Maranatha	0	1	3	1	0	6	1	0	1
Marlborough	0	0	0	0	0	0	0	0	0
Marymount	0	0	0	0	0	0	2	0	0
Mary Star of the Sea	1	0	13	0	0	1	0	0	0
Mayfield Sch./Holy Child	0	0	1	0	0	1	0	1	0
Montclair High	0	0	1	0	3	1	2	0	0
Montclair Prep.	0	0	0	0	0	0	0	0	0
Mount Carmel	0	0	0	0	0	0	0	0	2
Notre Dame Acad.	0	1	2	1	3	2	0	2	2
Notre Dame High	0	1	0	0	17	7	6	1	1
Oakwood	0	0	0	0	0	0	0	0	0
Our Lady of Loretto	0	2	0	1	0	0	0	0	0

CSUs Chosen by Private School Graduates

High School	DH	Full	LB	LA	NR	Pom	SD	SLO	Son
Pacific Christian	0	0	2	0	1	0	1	0	1
Pacific Hills	0	0	0	0	0	0	0	0	0
Paraclete	0	1	3	0	11	2	1	4	2
Pius X	1	1	3	2	0	1	0	0	0
Polytechnic	0	0	1	0	0	0	0	0	0
Pomona Catholic	1	4	0	1	0	9	0	0	0
Princeton College Prep.	0	0	0	0	0	0	0	0	0
Providence	0	3	0	0	3	2	0	0	0
Ramona Convent	0	0	9	8	2	8	1	0	0
Regina Caeli	0	0	0	0	0	0	0	0	0
Ribet Acad.	0	0	0	0	2	1	1	0	0
Sacred Heart	0	1	4	11	1	5	0	1	0
San Fernando Acad.	0	0	0	0	1	0	0	0	0
San Gabriel Acad.	0	0	0	1	0	1	0	0	0
San Gabriel Mission	0	0	4	11	0	8	0	0	0
Santa Monica Girls	0	0	0	0	0	0	0	0	0
Sherwood Oaks	0	0	0	0	10	0	0	0	0
Southwestern Acad.	0	0	1	0	0	0	0	0	0
St. Anthony	0	0	21	1	0	1	0	1	0
St. Bernard	0	1	13	4	7	0	3	1	0
St. Francis	0	1	4	0	7	5	0	0	1
St. Genevieve	0	0	1	0	15	0	1	0	0
St. John Bosco	1	19	29	2	1	4	2	0	0
St. Joseph	2	20	27	0	6	0	0	1	1
St. Lucy's Priory	0	27	8	2	1	19	2	0	0
St. Mary's Acad.	2	2	4	0	6	2	2	0	0
St. Matthias	1	0	7	2	0	1	0	0	0
St. Michael's	0	0	0	0	0	0	0	0	0
St. Monica	2	0	3	0	4	2	1	0	0
St. Paul	3	18	15	2	1	6	4	0	0
Valley Christian	0	5	9	1	1	1	2	1	0
Valley Torah Center	0	0	0	0	6	0	0	0	0
Verbum Dei	2	0	1	3	1	0	1	0	0
Village Christian	0	0	0	0	0	0	0	0	0
Webb	0	0	0	0	0	0	0	0	0
Western Christian	0	8	0	0	0	8	0	0	0
Westridge	0	0	0	0	0	0	0	0	0
West Valley Christian	0	0	0	0	0	0	0	0	0
Yeshiva University	0	0	0	0	1	0	0	0	0

Source: California Secondary Education Commission. The chart shows the most popular choices of 1998 local public high school graduates, not all Cal State universities. The state does not track graduates enrolling in private or out-of-state colleges. **Key**: DH (Dominguez Hills), Full (Fullerton), LB (Long Beach), LA (Los Angeles), NR (Northridge), Pom (Pomona), SD (San Diego), SLO (San Luis Obispo), Son (Sonoma).

Directory of Private Schools

For reasons of space, this directory includes only schools with 100 or more students. To attain a complete directory of private schools in the county, call the California Department of Education at 1-800-995-4099.

In California, tuition ranges widely in private schools. Many Catholic elementaries charge from about $2,000 to $3,000. Some non-denominational schools go as high as $11,000.

High schools range from $5,000 to $12,000. Discounts are often given for siblings. If strapped, ask about financial help.

Many schools offer family rates. Religious schools often charge more for non-members. Day care costs extra.

Alhambra
All Souls Elem., 29 S. Electric Ave., (626) 282-5695, Enroll: 199, K-8th.
Emmaus Lutheran, 840 S. Almansor, (626) 289-3664, Enroll: 250, K-8th.
Leeway, 9 N. Almansor St., (626) 308-4521, Enroll: 104, K-12.
Oneonta Montessori, 2221 Poplar Blvd., (626) 284-0840, Enroll: 103, K-6th.
Ramona Convent Secondary, 1701 W. Ramona Rd., (626) 282-4151, Enroll: 560, 7th-12th.
St. Therese Elem., 515 N. Vega St., (626) 289-3364, Enroll: 297, K-8th.
St. Thomas More Catholic Elem., 2510 S. Fremont Ave., (626) 284-5778, Enroll: 272, K-8th.

Altadena
Pasadena Waldorf, 209 E. Mariposa St., (626) 794-9564, Enroll: 248, K-8th.
Sahag-Mesrob Armenian Christian, 2501 N. Maiden Ln., (626) 798-5020, Enroll: 236, K-8th.
St. Elizabeth Elem., 1840 N. Lake Ave., (626) 797-7727, Enroll: 280, K-8th.
St. Mark's Elem., 1050 E. Altadena Dr., (626) 798-8858, Enroll: 207, K-6th.

Arcadia
Annunciation Elem., 1307 E. Longden Ave., (626) 447-8262, Enroll: 288, K-8th.
Arcadia Christian, 1900 S. Santa Anita Ave., (626) 574-8229, Enroll: 419, K-8th.
Barnhart Elem., 226 W. Colorado Blvd., (626) 446-5588, Enroll: 258, K-8th.
Holy Angels Elem., 360 Campus Dr., (626) 447-6312, Enroll: 286, K-8th.
Rio Hondo Prep., 5150 Farna Ave., (626) 444-9531, Enroll: 181, 6th-12th.

Artesia
Our Lady of Fatima, 18626 S. Clarkdale Ave., (562) 865-1621, Enroll: 302, K-8th.

Azusa
Light & Life Christian, 777 E. Alosta Ave., (626) 969-0182, Enroll: 154, K-6th.
St. Frances of Rome Elem., 734 N. Pasadena Ave., (626) 334-2018, Enroll: 283, K-8th.

Baldwin Park
St. John the Baptist, 3870 Stewart Ave., (626) 337-1421, Enroll: 577, K-8th.

Bell Gardens
Bell Gardens Christian Elem., 6262 E. Gage Ave., (323) 773-3968, Enroll: 151, K-8th.
St. Gertrude Elem., 6824 Toler Ave., (562) 927-1216, Enroll: 306, K-8th.

Bellflower
Adventist Union-Bellfower Elem., 15548 Santa Ana Ave., (562) 867-0718, Enroll: 117, K-8th.
Bellflower Christian Elem., 17408 Grand Ave., (562) 403-3153, Enroll: 522, K-6th.
St. Bernard Elem., 9626 Park St., (562) 867-9410, Enroll: 311, K-8th.
St. Dominic Savio Elem., 9750 Foster Rd., (562) 866-3617, Enroll: 356, K-8th.
St. John Bosco High, 13640 S. Bellflower Blvd., (562) 920-1734, Enroll: 1,108, 9th-12th.
Woodruff Christian, 16400 Woodruff Ave., (562) 867-8594, Enroll: 240, K-6th.

Beverly Hills
Good Shepherd Elem., 148 S. Linden Dr., (310) 275-8601, Enroll: 280, K-8th.
Hillel Hebrew Acad., 9120 W. Olympic Blvd., (310) 276-6135, Enroll: 673, K-8th.
Page Private, 419 S. Robertson, (323) 272-3429, Enroll: 130, K-6th.

Temple Emanuel Comm. Day, 8844 Burton Way, (310) 288-3737, Enroll: 274, K-8th.

Burbank
American Lutheran Elem., 755 N. Whitnall Hwy., (818) 846-0295, Enroll: 159, K-5th.

Alternative Schools of California, 704 S. Main St., (818) 846-8990, Enroll: 149, K-12th

Bellarmine-Jefferson High, 465 E. Olive Ave., (818) 972-1403, Enroll: 366, 9th-12th.

First Lutheran Elem., 1001 S. Glenoaks Blvd., (818) 848-3076, Enroll: 135, K-6th.

Providence High, 511 S. Buena Vista St., (818) 846-8141, Enroll: 561, 9th-12th.

St. Finbar Elem., 2120 W. Olive Ave., (818) 848-0191, Enroll: 269, K-8th.

St. Francis Xavier Elem., 3601 Scott Rd., (818) 767-2071, Enroll: 310, K-8th.

St. Robert Bellarmine Elem., 154 N. Fifth St., (818) 842-5033, Enroll: 338, K-8th.

Calabasas
Viewpoint, 23620 Mulholland Hwy., (818) 591-9153, Enroll: 690, K-8th.

Canoga Park
Agbu Monoogian-Demirdjian-Apos., 6844 Oakdale Ave., (818) 883-2428, Enroll: 849, K-12th.

Canoga Park Lutheran, 7357 Jordan Ave., (818) 348-5714, Enroll: 191, K-8th.

Faith Baptist, 7644 Farralone Ave., (818) 340-6131, Enroll: 1,211, K-12th.

Our Lady of the Valley Elem., 22041 Gault St., (818) 592-2894, Enroll: 281, K-8th .

St. Joseph the Worker Elem., 19812 Cantalay St., (818) 341-6616, Enroll: 315, K-8th.

St. Martin-in-the-Fields Parish Day, 7136 Winnetka Ave., (818) 340-5144, Enroll: 125, K-6th.

West Valley Christian Acad., 7911 Winnetka Ave., (818) 882-3242, Enroll: 391, K-6th.

Canyon Country (Santa Clarita)
Pinecrest Sch.-Children's Ctr., 16530 Lost Canyon Rd., (661) 298-2127, Enroll: 131, K-6th.

Santa Clarita Christian, 27249 Luther Dr., (661) 252-7371, Enroll: 569, K-12th.

Carson
Carson Christian, 218 S. Avalon Blvd., (310) 538-5370, Enroll: 104, K-12th.

Peninsula Christian, 22507 S. Figueroa, (310) 328-4541, Enroll: 101, K-8th.

St. Philomena Elem., 21832 S. Main St., (310) 835-4827, Enroll: 308, K-8th.

Cerritos
Concordia Lutheran, 13633 183rd St., (562) 926-7416, Enroll: 102, K-6th.

Valley Christian High, 10818 Artesia Blvd., (562) 865-0281, Enroll: 737, 9th-12th.

Valley Christian Middle, 18100 Dumont St., (562) 865-6519, Enroll: 285, 7th-8th.

Chatsworth
Chaminade College Prep., 19800 Devonshire St., (818) 363-8127, Enroll: 636, 6th-8th.

Chatsworth Hills Acad., 21523 Rinaldi St., (818) 998-4037, Enroll: 245, K-8th.

Egremont , 19850 Devonshire St., (818) 363-7803, Enroll: 145, K-6th.

Phillips Acad., 19750 Mayall St., (818) 993-4144, Enroll: 285, K-8th.

Santa Susana Sch. Inc., 22280 Devonshire St., (818) 709-9854, Enroll: 113, K-5th.

Sierra Canyon, 11052 Sierra Canyon Way, (818) 882-8121, Enroll: 667, K-8th.

St. John Eudes Elem., 9925 Mason Ave., (818) 341-1454, Enroll: 303, K-8th.

Claremont
Foothill Country Day Elem., 1035 W. Harrison Ave., (909) 626-5681, Enroll: 180, K-8th.

Our Lady of the Assumption, 611 W. Bonita, (909) 626-7135, Enroll: 522, K-8th.

Webb School, 1175 W. Base Line Rd., (909) 626-3587, Enroll: 340, 9th-12th.

Western Christian Sch., 3105 Padua Ave., (909) 624-8291, Enroll: 405, K-8th.

Compton
First Christian Day of Compton, 225 S. Santa Fe Ave., (310) 631-9534, Enroll: 201, K-8th.

Optimal Christian Acad., 1300 E. Palmer Ave., (310) 603-0378, Enroll: 325, K-8th.

150 PRIVATE SCHOOLS

Our Lady of Victory Elem., 601 E. Palmer Ave., (310) 631-1320, Enroll: 301, K-8th.
Queen of Angels Acad., 823 E. Compton Blvd., (310) 515-3891, Enroll: 191, 9th-12th.
St. Albert the Great Elem., 804 E. Compton Blvd., (310) 323-4559, Enroll: 651, K-8th.
St. Timothy's Episcopal, 312 S. Oleander Ave., (310) 638-6319, Enroll: 128, K-8th.

Covina
Sacred Heart Elem., 360 W. Workman Ave., (626) 332-7222, Enroll: 321, K-8th.
Sonrise Christian, 1220 E. Ruddock, (626) 331-0559, Enroll: 557, K-8th.
Sonrise Christian, 800 N. Banna Ave., (626) 332-1907, Enroll: 314, K-2nd.
St. Louise de Marillac Elem., 1728 Covina Blvd., (626) 966-2317, Enroll: 306, K-8th.
Western Christian, 1115 E. Puente, (626) 967-0733, Enroll: 434, 7th-12th.

Culver City
Echo Horizon, 3430 Mcmanus Ave., (310) 838-2442, Enroll: 257, K-6th.
Ed. Resource and Svcs, 10101 W. Jefferson Blvd., (310) 838-1200, Enroll: 151, K-12th.
Ohr Eliyahu Acad., 5950 Stoneview Dr., (310) 559-3330, Enroll: 125, K-8th.
St. Augustine Catholic Elem., 3819 Clarington Ave., (310) 838-3144, Enroll: 295, K-8th.
Willows Comm., 8509 Higuera St., (310) 815-0411, Enroll: 279, K-8th.

Diamond Bar
Mt. Calvary Lutheran, 23300 E. Golden Springs, (909) 861-2740, Enroll: 320, K-8th.

Downey
Calvary Chapel Christian, 12808 Woodruff Ave., (562) 803-6556, Enroll: 1,190, K-12th.
Creative Beginnings Elem., 8033 Third St., (562) 861-1499, Enroll: 129, K-5th.
Good Shepherd Lutheran Elem., 13200 Clark Ave., (562) 803-4918, Enroll: 135, K-8th.
Keystone Acad., 8615 Florence, No. 207, (562) 862-7134, Enroll: 195, K-12th.
Kirkwood Ed. Ctr., 11115 Pangborn, (562) 861-4419, Enroll: 134, K-3rd.

Our Lady of Perpetual Help Elem., 10441 S. Downey Ave., (562) 869-9969, Enroll: 297, K-8th.
St. Matthias High, 7851 E. Gardendale St., (562) 861-2271, Enroll: 433, 9th-12th.
St. Mark's Elem., 10354 Downey Ave., (562) 869-7213, Enroll: 127, K-8th.
St. Raymond Elem., 12320 S. Paramount Blvd., (562) 862-3210, Enroll: 325, K-8th.

Duarte
Anita Oaks, 822 Bradbourne Ave., (626) 301-1354, Enroll: 232, K-8th.

El Monte
Nativity, 10907 St. Louis Dr., (626) 448-2414, Enroll: 295, K-8th.
Pearl Prep., 4900 Kings Row, (626) 442-7737, Enroll: 116, 1st-5th.
Santa Anita Christian Acad., 4434 Santa Anita Ave., (626) 443-1128, Enroll: 110, K-12th .

El Segundo
St. Anthony Elem., 233 Lomita St., (310) 322-4218, Enroll: 283, K-8th .

Encino
Bethel Lutheran, 17500 Burbank Blvd., (818) 788-2663, Enroll: 132, K-6th.
Crespi Carmelite High, 5031 Alonzo Ave., (818) 345-1672, Enroll: 475, 9th-12th.
Holy Martyrs Elem. & Ferrahian High, 5300 White Oak Ave., (818) 784-6228, Enroll: 310, 5th-12th.
Our Lady of Grace, 17720 Ventura Blvd., (818) 344-4126, Enroll: 301, K-8th.
St. Cyril of Jerusalem Elem., 4548 Haskell Ave., (818) 501-4155, Enroll: 307, K-8th.
Valley Beth Shalom Day Elem., 15739 Ventura Blvd., (818) 788-2199, Enroll: 294, K-6th.
Westmark, 5461 Louise Ave., (818) 986-5045, Enroll: 234, 2nd-12th.

Gardena
Calvary Christian Acad., 2818 Manhattan Beach Blvd., (310) 327-3094, Enroll: 540, K-8th.
Gardena Valley Christian, 1473 W. 182nd St., (310) 327-4987, Enroll: 344, K-8th.
Junipero Serra High, 14830 S. Van Ness Ave., (310) 324-6675, Enroll: 391, 9th-12th.

Maria Regina Elem., 13510 S. Van Ness Ave., (310) 327-9133, Enroll: 295, K-8th.
St. Anthony of Padua, 1003 W. 163rd St., (310) 329-7170, Enroll: 272, 1st-8th.

Glendale
Chamlian Armenian, 4444 Lowell Ave., (818) 957-3399, Enroll: 500, 1st-8th.
First Lutheran, 1300 E. Colorado St., (818) 244-7319, Enroll: 138, K-6th
Glendale Adventist Acad., 700 Kimlin Dr., (818) 244-8671, Enroll: 689, K-12th.
Holy Family Elem., 400 S. Louise St., (818) 243-9239, Enroll: 316, K-8th.
Holy Family Girls High, 400 E. Lomita Ave. , (818) 241-3178, Enroll: 265, 9th-12th.
Incarnation Elem., 123 W. Glenoaks Blvd., (818) 241-2269, Enroll: 294, K-8th.
Salem Lutheran Elem., 1211 N. Brand Blvd., (818) 243-8264, Enroll: 192, K-6th.
Tobinworld, 920 E. Broadway, (818) 247-7474, Enroll: 264, K-12th.
Zion Lutheran, 301 N. Isabel St., (818) 243-3119, Enroll: 173, K-6th.

Glendora
Foothill Christian, 901 S. Grand Ave., (626) 335-4035, Enroll: 234, K-8th.
Foothill Christian, 242 W. Baseline Rd., (626) 914-1849, Enroll: 472, K-8th.
Hope Lutheran Elem., 1041 E. Foothill Blvd., (626) 335-5315, Enroll: 191, K-8th.
St. Dorothy's Elem., 215 S. Valley Ctr., (626) 335-0772, Enroll: 308, K-8th.
St. Lucy's Priory High, 655 W. Sierra Madre Ave., (626) 335-3322, Enroll: 889, 9th-12th.

Granada Hills
De La Salle, 16535 Chatsworth St., (818) 363-2270, Enroll: 602, K-8th.
Granada Hills Baptist Elem., 10949 Zelzah Ave., (818) 360-2104, Enroll: 175, K-6th.
Hillcrest Christian, 17531 Rinaldi, (818) 368-7071, Enroll: 764, K-12th.
Our Savior's First Lutheran, 16603 San Fernando Mission Blvd., (818) 368-0892, Enroll: 126, K-6th.
St. Euphrasia Elem., 17637 Mayerling St., (818) 363-5515, Enroll: 287, K-8th.

Hacienda Heights
Hacienda Christian, 15518 E. Gale Ave., (626) 336-0723, Enroll: 118, K-8th.
St. Mark's Lutheran Elem., 2323 Las Lomitas, (626) 968-0428, Enroll: 766, K-8th.

Harbor City (Near San Pedro)
Gateway Christian, 25500 S. Vermont Ave., (310) 326-3018, Enroll: 191, K-12th.

Hawthorne
Acacia Baptist Day, 4712 W. El Segundo Blvd., (310) 676-4543, Enroll: 132, K-8th.
Atherton Christian, 2627 W. 116 St., (323) 752-0228, Enroll: 131, K-6th.
Light & Life Christian, 14204 Prairie Ave., (310) 263-2790, Enroll: 178, K-12th.
St. Joseph Elem., 11886 Acacia Ave., (310) 679-1014, Enroll: 557, K-8th.
Trinity Lutheran, 4783 130th St., (310) 675-3379, Enroll: 218, K-8th.

Hermosa Beach
Hope Chapel Acad., 2420 Pacific Coast Hwy., (310) 374-4673, Enroll: 204, K-12th.
Our Lady of Guadalupe Elem., 340 Massey Ave., (310) 372-7486, Enroll: 260, K-8th.

Hollywood
Blessed Sacrament, 6641 Sunset Blvd., (323) 467-4177, Enroll: 318, K-8th.
Hollywood Little Red Schoolhouse, 1248 N. Highland Ave., (323) 465-1320, Enroll: 173, K-8th.

Huntington Park
St. Matthias Elem., 7130 Cedar St., (323) 588-7253, Enroll: 311, K-8th.
Huntington Park Baptist Elem., 2665 Clarendon, (323) 587-5387, Enroll: 132, K-8th.

Inglewood
Calvary Christian Elem., 2400 W. 85th St., (323) 752-7594, Enroll: 313, K-8th.
Good Shepherd Lutheran Elem., 901 S. Maple St., (310) 671-0427, Enroll: 103, 1st-8th.
Inglewood Christian Elem., 215 E. Hillcrest Blvd., (310) 671-7666, Enroll: 297, K-8th.
K. Anthony's Elem., 8420 Crenshaw Blvd., (323) 758-1187, Enroll: 223, 2nd-6th.

K. Anthony's Middle, 1003 Prairie Ave., (310) 671-5231, Enroll: 130, K-1st.
South Bay Lutheran High, 3600 W. Imperial Hwy., (310) 672-1101, Enroll: 135, 9th-12th.
St. John Chrysostom Elem., 530 E. Florence Ave., (310) 677-5868, Enroll: 293, K-8th.
St. Mary's Acad. of Los Angeles, 701 Grace Ave., (310) 674-8470, Enroll: 363, 9th-12th.
Westside School, 3600 W. Imperial Hwy., (310) 680-9452, Enroll: 150, K-8th
Wilders Prep. Acad., 336 E Spruce Ave., (310) 671-7585, Enroll: 222, K-8th.
Wiz, 121 W. Arbor Vitae, (310) 671-4246, Enroll: 100, K-6th

La Cañada Flintridge
Crestview Prep., 140 Foothill Blvd., (818) 952-0925, Enroll: 242, K-6th.
Delphi Acad., 4490 Cornishon, (818) 952-0909, Enroll: 249, K-12th.
Flintridge Prep., 4543 Crown Ave., (818) 790-1178, Enroll: 507, 7th-12th.
Flintridge Sacred Heart Acad., 440 St. Katherine Dr., (626) 685-8300, Enroll: 406, 9th-12th.
Learning Castle, 4490 Cornishon Ave., (818) 952-8008, Enroll: 196, K-8th.
Renaissance Acad., 4490 Cornishon, (818) 952-3055, Enroll: 126, K-12th.
St. Bede the Venerable Elem., 217 Foothill Blvd., (818) 790-7884, Enroll: 277, K-8th.
St. Francis High, 200 Foothill Blvd., (818) 790-0325, Enroll: 605, 9th-12th.

La Crescenta-Montrose
Armenian Sisters Acad., 2361 Florencita Dr., (818) 249-8783, Enroll: 299, K-8th.
Crescenta Valley Adventist, 6245 Honolulu Ave., (818) 249-1504, Enroll: 194, K-8th.
Holy Redeemer Elem., 2361 Del Mar Rd., (818) 541-9005, Enroll: 238, K-8th.
Montrose Christian Montessori, 2545 Honolulu Ave., (818) 249-2319, Enroll: 201, K-6th.
St. James the Less Elem., 4635 Dunsmore Ave., (818) 248-7778, Enroll: 286, K-8th.

La Mirada
Beatitudes of Our Lord Elem., 13021 S. Santa Gertrudes Ave., (562) 943-3218, Enroll: 287, K-8th.

Brethren Elem.-Jr. High, 12200 Oxford Dr., (562) 947-9997, Enroll: 310, K-8th.
St. Paul of the Cross Elem., 14030 Foster Rd., (562) 921-2118, Enroll: 308, K-8th.

La Habra Heights
Heights Christian Jr. High, 1225 Hacienda Blvd., 562 694-3304, Enroll: 180, 7th-8th

La Puente
Bishop Amat Memorial High, 14301 Fairgrove Ave., (626) 962-2495, Enroll: 1,605, 9th-12th.
St. Joseph Elem., 15650 E. Temple Ave., (626) 336-2821, Enroll: 247, 1st-8th.
St. Louis of France, 13901 E. Temple Ave., (626) 918-6210, Enroll: 316, K-8th.
Sunset Christian, 400 N. Sunset, (626) 336-1206, Enroll: 133, K-8th.

La Verne
Calvary Baptist, 2990 Damien Ave., (909) 593-4672, Enroll: 143, K-12th.
Damien High, 2280 Damien Ave., (909) 596-1946, Enroll: 1,097, 9th-12th.
Lutheran High, 3960 Fruit St., (909) 593-4494, Enroll: 152, 9th-12th.

Lakewood
Southwestern Longview Pvt., 4747 Daisy Ave., (562) 422-1582, Enroll: 189, K-12th.
St. Joseph High, 5825 Woodruff Ave., (562) 925-5073, Enroll: 830, 9th-12th.
St. Pancratius Elem., 3601 St. Pancratius Pl., (562) 634-6310, Enroll: 304, K-8th.
St. Timothy Lutheran, 4645 Woodruff Ave., (562) 421-3960, Enroll: 110, K-6th.

Lancaster
Antelope Valley Adventist, 45045 N. Date Ave., (661) 942-6552, Enroll: 106, K-10th.
Antelope Valley Christian, 3700 W. Ave. L, (661) 943-0044, Enroll: 266, K-12th.
Bethel Christian Acad., 3100 W. Ave. K, (661) 943-2224, Enroll: 535, K-12th.
Desert Christian, 44648 N. 15th St. West, (661) 948-5071, Enroll: 1,586, K-12th.
Grace Lutheran Elem., 856 W. Newgrove, (661) 948-1018, Enroll: 171, K-8th.
Heritage Christian, 43748 Adler Ave., (661) 945-4231, Enroll: 135, K-12th.

Lancaster Baptist, 4020 E. Lancaster Blvd., (661) 946-4663, Enroll: 351, K-12th.
Lancaster Christian, 44339 N. Beech, (661) 942-2137, Enroll: 135, K-8th.
Paraclete High, 42145 N. 30th St. W., (661) 943-3255, Enroll: 709, 9th-12th.
Pinecrest Sch.-Children's Ctr., 2110 W. Ave. K, (661) 723-0366, Enroll: 144, K-6th.
Sacred Heart Elem., 45002 N. Date Ave., (661) 948-3613, Enroll: 314, K-8th.
Seton School, 44751 Date Ave., (661) 948-8881, Enroll: 715, K-12th

Lomita
Coastal Acad., 25501 Oak Ave., (310) 644-0433, Enroll: 188, K-12th.
St. Margaret Mary, 25515 Eshelman Ave., (310) 326-9494, Enroll: 329, K-8th.

Long Beach
Bethany Baptist Elem., 2244 Clark Ave., (562) 597-2814, Enroll: 205, K-6th.
Bethany Lutheran, 5100 Arbor Rd., (562) 420-7783, Enroll: 438, K-8th.
First Baptist Church, 1000 Pine Ave., (562) 432-8447, Enroll: 192, K-12th.
First Baptist Church of Lakewood Elem., 5336 Arbor Rd., (562) 425-3358, Enroll: 291, K-6th.
Gethsemane Baptist Christian, 6095 Orange Ave., (562) 422-4206, Enroll: 135, K-12th.
Holy Innocents Elem., 2500 Pacific Ave., (562) 424-1018, Enroll: 323, K-8th.
Light & Life Christian, 5951 Downey Ave., (562) 630-6096, Enroll: 187, K-6th.
Long Beach Brethren Elem., 3601 Linden Ave., (562) 595-1674, Enroll: 265, K-6th.
Los Altos Brethren, 6565 Stearns St., (562) 430-6813, Enroll: 154, K-6th.
Nazarene Christian, 5253 Los Coyotes Diagonal, (562) 597-3900, Enroll: 120, K-7th .
Oakwood Acad., 2951 Long Beach Blvd., (562) 424-4816, Enroll: 102, K-6th.
Our Lady of Refuge, 5210 Los Coyotes Diagonal, (562) 597-0819, Enroll: 278, K-8th.
Pacific Christian, 2474 Pacific Ave., (562) 424-7724, Enroll: 117, Un-graded.
Parkridge Private, 3588 Long Beach Blvd., (562) 424-5528, Enroll: 105, K-12th.
St. Anthony Elem., 855 E. Fifth St., (562) 432-5946, Enroll: 284, K-8th.
St. Anthony High, 620 Olive Ave., (562) 435-4496, Enroll: 324, 9th-12th.
St. Athanasius Elem., 5369 Linden Ave., (562) 428-7422, Enroll: 245, K-8th.
St. Barnabas Elem., 3980 Marron Ave., (562) 424-7476, Enroll: 290, K-8th.
St. Cornelius Elem., 3330 Bellflower Blvd., (562) 425-7813, Enroll: 335, K-8th.
St. Cyprian Elem., 5133 Arbor Rd., (562) 425-7341, Enroll: 280, K-8th.
St. Joseph Elem., 6200 E. Willow St., (562) 596-6115, Enroll: 300, K-8th.
St. Lucy Elem., 2320 Cota Ave., (562) 424-9062, Enroll: 294, K-8th.
St. Maria Goretti, 3950 Palo Verde Ave., (562) 425-5112, Enroll: 311, K-8th.
Westerly Sch. of Long Beach, 2950 E. 29th St., (562) 981-3151, Enroll: 182, K-8th.

Los Angeles
Alex Pilibos Armenian, 1615 N. Alexandria Ave., (323) 668-2661, Enroll: 706, K-12th.
All Saints Elem., 3420 Portola Ave., (323) 225-7264, Enroll: 274, K-8th.
Alpha Presch. Elem., 5252 W. Adams Blvd., (323) 935-1293, Enroll: 121, K-6th.
Alternative Ed. Lrng Ctr., 4218 Hooper ave., (323) 233-7386, Enroll: 342, K-12th.
Ascension Elem., 500 W. 111th Pl., (323) 756-4064, Enroll: 194, K-8th.
Assumption Elem., 3016 Winter St., (323) 269-4319, Enroll: 194, K-8th.
Bais Chaya Mushka Chabad, 9017 W. Pico Blvd., (310) 859-8840, Enroll: 232, K-12th.
Bais Yaakov Sch. for Girls, 461 N. La Brea Ave., (323) 938-3231, Enroll: 235, 9th-12th.
Berkeley Hall, 16000 Mulholland Dr., (310) 476-6421, Enroll: 209, K-9th.
Bishop Conaty-Our Lady of Loretto, 2900 W. Pico Blvd., (323) 737-0012, Enroll: 445, 9th-12th.
Bishop Mora Salesian High, 960 S. Soto St., (323) 261-7124, Enroll: 405, 9th-12th.

154 PRIVATE SCHOOLS

Brentwood, 100 S. Barrington Pl., (310) 476-9633, Enroll: 961, K-12th.
California Tech. University, 1717-1/2 W. Century Blvd., (323) 777-6656, Enroll: 221, K-12th.
Cathedral Chapel Elem., 755 S. Cochran Ave., (323) 938-9976, Enroll: 281, K-8th.
Cathedral High, 1253 Bishops Rd., (232) 225-2438, Enroll: 533, 9th-12th.
Cecil L. Murray Ed. Ctr., 2400 S. Western Ave., (213) 730-2535, Enroll: 165, K-8th.
Cheder Menachem, 7215 Waring Ave., (323) 965-1772, Enroll: 185, K-8th.
Cheder of Los Angeles, 348 N. La Brea, (323) 935-9724, Enroll: 130, K-8th.
Christ the King Elem., 617 N. Arden Blvd., (323) 462-4753, Enroll: 240, K-8th.
Communion Christian Acad., 4729 W. Slauson Ave., (323) 290-0022, Enroll: 146, K-6th.
Community Pre-School, 650 E. 135th St., (310) 538-1387, Enroll: 100, K-4th.
Creative Lrng. Ctr., 1729 W. Martin Luther King Blvd., (323) 294-1444 Enroll: 143, K-6th.
Culver Christian, 11312 Washington Blvd., (310) 391-6963, Enroll: 162, K-6th.
Culver City Adventist, 11828 W. Washington Blvd., (310) 398-3305, Enroll: 140, K-8th.
Curtis Sch. Foundation, 15871 Mulholland Dr., (310) 476-1251, Enroll: 511, K-8th.
Daniel Murphy High, 241 S. Detroit St., (323) 935-1161, Enroll: 368, 9th-12th.
Divine Saviour Elem., 624 Cypress Ave., (323) 222-6077, Enroll: 276, K-8th.
Dolores Mission, 170 S. Gless St., (323) 881-0001, Enroll: 230, K-8th.
E. Los Angeles Light & Life Christian, 207 Dacotah St., (323) 269-5236, Enroll: 143, K-8th.
Escuela de Montessori, 8820 Sepulveda Eastway, (310) 645-4775, Enroll: 121, K-6th.
First Church of God Christian, 2941 W. 70th, (323) 753-7541, Enroll: 440, K-8th.
First Luthern Elem., 3119 Sixth St., (213) 380-6023, Enroll: 158, K-6th.

Fountain Day Sch., 1128 N. Orange Grove Ave., (323) 654-8958, Enroll: 158, K-5th.
Frederick K.C. Price III Elem.-Secondary, 7901 S. Vermont Ave., (323) 758-3777, Enroll: 216, K-12th.
Golden Day Schools, 4508 Crenshaw Blvd., (323) 296-6280, Enroll: 138, K-12th.
Harvard-Westlake, 700 N. Faring Rd., (310) 274-7281, Enroll: 740, 7th-9th.
Holy Angel Montessori, 3339 W. Temple St., (323) 669-0948, Enroll: 126, K-6th.
Holy Name of Jesus Catholic Elem., 1955 W. Jefferson Blvd., (323) 731-2255, Enroll: 306, K-8th.
Holy Spirit Elem., 1418 S. Burnside Ave., (323) 933-7775, Enroll: 153, K-4th.
Holy Trinity Elem., 3716 Boyce Ave., (323) 663-2064, Enroll: 275, 1st-8th.
Immaculate Conception Elem., 830 Green Ave., (213) 382-5931, Enroll: 311, K-8th.
Immaculate Heart High, 5515 Franklin Ave., (323) 461-3651, Enroll: 727, 6th-12th.
Immaculate Heart of Mary Elem., 1055 N. Alexandria Ave., (323) 663-4611, Enroll: 326, K-8th.
John Thomas Dye Elem., 11414 Chalon Rd., (310) 476-2811, Enroll: 305, K-6th.
Le Lycee Francais de Los Angeles, 10631 Pico Blvd., (310) 553-7444, Enroll: 183, K-1st.
Le Lycee Francais de Los Angeles, 3261 Overland Ave., (310) 836-3464, Enroll: 904, 2nd-12th.
Leon Garr Learning Inst., 5101 S. Western Ave., (323) 295-1399, Enroll: 106, K-5th.
Little Citizens Westside Acad., 4256 S. Western Ave., (323) 293-9775, Enroll: 126, lst-8h.
Los Angeles Adventist Acad., 846 E. El Segundo Blvd., (323) 321-2585, Enroll: 294, K-12th.
Los Angeles Christian, 1620 W. 20th St., (323) 735-2867, Enroll: 149, K-8th.
Loyola High, 1901 Venice Blvd., (213) 381-5121, Enroll: 1,173, 9th-12th.
Lycee Int'l De Los Angeles, 4155 Russell Ave., (323) 665-4526, Enroll: 308, K-12th.

PRIVATE SCHOOLS 155

Maimonides Acad., 310 N. Huntley Dr., (310) 659-2456, Enroll: 313, K-8th.
Marcus Garvey, 2916 W. Slauson Ave., (323) 291-9790, Enroll: 226, K-12th.
Marlborough, 250 S. Rossmore Ave., (323) 935-1147, Enroll: 525, 7th-12th.
Marymount High, 10643 Sunset Blvd., (310) 472-1205, Enroll: 379, 9th-12th.
Mid-Wilshire Christian, 221 S. Juanita Ave., (213) 389-1035, Enroll: 144, K-6th.
Milken Comm. HS of Stephen S. Wise Temple, 15500 Steven S. Wise Dr., (310) 889-2206, Enroll: 1,488, K-12th.
Miracle Baptist Christian, 8300 S. Central Ave., (323) 582-3898, Enroll: 303, K-8th.
Mirman Sch. for Gifted Children, 16180 Mulholland Dr., (310) 476-2868, Enroll: 351, Ungraded.
Montecito Park Baptist, 333 E. Ave. 43, (323) 222-2310, Enroll: 102, K-12th.
Mother of Sorrows, 100 West 87th Pl., (323) 758-6204, Enroll: 199, K-8th.
Mt. Calvary Christian, 3770 Santa Rosalia Dr. (323) 295-2675, Enroll: 163, K-6th.
Nativity Elem., 943 W. 57th St., (323) 752-0720, Enroll: 317, K-8th.
New Life Acad., 3202 W. Adams Blvd., (323) 731-1224, Enroll: 208, K-8th.
Normandie Christian of Los Angeles, 6306 S. Normandie Ave., (323) 752-3122, Enroll: 157, K-6th.
Notre Dame Acad., 2911 Overland Ave., (310) 287-3895, Enroll: 310, K-8th.
Notre Dame Acad. Girls' High, 2851 Overland Ave., (310) 839-5289, Enroll: 477, 9th-12th.
Oaks, 6817 Franklin Ave., (323) 850-3755, Enroll: 145, K-6th.
Operation Fresh Start Learning Ctr., 4218 Hooper Ave., (323) 233-2713, Enroll: 263, K-12th
Optimist High, 6957 N. Figueroa St., (323) 344-4250, Enroll: 180, 7th-12th.
Our Lady Help of Christians Elem., 2024 E. Darwin Ave., (323) 222-3912, Enroll: 288, K-8th.
Our Lady of Guadalupe Elem., 436 N. Hazard Ave., (323) 269-4998, Enroll: 272, K-8th.
Our Lady of Guadalupe-Rosehill, 4522 Browne Ave., (323) 221-8187, Enroll: 277, K-8th.
Our Lady of Loretto Elem., 258 N. Union Ave., (213) 483-5251, Enroll: 347, K-8th.
Our Lady of Lourdes, 315 S. Eastman Ave., (323) 526-3813, Enroll: 282, K-8th.
Our Lady of Soledad Elem., 4545 Dozier St., (323) 261-1083, Enroll: 240, K-8th.
Our Lady of the Rosary of Talpa, 411 S. Evergreen Ave., (323) 261-0583, Enroll: 283, K-8th.
Our Mother of Good Counsel, 4622 Ambrose Ave., (323) 664-2131, Enroll: 309, K-8th.
Pacific Christian High, 625 Coleman Ave., (323) 254-7161, Enroll: 133, 5th-12th.
Pacific Hills, 8628 Holloway Dr., (310) 276-3068, Enroll: 275, 6th-12th.
Page Private-Hancock Park Campus, 565 N. Larchmont Blvd., (323) 463-5118, Enroll: 253, K-8th.
Perutz Etz Jacob Hebrew Acad., 7951 Beverly Blvd., (323) 655-5766, Enroll: 144, K-8th.
Pilgrim, 540 S. Commonwealth Ave., (213) 385-7351, Enroll: 340, K-12th.
Precious Blood Elem., 307 S. Occidental Blvd., (213) 382-3345, Enroll: 236, K-8th.
Rabbi Jacob Pressman Acad. of Temple Betham, 1039 S. La Cienega Blvd., (310) 652-2002, Enroll: 318, K-8th.
Redeemer Alt., 900 E. Rosecrans Ave., (310) 639-8983, Enroll: 152, K-7th.
Redeemer Baptist Elem., 10792 National Blvd., (310) 475-4598, Enroll: 162, K-6th.
Resurrection Elem., 3360 Opal St., (323) 261-5750, Enroll: 244, K-8th.
Ribet Acad., 2911 San Fernando Rd., (323) 344-4330, Enroll: 577, K-12th.
Sacred Heart Elem., 2109 Sichel St., (323) 225-4177, Enroll: 323, K-8th.
Sacred Heart High, 2111 Griffin Ave., (323) 225-2209, Enroll: 362, 9th-12th.
Samuel A. Fryer Yavneh Hebrew Acad., 5353 W. 3rd St., (323) 931-5808, Enroll: 322, K-8th.
San Antonio de Padua Elem., 1500 E. Bridge St., (323) 221-6970, Enroll: 259, K-8th.
San Miguel Elem., 2270 E. 108th St., (323) 567-6892, Enroll: 298, K-8th.

156 PRIVATE SCHOOLS

Santa Isabel, 2424 Whittier Blvd., (323) 263-3716, Enroll: 298, K-8th.
Santa Teresita Elem., 2646 Zonal Ave., (323) 221-1129, Enroll: 305, K-8th.
Shalhevet High, 910 S. Fairfax Ave., (323) 930-9333, Enroll: 200, 9th-12th.
Sinai Akiba Acad., 10400 Wilshire Blvd., (310) 475-6401, Enroll: 534, K-8th.
St. Agnes Elem., 1428 W. Adams Blvd., (323) 734-6441, Enroll: 330, K-8th.
St. Aloysius Elem., 2023 E. Nadeau St., (323) 582-4965, Enroll: 268, K-8th.
St. Alphonsus Elem., 552 S. Amalia Ave., (323) 268-5165, Enroll: 273, K-8th.
St. Anastasia Elem., 8631 S. Stanmoor Dr., (310) 645-8816, Enroll: 303, K-8th.
St. Anselm Elem., 7019 S. Van Ness Ave., (323) 759-9371, Enroll: 270, K-8th.
St. Bernadette Elem., 4196 Marlton Ave., (323) 291-4284, Enroll: 265, K-8th.
St. Bernard Elem., 3254 Verdugo Rd., (323) 256-4989, Enroll: 274, K-8th.
St. Brendan Catholic Elem., 238 S. Manhattan Pl., (213) 382-7401, Enroll: 312, K-8th .
St. Casimir Elem., 2714 St. George St., (323) 661-9200, Enroll: 271, 1st-8th.
St. Cecilia Elem., 4224 S. Normandie Ave., (323) 293-4266, Enroll: 305, K-8th.
St. Columbkille's Elem., 131 W. 64th St., (323) 758-2284, Enroll: 255, K-7th.
St. Dominic Elem., 2005 Merton Ave., (323) 255-5803, Enroll: 511, K-8th.
St. Eugene Elem., 9521 S. Haas Ave., (323) 754-9536, Enroll: 300, K-8th.
St. Frances X. Cabrini, 1428 W. Imperial Hwy., (323) 756-1354, Enroll: 291, K-8th.
St. Francis of Assisi Elem., 1550 Maltman Ave., (323) 665-3601, Enroll: 263, K-8th.
St. Gerard Majella, 4451 Inglewood Blvd., (310) 397-9489, Enroll: 276, K-8th.
St. Gregory Nazianzen Elem., 911 S. Norton Ave., (323) 936-2542, Enroll: 279, 1st-8th.
St. Ignatius of Loyola Elem., 6025 Monte Vista St., (323) 255-6456, Enroll: 312, K-8th.
St. James Wilshire Elem., 625 S. St. Andrews Pl., (213) 382-2315, Enroll: 305, K-6th.
St. Jerome Elem., 5580 Thornburn St., (310) 670-1678, Enroll: 312, K-8th.
St. Joan of Arc Elem., 11561 Gateway Blvd., (310) 479-3607, Enroll: 214, 1st-8th.
St. John the Evangelist Elem., 6028 S. Victoria Ave., (323) 751-8545, Enroll: 271, K-8th.
St. Lawrence of Brindisi Elem., 10044 Compton Ave., (323) 564-3051, Enroll: 298, K-8th.
St. Malachy Catholic Elem., 1200 E. 81st St., (323) 582-3112, Enroll: 235, K-8th.
St. Martin of Tours Elem., 11955 Sunset Blvd., (310) 472-7419, Enroll: 266, K-8th.
St. Mary Catholic Elem., 416 S. St. Louis St., (323) 262-3395, Enroll: 312, K-8th.
St. Mary Magdalen Elem., 1223 Corning St., (310) 652-4723, Enroll: 120, 5th-8th.
St. Michael's Elem., 1027 W. 87th St., (323) 752-6101, Enroll: 261, K-8th.
St. Odilia Elem., 5300 S. Hooper Ave., (323) 232-5449, Enroll: 218, K-6th.
St. Paul the Apostle, 1536 Selby Ave., (310) 474-1588, Enroll: 537, K-8th.
St. Paul's Elem., 1908 S. Bronson Ave., (323) 734-4022, Enroll: 287, 1st-8th.
St. Raphael Elem., 924 W. 70th St., (323) 751-2774, Enroll: 285, K-8th.
St. Teresa of Avila Elem., 2215 Fargo St., (323) 662-3777, Enroll: 306, K-8th.
St. Thomas the Apostle Elem., 2632 W. 15th St., (323) 737-4730, Enroll: 319, K-8th.
St. Timothy Elem., 10479 W. Pico Blvd., (310) 474-1811, Enroll: 210, K-8th.
St. Turibius Elem., 1524 Essex St., (213) 749-8894, Enroll: 282, K-8th.
St. Vincent Elem., 2333 S. Figueroa St., (213) 748-5367, Enroll: 307, K-8th.
Star Christian, 2120 Estrella Ave., (213) 746-6900, Enroll: 185, K-6th.
Sycamore Grove Elem., 4900 N. Figueroa St., (323) 255-6550, Enroll: 118, K-8th.
T.C.A. Arshag Dickranian Armenian, 1200 N. Cahuenga Blvd., (323) 461-4377, Enroll: 324, K-12th.
Temple Israel of Hollywood Day, 7300 Hollywood Blvd., (323) 876-8330, Enroll: 140, K-6th.
Torat-Hayim Hebrew Acad., 1210 La Cienega Blvd., (310) 652-8349, Enroll: 200, K-8th.

Transfiguration Elem., 4020 Roxton Ave., (323) 292-3011, Enroll: 280, K-8th.
Turningpoint, 1300 N. Sepulveda Blvd., (310) 476-8585, Enroll: 164, K-6th.
United World Int'l Lrng. Ctr., 5125 Crenshaw Blvd., (323) 293-6127, Enroll: 180, K-9th.
Verbum Dei High, 11100 S. Central Ave., (323) 564-6651, Enroll: 180, 9th-12th.
Vista, 3200 Motor Ave., (310) 836-1223, Enroll: 118, K-12th.
Victory Baptist Day Elem., 892 E. 48th St., (323) 231-2424, Enroll: 137, K-8th.
Visitation Elem., 8740 S. Emerson Ave., (310) 645-6620, Enroll: 284, K-8th.
West Angeles Christian Acad., 3010 S. Crenshaw Blvd., (323) 731-2567, Enroll: 219, K-8th.
Westchester Lutheran, 7831 S. Sepulveda Blvd., (310) 670-5422, Enroll: 455, K-8th.
West Los Angeles Baptist, 1609 S. Barrington Ave., (310) 826-2050 Enroll: 104, 7th-12th.
Westland, 16200 Mulholland Dr., (310) 472-5544, Enroll: 129, K-6th.
Westminster Acad., 1495 Colorado Blvd., (323) 257-7576, Enroll: 226, K-8th.
White Mem. Adventist Elem., 1605 New Jersey St., (323) 268-7159, Enroll: 273, K-8th.
Wildwood Elem., 12201 Washington Pl., (310) 397-3134, Enroll: 284, K-6th.
Wilshire Elem., 4900 Wilshire Blvd., (323) 939-3800, Enroll: 161, K-6th.
Windward, 11350 Palms Blvd., (310) 391-7127, Enroll: 419, 7th-12th.
Woodcrest Nazarene Christian, 10936 S. Normandie Ave., (323) 754-4933, Enroll: 229, K-6th.
Yeshiva Gedolah, 5822 W. 3rd St., (323) 938-2071, Enroll: 105, 9th-12th.
Yeshiva Rav Isacsohn-Torah Emeth, 540 N. La Brea Ave., (323) 549-3180, Enroll: 938, K-8th.
Yeshiva University High, 9760 W. Pico Blvd., (310) 772-2480, Enroll: 332, 9th-12th.

Lynwood
St. Emydius Elem., 10990 California Ave., (310) 635-7184, Enroll: 563, K-8th.

St. Philip Neri, 12522 Stoneacre Ave., (310) 638-0341, Enroll: 315, K-8th.

Malibu
Our Lady of Malibu Elem., 3625 S. Winter Cyn. Rd., (310) 456-8071, Enroll: 207, K-8th.

Manhattan Beach
American Martyrs, 1701 Laurel Ave., (310) 545-8559, Enroll: 459, K-8th.
Community Baptist Christian Acad., 1243 Artesia Blvd., (310) 374-3118, Enroll: 215, K-8th.

Maywood
St. Rose of Lima, 4422 E. 60th St., (323) 560-3376, Enroll: 265, K-8th.

Mission Hills
Bishop Alemany High, 15101 San Fernando Mission Blvd., (818) 365-3925, Enroll: 1,534, 9th-12th.

Monrovia
Excellence in Ed. Acad., 527 Franklin Pl., (626) 357-4443, Enroll: 308, K-12th.
First Lutheran Elem., 1323 S. Magnolia, (626) 357-3596, Enroll: 146, K-8th.
Immaculate Conception Elem., 726 S. Shamrock Ave., (626) 358-5129, Enroll: 263, K-8th.

Montebello
Cantwell Sacred Heart of Mary High, 329 N. Garfield Ave., (323) 887-2066, Enroll: 437, 9th-12th.
Montebello Christian, 136 S. Seventh St., (323) 728-4119, Enroll: 285, K-8th.
Our Lady of the Miraculous Medal, 840 N. Garfield Ave., (323) 728-5435, Enroll: 594, K-8th.
St. Benedict Elem., 217 N. Tenth St., (323) 721-3348, Enroll: 557, K-8th.

Monterey Park
Belmont College Prep., 113 Avondale Ave., (626) 307-2219, Enroll: 107, 9th-12th.
New Ave. Ed. Ctr., 126 N. New Ave., (626) 280-5536, Enroll: 402, K-8th.
St. Stephen Martyr, 119 S. Ramona Ave., (626) 573-1716, Enroll: 438, 1st-8th.
St. Thomas Aquinas, 1501 S. Atlantic Blvd., (323) 261-6583, Enroll: 249, K-8th.

North Hills
Holy Martyrs Armenian Elem., 16617 Parthenia Ave., (818) 892-7991, Enroll: 202, K-4th.

158 PRIVATE SCHOOLS

Los Angeles Baptist High, 9825 Woodley Ave., (818) 894-5742, Enroll: 907, 7th-12th.
Our Lady of Peace, 9022 Langdon Ave., (818) 894-4059, Enroll: 289, K-8th.
Valley Presbyterian Elem., 9240 Haskell Ave., (818) 894-3674, Enroll: 377, K-6th.

North Hollywood

Adat Ari El Day Elem., 12020 Burbank Blvd., (818) 766-4992, Enroll: 293, K-6th.
Campbell Hall, 4533 Laurel Cyn. Blvd, (818) 980-7280, Enroll: 902, K-12th.
Country, 5243 Laurel Canyon Blvd., (818) 769-2473, Enroll: 172, K-6th.
Harvard-Westlake, 3700 Coldwater Cyn. Ave., (818) 980-6692, Enroll: 809, 10th-12th.
Laurel Hall, 11919 Oxnard St., (818) 763-5434, Enroll: 563, K-8th.
Oakwood Elem., 11230 Moorpark St., (818) 752-4444, Enroll: 283, K-6th.
Oakwood Secondary, 11600 Magnolia Blvd., (818) 752-4400, Enroll: 462, 7th-12th.
St. Charles Borromeo, 10850 Moorpark St., (818) 508-5359, Enroll: 298, K-8th.
St. Jane Frances de Chantal, 12950 Hamlin St., (818) 766-1714, Enroll: 300, K-8th .
St. Patrick's Elem., 10626 Erwin St., (818) 761-7363, Enroll: 306, K-8th.
St. Paul's First Lutheran, 1330 McCormick St., (818) 763-2892, Enroll: 178, K-8th.
Valley Torah High, 12003 Riverside Dr., (818) 984-1805, Enroll: 242, 9th-12th.
Wesley, 4382 Tujunga Ave., (818) 508-4542 Enroll: 129, K-8th.

Northridge

Abraham Joshua Heschel Day, 17701 Devonshire St., (818) 368-5781, Enroll: 458, K-8th.
Abraham Joshua Heschel Day Sch., 29646 Agoura Rd., (818) 707-2365, Enroll: 163, K-6th.
Casa Montessori, 17633 Lassen St., (818) 886-7922, Enroll: 126, K-6th.
First Lutheran Elem.-Middle, 18355 Roscoe Blvd., (818) 885-1655, Enroll: 172, K-8th.
First Presbyterian Church of Granada Hills, 10400 Zelzah Ave., (818) 368-7254, Enroll: 192, K-5th.

Highland Hall, 17100 Superior St., (818) 349-1394, Enroll: 335, K-12th.
Our Lady of Lourdes, 18437 Superior St., (818) 349-0245, Enroll: 317, K-8th.
Pinecrest Elem., 17081 Devonshire St., (818) 368-7241, Enroll: 521, K-6th.
San Fernando Valley Acad., 17601 Lassen St., (818) 349-1373, Enroll: 201, K-12th.
St. Nicholas, 9501 Balboa Blvd., (818) 886-6751, Enroll: 315, K-8th.
Trinity Christian, 20040 Parthenia, (818) 998-5797, Enroll: 145, K-6th.

Norwalk

Baptist Christian Schools, 12226 Alondra Blvd., (562) 926-5541, Enroll: 117, K-6th.
Brethren Elem., 11005 Foster Rd., (562) 863-6282, Enroll: 272, K-6th.
Nazarene Christian Elem., 15014 Studebaker Rd., (562) 863-1738, Enroll: 210, K-8th.
New Harvest Christian, 11364 E. Imperial Hwy., (562) 929-0774, Enroll: 206, K-12th.
Norwalk Christian, 11129 Pioneer Blvd., (562) 863-5751, Enroll: 150, K-8th.
Pioneer Baptist Elem., 11717 Pioneer Blvd., (562) 863-5817, Enroll: 152, K-12th.
St. John of God Elem., 13817 S. Pioneer Blvd., (562) 863-5721, Enroll: 303, K-8th.
St. Linus Elem., 13913 Shoemaker Ave., (562) 921-0336, Enroll: 311, K-8th.
Trinity Christian, 11507 Studebaker Rd., (562) 864-3712, Enroll: 257, K-8th.

Pacific Palisades

Archer Sch. for Girls, 11725 Sunset Blvd., (310) 873-700, Enroll: 219, 6th-12th.
Calvary Christian, 701 Palisades Dr., (310) 573-0082, Enroll: 336, K-8th.
Corpus Christi Elem., 890 Toyopa Dr., (310) 454-9411, Enroll: 314, K-8th.
St. Matthew's Parish, 1031 Bienveneda Ave., (310) 454-1350, Enroll: 275, K-8th.
Village, 780 Swarthmore Ave., (310) 459-8411, Enroll: 266, K-6th.

Pacoima

Guardian Angel Elem., 10919 Norris Ave., (818) 896-1113, Enroll: 249, K-8th.

Mary Immaculate Elem., 10390 Remick Ave., (818) 834-8551, Enroll: 281, K-8th.
Panorama Baptist Elem., 8755 Woodman Ave., (818) 892-8700, Enroll: 255, K-6th.

Palmdale
Pinecrest, 2320 E. Avenue R, (661) 265-0045, Enroll: 130, K-6th.
St. Mary Elem. Catholic, 1600 E. Ave. R-4, (661) 273-5555, Enroll 333, K-8th.
Westside Christian, 40027 N. 11th St. West, (661) 947-4452, Enroll: 252, K-8th.

Palos Verdes Estates
Int'l Bilingual-Los Angeles, 300 Paseo Del Mar, No. B, (310) 373-0430, Enroll: 105, K-9th.
Rolling Hills Prep., 300 Paseo Del Mar, No. A, (310) 791-1101, Enroll: 224, 6th-12th.

Palos Verdes Peninsula
Chadwick, 26800 S. Academy Dr., (310) 377-1543, Enroll: 725, K-12th.

Panorama City
St. Genevieve Elem., 14024 Community St., (818) 892-3802, Enroll: 662, K-8th.
St. Genevieve High, 13967 Roscoe Blvd., (818) 894-6417, Enroll: 370, 9th-12th.

Paramount
Our Lady of the Rosary Elem., 14813 S. Paramount Blvd., (562) 633-6360, Enroll: 310, K-8th.

Pasadena
Assumption of the Blessed Virgin Mary, 2660 E. Orange Grove Blvd., (626) 793-2089, Enroll: 298, K-8th.
Chandler Elem., 1005 Armada Dr., (626) 795-9314, Enroll: 423, K-8th.
High Point Acad., 1720 Kinneloa Cyn. Rd., (626) 798-8989, Enroll: 350, K-8th.
La Salle High, 3880 E. Sierra Madre Blvd., (626) 351-8951, Enroll: 759, 9th-12th.
Living Way Christian Acad., 2495 E. Mountain St., (626) 791-7295, Enroll: 144, K-8th.
Mayfield Jr. Sch. of the Holy Child Jesus, 405 S. Euclid Ave., (626) 796-2774, Enroll: 425, K-8th.
Mayfield Sr. Sch. of the Holy Child Jesus, 500 Bellefontaine St., (626) 799-9121, Enroll: 258, 9th-12th.
New Horizon, 651N Orange Grove Blvd., (626) 795-5186, Enroll: 189, K-8th.
Pasadena Christian, 1515 N. Los Robles, (626) 791-1214, Enroll: 536, K-8th.
Pasadena Towne & Country Elem., 200 S. Sierra Madre Blvd., (626) 795-0658, Enroll: 277, K-8th.
Polytechnic, 1030 E. California Blvd., (626) 792-2147, Enroll: 819, K-12th.
San Marino Montessori, 444 S. Sierra Madre Blvd., (626) 577-8007 Enroll: 105, K-6th.
Sequoyah Elem., 535 S. Pasadena Ave., (626) 795-4351, Enroll: 170, Un-graded.
St. Andrew Elem., 42 Chestnut St., (626) 796-7697, Enroll: 293, K-8th.
St. Gregory Armenian Sch., 2215 E. Colorado Blvd., (626) 578-1343, Enroll: 177, K-8th.
St. Philip the Apostle, 161 S. Hill Ave., (626) 795-9691, Enroll: 414, K-8th.
Walden School of Pasadena, 74 S. San Gabriel Blvd., (626) 792-6166, Enroll: 190, K-6th.
Waverly, 67 W. Bellview, (626) 792-5940, Enroll: 172, K-6th.
Westridge, 324 Madeline Dr., (626) 799-1153, Enroll: 475, 4th-12th.

Pico Rivera
Armenian Mesrobian, 8420 Beverly Rd., (323) 723-3181, Enroll: 259, K-12th.
St. Hilary Elem., 5401 S. Citronell Ave., (562) 942-7361, Enroll: 372, K-8th.
St. Marianne de Paredes Elem., 7911 Buhman St., (562) 949-1234, Enroll: 293, K-8th.

Playa Del Rey
St. Bernard High, 9100 Falmouth Ave., (310) 823-4651, Enroll: 639, 9th-12th.

Pomona
Arrow Hwy. Christian Elem., 305 E. Arrow Hwy., (909) 624-1455, Enroll: 137, K-8th.
City of Knowledge, 3285 N. Garey Ave., (909) 392-0251 Enroll: 166, K-12th.
First Baptist Elem., 521 N. Garey, (909) 622-1053, Enroll: 231, K-8th.
Oak Tree Day, 456 W. Orange Grove, (909) 623-5164, Enroll: 143, K-8th.
Pomona Catholic Girls' High, 533 W. Holt Ave., (909) 623-5297, Enroll: 323, 9th-12th.

160 PRIVATE SCHOOLS

St. Joseph Elem., 1200 W. Holt Ave., (909) 622-3365, Enroll: 324, K-8th.
St. Madeleine Elem., 935 E. Kingsley Ave., (909) 623-9602, Enroll: 292, K-8th.

Rancho Palos Verdes
Christ Lutheran Elem., 28850 S. Western Ave., (310) 831-0848, Enroll: 420, K-8th.
Peninsula Montessori Elem., 28915 Northbay Rd., (310) 544-3099, Enroll: 188, K-5th.
St. John Fisher Elem., 5446 Crest Rd., (310) 377-2800, Enroll: 273, K-8th.

Redondo Beach
Carden Dominion, 320 Knob Hill, (310) 316-4471, Enroll: 134, K-6th.
Coast Christian Schools, 525 Earl Lane, (310) 370-5847, Enroll: 339, K-12th.
Riviera Hall Lutheran, 330 Palos Verdes Blvd., (310) 375-5528, Enroll: 214, K-8th.
South Bay Faith Acad., 101 S. Pacific Coast Hwy., (310) 379-8242, Enroll: 266, K-12th.
St. Lawrence Martyr Elem., 1950 S. Prospect Ave., (310) 316-3049, Enroll: 309, K-8th.

Reseda
First Baptist Church of Reseda, 18644 Sherman Way, (818) 881-9828, Enroll: 190, K-6th.
Kirk o' the Valley, 19620 Vanowen, (818) 344-1242, Enroll: 135, K-5th.
New Horizon Christian, 8055 Reseda Blvd., (818) 885-8202, Enroll: 103, K-6th.
St. Catherine of Siena, 18125 Sherman Way, (818) 343-9880, Enroll 312, K-8th.

Rolling Hills Estates
Nishiyamato Acad. of California, 3011 Palos Verdes Dr. North, (310) 544-6880, Enroll: 138, K-9th.
Rolling Hills Country Day Elem., 26444 Crenshaw Blvd., (310) 377-4848, Enroll: 387, K-8th.

Rosemead
Don Bosco Tech. Inst., 1151 San Gabriel Blvd., (626) 940-2000, Enroll: 882, 9th-12th.

San Dimas
Holy Name of Mary, 124 S. San Dimas Cyn. Rd., (909) 599-1243, Enroll: 311, K-8th.

Sonrise Christian, 1400 W. Covina Blvd., (909) 599-5958, Enroll: 125, K-5th

San Fernando
Calvary Baptist Christian, 12928 Vaughn St., (818) 899-8206, Enroll: 150, K-10th.
First Lutheran, 777 N. Maclay Ave., (818) 361-4800, Enroll: 171, K-6th.
Santa Rosa De Lima, 1309 Mott St., (818) 361-5096, Enroll: 274, K-8th.
St. Ferdinand Elem., 1012 Coronel St., (818) 361-3264, Enroll: 310, K-8th.

San Gabriel
Clairbourn, 8400 Huntington Dr., (626) 286-3108, Enroll: 364, K-8th.
San Gabriel Acad., 8827 E. Broadway, (626) 292-1156, Enroll: 643, K-12th.
San Gabriel Christian Elem., 117 N. Pine St., (626) 287-0486, Enroll: 658, K-8th.
San Gabriel Mission Elem., 416 S. Mission Dr., (626) 281-2454, Enroll: 274, K-8th.
San Gabriel Mission High, 254 S. Santa Anita St., (626) 282-3181, Enroll: 344, 9th-12th.
St. Anthony Elem., 1905 S. San Gabriel Blvd., (626) 280-7255, Enroll: 591, K-8th.

San Marino
Southwestern Acad., 2800 Monterey Rd., (626) 799-5010, Enroll: 163, 1st-12th.
Sts. Felicitas and Perpetua, 2955 Huntington Dr., (626) 796-8223, Enroll: 297, K-8th.

San Pedro
Holy Trinity Elem., 1226 W. Santa Cruz St., (310) 833-0703, Enroll: 601, K-8th.
Mary Star of the Sea-Elem., 717 S. Cabrillo Ave., (310) 831-0875, Enroll: 300, K-8th.
Mary Star of the Sea-High, 810 W. 8th St., (310) 547-1138, Enroll: 440, 9th-12th.
St. Peter's Episcopal Day, 1648 W. Ninth St., (310) 833-7355, Enroll: 144, K-6th.

Santa Clarita
Advantage Prep. Schools, 22589 W. Hickory Pl., (661) 296-5466, Enroll: 247, K-12th.
Cornerstone Christian, 27945 Oakgale, (661) 251-9732, Enroll: 257, K-12th.

Our Lady of Perpetual Help Elem., 23225 W. Lyons Ave., (661) 259-1141, Enroll: 324, K-8th.

Santa Fe Springs
Santa Fe Springs Christian, 11457 E. Florence Ave., (562) 868-2263, Enroll: 248, K-8th.
St. Paul High, 9635 S. Greenleaf Ave., (562) 698-6246, Enroll: 913, 9th-12th.
St. Pius X Elem., 10855 S. Pioneer Blvd., (562) 864-4818, Enroll: 302, K-8th.

Santa Monica
Carlthorp, 438 San Vicente Blvd., (310) 451-1332, Enroll: 281, K-6th.
Crossroads, 1714 21st St., (310) 829-7391, Enroll: 1,121, K-12th.
Lighthouse, 1220 20th St., (310) 829-1741, Enroll: 196, K-12th.
New Roads, 3131 Olympic Blvd., (310) 828-5582, Enroll: 149, 9th-12th.
Pilgrim Lutheran Elem., 1730 Wilshire Blvd., (310) 829-2239, Enroll: 146, K-8th.
Pluralistic, 1454 Euclid St., (310) 394-1313, Enroll: 165, Ungraded.
Santa Monica Montessori, 1909 Colorado Ave., (310) 829-3551, Enroll: 114, K-8th.
St. Anne Elem., 2015 Colorado Ave., (310) 829-2775, Enroll: 174, K-8th.
St. Monica Elem., 1039 Seventh St., (310) 451-9801, Enroll: 295, K-8th.
St. Monica High, 1030 Lincoln Blvd., (310) 394-3701, Enroll: 598, 9th-12th.
Westside Waldorf, 1229 4th St., (310) 576-0788, Enroll: 102, K-4th.

Saugus (Santa Clarita)
Canyon Oaks Ranch, 36491 Bouquet Canyon Rd., (661) 270-0209, Enroll: 178, 4th-12th.

Sherman Oaks
Buckley, 3900 Stansbury Ave., (818) 783-1610, Enroll: 692, K-12th.
C. & E. Merdinian Armenian Evang., 13330 Riverside Dr., (818) 907-8149, Enroll: 245, K-8th.
Emek Hebrew Acad., 15365 Magnolia Blvd., (818) 783-3663, Enroll: 511, K-8th.
New School for Child Development, 13130-50 Burbank Blvd., (818) 781-0360, Enroll: 411, K-12th.
Notre Dame High, 13645 Riverside Dr., (818) 501-2300, Enroll: 1,139, 9th-12th.

St. Francis de Sales, 13368 Valleyheart Dr., (818) 784-9573, Enroll: 314, K-8th.

Sierra Madre
Alverno High, 200 N. Michillinda Ave., (626) 355-3463, Enroll: 228, 9th-12th.
Bethany Christian Elem., 93 N. Baldwin, (626) 355-3527, Enroll: 271, K-8th.
Gooden Elem., 192 N. Baldwin Ave., (626) 355-2410, Enroll: 154, K-8th.
Marantha High, 160 N. Canon Ave., (626) 355-4242, Enroll: 490, 9th-12th.
St. Rita Elem., 322 N. Baldwin Ave., (626) 355-6114, Enroll: 299, K-8th.

So. Pasadena
Almansor Ctr., 1955 Fremont Ave., (323) 257-3006 Enroll: 128, K-12th.
Holy Family Catholic Elem. , 1301 Rollin St., (626) 799-4354, Enroll: 308, K-8th.

South El Monte
Epiphany, 10915 Michael Hunt Dr., (626) 442-6264, Enroll: 290, K-8th.

South Gate
Faith Christian Acad., 9605 State St., (323) 564-3976, Enroll: 124, K-12
Redeemer Lutheran, 2626 Liberty Blvd., (323) 588-0934, Enroll: 118, K-8th.
St. Helen Elem., 9329 Madison Ave., (323) 566-5491, Enroll: 338, K-8th.

Sun Valley
Grace Community, 13248 Roscoe Blvd., (818) 909-5611, Enroll: 289, K-9th.
Our Lady of the Holy Rosary, 7802 Vineland Ave., (818) 765-4897, Enroll: 327, K-8th.
Village Christian, 8930 Village Ave., (818) 767-8382, Enroll: 1,937, K-12th.

Sunland
Sunland Christian, 10489 Sunland Blvd., (818) 951-9652, Enroll: 415, K-12th.

Sylmar
First Lutheran High, 13361 Glenoaks Blvd., (818) 362-9223, Enroll: 173, 7th-12th.
Foothill Baptist Day, 13550 Herron St., (818) 367-8164, Enroll: 126, K-6th.
Hathaway, 8955 Gold Creek Rd., (818) 896-2474, Enroll: 109, K-12th.
Los Angeles Lutheran High, 13570 Eldridge Ave., (818) 362-5861, Enroll: 277, 7th-12th.
St. Didacus Elem., 14325 Astoria St., (818) 367-5886, Enroll: 308, K-8th.
Sylmar Light & Life Christian, 14019 Sayre St., (818) 362-9497, Enroll: 179, K-6th.

162 PRIVATE SCHOOLS

Tarzana
Woodcrest, 6043 Tampa Ave., (818) 345-3002, Enroll: 154, K-6th.

Temple City
First Lutheran Elem., 9123 E. Broadway, (626) 287-0968, Enroll: 121, K-8th.
St. Luke Elem., 5521 N. Cloverly Ave., (626) 291-5959, Enroll: 285, K-8th.
U.S. Arts Education Ctr., 9451 1/2 Las Tunas Dr., (626) 287-7204, Enroll: 114, K-12th.

Topanga
Calmont, 1717 Old Topanga Cyn. Rd., (310) 455-3725, Enroll: 125, K-8th.

Torrance
Ascension Lutheran Elem., 17910 S. Prairie, (310) 371-3531, Enroll: 217, K-8th.
Bishop Montgomery High, 5430 Torrance Blvd., (310) 540-2021, Enroll: 1,251, 9th-12th.
First Lutheran Christian Elem., 2900 Carson St., (310) 320-0117, Enroll: 423, K-8th.
Nativity Elem., 2371 W. Carson St., (310) 328-5387, Enroll: 290, K-8th.
South Bay Jr. Acad., 4400 Del Amo Blvd., (310) 370-6215, Enroll: 212, K-10th.
St. Catherine Laboure Elem., 3846 Redondo Beach Blvd., (310) 324-8732, Enroll: 561, K-8th.
St. James Elem., 4625 Garnet St., (310) 371-0416, Enroll: 309, K-8th .

Tujunga
Mekhitarist Armenian, 6470 Foothill Blvd., (818) 353-3003, Enroll: 248, K-9th
Our Lady of Lourdes, 7324 Apperson St., (818) 353-1106, Enroll: 273, K-8th.
Trinity Christian Schools, 7754 McCroarty St., (818) 352-7980, Enroll: 250, K-8th.

Valencia (Santa Clarita)
Pinecrest Sch.-Valencia, 25443 N. Orchard Village Rd., (661) 255-8080, Enroll: 213, K-6th.
Sunshine Acad., 23720 Wiley Canyon, (661) 254-6855, Enroll: 125, K-2nd.

Valinda
St. Martha's Elem., 440 N. Azusa Ave., (626) 964-1093, Enroll: 277, 1st-8th.

Van Nuys
Fairfield Elem., 16945 Sherman Way, (818) 996-4560, Enroll: 137, K-8th.
First Lutheran Elem., 6952 Van Nuys Blvd., (818) 786-3002, Enroll: 145, K-6th.
Grace Christian Acad., 6510 Peach Ave., (818) 786-3515, Enroll: 137, 1st-12th.
Laurence/2000, 6428 Woodman Ave., (818) 782-4001, Enroll: 220, K-6th.
Montclair College Prep., 8071 Sepulveda Blvd., (818) 787-5290, Enroll: 438, 6th-12th.
Pinecrest Elem., 14111 Sherman Way, (818) 988-5554, Enroll: 366, K-6th.
St. Bridget of Sweden, 7120 Whitaker Ave., (818) 785-4422, Enroll: 270, 1st-8th.
St. Elisabeth, 6635 Tobias Ave., (818) 779-1766, Enroll: 303, K-8th.
Valley Sch.-Indiv. Trng., 15700 Sherman Wy., (818) 786-4720, Enroll: 289, K-8th.

Venice
First Lutheran School of Venice, 815 Venice Blvd., (310) 823-9367, Enroll: 112, K-8th.
St. Mark Elem., 912 Coeur d'Alene Ave., (310) 821-6612, Enroll: 303, K-8th.

Walnut
Southlands Christian Schools, 1920 S. Brea Canyon Cutoff Rd., (909) 598-9733, Enroll: 845, K-12th.

W. Hollywood
Ctr. for Early Ed., 563 N. Alfred St., (323) 651-0707, Enroll: 371, K-6th.

W. Covina
Christ Lutheran Elem., 311 S. Citrus Ave., (626) 967-7531, Enroll: 276, K-8th.
Immanuel First Lutheran, 512 S. Valinda Ave., (626) 919-1072, Enroll: 201, K-8th.
South Hills Acad., 1600 E. Francisquito Ave., (626) 919-2000, Enroll: 614, K-8th.
St. Christopher Elem., 900 W. Christopher St., (626) 960-3079, Enroll: 297, K-8th.
W. Covina Christian Elem., 763 N. Sunset Ave., (626) 962-7089, Enroll: 528, K-8th.

West Hills
Chaminade College Prep., 7500 Chaminade Ave., (818) 347-8300, Enroll: 1,064, 6th-12th.

Shepherd of the Valley Lutheran Elem., 23838 Kittridge St., (818) 347-6784, Enroll: 179, K-6th.
West Valley Christian Church, 22944 Enadia Way, (818) 884-7245, Enroll: 134, K-5th.
West Valley Christian Church, 23834 Highlander Rd., (818) 884-4710, Enroll: 153, 6th-12th.

West Los Angeles
St. Sebastian Elem., 1430 Federal Ave., (310) 473-3337, Enroll: 243, K-8th.

Westchester
Westchester Neighborhood Elem., 5520 Arbor Vitae St., (310) 649-1959, Enroll: 208, K-8th.

Westlake Village
St. Jude the Apostle, 32036 W. Lindero Canyon Rd., (818) 889-9483, Enroll: 292, K-8th.

Whittier
Brethren Christian Schools, 8101 S. Vicki Dr., (562) 699-5913, Enroll: 118, K-6th.
Broadoaks Sch. of Whittier College, 13447 Philadelphia St., (562) 907-4250, Enroll: 167, K-6th.
Carden School of Whittier, 11537 Grovedale Dr., (562) 694-1879, Enroll: 401, K-8th.
Faith Lutheran Elem., 9920 S. Mills Ave., (562) 941-0245, Enroll: 153, K-8th.
Painter Ave. Christian, 4512 Workman Mill Rd., #C210, (562) 945-0073, Enroll: 148, K-12th.
Palm View Christian, 7106 Sorensen Ave., (562) 693-3746, Enroll: 171, K-8th.
Plymouth Christian Elem., 12058 Beverly Blvd., (562) 695-0745, Enroll: 119, K-6th.
Primanti Montessori School, 10947 S. Valley Home Ave., (562) 943-0246, Enroll: 116, K-8th.
St. Bruno Elem., 15700 Citrustree Rd., (562) 943-8812, Enroll: 322, K-8th.
St. Gregory the Great, 13925 Telegraph Rd., (562) 941-0750, Enroll: 319, K-8th.
St. Mary of the Assumption-Elem., 7218 S. Pickering Ave., (562) 698-0253, Enroll: 578, K-8th.
Trinity Lutheran Elem., 11716 E. Floral Dr., (562) 699-7431, Enroll: 194, K-8th.

Whittier Christian Elem., 6548 S. Newlin Ave., (562) 698-0527, Enroll: 305, K-6th.
Whittier Christian, 911700 Maybrook Ave., (562) 947-3757, Enroll: 519, K-6th.

Wilmington
Holy Family Elem., 1122 E. Robidoux St., (310) 518-1440, Enroll: 201, K-8th.
Pacific Harbor Christian, 1530 Wilmington Blvd., (310) 835-5665, Enroll: 206, K-8th.
Sts. Peter & Paul, 706 Bay View Ave., (310) 834-5574, Enroll: 281, K-8th.
Wilmington Christian, 24910 S. Avalon Blvd., (310) 834-1448, Enroll: 123, K-6th.

Woodland Hills
Castlemont-Encino Camps, 19722 Collier St., (818) 348-9070, Enroll: 336, K-6th.
Kadima Hebrew Acad., 5717 Rudnick Ave., (818) 346-0849, Enroll: 281, K-8th.
Louisville High, 22300 Mulholland Dr., (818) 346-8812, Enroll: 495, 9th-12th.
Lycee Int'l de Los Angeles, 5724 Oso Ave., (818) 883-1966, Enroll: 139, K-9th.
Pinecrest, 5975 Shoup Ave., (818) 348-4314, Enroll: 656, K-8th.
St. Bernardine of Siena Elem., 6061 Valley Circle Blvd., (818) 340-2130, Enroll: 327, K-8th.
St. Mel Elem., 20874 Ventura Blvd., (818) 340-1924, Enroll: 596, K-8th.
West Valley Hebrew Acad., 5724 Oso Ave., (818) 712-0365, Enroll: 164, K-8th.

BUY 10 OR MORE & SAVE!

If your order adds up to 10 or more, the price drops to $5.95 per book. You also save on shipping. Fill out form and send with check to: McCormack's Guides, P.O. Box 1728, Martinez, CA 94553. Or fax to (925) 228-7223.

Visa and MasterCard accepted on phone orders. **VISA** **MasterCard** **1-800-222-3602**

Next to title, write in number of copies ordered and total below:

No.	McCormack's Guide Title	Single	Bulk
___	Alameda County 2001	$13.95	$5.95
___	Contra Costa & Solano 2001	$13.95	$5.95
___	Los Angeles County 2001	$13.95	$5.95
___	Marin, Napa & Sonoma 2001	$13.95	$5.95
___	Orange County 2001	$13.95	$5.95
___	Riverside, San Bernardino 2001	$13.95	$5.95
___	Sacramento & Central Valley 2001	$13.95	$5.95
___	San Diego County 2001	$13.95	$5.95
___	San Francisco & San Mateo 2001	$13.95	$5.95
___	Santa Barbara, Ventura 2001	$13.95	$5.95
___	Santa Clara/Silicon Valley 2001	$13.95	$5.95

_____ Books @ $_____ (Price) = $_____

CA sales tax (8.25%) _____

Shipping* _____

Total Amount of Order: $_____

* For orders of 10 or more, shipping is 45 cents per book. For orders of fewer than 10, shipping is $4.50 for first book, $1.50 per book thereafter.

Paid by (circle one) Check/MC/Visa or Bill Us

Name _____

Company _____

Address _____

City _____ State ____ Zip _____

Phone: (____) _____ Fax: (____) _____

☐ **Check here to receive advertising information**

bookinfo@mccormacks.com • www.mccormacks.com

Chapter 5

LOS ANGELES COUNTY
City & Town Profiles

THE FOLLOWING PROFILES cover about 125 towns and cities. The profiles are far from the last word on these places but they will at least help you identify where you might like to settle. Realtors and chambers of commerce can provide more detailed information.

Many chambers scrape by on meager funds. When you call for information, offer to send in $10 for an information packet. It will make your request all the more agreeable. Some chambers charge $15 or more for their packets.

City halls, particularly planning departments, can provide information on zoning and upcoming construction. Often Realtors will have this information. Libraries and city halls usually carry booklets or flyers on recreational activities. Check with the schools for attendance and registration information. See Chapter Five.

Picking a place to live often comes down to working out the best compromise. The more information you gather, the more likely your choice will be intelligently made.

If your child's education comes first, refer to the school scores and try to find a high-scoring neighborhood within your means. Or plan your budget to include a private school you like. Academic rankings compare California schools to each other. A school scoring in the 90th percentile is in the top 10th percent in state; in the 10th percentile, the lowest 10th percent. See Chapter 2 for all school rankings.

You're young or divorced or just plain poor and would love to own a home. Many towns have modestly priced houses but the traffic on your street might be a little heavier or the crime a little higher than found in other locations.

If you have your heart set on one town but can't find what you want in a certain neighborhood, try another. Many towns offer a variety of housing.

Finally, if you buy a home then make unpleasant discoveries — you really can't stand the commute — look for alternatives: Car pooling, buses, commuter rail; perhaps a job closer to home. Happy hunting!

Copyright © 2001 McCormack's Guides. No reproduction without permission.

AGOURA HILLS

UPPER-MIDDLE class bedroom community located off Highway 101 on the west side, near Ventura County. Good selection of large, new homes. School rankings high, crime low. Population 22,143. Until the 1960s, Agoura Hills rounded up cows and horses and had little to do with city life. Then its mini-boom came — 858 residential units that decade, 2,701 in the 1970s and about 3,270 units in the 1980s. In the last decade, development slowed to just 120 single homes.

By the 1970s, L.A. was outgrowing the three-bedroom home and moving up to four. Agoura Hills rode this wave. Among owner-occupied homes, the four-bedroom home leads all, followed by the three-bedroom, then the five-or-more-bedroom, the 1990 census reported. For a description of an average home: two-story, sandy-colored stucco sides, red-tile roof, walk-in closets, plenty of light, 2.5 to 3 bathrooms. Modern. Nice. Streets clean. Utility lines underground. Enough open space to give a country feeling. Some residents trying to limit development. Since 1990, town has added about 1,800 residents.

Agoura Hills, off Grey Rock Road and Fountainwood Street, rises into executive homes, large with custom touches (stone facing, columns, brick driveways) and views of countryside. But much of the city was built on fairly flat land. For horse lovers, "Old Agoura," off Kanan Road, still has ranches. On the eastern border, a small subdivision pops up, three- and four-bedroom homes, off Liberty Canyon Road. The state in 2000 counted 7,043 housing units: 5,140 single homes, 1,060 single attached, 834 multiples, 9 mobiles.

Served by the Las Virgenes Unified School District, which is using a $93 million bond to renovate schools and build an elementary school and a middle school. School rankings land in the top 20 percent statewide and many schools are scoring in the top 10 percent.

Zero homicides in 1999, 1998 and 1997. The counts for previous years are 0, 1, 0, 0, 1, 2, 0. Agoura Hills contracts with the sheriff for police protection.

Golf course in town, several within a short drive. About a half-dozen city parks. Large regional park on south side. Neighborhood shopping centers. Library. Large schools provide playing fields. Recreation center. Usual sports.

About 33 miles from downtown L.A., a long haul, but clean industry and office parks are discovering this side of the county, which makes for a shorter commute. Ten miles to San Fernando Valley, which has many jobs. Several park-and-ride lots. Chamber of commerce (818) 889-3150.

ALHAMBRA

Downtown L.A.
Alhambra
L.A. International Airport
Long Beach

MIDDLE-CLASS, BEDROOM CITY located about eight miles northeast of downtown L.A., between Monterey Park and San Marino. School rankings low-middle to high. Crime rate low. Population 92,809.

Alhambra started the 1940s with 6,887 residential units and added 5,327 units in that decade and 5,037 homes and apartments in the 1950s. About 57 percent of the current housing predates 1960, which means, because Alhambra was built for the middle class, thousands of two- and three-bedroom homes. Alhambra also has its share of the new and the big but very little leaps up the scale. The 1990 census counted only 797 four-bedroom homes and 165 homes with five or more bedrooms. Apartment units and single homes are about evenly divided. Many of the apartment complexes have been built on deep, narrow lots, a common pattern in L.A. County. In and about the downtown, the bungalows and older homes can be found. In the 1990s, Alhambra built 625 units, almost all of them apartments or condos.

Well-kept city, streets cleaned, lawns watered, many of the oldest homes preserved. On many blocks, palms, magnolias and maples dapple homes and lawns and soften the sunlight. The east side offers probably the best selection of single homes but these units can be found all over. The west side rises into gentle hills. North side borders two upscale towns: San Marino and South Pasadena. The state in 2000 counted 30,223 housing units: 12,628 single homes, 2,954 single attached, 14,621 multiples, 20 mobiles.

Served by an elementary and a high school district, both called Alhambra. Overall scores for both land a little above and below the 50th percentile, state comparison, and vary by neighborhood. Alhambra High in math is scoring in the 90th percentile. In 1999, voters passed a $22 million bond to renovate the elementary schools.

Four homicides in 1999. The counts for previous years are 8, 3, 4, 3, 3, 3, 7, 8, 3. Alhambra has its own police department.

Golf course, five parks. Annual 8K run. Farmers' market. Large library. Movie-plex. Three swimming pools, two gyms. Seniors center. Many activities for kids and adults. Borders Cal State University.

Large county public works complex. Buses. Interstate 10 cuts across the south side, making freeway access to downtown convenient. Parkways and other wide arterials move traffic. The city is improving downtown. Large auto row, a good source of tax revenue. Chamber of commerce (626) 282-8481.

ALTADENA

BEDROOM COMMUNITY located north of Pasadena in the foothills of the San Gabriel Mountains. Mix of low-, middle- and high-income homes. Unincorporated. A town, not a city. Estimated population 45,000.

School rankings middling. Crime not tracked by the FBI but the demographics say suburban average, with the low-income neighborhoods probably suffering more incidents than the high-income sections. Patrolled by sheriff's deputies. Sheriff's substation.

Altadena, started in the 1880s, is one of the oldest communities in the county and offers housing styles across 100 years. About one-fifth of the town, according to the 1990 census, was built before 1940. Single homes make up about 75 percent of the housing stock. Locals try to preserve oldest homes. The town starts about the 800-foot level and rises to about 2,000 feet. This gives Altadena a genuine feeling of being "alta," Spanish for high. The "dena" was lifted from Pasadena.

Lake Avenue, which runs north to south, roughly divides the housing styles of the town. West of Lake, the homes are a mix of low- and middle-income units interspersed with residences that jump up the scale.

East of Lake, you will find some of the loveliest homes in the county: mansions and large ranchers, exquisitely maintained, many of them positioned on hills and small ravines to command views. Loads of trees and shrubs and hedges and foliage. Plenty of shade. Pleasing neighborhoods. Altadena is a town that needs to be driven to appreciate its housing diversity. Many of the older, smaller homes are in great shape. Some of the homes that were built in later decades are not.

Education is provided by the Pasadena Unified School District. Rankings, state comparison, for Burbank and Altadena Elementary schools run generally from the 20th to the 50th percentile. District is creating magnet programs and it passed a $240 million bond to renovate all schools. Work underway.

Golf course, about a half-dozen parks, Christmas parade and tree lighting. Altadena has its own shops and services and neighboring Pasadena offers a great variety of cultural and artistic activities.

About 14 miles to downtown L.A. Freeways can be picked up in Pasadena. Close to Caltech, Altadena is attracting high-tech businesses. Chamber of commerce (626) 794-3988.

ARCADIA

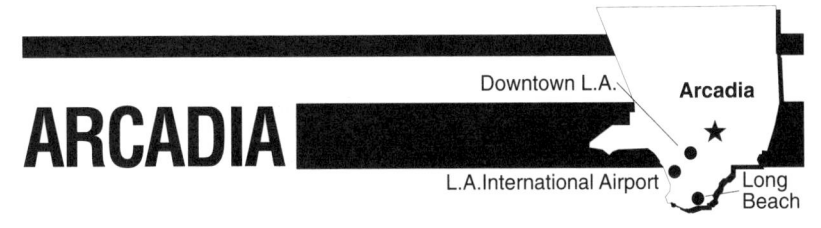

PRESTIGE BEDROOM CITY. Built on mostly level land that rises into the foothills of the San Gabriel Mountains. Home to Santa Anita, one of the premier race tracks of the West Coast. Crime low. School scores high. Population 54,013.

Housing runs from very nice to knockout. Single homes outnumber apartments three to one and many homes fall in the estate class. Lawns are well-cared-for, landscaping tastefully done and almost everything shows a lot of attention to detail. Trees, trees, trees. Handsome leafy city. City was founded in 1903 by Elias "Lucky" Baldwin, gambler and speculator, big thinker. His estate was converted to a public arboretum.

In its foothill neighborhood and around town, Arcadia built many large ranchers or upscale tract models popular in the 1950s and 1960s. The estate homes generally can be found above Foothill Boulevard and west of Santa Anita Avenue. Most of the apartments are located on the west side below Huntington Drive, mixed in with single homes. As you move east below Huntington Drive, the homes become a little plainer. Almost all, however, fall into category of upscale middle. State in 2000 counted 19,961 units: 11,796 single homes, 1,404 single attached, 6,749 multiples, 12 mobiles. In 1990s, Arcadia increased population by about 5,700 and built about 500 more homes.

Education by Arcadia school district. Scores in 80th and 90th percentiles, among highest in state and indicate solid community and parental support for education. Bond passed to renovate schools. A few streets are in other school districts. Check with schools for precise borders. Arcadia High often wins the regional National Science Bowl. Every year in California only about two dozen high schools break the 600 mark in the math SAT. Arcadia High always makes the list; in 1998 hitting 619, in 1999, going higher, 628.

Zero homicides in 1999. The counts for previous years are 0, 1, 0, 1, 1, 2, 2, 1, 1. Arcadia has its own police department.

Horse racing, library, 18 parks, movies, two golf courses, community center, two public swimming pools. Also equestrian trails. Mall with a Nordstrom. Hotels. About 3,500 swimming pools in city.

About 17 miles to downtown L.A. Easy access to Foothill Freeway, Arcadia borders Pasadena, which has many jobs. Race track and Methodist Hospital are largest employers. Chamber of commerce (626) 447-2159.

ARTESIA

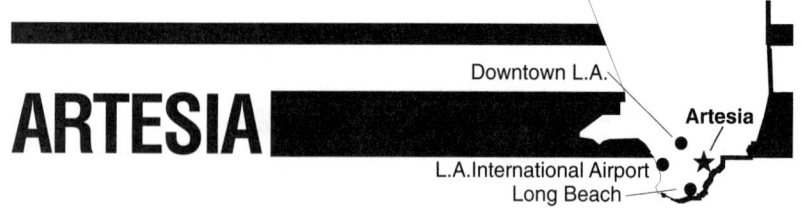

Downtown L.A.
Artesia
L.A. International Airport
Long Beach

SMALL BEDROOM CITY bordered on three sides by Cerritos, an upscale middle-class city. Both are located a few miles north of Long Beach. Artesia has its modest homes but its newer housing seems to be stepping up in quality.

Crime suburban average on the low side. School rankings middling. Population 17,132. In the 1990S, Artesia added about 1,700 residents and increased its housing stock by about 50 units.

Artesia's not easy to classify. About 15 percent of its housing was built before 1950 and about 25 percent in the 1950s. This gives it a nice chunk of smaller, older housing, some of it starting to fade.

But almost side-by-side with the older housing, large new homes, some of them custom designed, have been erected and Artesia has its blocks that come across as middle-class comfortable.

Cerritos, its neighbor, has a good deal of new middle-class-plus housing and this may be having the effect of pushing Artesia's new housing up the scale.

The state in 2000 counted 4,584 housing units: 3,202 single homes, 311 single attached, 974 multiples, 97 mobiles.

Education by the ABC Unified School District, which also includes Cerritos. State rankings for Neimes and Burbank Elementary schools land in the 40th to the 60th percentile, for Artesia High, in the 40th and 50th percentiles. Voters in 1997 approved a $25 million bond to renovate the schools; work is about half done.

Two homicides in 1999. The counts for previous years are 7, 1, 0, 3, 1, 3, 4, 6, 1. Artesia contracts with the sheriff's department for police protection.

Library, three parks, close to Cerritos Community College, which offers many classes and activities at low prices. Town borders upscale mall with a Nordstrom and Macys.

About 19 miles to downtown L.A. Highway 91 crosses the city and Interstate 605 is located a few miles to the west. For the lucky residents who work in the Long Beach area, which has many jobs, the commute will be short.

Town was named by Artesia Water Company, which in the 19th century drilled artesian wells for farmers.

Chamber of commerce (562) 924-6397.

AZUSA

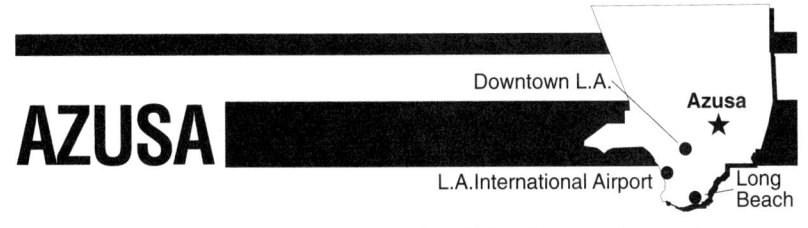

BEDROOM CITY in the foothills of the San Gabriel Mountains, on the east side of L.A. County. The name has an Indian origin but local residents and many others genially interpret it to mean "everything from A to Z in the USA."

School rankings low to fairly high. Crime about suburban average. Population 46,261. Added about 5,000 people in the 1990s and built about 300 units.

Formerly a citrus center, Azusa switched to bedroom status during the 1940s when 1,084 residential units were built and the city more than doubled in size. The 1950s saw the construction of 3,100 units and in each of the following three decades about 2,500 to 2,900 homes and apartments were built. A lot of the old and new.

Developers aimed mainly at the low-middle side of the market, two- and three-bedroom homes, blue-collar workers, veterans getting started in the housing market. Azusa is a well-cared-for town but not a glamour town. Very little jumps up the scale, even near the golf course in the foothills. The state in 2000 counted 13,502 housing units: 5,665 single homes, 1,966 single attached, 5,278 multiples, 593 mobiles.

Education by the Azusa Unified School District. Rankings by school, state comparison, land generally in the 20th to 40th percentiles. In discussion, bond measure to renovate schools.

Citrus Community College, just over the east border in Glendora, offers hundreds of classes and activities at low prices, about $36 for an average academic class. A big plus for both towns. Azusa also has a private university.

One homicide each in 1999, 1998 and 1997. Counts for previous years are 4, 3, 2, 4, 1, 2, 5. Azusa has own police department.

Aquatic center, recreation center, golf course, seven parks, tennis and basketball courts. Library. Farmers market. A lot of open space. Azusa backs up to the Angeles National Forest. On the east side of town, large nurseries (about 600 acres) grow thousands of plants and this contributes to the country feeling.

On the northwest side of town is the floodplain of the San Gabriel River. Section supplies sand and gravel for building.

Interstate 210 crosses the town, easy access to connecting freeways but it's 25 miles to downtown L.A. Metroliner (commuter rail) to downtown. Neighboring Irwindale has many jobs. Chamber of commerce (626) 334-1507.

BALDWIN HILLS
View Park, Windsor Hills, Ladera Heights

BALDWIN HILLS is an unincorporated pocket of land about 5 miles in from the ocean, near Culver City. Most of the hills lack housing and include many active oil wells and a large regional park with views of L.A. Basin.

To the east of the hills and buffered from the oil derricks are three unincorporated neighborhoods that are sometimes wrapped into "Baldwin Hills": View Park, Windsor Hills and Ladera Heights.

In 1994, the Southern California Assn. of Governments counted 6,558 residents in Ladera Heights, and 12,218 residents in View Park-Windsor Hills.

The housing in the three neighborhoods, most of it built after 1950, mixes styles and sizes. Many of the units are built on view lots. Some of the homes and apartments go up the scale but most are built for the middle class.

Slauson Avenue and La Cienega Boulevard bisect the neighborhoods and feed into nearby freeways. L.A. International Airport is about three miles to the south. Plenty of jobs in this region and many residents probably enjoy a short commute.

Served by the Los Angeles Unified School District Educational pluses include the West Los Angeles Community College.

School rankings for the 54th Street Elementary generally ran well above the 50th percentile. Rankings for Windsor Hills Elementary land in the 50th to 60th percentiles.

Regional Park includes a lake and hiking trails. Two other parks are located in the neighborhoods and the community college offers many recreational activities for residents. Library. Close enough to the Pacific to make the beaches a convenient playground.

On the northeast side of View Park can be found the Baldwin Hills-Crenshaw Plaza, a shopping mall.

BALDWIN PARK

BLUE-COLLAR, MIDDLE-INCOME city that built most of its housing between 1950 and 1990 and offers a lot of housing choices, especially in single homes. They make up over 75 percent of Baldwin Park's housing. Population 77,124.

School rankings run from low to high.

Baldwin Park started its housing boom in the 1950s when it constructed 4,763 units. In the following decade it erected 3,511 units and in the 1970s, 2,145 units. In the 1980s another boom surfaced, 4,165 units. In the last decade, construction dropped to fewer than 300 units. Baldwin Park is about built out.

For the most part, Baldwin Park built for blue-collar America, veterans starting out in their first homes, generally two and three bedrooms. Some of this housing is faded but for every home that needs some paint applied and shrubs trimmed, you'll see two or three that show loving attention.

The state in 2000 counted 17,472 housing units: 11,705 single homes, 1,632 single attached, 3,733 multiples, 402 mobiles.

The children are educated in the schools of the Baldwin Park Unified School District. Scores, state comparison, land generally in the 20th to 40th percentile. District voters in 1996 okayed $26 million bond for renovation of schools. Work continuing.

Seven homicides in 1999, eight in 1998 and 1997. The counts for previous years are 12, 7, 7, 8, 12, 11, 8. In the older sections of town, security bars and doors are used by many.

Community center with indoor pool. Seven parks. Boys and Girls Club. Summer concerts. Seniors center. Sports programs for kids, adults.

Two freeways, Interstates 10 and 605. Many local jobs, especially in the nearby City of Industry. About 18 miles to downtown L.A. Metrolink (commuter rail) to downtown. Local stores include a Target and a Home Depot. Kaiser Medical Center.

Baldwin Park introduced the world to the first drive-through restaurant, an In-N-Out Burger. Town calls itself the "Hub of the San Gabriel Valley." Named after Elias "Lucky" Baldwin, pioneer developer, speculator, gambler.

Chamber of commerce (626) 960-4848.

BEL AIR ESTATES
Beverly Glen

NEIGHBORHOODS to the immediate west of Beverly Hills, just north of UCLA. Prestigious. Home to stars and some of the biggest wigs in entertainment and politics (Ronald Reagan). Crime low. School rankings high. Population about 21,000.

Beverly Hills mixes the posh with the plain below Sunset Boulevard but above Sunset, in the foothills of the Santa Monica Mountains, homes range from the way upscale to the knockout. Bel Air Estates and Beverly Glen (also called Beverly Crest) are also located north of Sunset Boulevard in the foothills. Homes, many hidden behind hedges, tend to mansions or executive homes. Large pools. Lovely gardens. Spectacular views from some homes.

Three main roads serve these neighborhoods: Benedict Canyon Drive, Beverly Glen Road and Bellagio-Roscomare Drive. From these thoroughfares, short, often dead-end streets spin off. All three roads wind and twist up to the top of the ridge where they hook into Mulholland Drive.

As Benedict Canyon and Beverly Glen move toward Mulholland, middle-class homes, three and four bedrooms, showing much care, appear. Sometimes the modest and the rich live within shouting distance. Many of the homes are built on mesas or shelves carved into the hills or in ravines thick with brush and trees. Bel Air Estates is more clearly defined than Beverly Glen. But neither has municipal boundaries.

Bel Air Estates and Beverly Glen are neighborhoods of the City of Los Angeles, governed by the L.A. City Council (but in reality local groups exert great influence) and protected by L.A. police. Both towns are served by the Los Angeles School District. Roscomare Elementary scores in high 90s, Revere Magnet in the 70th percentiles.

No government agency tracks crime here but rich neighborhoods usually have very low crime. Private security beefs up police protection.

Two golf courses. Large parks nearby. Many homes have swimming pools. UCLA. Restaurants, shops in Beverly Hills. University of Judaism. New Getty museum across the freeway to west.

About 14 miles to downtown L.A. Interstate 405 near by. Studios and entertainment complexes are located on both sides of the hills. Short commute for many. Almost no businesses so no chamber of commerce.

BELL

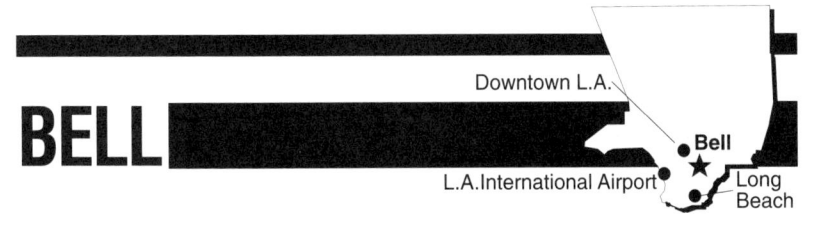

Downtown L.A.
L.A. International Airport
Bell
Long Beach

SMALL BLUE-COLLAR CITY located about five miles southeast of downtown L.A., near South Gate. Schools score low. Short commute. Population 38,044.

If you're short of money and want to buy a home, Bell is a good place to start.

About one-fourth of its housing was built before 1950. In the 1950s and 1960s, the city went on a splurge and constructed about 50 percent of its current housing stock. Housing starts fell off to about 1,000 units in 1970s, about 600 in 1980s and dwindled to about 50 in the 1990s.

Bell's housing follows a pattern seen in some of the older communities in the county. Many of the homes are small. Among owner-occupied units, the two-bedroom home is the most prevalent, the 1990 census reported. Many homes are clustered one behind the other on deep lots, served by one driveway.

In appearance, Bell is a mixed bag. Many homes are kept up and well-maintained and some are not. Security doors are popular but many windows go without security bars.

The small size of the town, 26 blocks east to west and 10 blocks north to south, gives residents the chance to know each other and creates a governing climate that can readily address problems.

The state in 2000 counted 9,453 housing units: 3,557 single homes, 1,080 single attached, 4,387 multiples, 429 mobiles.

Education provided by the Los Angeles Unified School District. Sample rankings, state comparison, put Corona Avenue Elementary in the 10th percentile and Bell High in the 30th percentile.

Library, public swimming pool at the high school, typical sports and activities. Five parks. Community Center. Several of the parks were built next to the schools, which makes it easier for the kids to play.

One homicide in 1999. The counts for previous years are 3, 9, 3, 3, 7, 8, 6, 7, 6.

Bell is located in an area with many industrial and professional jobs. This means a short commute for many residents. Town used to be called Obed.

Chamber of commerce (323) 560-8755.

BELLFLOWER

LOCATED NORTH of Long Beach, Bellflower offers housing that spans the last century. Population 68,345. Schools score from low-middle to high. Town took name from an apple that grew in region.

Bellflower started the 1950s with about 4,600 housing units, about 20 percent of its current housing stock. In the 1950s, it added 7,147 homes and apartments and in the 1960s, 4,560 residential units. In the 1970s and 1980s, the city built about 8,000 units equally divided between the decades. In the 1990s, housing construction fell to about 300 units. Bellflower built for the middle class. Among owner-occupied homes, the three-bedroom model dominates.

Bellflower has a layout that shows up in several other communities in L.A. County. Much of the city is subdivided into large lots that once contained a single home but in following years have added, out back, other homes and apartments. In some places, the single home blends into an apartment complex. Typically, one driveway serves all the residential units. Some large lots contain just one home and this gives parts of Bellflower a country feeling.

In appearance, the city shows a lot of care. The homes are in good repair, the yards tended. The state in 2000 counted 24,400 housing units: 11,513 single homes, 1,727 single attached, 9,623 multiples, 1,537 mobiles.

Education is provided by Bellflower Unified School District. Most schools are scoring in the 20th to 40th percentiles. Cerritos Community College is located a few miles to the east and provides many classes and recreational activities at a low price.

Eight homicides in 1999. The counts for previous years are 4, 4, 7, 10, 6, 4, 9, 4, 2. Bellflower contracts with the sheriff's department for police protection.

Cultural and recreational offerings include five parks, tennis courts, swimming pools, a 9-hole golf course, horse trails, a bowling alley, sports leagues, social clubs and a symphony orchestra. Several hospitals, including a Kaiser.

Four freeways in or near the city make it easy for residents to hit the road. About 18 miles to downtown L.A. A short commute for those who have local jobs, many of which can be found in Long Beach. Chamber of commerce (562) 867-1744.

BELL GARDENS

SMALL BEDROOM CITY, low to middle income, located about 10 miles southeast of downtown L.A. Population 45,733.

Crime worrisome. School rankings low-middling.

Bell Gardens started booming in the 1940s, when it tripled its housing stock, and swung into high gear in the 1950s — 2,686 units built. The following decade saw 2,165 housing starts and then, in the 1970s, a drop to 979 starts. In the 1990s, it built about 125 units.

The boom-year housing was aimed at veterans buying their first home. Among owner-occupied units, the 1990 census reported, two- and three-bedroom homes were the most popular. Bell Gardens also has about 200 four-bedroom homes.

Some of this housing is showing its age, and the level of care varies from street to street.

Bell Gardens is one of those cities that favored deep-lot housing. The homes or apartments are built on one lot served by one driveway.

Many of the original residents have taken their equity and moved up and out, creating a situation that welcomes newcomers and first-time buyers.

The state in 2000 counted 9,661 housing units: 4,020 single homes, 1,908 single attached, 3,302 apartments or condos, 431 mobiles.

The children are educated in the schools of the Montebello Unified District. Academic rankings often fall below the 20th percentile. Voters passed bond in 1998 to renovate schools. Work underway.

Overall crime rate runs suburban average but violent crime is higher than what's found in many suburban cities. Five homicides each in 1999 and 1998, six in 1997. The counts for previous years are 5, 10, 7, 8, 5, 6, 7. Many homes have security doors and window bars.

Library. Four parks, including a large regional park on the south side. Golf course.

Interstate 710 runs up the west side of the city, Interstate 5, the east side. Buses. Straight shot to downtown L.A.

Many local jobs, which means short commutes for residents. Close to commute rail station. Chamber of commerce (323) 560-8755.

BEVERLY HILLS

A CITY CELEBRATED for its wealth, stars and panache. In appearance, as good as its reputation, a lovely looking city. Homes extremely well-maintained, lawns putting-green quality, streets immaculate, a town with a lot of pride. About seven miles to Pacific. Population 35,096.

Founded by Mary Pickford, Douglas Fairbanks, Tom Mix, Rudolph Valentino, Harold Lloyd, Will Rogers and a few others. Pressured to annex to L.A., they voted in 1923 to form their own city. At that time, Beverly Hills had about 800 homes. Fairbanks used to step out in his backyard and shoot coyotes. Pioneer developer hailed from Beverly Farms, Massachusetts. For a rich city, Beverly Hills is surprisingly diverse in housing. The state in 2000 counted 15,890 housing units: 5,674 single homes, 220 single attached, 9,991 multiples, 5 mobiles. In the 1990s, about 170 new homes were built and the population increased by 3,000.

Santa Monica Boulevard divides the town about middle. Just about all the commercial and all the apartments are found south of Santa Monica. Many of the houses and apartments below Santa Monica Boulevard predate World War II and follow a Spanish style. South of the boulevard, the land flattens or slopes gently. North of the boulevard, Beverly Hills rises into hills and large homes. Visually accessible city. You can see from the street many of the mansions of old and new Beverly Hills but as you rise into the hills, high walls and hedges hide many of the more opulent homes. Hill homes are positioned to command views of the Basin or the Pacific. Strict controls on signs, parking.

Served by the Beverly Hills Unified School District. State rankings in the 90th percentile, the top 10 percent of California schools. Bond passed in 1994 to raise $77 million to renovate schools. Parents chip in for school programs. UCLA is located about a mile west.

One homicide in 1999. Counts for previous years are 0, 1, 0, 0, 3, 1, 0. Beverly Hills has own police. Many homes have private security.

About eight parks. Library. Three large country clubs are located near the city. First-class shopping, hotels, restaurants on Rodeo Drive and Wilshire Boulevard. All this pumps revenue into city coffers and helps fund services. Star-gazing throughout the city. About 12 million visitors a year. About two miles to freeway. For those working in the movie industry, a drive of five to 15 miles to many of the studios and media facilities. Beverly Hills has its own movie-media firms. Chamber of commerce (310) 248-1000.

BRADBURY

MORE A NEIGHBORHOOD than a city. Rich, secluded, many streets closed to the public. Located in the foothills of the San Gabriel mountains, just above the City of Duarte. Population: 965.

Up until about 25 years ago, it was easy in California for neighborhoods and small towns to incorporate themselves as legal cities and take control of their zoning, planning, taxes and expenditures. Now it's much harder.

During the boom years following World War II, suburbia galloped across the countryside, pleasing developers and countless buyers but also upsetting many. Some groups wanted to retain the flavor and habits of their small towns or a certain way of life.

Bradbury residents wanted to keep the rural horse-country atmosphere they had come to love and to avoid tract housing. So they incorporated the neighborhood in 1957. Building restrictions were tightened in 1998.

Behind the gates, the housing runs to custom homes, many on five-acre lots. The majority of breadwinners are managers or professionals.

The state in 2000 counted 302 housing units: 291 single homes, five single attached, six multiples, zero mobiles. In 1990s, 21 homes were built and population increased by 135.

The few children attend public schools in the Duarte Unified District. Academic rankings land above and below the 50th percentile. Bond passed to renovate schools.

Police protection by private patrols and the sheriff's department. Zero homicides between 1995 and 1999. Duarte has a few streets open to the public and occasionally will report a burglary or theft. But the crime rate is one of the lowest in L.A. County and the state.

About 21 miles to downtown L.A., possibly the only drawback to the town. The Foothill Freeway (I-210) can be picked up in Duarte.

For recreation, many families supply their own. Stores in Duarte. Bradbury is about eight miles east of Pasadena, which offers much in the way of shopping, culture and amusements.

No businesses. No chamber of commerce.

For information, call city hall at (626) 358-3218.

BRENTWOOD

PRESTIGE TOWN, located mostly in the foothills of Santa Monica Mountains. One of the movie-entertainment towns. Part of City of Los Angeles. Home to new Getty Museum and Mount Saint Mary's College.

Used to be home to O.J. Simpson and during trial reporters poured over and analyzed Brentwood. Simpson gave up home, moved away, home demolished. Crime ratings for the town are not tracked but probably are very low. Rich communities almost always have low crime.

Brentwood is situated immediately west of Interstate 405 (San Diego Freeway) and is split about its middle by Sunset Boulevard. The Brentwood Country Club is located on its south side, Mount St. Mary's College and the new Getty Museum on its north side, and Topanga State Park on the west side. San Vincente Boulevard on the south defines housing patterns. Below San Vincente, mostly apartments; above San Vincente, mostly single homes. Beverly Hills is about four miles to the east, the Pacific about four miles to the west. Population, 1994 count, was put at 28,649.

Brentwood has its mansions, some gigantic. It has its homes that hang off the hills or sit on mesas and command great views of the countryside and for some, the Pacific. But for the most part, Brentwood was built for upscale professionals. The typical home is probably a three- or four-bedroom rancher, two-car garage, built in the 1950s or 1960s. Many of Brentwood's streets meander around and over the hills. Trees and shrubs are plentiful. Country feeling. Many homes front the street; some hide behind hedges or gates. Lot of attention paid to lawns, landscaping and appearances.

Education by Los Angeles School District. State rankings: Brentwood Science Magnet, 70th to 90th percentiles, Revere Junior High, 70th percentiles.

Patrolled by L.A. police. Many homes have medallions indicating protection by security services. Residents led fight to suppress leaf blowers.

Several regional parks nearby. Two golf courses. Lots to do in Santa Monica. UCLA close by. Short drive to the Pacific.

About 15 miles to downtown L.A. Freeway all the way, Interstate 405 to Santa Monica Freeway. Many jobs in Hollywood and West L.A. Getty Museum built tram from parking lot to museum. Chamber of commerce (310) 442-9784.

BURBANK

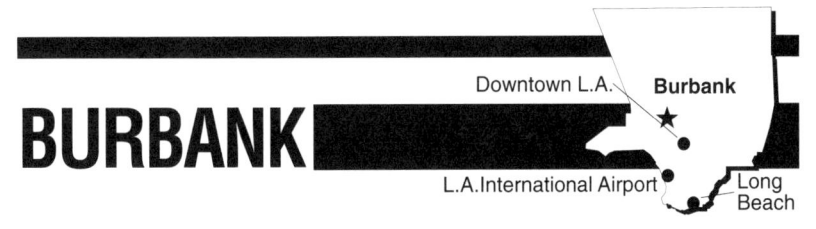

MOVIE-ENTERTAINMENT CITY located in the San Fernando Valley just over the hills from Hollywood. Home to Disney, NBC and Warner Brothers studios, and to the largest airport serving the San Fernando Valley.

School rankings generally high. Crime about suburban average. Population 106,480.

Burbank is one of the oldest "suburban" towns in L.A. County. About 60 percent of its housing was built before 1960. The homes tend to two and three bedrooms, housing built mainly for the GIs returning after World War II.

Other communities with this type housing have gone into decline. From its appearances, Burbank has not. It is a cared-for town where residents take pride in sprucing up their homes. Even in the middle of August, with the sun glaring down, many lawns will be lustrous green.

The state in 2000 counted 43,001 housing units: 19,551 single homes, 1,554 single attached, 21,844 multiples, 52 mobiles. In the 1990s, Burbank increased its population by 13,000 and its housing stock by 1,800 units, most of them apartments.

The great majority of Burbank was built on flat land and laid out on a grid pattern, the standard layout of old suburbia. On the northeast side, some streets rise into the hills and here you will find new and bigger homes and the "best" neighborhoods. But Burbank straddles the middle, avoiding the very high and the very low income, and its school and crime figures tell the same story.

Served by Burbank Unified School District. Almost all schools score at or above the 50th percentile, a few in the 70th. These scores suggest stable neighborhoods, middle-class-plus demographics and good support of education. Bond passed in 1998 to renovate schools; work continuing.

Two homicides in 1999, four in 1998, and zero in 1997. Counts for previous years are 4, 6, 5, 5, 7, 6, 2.

Golf course, equestrian center, 17 parks, bike trails, Woodbury University. With so many movie and entertainment people clustered here, the local economy has thrown up many first-class restaurants, shops and diversions. Lively downtown. Also many businesses and manufacturing firms. Arguments over expansion of airport facilities. One of best commutes in L.A. because of many local jobs. Two freeways, Metrolink (commuter rail). Check out noise from airport. Buses. Chamber of commerce (818) 846-3111.

CALABASAS

UPSCALE TO WEALTHY city in foothills of Santa Monica Mountains, on the west side of San Fernando Valley. Many neighborhoods are protected by guards and gates. School rankings very high. Crime very low. Population 20,455.

Calabasas started as a stage stop and rough-and-ready frontier town. Vigilantes hung desperadoes and other offenders from large oak. The town then mellowed into a farm burg. Warner Brothers owned 1,200 acres in region, backdrop for countless movies. As L.A. and the movie-entertainment towns grew and the freeways were constructed, what was inaccessible and out-of-touch became the opposite and, after some time, highly desirable.

Until 1991, the Calabasas region was under the control of the county government, which gave the OK to apartment complexes, everyday single homes, luxury homes, condos, stores, shops, some office complexes, even a small mobile home park. But developers aimed a lot at the upper end. Many of the homes run to four and five bedrooms and two stories. The off-the-chart stuff runs to something Nero might have built — large custom homes, some perched on mesas with great views. Ravines and canyons divide the city and encourage a sense of separate neighborhoods. In 1991, Calabasas voted to incorporate itself as a legal city, bringing development under local control.

Name derives from Spanish for "Pumpkins" or Indian for "Where the wild geese fly." Calabasas rolls over hills and, on its south, borders the rugged mountains that extend to Malibu. Country feeling. Also on the south side, miles of open space. Possibly some relief from smog. Some claim ocean breezes clean the air. State in 2000 counted 8,235 housing units: 5,276 single homes, 945 single attached, 1,666 multiples, 348 mobiles. Single homes make up almost all new construction.

Served by Las Virgenes School District, which includes Hidden Hills. Bond passed in 1997 to renovate and build schools. State rankings in 80th and 90th percentiles. Calabasas High scores in the high 90s.

Zero homicides 1999. Counts for previous years are 0,1, 0, 0, 1, 1, 0. Calabasas contracts with sheriff's department for police protection. Private security services much in use. Sheriff's substation.

Horse country. Swimming center. Golf course. Gun club. Library. Local shops, restaurants. Short drive to Ventura Boulevard, a shopping-dining cornucopia. About 26 miles to downtown L.A. but many residents work nearby. Highway 101 skirts the north side. Chamber of commerce (818) 222-5680.

CANOGA PARK
West Hills

LOCATED AT THE WEST END of the San Fernando Valley, on the border of Ventura County. Bedroom communities. Housing runs from a few low-income units to many in the middle and upper middle. Population combined, about 70,000. Crime rate unknown. School rankings, low-middle to high.

Both are towns of the City of Los Angeles. Until recently, West Hills was included in Canoga Park and the two are partners in the chamber of commerce. Children in both towns are educated by L.A. Unified School District.

West Hills, built on ravines and hills at the extreme west, contains some of the newest housing in the Valley. The homes run to two-story units, tile roofs, four and five bedrooms. Some places with views start at over $500,000. The lower hills contain homes built generally over the last 25 years. Many include at least four bedrooms. Some have three-car garages. Nothing custom, all tract but nice in a modern suburban way.

Going east, you enter Canoga Park. Many of the homes fall into the three-bedroom models of 40 years ago, and some are smaller. Many show a lot of care, some show little. Toward the center of town, the homes become smaller and appearances fall off. Generalizations are difficult because neighborhoods change within a few blocks, and even a block with rundown homes may have sitting in its middle a new stucco-tile job worth $400,000.

State school rankings reflect the jumbled nature of the towns. Welby Way Elementary (West Hills), 90th percentiles; Capistrano Elementary, 20th to 60th percentiles; Canoga Park Elementary, 10th percentiles; Canoga Park High School, 40th to 50th percentiles.

Patrolled by L.A. police. West Hills and most of Canoga Park do without security doors and window bars and probably have crime rates that fall into the range of suburban average. Where the bars and security doors turn up, extra precautions might be necessary.

About 10 parks. Two shopping malls. Two rec centers. Horticultural park.

About 26 miles to downtown L.A. Highway 101 can be picked up by driving south 2-3 miles. Metrolink station (commuter rail) at Chatsworth. Park-and-ride lots at the malls. Chamber of commerce (818) 884-4222.

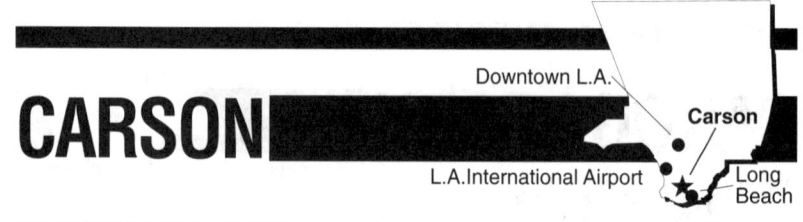

CARSON

Downtown L.A., Carson, L.A. International Airport, Long Beach

BEDROOM COMMUNITY west of Long Beach, on its north side. Home to California State University-Dominguez Hills. Population 93,196. School rankings low-middling.

Carson started its housing boom in the 1950s but at a slightly later date than other L.A. cities. Carson built 5,006 homes in the 1950s and almost double that in the 1960s. In the 1970s and 1980s it continued to add homes and in the 1990s it built about 650 units, about half of them single homes.

As a result, homes are a little bigger and a little better-appointed than found elsewhere and, in general, Carson presents a nice suburban face. Lawns are green and trim, homes in good repair. Carson looks "new." Near the university, the homes step up in quality, four and five bedrooms, many two-story units. Landscaping is a notch above what is found in other parts of the city. The state in 2000 counted 25,095 housing units: 17,583 single homes, 1,926 single attached, 3,027 multiples, 2,559 mobiles.

Served by L.A. Unified School District. Sample rankings: Dolores Elementary School, 40th to 60th percentile; Carson High School, 30th to 40th percentiles. School for high I.Q. kids: Academy of Math and Sciences. Cal State university is a great plus. It waves the flag for academic values, provides extension classes for the community and benevolently influences Carson life.

Many homes, even on obviously middle-class streets, are protected by security doors and windows. Not on every street. Carson's neighborhoods vary but the city seems attentive to security. Nine homicides in 1999, eight homicides in 1998, 10 in 1997. The counts for previous years are 19, 15, 17, 10, 12, 7, 6. Police protection is provided by the sheriff's department under contract with the city.

The university also works with local businesses and industries. Carson and Long Beach have created thousands of jobs for local residents.

Sports complex, community center, two golf courses, about a dozen parks, community colleges close by, jogging and recreation at university, Carson Center for conventions, banquets. Several large hotels. Six miles to the ocean. Large Ikea furniture store in South Bay Pavilion (mall).

About 18 miles to downtown L.A. Four freeways run through or border Carson and provide quick access. Light rail to Long Beach and downtown L.A. Buses. About 10 miles to L.A. International Airport. About 6,000 local jobs. Chamber of commerce (310) 522-5595.

CERRITOS

FAIRLY NEW, MIDDLE-CLASS-PLUS bedroom city located about two miles northeast of Long Beach. Exceptionally well-maintained. A handsome suburb. School rankings among the tops in the state. Population 58,063.

Cerritos is a late bloomer. It did not get its start until the late 1960s and the 1970s. In the latter decade, it built 10,504 residential units (great majority single homes) or about two-thirds of its current housing. The U.S. came out of World War II fearing that the Depression would return. As prosperity took hold in the 1950s and 1960s, the homes and garages grew bigger, the closets larger, the kitchens better equipped, the decorative touches nicer (but lot sizes shrunk).

Coming to life when it did, Cerritos presents a more modern, more upscale look than its neighbors. Utility lines have been placed underground and median strips planted. The city has been divided into neighborhoods (Shadow Park, Rancho Cerritos) and walls surround each section. This dampens noise and reduces the number of vehicles on residential streets. One mall greets shoppers with a waterfall that cascades over boulders. A second mall has a Nordstrom, a Sears and Mervyn's.

Rare for an L.A. County suburb, four-bedroom homes outnumber three bedrooms in Cerritos. If you want a large home, this is a good place to look. Many homes ascend to two stories. The state in 2000 counted 15,512 housing units: 13,288 single homes, 1,225 single attached, 995 multiples, 4 mobiles. In the 1990s, Cerritos built around 150 residences.

Education by ABC District, which also serves Lakewood, Hawaiian Gardens and Artesia. Sample rankings for Cerritos schools: Wittman Elementary, high 90s; Carmenita Junior High, 90s and Whitney High, 99th percentile. In 1999, 22 high schools in California scored over 600 on the math SAT. The ABC district had two of them, Whitney (academic magnet school for district), 684 (highest in the state), and Cerritos, 608. Voters in 1997 approved a $25 million bond to renovate schools. Work under way. According to one study, one of the most ethnically diverse cities in U.S. Schools and city work to promote harmony among all.

Zero homicides in 1999. Counts for prior years are 3, 0, 1, 3, 1, 5, 5, 1, 2.

Performing arts center. Seniors center. Large new library. About 18 parks (a lot). Golf course. Community college. Highway 91 and I-605. About 18 miles to downtown L.A. Many local jobs. AT&T and UPS, major employers. Buses. Chamber of commerce (562) 404-1806.

CHATSWORTH

AFFLUENT town in northwest corner of San Fernando Valley. Boulder and horse country. Where many movies — by one count about 2,000 — particularly Westerns, were shot. Estimated population: 64,000.

School rankings middling to high. Crime not tracked by FBI but probably suburban average on the low side. Chatsworth is a little secluded and this will help keep crime down. Patrolled by Los Angeles police.

Highway 118 on the north, Plummer Avenue on the south and Topanga Canyon Boulevard down the middle. That's an approximate fix on Chatsworth, which is a town of the City of Los Angeles and does not have legal boundaries.

Horse ranches, large homes and upscale subdivisions can be found on the north side of Chatsworth and in its western hills. Some of the homes are giant custom creations with great views. Many fall in the range of comfortable upscale, two stories, five or six bedrooms, nicely appointed and decorated.

Off Devonshire Street, the homes run to three, four and five bedrooms, some everyday tract, others up the scale, two-story, four-car garage — pleasing to the eye in a suburban way. Chatsworth has apartments, also quite presentable. Many are located along or near Owensmouth Avenue.

Education by Los Angeles Unified School District. Sample academic rankings, Chatsworth Park Elementary, 50th and 60th percentiles; Chatsworth High School, 60th and 70th percentiles. Bond passed to renovate schools. Several private schools in the town.

Unlike many valley towns, Chatsworth has a strong business-industry base, most of it located along Plummer Avenue on the south side, away from homes. Large business park.

Library, several large parks, horse trails. Many homes have pools. Close to California State University, Northridge; many classes, activities. Town name comes from estate of English duke.

About 31 miles to downtown L.A. This is a good town to have a local job. But Metrolink (commuter rail) offers a convenient alternative to the freeway.

If you want the feel of the country, Chatsworth on its north side does it as well as any suburb in L.A. County. Chamber of commerce (818) 341-2428.

CLAREMONT

COLLEGE TOWN on east border of county. Pretty, well-kept, many trees, loaded with activities, many of them related to the city's five colleges and educational institutions. Mountains in background. School rankings middling to high, crime low. Population 35,968.

Claremont is home to a complex consisting of Harvey Mudd, Pitzer, Claremont McKenna, Claremont Graduate, Pomona and Scripps colleges. Their presence and the type of residents they draw — graduate and undergraduate students, ministers, professors and professionals — give the town a collegiate air on the scrubbed and well-groomed side. Claremont has a quaint downtown with shops and restaurants that border the colleges. Much interest in preserving older buildings.

Housing a mix of old and new. On west side near the colleges you'll find the older neighborhoods. As you move north towards the hills, the housing gets newer and bigger. North of Baseline Road some streets ascend into hills and provide vistas of the San Gabriel Valley. Around Mt. Baldy Road, the lots get bigger still and some homes jump into the executive class, large and impressive. For the most part, Claremont was built for middle-class professionals. Several senior complexes. Some lower-income units near the freeway. The state in 2000 counted 11,507 housing units: 8,238 single homes, 894 single attached, 2,372 multiples, 3 mobiles. In the 1990s, Claremont's population increased by 3,400 and its housing stock by 632, most of them apartments.

Educated by the Claremont Unified School District. Scores a mix, reflecting the diverse demographics of the town. Claremont High scores in 80th to 90th percentiles. Oakmont Elementary scores in 50th percentiles. Voters in 2000 approved $49 million bond to renovate schools.

Zero homicides each in 1999. The counts for previous years are 0, 0, 1, 1, 1, 3, 0, 0, 2. Claremont has its own police department.

Downtown L.A. is a long 30 miles to the west but Claremont has Metrolink (commuter rail) service to L.A. and San Bernardino. Freeway on south of town. About eight miles to Ontario Airport.

Activities galore. The city runs programs for all ages with activities ranging from dance to tennis to chess to knitting. Usual sports. Many activities associated with the colleges: concerts, readings, plays, exhibits, etc. Botanical garden, senior center, modern library, heritage tours. Golf course, 14 parks. Chamber of commerce (909) 624-1681.

COMMERCE

Downtown L.A.
Commerce
L.A. International Airport
Long Beach

LIKE ITS NAME SUGGESTS, this city is devoted to commerce (and industry), about 1,500 businesses, but it's also home to 13,371 residents, almost all of them living in two neighborhoods divided by Atlantic Boulevard.

School rankings low to middling. Commerce formed itself into a legal city in 1960 to get control of its taxes and planning. As part of the incorporation package, the new city included four libraries, an inducement for residents to vote yes. City offers great package of amenities.

Commerce erected about 57 percent of its current housing between 1940 and 1970. Among single homes, two- and three-bedroom units run neck and neck. The housing was aimed at blue-collar workers: plain, easy to build, affordable. Here and there you'll find homes with four bedrooms. Some deep lots have homes out back.

Housing care mixed. Some people take a lot of care. No graffiti (city runs a cleanup program.) The state in 2000 counted 3,453 housing units: 1,968 single homes, 541 single attached, 942 multiples, 2 mobiles. In the 1990s, the town's housing stock increased by 125 units and its population by 1,200.

Children attend schools run by the Montebello Unified School District. Sample rankings: Bandini Elementary, 20th to 40th percentile; Rosewood Park Elementary, 10th percentile. In 1998 voters passed a bond to renovate schools.

Three homicides each in 1999 and 1998. Counts for previous years are 4, 4, 2, 10, 1, 4, 1, 1. Commerce has one of the highest crime rates in county, the mischief mainly of burglars and thieves. The low population throws off the statistics. But this is a town for precautions. Some homes use security doors and window bars. City contracts with sheriff's department to provide police protection. Two sheriff's substations.

Seniors center, community center, aquatorium (two pools, wading pool, sauna), three parks, shooting range. Classes and activities for adults and children. People working (but not living) in Commerce can purchase a pass for the aquatorium. Large casino.

About six miles east of downtown L.A. Interstates 5 and 710 bisect the town. Commerce has its own bus system (no fares). Metrolink (commuter rail). Buses to downtown L.A. All in all, a great commute. Many jobs in town. Commerce is working to attract even more businesses. Buildings include former tire factory, now office-retail complex, with a facade inspired by palace of Assyrian king. Chamber of commerce (323) 728-7222.

COMPTON

BEDROOM CITY located about 12 miles south of Los Angeles downtown. School scores low. Nonetheless, a community that provides needed housing for low-income residents. Population 97,966.

The state tallied 54 homicides in 1999, 48 homicides in 1998 and 16 in 1997. The counts for previous years are 72, 79, 81, 62, 58, 87, 78. Crime remains worrisome.

Served by Compton Unified School District. A few schools score above the 20th percentile. Most score below. State intervened to renovate and run schools, improve teaching, buy books. Extra funding to help kids and improve programs. Educators are watching Compton to see if state intervention helps.

These problems notwithstanding, Compton in many ways is a "working" community. It provides low-cost housing for the low-income and for immigrants getting started in this country.

When you drive into town, you will see graffiti, steel security doors, bars on windows, derelict cars, empty lots and many homes rundown and in need of repair. But you'll also see homes that have been kept up and people repairing roofs, painting exteriors and making improvements. On the west side a townhouse subdivision was recently constructed. You'll also find, hidden away on narrow roads, small farms with cows, chickens and gardens.

Compton started its boom in the 1940s when 5,878 housing units were built. The 1950s saw the construction of 7,891 units and in 1960s, 3,619 units. In 1970s, housing starts dropped to 1,086 units and in 1980s they rose to 2,488 units. All this translates into a lot of housing choices. The state in 2000 counted 23,471 housing units: 16,026 single homes, 1,493 single attached, 5,370 multiples, 582 mobiles. In the 1990s, Compton increased its population by 7,500 and its housing stock by 230 units.

On weekends, soccer teams in flashy uniforms take over Compton's playing fields. Compton Community College waves the flag for education and provides many courses and activities for low fees— a plus for the community. California state university about a mile to the south.

Bordered by five freeways, a commute plus. About 20 minutes to downtown L.A. or to Long Beach, both job centers. Buses. Compton has small airport on west side. Chamber of commerce (310) 631-8611.

COVINA

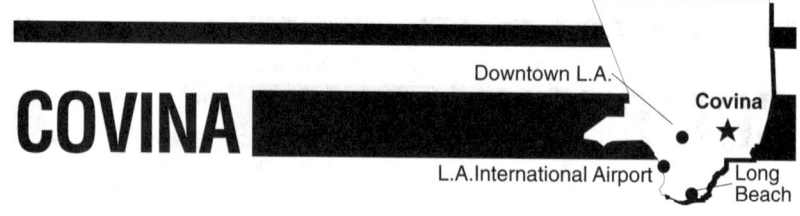

MIDDLE-CLASS CITY in the east county. It lies between the San Jose hills and the San Gabriel Mountains, a sort of cove, one pioneer supposedly thought. In its early days, it had vineyards. And so the name: cov + vina. Another version spins off an Indian name. Crime rate low. School rankings low to high. Population 47,988.

In housing, Covina is a city that can almost be defined by one statistic. About 64 percent of its housing was built in the 1950s and the 1960s. At that time, the favorite was the three-bedroom, two-bathroom home with the garage attached to the house, often set off at an angle to the driveway.

With variations, that's what you'll find all over Covina. Some streets mix in newer homes, slightly bigger. Near the downtown and on the west side, you'll find cottages and bungalows and larger custom homes. But even here the three-bedroom home shows up. Some tract models rise into two-stories and four bedrooms, and a smaller number into five or more bedrooms. The state in 2000 counted 16,346 housing units: 9,162 single homes, 1,179 single attached, 5,483 multiples, 522 mobiles. In the 1990s, Covina's population increased by 4,500 and housing by 200 units.

Nice-looking town. Homes in good repair, lawns mowed, shrubs trimmed. Palm trees line — what else? — Palm Drive. Downtown fixed up: bookstore, movie house converted to community theater, restaurants, sidewalk cafes, antique shops. Used to be famous for its oranges. Rich soil, great for growing.

Education by the Covina-Valley Unified School District, which will vote on an improvement bond in June 2001. Most schools score just below or just above the 50th percentile. Charter Oak Unified School District also serves the area. Its overall scores also hover about the 50th percentile. Two community colleges in nearby towns.

Four homicides in 1999. The counts for previous years are 1, 1, 7, 2, 2, 10, 2, 1, 2. Covina has its own police department.

Interstates 210 and 10 run to the north and south of the town. Downtown L.A. is a long 23 miles to the west. Metrolink (commuter rail). Buses. Covina has landed a bunch of small and mid-sized industries, offices and stores and this cuts the commute for many while boosting the tax base.

Library. Seniors center. Historical museum. About a dozen parks. Usual sports. Farmers market. Horseback riding. Christmas parade. Chamber of commerce (626) 967-4191.

CRENSHAW
Leimert Park, W. Adams

NEIGHBORHOODS OR TOWNS of the City of L.A., located on the west side. This section stretches from Arlington Avenue to the Baldwin Hills area. Estimated population, about 163,000. School rankings generally below the 50th percentile. Crime ratings unknown.

As you move west along Exposition Boulevard from University of Southern California, home quality falls off a bit then steadily improves and by Arlington Avenue, the neighborhoods come across as middle-class presentable. The homes are old, generally cottages and bungalows, but in good repair and the lawns and shrubs are tended. Tall palm trees line many streets and charm the eye. Many homes have security doors. In many sections of the L.A. Basin, these doors have become a routine item but they may indicate concerns about crime. Patrolled by L.A. police.

Leimert Park is a compact, middle-class community at the base of hills. Two- and three-bedroom homes. Clean. Well-maintained. On one street, giant fir trees, planted on both sides of the street and in the median strip, cast pleasant shadows over all. Small shops, art galleries. Quaint.

Crenshaw lies generally to the west of the Baldwin Hills-Crenshaw Mall and rises from flat lands into hills. The flats contain many apartments; the hills, upscale single homes with views of downtown L.A. In a suburban way, a nice-looking neighborhood.

Served by Los Angeles Unified School District. Sample academic rankings: Vermont Avenue Elementary, 10th percentile; Foshay Learning Center, lower grades, 10th to the 60th percentiles; Crenshaw High, 30th percentiles. Several magnet schools.

About a dozen parks. Recreation through City of L.A. About 10 miles to the Pacific and its beaches. Science Center at Exposition Park.

These neighborhoods are about seven miles from downtown L.A. and five miles from L.A. International Airport, both jobs centers. Compared to other towns, commute falls into the category of "not that bad." Interstate 405 on the east, I-10 on the north. Chamber of commerce (323) 292-7000.

CUDAHY

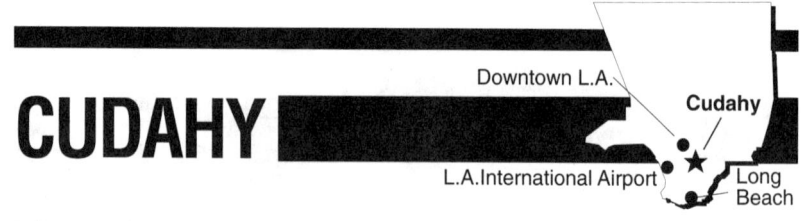

Downtown L.A.
Cudahy
L.A. International Airport
Long Beach

LOW-INCOME CITY located about eight miles southeast of downtown L.A. School rankings low. Population 25,857. Town was named after meat packer Michael Cudahy, who owned a local ranch.

Cudahy by map and Cudahy by population seem mismatched. A standard street map will show a mostly rectangular city with about six streets running in either direction and lot sizes that suggest warehouse and industrial buildings, and almost nothing providing housing for 26,000 people.

The streets are in fact residential streets. Cudahy is one of about a half-dozen L.A. County cities that was subdivided into large lots, sometimes one or two football fields deep.

Homes and apartments, served usually by one driveway, are built on these lots. Some lots will show a home up front and two or three behind. Some will have a dozen or more homes. Or an apartment complex. Some will be empty.

The quality is also uneven. Some homes and apartments need repairs and better care. Some are brand new and well kept. Renters outnumber home owners about five to one, the 1990 census reported. Warehouses and trucking firms can be found on the south side.

The state in 2000 counted 5,547 housing units: 1,631 single homes, 1,187 single attached, 2,309 multiples, 420 mobiles. In the 1990s, Cudahy's population increased by 3,000 and its housing stock by 130 units.

Served by Los Angeles Unified School District, which in 1997 passed $2.4 billion bond to renovate and build schools. Sample academic rankings: Hughes Elementary, 20th percentile; Elizabeth Elementary, lower grades, 10th percentiles; upper 30th percentile.

One homicide in 1999. Counts for previous years are 2, 3, 1, 2, 4, 3, 2, 5, 5. Security doors spotted around town. Some complexes protect themselves with security gates.

Library. Three parks, one with a sports complex. New teen center, fitness center and boxing center. Small cities, like Cudahy, often do better than large cities on making improvements because they are in close contact with their residents and quicker to respond to civic needs.

Buses to downtown. Interstate 710 on the east side. Metrolink (commute rail) station in nearby Commerce. City hall (323) 773-5143.

CULVER CITY

BEDROOM CITY famous for its movies. Where "Gone With The Wind" and the "Wizard of Oz" were shot. Still big part of the movie-entertainment scene. Calls self "Heart of Screenland." Located about three miles south of Beverly Hills and about five miles east of Santa Monica. Population 42,776.

Culver City is a disjointed town, split by a creek. Parts of the city blend into nearby neighborhoods. The western side wiggles down Washington Boulevard in a shape that looks like a dog.

The city started 1940 with 1,827 residential units. In that decade it built 3,194 homes and apartments and in the 1950s, 4,089 units. The 1960s saw the construction of 3,029 units and the 1970s, 3,968 units. In the 1980s, housing starts fell to 836, and in the 1990s, the city constructed about 370 units, most of them apartments. The numbers indicate that Culver City is about out of untapped residential land.

Culver City was built for the middle class at a time when two- and three-bedroom homes were the vogue. The streets are clean, homes are generally kept up, the town seems to get a lot of the old tender loving. Some streets are decorated with old-fashioned lights. A small neighborhood on the south rises into hills with view homes. The state in 2000 counted 17,312 housing units: 6,473 single homes, 1,475 single attached, 9,202 multiples, 162 mobiles.

Zero homicides in 1999. The counts for previous years are 4, 3, 4, 3, 4, 4, 2, 6, 0. Culver City fields its own police department.

Educated by Culver City Unified School District. Many schools are scoring just above the 50th percentiles and a few in the 70th. Voters in 1997 approved $40 million bond to renovate schools. Work is almost complete.

Library, about a dozen parks, Fox Hills Mall. West Los Angeles Community College. About four miles from the Pacific Ocean. Large regional park nearby. Regional mall. Rejuvenated downtown. New civic center. Costco. Best Buy. Two medical centers.

Short hop to the Santa Monica Freeway, which leads to downtown L.A., 11 miles to the east. Five miles to LAX. Culver City has a good jobs base, which means a short commute for many. Sony Pictures studio.

Holy Cross Cemetery: John Candy, Rita Hayworth, Gary Cooper, Bing Crosby, Jimmy Durante, Bela Lugosi, Mario Lanza, Rosalind Russell. Chamber of commerce (310) 287-3850.

DIAMOND BAR

Downtown L.A. — Diamond Bar
L.A. International Airport — Long Beach

MIDDLE-CLASS TO RICH community built over hills, mesas and valleys. Many homes have sweeping views. Located in east county on border of San Bernardino County. Single homes make up over 85 percent of housing. Population 59,101. Diamond Bar got its start in 1956 when a developer purchased 8,000 acres and laid out a "master plan" for community. All California cities are "planned," even those built during the gold rush. Many of the older cities, however, were developed piecemeal and had as their center the railroad depot. This often skewed the town's modern development. Master-plan cities recognize the importance of the freeway and try to do an intelligent job, in a unified way, of mixing homes, roads and businesses.

In its northern sector, Diamond Bar has erected middle-class homes and condos. Many are positioned for views. On the east side of town, south of Grand Avenue, executive homes hide behind security gates. Some of these homes are gorgeous affairs that run down the ridgelines and command great views. West of Diamond Bar Boulevard, most of the housing runs to middle-class plus, all in good shape. On the west side of town, an older subdivision will be found, along with a mobile home park. Over 80 percent of the town was built in the last 25 years — a lot of the new. The state in 2000 counted 18,043 housing units: 12,750 single homes, 2,667 single attached, 2,358 multiples, 268 mobiles. In the 1990s, the city built about 380 units, most of them single homes. Population increased by nearly 5,500.

Walnut Valley School District. Many schools score in 80th and 90th percentiles. Voters in 2000 approved a $50 million renovation bond. Some neighborhoods are in Pomona District where scores vary widely but the Diamond Bar elementary schools are scoring in the 80th and 90th percentiles. Pomona district in 1998 passed a bond to renovate schools. Cal Poly (state university) and community college are located nearby.

Diamond Bar has its own jobs, including a large Insurance complexes, and it borders City of Industry, major job center. Also many jobs around Ontario Airport. Short drive to Orange County. Highways 57 and 60 split the town. About 31 miles to downtown L.A. Park and ride lots.

Zero homicides in 1999 and 1998, three in 1997. The counts for previous years are 2, 2, 1, 2, 0, 3, 4.

One golf course, another located nearby. Large regional park. City runs recreation programs that include bowling, fitness, horseback riding, tennis, kids music, ballet and more. Seniors center. Chamber of commerce (909) 595-5222.

DOWNEY

Downtown L.A.
Downey
L.A. International Airport
Long Beach

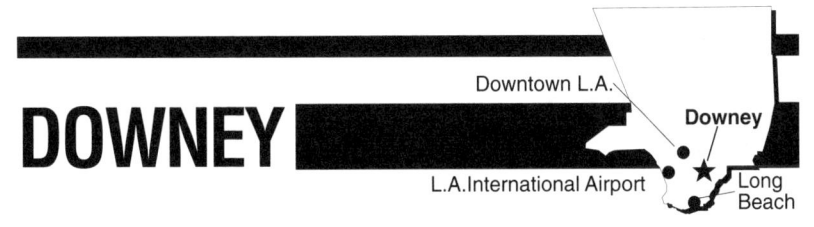

MIDDLE TO MIDDLE-PLUS CITY that used to be an aerospace center and is undergoing major changes. The largest firm, Boeing, which employed about 2,800, closed a few years ago. The property was taken over by the city and is to be developed. Population 102,103. School rankings bounce all over but many are well above the 50th percentile.

Like many L.A. cities, Downey got its boom in the years right after World War II. The city built about 44 percent of its current housing in one decade alone, the 1950s. When you add the housing built over the two following decades, you have about 75 percent of all of Downey's housing. The three-bedroom home with family room was the favorite of this era. The 1990 census disclosed that among owner-occupied units in Downey the three-bedroom home made up about 55 percent of the total. The two-bedroom home followed with 27 percent of the total.

This conjures up a picture of Downey as a typical suburb with tract homes laid down one after the other. In reality, the town comes across as prettier. Downey's demographics show that it attracted many executives and professionals. Many of the homes have been teased upscale with brick facing, imaginative landscaping and custom touches. The styles include colonials, Tudors and some homes that in size and appointments rise into mini-mansions. Downey also has its plain housing but the level of care throughout the city appears high. The state in 2000 counted 34,612 housing units: 20,106 single homes, 1,368 single attached, 12,939 multiples, 199 mobiles. In the 1990s, Downey's housing stock increased by about 310 units and its population by 10,500.

Educated by the Downey Unified School District. Many schools are scoring from the 50th to the 80th percentile.

Nine homicides in 1999. Counts for previous years are 6, 7, 7, 7, 9, 3, 5, 8, 1. Downey has own police department. Here and there you'll find security doors and windows but many homes go without them.

Movies, roller-skating rink, two golf courses, 11 parks, 10 playgrounds, civic theater, fishing lakes, two museums, senior center, bowling alley — Downey appears to do very well in the recreation department. Medical center.

Interstates 105 and 5 to downtown L.A., about 13 miles to northwest. Metrolink (commuter rail) in nearby towns. Chamber of commerce (562) 923-2191.

DOWNTOWN L.A.

Downtown L.A.
L.A. International Airport
Long Beach

Westlake, Boyle Heights, Chinatown

HEART OF THE CITY of L.A. Where hotels, office and government buildings, civic center are located. Bustling, changing, diverse. Many apartment buildings but also many single homes. School rankings on the low side. A good place to get a start in L.A.

Westlake is the neighborhood to immediate west of downtown. It includes MacArthur Park, backdrop to many movies. The city planning department in 1994 put the population at 103,225. Boyle Heights, 1994 population 92,489, is located just east of the downtown and blends into the unincorporated neighborhood of East L. A. Chinatown is a small neighborhood located just north of the downtown, population about 10,000. Many Chinese restaurants and stores. A few guide books will break out a "Little Tokyo," a few blocks south and east of the civic center. Some neighborhoods in L.A. start out as the first home for a particular group, win a name designation and then many residents and their descendants move on, leaving behind some compatriots, the neighborhood tag and a focal point for celebrations, restaurants, cultural centers.

Downtown L.A., like Manhattan, is built up, up, up. But, unlike Manhattan, once you get away from the central core L.A. descends into low-profile apartment buildings, two to four stories (some higher) and single homes.

The 1990 census divided Westlake into 88 percent apartments, 8 percent single homes (the remaining were group quarters, such as hotels). Boyle Heights was divided 58 percent apartments and 41 percent single homes.

Central City, with a current population of about 48,000, split 64 percent apartments, 4 percent single homes (the rest group quarters).

Served by L.A. Unified School District. Sample rankings: Ann Street Elementary and Berendo Middle, 10th percentile; Roosevelt High, 20th-30th percentile.

For information about crime, see profile of City of L.A. and last chapter.

Main library. Parks. El Pueblo de Los Angeles and Olivera Street (first Spanish settlement). Museums. Concert halls. New sports arena, Catholic cathedral under construction. Both are expected to boost fortunes of downtown. Buses travel all around these neighborhoods. Many jobs. Short commute. Chamber of commerce (213) 580-7500.

DUARTE

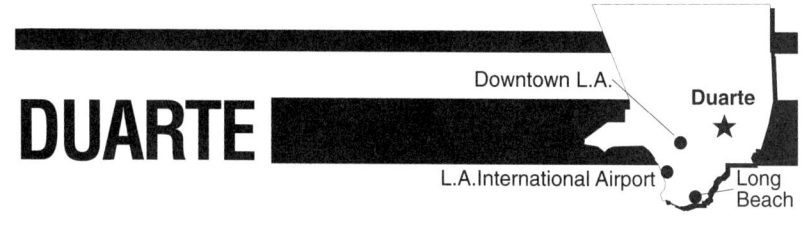

BEDROOM CITY in the foothills of the San Gabriel Mountains. Generally middle class. Well-cared-for. Spruced up downtown. In 1998, passed a $43 million bond to renovate schools. Crime low. Population 23,000.

Duarte is a pretty town that slopes up to the San Gabriel Mountains then moves into the foothills. Ordinarily, this would push the housing way up the scale. But Duarte even in its hill neighborhoods was built for the middle class. Some homes expand to a second floor and a third car in the garage but that's about it for opulence.

The city is divided by Interstate 210. South of the freeway, the homes on some streets run to old and small. Maintenance is still generally good but a few homes have faded in appearances.

North of the freeway, the homes are newer, the quality of care higher. Some of the hill homes have views.

The state in 2000 counted 6,906 housing units: 4,204 single homes, 935 single attached, 1,556 multiples, 211 mobiles. In the 1990s, Duarte's housing increased by 135 units and its population by 2,300 people.

North of the freeway, the schools score higher, a reflection of the town's demographics. Duarte school district also educates children from outside city limits. School rankings bounce all over, a reflection of the district's diverse demographics. Three schools score below the 50th percentile and one school scores well above while another straddles the middle.

One homicide in 1999. The counts for previous years are 1, 1, 1, 0, 0, 1, 4, 2, 0. City contracts with the sheriff's department to provide police protection.

Swim center. Fitness center. Nine-hole golf course. Seniors center. City runs after-school programs for kids and provides child care. About dozen parks. Hiking and horse trials. Large regional parks near by. Library. Museum. Performing arts center.

Two medical centers: City of Hope and Santa Teresita. City is using redevelopment (tax allocations) to spruce up downtown and get rid of the dilapidated. About 20 miles to downtown L.A., a grueling commute for those who have to make it. But many jobs can be found in Pasadena, about eight miles to the west. Chamber of commerce (626) 357-3333.

EAST L.A.

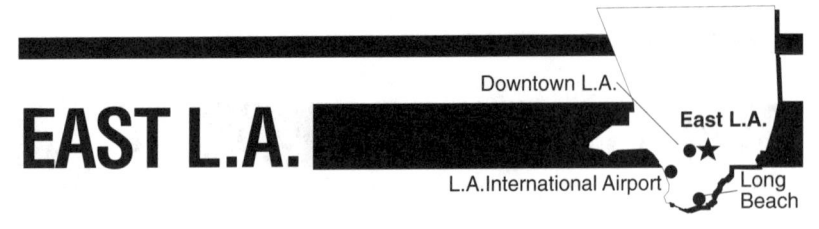

Downtown L.A.
East L.A.
L.A. International Airport
Long Beach

LARGE UNINCORPORATED COMMUNITY to the immediate east of downtown L.A. Housing over hills and flatlands. Also known as "East Los." Population, 1994 figures, 131,647.

School scores generally low. Crime not tracked by the FBI but many homes have security doors and window bars.

East Los Angeles has some of the oldest housing and one of the best commutes in the county. It's a popular place for immigrants seeking to get a toehold in L.A.

But it also has a solid foundation of home ownership. Over one-third of the residential units, mostly two- and three-bedroom homes, are owner occupied, the 1990 census reported.

Appearances vary by block. Some suffer from graffiti and litter, others are relatively clean. Some houses are kept up and in good repair; others aren't. Lively business section. Many shops. On weekends, the streets are crowded with shoppers.

Homes in the northern section, known as City Terrace, are draped over hills with narrow streets. The rest of East L.A. is generally flat.

Educated by the Los Angeles School District. Sample rankings: Belvedere, 10th to 25th percentiles; Eastman Avenue Elementary, 20th percentiles; Garfield High, 30th percentiles. Several magnet schools also serve the neighborhood. A large California state university and a community college border East L.A. Many classes and activities. Both encourage residents to take an interest in education.

Being unincorporated, East Los Angeles is governed by the county board of supervisors and its departments. Patrolled by sheriff's deputies. Over last 30 years, several efforts have been made to incorporate the neighborhood as a city but all have failed.

About 10 parks, including Belvedere, a half-mile square. Several libraries. Outdoor murals. Shopping along Cesar Chavez Boulevard and in downtown.

About four miles from downtown L.A. Buses. Metrolink (commute rail) station at the university. Four freeways cross the community. Great commute.

Chamber of commerce (323) 722-2005.

ECHO PARK
Silver Lake, Los Feliz

NEIGHBORHOODS of the City of Los Angeles, located northwest of downtown L.A. Section includes Chavez Ravine (Dodger Stadium), Elysian Park, and streets below and to west of Griffith Park. Estimated population 100,000. Good commute. These neighborhoods defy easy labeling. They mix housing styles or they border neighborhoods different in quality.

Echo Park, near Dodger Stadium, has many old, small homes. Quality uneven. Some streets sparkle, some fizzle, and even on the same block, upkeep will vary. Number of Victorians preserved.

Silver Lake, located around the lake, steps way up in quality and on many streets comes across as middle-class plus. Old Hollywood movie leaders used to make their homes here.

Both Echo Park and Silver Lake meander over hills. Many homes have views of L.A. Basin or lake. Some hill streets are narrow. The 1990 census divided residential units in Echo Park-Silver Lake into 41 percent single homes, 59 percent apartments.

Los Feliz is a prestige neighborhood that scoots around Griffith Park and flows into the upscale Hollywood hills. Many of the homes run to two-story, four- and five-bedroom units. Some can be classified as palatial. Many homes are built in ravines; no views. Others have great vistas.

In many locations, if you drive five or ten blocks these neighborhoods change, often dramatically. Some streets, usually near commercial thoroughfares, will have stores and homes with security doors. A few blocks away, these devices disappear. No reading on crime but many streets appear middle-class safe. Many residents use private security services. Patrolled by L.A. police.

Served by L.A. Unified School District. Sample academic rankings: Los Feliz Elementary, 20th to 40th percentile; King Middle, 20th percentile; Marshall High, 40 to 50th percentile.

Parks and open space galore, thanks to the two large parks. L.A. City College close by. Many classes, activities. Libraries. Close to movie-entertainment studios. Santa Monica Boulevard runs straight to Hollywood. Three to five miles to downtown L.A. Highway 101 and Interstate 5 to downtown. Buses. Chamber of commerce (213) 580-7500.

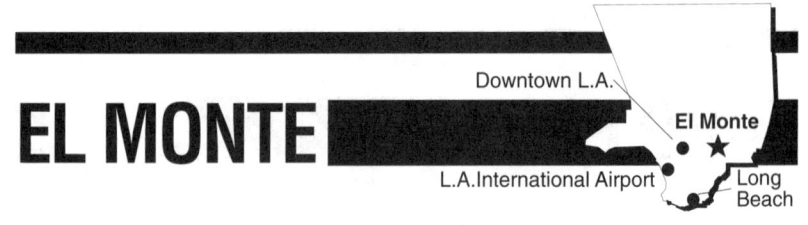

EL MONTE

Downtown L.A. • El Monte ★ • L.A. International Airport • Long Beach

BEDROOM CITY located about 12 miles east of downtown L.A. Great variety of single homes. Country feeling in some neighborhoods. School rankings low to high. Population 119,992.

Like about a half-dozen other cities in L.A. County, El Monte went in for deep-lot housing. Scattered around the town are lots roughly about the size of a football field. Some have just one home and a lot of open space. Others have four or six or eight or more homes, served by one driveway. Some of the newer "complexes" will be protected by gates.

In some instances, modern homes (stucco, tile roofs, two stories) will be set down across from shacks or old, small homes. On other streets, toward the center of town, El Monte runs to everyday suburban tract with three-bedroom homes but even here the unexpected enters. A few of these streets are almost entirely shaded by trees. And this combined with the good upkeep of the homes creates a pleasing impression.

El Monte's boom started in war years. Between 1940 and 1970, about 60 percent of its housing stock was constructed, single homes outnumbering apartments by two to one. Mobile home park can be found on the south side, near the San Gabriel River. The state in 2000 counted 28,004 housing units: 14,956 single homes, 2,943 single attached, 8,583 multiples, 1,522 mobiles. In the 1990s, El Monte's population increased by 14,000 people and its housing stock by 860 units.

Served by the El Monte elementary and high school districts and by the Mountain View Elementary District. Sample rankings: Gidley Elementary, 30th to 60th percentiles; Shirpser Elementary, 20th percentiles; Arroyo High School, 40th to 50th percentiles. In 1999, the El Monte Elementary District passed a $40 million bond to renovate its schools.

Eight homicides in 1999. The counts for previous years are 11, 7, 9, 30, 16, 19, 17, 13, 9. Many California cities of El Monte's size fall into a category of what might be called "suburban safe." Their homicides run maybe four to ten a year. So El Monte's homicides are of some concern but they fall below what's found in inner cities. El Monte has its own police department.

Library, community center, seniors center, eight parks, swimming pool. Close to large regional parks and several golf courses.

Metrolink (commuter rail) to downtown L.A. Interstate 10 crosses the center of city. Easy freeway access. Buses. Internal trolleys. Small airport at north end of town. Chamber of commerce (626) 443-0180.

EL SEGUNDO

LOCATED SOUTH of L.A. International Airport. El Segundo in name and situation turns some people off but once you get beyond this, you'll find a charming little city. Population 16,864. The name means "The Second." In this instance the second Standard Oil Refinery, built in 1917. Standard, now Chevron, remains a big presence, controlling on the south side about half of El Segundo. Down through the years, a small community covering about 550 acres grew up between the refinery and the airport and, because the town had a strong tax base and corporate sponsors, it did an excellent job of installing parks and amenities.

El Segundo has a library, recently renovated, a seniors center, a swimming pool, a driving range, a golf course and about half-dozen parks. The city rec department offers many activities for children, teens and adults. Secluded, intimate town, close to everything, but buffered by the airport and the major industries, seemingly stuck off by itself. It's on the Pacific and has a short drive to some of the finest beaches in L.A. County.

It has its own school district, including one elementary, one middle, and one high. Scores generally run from the 80th to 90th percentile. This indicates strong support for education. $24 million bond passed in 1997 to renovate schools. Center Elementary in 2000 was split into Center Street Elementary and Richmond Street Elementary schools. The town also has a parochial school.

Zero homicides between 1995 and 1999. Counts for previous years are 1, 1, 0, 1, 2. City has own police department.

About 25 percent of the town's housing was built before 1950. About 40 percent was built between 1950 and 1970 and the rest over the last 30 years. The great majority of the single homes have two or three bedrooms. About two dozen homes are positioned along the beach bluffs to command views of the ocean. The rest of the town is built along gently sloping land away from the beach. The state in 2000 counted 7,362 housing units: 3,181 single homes, 293 single attached, 3,887 multiples (many of them hotel rooms), one mobile. In the 1990s, El Segundo's population increased by 1,500 people and its housing stock by 175 units.

Short commute for many because town is surrounded by and includes job-producing offices and industries. Several major hotels. For commuters to downtown L.A., the drive is about 20 miles. Check out the plane noise. Chamber of commerce (310) 322-1220.

ENCINO
Tarzana

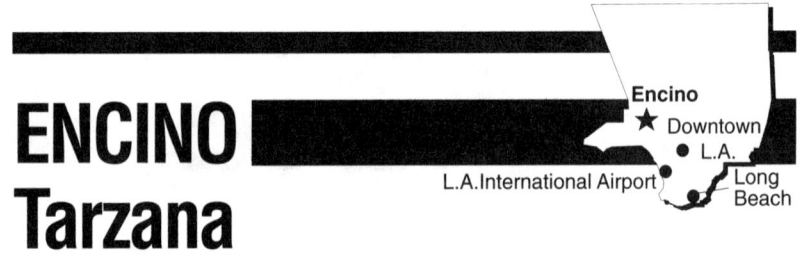

Encino ★
Downtown L.A. ●
L.A. International Airport ●
Long Beach

UPSCALE COMMUNITIES, located on north side of Santa Monica mountains, facing the San Fernando Valley, close to the movie-entertainment businesses.

Tarzana was named after Tarzan; Edgar Rice Burroughs, author of Tarzan books, lived here. Encino is home to some stars. Al Jolson was one of its first honorary mayors. Estimated population for both towns, 65,000.

Both are towns of the City of Los Angeles and patrolled by the L.A. police. Both are educated by the Los Angeles Unified School District. Crime not tracked by FBI but demographics say low. A few homes and a few upscale developments hide behind security gates and tall hedges and many homes subscribe to security services.

Although well-to-do, these towns favor the three- and four-bedroom designs that proved so popular after World War II. Many homes are one story. Where they differ from other towns is in quality of appearance (lot of care) and in luxury mix.

On some streets, the first, second and third homes might be described as middle-class nice, the fourth as a mansion. Generally, the higher the elevation the bigger and better the home but even in the flatlands Tarzana and Encino have some gorgeous homes, with striking designs.

Some hill homes, supported by steel beams, are built out over steep ravines — quintessential L.A.

As you near Ventura Boulevard, apartments and condos enter and older, smaller homes. This explains the hodgepodge scores. The schools mix kids from various demographic backgrounds.

Sample national rankings: Encino Elementary, 50th to 60th percentile; Wilbur Avenue Elementary, 70th to 90th percentile; Tarzana Elementary, 40th to 50th percentile.

Both towns straddle Ventura Boulevard, which has restaurants, shops, bookstores, movies, tall office buildings and a little to the north, the Promenade Mall. Six golf courses in or near these towns. About half-dozen parks,

GARDENA

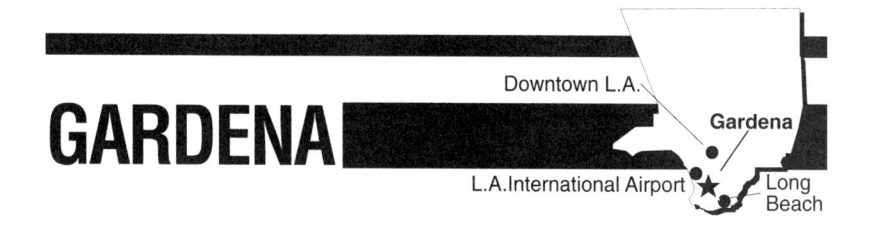

BEDROOM CITY, located about 15 miles south of downtown L.A. In overall appearance plain but well kept. Many trees. School rankings low. Population 59,557. Many people of Japanese descent settled here before World War II, were interned during the war and returned afterwards. Gardena has a sister-city relationship with a Japanese city and has attracted many businesses from Japan.

Another city that boomed during and immediately after World War II. Gardena built 2,439 residential units in the 1940s, 6,987 units in the 1950s and 3,771 in the 1960s — in total about 63 percent of its current housing. In the 1970s and 1980s, Gardena erected, respectively, 2,420 and 2,846 units, a nice chunk of the new and fairly new.

But in housing style, the town stayed close to the most popular postwar model, the three-bedroom home. It makes up almost 50 percent of all owner-occupied homes, followed by the two-bedroom home, 29 percent. Apartments and single homes post almost equal numbers. In the 1990s, Gardena's population increased by 9,700 people and its housing stock by 2,000 units, about half of which were single homes.

While many cities are clean, Gardena is perhaps a little cleaner and a little better maintained than others. The trees help. City hall presents a nice face. The library is first class. The state in 2000 counted 21,054 housing units: 8,959 single homes, 1,033 single attached, 9,894 multiples, 1,168 mobiles.

Education by the Los Angeles Unified School District. Sample academic rankings: Gardena Elementary, 10th to 20th percentile; Peary Middle, 20th percentile; Gardena High School, 30th percentile.

Four homicides in 1999. The counts for previous years are 6, 8, 6, 8, 14, 7, 13, 7, 10. The town has its own police department.

About a half-dozen parks. Community center. Community gym. Swim center. Seniors center. El Camino Community College on southern border. About eight miles to the ocean. A town where you've got to know when to hold and to fold. Among the largest employers, two card casinos, which also stage Las Vegas-type shows and pump millions in taxes into city coffers.

Interstate 110 on the east side, Interstate 105 on the north. Highway 91 on the south, Interstate 405 a few miles to west. About six miles to L. A. International Airport. Many airport-related jobs and this probably means a short commute for many residents. Chamber of commerce (310) 532-9705.

GLENDALE

Downtown L.A. — Glendale — L.A. International Airport — Long Beach

HANDSOME, DYNAMIC CITY built on and around two mountain ranges. Loaded with view homes and housing choices. Pretty, clean and well maintained. School rankings generally middling to high. Population 203,734. Third most-populous city in L.A. County. Thriving downtown.

Glendale starts with gentle hills in its southern section, levels out for its downtown, then rises into the Verdugo Mountains, levels out again before rising into the San Gabriel Mountains. All these hills, mesas and ravines make for view home sites and enhance the attractiveness of the town. Home construction in the hills north of the downtown started just before World War II. Housing styles reflect the era. But almost all fall into the category of professional, four or five bedrooms, tastefully landscaped, showing much care. Above Chevy Chase Drive, east of Highway 2, you'll find some of the newest homes in Glendale, many of them two story, stucco sides and red-tile roofs. Above Foothill Boulevard, on north side, many homes were constructed between 1950 and 1970. Generally they run to three and four bedrooms. At top, Skyview Estates, a cluster of new homes. Glendale also has its older homes, from 19th century and early 1900s. For middle-class housing, drive Verdugo Road at the base of the Verdugo Mountains. Most of the apartments can be found in the downtown, south of the Ventura Freeway. The state in 2000 counted 73,774 housing units: 26,065 single homes, 3,449 single attached, 44,228 multiples, 32 mobiles. In the 1990s, Glendale's population increased by 24,000 people and its housing stock by 1,660 units, most of them apartments or condos.

Glendale School District. Scores range from 30th to 90th percentiles reflecting the varying demographics of the neighborhoods. Magnet high school boosts science. Two new schools opened in 1998, part of 1996 bond measure. Community college.

Three homicides in 1999. Counts for previous years are 2, 6, 14, 8, 5, 9, 7.

Many activities for kids, adults. Two dozen parks. Three golf courses. Glendale symphony. Downtown thrives as a cultural-shopping center with festive night life: classy theater, book stores, restaurants, shops, movie plex. About 14 high-rise buildings. One library has world's largest collection of books on cats. First-class shopping at Galleria (Nordstrom, Macys). Forest Lawn Cemetery on south side: W.C. Fields, Humphrey Bogart, Jean Harlow.

About seven miles to downtown L.A. Three freeways cross town. Metrolink (commuter rail). Chamber of commerce (818) 240-7870.

GLENDORA

MIDDLE TO UPPER-MIDDLE bedroom city located in foothills of San Gabriel Mountains, in the East County. School rankings high, crime low, town well maintained. Population 53,761.

Glendora illustrates a common pattern in many foothill towns. Generally the higher the elevation, the newer the homes, the better the views, the higher the prices. Always there are exceptions. Glendora has some older, smaller homes in its "higher" neighborhoods but they show much care and attention to detail. On the south side, some small hills rise near the Foothill Freeway (Highway 210) and here you also will find upscale housing.

For the most part, Glendora housing runs to middle-class suburban, much of it constructed in the 1950s and 1960s, when Glendora built about 60 percent of its current housing. Foothill Boulevard is a good dividing line. South of Foothill, you will find the older and smaller (generally three bedrooms), north of Foothill, the newer and bigger. For the old and the quaint, drive the west neighborhoods around Pennsylvania Avenue and the streets near the civic center.

Well-cared-for town and in a suburban way, pretty. It has a sign ordinance to discourage the garish, and residents take pride in keeping up their homes. The state in 2000 counted 17,513 housing units: 12,785 single homes, 1,142 single attached, 2,713 multiples, 873 mobiles. In the 1990s, Glendora's population increased by 6,000 people and its housing stock by 635 units.

Served by Glendora Unified School District. Scores land in the top 20 percent in the state. Voters in 2000 approved a $21 million bond, the money to spent to renovate schools and build a new pool and gym at high school.

Citrus Community College, on the west side, sweetens the educational offerings and fields many sports and cultural activities. Glendora used to grow a lot of lemons and oranges.

Zero homicides in 1999 and 1998, one in 1997, and one in 1996. The counts for previous years are 0, 3, 0, 1, 0, 1.

Seniors center, two golf courses, wilderness park, Angeles National Forest (miles of open space), well-stocked library, 10 parks, including a sports park and an equestrian park.

Twenty-six miles to downtown L.A., probably main drawback to the town. But jobs in nearby towns are plentiful. Chamber of commerce (626) 963-4128.

GRANADA HILLS
Knollwood, North Hills

GRANADA HILLS is a bedroom town that straddles Highway 118 on the north side of the San Fernando Valley, just west of Interstate 5. South of Highway 118 the housing runs to middle income. North of Highway 118, the housing becomes newer and rises in size and quality. Estimated population, 46,000. Knollwood, a country-club subdivision located north of the freeway, is generally considered part of Granada Hills.

North Hills, estimated population 50,000, is located south of Highway 118 and south of Granada Hills. North Hills used to be called Sepulveda and maps and guides will frequently still use this name.

Crime not tracked by FBI but probably suburban average south of Highway 118 and low above the highway. Some upper-income neighborhoods hire security services to augment L.A. police.

South of Highway 118, Granada Hills, North Hills and Northridge glide into one another and except for the occasional street sign and vague map designation the communities are almost indistinguishable. North Hills also jumps over Interstate 405 and blends in with Panorama City.

All three boomed in the decades following World War II. All favored middle-class tract homes, mostly three bedrooms. All are towns of the City of Los Angeles and served by the Los Angeles Unified School District. In housing appearances, south of the freeway, North Hills, on a few streets, might lag a little behind Granada Hills but generalizations here invite arguments. Too many similarities. North of the freeway, hills and dales appear, creating view lots. This section was developed later and presents a more modern face.

Sample school rankings: Monroe High School (North Hills), 40th percentiles; Haskell Elementary (Granada Hills), 50th to 70th percentiles; Granada Elementary, 50th percentiles; Granada Hills High, 80th percentiles. Several schools have magnet programs. Following 1994 earthquake, Van Gogh Elementary was rebuilt as high-tech campus.

Two golf courses. Parks and recreation centers scattered around. Close to Cal State University, Northridge, and all it offers.

About 21 miles to downtown L.A. but within 10 to 15 miles of the job centers at Burbank and Van Nuys. Metrolink (commuter rail) at Northridge. Buses. Chamber of commerce (818) 368-3235.

HACIENDA HEIGHTS
Rowland Heights

TWO UNINCORPORATED COMMUNITIES located side by side in eastern L.A. County. School rankings high. Hacienda Heights, estimated population 63,000, and Rowland Heights, estimated population 47,000, are located in flatlands and rolling hills just south of the City of Industry. Being unincorporated they are governed by the County Board of Supervisors and patrolled by sheriff's deputies. No crime stats available but school rankings are a good measure of crime problems. Generally the higher the rankings, the lower the crime. These two communities come across as suburban safe.

Hacienda Heights started to boom in the 1950s but got most of its housing in the 1970s and 1980s. Rowland Heights followed a similar pattern except its boom did not begin until the 1960s. These were decades of prosperity when homes started to grow bigger. Although the three-bedroom home remains the most popular unit, both communities have thousands of four-bedroom homes.

There is a lot of sparkle to these towns because they are so new and well-cared-for. In parts of Hacienda Heights, near Highway 60, some older faded housing can be found. Both communities offer hill homes, some almost mansions, with views of countryside. In Hacienda Heights, one of the largest Buddhist temples in world. Striking building. Many residents in Hacienda Heights want to incorporate the neighborhood into a legal city. A vote may come in 2002.

Hacienda Heights children attend Hacienda-La Puente Unified School District. Scores vary widely but many of the Hacienda Heights schools are landing in the 80th to 90th percentiles. Voters in 2000 approved a $100 million bond to renovate district schools.

Rowland Heights is served by the Rowland Unified School District, which also educates children from other towns. Most of the schools are landing in the 40th to 60th percentile, some higher. Rowland High is scoring in the 80th percentiles. Rowland voters in 2000 approved a $70 million renovation bond.

Highway 60 to downtown L.A., 22 to 25 miles to the east. City of Industry has many jobs, which means a short commute for many residents. Orange County and its job centers are just over the hills to south. Metrolink (commuter rail) to downtown L.A. About six parks in each community, including a regional park that divides the two. Rowland Heights has a golf course on its west side. Shopping at Puente Hills Mall. Library in Hacienda Heights.

HAWAIIAN GARDENS

SMALL BEDROOM CITY, low income, located east of Long Beach on the border of Orange County.

School rankings low but school district offers many choices. Population 15,205.

Hawaiian Gardens built about 75 percent of its current housing between 1940 and 1970. For the most part the city built for working-class families trying to get a toehold in the housing market. Among owner-occupied units, two-bedroom homes dominate.

Housing styles mix the old and the new. Many homes have security doors and window bars. Many look faded. But Hawaiian Gardens also has its homes and apartments where people take pride in appearances.

The state in 2000 counted 3,578 housing units: 1,546 single homes, 430 single attached, 1,351 multiples, 251 mobiles. In the 1990s, Hawaiian Garden's population increased by 1,800 people and its housing stock by 60 units.

Zero homicides in 1999, two in 1998, and three in 1997. The counts for previous years are 1, 3, 0, 3, 5, 8, 4. Hawaiian Gardens has its own police department.

Served by the ABC Unified School District. Sample rankings: Hawaiian Elementary School, 10th percentile; Fedde Middle School, 10th percentile.

The ABC District also serves Lakewood and Cerritos, middle-class towns, higher academic rankings. The kids all come together at the high schools and scores come up. This means that Hawaiian Gardens kids will have a lot of variety in their educational choices and programs. Voters in ABC district in 1997 approved $25 million bond to renovate schools.

Four parks, library, close to a large regional park with a nature center and a golf course.

A long way from downtown L.A., 22 miles, but the Long Beach area offers many jobs and this means a short commute for the lucky ones with these jobs. Hawaiian Gardens is close to many of the job centers of Orange County. Interstate 605 runs up the east side of the city.

With its older, smaller housing, Hawaiian Gardens remains a good town to get started in home ownership if you have little money.

Chamber of commerce (562) 421-1632.

HAWTHORNE

BEDROOM-APARTMENT COMMUNITY located about two miles southeast of L.A. International Airport and about four miles in from the Pacific. Population 80,459.

Blue-collar, middle-class town. School rankings low to middling to high.

Lower-income housing is located near the north. As you move south, the housing shows itself better in quality and appearance. Many streets well-cared-for.

Hawthorne offers a good deal of variety in its housing. Between 1950 and 1990, it built 4,000-6,000 residential units every decade. It is primarily a renter's town, apartments outnumbering single homes by about two to one.

The state in 2000 counted 29,593 housing units: 8,477 single homes, 1,812 single attached, 19,094 multiples, 210 mobiles. In the 1990s, Hawthorne's population increased by 9,000 people and its housing stock by 280 units.

Served by three school districts. Scores in Hawthorne Elementary District land in the 20th and 30th percentiles. Scores at Hawthorne High, part of Centinela Valley District, fall into the 30th percentiles. This district in 2000 approved a $50 million bond to renovate schools. Highest scores, 60th and 70th percentiles, are to be found in Wiseburn Elementary District, on the west side of town. Wiseburn district voters in 2000 approved a $35 million renovation bond. Another school to open in 2001. Southwest community college is located just outside city limits, a nice plus for the town.

Because of the proximity to the airport and local industries, many residents have a commute of only a few miles. Downtown L.A. is 25 miles to the east. Highway 105 recently opened. Down its middle travels a light rail that runs trolleys west to a spot near the airport and east to Norwalk, with connections to downtown L.A. and Long Beach.

Eight homicides in 1999. The counts for previous years are 9, 11, 14, 16, 21, 12, 18, 6, 10. Hawthorne has its own police department.

Incorporated as a city in 1929, Hawthorne has been building its parks and recreation facilities for decades. Two libraries. About 10 parks. Golf course. Town was named after Nathaniel Hawthorne, author of "The Scarlet Letter."

Penneys. Two medical centers. Park and ride lots. Hawthorne has a large municipal airport on its north side. If you are thinking of moving in, check out the airplane noise. Chamber of commerce (310) 676-1163.

HERMOSA BEACH

SMALL RESORT TOWN on the Pacific, about five miles south of L.A. International Airport. Pretty. Well kept. Population 19,631. Crime low. School rankings high.

Hermosa Beach runs about 15 blocks east to west and about 40 blocks north to south. The Pacific Coast Highway runs down its middle. Residential units to the west of Pacific Coast Highway mix single homes with apartments, many of them with good views of the Pacific. L.A. beaches generally rise into small bluffs and these allowed builders to position homes and apartments to catch what everybody wants — a view of the sun sinking into the Pacific. Many of the units here are small and lend themselves to vacation rentals. Streets are narrow. In the summer, the town is filled with college students.

The beach is great: flat, full of sand, miles long, ideal for sunbathing, volleyball and Frisbee tossing. A promenade runs along the beach and extends into several other towns. Restaurants, shops and supermarkets can be found along Pier Avenue and the Pacific Coast Highway. East of Pacific Coast Highway the hills rise into neighborhoods with middle-class tract homes.

Between 1940 and 1990, Hermosa Beach built between 1,000 to 2,000 units in every decade. Among owner-occupied units, two and three bedrooms run neck and neck. Most of the homes and apartments run to middle-class presentable. But a fair number of homes, especially those with ocean views, have many custom touches. The state in 2000 counted 9,813 housing units: 3,969 single homes, 943 single attached, 4,824 multiples, 77 mobiles. In the 1990s, Hermosa Beach added 125 single homes.

Zero homicides in 1999, 1998, and 1997. The counts for previous years are 0, 1, 0, 1, 0, 0, 0. Hermosa Beach has its own police department.

Hermosa Beach Elementary District, which has two schools, scores in 90th percentiles. Teens have choice of Mira Costa High in Manhattan Beach District or Redondo High in Redondo Beach district. In 2000, voters in both districts approved renovation bonds, Manhattan Beach $26 million, Redondo $55 million. Mira Costa scores in 90th percentiles, Redondo High 80th.

Fishing pier, about half-dozen parks, library, a good mix of restaurants, movies, the beach and all it offers. Skate park.

About 21 miles to downtown L.A. but many residents probably work in or near the L.A. airport, a 15-minute drive. About three miles to Interstate 405. Chamber of commerce (310) 376-0951.

HIDDEN HILLS

PRESTIGE GATED CITY in the Santa Monica Mountains, near Woodland Hills, facing San Fernando Valley. Crime low, school rankings high. Kind of town where if you have to ask how much, you don't belong. Population 2,052.

For a city, Hidden Hills has one of the highest, if not the highest, average incomes in the county. Of the 467 homes singled out for a special count by the 1990 census, 454 or 97 percent were worth $500,000 or more. About half the homes have nine or more rooms, reported the census. Locals call the homes "country estates." No street lights, no sidewalks. Lots of trees and foliage. Country feeling. Many homes have pools and tennis courts. Community pool. Horse country. Trails meander through town. Golf course nearby.

To head off a proposed extension of Burbank Boulevard, Hidden Hills incorporated as city in 1961, just before the state passed laws to make it harder for small communities with no businesses to make themselves legal cities. As a legal city, Hidden Hills has control over its planning, police protection and civic affairs. The town in reality is run by a city government and a homeowners association. Tough rules on what can be built. Covenants and restrictions.

Slow-growing. According to state statistics, Hidden Hills added 62 single homes in the 1980s and 50 homes in the 1990s. The state in 2000 counted 577 housing units: 570 single homes, 6 single attached, 1 multiple, 0 mobiles. In the 1990s, Hidden Hills' population increased by 225 people.

Security gates and guards at entrances to Hidden Hills. Patrolled. Many neighborhoods in this part of L.A. county, for reasons of safety and privacy, are gated and employ private security firms. This does not mean that they are crime free. Teens will still get into mischief, domestic disputes will break out. But it does mean that compared to other places, these high-security towns and neighborhoods will have much lower crime. Zero homicides in 1994 through 1999.

Served by Las Virgenes School District, which is using a $93 million bond to renovate schools, open a new middle school in 2002 and relocate and open an elementary school in 2003. District includes Calabasas and Agoura Hills, also upscale. Many schools in district are scoring in the top 20 percent of state which indicates strong community and parental support for education. Round Meadow Elementary School, located at the top of Hidden Hills, lands in the 80th to 90th percentile.

No chamber of commerce. City hall (818) 888-9281.

HOLLYWOOD
Hollywood Hills

FABLED MOVIE CAPITAL of the world, still a media-entertainment center. Favorite spot for tourists. Estimated population 208,000. In housing, divided between the plain and the upscale. Over three-fourths of the residential units are apartments. Many of the single homes are located in the hills.

A "town" of the City of L.A., governed and policed by the City of L.A. Melrose Avenue marks the southern boundary, the famous Hollywood sign in the hills the northern boundary, La Brea Avenue the western boundary and just beyond Vermont Avenue the eastern boundary. Moving north from Melrose, Hollywood rises gently until it reaches the hills and then ascends dramatically. For our purposes, we include the hill neighborhoods above Hollywood and Sunset boulevards, up to Beverly Hills and West Hollywood.

South of Hollywood Boulevard, the housing consists mainly of apartment complexes. Many of them were built in the 1950s and 1960s and show their age. As you move west towards Beverly Hills, the apartments become a little cleaner, the streets a little spiffier, the landscaping a little more imaginative.

The single homes found in the hills above Sunset and Hollywood boulevards command views of the countryside and sometimes the ocean. These are considered choice neighborhoods, home to many who work in the entertainment industries. Great variety of shapes and size in homes — some mansions, most homes for professionals.

Served by the L.A. Unified School District. Sample rankings: Cheremoya Elementary, 10th to 30th percentiles; Melrose Elementary, 20th to 40th percentiles; Hollywood High, 30th to 40th percentiles.

Crime stats not available but prudence indicates extra care in run down sections. Renewal efforts are under way to return town to its glory days. Move also afoot to pull out of L.A. and incorporate Hollywood as a city.

Hollywood has too many attractions to list but among them are the Chinese Theater, the Walk of Fame with the names of over 2,000 stars, Hollywood Bowl, and Griffith Park where James Dean and Sal Mineo played out the planetarium scene from "Rebel Without a Cause." Libraries, parks.

Highway 101 divides the town and leads directly to downtown L.A., seven miles to east. Many local jobs. Subway to downtown. Buses. Chamber of commerce (323) 469-8311.

HUNTINGTON PARK

SMALL CITY located about five miles south of downtown L.A. near the cities of Vernon and Bell. School rankings low. Lively shopping section. Population 63,626.

Huntington Park got its housing boom from 1940 to about 1970 when about 2,600 residential units, a mix of apartments and single homes, were constructed every decade.

For the most part, the single homes ran to two and three bedrooms and were aimed at veterans and people just getting into the housing market.

Huntington Park remains a good place to pick up a home for a reasonable price and is popular with immigrants.

The state in 2000 counted 14,878 housing units: 4,921 single homes, 1,807 single attached, 8,139 multiples, 11 mobiles. In the 1990s, Huntington Park's population increased by 7,500 people and its housing stock by 340 units.

Education by Los Angeles Unified School District. Sample rankings: Miles Avenue Elementary, 20th and 30th percentile; Gage Middle School, 10th percentile; Huntington Park High, 30th percentile.

Six homicides in 1999, thirteen in 1998, and eight in 1997. The counts for previous years are 4, 11, 8, 9, 8, 14, 12. Many homes have security doors. Huntington Park has its own police department.

Library. Six parks, including a large municipal park, and the usual recreation activities: baseball, soccer, etc. On weekends, downtown streets are filled with shoppers. Lively section.

Five minutes to downtown L.A. Close to Interstate 110. Buses. Light rail a few miles to east. Many jobs in and near downtown and in nearby Vernon and Commerce.

On weekends, residents take to the shops, restaurants and stores along Pacific Boulevard.

Town's developer chose name to honor Henry E. Huntington, his friend and one of the richest men in country.

Chamber of commerce (323) 585-1155.

INDUSTRY

Downtown L.A.
Industry
L.A. International Airport
Long Beach

A LONG, NARROW CITY running east to west, Industry is what its name implies: a place where businesses, industries, service firms and offices have collected. Located in the east county, near La Puente.

About 700 people live in the community but you would be hard pressed to find them. The landscape is dominated by warehouses, office complexes, etc. Some open spaces are planted for farming.

The state in 2000 counted 134 housing units: 117 single homes, 5 single attached, 6 multiples, 6 mobiles.

Until about 1960, California law made it easy for any organized landowning group to establish a city. Within L.A. County, about a half-dozen "cities" were formed to give business interests control over planning, zoning and municipal taxes. Only in a remote way can they be considered residential communities.

Industry's few children are educated in the Hacienda-La Puente Unified School District. District scores bounce all over the place, from low to high. Voters in 2000 approved a $100 million bond to renovate district schools.

Zero homicides in 1999, one in 1998, and zero in 1997. The counts for previous years are 4, 2, and 7. Cities like Industry often have statistically skewed crime rates and unusual crime patterns. The towns attract thousands of outsiders during the day and few at night. Sometimes crime spills over from other communities. About 90 percent of Industry's crime falls under category of theft in one form or another. Sheriff's substation in town.

For a business-industrial town, a nice-looking place. The streets are clean, the buildings painted, the shrubs and lawns tended to. A fair amount of open land gives a spacious quality to the town. For amusement, one shopping plaza, a museum, an equestrian center, a golf course and a large hotel.

Jobs galore. For all its problems with commuting, Los Angeles has many jobs outside of the downtown. Industry makes the commute easy for residents who live in the east county. Twenty miles to downtown L.A. Served by Metrolink (commuter rail).

The Manufacturers Council serves as a chamber of commerce (626) 968-3737.

INGLEWOOD

BEDROOM CITY located just east of L.A. International Airport and in the flight path of many planes. Population 121,035. Home to Hollywood Park, a large horse-racing track, and to the Forum, which hosts concerts, boxing matches and other events.

Homicides are down but crime is still troublesome, school scores low to high. Many streets show a lot of care: homes in good repair, streets cleaned, graffiti rare. Some of the newer tracts are gated and you will find new middle-class housing right in the center of the town. When the jumbo jets glide in overhead, you brace yourself for a roar of noise. The noise certainly is there but suppressed and it may not be irritating to many residents.

Served by Inglewood Unified School District. Scores land generally in the 30th to 60th percentile and some schools land in the top 20 percent of state. In 1998 district voters passed $131 million bond to build and renovate schools.

Sixteen homicides in 1999, thirty-five in 1998, and twenty-five in 1997. The counts for previous years are 27, 40, 46, 45, 37, 46, 55. Many homes have bars on windows and security doors. Inglewood has its own police department.

Inglewood varies markedly in the quality of neighborhoods. Some sections, particularly those on the east side, have lower crime than others. Inglewood is using code enforcement officers to discourage graffiti and to keep the streets clean of debris and derelict cars and to improve appearances.

The state in 2000 counted 39,102 housing units: 13,683 single homes, 2,744 single attached, 22,398 multiples, 277 mobiles. In the 1990s, Inglewood's population increased by 11,400 and its housing stock by 400 units.

In the 1940s, Inglewood constructed 6,131 residential units; in the 1950s, 10,054 units and in the 1960s, 8,287 units. These three decades account for two-thirds of all of the housing units in the city. Among single homes, two and three bedrooms dominate.

Social amenities include Boys and Girls Club, after-school activities for the kids, Little Theater, a seniors center, and 13 parks, plus all the activities associated with the race track and Forum. L.A. International Airport and the surrounding communities are loaded with industries and jobs. High rises near freeway. Many residents have a short commute. Interstates 405 and 105 tie into freeway system. Distance to downtown L.A. is 13 miles. Buses. Light rail (with connections) to downtown L.A. Chamber of commerce (310) 677-1121.

IRWINDALE

IF YOU WANT INTIMACY, look here. Population 1,202. Crime low, school rankings hard to break out because the kids are mixed in with children from other towns.

Irwindale is synonymous with rocks. By one estimate, the quarries on the west side of the city have supplied about two-thirds of the rock, gravel and aggregate used to build L.A. County. The city also has a fair number of industries and warehouses.

Irwindale incorporated itself as a legal city in 1957 for a variety of reasons: to get control of local taxes, to head off annexation by neighboring Duarte, to get some revenue to fill potholes and build sidewalks, and to put some money back in the town.

If you have a great tax base, which Irwindale does, you can afford to shell out for arts and crafts and amusements. Irwindale has a large park, a swimming pool, a gym, a library, a community center with seats for everyone in town. Large regional parks nearby. Short drive to the San Gabriel Mountains. Removed from the residential neighborhoods is a speedway.

Irwindale has its own police department, one officer for every 50 residents. Two homicides in 1999, zero in 1998, 1997, 1996, 1995 and 1994.

The housing generally is middle-class tract, well-cared-for but nothing fancy, most of it clustered around city hall. The state in 2000 counted 304 housing units: 272 single homes, 7 single attached, 19 multiples, 6 mobiles. In the 1990s, Irwindale's population increased by 150 people and its housing stock by 22 units.

Served by Covina Valley School District. The elementary school in town, Merwin, scores in the 40th and 50th percentiles. Irwindale, through scholarships, rewards kids who work at academics and go to college. City provides free busing to schools. Up for vote in 2001: a $50 million renovation bond.

For the future, Irwindale hopes to shape some of the older quarries into more land for businesses and industry.

Bisected by Interstates 605 and 210. Good freeway access. About 20 miles to downtown L.A. but if you can't find a local job in this burg, God or nature probably doesn't want you to work.

Named after Irwin, a fellow who in the 19th century figured out a way to irrigate most of the town. Chamber of commerce (626) 960-6606.

LA CAÑADA FLINTRIDGE

PRESTIGE CITY in foothills of San Gabriel Mountains next to Pasadena. Has some of the finest mansions in L.A. County. Crime low, school scores among highest in state. Home to Jet Propulsion Lab. Population 21,103.

La Cañada Flintridge defies one of the fundamentals laws of development: It did not build its best homes on its highest elevations.

When a rich politician named Flint wanted to create an estate village in the 1920s, he chose flat and rolling land below Foothill Boulevard. There the wealthy built their mansions, gorgeous buildings, some visible from the road, many hidden behind tall hedges. The mansion neighborhood also has its modern homes, large, pretty and well appointed. Some of them have views.

After World War II, the land above Foothill Boulevard, known as Alta Cañada, was developed. Housing was built for professionals and managers. Many of the homes are four- and five-bedroom ranchers or Eichlers (a 1950 design that made innovative use of windows and atriums) or tract models of that era. At the top of the hills, you'll find executive homes, two stories, six, seven and eight rooms. In 1976, the two communities joined in the city of La Cañada Flintridge. The state in 2000 counted 7,042 housing units: 6,567 single homes, 209 single attached, 264 multiples, 2 mobiles. In the 1990s, La Cañada Flintridge's population increased by 1,700 and its housing stock by 125 units.

La Cañada Unified School District. Scores usually run above the 95th percentile or top 5 percent in the state. Residents back schools through fundraisers. Voters in 1999 approved bonds for renovation and a new high school library. Scores and bond indicate a high level of support for education.

Two homicides in 1999, one each in 1998 and 1997, and zero in 1996. The counts for previous years are 1, 0, 0, 0, 0, 1. One of the lowest crime rates in the county. Police protection is provided by the sheriff's department.

Two golf courses, library, YMCA. Descanso, a park famous for its botanical gardens, is located on the west side. Angeles National Forest. Residents have fund to buy land and place it in preserve; no development.

About 13 miles to downtown L.A. Many jobs in nearby Pasadena. Interstate 210 and Highway 2 touch the town and provide easy access for drivers. Park-and-ride lot. Chamber of commerce (818) 790-4289.

LA CRESCENTA

SMALL UNINCORPORATED TOWN squeezed in between Glendale and La Cañada Flintridge. Pretty, upscale. Located in the foothills of San Gabriel Mountains. Estimated population (1994 count) 17,621.

School rankings high. Crime figures unavailable but the demographics, appearance and out-of-the-way location suggests low crime. No graffiti, no security bars or windows. Patrolled by sheriff's deputies. Sheriff's substation in town.

La Crescenta was built for the middle managers and young professors of 30 or 40 years ago. Town started in the 1950s with about 2,200 residential units and in that decade built about 2,000 units, mostly single homes. In the 1960s the housing starts dropped to 1,282 and in the following decade to 595. The 1980s added 600 units.

The older, smaller homes will generally be found around Foothill Boulevard. As you move into the hills, housing quality improves but doesn't make a dramatic leap. The town in general looks good. The houses are well kept, the lawns mowed, the shrubs trimmed and it's obvious that a lot of attention is paid to keeping up appearances.

Some homes in the upper elevations have views.

Children attend schools in the Glendale Unified School District. Schools in the La Crescenta area score among the top 10 percent in the state. Glendale district has passed a bond to build and renovate schools. In 1998, the district opened a magnet high school that emphasizes science. Crescenta Valley High School to be rebuilt by 2003.

About 12 miles to downtown L.A. Easy access to Interstate 210, which bisects the town just below Foothill Boulevard.

On the south side of La Crescenta is a small neighborhood called Montrose and some books identify the town as La Crescenta-Montrose.

Because of its higher elevation, La Crescenta escapes some of the L.A. smog. Clark Gable and Carole Lombard used to have a cabin in town.

Three parks, two libraries, golf courses in nearby communities, recreational activities connected with the schools.

Chamber of commerce (818) 248-4957.

LA HABRA HEIGHTS

PRESTIGE COMMUNITY located in the east county, on the Orange County border. Built over hills. Country feeling. Many homes have views. Bougainvillea spills over hedges, brightening the roads.

Crime rate one of the lowest in Southern California. School rankings high but muddied by attendance setup. Schools are spread over four districts and two counties. Population 6,896.

The Puente Hills divide the San Gabriel Valley of Los Angeles County from Orange County. La Habra Heights is situated about the middle of the hills. Its neighbor to the south is the City of La Habra, which is part of Orange County. La Habra ... La Habra Heights ... some people confuse the two. The first is a blue-collar, middle-class city with stores; the second, an upscale community with almost no businesses (the main exception: the golf course). Added to the confusion, the two towns share part of one school district.

La Habra Heights cultivates a style that might be called country secluded. Many streets have no sidewalks. Hedges or small groves of orange or avocado trees hide many homes. Some homes have gates. Having no stores, the town draws little commercial traffic. The roads curve and wind over hills and valleys thick with oak, manzanita and brush. The 1990 census counted 2,002 owner-occupied units. Three-bedroom homes accounted for about 42 percent of this total, four-bedroom homes about 34 percent and five-or-more-bedroom units, about 13 percent or 268 homes. Some homes are knockouts: large, tastefully decorated. Many others fall into the category of upscale nice. A few homes are small working ranches. La Habra Heights is horse country. The state in 2000 counted 2,236 housing units: 2,209 single homes, 18 single attached, 7 multiples, 2 mobiles. In the 1990s, La Habra Heighs' population increased by 670 people and its housing stock by 75 homes.

Served by four school districts, two elementary, two secondary. The two elementary schools in the Lowell district that serve part of La Habra Heights are scoring generally in the top 10 percent in the state. For a fix on a particular address, phone the Lowell district at (562) 943-0211.

Zero homicides in 1999, 1998, 1997, one in 1996, zero in 1994 and 1995.

Golf course. Many homes have swimming pools. One park. Horse trails. For the unusual, a large Buddhist temple, just over the northern border.

Main drawback if you work in downtown L.A: 24 long miles. Highway 60 can be picked up north of the city. City hall (562) 694-6302.

LAKEWOOD

Downtown L.A., Lakewood, L.A. International Airport, Long Beach

BEDROOM COMMUNITY bordered by Long Beach. Well maintained, loaded with trees. Population 80,952. School rankings low to high. Large parks scattered around the city. Served by four school districts.

Lakewood came to life right after World War II when freeways, the GI bill and general prosperity created a boom in housing. In the 1950s, Lakewood built 15,621 residential units or 57 percent of its current housing. Single homes outnumber apartments five to one. The 1990 census disclosed that 83 percent of the residential units were owner-occupied, a good sign of social stability. Two-thirds of Lakewood's single homes are three-bedroom units. Nothing fancy: tract homes, one- and two-car garages, small porches, lawns.

In appearance, Lakewood comes off as pretty because large shade trees line many of the streets and soften the sun's glare and the tract lines of the town. The lawns are mowed, the shrubs trimmed, the exteriors kept up — a nice-looking burg. The state in 2000 counted 27,380 housing units: 22,279 single homes, 598 single attached, 4,404 multiples, 99 mobiles. In the 1990s, Lakewood's population increased by 7,400 people and its housing by 400 units.

The four school districts are ABC, Long Beach, Bellflower and Paramount. Lakewood residents have voted to pull out of these districts and form their own, and won state approval. But the other districts are contesting this. Another ruling, to be made in 2001, may clarify matters. In recent years, Long Beach, Paramount and ABC districts have approved renovation bonds.

Lakewood High scores in the 60th percentiles, Aloha Elementary the 40th percentiles, Foster Elementary the 70th to 80th percentiles, Lakewood Elementary in 20th percentiles. At least one school follows a year-round schedule. Other educational pluses include, just over the border in Long Beach, a community college and a little farther to the south, a state university.

Four homicides in 1999, one in 1998, and three in 1997. The counts for previous years are 2, 6, 5, 3, 5, 5, 1. Some security doors, not many. Lakewood contracts with the L.A. County Sheriff's Office to provide police protection.

Three libraries, 13 parks, movie theaters, swim pavilion, and along the San Gabriel River, riding stables. Lakewood Country Club. City runs many sports for children and teens. Lakewood Center Mall includes Pennys, Mervyn's.

Interstate 605 runs through Lakewood. Buses. About 20 miles to downtown L.A. Many jobs in Long Beach. Chamber of commerce (562) 920-2120.

LA MIRADA

Downtown L.A.
La Mirada
L.A. International Airport
Long Beach

MIDDLE TO MIDDLE-PLUS city located on the east side, on the Orange County border, near Sante Fe Springs and Cerritos. Well kept. Large private university. Mix of mature and young suburbia. School rankings generally high. Population 49,918.

About six or seven out of every ten residential units in La Mirada were built between 1950 and 1970. La Mirada favored the three-bedroom, one-story home with the garage in the house, usually set off at angle to the driveway. Many of the homes have decorative touches: pseudo-bird nests, A-framed windows. In the late 1980s, on the south side of the city, off Hillsborough Drive, in the Coyote Hills, a second boom started featuring the look of modern suburbia: sandy stucco, red-tile roofs, two stories, four and five bedrooms. Many homes have views of the San Gabriel Valley and Mountains.

A seniors complex is located off Santa Gertrudes Avenue on the east side of the city. On the north side of La Mirada Park, a small number of horse ranches can be found. In the center of town sits Biola University, trees, green lawns, pretty campus. On the south side, away from the homes, an industrial-business park is located.

Not a glamorous town but certainly a pretty one. With few exceptions, the homes and lawns reflect care and attention. Trees are plentiful; near the university one street is lined with tall pines. Streets are clean. New neighborhoods sparkle. The state in 2000 counted 15,136 housing units: 12,224 single homes, 521 single attached, 2,241 multiples, 150 mobiles. In the 1990s, La Mirada's population increased by 9,500 people and its housing stock by 1,800 units, about three-fourths of them single homes.

Served by Norwalk-La Mirada Unified School District. Sample rankings: Benton Middle, 50th percentiles; Escalona Elementary, 70th percentiles; La Mirada High, 50th percentiles. The rankings say middle class plus. In recent years, the town has added an elementary school and a middle school.

Three homicides in 1999, one in 1998, and zero in 1997. Counts for previous years are 2, 2, 6, 2, 1, 2, 3. La Mirada has its own police department.

About 10 parks, several of them large. One golf course in town, two nearby. Performing arts center. Library. Activities associated with the university. Many classes and activities for kids.

I-5 cuts through the town on south side. Metrolink (commuter rail) to downtown L.A., 20 miles to east. Chamber of commerce (714) 521-1700.

LANCASTER

HIGH-DESERT CITY bordering Edwards Air Force Base. Good selection of homes and apartments at modest prices and rents. Population 132,402.

Lancaster and Palmdale, neighbors, are frequently tied together as "Antelope Valley." Both are large with plenty of room to grow. Summer days hot, summer evenings mild, winters cool to frosty, no smog. Asthmatics like the clean air of the high desert. Desert vegetation: cactus, sagebrush, poppy.

Lancaster has been building steadily since 1950s and like Palmdale enjoyed a housing spurt in the 1980s and 1990s. You'll find housing styles of two and three bedrooms, popular between 1950 and 1970, and the larger homes in vogue after 1970. Some older units look a little frayed but for the most part Lancaster is well maintained. Over forty percent of the housing was built over the last fifteen years. New housing runs three to five bedrooms, two-car garages, two or three bathrooms. The great majority are two-story. Many trees. Desert land being cheaper, homes in Palmdale and Lancaster go for what would be considered bargains in other cities. The state in 2000 counted 42,927 housing units: 27,476 single homes, 942 single attached, 10,262 multiples, 4,247 mobiles. In the 1990s, Lancaster's population increased by 35,000 people and its housing stock by 6,700 units, 80 percent of them single homes.

Education by Lancaster Elementary District, scores 20th to 50th percentiles. Teens move up to Antelope Valley High district, which includes Lancaster High, scores in 50th percentiles. Some children attend schools in Westside elementary district, 60th to 80th percentiles. In recent years, Westside and Lancaster districts have won bonds to build and renovate schools. Many schools run year-round schedules. Community College. Baptist college.

Five homicides in 1999. Counts for previous years: 8, 7, 12, 9, 10, 7, 10, 14, 4.

"Cradle of Aerospace Technology" — Edwards Air Force Base, where Chuck Yeager broke the sound barrier and space shuttle lands. Walk of Honor along Lancaster Boulevard honors with monuments the pioneering test pilots. Many aerospace jobs. Many distribution firms. Highway 14 to San Fernando Valley. Metrolink (commuter rail). Buses. About 70 miles to L.A. International, about 50 miles to Burbank Airport. Commercial flights from Palmdale Airport.

Ballooning, sky diving, gliders, off-road vehicle areas, fishing, hiking, golf, tennis, swimming, sports center, movie plex, 21 screens, racing tracks, performing arts center, fair grounds. Chamber of commerce (661) 948-4518.

LA PUENTE

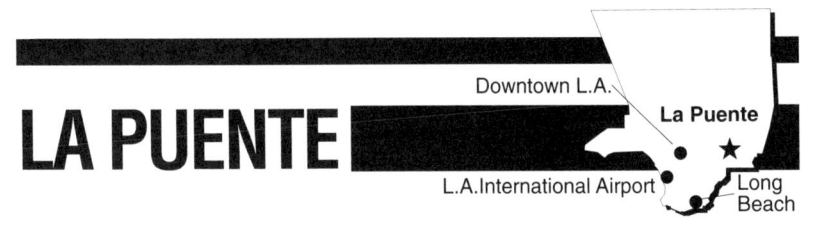

WORKING-CLASS CITY that borders a job center, the City of Industry. School rankings low to middling. Population 42,189.

La Puente got most of its housing in the 1950s when 4,634 residential units were constructed, almost half of the city's current housing stock.

Three-bedroom homes dominated and many are now showing wear but La Puente has some new housing, located east of Glendora Avenue. This is a good town if you are low on money and want to get a start in the housing market.

The state in 2000 counted 9,710 housing units: 6,308 single homes, 521 single attached, 2,798 multiples, 83 mobiles. In the 1990s, La Puente's population increased by 5,200 people and its housing stock by 425 units.

Served by the Hacienda-La Puente Unified School District, which in 2000 approved a $100 million bond to renovate schools. The district includes several towns and has academic rankings low-middling to high. Also served by the Bassett Unified School District. Bassett is thinking about asking its voters to approve a bond.

Sample rankings from the Hacienda-La Puente district: California Elementary, 30th percentile; Temple Academy, 20th percentile; La Puente High, 30th percentile.

Sample rankings from Bassett district: Erwin Elementary, 20th to 30th percentile; Bassett High, 20th to 30th percentile.

Some children attend schools in the Rowland Unified School District.

Four homicides in 1999, seven in 1998, and three in 1997. The counts for previous years are 6, 9, 8, 8, 13, 10, 12.

Library, several parks, many activities at the schools.

For those who have a local job, great commute. One of the pluses for La Puente: Metrolink (commuter rail) nearby. Short drive to Highway 60 and freeway system. 19 miles to downtown L.A.

LA VERNE

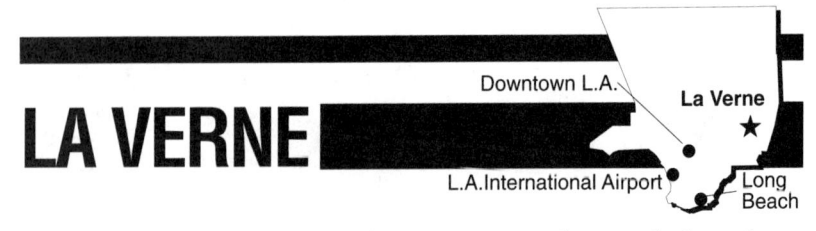

UNUSUAL NAME but a pretty bedroom town, somewhat upscale, located at the foot of the San Gabriel Mountains in the east county. School scores fairly high, crime low. Well known for its University of La Verne. Population 34,802.

La Verne was founded in 1887 when the Santa Fe Railroad came through and a boom town sprang up and then went bust after building a large hotel. A few years later, the German Baptist Brethern bought the hotel, reopened it as a college and organized a church that attracted more brethern. From then the town grew as a citrus center. The name La Verne is a French derivation of "growing green" or "spring like." Starting downtown near the university, you'll find La Verne's oldest homes, some of them bungalows, a pleasing reminder of a quieter past. As you move towards the hills, the homes get newer, bigger and better appointed. Many of them remain in the category of middle-class nice.

La Verne's boom started around 1960 when three-bedroom homes were expanding to four, two-car garages were easing into three, closets were getting bigger. About 60 percent of the town's housing was built between 1960 and 1980 and another 25 percent between 1980 and 2000. Above Baseline Road and into the hills, view homes have been constructed and some gated subdivisions. This section also contains, in La Verne and on its east and west borders, three golf courses. The state in 2000 counted 11,632 housing units: 7,439 single homes, 585 single attached, 1,853 multiples, 1,755 mobiles. In the 1990s, La Verne's population increased by 4,000 people and its housing stock by 540 units, most of them single homes.

Children attend the Bonita Unified School District, which also serves San Dimas. La Verne's rankings run from the 60th to the 90th percentiles, which reflects well on the town's academic values. Renovation bond under discussion. La Verne is close to the Claremont colleges and Cal Poly.

Zero homicides in 1999, 1998 and 1997. The counts for previous years are 5, 1, 0, 2, 0, 0, 1.

Little League, football, typical sports and activities. Historical society, social clubs, library, close to the colleges and the activities they offer. Close also to Mt. Baldy, skiing, hiking and camping. Roller hockey arena.

Thirty-one miles to downtown L.A. Two freeways help but still a long commute. Foothill Transit buses and Metrolink (commuter rail) stations nearby. Short drive to airport at Ontario, which may be the true job center for La Verne. Chamber of commerce (909) 593-5265.

LAWNDALE

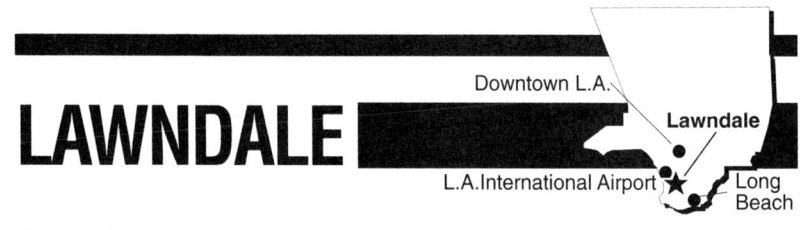

BLUE-COLLAR, white-collar city located on the west side, between Torrance and Hawthorne. Population 30,862.

Elementary school rankings land generally in the 10th to 60th percentiles. Lawndale Elementary School District in 1998 passed a bond to build and renovate schools. Middle school to open new gym in 2001. Teens attend schools in Centinela Valley High School District, which in 2000 okayed a $50 million renovation bond. Sample rankings: Leuzinger High, 20th percentile.

Lawndale started its boom in the 1940s when it built about 1,600 residential units. In the 1950s, housing starts jumped to 2,457 units and in the 1960s dropped to 1,859 units. The 1970s posted 1,062 units and the 1980s rose to about 2,300 units. In the 1990s, Lawndale's population increased by 3,400 people and its housing stock by 390 units.

So what you have is an old-new suburb that has built steadily over 60 years and this means a good choice of housing styles aimed at people who can afford a mortgage of $1,000 to $2,000 a month or rents of $750 to $1,100 a month.

In housing, Lawndale favored single homes two to one over apartments. Among owner-occupied units, the numbers divide about evenly between two- and three-bedroom homes. In total housing, the two-bedroom unit outnumbers the three by about two to one, the census reported.

Lawndale is built on flat land. Streets are clean. Many homes are well-cared-for. Not a fancy city. Much of it was designed for veterans getting into the housing market and it remains a good town to get a start in housing.

The state in 2000 counted 10,166 housing units: 5,287 single homes, 1,263 single attached, 3,349 multiples, 267 mobiles.

One homicide in 1999, two each in 1998 and 1997. Counts for previous years are 5, 2, 4, 2, 5, 1, 7. Lawndale contracts with the sheriff's department for police services.

Lawndale is about five miles from L.A. International Airport, which has many jobs. This probably means a short commute for many residents. Interstate 405 bisects the city. Lawndale runs its own bus system.

Three parks. Playing fields at schools. Library. Close to golf course and community college (many classes, activities). Chamber of commerce (310) 679-3306.

LOMITA

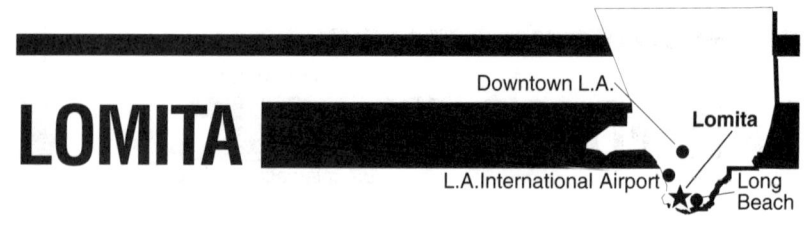

SMALL, MIDDLE-CLASS COMMUNITY squeezed in between Torrance, Rolling Hills Estates and City of L.A. Name translates to "Little Hill." Most of Lomita is flat but the southern section rises into hills. Population 20,951.

School rankings middling to high. Crime low. Tidy town, clean, housing kept in good repair.

Part of the L.A. Unified School District. Scores range from the 50th percentiles at Eshelman Elementary to the 50th and 70th percentiles at Lomita Fundamental. Teens attend Narbonne High School, rankings 50th to 70th percentile. Community colleges nearby

Another town that blossomed after World War II. Two-thirds of the town's residential units were built between 1950 and 1980. Homes and apartments in the flatlands reflect the modest but sturdy styles of that era. Among owner-occupied homes, two- and three-bedroom units, in about equal numbers, dominate.

As you move south into the hills, home quality rises. The landscaping is a little more extensive, the decorative touches a little nicer. Some homes are customized, some have views, but Lomita was built almost entirely for the middle class. Lomita measures about one mile east to west and, about two miles north to south — an intimate place.

The state in 2000 counted 8,301 housing units: 4,029 single homes, 742 single attached, 3,014 multiples, 516 mobiles. In the 1990s, Lomita's population increased by 1,500 people and its housing stock by 25 homes.

One homicide in 1999. Counts for previous years are 2, 0, 0, 0, 2, 0, 1, 0, 2. Lomita contracts with sheriff for protection. Sheriff's substation in town.

Five parks, tennis courts, a wading pool, a public library and a railroad museum. Five miles to the beaches. Usual sports. Two shopping plazas just outside city limits.

Downtown L.A., 22 miles to the north. Interstate 110 near by. Many jobs in Long Beach. Torrance Municipal Airport borders Lomita. Check out the plane noise.

Jim Thorpe, one of the most famous athletes of the 1920s, lived in Lomita. A plaque at city hall celebrates his achievements. In its salad days, Lomita boasted it was "The celery capital of the world." Chamber of commerce (310) 326-6378.

LONG BEACH

Downtown L.A.
L.A. International Airport
Long Beach

SECOND MOST-POPULOUS CITY in L.A. County and a major city in its own right. Population 457,608.

Great choice of housing. Many recreational choices. Large port. Marinas. Long Beach is adjusting to the end of the Cold War and the loss of many defense jobs but is still a major job center. City has taken over port facilities left by Navy when it closed base. New shopping center in this area.

Large regional airport. Direct flights to Phoenix, Salt Lake, Las Vegas, Chicago.

Education by Long Beach district, enrollment 92,000 students. The district uses magnet schools to encourage ethnic mixing. Overall rankings bounce all over but some schools are above the 50th percentile and some are even in the 90th. Scores tend to reflect neighborhood demographics. Middle- and high-income neighborhoods usually post middle to high scores. Bond passed to renovate and build schools.

Two community college campuses. Large state university, enrollment 31,000, greatly enriches the city's life. Through its extension program, many classes are open to the public.

Long Beach has been building its housing for well over 100 years. Most of the housing came in spurts: from 1920 to 1950, when the population went from 56,000 to 251,000; in the 1950s when the city added 93,000 residents; and between 1980 and 1990 when the population jumped by 68,000. In the 1990s, Long Beach's population increased by about 28,000 people and its housing stock by 1,750 units.

Housing built over a long period usually means many choices and diverse demographics with prices across the spectrum, low, middle and high. Long Beach has many homes that are old and small (two-bedroom) but in a good shape. For people low in funds but wanting to buy a home, Long Beach opens the door. The city, for the most part, built for the blue and white-collar middle class. But several large neighborhoods jump up the scale.

Low-income neighborhoods tend to border the downtown. As you move north, the housing improves in quality and becomes newer.

North and east sides of the town are generally middle class. Many three-bedroom homes. Some streets stand out for quality of care. A west-side neighborhood seems to make a transition from low income to middle class.

South of the university, moving towards the water, the housing steps up in appointments, size and newness. Down on the water, you'll find many older homes, well-maintained, charming, almost an artists' colony. The Naples neighborhood is built on and around islands.

Graffiti rare, even in the low income neighborhoods. Lawns tended. Many streets are lined with sycamores, palms, magnolias and other trees.

The state in 2000 counted 172,089 housing units: 69,287 single homes, 8,261 single attached, 92,275 multiples, 2,266 mobiles.

Forty-six homicides in 1999 and 38 in 1998. Counts for previous years are 38, 57, 95, 80, 80, 126, 104, 94, 106. Like many large cities, Long Beach suffers crime problems in some of its poorer neighborhoods but crime in middle- and upper-income neighborhoods probably runs to suburban average. Long Beach officer shot to death in 2001; fellow officer wounded. City shocked.

About 24 miles to downtown L.A. At peak hours, these are congested miles but the many local jobs ease the commute for residents. Short drive to job centers of Orange County. Long Beach light rail ties into the L.A. Metro Line to downtown L.A. Four freeways run through the city.

Many activities, sports, things to do. Five golf courses, 40 tennis facilities, about 3,400 boat slips. About four dozen parks, several on the Pacific. Theater, restaurants, night life in downtown, which has convention center, high-rise office buildings, major hotels. New aquarium in the downtown, one of largest in the country.

Tourists flock to see Queen Mary, docked in Long Beach Harbor. The ship also serves as a hotel and meeting center.

Chamber of commerce (562) 436-1251.

LOS ANGELES

Los Angeles ★
L.A. International Airport • Long Beach

DIVERSE AND CHANGING CITY, housing for rich, poor and middle class. Population 3,822,955. School scores high in some neighborhoods and low in others. Many children transfer out of their neighborhood schools. Crime low, high or middling, depending on location. Fewer homicides in recent years.

For ease of understanding, Los Angeles should be split into two regions: the Basin and the San Fernando Valley, also known as the Valley. The two are divided by the Santa Monica Mountains. See maps on pages 7, 10, and 11. The Basin covers the south, the Valley the north.

Some cities have neighborhoods or districts; Los Angeles has "towns." Some guides will call them "villages." When some event or crime happens, rarely will reporters say ... "In Los Angeles today ...." Rather they will say, "In Hollywood (or Silver Lake or Van Nuys or Northridge)...." All are towns of the City of Los Angeles. All are "profiled" in this chapter.

Basin towns include San Pedro, Wilmington, Watts, South Central L.A., Southeast L.A., Hollywood, Hancock Park, Venice, Mar Vista, Pacific Palisades, Brentwood, Bel Air Estates, the downtown, Boyle Heights, Crenshaw, Leimert Park, Highland Park, Eagle Rock, Echo Park, Silver Lake, Los Feliz.

The Valley towns include North Hollywood, Studio City, Northridge, Encino, Sherman Oaks, Toluca Lake, Van Nuys, Reseda, Woodland Hills, West Hills, Chatsworth, Porter Ranch, Granada Hills, Sylmar, Pacoima, Sunland-Tujunga, Sun Valley and Panorama City.

In its formative years, the City of L.A. got control of the water and told outlying towns that if they wanted any, they would have to join the City of L.A. Much grumbling but they did. The grumbling remains. L.A. and its towns are forever arguing about how power should be divided and a serious effort is being made to split off the San Fernando Valley into a new city. Hollywood and Venice are also trying to break away and form their own cities.

Like other cities in the county, Los Angeles about World War II started to boom in residential construction. The city began the 1940s with about 226,000 residential units. In that decade, it added 190,656 units and in the 1950s, 270,619 units. In the 1960s, the city built 231,415 homes and apartments and in the 1970s it erected 179,996 units. The 1980s saw housing starts rise to about 200,000. In the 1990s, housing starts dropped to 33,340, very low, and an indication that in many parts Los Angeles is built out — but not up. There's a movement to erect more high-rise apartment buildings.

As the figures show, Los Angeles offers a wide selection of the old and the new. And of housing styles and sizes. Among owner-occupied units, the three-bedroom home dominates, followed by the two-bedroom home, the 1990 census reported. Los Angeles has about 68,000 four-bedroom homes and about 20,000 homes with five or more bedrooms, the census reported.

The state in 2000 counted 1,333,421 housing units: 518,544 single homes, 79,178 single attached, 728,033 multiples, 7,666 mobiles.

For public education, Los Angeles children attend the Los Angeles Unified School District, second largest in the nation, about 696,000 pupils. In 1997, voters passed a $2.4 billion bond to renovate schools and open new ones. State is chipping in millions for new schools. The great majority of students attend neighborhood schools but the district encourages and supports (with free busing) transfers to mix the kids better ethnically. See Chapter 3, How Public Schools Work.

Homicides totaled 425 in 1999, 426 in 1998, and 576 in 1997. The counts for previous years are 709, 849, 845, 1,076, 1,094, 1,027, 983. Los Angeles has its own police department. For a breakout of homicides by neighborhood, see last chapter.

Personal safety is a big issue in L.A. and a complicated one. Big-city rules apply: take care, be wary, install good locks and security doors, if you think them necessary. Avoid neighborhoods and situations that you think unsafe. But don't cross off L.A. because of its reputation. If you went by security doors, which are in wide use, L.A. would appear to be the most crime-ridden city in the nation. But its overall crime rate runs suburban average. L.A. homicides slightly exceed everyday suburbia but they're lower than what's found in such cities as Chicago, Little Rock, Washington D.C. and Atlanta. Many parts of Los Angeles are quite safe, many in range of suburban safe, a few unsafe. Besides security devices, many residents, especially in the high-income sections, subscribe to security services.

Recreational offerings plentiful. Libraries, parks, playgrounds, beaches, museums. Big-city energy. Recently opened Getty Museum, near Brentwood. Many sections of city being renovated. Big projects on the horizon: overhauling and expanding port, building high-speed rail service to port, expanding L.A. International Airport.

City government is run by a mayor, Richard Riordan, and 15 council members, elected by district. Council members are strong in determining policy for their districts.

If the San Fernando Valley pulls out of the City of Los Angeles, this might force extensive changes in how L.A. is governed. Chamber of commerce (213) 580-7500.

LYNWOOD

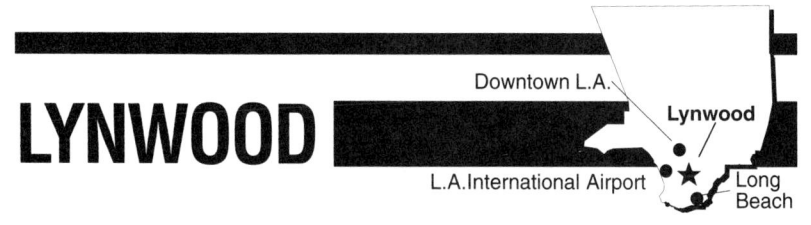

BEDROOM CITY, an older suburb. Located about 11 miles south of downtown L.A. School rankings low to middling. Population: 69,328.

About 75 percent of Lynwood's current housing was built between 1940 and 1970 and when you include the units constructed before World War II, about 85 percent predates 1970.

Lynwood's boom started in the 1940s, an era that favored two-bedroom homes. About the 1950s, small three-bedrooms started to become popular and in the late 1950s and 1960s these homes grew a little larger and often added a second bathroom. Lynwood built 3,928 residential units in the 1940s and 4,564 in the 1950s. In the 1960s, the town added 2,632 units.

Among the owner-occupied, two-bedroom units make up the biggest block, followed by three-bedroom, then one-bedroom and then four-bedroom (about 300 homes), the census reported. In its housing, Lynwood aimed at people coming into the market for the first time and it remains a good town to secure a plain but affordable home.

Individually, the homes and apartments show loving care but empty lots and many security doors and windows suggest problems. The state in 2000 counted 14,763 housing units: 8,425 single homes, 1,068 single attached, 5,185 multiples, 85 mobiles. In the 1990s, Lynwood's population increased by 7,400 people and its housing stock by 240 units.

Education by Lynwood Unified School District. Academic rankings range from the 10th to the 40th percentile. New high school, middle school and elementary school.

Twelve homicides in 1999. The counts for previous years are 15, 25, 20, 25, 25, 22, 19, 23, 23. Overall crime rate runs to suburban average but homicides are high. City contracts with sheriff's department for police protection.

Interstate 105 cuts across Lynwood and Interstate 710 runs up its east side. Good access to freeway system. Light rail to L.A. International Airport and, with transfer, to downtown L.A. Lynwood uses traffic circles, a rarity.

Indoor swim center. Several parks. Venus and Serena Williams learned their tennis on the courts of Lynwood High School.

One of the first landowners had a wife named Lynne with a maiden name of Wood. Chamber of commerce (310) 537-6484.

MALIBU

Downtown L.A. — Malibu — L.A. International Airport — Long Beach

CITY OF FAME AND THE FAMOUS. On the Pacific. One of longest shorelines in California, about 27 miles. Home to movie stars and magnates but mostly to upper-middle professionals. Residences from opulent to middle to somewhat ratty (at least on outside). Great views of Pacific. School rankings among highest in state. Crime low suburban average. Population 13,324.

Several forces influenced Malibu's residential development. A good deal of the town was erected before tough building and zoning codes were passed. This pretty much left quality and positioning up to developers and individual owners. Their tastes varied. Shore homes on the south side look worn and pinched. Malibu incorporated as a city in 1990 in large part because it wanted to bring development under control. Anything built now faces stricter rules.

Malibu backs up against the Santa Monica Mountains. The terrain, especially in south, is steep. Home pads are small. As you move north, terrain eases off, creating mesas ideal for large homes pointed toward the Pacific.

The civic center, main supermarket and many stores are located near Malibu Lagoon where the land levels off. Beaches, with exceptions, are not deep. Many homes on south side are built on pilings washed by ocean waves. On the Riviera (a neighborhood) homes sit on high bluff overlooking Pacific, and often away from Pacific. To be near the ocean is not necessarily to have the best view. All this notwithstanding, this city is unusually blessed with its mountains, hills and shore. When Malibu kids square off for soccer on a shore mesa, backdrop is wide Pacific. The state in 2000 counted 6,294 housing units: 3,856 single homes, 554 single attached, 1,197 multiples, 687 mobiles.

Served by the Santa Monica-Malibu School District. Scores in 80th to 90th percentile. Bond passed to improve schools and build classrooms and gym at Malibu High. In both communities, good support for schools.

Zero homicides in 1999. Counts for previous years are 0, 1, 1, 0, 2, 4. Richer homes and streets have security guards and gates. Malibu likes privacy.

Beaches galore. Horse ranches. Large regional parks along the shore and in the mountains. Restaurants. Shops. Pepperdine University sits in the middle of Malibu, a lovely campus. For the city lights, Santa Monica is close by. Highway 1 often gets snarled and occasionally washed out by slides. Back roads to San Fernando Valley. About 25 miles to downtown L.A. Chamber of commerce (310) 456-9025.

MANHATTAN BEACH

BEDROOM, RESORT COMMUNITY on the Pacific, two miles south of L.A. International Airport. Upscale, professional, school scores very high, crime low. Population 36,124.

A pretty town, kept in good repair. Most of the housing was built in the 1950s when Manhattan Beach doubled its population from 17,000 to 34,000. In the 1990s, Manhattan Beach's population increased by 4,100 people and its housing stock by 600 units.

Manhattan Beach housing can be divided into the units close to the beach and units east of Sepulveda Boulevard, the east-west divider. On the east side, the homes run to 1950s to 1960s models, standard tract, three-bedroom units. Lawns are mowed, hedges trimmed. Near the golf course some upscale homes have been placed behind gates. West of Sepulveda, you'll find similar tract homes but as you near the beach they rise slightly in appointments. At the beach, a bluff descends to the ocean. Homes are positioned on this bluff to command views of the Pacific. Housing styles are a little more customized. Every once in a while, a home jumps up the scale but we're talking middle-class-plus for the town. The state in 2000 counted 15,293 housing units: 10,097 single homes, 1,237 single attached, 3,956 multiples, 3 mobiles.

Served by Manhattan Beach Unified School District, which in 1995 passed a bond to renovate all schools and build a middle school (done in 1998). Every school is scoring in the top 10 percent of the state and several in top 5 percent. Voters in 2000 approved a $26 million bond to renovate high school.

Zero homicides in 1999. The counts for previous years are 1, 2, 2, 1, 0, 1, 0, 0, 0. Manhattan Beach has its own police department.

Ten parks, golf course, racquetball and tennis courts, usual sports, library, community centers, jazz concerts, art festivals, small theater and more. The jewel of the town is the beach, over two miles in length, and it is an accessible beach. Many California beaches are blocked by cliffs or rocky shores.

Homes line beach, restaurants cluster along Manhattan Beach Boulevard. Fishing pier. On summer days, volleyball players, surfers and swimmers are out in force. Come evening, people stroll the promenade watching the golden sunset. Leaf blowers banned. About 22 miles to downtown L.A. How the town got its name: two landowners flipped coin; winner from New York City.

Airport industries, studios provide thousands of jobs. Chamber of commerce (310) 545-5313.

MAR VISTA
Marina Del Rey, Venice

LOCATED ON THE WEST, on or near the ocean. Mix of low-middle and middle-class upscale. Artsy. Many apartments, beach homes. Academic rankings low to fairly high.

Mar Vista and Venice, located just south of Santa Monica, are towns of City of L.A. Venice is on the ocean, Mar Vista is east of Venice and is often coupled with Palms, a neighborhood to its east. L.A. in 1994 counted 40,410 residents in Venice and 104,104 residents in Mar Vista-Palms.

Mar Vista, more middle class than Venice, is built over flat lands and gentle hills. Some homes have views of downtown L. A. Many of the homes show much care. School scores come in higher than the other neighborhoods.

As you move toward the ocean and into Venice the homes and apartments become older and on some blocks rundown. Generalizations are dangerous because the next street over may look great. Venice is famous for its canal neighborhood: homes built on canals. Ducks and bridges and rowboats and balconies with flowers, all charming. But this section accounts for only a small number of homes. Many of the homes and apartments are oriented toward the ocean and in many spots Venice comes across as an old but still lively resort town, a favorite of artists and of the live-and-let-live persuasion. Many residents are unhappy with L.A. City government and are trying to incorporate Venice into a legal city, with control over local affairs.

Marina Del Rey, located just south of Venice, is a "county" town, unincorporated, patrolled by sheriff's deputies. Population, 7,500-8,500. This is town of boats — about 6,000 slips — and apartment dwellers. Venice and Marina Del Rey attract many single people.

Served by the L.A. Unified School District. Sample rankings: Mar Vista Elementary, 50th to 70th percentile; Marina Del Rey, 20th percentile; Venice High School, 40th to 60th percentile.

Great beaches, including Muscle Beach. Boating. About a half-dozen parks. Golf course, restaurants, shops. Fishing pier. Interstate 405 close by. Venice Boulevard works as a parkway. Many entertainment and high-tech firms close by. Check out noise from Santa Monica airport. Marina Del Rey C of C (310) 645-5151. Venice C of C (310) 396-7016.

MAYWOOD

BLUE-COLLAR TOWN, located about five miles southeast of downtown L.A. School scores low. Population: 30,408.

Maywood is an uneven town. On many streets some homes will show a lot of care and the neighboring units show little care.

About one-third of the city's residential units were built before 1950, a time when tract housing favored two bedrooms.

Another forty percent or so of the housing was built between 1950 and 1970.

The town measures 15 blocks east to west and 11 blocks north to south. This smallness and the fact Maywood is a legal city, with its own government structure and police department, gives it a good chance to deal with its challenges.

The state in 2000 counted 6,654 housing units: 2,701 single homes, 978 single attached, 2,963 multiples, 12 mobiles. In the 1990s, Maywood's population increased by 2,800 people. Its housing stock remained stable.

Served by the Los Angeles Unified School District. Sample academic rankings: Fishburn and Loma Vista Elementary schools, 10th percentile.

Zero homicides in 1999, seven in 1998, and three in 1997. The counts for previous years are 4, 1, 6, 6, 3, 4. Overall crime, as recorded by FBI, is low but as the figures indicate, in some years violent crimes run higher than what's found in many suburban cities.

Two parks, one with a swimming pool. Library. Typical sports.

Situated close to downtown L.A. and near major industrial cities and having many industries of its own, Maywood offers its residents local jobs and a short commute. Buses. Commute rail station nearby; leads to downtown L.A. Interstate 710 runs up the east side of the city.

In the 1920s, when Maywood was incorporating as a city, a contest was held to name the town. Residents chose ... you know what.

Chamber of commerce (323) 562-3373.

MISSION HILLS
Panorama City

BEDROOM COMMUNITIES located on the north side of the San Fernando Valley. Housing runs from low-middle to middle and includes many of the two- and three-bedroom homes built just after World War II.

Mission Hills is pretty flat. Panorama City is not a legal "city." Both are towns of the City of Los Angeles and patrolled by L.A. police. Both are served by the Los Angeles Unified School District.

Mission Hills and Panorama City blend into each other and the surrounding towns of North Hills and Pacoima. Adding to the confusion some guides still call North Hills by its old name, Sepulveda.

We are placing Mission Hills in the triangle formed by the meeting of I-405, I-5 and, at the south, Highway 118. Estimated population, about 15,000. At the center is the San Fernando Mission, established in 1797 and rebuilt several times. A source of pride for local residents. Much of the housing in Mission Hills was built in the 1950s, generally three-bedroom tract. The town includes two parks, a cemetery attached to the mission, Holy Cross Medical Center and several private schools.

Panorama City, for this book, includes everything north of Roscoe Boulevard, between I-405, I-5 and, at the north, Highway 118. North of Roscoe on the west side, you will find many apartment complexes and north of Plummer Street a mix of ranchettes (deep lots), and old and small and new and fairly big single homes. Near Devonshire Street (and Mission Hills) the homes tend to be middle-class standard, well maintained. East of Workman, the housing runs to single homes, circa late 1940s and 1950s. Some houses have been kept up, some haven't. Some have security bars and doors.

Sample school rankings: Langdon Elementary, 10th percentile; Burton Street Elementary, 10th percentile.

Crime rate unknown but probably of concern in neighborhoods with security doors and window bars. Parks, rec centers, shopping mall. Close to community college and Cal State Northridge. Land used to be owned by Panorama Dairy and Sheep Ranch. About 20 miles to downtown L.A. Metrolink (commuter rail) stations at Northridge and San Fernando. Buses. Several freeways. Mission Hills Chamber of Commerce (818) 361-8888.

MONROVIA

MIDDLE TO UPPER-MIDDLE city located in foothills of San Gabriel Mountains, east of Pasadena. Mixes old and new nicely. School rankings land just below 50th percentile. Crime suburban average. Population: 41,037.

Monrovia started the 1940s with about 3,000 residential units built over a half century. In the 1940s, the city constructed 2,022 units and in the 1950s, 2,785 units. Over the next 30 years, Monrovia added about 1,700 to 2,000 units a decade. Compared to many other L.A. County cities, its development has been more even and gradual.

Generally the higher the elevation, the larger, the newer, the more expensive the homes. Off North Myrtle Avenue and its spin-off meandering streets, you'll find large ranchers, two-story executive homes and homes that start with a tract design but incorporate custom touches. Some homes have views. In the hill neighborhoods you also find the professionals' homes of the prewar years, some of them looking like they stepped out of old-moneyed New England, many of them modest, all well maintained.

South of Foothill Boulevard, the homes step down a notch to every day suburban but even here, on the west side, the old (including some Victorians) is mixed pleasantly with the 1950s and 1960s housing. Commercial and industrial buildings are located on the south side.

Downtown has been spruced up with brick crosswalks, trees and awnings. The high school has a bell tower and shows a lot of tender loving. Some streets are planted with tall pines. Some streets have old-fashioned lights. For its beautification and social efforts, Monrovia in 1995 was named an "All-American City." State in 2000 counted 14,517 units: 7,751 single homes, 1,560 single attached, 4,952 multiples, 254 mobiles. In 1990s, Monrovia's population increased by 5,300 people and its housing stock by 600 units.

Monrovia School District. Sample rankings: Bradoaks, 30th to 50th percentiles; Clifton Middle, 50th percentiles; Monrovia High, 50th and 60th percentiles. Bond passed to renovate schools. New gym at Santa Fe Middle.

Zero homicides in 1999, 1998 and 1997. The counts for previous years are 8, 4, 0, 1, 1, 6, 4. Monrovia has its own police department.

Library. Two museums. Community center. Swim center. About six parks. Summer concerts. Arts festival. Movies. Christmas parade. About 19 miles to downtown L.A. Buses. Interstate 210. Name inspired by pioneer rancher, William Monroe. Chamber of commerce (626) 358-1159.

MONTEBELLO

Downtown L.A.
Montebello

BEDROOM CITY that rises from flatlands to hills. Located about nine miles east of downtown L.A. Crime suburban average. School rankings low-middling. Population: 64,952.

The decisive battle of the war that secured California from Mexico was fought in Montebello. A cannon and a historical marker commemorate the event. When oil was discovered about World War I, Montebello turned into a boom town. In the hills, derricks still pump away.

Montebello started the 1940s with about 1,000 residential units. In the Forties, it built 3,370 units; in the Fifties, 4,028 units; the Sixties, 4,637 units; the Seventies, 3,993 units, and the Eighties, 2,080 units. In the 1990s, the city's population increased by 5,400 people and the housing stock by 125 units. So what you have is a fair amount of old suburban mixed with a fair amount of new suburban. Single homes run slightly ahead of apartment units.

The old suburban starts on the south side, then blends into the older downtown, then newer homes and apartments show themselves as Montebello moves into the hills. The north side has a regional mall on the east and a golf course-country club on the west. Many of the apartment complexes can be found along Lincoln Avenue, on the north.

The three-bedroom home, among owner-occupied units, leads in housing styles, followed by the two-bedroom, then the four-bedroom (about 1,250 of them). The older streets show some security doors, the newer ones do not. Overall maintenance is good, particularly on the hill streets. The state in 2000 counted 19,317 housing units: 9,250 single homes, 1,387 single attached, 8,473 multiples, 207 mobiles.

Education by the Montebello Unified School District, which includes neighboring towns. Sample rankings: Greenwood Elementary, 20th to 30th percentiles; Washington Elementary, 20th to 40th percentiles; Montebello High School, 20th and 30th percentiles. Bond passed to renovate schools.

Four homicides in 1999, five in 1998, and six in 1997. The counts for previous years are 7, 6, 3, 4, 4, 5. Montebello has its own police department.

Cultural arts center. Two libraries. Swim center. About eight parks. Regional park with nature center, horseback riding. Golf. Seniors center.

Highway 60 runs along the north border and leads straight to downtown L.A. Metrolink (commuter rail). Chamber of commerce (323) 721-1153.

MONTEREY PARK

A MIDDLE-CLASS CITY located about eight miles east of downtown L.A. Academic rankings generally high. Population: 67,409.

Monterey Park is built on hills, valleys, mesas and flat land. Single homes outnumber apartment units about two to one. Housing styles follow a pattern common to many communities in the county. About 1,000 residential units predate World War II. In the 1940s, Monterey Park about tripled in size, adding 2,851 units and in the 1950s it cut loose with 5,594 units and in the 1960s with 3,725 units. In the 1970s, housing starts eased off to 3,725 units and in the 1980s, they dropped to 2,694 homes and apartments. In the 1990s, Monterey Park's population increased by 6,700 people and its housing stock by 425 units.

Housing in the 1940s and early 1950s favored two-bedroom homes and as the postwar prosperity caught on moved up to three bedrooms. In the 1970s, four-bedroom homes started to appear. Three-bedroom homes, the last census reported, make up 47 percent of the owner-occupied units, two-bedroom, 27 percent, four-bedroom, 13 percent, and five-or-more-bedroom, 3 percent.

Pretty city. Many of the homes have views (Ridgecrest Street some of the best). Residents have indulged a fondness for gardening and topiary. One neighborhood greets visitors with a waterfall that cascades over blue tiles.

The apartments are clustered generally in their own sections. Some complexes, on the east side, were built on deep lots with small street fronts. The state in 2000 counted 20,720 housing units: 11,572 single homes, 1,978 single attached, 7,111 multiples, 59 mobiles.

Served by four school districts: Alhambra, Montebello, Garvey Elementary, Los Angeles. Sample rankings: Brightwood Elementary, 60th to 90th percentile; Monterey Highlands Elementary, 60th to 70th percentile; Monterey Vista Elementary, 50th to 60th percentile. Many schools are scoring in top 25 percent of state. Community college and state university. Montebello, Garvey and Los Angeles districts have passed bonds to renovate schools.

Four homicides in 1999. The counts for previous years are 2, 3, 1, 3, 6, 6, 2, 7, 0. Monterey Park has its own police department.

Thirteen parks. Two public swimming pools. Library. Two golf courses.

Short commute to downtown L.A. Monterey Park also has an office park (west side) and many jobs can be found in nearby towns. Buses. Metrolink (commuter rail). Chamber of commerce (626) 570-9429.

NORTHEAST L.A.

El Sereno, Montecito Heights, Cypress Park, Mount Washington, Glassell Park, Highland Park, Eagle Rock

NEIGHBORHOODS JUST NORTH of downtown L.A. and part of the City of L.A. Commutes from five to nine miles. School rankings low-middle to fairly high. Estimated population about 239,000.

Home to a large Cal State University and Occidental College. A real mix. Low-income neighborhoods sit side-by-side with middle and upper neighborhoods. Often a drive of just a few blocks will show a dramatic change in housing quality. Some new housing, including a gated hilltop condo complex.

For the middle- and upper-income housing, take a spin up Mount Washington Drive. Here you will find lovely homes, many artistically done. Great views of downtown L.A. Plenty of trees, shrubs and foliage. Favorite neighborhood of writers, artists.

Also in the middle-class way, the neighborhoods around Occidental College, Eagle Rock in general, and the hill sections. Some hill neighborhoods on the east side, however, have old, worn housing built on narrow streets.

For the low-income, drive the streets around Broadway.

Sample school rankings: Eagle Rock Elementary, 50th to 60th percentile; Lincoln High School, 30th percentile; El Sereno Elementary, 10th to 20th percentile. Several magnet schools.

Many parks, activities, especially from the college and university, close to downtown and all it offers, operas, movies, etc.

Crime figures not available but the presence of security doors and bars, especially in the low-income neighborhoods, indicate concerns about crime. As you move north into Eagle Rock, security devices become fewer.

Short commute to downtown, a big selling point. Buses, Metrolink (commuter rail) for some residents. Highway 110, Highway 2 and, a ghost from the past, Route 66.

Los Angeles Chamber of Commerce (213) 580-7500.

N. HOLLYWOOD
Valley Village, Sun Valley

NORTH HOLLYWOOD IS LOCATED in the San Fernando Valley, bordering Burbank on the west, miles away from the real Hollywood but very much in the movie-entertainment culture. It is home to Universal Studios and close to the Warner, NBC and Disney studios.

Sun Valley is the town immediately north of North Hollywood. Estimated population, 79,000. Valley Village is the town just south of North Hollywood. Its northern border is approximately Chandler Boulevard. Many guides and maps include Valley Village in North Hollywood. Estimated population for both is 124,000. All three are towns of the City of Los Angeles and are patrolled by L.A. police. All are educated by the L.A. Unified School District.

For a rough guide, the housing north of Chandler Boulevard tends to be low income and old, immediate postwar. Many of the homes need paint, have burned-out lawns and are in need of repairs. Not all the housing. You will always find homes that have been kept up and well maintained. The apartment complexes here present a good face. The same for Sun Valley, a mix of old and (a few) new homes and apartments. Many security doors and gates. Care of homes is uneven. Some get good care, some don't. Many two-bedroom homes. Jets (Burbank Airport) land and take off over Sun Valley.

South of Chandler Boulevard (Valley Village) the housing moves into the middle class and, on some streets, into the upper middle. The homes are very well-kept, the lawns tended, etc.

Schools mix kids from high- and low-scoring neighborhoods. Sample rankings: North Hollywood High, 40th to 60th percentile; Colfax Elementary, 30th to 70th percentile; Sun Valley Middle, 10th percentile.

No crime figures available but as crime follows demographics you can expect more in the low-income neighborhoods. Local groups are working to overhaul the older housing and business strips.

Libraries, senior centers, art festivals, parks, community college, many activities and restaurants, the usual trappings of Valley suburbia.

Burbank Airport. Two freeways. About 13 miles to downtown L.A. Metrolink (commuter rail). Buses. Chamber of commerce (818) 508-5155.

NORTHRIDGE

MIDDLE- TO UPPER MIDDLE-INCOME town built around California State University in San Fernando Valley. Pretty in a suburban way. One of the intellectual-cultural centers of the Valley. Site of 1994 earthquake. Estimated population 55,000.

Crime not tracked by FBI but the demographics say suburban average. Neighborhoods in Northridge generally go without security doors. Patrolled by L.A. Police Dept. Northridge is one of the towns of the City of Los Angeles. School rankings middling to high.

Northridge starts at Roscoe Avenue and moves north into foothills of the Santa Susana Mountains, passing on both sides of the university. The city planning department counts about 18,000 residential units, the majority of them single homes.

In prices and style and decorative touches, Northridge is aimed at professionals and middle managers. With the exception of some custom executive homes, the housing runs to suburban tract, three, four and five bedrooms, almost all very well maintained. The neighborhoods vary in quality but not by much. Northridge is the kind of town that attracts both a Starbucks Coffee and a Barnes and Noble Bookstore.

Apartments and student housing can be found around the university, which has dorms. Northridge appears to have made an almost complete recovery from the 1994 quake. Billions were pumped into the neighborhood to repair and upgrade housing.

Served by Los Angeles Unified School District. Sample academic rankings: Calahan Elementary, 50th to 80th percentiles; Darby Elementary, 40th to 70th percentiles; Granada Hills High School, 70th to 90th percentiles. Balboa, an elementary for "gifted" children, scores in the 99th percentile, among the tops in the state and nation.

About a half-dozen parks, some large. Nearby golf course. Many activities at the university. Northridge Fashion Mall will please shoppers. Barbara Stanwyck, movie star, used to own a horse ranch in the vicinity. Its name was Northridge Farms, hence the town's name.

About 24 miles to downtown L.A. Northridge is one of the few Valley towns where you have to drive a few miles to reach a freeway. But Metrolink (commuter rail) runs through Northridge to downtown L.A. Buses. Chamber of commerce (818) 349-5676.

NORWALK

Downtown L.A.
Norwalk
L.A. International Airport
Long Beach

BEDROOM CITY, one of the older suburbs. Located in southeast county, near border with Orange County. Academic rankings low to middling. Population: 104,473.

Norwalk's building spree started in the 1940s and exploded in the 1950s. About 60 percent of the city's current housing was built in these two decades. Most of the units were single homes, two and three bedroom, the one-story style that swept over L.A. County in the postwar years. Many of the homes were snapped up by veterans, making use of the GI Bill.

Norwalk also has about 1,700 four-bedroom homes and about 200 homes with five or more bedrooms, the 1990 census reported. By far the dominant style is the two- and three-bedroom unit, sturdy and plain, little ornamentation. Some streets are a little faded but Norwalk generally comes across as well maintained, lawns mowed, bushes trimmed, etc. Many of the original residents have taken their equity and moved along, replaced by others seeking to get a start in the housing market. Norwalk offers affordable homes. The state in 2000 counted 27,697 housing units: 20,018 single homes, 1,221 single attached, 5,985 multiples, 473 mobiles. In the 1990s, Norwalk's population increased by about 10,200 people and its housing stock by 450 units.

Served by Norwalk-La Mirada Unified School District. Sample academic rankings: Moffitt Elementary, 20th to 30th percentiles; Lampton Middle School, 40th to 50th percentiles; Norwalk High School, 30th to 40th percentiles.

Ten homicides in 1999. Counts for previous years are 16, 8, 14, 16, 10, 6, 7, 10, 11. Security doors here and there around town. Norwalk contracts with the sheriff's department to provide police protection.

Two libraries. Sports complex. Seniors center. About 14 parks. Shopping mall. Cerritos Community College, on south border, offers many classes and activities for fees that run about $36 a class.

Interstates 5 and 605 run through the town. Downtown L.A. 16 miles to northeast. Metrolink (commuter rail) to downtown L.A. and Orange County. On west side, new light-rail service to L.A. Airport and downtown L.A.

When the railroad was built in the late 1800s, the tracks crossed a road called the "North Walk." From this came the Norwalk Station and ultimately the town's name. Chamber of commerce (562) 864-7785.

PACIFIC PALISADES
Pacific Highlands

PRESTIGE COMMUNITIES located on or near the Pacific just north of Santa Monica. Many homes have great views of the Pacific. Estimated population: 27,000. School rankings run from the 70th to 90th percentiles. Crime not tracked by the FBI but high-income towns generally have low crime and these neighborhoods do not appear to be an exception.

Home to the J. Paul Getty Museum (the first, now closed for renovation) and the Self-Realization Fellowship Lake Shrine. Just outside city limits is the ranch of Will Rogers, the cowboy humorist. It is now included in a State Park (but still fields polo matches).

Pacific Palisades starts with palisades (high bluffs) that run about three miles along the Pacific shore then level off into small mesas. In the mesa neighborhoods, the housing mixes the old, the fairly old and occasionally the new. Homes along the edge of the bluff and some ravine homes have views of the Pacific. The rest are within walks of five to ten blocks to the beaches. The homes show a lot of care, the landscaping is nicely done, the streets attractive. The tenor is upper-middle-class to well-to-do (with exceptions, notably, a small mobile home park squeezed into a ravine).

Moving east on Sunset Boulevard, you pick up Palisades Drive, which gradually and then abruptly rises into the hills. This section is called Pacific Highlands. It consists of condos, executive homes and mansions, many of which have views of the countryside and Pacific. Many new homes here. Returning to Sunset Boulevard, as you travel east, other streets spin off of Sunset into the hills. The housing here is older but still upscale and many of the homes command sweeping views.

Served by the Los Angeles School District. Sample rankings: Marquez Elementary, upper 90th percentile; Revere Middle, 70th percentile; Palisades High School, 80th percentile.

If commuting to Hollywood ... a snap. But if your destination is downtown L.A. you've got 19 tough miles before you. Pacific Palisades is a town of the City of Los Angeles but residents, through civic groups, exercise much local control. Patrolled by L.A. police. Many beach activities. Typical sports for kids. Golf course-country club on south side. Chamber of commerce (310) 459-7963.

PACOIMA
Arleta, Lake View Terrace

LOW- TO MIDDLE-INCOME TOWNS located at the northeast side of the San Fernando Valley in the foothills of the San Gabriel Mountains. Pacoima is bordered by the City of San Fernando on the north and by Interstate 5 on the west.

Arleta is situated on the west side of Pacoima, and Lake View Terrace on the east side.

All are towns or neighborhoods of the City of Los Angeles. Education by the Los Angeles Unified School District, which has passed a bond to renovate its schools.

This is a situation, especially with Arleta-Pacoima, where boundaries blend into one another. The city planning department in 1994 gave this section a population of 92,537.

Many of the Pacoima-Arleta homes were built right after World War II. Some show loving care, many do not. Some people keep their lawns green, others parks their cars on the lawn. Security doors and window bars are common in many neighborhoods. Los Angeles police provide protection.

As you move toward the hills, the housing improves a little in size and quality and above Foothill Boulevard moves into the fairly new and middle class.

Sample academic rankings: Haddon Elementary, 10th percentile; Pacoima Elementary, below the 10th percentile; Pacoima Middle, 10th to 20th percentile.

Library, seniors center. Recreation center. Large regional park with golf course around Hansen Lake. About half-dozen parks. Close to the Angeles National Forest.

Three freeways. About 19 miles to downtown L.A. Metrolink (commuter rail) in San Fernando. Regional airport. If moving to area, check the plane noise.

Arleta Chamber of Commerce (818) 830-0900.

PALMDALE

HIGH-DESERT CITY. Situated on flat land ascending on its outskirts into craggy buttes and mountains. Summer days hot, summer evenings mellow, winters mild to chilly with occasional frosts. Clean air, no smog.

City of young families. Many new homes priced well below what's found in other cities. In size, one of the biggest cities in the county, over 100 square miles. Plenty of room to grow. Population: 122,392.

School rankings middling. Closely tied to neighboring city of Lancaster in region known as "Antelope Valley." Both famous for aerospace. Boeing, Lockheed Martin, Northrup-Grumman have plants and facilities in Palmdale.

Between 1950s and 1980s Palmdale added 1,400 to 2,000 homes and apartments per decade. In 1980s the city boomed with the construction of 14,712 residential units, and the growth continues. State in 2000 counted 39,468 housing units: 30,489 single homes, 574 single attached, 6,436 multiples, 1,969 mobiles. In the 1990s, Palmdale's population increased by 53,400 people and its housing stock by 15,000 units, almost all of them single homes.

Housing in central city runs mainly three-bedroom, one-two baths, two-car garages, 50s-60s, kept in good repair, tall trees for bowered look. New homes favor three-five bedrooms, two-three car garages, two-three baths, two-story, desert-sand stucco, red-tile roofs, small lots. Some homes rise into buttes (pointed hills) to command views. Many subdivisions are surrounded by sound walls, some gated. No graffiti, streets clean. Many homes favor lawns; some prefer desert plants: cacti, Joshua trees, sagebrush. German settlers, mistaking Joshua trees for palms, first called area, "Palmethal" (Palm Valley).

Antelope Valley Mall. Striking new civic center: red tiles, adobe texturing, mosaics, fountain, desert flowers. Library with large childrens' section.

Education by Palmdale Elementary District and Antelope Valley High School District. Rankings for the elementary district place just below or in the 50th percentile. Palmdale High scores right about the 50th percentile. Every year or so, a school is opened to meet rising enrollments.

Palmdale contracts with sheriff for police protection. Six homicides in 1999, seven in 1998. Counts for previous years are 6, 6 , 7, 7, 8, 11, 4, 4.

Skiing in nearby mountains. Cultural Art Center, Performing Arts Center, many civic groups and sports and activities. For commute, see Lancaster. Chamber of commerce (661) 273-3232.

PALOS VERDES ESTATES

PRESTIGE CITY, located on the Pacific. One of the choicest locations in California. Homes run from the well-to-do to the opulent. School rankings very high, crime low. Population: 14,742.

Palos Verdes Estates is clustered with three other communities on a blunt, hilly peninsula west of Long Beach. The others are: Rancho Palos Verdes, Rolling Hills Estates and Rolling Hills. They comprise one of the richest and most scenic sections of the county. All are residential communities. They have shops and one major shopping plaza but no hotels, hospitals or major industries. They are legal cities in control of their planning, zoning and civic affairs. The state in 2000 counted in Palos Verdes Estates 5,211 housing units: 4,812 single homes, 35 single attached, 363 multiples, 1 mobile. In 1990s, the city's population increased by 1,230 and its housing stock by 80 single homes.

Although Palos Verdes Estates has its mansions, especially on the Pacific, much of the housing consists of large, single-family homes, well maintained but not opulent, many of them commanding views of the Pacific. Back from the shore, the town rises into gentle hills with meandering horse trails. On the east side: the Palos Verdes golf and tennis clubs. About 850 acres have been dedicated as permanent park land. The city's population rose in the 1970s, dropped in the 1980s and will probably stabilize at 14,000-15,000 residents.

Served by Palos Verdes Unified School District, scores usually in the top 10 percent of the state. In 1998, the high school, which usually ranks in the state's top 5 percent, scored 618 on math SAT, one of 22 schools in state to crack 600. Did it again in 1999, math 614. Voters in 2000 okayed $52 million bond to renovate the schools. Good support for academics and education.

Zero homicides in past seven years. The counts for previous years are 1, 2, 0. The four cities contract with the L.A. Sheriff's Department to provide police protection. Overall crime rate very low. Private security used by many.

Golf, tennis, swimming, usual sports for children, little theater, ballet, chamber music society, art exhibits, botanical garden, Wayfarer Chapel (designed by Frank Lloyd Wright), whale watching, hiking trails, food and wine festival, ice skating. Upscale shopping at mall in Rolling Hills Estates.

The fly in the ointment: 23 miles to downtown L.A. But the job centers of Long Beach and L.A. Airport are within 10 to 15 miles. Interstate 110 can be picked up in Long Beach. Chamber of commerce (310) 377-8111.

PARAMOUNT

Downtown L.A. — Paramount — L.A. International Airport — Long Beach

BEDROOM-INDUSTRIAL CITY located on the north side of Long Beach. School rankings low to middling. Population: 55,978.

Paramount's housing boom started in the 1940s with 1,784 residential units, jumped to 2,692 units in the following decade and to 3,126 units in the 1960s — in total about 50 percent of its current housing stock.

Among owner-occupied homes, the one-story, two-bedroom unit was the favorite style, followed by the three-bedroom. The homes were modestly priced and aimed at people trying to get into the housing market.

Many homes have been kept up; some haven't. Paramount is sharpening the town's appearance with planted median strips, a public fountain and outdoor art.

Paramount also has new and fairly new housing, including some townhouses. The state in 2000 counted 14,683 housing units: 5,957 single homes, 1,743 single attached, 5,484 multiples, 1,499 mobiles. In the 1990s, Paramount's population increased by 8,300 and its housing stock by about 950 units.

Served by the Paramount Unified School District, rankings in the 10th to 30th percentile. The district in 1998 passed a $35 million bond to build and renovate schools.

Eleven homicides in 1999, seven in 1998, and ten in 1997. The counts for previous years are 5, 14, 16, 13, 7, 9, 16. Security doors have been installed on many homes. Paramount contracts with the sheriff's department to provide police protection.

One of the most popular swap meets in the west. Wal-Mart. About a half-dozen parks. Golf course. Library. Medical center.

About 17 miles to downtown but many jobs are to be had in Paramount (which has an oil refinery) and Long Beach. This means a short commute for many. Four freeways surround the town. Easy access to all four. Light rail to L.A. Airport and, with connection, to downtown L.A.

In the late 1800s, Paramount, with plenty of flat land, was decorated with dairy farms and where there are cows and cattle, there is hay. One of the hay markets was called Paramount.

Chamber of commerce (562) 634-3980.

PASADENA

DYNAMIC, COSMOPOLITAN CITY in foothills of San Gabriel Mountains. Housing a mix of plain, middle, middle-plus and gorgeous. School rankings bounce all over. Population 143,874.

One of the prettiest cities in the county. Set in the foothills of the San Gabriel Mountains.

Home of California Institute of Technology (Nobel winners), which manages the famed Jet Propulsion Lab.

First-class museums, including the Norton Simon — paintings by Rembrandt, Rubens, Renoir, etc. Also Pacific Asia Museum.

Home of Rose Bowl, where two of the best college football teams in nation face off on New Year's Day. Game is preceded by the Tournament of Roses Parade, one of the most famous in country.

Community college, art college, top-notch playhouse that has showcased many talents who later made it big in the movies.

Most libraries (10), per capita, of any city in the county. Historic district, popular with tourists. Lively downtown and night life, concentrated along Colorado Boulevard. Movie houses, bookstores, restaurants, boutiques — all there. Arts college. Music school.

Many lovely homes and neighborhoods. Mansions built for the old rich. Custom homes for the new rich. Many "ordinary homes" lovingly and landscaped and appointed.

Many businesses, which shortens commute for residents. Luxury hotels, including a Doubletree, a Hilton and a Ritz-Carlton.

So much does Pasadena have, many people assume it is the province solely of the affluent. It isn't. Pasadena has its low-income neighborhoods and demographics that run the spectrum. This explains the mix of school scores and crime that on some streets runs to "be careful."

Children attend the schools of the Pasadena Unified School District, enrollment about 23,000. The district also educates children in Sierra Madre and Altadena. Several years ago, voters approved a $240 million bond to renovate and equip for high-tech all the schools in the district. Work is being done now. Many schools score at or below the 50th percentile.

Pasadena and neighboring cities have many private schools that in total enroll almost 10,000 students.

Incorporated as a city in 1886, Pasadena has been building homes for well over 100 years. The city has always attracted the wealthy and the affluent but rare is the city that can afford to build only for the rich. Someone has to staff the local stores and businesses, maintain the roads, teach in the schools, patrol the streets and so on. Along with mansions, Pasadena erected modest homes and apartments.

By 1940, Pasadena had evolved into an affluent but rounded city of 82,000 inhabitants. In the 1940s, Pasadena has a small boom in housing and boosted its population by about 25,000. In the following decades, the city gradually increased its housing and its population and by 1990 claimed about 132,500 residents. In the 1990s, Pasadena's built about 1,200 housing units and added 12,300 inhabitants.

The state in 2000 counted 54,252 housing units: 25,057 single homes, 3,621 single attached, 25,550 multiples, 24 mobiles.

About one fourth of the city's housing predates World War II. About 40 percent was erected between 1940 and 1970. As the housing has grown older and in some places run down, it has become more affordable and this has changed the demographics of the town.

The mansions can be found on the south and west side, below Colorado Boulevard. The upscale middle housing is located around the Rose Bowl and off Loma Road, on the west side. Some of the low-income can be found north of Colorado Boulevard near Fair Oaks Boulevard. Outside of this, generalizations become useless. Some streets show want of care; a few blocks away, the houses sparkle. Less this seem pessimistic, Pasadena in probably all its neighborhoods will strike the casual visitor as quite presentable, if not lovely.

Two homicides in 1999. The counts for previous years are 10, 12, 14, 12, 16, 27, 18, 15, 13. Pasadena has its own police department.

Three golf courses in town, several more in region. About 20 parks. Many activities for adults and children. Aquatics center. Many cultural pursuits. Usual sports.

In planning, a large complex that combines offices, apartments, parking, condos, retail stores and a cultural arts center-auditorium. On the west side of the downtown.

About 10 miles to downtown L.A. Two freeways. Chamber of commerce (626) 795-3355.

PICO RIVERA

BLUE-COLLAR CITY located about eleven miles southeast of downtown Los Angeles between the cities of Whittier and Montebello. Population: 65,202. School rankings low to middling.

Pico Rivera, named after one of the famous Californio landowners, is located between the San Gabriel and the Rio Hondo rivers. It's a level town, measuring about two miles wide and four miles long.

The city started 1950 with about 3,200 housing units, then exploded into the tremendous growth that followed World War II. In the 1950s it built 8,224 units and in the 1960s, 2,023 units. Construction then dropped to 1,149 units in the 1970s and 1,659 units in the 1980s.

Single homes, two and three bedrooms, circa 1950s, make up the most popular style. Some homes have been neglected but many show a lot of care.

The state in 2000 counted 16,688 housing units: 12,606 single homes, 706 single attached, 2,903 multiples, 473 mobiles. In the 1990s, the city's population increased by 6,000 people and its housing stock by 375 units.

Served by the El Rancho Unified School District. Rankings land in the 20th to 50th percentile. When enrollment dropped decades ago, the district closed schools but kept them. When kids made a comeback, some of the schools were reopened.

Nine homicides in 1999, eight in 1998, and nine in 1997. The counts for previous years are 12, 12, 14, 8, 15, 5, 5. Pico Rivera contracts with the L.A. County Sheriff's Office for police protection.

Six parks, two libraries, swimming center, nine-hole golf course, tennis and handball courts. Just north of town is a large park that has a sports arena, fishing, archery, model boating, nature study and horse riding.

Like many older communities, Pico Rivera is using redevelopment (tax investment) to improve its commercial areas. Northrup-Grumman, which not too long ago employed 4,000 in Pico Rivera, closed in 2000. Cold War is over.

Freeways north and south of town. Quick commute to downtown L.A. Many local jobs.

Chamber of commerce (562) 949-2473.

PLAYA DEL REY
Westchester

EASILY OVERLOOKED neighborhoods-towns, located on the west side, just north of L.A. International Airport. Middle class, middle plus. Well maintained. Pretty. Great beaches. Site of Loyola Marymount University. Part of the City of L.A. School rankings middling plus. Crime not tracked but probably suburban average. Estimated population, 50,000. Many new homes going up near Jefferson Boulevard.

On a map, Playa Del Rey and Westchester come across as something to be avoided. L.A. Airport on their southern border looms large and, one might conclude, loud. The planes certainly can be heard but as they do not take off or land over Playa Del Rey and Westchester, the sound is somewhat muted.

Playa Del Rey, located to the west, rises and falls and levels out over gentle hills and mesas. Resort atmosphere on some streets, the influence of the ocean. A fair number of homes jump up the scale, two story, balconies. Wherever possible, the homes try to grab a sunset view. Big sandy beach that stretches for miles, one of hidden treasures. L.A. airport glides right into the ocean — no homes, apartments or people on its west side — but it does have a great beach, accessible to residents of Playa Del Rey-Westchester (and El Segundo). An estuary-boat channel on the north isolates these neighborhoods from Venice-Santa Monica, increasing the feeling of seclusion.

Moving east toward Westchester the housing turns to tract homes built in the 1950s and 1960s. Some of the newer homes climb into two stories and four bedrooms and a small number of homes were custom built. Overall impression: middle to upper middle. Lot of attention to keeping up homes. Patrolled by L.A. police. Many homes do without security doors.

Served by L.A. School District. Sample rankings: Loyola Village Elementary, 60th to 70th percentiles; Paseo Del Rey Fundamental, 50th to 80th percentile; Wright Middle, 40th to 50th percentile; Westchester High, 40th to 50th percentile. Several magnet programs.

Golf course, rec center, four parks. Beaches to die for. Sports, activities and cultural events associated with Loyola-Marymount U. Many jobs in or near the airport and Hughes plant. Close to Interstate 405. Buses. Chamber of commerce (310) 645-5151.

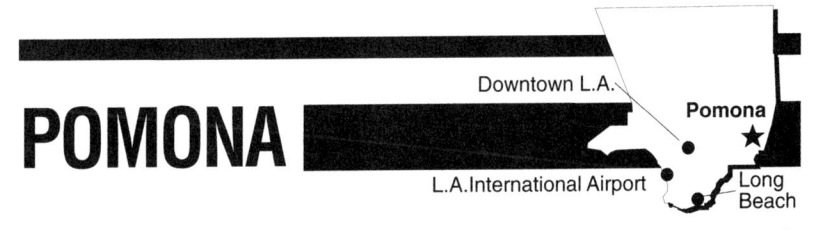

POMONA

Downtown L.A.
Pomona
L.A. International Airport
Long Beach

LARGE CITY ON EASTERN BORDER of county. Home to Cal Poly, one of the top public universities of the state. School rankings low-middle to high. Population 147,656.

A city in transition. Pomona had its boom between 1940 and 1970 when over 50 percent of its housing was built. These homes, generally located in the east and central part of town, are showing their age. But many are middle-class presentable and reflect a lot of attention. Efforts, including tax incentives, are being made to rejuvenate Pomona's downtown, which has a nice civic complex and many shops.

West of Highway 71, in the Phillips Ranch neighborhood, the housing moves up the scale into middle-class professional and the streets ascend into gentle hills. Some homes have views. On the northwest side near McKinley Avenue another middle-class neighborhood can be found.

The state in 2000 counted 39,330 housing units: 23,654 single homes, 2,847 single attached, 10,993 multiples, 1,836 mobiles. Three-bedroom units dominate the single homes but Pomona has a nice chunk of about 4,000 four-bedroom homes. In the 1990s, the city's population increased by 16,000 and its housing stock by 870 units.

Served by Pomona Unified School District. Many schools in the old town are scoring well below the 50th percentile but schools in the newer areas are scoring in the 80th to 90th percentiles, the top 20 percent of state. In 1998, a $50 million bond was passed to renovate schools. Cal Poly waves the flag for local education and helps with some programs.

Twenty six homicides in 1999. The counts for previous years are 16, 34, 19, 32, 39, 40, 39, 25, 34. Many homes in older Pomona have security doors and windows, an indication of concerns about crime. Civic leaders are working on prevention programs. Pomona has its own police department.

About 20 parks. Regional park with lake and golf course on the northern border. County fair at Fairplex, 487 acres, draws about two million people every summer. Fairplex also runs trade shows, sporting events year round. Usual sports and activities for kids and adults.

If you drive to downtown L.A., about 30 miles due west, our sympathies, a long haul. But Metrolink (commuter rail) can be picked up nearby. Short drive to Ontario Airport. Three freeways and an expressway help speed things along. Chamber of commerce (909) 622-1256.

PORTER RANCH

UPSCALE COMMUNITY located in foothills of Santa Susana Mountains, in San Fernando Valley, above Northridge. Crime low. School rankings high. Lot of the new. Home prices start at $450,000. Population: 18,000 plus.

Porter Ranch started building about 20 years ago, favoring single homes, three and four bedroom, built over hills and ravines and incorporating the touches of modern suburbia, for example, utility lines undergrounded, roofs using fire-retardant tiles, arterial traffic buffered from residential streets.

The first homes were built on public streets. The later homes and the homes going up now were placed behind gates with guards. Sales agents make a point of noting that Porter Ranch offers safety and security and a family style of life. The first homes fall into the category of upscale middle. The homes being built now jump up a notch or two. Porter Ranch is built around a golf course and backs up to open hills. Real feeling of country. Many of the homes are built on hills or mesas and have views of the Valley.

Some guides lump Porter Ranch in with Northridge. A freeway (Highway 118) separates the two and Porter Ranch does have its own identity. But in other ways the connection makes sense. Both are towns of the City of L.A., their demographics are close, and they shop the same mall, Northridge. The state university at Northridge kind of functions as the intellectual center of the North Valley and Northridge attracts certain stores (Barnes and Noble, Starbucks) that Porter Ranch people would find enticing. Porter Ranch also gets connected to Chatsworth.

Served by L.A. Unified School District. Sample rankings: Castlebay Elementary, scores in the 80th to 90th percentile, which translates to top 15 percent in state. Bond passed to renovate schools.

Patrolled by L.A. police. No stats are broken out but the demographics place the crime rate on the low side and the private security and gates work to keep crime low.

Golf course, tennis courts. Long canyon park that extends into Northridge. Several smaller parks. Library. Country club.

About 20 miles to downtown L.A. Easy access to the freeway. Metrolink (commute rail) station at Northridge.

To reach Porter Ranch, take the Tampa Avenue exit off of Highway 118 and drive north.

RANCHO PALOS VERDES

ONE OF FOUR PRESTIGE BEDROOM CITIES clustered on a peninsula just west of Long Beach. One of the prettiest locations in the county. Ocean views, upscale homes. Schools score high, crime low. Population: 44,933.

The Palos Verdes Peninsula encompasses Rancho Palos Verdes, Palos Verdes Estates, Rolling Hills and Rolling Hills Estates. The four cities are built over hills with great views of the Pacific and Santa Catalina Island. From their beginning, their housing has been aimed at affluent professionals and the rich.

Rancho Palos Verdes started 1950 with fewer than 500 homes. In the 1950s, it constructed 3,221 units; in the 1960s, 6,690 units, in 1970s, 4,186. These three decades account for 90% of the homes found in the community. Housing types range from flat-top Eichlers (plenty of glass) to 50's-60's traditional tract to 80's four- and five-bedroom, two-story homes.

On some streets, the houses jump off the scale: mansions, beautiful creatures often commanding particularly advantageous views of the ocean but there are many everyday, slightly upscale homes in this community. Some neighborhoods hide behind gates. In the hills the roads twist and turn and the houses sit atop hills or little mesas with views of the ravines, the ocean and countryside. All in all, a lovely place. Bring money. The state in 2000 counted 15,742 housing units: 12,137 single homes, 1,113 single attached, 2,487 multiples, 5 mobiles. In the 1990s, the city's population increased by 3,300 people and its housing stock by 271 homes.

Served by the Palos Verdes Peninsula Unified School District. School rankings are among the highest in the state. Voters in 2000 okayed $52 million renovation bond. A small portion of the city is served by the Los Angeles Unified School District. See Palos Verdes Estates.

One homicide each in 1999 and 1998. Counts for previous years are 0, 1, 0, 3, 1, 1, 0, 0. The four cities contract with the sheriff for police protection.

Rancho Palos Verdes, like its neighbors, imposes strict controls on planning and development. The four communities share many recreational activities. These include golfing, horseback riding, kids' sports, arts, chamber music, ballet, ice skating, whale watching, etc.

If your commute is to downtown L.A., 27 miles yonder, the road is long and often congested. But jobs are plentiful in Long Beach and near the L.A. airport. Chamber of commerce (310) 377-8111.

REDONDO BEACH

OCEAN CITY that angles inland. Located about seven miles south of L. A. International Airport. Bedroom community. Middle to upper-middle class. Crime rate low. School rankings fairly high. Population: 67,638.

Although a Pacific county, L.A. has few resort cities, miles of beach being narrow and inaccessible or given over to shipping and industry. Redondo Beach is a resort city. It has about two miles of beach, loaded with sand, ideal for swimming, surfing, sunbathing and beach games, such as volleyball. Throughout the day and in the evening, visitors and residents stroll or rollerblade the promenade. Lovely sunsets.

At the shore, single homes are blended with apartment buildings. As you move back a bit, the single homes increase in number, many of them angled to see the sun set. On the north side, the City of Hermosa Beach takes over the beach and Redondo Beach continues behind Hermosa Beach. This northern neighborhood, suburban in character, consists mainly of single homes with some apartments. Redondo Beach started its boom in the late 1940s and added 7,001 residential units in the 1950s. Over the next 40 years, the city built 5,000 to 6,000 units in every decade. Among owner-occupied units, the 1990 census tallied 238 homes with five or more bedrooms, 1,497 with four bedrooms, 6,392 with three bedrooms and 3,400 with two bedrooms. Maintenance and the level of care throughout the city are generally high. The state in 2000 counted 29,164 housing units: 11,262 single homes, 4,065 single attached, 13,745 multiples, 92 mobiles. In the 1990s, the city's population increased by 7,500 people and its housing stock by 950 units.

Served by Redondo Beach Unified School District, which in 2000 okayed a $55 million renovation bond. Scores land in the 70th to 90th percentile. All Redondo High freshmen are given laptop computers but the following year they have to give them up to new freshman. School got a grant for the laptops. District reportedly has excellent arts program.

One homicide in 1999. The counts for previous years are 1, 3, 0, 4, 0, 4, 0, 5, 2. Redondo Beach has its own police department.

New library with reading room for children. Rebuilt fishing pier. Performing arts center. Seniors center. About 15 parks, marina. Many activities. Usual sports. Many restaurants, cafes, shops. Where surfing was introduced to the U.S. mainland (from Hawaii). About 23 miles to downtown L.A. Interstate 405 to east. Local jobs in or near airport. Chamber of commerce (310) 376-6911.

RESEDA
Winnetka

Reseda ★ Downtown • L.A.
L.A. International Airport — Long Beach

SAN FERNANDO VALLEY bedroom towns. Reseda starts about two miles west of Van Nuys Airport. Winnetka is the town immediately west of Reseda. After Winnetka, moving west, comes Canoga Park.

Both Reseda and Winnetka are towns of the City of Los Angeles and both are served by the Los Angeles Unified School District.

Reseda (including West Van Nuys) has an estimated population of 85,000. The 1990 census includes Winnetka, which covers about 18 blocks, in with other towns. Depending on where the lines are drawn, its population runs from 30,000 to 60,000.

Reseda and Winnetka got their booms right after World War II and both built for the blue-collar middle class. The land here is flat and ideal for tract housing. Homes run to two- and three-bedroom units, with typically the garage out front and offset at an angle to the house. Apartment complexes have that "Lanai Kai" look, popular in the 1950s and 1960s.

In overall appearances, both towns come off pretty good. The homes often show their age but the lawns are mowed, the shrubs trimmed and so on. Residents work to keep up appearances. Some streets are faded. Some homes have security doors. Many homes use gates, behind which vehicles are placed. Some new homes are going up, three and four bedroom.

Sample school rankings: Fullbright Elementary (Winnetka), 20th to 30th percentile; Reseda Elementary, 20th to 30th percentile; Reseda High School, 40th to 50th percentile. Garden Grove Elementary, 20th to 30th percentile.

About a half-dozen parks. Several recreation centers. Close to California State University-Northridge and all it offers. Pierce Community College borders Winnetka on the south. Many classes, activities, low fees.

About 22 miles to downtown L.A. Interstate 405 can be picked up in Van Nuys. Also at Van Nuys, Metrolink (commuter rail) to downtown L.A.

Winnetka, Reseda and many of the towns of the San Fernando Valley flow into one another. Some towns define their borders along historical lines, others are using zip codes or census tracts. This sometimes confuses addresses where the towns "meet." Chamber of commerce (818) 345-1920.

ROLLING HILLS

LEGALLY A CITY but in reality a cluster of estate homes, about 680 in number. Population: 2,066.

Prestigious, pretty, located in one of the nicest sections of L.A. County, the Palos Verdes Peninsula.

In the old days, which was only a few decades ago, any community with enough ambition could form itself into a city under the easy incorporation laws of the state. Rolling Hills, probably to control development, incorporated in 1957.

Gated community, surrounded by a fence. Casual visitors cannot enter. The town is governed by the city council and the homeowners association. About 70 percent of the homes were erected between 1950 and 1980.

Some homes are pointed towards downtown L.A. and have views of the San Gabriel Mountains and the L.A. Basin. Other homes command views of the Pacific. About half of the homes have nine or more rooms, the 1990 census reported. In the 1990s, the city's population increased by 195 people and its housing stock by eight homes.

Served by Palos Verdes Peninsula Unified School District, which also includes the communities of Rancho Palos Verdes, Palos Verdes Estates and Rolling Hills Estates. Voters in 2000 approved a $100 million bond to renovate district schools. School rankings are among the highest in the state. See Palos Verdes Estates for more on schools.

Zero homicides in 1999, 1998, 1997, 1996, 1995 and 1994. For a "city," one of the lowest crime rates in the state. The local cities contract with the L.A. County Sheriff's Office for police protection. Rolling Hills augments this with its own security guards.

For recreation, see Rancho Palos Verdes. Rolling Hills loves the horses. Stables and trails are found throughout the community.

No stores but a large shopping mall is located in the adjoining town. Also golf course. Chamber of commerce for region, (310) 377-8111.

Interstate 110 can be picked up a few miles east of the city.

Rolling Hills occasionally shows up in surveys of the richest cities in the U.S.

ROLLING HILLS ESTATES

ONE OF FOUR PRESTIGIOUS COMMUNITIES located on a hilly peninsula west of Long Beach. Many homes command views of the L.A. Basin or the Pacific and Catalina Island.

All are upscale communities with homes that range from everyday suburban (but often extensively improved) to opulent. All share the same school district.

All contract with the sheriff's department to provide police protection. Each town has its own recreational activities but they share many activities. School scores very high, crime low. Zero homicides in 1999, 1998, 1997, 1996, 1995 and 1994. Rolling Hills Estates population: 8,787.

Rolling Hills Estates got its boom in the 1950s when 1,036 homes were constructed. The following decade housing starts dropped to 622 units and in the 1970s the city built 776 units. In the 1980s new homes dropped to 278 and in the 1990s to 130 homes. As a legal city, Rolling Hills Estates controls its own planning.

The state in 2000 counted 3,005 housing units: 2,351 single homes, 598 single attached, 54 multiples, 2 mobiles.

Rolling Hills Estates winds through and around the communities of Palos Verdes Estates, Rancho Palos Verdes and Rolling Hills. All are noted for their tight building controls.

Served by the Palos Verdes Peninsula Unified School District. All the schools score in either the top 10 percent or top 5 percent in state. This indicates strong parental interest in education. See Palos Verdes Estates.

Rolling Hills Estates differs from its sister communities in one major aspect: It has stores, banks, boutiques and an upscale shopping section. This gives it what the others lack, a tax base to fund local amenities. The commercial area is buffered from the homes and with its restaurants functions as the social and business center for the peninsula. Among the stores, Saks Fifth Avenue, Williams-Sonoma, Talbots, Restoration Hardware, Gap.

Six parks, 25 miles of horse trails and 10 miles of bicycle paths. City hall has a hitching post. Tennis club, stables, three golf courses on peninsula, swimming, arts, many activities (See also Rancho Palos Verdes). Chamber of commerce (310) 377-8111.

ROSEMEAD

Downtown L.A.
Rosemead
L.A. International Airport
Long Beach

LOW-MIDDLE TO MIDDLE-INCOME CITY located about 11 miles east of downtown L.A. School rankings above and below the 50th percentile. Population: 57,328.

Except for some small hills to the south, Rosemead was built over flat land. It doubled its residential units during the 1940s and boomed in the 1950s. About 55 percent of the homes and apartments predate 1960.

Many of Rosemead's neighborhoods blend the old with the new. Developers aimed at the blue-collar middle class and people buying their first home. Much of the housing can be described as suburban practical. Among owner-occupied units, three-bedroom homes edge out two-bedroom homes by about 150 units, the 1990 census reported. Homes and streets are generally well kept, the lawns mowed, etc. But this is a town that has not overindulged landscaping and decorative touches. It remains what it started out: affordable housing. On the south side, in the hills, many of the newer homes have been built, some four-bedroom and bigger. Older neighborhoods have some of the newer and bigger. The state in 2000 counted 14,345 housing units: 9,778 single homes, 1,838 single attached, 2,340 multiples, 389 mobiles. In the 1990s, the city's population increased by 5,700 people and its housing by 211 units.

Education by Garvey Elementary District, Rosemead Elementary District and El Monte High District. Sample rankings: Duff Elementary, 20th to 30th percentile; Shuey Elementary, 60th to 80th percentile; Rosemead High, 50th to 70th percentile. Don Bosco, Catholic tech school, on south side. In 2000, Garvey passed a $15 million bond and Rosemead a $30 million bond, both for renovation.

Eight homicides in 1999. The counts for previous years are 3, 4, 7, 6, 10, 8, 9, 7, 5. Rosemead's overall crime rate is fairly low but the number of homicides is slightly higher than what's found in many suburban cities. Rosemead contracts with the sheriff's department to provide police protection.

Sports complex, two public swimming pools, library, six parks, 10 playgrounds. Regional park with golf course. City sponsors sports and activities for kids and adults. Two community centers. Shopping mall.

Interstate 10 splits the city. Easy access to freeways and short hop to downtown L.A. Buses. Metrolink (commuter rail) station in bordering El Monte. Southern California Edison is headquartered in Rosemead, thousands of jobs. Chamber of commerce (626) 288-0811.

SAN DIMAS

MIDDLE- TO UPPER MIDDLE-CLASS bedroom community located in the east county at the foot of the San Gabriel Mountains. Horse country. San Dimas flattens out at its center and at its southern and northern ends rises into hills. Population 37,357. School rankings middling to high, crime low.

Farm country until about 1960, famous for its lemons, San Dimas built about 2,300 residential units in the 1960s and 4,100 units in the 1970s. This late start on suburbia gives much of the town a new look.

But there are housing choices. In or near the downtown you will find cottages and rambling bungalows that look as though they came out of the Midwest. As you move towards the northern hills, the housing glides into middle-class tract, nicely done, and near and above Baseline Road ascends a little up the scale. You will also find some horse ranches here.

Below the downtown, which is generally flat, San Dimas rises into gentle hills upon which are built large and affluent homes centered around the Via Verde Country Club. San Dimas has its older, smaller housing but in general the town comes across as middle-class-plus with a fair number of homes crossing into the executive class. Several senior complexes. The state in 2000 counted 12,077 housing units: 7,485 single homes, 1,765 single attached, 1,927 multiples, 900 mobiles. In the 1990s, the city's population increased by 5,000 people and its housing stock by 600 units, about half of them single homes.

The children are educated by the Bonita Unified School District, which also serves La Verne. Scores land generally in the 50th to 80 percentiles. A construction bond may be attempted in 2001.

Zero homicides in 1999, 1998, 1997. Counts for previous years are 0, 2, 0, 0, 0, 3, 2. Overall crime rate is low. Police protection by sheriff's department.

Five golf courses are located in or near San Dimas. The city borders a large regional park with a reservoir and a "Raging Waters." Equestrian trails wind through the town. Half dozen parks, one long and narrow along creek.

San Dimas, which calls itself the "home of the modern pioneer," plays up the Old West theme with wooden sidewalks in the downtown. Library, seniors' center. Annual exhibit of western art.

Two freeways crisscross San Dimas making access convenient but it is about 30 miles to downtown L.A. Buses and Metrolink (commuter rail). About 14 miles to the airport at Ontario. Chamber of commerce (909) 592-3818.

SAN FERNANDO

Downtown L.A.
San Fernando
L.A. International Airport
Long Beach

SMALL CITY located on the east side of the San Fernando Valley. In an older suburban way, pretty. Shows a high level of care. Population 24,722. School rankings low.

About 17 percent of San Fernando's housing was built before World War II. About 47 percent was constructed between 1940 and 1960. To state this another way, about two-thirds of the city predates 1960 and this makes San Fernando an old suburb. And a modest one. Two-bedroom units outnumber three-bedroom. If you took these numbers and applied them to other towns, the adjectives "rundown" and "worn out" might round out the description.

To the credit of its government, civic leaders and residents, San Fernando comes across as quite presentable. The streets are clean, the housing generally in good repair. Mission Street, decorated with palm trees, gladiolus and other flowers, makes a lovely entrance to the city. Along Orange Avenue, you'll find the larger homes of the city. Downtown has been spruced up with brick and paint and revamped to encourage pedestrian shopping.

San Fernando is not problem free. Some homes resort to security doors and window bars. School rankings are worrisome. But the city gives the impression of having the energy to deal with problems and to shape its future.

The state in 2000 counted 5,991 housing units: 3,825 single homes, 523 single attached, 1,538 multiples, 105 mobiles. In the 1990s, the city's population increased by 2,150 people and its housing stock by 200 units.

Education provided by the Los Angeles Unified School District. Sample national academic rankings: O'Melveny Elementary, 10th percentile; Gridley Elementary, 10th percentile; San Fernando High, 20th to 40th percentile.

One homicide in 1999, two in 1998, and four in 1997. Counts for previous years are 2, 2, 2, 3, 3, 6, 3. San Fernando has its own police department.

Library. Four parks. Usual sports and activities for kids and adults. Close to Mission Community College, many job and vocational classes. Close also to the San Fernando Mission, founded by Father Junipero Serra. Government buildings damaged in 1994 quake. Repaired, strengthened, reopened in 1998. Community hospital.

About 21 miles to downtown L.A. Interstates 5 and 210 and Highway 118 border the city. Easy access to freeway system. Metrolink (commuter rail) to downtown L.A. Park and ride lot. Chamber of commerce (818) 361-1184.

SAN GABRIEL

MISSION CITY. Pretty. Well-cared-for. Built on flat land but mountains six miles to north make presence felt. Mix of low, middle and upper income. School rankings across spectrum. Population 41,604.

Father Junipero Serra opened the San Gabriel Mission in 1771. A few years later floods destroyed the building and in 1776, at a different site, a second mission was erected. Restored, it attracts thousands of visitors every year and may have inspired residents to pay extra attention to appearances. Local lad who made good, George Patton, dashing World War II general.

San Gabriel can be divided at the mission or Main Street. To the north, the homes are better appointed, larger, and in an old-fashioned way, upscale, as if the neighborhood was built for managerial class of 50 or 60 years ago. The north side borders San Marino, an affluent community, and has a golf course with country club. The north side also has its small homes but they show a high level of care. Below the mission, the homes and apartments run to middle class and at the south end, to low income and middle class. On some blocks, here and there a new home will jump up the scale but for the most part the homes are small. About 42 percent of the housing stock predates 1950 and about 30 percent of the town's housing was built between 1950 and 1970. San Gabriel has its new but it is an old town. Among owner-occupied units, as reported in 1990 census, the three-bedroom home was the most popular style, followed by the two, and then by four-plus. Some apartment buildings use a Spanish motif: sandy stucco and red tiles. State in 2000 counted 12,891 units: 7,216 single homes, 888 single attached, 4,757 multiples, 30 mobiles. In the 1990s, the city's population increased by 4,500 people and its housing stock by 155 units.

Children attend schools in San Gabriel district and Alhambra High district Sample rankings: McKinley Elementary, 50th to 70th percentile; Wilson Elementary, 60th to 70th; San Gabriel High, 50th; Gabrielino High, 50th to 70th. Check school boundaries if looking at homes at northeast side and in unincorporated land. Might be San Marino district.

One homicide each in 1999. The counts for previous years are 1, 2,1, 4, 4, 4, 1, 1, 3. San Gabriel has its own police department.

Two golf courses in or near town. Many activities associated with mission. Swimming pool. Four parks, two rec centers. Small theater. Civic auditorium. Skating rink. City hall sponsors many classes, activities. Interstate 10 runs along south side of town. Park-and-ride lot. Buses. About 10 miles to downtown L.A. Chamber of commerce (626) 576-2525.

SAN MARINO

PRESTIGE CITY located south of Pasadena. Famous for its Huntington Library, Art Collections and Botanical Gardens. School rankings among the highest in the state. Overall crime rate very low. Population 14,006.

Although rich with more than its share of mansions, San Marino is not a showy town. Palms grace some of the median strips, lawns are putting-green quality, shrubs and trees show the gardener's care, everything appears very presentable. But rarely overwhelming. Many homes fall into the category of upscale professional.

The 1990 census counted 687 homes with five or more bedrooms (mansions or executive homes) and 1,095 four-bedroom homes and 1,761 three-bedroom homes. South of Huntington Drive, the homes run to custom tract, nicely done. North of Huntington Drive, many homes step up in size and quality. Lovely city. About 47 percent of the homes were built before World II and about 45 percent between 1940 and 1960 — in total 92 percent of the current housing. No apartment buildings. No industries. Service stores and shops are located along Huntington Drive. The state in 2000 counted 4,472 housing units: 4,435 single homes, 20 single attached, 13 multiples, 4 mobiles. In the 1990s, the city's population increased by 1,050 people and its housing stock was unchanged.

Served by San Marino Unified School District, scores in the top 5 percent. Much attention paid to schools and education. Every year, high school breaks 600 mark in math SAT, and in 1999 hit 650, second highest in state. Two bonds passed to renovate schools. Parcel tax for school programs. High school is being rebuilt. Every school in the district is being remodeled and renovated. Parents' group sponsors classes in Chinese language, culture. Civic group raises about $700,00 annually for schools.

Zero homicides in 1999, 1998, and 1997. Counts for previous years are 0, 5, 2, 0, 0, 0, 1. Five homicides concerned a domestic incident, arson. San Marino has its own police department, fire department and paramedic service. One park. Library. Sports fields at the schools. Many homes have own recreation, pools. Golf course to the south.

Henry Huntington, nephew of a Big Four railroad magnate, helped his uncle run his business and later took over and expanded firm. He and wife Arabella loved and collected rare books and art, which they housed at their San Marino estate. Chamber of commerce (626) 286-1022.

SAN PEDRO
Wilmington

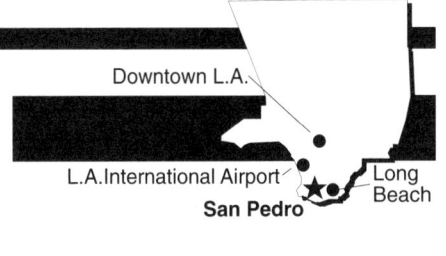

Downtown L.A.
L.A. International Airport
San Pedro
Long Beach

TWO QUITE DIFFERENT TOWNS, part of the City of L.A., located next to each other on the south side near Long Beach.

San Pedro, estimated population 72,000, borders Rancho Palos Verdes, a high-income community, and absorbs some of its character, especially on the west side. The homes here are middle-class-plus, some of them built on streets rising gently into the hills and offering views of the Pacific.

As you move east towards Long Beach, homes become smaller and older, more middle and working class, generally well-cared-for, some new homes and apartments mixed in. Some old homes are being customized and parts of town hint at the artistic, as if San Pedro is nurturing an artists' colony. On the east side, as land descends to water, terrain creates view lots.

San Pedro is bordered on two sides by water, either the Pacific or the ship channel, and the town clearly benefits from the ocean exposure. Several parks, one a public beach, decorate shoreline and other parks are scattered throughout city.

Wilmington, estimated population 40,000, borders a large oil refinery. This has probably driven down property values but at the same time created affordable housing. The housing below the Pacific Coast Highway tends to be old and plain, apartments and small homes built mostly right after World War II. North of Pacific Coast Highway housing quality steps up a bit.

Many homes have security doors and windows.

Both towns are served by the Los Angeles Unified School District. San Pedro High School shows rankings in the 50th to 70th percentile. Wilmington Middle School shows rankings in the 10th percentile. Educational pluses include Harbor Community College, located next to a large park in Wilmington.

The towns are 20 to 25 miles south of downtown L.A. Many local jobs. Easy access to Interstate 110.

Typical sports, many activities associated with the ocean, fishing, boating, etc. Among the unusual, a Civil War museum. San Pedro Chamber of Commerce: (310) 832-7272. Wilmington Chamber of Commerce (310) 834-8586.

SANTA CATALINA
Avalon

SANTA CATALINA ISLAND, usually called Catalina, is located about 21 miles out to sea, due south of Long Beach. It has a small city called Avalon, 3,608 residents.

Avalon is a pretty town with a large harbor that attracts many tourists and boaters. The city has beaches, hotels, bed-and-breakfast inns, condominiums, shops and places to rent boats, bicycles and equipment to enjoy the island and the waters offshore (snorkeling, etc.). Trails meander around the island, which has interesting flora and fauna, over 100 species of birds, and a botanical garden. Great sport fishing.

On summer weekends, the population sometimes rises to 10,000. Ferries, pleasure boats and planes connect Catalina Island with the mainland.

Education is provided by the Long Beach Unified School District. Avalon School has a rare configuration: it goes from kindergarten to the 12th grade; enrolls about 730. Scores range from the 30th to the 50th percentile. Bond passed to renovate and build schools.

Avalon has been slowly adding apartments and homes. Between 1980 and 1990 the population increased by 44 percent. Many of the units are rentals. Avalon has adopted a policy of slow and controlled growth.

The state in 2000 counted 2,203, housing units: 476 single homes, 452 single attached, 1,270 multiples, 5 mobiles. In the 1990s, the city's population increased by 700 people and its housing stock by 315 units, most of them apartments.

Zero homicides in 1994, 1995, 1996, 1997, 1998, and 1999. Overall crime rate is high but violent crime is low. Resort towns have many stores and this usually means many thefts, which pushes up the crime rate.

About 85 percent of Santa Catalina Island has been placed in a nature conservancy. If you want a home where the buffalo roam, Santa Catalina can oblige. It has a small herd. Also has deer, foxes and wild pigs.

The sales tax for Los Angeles County is 8 cents per dollar spent. In Avalon it is 8.5 cents. The city tacked on a half-cent to pay for local projects.

Visitors Bureau (310) 510-7649.

SANTA CLARITA
Canyon Country, Newhall, Saugus, Sulphur Springs, Valencia

INLAND BEDROOM CITY, located off of Interstate 5. Many new homes and more coming. One of the fastest growing communities in the county. Population 151,260. Location of Six Flags Magic Mountain.

Following World War II, veterans poured into the San Fernando Valley. Miles upon miles of farm land were turned to tract housing. The boom continued into the 1970s when the Valley started to run out of land. The Valley also attracted many industries, foremost defense and entertainment, and this meant local jobs. Meanwhile, the freeway networks were extended and improved.

The San Fernando Valley is ringed by hills and mountains that often trap or slow the circulation of the air — smog. Just over the ridge were five small communities — Saugus, Newhall, Valencia, Sulphur Springs and Canyon Country — that offered country living and cleaner air and with the new freeways and the Valley jobs an endurable commute.

More people settled in the communities. Developers responded to the demand, building large master-planned neighborhoods with wide internal roads that moved traffic quickly to freeway ramps. The projects, at their inception, allotted land for schools, parks and shopping centers, used walls and clever layouts to keep arterial traffic away from residential streets, and, compared to the 1950s and 1960s tracts, did a better job of making suburbia pleasing and inviting.

As the population increased, arguments over local control and pace of development surfaced — an old story in fast-growing towns — and in 1987 the five communities incorporated themselves into the City of Santa Clarita.

Because they had been around so long, however, the communities retained their identities. If asked, many residents will say they live in Saugus, Valencia or Newhall. The last two — Sulphur Springs and Canyon Country — are not as well known as the first three. The media also uses Saugus, Newhall, etc.

Accurately speaking, however, these are no longer towns or communities. They are neighborhoods of Santa Clarita. The city government does the planning, contracts with the sheriff for police protection, repairs the streets, maintains the parks, and sponsors many of the recreation and cultural activities.

The school districts, which predated the city, are still intact. Children attend schools in the Newhall elementary district or the Saugus elementary district or the Sulphur Springs elementary district. They then move up to the William S. Hart High School District, which covers grades 7-12. Hart was a star of the silent screen. He played the steely-eyed hero who always got the girl and vanquished the villains. He owned a local ranch, part of which has been set aside as park with a museum.

Santa Clarita also benefitted from three other forces. Its homes, many of them two-story, four-bedroom, were often priced cheaper than homes in other communities in L.A. County. By the 1970s and 1980s, many Valley and L.A. residents had built up a fair amount of equity in their homes. They took this equity and bought into Santa Clarita.

And Santa Clarita benefitted from the reputation and demographics it developed. Many of the new residents were middle-class professionals, often with young families. School scores generally follow demographics. Many Santa Clarita schools are scoring in the 70th, 80th and 90th percentiles, among the top 30 percent in the state. In 1999, Newhall district voters approved a $35.5 million bond for new schools, three of them to be built over the next three years. Hart district in 2000 narrowly lost a bond vote but is applying for state funds to build four schools. Many schools are on year-round schedules.

Crime follows demographics. Santa Clarita's crime rate is very low. Two homicides in 1999. Counts for previous years are 6, 2, 2, 2, 2, 4, 0, 4, 4, 2, 1.

In the 1980s, Santa Clarita built about 19,000 residential units and in the last decade 11,000. The great majority of the housing follows modern tract designs but the old towns have cottages and bungalows and Sulphur Springs, with its horse estates, goes way up the scale. The state in 2000 counted 51,966 housing units: 29,846 single homes, 5,989 single attached, 13,935 multiples, 2,196 mobiles.

Santa Clarita is spread over flats, hills and mesas in a large valley. Many homes have views of countryside. Big city. Country atmosphere. Summers hot but the heat dry; low humidity. In spring, winter and fall the weather mellows but because the countryside is dry, the feel of desert is strong. Clean town. Utility lines undergrounded in many sections. Many arguments over how many more homes should be built in the region.

Three libraries, hike-bike trails, bookstores, movie plexes. Dozen parks plus regional parks. Many kids' sports, activities. Little theater. Community college, arts college (founded by Walt Disney and Disney people in 1997 put up $25 million for concert hall), private college. Restaurants. Golf courses. Oil wells, office parks. Hyatt hotel. Regional mall. Jobs in San Fernando Valley, drive of 5 to 15 miles. Many jobs in Palmdale and Lancaster. Metrolink (commute rail). I-5 freeway. Chamber of commerce (661) 259-4787.

SANTA FE SPRINGS

BEDROOM-INDUSTRIAL TOWN located about 14 miles southeast of downtown L.A. School rankings are hard to break out because the city is served by three school districts but they run generally from low to middling. Population 16,463.

Santa Fe Springs clusters almost all of its homes and apartments on its west side and leaves the rest to business and industry, including an oil refinery. Town used to be an oil boomer. A large mall can be found on the east side.

The city blossomed in early 1900s when oil was discovered. After the wells slowed, industry and commerce moved in. Housing revved up in the 1940s when 346 residential units were built and opened the throttle in the following decade, 2,530 units, mostly single homes. The 1960s produced 420 units, the 1970s and 1980s, 700-750 units apiece. Among owner-occupied units, the three-bedroom home leads all, then the two bedroom, and then the four bedroom. Sante Fe Springs was built mainly for veterans and blue-collar workers. Housing is generally well maintained. Some homes have security doors.

Industrial-commercial towns often have deep tax pockets and occasionally fund sports and community buildings a cut above what's found elsewhere. Santa Fe Springs has some of biggest school grounds in L.A. County. The state in 2000 counted 4,663 housing units: 3,042 single homes, 265 single attached, 1,235 multiples, 121 mobiles.

Served by the Little Lake and Los Nietos Elementary districts and by Whittier Union High District. Sample rankings: Lakeview Elementary, 30th to 60th percentiles; Rancho Santa Gertrudes Elementary, 10th to 30th percentiles; Santa Fe High, 40th to 50th percentiles. Little Lake district in 2000 passed a $34 million bond to build classrooms; Whittier High district in 1999 passed a $98 million renovation bond.

Three homicides in 1999. Counts for previous years are 3, 7, 5, 4, 5, 3, 5, 1, 2. Overall crime rate is above suburban average but business-commerce cities often have distorted statistics. But take care. Santa Fe Springs contracts with sheriff for police protection.

Library. Swim Center. About seven parks. The schools are used for sports and recreation. Community college in nearby town.

Interstates 5 and 605 touch the city. Many local jobs means short commute for some residents. Chamber of commerce (562) 944-1616.

SANTA MONICA

BEACH CITY located west of Beverly Hills. Favorite town for the young and upcoming. Apartments outnumber single homes by four to one. Rents high.

Pretty, well tended, popular with professionals. Spiffed-up downtown, restaurants, festivals, linear park on bluff overlooking Pacific, a lot of people out in the sun having fun. Attracts many tourists. Population: 96,528.

One of the most famous beach cities in U.S. Frequently pops up in movies. Fishing pier, three miles of beach, a promenade, a built-up downtown. Loaded with amusements. Situated a short distance from the movie and entertainment industries. Has and has an enviable base of info-tech firms, including RAND, one of first think tanks. Liberal, activist, engaging.

If you are interested in a single home, look to the neighborhood north of Montana Avenue. There you will find upper-middle-class homes, nicely appointed, in good repair, streets clean and lined with trees.

South of Montana and throughout the rest of the city, apartments take over. Most of the apartments can be found in three- and four-story buildings, generally nice looking. The state in 2000 counted 49,479 housing units: 9,126 single homes, 1,804 single attached, 38,293 multiples, 256 mobiles. In the 1990s, the city's population increased by 9,600 people and its housing stock grew by 1,726 apartments. Santa Monica has rent control; for details call (310) 458-8751. Some high-rise buildings and homes on bluffs have ocean views but most of Santa Monica is built on flat land away from beach.

Served by Santa Monica-Malibu Unified School District. Rankings in the 60th to 90th percentile. Bond, parcel tax passed. All schools to be renovated. High school to add music room, more classes. Santa Monica Community College is considered one of the best in the state, especially in transfers to four-year universities. Many classes-activities.

One homicide in 1999. Counts for previous years: 12, 1, 3, 8, 8, 9, 7, 14, 6. City police department. Crime lowest on north side, in single homes.

Recreational and cultural activities are too numerous to mention. This town amuses itself very well. Large regional library. Open-air pedestrian mall.

Santa Monica Freeway straight to downtown L.A., 16 miles to east. West Los Angeles has many jobs and Santa Monica alone claims 76,000-plus jobs. Airport on south side. Chamber of commerce (310) 393-9825.

SHERMAN OAKS
Studio City, Toluca Lake, Universal City

THE SANTA MONICA MOUNTAINS, shaped like a blunt spear, divide the L.A. Basin from the San Fernando Valley. Where the spear nears its tip and the mountains descend into hills, you'll find the movie-entertainment towns and cities. On the south side of the hills, Beverly Hills, Hollywood, Bel Air, Brentwood. On the north side, facing the San Fernando Valley, with an estimated population of 66,000, Toluca Lake, Sherman Oaks and Studio City.

Going from east to west, Toluca Lake is a favorite address of old Hollywood and has a small number of large estate homes hidden behind tall hedges. The rest of the housing runs to apartments and well-cared-for tract homes for professionals and managers. Universal City (not a city but a studio-entertainment complex) is located just south of Toluca Lake. Yes there is a lake, small and privately owned. Also Lakeside Country Club.

Studio City and Sherman Oaks are divided between flat land and hills. Ventura Boulevard runs through both and is lined with restaurants, shops and all sorts of stores. South of Ventura Boulevard, the hills start. Homes constructed in the lower hills tend to upscale professional, three to five bedrooms, tastefully decorated and landscaped, very well maintained. Some homes have views. Some deserve to be called mansions. North of Ventura, the homes also run to middle-class-plus, interspersed with apartment complexes, especially along such arterials as Laurel Canyon, Coldwater Canyon and Woodman. All three are towns of the City of Los Angeles and patrolled by L.A. police. Crime figures are unavailable but upper-income towns usually have low crime. Many homes subscribe to private security services. Following 1994 earthquake, many apartment complexes in Sherman Oaks were refurbished.

L.A. Unified School District. Sample rankings: Millikan Middle, 30th to 50th percentiles; Toluca Lake Elementary, 30th to 40th percentiles; Carpenter Elementary, 80th to 90th percentiles. Disney and Warner studios, several large hotels. About 10 to 13 miles to downtown L.A. Highway 101. Close to Burbank Airport and Metrolink (commuter rail). Several parks, two golf courses and a large equestrian center. Ventura Boulevard jumps after dark. Chamber of commerce (818) 906-1951.

SIERRA MADRE

SMALL, SOMEWHAT AFFLUENT city located in the foothills of the San Gabriel Mountains, just east of Pasadena. Out-of-the-way charmer. No traffic lights. Volunteer firefighters. Population 11,719.

Sierra Madre started in the late 1800s when a promoter tried to build a utopian community, called Nature's Sanitarium, on 1,000 acres. The town enjoyed a reputation for clean air and attracted other sanitoriums. Down through the decades, the town has cherished its offbeat ways and is often talked of as an artists' colony with a lot of community spirit. You've seen the town in some movies, among them, the first "Invasion of the Body Snatchers."

Sierra Madre did not grow as quickly as other L.A. County towns and this slower pace may have given it time to digest its growth. The city started 1940 with 1,512 residential units, added 608 that decade, 1,223 in the 1950s, and 685 in the 1960s. Housing starts fell to 439 in the 1970s and to 391 in the 1980s. In the 1990s, the city's population increased by 950 people and its housing stock by 50 units.

Sierra Madre rises into the hills. Many view lots. Also many nice homes that run to the upscale middle class, four or more bedrooms. But also many two- and three-bedroom homes. In some sections, the streets narrow to one lane and the houses seemed shoehorned onto the lots, reflecting the difficulty of building on steep terrain (but great views). Three-bedroom homes, among owner-occupied units, come in first, 47 percent of total, followed by two-bedroom, 28 percent, then four-bedroom, 18 percent, the 1990 census reported. Lots of trees and foliage. Overall, a well-kept town. Shops and stores along Sierra Madre Boulevard. The state in 2000 counted 4,919 housing units: 3,393 single homes, 296 single attached, 1,225 multiples, 5 mobiles.

Children attend Pasadena district schools. Almost all the schools are in Pasadena and Altadena. Sample ranking, Sierra Madre Elementary, 40th to 50th percentiles. Some parents want to de-annex and join higher-scoring Arcadia district but they were turned down. In 1997 Pasadena district passed $240 million bond to renovate all its schools. Work still being done.

Zero homicides in 1999, 1998, 1997, 1996. The counts for previous years are 0, 0, 1, 0, 0, 0. Crime rate very low. Town has its own police department.

Three parks. Library. Wisteria festival. Close to Pasadena amusements. About 17 miles to downtown L.A. Interstate 210 is located about a mile south of the city. Chamber of commerce (626) 355-5111.

SIGNAL HILL

HILL CITY surrounded by Long Beach. Legend has it the Indians set signal fires on the summit.

City used to be famous for its oil wells. The wells are still pumping but these days Signal Hill is evolving into more of a residential city. Population 9,247.

Signal Hill is one of the few communities to escape the housing boom that followed World War II. Sitting atop oodles of oil, the land was considered too valuable for housing and it was only after the oil started to dry up that housing made a modest appearance.

When you drive Signal Hill you see a mix of apartments and single homes that stretch back to the 1920s. Between 1940 and 1970, the town built 300 to 500 residential units a decade. In the 1970s, this jumped to 737 and in the 1980s to about 1,158 units. Almost all of the housing is aimed at the middle class. Many apartments. In the 1990s, the city's population increased by 875 people and its housing stock by 130 single homes.

The homes and streets are generally in good shape. Most of the housing is clustered at the bottom of the hills. The hill units command views of the countryside.

The state in 2000 counted 3,802 housing units: 969 single homes, 475 single attached, 2,357 multiples, 1 mobile.

Served by the Long Beach Unified School District. Sample ranking: Signal Hill Elementary, 40th to 60th percentiles. Long Beach district in 1999 passed a $295 million bond to build and renovate schools.

A community college borders Signal Hill, a plus for the city. These institutions offer many classes and activities for low fees.

Zero homicides in 1999, two in 1998 and 1997, and one in 1996. Zero homicides in 1995 and 1994. City has its own police department.

Two parks, usual sports activities.

Twenty-three miles to downtown L.A., a long haul but the Long Beach area has many jobs and this means a short commute for many residents. San Diego Freeway (I-405) touches the north side of city. Light rail, just over the west border, runs to the downtowns of L.A. and Long Beach.

Chamber of commerce (562) 424-6489.

S. CENTRAL
Southeast L.A., Watts, Florence, Walnut Park

NEIGHBORHOODS OR TOWNS located south of downtown L.A. and extending to about Interstate 105 or the Imperial Highway.

School scores are low, crime a problem. The shortcomings acknowledged, these are also functioning neighborhoods. They provide much in the way of low-cost housing, and they include many people who hold jobs and keep up their homes. They encompass the University of Southern California (USC), which is working to improve its immediate neighborhood, and the Coliseum.

Some blocks come across as quite presentable: roses planted, shrubs trimmed, even topiary cultivated, graffiti absent or painted over. Others are struggling: lots littered, paint flaking, here and there a few homes boarded up, men drinking on the corner. A good deal falls in between.

These neighborhoods are changing and becoming more ethnically diverse, a first stop for many immigrants. On weekends, soccer, not baseball, is often the game of choice.

Many of the single homes were built just before or just after World War II and favor the two-bedroom style. Watts has public housing complexes.

Both South Central and Southeast L.A. are part of the City of Los Angeles and patrolled by L.A. police.

The City Planning Department divides the south side into Southeast L.A. (including Watts) and South Central L.A. Main Street is a good demarcation line. Everything to the west lies in Central, everything to the east of Main lies in the Southeast.

In 1994, the city counted 253,098 residents in Central and 235,638 in Southeast.

The 1990 census tallied 61,609 housing units in Southeast L.A., of which about 50 percent were single-family homes and 32 percent owner-occupied. For South Central, the census counted 81,725 housing units, of which 43 percent were single-family homes and 33 percent were owner-occupied.

Florence and its smaller neighbor, Walnut Park, are unincorporated towns, governed by the county board of supervisors and patrolled by sheriff's deputies. The combined population for both is about 72,000 (1990 census). Single homes in these sections favor first two bedrooms, then three. About 25 percent of Florence's housing predates World War II, about 23 percent was built in the 1940s and about 19 percent in the 1950s. About 38 percent of all housing units are owner-occupied.

All these towns are served by the Los Angeles Unified School District. Sample rankings: 75th Street Elementary and Markham Middle, both below the 10th percentile; Fremont High, 10th to 20th percentiles.

Several magnet or special schools located on the south side. They include the USC Performing Arts and the King-Drew Medical Magnet in Watts.

School district has passed $2.4 billion bond to renovate and build schools.

Security gates and often window bars are quite common in these neighborhoods and come across as a standard household equipment. In recent years, homicides and crime numbers have been dropping in these neighborhoods — a good sign. But still, be wary. See profile of City of L.A. for statistics of crime by sections of the city.

About two dozen parks. Rec centers, libraries. Close to downtown and all it offers. One of the best commutes in the county. Buses. Light rail. Interstate 110. Summing up: problems and pluses. Affordable housing.

Chamber of commerce (213) 580-7500.

SOUTH EL MONTE

LOW-MIDDLE-INCOME TOWN located just east of Rosemead and about 12 miles from downtown L.A. Population 22,717.

Academic rankings are hard to break out because the three school districts also serve other cities.

South El Monte built over two-thirds of its current housing between 1940 and 1960 and went in for a style favored by veterans entering the housing market: two- and three-bedroom homes. Appearances are mixed: Many of the homes and yards have been kept up, some haven't.

South El Monte is a transition town. After residents build a little equity, they often move up and out, making way for others entering the housing market. Single homes outnumber apartments by about four to one. The state in 2000 counted 4,847 housing units: 3,108 single homes, 314 single attached, 847 multiples, 578 mobiles. In the 1990s, the city's population grew by 1,900 people and its housing stock was unchanged.

Education by the El Monte elementary district, which passed a $40 million renovation bond in 1999, and the El Monte high school district, which also educates children from Rosemead, El Monte, Arcadia and Temple City, or unincorporated neighborhoods near these cities. Some schools are in the Mountain View school district.

Sample rankings: Loma Elementary, generally below the 10th percentile; South El Monte High School, 30th to 40th percentile.

Two homicides in 1999, four in 1998 and 1997. The counts for previous years are 2, 5, 4, 4, 4, 1, 3. South El Monte contracts with the sheriff's department for police services.

Library. Three parks. Swimming pool. Seniors center. Childcare facility. Large regional parks on southern and western border of South El Monte: lakes, horse and hiking trails and golf course.

The name "El Monte" in old Spanish translates into marsh or wooded place, a reference to the regional park land, which is bordered or split by the Rio Hondo and the San Gabriel rivers.

The city is crisscrossed or close to four freeways. Metrolink (commuter rail) station nearby. Many local jobs, which means a short commute for residents. Chamber of commerce (626) 443-0180.

SOUTH GATE

ONE OF THE OLDER suburban cities. Generally well maintained. Located on flat land about 10 miles southeast of downtown L.A. Used to be home to several large factories, now closed, but town continues to add residents.

School rankings low to middling. Population 95,326.

One of its first subdivisions was named South Gate Gardens because it was located next to the south gate of an adjoining ranch. Name caught on.

South Gate started to boom in the 1940s. In that decade it built about 32 percent of its current housing and the 1950s added another 23 percent. When you throw in the housing constructed before World War II, you have a community where seven out of ten residential units predate 1960.

The postwar years favored two-bedroom and three-bedroom homes, small, plain homes aimed at veterans. In almost all the cities that blossomed after World War II, the three-bedroom home dominates owner-occupied units. In South Gate, the two-bedroom home leads, reflecting the early start the city got in the 1940s. At that time, two-bedroom units were in great demand.

In its modest way, South Gate is a handsome town. The streets are clean, many of the yards show much care, the trees are mature and leafy, their shade taking the edge off the summer heat. Some streets are almost completely shaded by trees.

The state in 2000 counted 23,029 housing units: 12,361 single homes, 2,215 single attached, 8,146 multiples, 307 mobiles. In the 1990s, the city added about 8,500 residents and its housing stock grew by 80 units.

Education by Los Angeles Unified School District. Sample academic rankings: Victoria Elementary, 10th to 20th percentiles; South Gate Middle 10th percentile and South Gate High, 20th to 40th percentiles.

Seven homicides in 1999, four in 1998, and eleven in 1997. The counts for previous years are 7, 15, 9, 11, 10, 11, 9. South Gate has its own police department. Security doors are employed on many homes in the city.

Library. Three parks, including one with golf course.

Interstate 710 on the east side of the city; Interstate 105 on the south side, about a mile over the town line. Also just over city limits: light rail to downtown L.A. and to L.A. airport. Chamber of commerce (323) 567-1203.

SOUTH PASADENA

Downtown L.A. — South Pasadena — L.A. International Airport — Long Beach

PRESTIGE CITY located — no surprise — just south of Pasadena. Built over hills. Many lovely homes. Winding streets. Crime rate low. School rankings high, among top 10 percent in the state. Population 25,997.

South Pasadena, also located next to San Marino, is a rounded town with bungalows, cottages, apartments, middle and upper-middle tract homes and mansions. The mansions are located on the north side of town, in a secluded neighborhood cut off from the rest of the city by the freeway.

Moving south toward the middle, the cottages, bungalows and some apartments appear, the older section of town, identified by the grid pattern of the streets. On the southwest side, off Indian Avenue, South Pasadena rises into hills with narrow streets. Many of the homes here are shoehorned onto steep lots. Moving east, the streets become wider, the homes bigger and better appointed, the look more modern in an upscale suburban way. Off Camino Verde, some homes grow even bigger, add a second story, and expand the garage to four stalls. The ridge and many of the hill homes are positioned for views. Moving further east, across Fremont Avenue, the housing moves into flat lands and apartments, bungalows and tract homes.

Handsome town. Lawns mowed, shrubs clipped, much attention to landscaping. Trees on many streets have had decades to grow. South Pasadena was incorporated as a city in 1888 and in parts exudes that old small-town charm. The state in 2000 counted 10,801 housing units: 4,870 single homes, 611 single attached, 5,318 multiples, 2 mobiles. In the 1990s, the city's population increased by 2,100 residents and its housing stock by 80 units.

Served by the South Pasadena Unified School District. Academic rankings land in 80th and 90th percentiles. In 1999, high school broke the 600 mark in math SAT, an achievement equalled only by 22 others in state. The high rankings indicate a lot of interest in and support of the schools. Bond passed in 1995 to renovate schools. High school is being expanded.

Zero homicides in 1999. The counts for previous years are 1, 1, 0, 0, 0, 0, 0, 1, 0. Overall crime rate is low. South Pasadena has own police department.

Library, golf course, YMCA, seniors center, dance center, five parks. Movies. Close to Pasadena and all its goodies.

About seven miles to downtown L.A. Highways 66 and 110 cut through town. Buses. Many jobs in Pasadena. State wants to run I-710 through South Pasadena. Residents vow, no way. Chamber of commerce (626) 799-7161.

STEVENSON RANCH

BEDROOM COMMUNITY, master planned, going up on 4,000 acres off of Interstate 5, just west of Santa Clarita in foothills. Country feeling. New.

About 8,000 homes, condos and apartments are planned, of which about 3,000 have been built. Stevenson Ranch is selling condos, cottages and single homes. All the single-home sections offer plans in three and four bedrooms and the higher-priced neighborhoods go to five bedrooms.

All communities are planned. Master-planned communities differ in that the planning is more extensive (where schools and parks and stores will be located) and being modern, they often do a better job than older communities in moving traffic to the freeway and in shielding residential streets from traffic.

No surprise — Stevenson Ranch looks good in a suburban way. Many of the homes have views. The streets are clean, the lawns well-cared-for, everything is new, new, new. A cascading waterfall greets residents at the entrance.

Served by Newhall school district, which in 1999 passed $35 million bond to build and renovate schools. Two schools in Stevenson Ranch, one new. Sample rankings, Stevenson Elementary, 80th to 90th percentiles. Children move up to Hart High School, 80th percentile. Another elementary school and a middle school and high school are planned. FBI doesn't track crime in unincorporated towns but the demographics say low. Private security augments efforts of sheriff's deputies.

Although separate from Santa Clarita, Stevenson Ranch benefits from its neighbor's ornaments, including a community college and the California Institute of Arts. And bookstores, shopping malls, restaurants, libraries. And sports leagues, for kids and adults. Within a short drive are golf courses, lakes, Six Flags Magic Mountain, a water park. Stevenson Ranch is building is own recreational facilities. Two parks.

Shopping mall to the south. About 1,000 acres have been placed in open space. Residents have formed town council. The probable future: Stevenson Ranch will annex to Santa Clarita or form its own city. Lot of housing to be constructed in region. Lot of arguments over pace and extent of development.

Although it has hazy days, the Santa Clarita Valley escapes the smog that afflicts L.A. Summer days are hot, summer evenings and the rest of the year generally comfortable. Humidity low. Real feel of the desert. Take McBean Parkway exit west off of Interstate 5. For info., call developer (800) 310-7262.

SUNLAND Tujunga

BLUE-COLLAR TOWNS in the foothills of the San Gabriel Mountains. Somewhat hidden. Country flavor. Estimated population: 53,000.

Many older homes. Good place to get into the housing market. School rankings middling. Crime not tracked by the FBI but it probably runs to suburban average. Some homes in low-income sections have security bars and doors.

Sunland and Tujunga, part of the City of Los Angeles, are two communities that became one as they grew into each other. They are located north of Highway 210 and just west of Glendale. North and south of Sunland-Tujunga the terrain rises into mountains and this gives the town a secluded air.

Tujunga used to be a legal city but, lacking water, it disbanded itself to join the City of Los Angeles, which controlled the water supply. Town was noted for its fresh air and mountain breezes; attracted many who had breathing problems. Development started to boom about World War II.

Most of the homes appear to have been built in the late 40s, and in the 50s and 60s. Two- and three-bedroom units. Many of them show good care and a few neglect. As you rise into some hills, the quality of the homes steps up slightly. But these are not upper-income towns.

Served by Los Angeles Unified School District. Sample rankings Sunland Elementary, 30th to 40th percentiles; Verdugo Hills High, 40th to 50th percentiles.

About a half dozen parks. Golf course. Sunland Rec. Center. Cultural center.

Patrolled by L.A. Police.

About 25 miles to downtown L.A. Many office jobs in nearby Glendale and Pasadena. Easy access to Highway 210.

Chamber of commerce (818) 352-4433.

SYLMAR

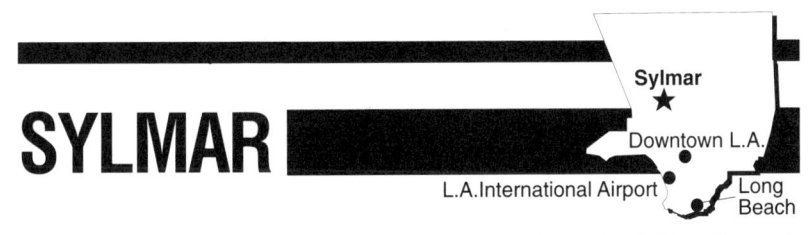

BEDROOM-RANCHETTE COMMUNITY located in the foothills at the north end of the San Fernando Valley, east of Interstate 5, above and bordering the City of San Fernando.

A mix of the old and the new, and the low and middle income. Changing. Country feeling. Mountains in the background. Estimated population 60,000. A town of the City of Los Angeles. Education by the Los Angeles Unified School District. School rankings, low to middle.

Sylmar is divided by Interstate 210. Above or north of this freeway, the homes run to the old and faded, many small and in need of care, to middle-class presentable, to new homes in the hills that jump a little up the scale: two stories, stucco, red-tile roofs, modern in design. Rare for L.A. County, there is, at the end of Gavina Avenue, a modest and new development of patio homes built on small lots with great views of the countryside. Usually new hill homes jump way up the scale.

Sylmar is on the outskirts of the San Fernando Valley. From the housing styles, it looks like it got a blip of houses about 40 years ago, then things settled down to slow growth and now, when the Valley has filled, development is heating up. South of Interstate 210, many of the homes run to horse setups on large lots. Empty lots are to be found around the town. The larger homes show good care in a relaxed way. Some appear to be working ranches. The rest of the housing here runs to small and old, two bedrooms, to the standard three-bedroom home. A mobile home park, behind gates, can be found just north of the freeway. Sylmar also has apartment complexes. Where the housing is old and in poor condition, security doors and window bars show up on some homes. Patrolled by L.A. police.

Sample state rankings: Herrick Elementary, 20th to 40th percentiles; Hubbard Elementary, 30th to 50th percentiles; Sylmar High, 20th to 40th percentiles. District passed $2.4 billion bond to build and renovate schools.

Mission Community College, a big plus. Community colleges charge little and provide all sorts of job and academic classes along with sports (tennis, aerobics, etc.) and cultural activities (drawing, dance, and so on). Four parks. Golf course. Swimming pool. Horseback riding. Hang gliding. Library.

Two freeways. A long way to downtown L.A. but many jobs can be found in the valley. UCLA has a large medical facility in Sylmar. Chamber of commerce (818) 367-1177.

TEMPLE CITY

"THE HOME OF THE CAMELLIAS." A neat-looking, middle-class city located northeast of downtown L.A. bordering Arcadia.

Crime low. School scores high. Population: 34,731.

Temple City built almost 75 percent of its current housing between 1940 and 1970. At that time, the two- and three-bedroom single-family home was the rage. And that's what you'll find mostly in Temple City: suburban tract homes of that era, well maintained.

The designs usually place the garage, wide enough for one big car, inside the house. Utility lines are overhead, either down the front of the street or at the rear of the lot. Single homes outnumber apartments by about six to one.

The trees are tall and full and with their shade soften the summer heat.

The state in 2000 counted 11,801 housing units: 9,477 single homes, 665 single attached, 1,650 multiples, 9 mobiles. In the 1990s, the city's population increased by 3,600 residents and its housing stock by 225 units, half of them single homes.

Education by Temple Unified School District, overall rankings in the 80th to 90th percentiles. In 1998, the district passed a $24 million bond to upgrade schools and add classrooms. The scores and the bond indicate strong support for schools.

Two homicides in 1999. The counts for previous years are 0, 0, 1, 0, 2, 0, 1, 1, 3. City contracts with sheriff's department for police protection. Sheriff's substation in town.

Crime rate well below suburban average. No graffiti. Every once in a while, you'll see a security door but for the most part the town feels safe without these doors or bars on windows.

Library, two parks. City hall runs recreational and cultural programs for kids and adults. Every February the city hosts a camellia festival which features a parade with floats and thousands of children.

Stores and shops along Rosemead Boulevard. Movies. First-class shopping, Nordstrom, etc., in Arcadia. Many cultural activities in nearby Pasadena.

About 13 miles from downtown L.A. Interstate 10 is located just south of the town and I-210 just north. Quick access to both on arterial streets.

Chamber of commerce (626) 286-3101.

TORRANCE

SOUTH COUNTY bedroom city. Located inland but small part touches Pacific. School rankings high. Sixth-most-populous city in county, 147,414 residents.

On south side, bordering Palos Verdes Estates, Torrance rises into small hills in a section called Hollywood Riviera. Views of flatlands and the Pacific.

Moving north on the east side, housing from the 1950s shows itself, mainly three-bedroom homes. Near Plaza de Amo, apartment complexes kick in. Then comes an "old town" with cottages. Then the Mobil refinery and assorted industries. North of 190th Street the homes return, generally three bedrooms. Moving to the west, more of the same, except the homes are a little newer and bigger. On the south side, near the ocean the homes in many instances date from the 1940s or earlier but they come across pleasing because many have been remodeled or given extra care or planted with exotic shrubs.

Torrance boomed in the 1950s when 20,010 residential units were built. It continued to boom in the 1960s (15,189 units) and the 1970s (8,098 units). In the latter decades, large homes became popular and this explains Torrance's upscale demographics. It built about 6,000 homes with four bedrooms and about 1,200 with five-or-more bedrooms. The three-bedroom home, however, leads all, about half of the owner occupied, the 1990 census reported. In the 1990s, Torrance increased its population by 14,300 and its housing stock by 1,431 units, over half of them single homes.

Level of care high. Some streets go all out with trees and flowers. Clean. On the east side, a few security doors pop up; not many. Airport on southeast side. Check noise. Oil refinery may bother some but it has greatly reduced pollutants. The state in 2000 counted 56,358 housing units: 30,300 single homes, 3,231 single attached, 21,746 multiples, 1,081 mobiles.

Served by Torrance Unified School District, rankings in 70th to 90th percentiles which indicates strong support for academics. District in 1998 passed $43 million bond to renovate and upgrade schools. Work is being done.

Three homicides in 1999. Counts for previous years are 3, 2, 3, 5, 3,12, 2, 2, 2. Torrance has its own police department. Two dozen parks. Cultural arts center. About five libraries. Two malls. El Camino Community College.

Interstate 405 on the north, Pacific Coast Highway on south. About 19 miles to downtown L.A. but many jobs in town and at Long Beach and L.A. airport, seven miles to north. Chamber of commerce (310) 540-5858.

VAN NUYS

BEDROOM TOWN located in the middle of the San Fernando Valley. Housing a mix of low income and middle class, and where Sherman Oaks comes in, a little upscale middle class. Homes make up about one-third of the residential units, apartments the rest. Large active airport. Estimated population 131,000.

School rankings low to middling. Crime not tracked by the FBI but security doors are common in low-income neighborhoods.

Van Nuys, like most of the San Fernando Valley, got its housing boom right after World War II and it shows many of the housing patterns common to the older suburbs. Homes that were built small and inexpensively have turned into low-income neighborhoods that attract many newcomers. Prices are quite affordable. But these areas tend to have low school scores and security bars and windows, indications of concerns about crime.

Homes that were built for the middle-class market seemed to have held their value. Van Nuys has many streets where lawns are watered and mowed, shrubs trimmed and appearances decidedly middle class. Neighborhood quality sometimes changes markedly within the space of a few blocks. When new homes are built, they often jump up the scale, two story, four-five bedrooms, tile roofs — a vote of confidence in the town.

Served by L.A. Unified School District. Sample state school rankings: Van Nuys Middle, 20th percentile; Grant High, 30th to 50th percentile. Los Angeles Valley Community College close by.

Patrolled by L.A. police. Some homes have medallions that indicate protection by private security services. Security devices (doors, gates, windows) vary in use. Sometimes they are found in middle-class neighborhoods.

Recreational opportunities are many, including the community college and a large park with two golf courses just south of the airport.

Van Nuys blends in with Sherman Oaks and wraps around the airport to ease into Reseda. Population estimates vary according to source. If shopping for homes near Van Nuys airport, check out the noise. Many of the larger jets use the Burbank Airport to the east of Van Nuys.

Quick access to Interstate 405. About 16 miles to downtown L.A., an exhausting drive during commute hours. Local jobs in the movie studios, the airports and the hotels. Metrolink (commuter rail) to the downtown. Buses. Chamber of commerce (818) 989-0300.

VERNON

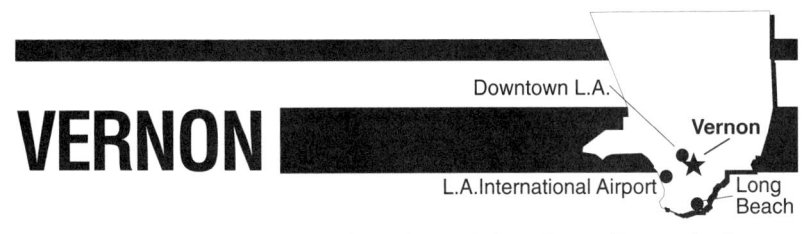

COMMERCIAL-INDUSTRIAL CITY located about four miles south of downtown L.A. Population 85. Two homicides in 1999. Zero homicides in 1998, 1997, 1996 and 1995, one in 1994.

Up until about 25 years ago, it was fairly easy for landowners to incorporate their business holdings into legal cities.

In doing so, they gained control over local taxes (this was before state Proposition 13 evened out taxes), planning, zoning laws, and usually the city government. In this way, they assured that the local government would always be friendly to their concerns.

Los Angeles County has about a half-dozen cities established mainly to serve business interests. Vernon is one. The city has about 1,400 firms employing over 50,000. And one church, Holy Angels Church for the Deaf, which works with the hearing impaired.

The state in 2000 counted 30 housing units: 11 single homes, 4 single attached and 15 multiples.

Vernon has its own police department, specializing in the protection of businesses. Crime rate is astronomical but misleading. The low population distorts the statistics.

If you want a business-industrial site close to the downtown, Vernon may fit the bill. It's close to rail lines and freeways and definitely congenial to business.

Chamber of commerce (323) 583-3313.

WALNUT

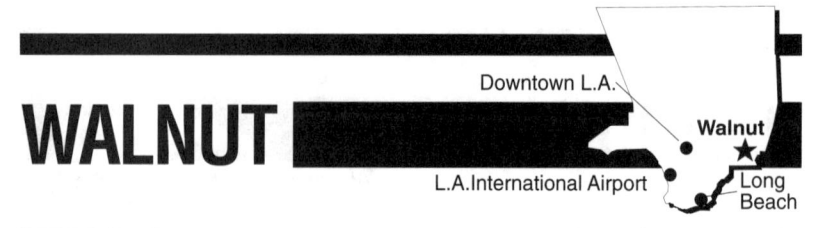

Downtown L.A.
L.A. International Airport
Walnut
Long Beach

BEDROOM CITY located just north of the City of Industry. New, pretty, a lot of sparkle, middle class to rich. Population 33,203. School rankings high, crime low.

Famous for its walnuts, the City of Walnut came to life as a suburban community in the 1960s when 1,128 homes were constructed. In the 1970s, the city added 2,131 units, in the 1980s, 4,456 homes and in the last decade, 503 homes.

To state this another way, about 82 percent of the town's homes and apartments were built in the last 30 years. The first units were built off Amar Road on the west side. These homes run three and four bedrooms, nothing showy but all well kept. As you move east beyond Lemon Avenue, the homes get newer and better appointed and on a few streets jump up to mansions of 5,000 to 11,000 square feet. Some look straight out of "Gone With the Wind" (before the Yankees struck).

Walnut and its residents have done an unusually good job in landscaping yards, median strips and roadways. Much of the town is built over gentle hills and this adds to the beauty. Much of the land remains in open space. Some slopes appear too steep to permit housing.

The state in 2000 counted 8,594 housing units: 8,099 single homes, 96 single attached, 215 multiples, 184 mobiles.

Served by the Walnut Valley Unified School District, which also includes parts of Diamond Bar. Rankings: 70th to 90th percentiles. Some children attend schools in the Rowland Unified School District. Sample rankings: Ybarra Elementary, 70th to 90th percentiles.

Zero homicides in 1999. The counts for previous years are 0, 1, 0, 1, 2, 2, 1, 2, 3. Overall crime rate very low.

Mount San Antonio Community College is located on the northeast side — a real plus for the city. Cal Poly is just over the hill, another plus. Horse trails wind through the community. At least seven parks. Kids and adults use the playing fields at the schools for the usual sports. Golf courses nearby.

Walnut's neighbor, the City of Industry, is a major job center in the county. Downtown L.A., 28 miles to west. Ontario Airport, 14 miles to east and John Wayne Airport, 25 miles to south. Chamber of commerce (909) 595-6138.

WEST COVINA

MIDDLE- TO UPPER-MIDDLE CITY that shows much care and attention to appearances. The kind of town where on Saturday mornings you'll see whole families out working on the lawn. Population: 107,631. School rankings middling.

Three homicides in 1999. The counts for previous years are 5, 8, 6, 10, 6, 5, 4, 11, 8. West Covina has its own police department.

West Covina is another town that burst to life in the 1950s when it built 12,195 homes, about 38 percent of its current housing stock. Housing starts fell off to 5,285 units in the 1960s, jumped to 8,129 in the 1970s and eased off to 4,000 units in the 1980s. In the 1990s, the city built about 800 units, almost all of them single homes.

On the east side, the land rises into the hills and here you will find upper-income homes, some in the executive class: five and six bedrooms or more, two stories, extensive landscaping, nicely done. This is the kind of neighborhood where you would expect a golf course and there is one, the South Hills Country Club. The rest of West Covina runs generally to three-bedroom homes. Many lawns will have trees, shrubs and rose bushes.

Older suburbs sometimes give up their charms. People start renting out their homes, the lawns die, the shrubs go ragged. This is not the case in West Covina. The city comes across as solid middle-class with a lot of interest in keeping up appearances. The state in 2000 counted 31,941 housing units: 20,829 single homes, 2,584 single attached, 8,242 multiples, 286 mobiles.

Education provided by the West Covina Unified School District. Many schools are scoring in the 40th and 50th percentiles. Voters in 2000 approved a $40 million renovation bond.

Senior center, youth center, 10 parks, 16 playgrounds, shopping at the West Covina Plaza. Mix of restaurants.

Used to be associated with Covina but incorporated in 1923 when locals became irate over proposal to build sewage plant in their sector. About 20 miles to downtown L.A., Metrolink (commuter rail). Chamber of commerce (626) 338-8496.

WEST HOLLYWOOD

RENTERS' CITY in the heart of movie land. Situated between Beverly Hills and Hollywood. Split by Santa Monica Boulevard. School rankings low to middling but many households don't have school-age kids.

The 1990 census counted about 2,700 kids under age 19 or about 7 percent of the population, very low. West Hollywood is an adults' town. Population 38,913.

What's the difference between West Hollywood, Hollywood and North Hollywood? Besides location and demographics, the first is a legal city in control of its own planning and local services and politics. The others are "towns" of the City of Los Angeles. West Hollywood voted itself into existence in 1984 in part because it wanted to set the tone of its politics, which can be described as liberal.

Almost all the housing in West Hollywood was erected before it became a city. Single homes can be found here and there but most of the housing runs to two- and three-story apartment complexes, generally well maintained. The city has major hotels and in or near its borders, high-rise apartments. And it has a good deal of commercial development in the city or close by, including movie studios, the Pacific Design Center, and the Beverly Center (a mall). The state in 2000 counted 24,125 housing units: 1,746 single homes, 816 single attached, 21,557 multiples, 6 mobiles. In the 1990s, the city's population increased by 2,800 and its housing stock by 300 apartments.

Served by the Los Angeles Unified School District. Sample academic rankings, West Hollywood Elementary, 10th to 20th percentiles; Laurel Elementary, 30th to 50th percentiles.

Two homicides in 1999. The counts for previous years are 3, 4, 2, 1, 2, 5, 6, 2, 3. West Hollywood contracts with the sheriff's department to provide police protection. West Hollywood in 1999 reported 144 robberies and 176 assaults, and for this reason, extra wariness is justified.

Four parks in or bordering city. Library. Recreation center. In an area loaded with things to do.

About nine miles to downtown L.A. Many local jobs, which means a short commute for many. Buses. Chamber of commerce (323) 650-2688.

WESTLAKE VILLAGE

UPSCALE BEDROOM CITY, located on west side of the county. School rankings among highest in the state. Crime low.

Westlake Village straddles L.A. County and Ventura County. The neighborhoods and roads flow into one another. In the middle of the community sits a lake and in the middle of the lake sits an island with streets and homes. Half of the island is in Ventura County, half in L.A. Westlake Village (L.A) is a legal city of L.A. County. It has its own city council. Westlake Village (Ventura) is a neighborhood of the City of Thousand Oaks. Children on the Ventura side attend schools in the Conejo Valley School District. Children on the L.A. side attend schools in the Las Virgenes District, which also includes some of the wealthiest communities in L.A. County.

The City of Westlake Village (L.A.), population 8,593, has a good mix of housing that includes some of the nicest homes in the county. On the north side, above Highway 101, you'll find a shopping center, an office park, and townhouses and single homes. South of Highway 101, the main part of Westlake Village enters, built over hills and flatlands. Dominant style here is the 1960s and 1970s tract home, many of them having four bedrooms. The landscaping shows special care, many of the homes have custom touches, such as brick or stone facing. Upscale professional. Many of the lake homes are oriented toward the water: plain fronts, little decoration, large rear patios or decks. Paddleboats on lake. Sound controls. Oaks preserved. Residents sensitive about too much development.

South of the lake the terrain ascends and here you'll find often modern three- and four-bedroom homes with views of the valley. Off of Ridgeford and Foxfields drives, you'll find the mansions, custom jobs, large, often ornate, some with views. Apartments or condos can be found near the freeway or near the dam, at the head of the lake. Nice-looking burg. Clean. Trees galore. The state in 2000 counted 3,211 housing units: 2,135 single homes, 642 single attached, 277 multiples, 157 mobiles.

Sample rankings: White Oak Elementary, 90th percentile. In 1997 bond was passed to renovate and build schools.

Zero homicides in 1999, 1998, 1997, 1996, 1995 and 1994, state reports. City contracts with sheriff for police protection. Five golf courses in or near the town. Horse and hiking trails. Usual sports. Fishing. About 35 miles to downtown L.A. Many jobs close by in movie-entertainment, high-tech firms. Highway 101. Chamber of commerce (805) 370-0035.

WESTWOOD
Century City, Cheviot Hills, Rancho Park

NEIGHBORHOODS east and west and south of UCLA, on the west side of the City of L.A. Mix of apartments, single homes. Upscale in old-fashioned way but with a modern edge. Collegiate. Lively. Lots to do. Academic rankings middling to high. Security sensitive but crime probably middle-class average.

Cheviot Park spins out over gentle hills to the south of the Rancho Park and Hillcrest golf courses. Homes were built just before and just after World War II and aimed at a market that can be described as middle to upper management. The landscaping shows extra care, many of the homes run to two stories, the look is modified East Coast, not Western, although here and there in these neighborhoods the Spanish Revival pops up.

Moving northwest around the golf course, Rancho Park flows in, perhaps a shade less prestigious but as you move north the housing quality improves. Near Wilshire Boulevard, high rises show themselves. In these neighborhoods skyscrapers exist side by side with single homes and three-story apartments. Above Wilshire Boulevard, more of the same but the quality will vary by block. All, however, fall into the category of upscale professional. Apartments near university for the students. Moving north, Bel Air enters, really upscale.

Century City is not a "city." It's a neighborhood with high-rise office buildings.

Served by L.A. Unified School District. Sample rankings: Warner Avenue Elementary, generally above the 95th percentile (very high); Emerson Junior High, 20th to 30th percentile; Westwood Elementary, 90th percentile; Hamilton High, 50th to 60th percentiles.

Protected by L.A. police. Many homes use private security. Security doors and window bars rare. Restaurants, bookstores, museums, college sports. First-run movies (often attended by stars). Two golf courses. Large park-rec center. About seven miles to Pacific. Striking Mormon temple.

Small, hidden cemetery off Wilshire: Marilyn Monroe, Truman Capote, Natalie Wood.

Santa Monica freeway (I-10) Freeway to the south, San Diego freeway (I-405) to the west. Buses. Close to movie-entertainment studios. Many people employed by university. Los Angeles Business Council (310) 475-4747.

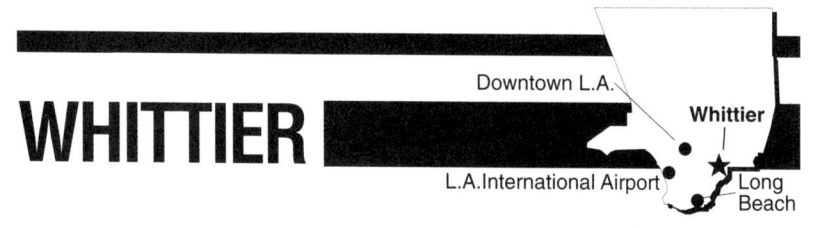

WHITTIER

Downtown L.A.
Whittier
L.A. International Airport
Long Beach

BEDROOM COMMUNITY in the east county. Where Richard Nixon was raised. Built for the middle class but some neighborhoods glide up the scale. One of the prettiest suburbs in L.A. County. Academic rankings bounce all over but many are high. Population 86,152.

Founded by Quakers in the late 1800s, Whittier was named after the poet John Greenleaf Whittier, himself a Quaker. For most of its early decades Whittier slumbered, a quiet burg with a rail line to downtown L.A. Came World War II and Whittier's population jumped from 16,115 to 23,433 in the war decade and by 1960 had risen to 33,663. Then it doubled itself in Sixties to 72,863 residents. About 60 percent of town was built between 1950 to 1970.

Timing is important because by the Sixties, homes had started to grow. Whittier has neighborhoods blanketed with that favorite, the three-bedroom home, but it also has sections where the homes are bigger, the attention to detail greater. These neighborhoods include a country-club subdivision. Some streets rise into gentle hills.

The downtown is anchored by an historic district and by Whittier College (Nixon's alma mater). In the summer, tall trees break out in orange blossoms. Restaurants, cafes and shops line the quaint, clean streets. The other neighborhoods, decked out with roses and birds of paradise, seem to take pride in keeping up appearances. Not to gild the lily, Whittier has its plain housing. The state in 2000 counted 29,224 units: 18,902 single homes, 1,261 single attached, 8,861 multiples, 200 mobiles.

Whittier is bordered by large and diverse neighborhoods. Whittier and East Whittier elementary school districts and the Whittier Union High District serve all. Sample academic rankings: Ocean View Elementary, 80th percentile; Evergreen Elementary, 20th to 30th percentile; La Serna High School, 60th to 80th percentile; Whittier High School, 40th percentile. Whittier district in 2000 approved a $30 million bond to renovate schools and build an elementary. Whittier High district in 1999 passed a $98 million renovation bond.

Four homicides in 1999, six in 1998, and five in 1997. The counts for previous years are 4, 4, 7, 5, 4, 6, 6. Whittier has its own police department.

About 15 parks. Many activities with the college and with community college. Small theater. Two libraries. Arts association. Seniors centers.

About 15 miles to downtown L.A. Interstate 605. Commuter rail station nearby. Chamber of commerce (562) 698-9554.

Wilshire District
Country Club Park, Hancock Park, Park La Brea

L.A. CITY neighborhoods immediately east of Beverly Hills. Mix of apartments, single homes. For most part, upscale. Hancock Park was the creme de la creme of old L.A. and still rates adjective, opulent. But in the peculiar nature of L.A., housing quality changes dramatically within the space of five or ten blocks.

School rankings high in the elementary grades. Crime statistics not broken out by neighborhood but probably low-middling. These neighborhoods, like much of L.A., are safety sensitive. Many homes and apartment complexes use security services or devices such as gates. Protected by L.A. police.

Wilshire Boulevard runs from the ocean to the downtown. The Wilshire District starts at the Beverly Hills border and runs east to about Western Avenue (although some extend it farther). This section is famous for its highrise offices (the Miracle Mile) and its museums, including the County Museum of Art, the Page Museum (fossils), Kaye Museum of Miniatures, the Petersen Automotive, the Craft and Folk Art. Eons ago mastodons, sloths and other ancients blundered into the La Brea tar pits.

Park La Brea, located just north of Wilshire, consists mainly of apartments, many of them in 18 buildings, about 14 stories high. These places are popular with people working in the entertainment industry.

Immediately east, straddling Third Street, is Hancock Park. Before World War II, this is where many of the big shots and first families lived and even today it attracts its share of the well-to-do. Mansions. Manicured lawns. Lovely landscaping. Anchored by the Wilshire Country Club. About 20 blocks to the southeast is Country Club Park, upscale but not in the mansion class.

Served by L.A. Unified School District. Sample rankings: Hancock Park Elementary, 90th percentile; Wilton Place Elementary, 30th to 60th percentile; Fairfax High, 40th to 50th percentile.

About 10 parks. Great shopping. Scads to do in and near Hollywood, a short distance to the north. Farmers Market (restaurants and shops). About seven miles to downtown L.A. Many local jobs. Santa Monica freeway (I-10) to south. Chamber of commerce (213) 580-7500.

WOODLAND HILLS

Woodland Hills — Downtown L.A. — L.A. International Airport — Long Beach

MIDDLE TO UPPER MIDDLE COMMUNITY, located on north side of Santa Monica mountains, roughly between Calabasas and Tarzana, and extending north to Canoga Park. An early developer, to woo buyers, planted over 100,000 pine, pepper, sycamore and eucalyptus trees in the hills.

Homes in the hills, homes in the flatlands. Includes Warner Center, former ranch of movie mogul Harry Warner, converted into an office-shopping center. Estimated population, 63,000.

A community of the City of Los Angeles. Served by Los Angeles Unified School District. Sample rankings: Woodland Hills Elementary, 90th percentile; El Camino Real High School, 80th and 90th percentile; Taft High School, 60th to 80th percentiles. About a dozen private schools in town.

Includes Pierce Community College, 402 acres. Many classes and activities, a plus for Woodland Hills.

A town of contradictions. Woodland Hills, where it has hills (south of Ventura Boulevard), lines up almost in a straight line with Encino, Tarzana and Calabasas, all affluent towns with opulent homes in their hills. But in the hill section of Woodland Hills, everyday three-bedroom homes dominate. This section was developed after World War II when there was a great demand for three-bedroom homes.

North of Ventura Boulevard, going toward Canoga, Woodland Hills is flat and if this sector were true to the valley pattern, it would be loaded with three- or four-bedroom homes built in standard tracts. Well, there are some tracts but many of the homes in this area are large ranchers, well appointed, cleverly landscaped, and situated on large lots.

In the hills, the streets meander around ravines. Many homes have views. Bring map. Lot of housing variety. The hills also have their upscale and large homes. Generally, if the home is new, it will be big, custom and pricey — what the market supports these days.

Woodland Hills straddles Ventura Boulevard, which has restaurants, coffee shops, boutiques, bookstores, movies and tall office buildings. One golf course. About four parks. Five other golf courses nearby.

Quick access to Highway 101 or Interstate 405, which scoots over the Santa Monica Mountains to West Los Angeles. Buses. About 25-30 miles to downtown L.A. Woodland Hills C of C (818) 347-4737.

Chapter 6

LOS ANGELES COUNTY
Newcomers Guide

Voter Registration

You must be at least 18 years old and a citizen. Go to the nearest post office and pick up a voter registration postcard. Fill it out and pop it into the mail box. Before every election the county will mail you a sample ballot with the address of your polling place. For more information, call the Registrar of Voters at (323) 260-2991.

Vehicle Registration and Smog Rules

California has the most stringent smog requirements in the country; you may have to shell out a few hundred or more dollars to bring your vehicle up to code. You have 20 days from the time you enter the state to register your vehicle. After that you pay a penalty and risk a ticket-fine.

For registration, go to any office of the Department of Motor Vehicles. Bring your smog certificate, your registration card and your license plates.

Driving Rules, Requirements and Tests

If going for a driver's license, ask to have the test booklet mailed to you or pick it up. Study it. Almost all the questions will be taken from the booklet.

To obtain a driver's license, you must be 16 years old, pass a state-certified Driver's Education (classroom) and Driver's Training (behind-the-wheel) course, and written and driving tests at DMV. Once you pass, your license is usually renewed by mail. Retesting is rare, unless your driving record is poor.

Teenagers older than 15 1/2 years who have completed driver's training can be issued a permit. New law restricts driving hours for young teens to daylight hours and, unless supervised, forbids them for six months to drive other teens. Law also requires more parental training and extends time of provisional license. Purpose is to reduce accidents. If no driver's education program has been completed, you must be at least 18 years old to apply for a license.

- Turning Rules: If signs don't say no, you can turn right on a red light (after making a full stop), and make a U-turn at an intersection.

- Stop for pedestrians. When school bus stops and flashes lights, stop, even if on opposite side of road.

Copyright © 2001 McCormack's Guides. No reproduction without permission.

- Insurance. Must have it to drive.
- Out-of-state applicants must supply proof of "legal presence," which could be a certified copy of a birth certificate. Foreign applicants must supply other documents.
- Department of Motor Vehicles offices are too numerous to list but call these numbers for addresses, forms, booklets and more information:
- Los Angeles (213) 744-2000.
- San Fernando Valley (818) 901-5500.
- East County (626) 962-3661.
- Long Beach area (310) 832-4160.

Garbage Service

The garbage fellows come once a week. Rates vary by city but average $15 to $25 a month. Many homes will receive recycling bins or carts for plastics, glass and cans. Carts that can be lifted by mechanical arms are becoming popular. Don't burn your garbage in the fireplace or outside. Don't burn leaves. Against law.

Property Taxes

Average property tax rate in California is 1.25 percent. If you buy a $250,000 home, your property tax will be $3,125. Once basic tax is established, it goes up very little in following years. "Average" needs to be emphasized. Some jurisdictions have tacked costs on to the property tax.

Property taxes are paid in two installments, due by April 10 and December 10. Generally, they are collected automatically through impound accounts set up when you purchase a home but check your sale documents carefully. Sometimes homeowners are billed directly.

Sales Tax

The rate varies by county. In L.A. County it is 8 percent. This means that if you buy $100 worth of goods, you will pay $108. Food, except when sold in restaurants, is not taxed.

State Income Taxes

See chart next page.

Cigarette-Tobacco Tax

New tax adds 50 cents to a pack of cigarettes. Many smokers load up on cigarettes in Nevada or Mexico or buy over the internet.

Mello-Roos Taxes

Some cities, to fund parks and lights and other amenities in new subdivisions, have installed what is called the Mello-Roos tax. Realtors are required to give you complete information on all taxes.

1999 California Tax Rate Schedule
Schedule X Single Married Filing Separate Returns

Taxable Income		Computed Tax	On Amount Over
Over	But not over		
$0	$4,831	$0.00 + 1.0%	0
$5,264	$12,477	$52.64 + 2.0%	$5,264
$12,477	$19,692	$196.90 + 4.0%	$12,477
$19,962	$27,337	$485.50 + 6.0%	$19,692
$27,337	$34,548	$944.20 + 8.0%	$27,337
$34,548	AND OVER	$1,521.08 + 9.3%	$34,548

Schedule Y Married Filing Jointly & Qualified Widow(er)s

Taxable Income		Computed Tax	On Amount Over
Over	But not over		
$0	$10,528	$0.00 + 1.0%	0
$10,528	$24,954	$105.28 + 2.0%	$10,528
$24,954	$39,384	$393.80 + 4.0%	$24,954
$39,384	$54,674	$971.00 + 6.0%	$39,384
$54,674	$69,096	$1,888.40 + 8.0%	$54,674
$69,096	AND OVER	$3,042.16 + 9.3%	$69,096

Schedule Z Heads of Households

Taxable Income		Computed Tax	On Amount Over
Over	But not over		
$0	$10,531	$0.00 + 1.0%	0
$10,531	$24,955	$105.31 + 2.0%	$10,531
$24,955	$32,168	$393.79 + 4.0%	$24,955
$32,168	$39,812	$682.31 + 6.0%	$32,168
$39,812	$47,025	$1,140.95 + 8.0%	$39,812
$47,025	AND OVER	$1,717.99 + 9.3%	$47,025

Example

Mr. And Mrs. Smith are filing a joint tax return with $125,000 on line 19 of form 540, using Schedule Y, here is how they figured their tax amount.

	Taxable Income	Computed Tax	On Amount Over
Using Schedule Y-	$69,096 and over	$3,042.16 + 9.3%	$69,096

They subtract the amount at the beginning of their range from their taxable income.

$125,000.00
-69,000.00
$ 55,904.00

They multiply the result from Step 2 by the percentage for their range.

55,904.00
x.093
$ 5,199.07

They round the amount from Step 3 to two decimals (if necessary) and add it to the tax amount for their income range. After rounding the result, they will enter $8,241 on their tax owed line.

$3,042.16
+5,199.07
$8,241.23

Copyright © 2001 McCormack's Guides. No reproduction without permission.

Grocery Prices

Item	Store one	Store two	Average
Apple Juice, 1 gal.	$4.25	$3.79	$4.02
Apple Pie, Mrs. Smith's	5.19	4.99	5.09
Apples, Red Delicious, 1 lb.	0.99	.99	.99
Aspirin, cheapest, 250 count	3.99	3.99	3.99
Baby Shampoo, Johnsons, 20 fluid oz.	4.99	4.89	4.94
Bacon, 1 lb. Farmer John Sliced	3.49	4.29	3.89
Bagels, store-made,	.59	.50	.55
Bananas, 1 lb.	.59	.59	.59
Beef, top round boneless roast, 1 lb.	3.39	4.19	3.79
Beef, ground round, 1 lb.,(15% fat)	2.29	2.49	2.39
Beer, Budweiser, 12-pack, cans	8.99	8.99	8.99
Beer, Coors, 12-pack, cans	8.99	8.99	8.99
Bisquick, 2 lbs. 8 oz.	2.49	2.69	2.59
Bleach, Clorox, 1 gal.	2.19	2.29	2.24
Bok Choy, 1lb.	.59	.99	.79
Bread, sourdough, Colombo 1.5 lb,	2.49	2.59	2.54
Bread, white, cheapest 1.5lb,	1.69	1.49	1.59
Broccoli, bunch	1.29	1.09	1.19
Butter, Challenge, 1 lb.	2.19	1.89	1.99
Cabbage, 1 lb.	.49	.49	.49
Cantaloupe, 1 lb.	.59	.49	.54
Carrots, fresh, 1 lb.	.39	.49	.44
Cat Food, store brand, small can	.39	.39	.39
Cereal, Grapenuts, 24 oz.	3.75	3.89	3.82
Cereal, Wheaties, , 18 oz.	4.29	4.59	4.44
Charcoal, Kingsford, 20 lbs.	8.49	8.29	8.39
Cheese, Mild Cheddar, 1 lb.	3.99	3.99	3.99
Chicken, breasts, boneless skinless, 1 lb.	1.99	1.99	1.99
Chicken-Foster Farms, whole, 1 lb.	1.29	1.19	1.24
Chili, Stagg, with beans, 15 oz. can	1.85	1.99	1.92
Cigarettes, Marlboro Lights, carton + sales tax	39.99	39.99	39.99
Coca Cola, 12-pack, 12 oz. cans	4.99	4.99	4.99
Coffee, Folgers, 1 lb.	3.89	3.99	3.94
Cafe latte, Starbucks, 1 cup,	2.50	2.50	2.50
Coffee, 1 cup, Starbucks, reg. or decaf.,	1.35	1.35	1.35
Cookies, Oreo, 20 oz. pkg.	3.59	3.59	3.59
Diapers, Huggies, size 2, (34-pack)	7.99	7.99	7.99
Dishwashing Liquid, Dawn, 28 oz.	3.49	3.39	3.44
Dog Food, Pedigree, 22-oz. can	1.49	1.29	1.39
Eggs, large, Grade AA, doz.	2.09	1.99	2.04
Flour, Gold Medal, 5 lbs.	1.99	1.99	1.99
Flowers, dozen roses	20.00	12.99	16.50
Flowers, carnations per bunch	3.99	3.34	3.67
Fresh Ginger	2.49	2.19	2.34
Frozen Dinners, Marie Callendar's	3.49	3.99	3.74
Frozen Yogurt, Dreyers, half gal.	5.29	5.29	5.29
Gerber's Baby Food, Fruit or Veg., 4 oz.	.51	.49	.50
Gerber's Baby Food, Meat, 2.5 oz.	.75	.79	.77
Gerber's Baby Food, Cereal, 4 oz.	.51	.49	.50
Gerber's Baby Food, Turkey, 2.5 oz.	.79	.79	.79
Gin, Gilbeys, 1.75 Ltr.	16.99	16.99	16.99
Granola Bars	3.29	3.29	3.29
Grapes, Red Seedless, 1 lb.	.99	1.49	1.24
Grapefruit, each	0.50	0.69	0.60

Copyright © 2001 McCormack's Guides. No reproduction without permission.

Grocery Prices

Item	Store one	Store two	Average
Ham, Armour, 1.5-lbs., canned,	$5.29	$5.99	$5.64
Ice cream, Dreyers, half gal.	5.29	5.29	5.29
Ice cream, Haagen Daz,	5.49	5.49	5.49
Instant Lunch	.65	.65	.65
Jam, Mary Ellen, 18 oz.	3.89	3.79	3.84
Kentucky Fried Chicken, 8 pc. family bucket,	15.14	15.14	15.14
Ketchup, Del Monte, 36 oz.	2.99	2.99	2.99
Kleenex, 160-count box	1.75	1.79	1.77
Kraft Macaroni & Cheese, family size, (14.5oz)	1.99	1.99	1.99
Laundry Detergent, Tide, 92 oz.	8.79	8.59	8.69
Lettuce, Romaine, head	.99	1.29	1.14
Margarine, I Can't Believe It's Not Butter, 1-lb. Tub	1.65	1.79	1.72
Mayonnaise, Best Foods, 1 qt.	3.99	3.89	3.94
Milk, Whole, half gal.	2.02	1.99	2.01
Mocha, Starbucks, 1 cup,	2.50	2.50	2.50
M&M Candies, plain, 1 lb.	2.89	2.99	2.94
Mushrooms, sliced, per 0.5 lb.	1.89	1.79	1.84
Olive Oil, cheapest, 17 oz.	5.09	2.49	3.79
Onions, yellow, 3 lbs.	1.79	1.39	1.59
Orange Juice, Tropicana, 64-oz. Original Style	3.99	3.99	3.99
Paper Towels, single pack	1.79	1.19	1.49
Peanuts, cocktail, Planter's, 12-oz. Jar	2.69	3.09	2.89
Peas, frozen, 10 oz.	1.39	.79	1.09
Peanut Butter, Jiff, 1 lb.	2.69	2.69	2.69
Popcorn, Orville Reddenbacher, 3-pack	2.69	2.79	2.74
Pork, chops, center cut, 1 lb.	3.99	3.99	3.99
Potato Chips, Lays, 12.25 oz.	2.99	2.99	2.99
Potatoes, 10 lbs.	1.99	1.99	1.99
Raisins, bulk, 24 oz.	3.09	3.19	3.14
Reese's Peanut Butter Cups, 10 pk.	1.49	1.49	1.49
Rice, cheapest, 5 lbs.	3.09	2.49	2.79
Salmon, fresh, 1 lb.	5.99	5.99	5.99
Seven-Up, 6-pack, cans	2.59	2.99	2.79
Soap, bar, Zest, 3-pack	2.69	2.29	2.49
Soup, Campbell, Chicken Noodle, 10-oz. Can .	.85	.85	.85
Soy Sauce, Kikkoman, 10 oz.	1.69	1.69	1.69
Spaghetti, cheapest, 2 lbs.	1.99	1.69	1.84
Sugar, cheapest, 5 lbs.	2.15	1.89	2.02
Tazo tea, Starbucks	1.10	1.10	1.10
Tea, Lipton's, 48-bag box	2.69	2.79	2.74
Toilet Tissue, 4-roll pack, cheapest	1.49	.50	1.00
Tomatoes, 1 lb.	1.29	.99	1.14
Toothpaste, Colgate, 6.4 oz.	2.59	2.99	2.79
Top Ramen	.33	.25	.29
Tortillas, cheapest, 12-count pack	1.19	.99	1.09
Tuna, Starkist, 6 oz.	.89	.89	.89
Turkey, ground, 1 lb.	2.99	1.69	2.34
Vegetable Oil, store brand, 64 oz.	3.45	3.99	3.72
Vegetables, frozen, 10 oz.	2.09	.79	1.44
Vinegar, store brand, 1 pint	.89	.69	.79
Water, 1 liter,	.79	.89	.84
Whiskey, Seagrams 7 Crown, 750ml.	10.89	10.99	10.94
Wine, White Zinfandel, 750 ml.	4.39	3.99	4.19
Yoplait Original Yogurt, single	.79	.79	.79

Copyright © 2001 McCormack's Guides. No reproduction without permission.

Fun & Games, Arts, Activities

Although city departments organize some activities, a great many others are sponsored by individuals or organizations with no connection to city hall.

Adult softball is often coordinated by city hall. Little League is not. Neither usually is Pop Warner football. Gymnastics shows up in many city catalogs. Swim teams do not. Usually parent clubs organize the clubs and run the meets. Same for soccer, which is well organized and played extensively in the county.

Tennis, often public; racquetball, invariably private. Volleyball and basketball, sometimes public; boating, private.

Nurturing Mind & Body

Some of the biggest public sponsors of activities are often some of quietest in announcing their services. Many school districts offer adult classes: computers, cardiopulmonary resuscitation, aerobics, etc. For want of money, the districts usually do one mailing of their schedules and that's it.

Community colleges offer conditioning and sports — tennis, swimming, etc. — for low prices and a great variety of cultural and business classes. You can take them one at a time. You don't have to enroll in programs or put yourself on a diploma track. The same for "extension" classes offered by universities.

Ignore city boundaries. You're a Lakewood resident but you want to play in a Long Beach softball team. Sign up. They don't care. Some places might charge a few bucks extra for outside residents.

Community Activities

For community activities, get the following:

- The activities calendar from city hall, if it has one.

(Continued on Next Page)

Disclosure laws

California requires Realtors to give detailed reports on every home sold, including information about earthquake faults. Megan's law applies: for home sales and rentals, sales agent must tell you where you can get names and addresses of registered sex offenders. Usually, this will be the local police department.

(FUN & GAMES, from Previous Page)

- The chamber of commerce publication for your town. This will give a list of the social clubs and many of the youth groups. If writing to a chamber, sent $5 with your request. Many chambers are run on peanuts; a few bucks speeds things along. See city profiles for chamber numbers.
- Adult school calendar. Call the local school district. In California, adult schools offer many business and self-improvement classes.
- The Boys and Girls Club activity list, if there's a club nearby.

Education and Culture

For educational and cultural activities, get the following:

- Schedule of classes from the closest community colleges. Classes-activities days and evenings. Fees are range from about $13 to $65 for a class or activity.
- Catalogs from the Extension Divisions of UCLA and the California State Universities. All offer classes to the public.

More Sources

- Flip through the Yellow Pages under the activity you're interested in. Sounds obvious but many people don't.
- Get the local paper. Almost all do a good job on "calendar of events."
- Ask the people directly involved. If you see kids kicking a soccer ball and your nipper wants to play the game, ask the kids or their coach if there's a league. If interested in little theater, call a playhouse and inquire about acting groups. Many small groups put out newsletters. Get on the mailing list.
- Disregard in some cases religious affiliation. The Young Men's Christian Assn. doesn't ask you for proof of baptism to take weight training.

Phones

General Telephone (GTE) serves Santa Monica and other towns in West Los Angeles. Pacific Bell generally serves every one else. Activation costs $35 to $50 (more if wiring has to be done).

GTE, phone 800-483-4000. Pac Bell, 800-310-2355. There are so many options today that it's hard to describe basic service but it can be had for less than $20. Direct line internet service is available in many towns.

Water and Power

For water and electricity, the L.A. Dept. of Water and Power (213) 367-

4211. Depending on where you live, electricity may be provided by The Edison Company (800) 655-4555. For gas, Southern California Gas Company (800) 427-2200. Many homes are heated with natural gas.

Age Limitations

You must be 18 to vote and smoke and 21 to drink alcohol. Watch the booze. Drunk-driving law is so stringent that even a drink or two can put you in violation. How to tell whether you're maturing: clerks are supposed to ask you for ID if you look under 27 for smokes and under 30 for booze.

Smoking

In 1998, a state law took effect forbidding smoking in saloons, one of the last bastions of smoking. Bars in restaurants generally comply. Saloons sporadically enforce but many people refrain from smoking and those that do, often hide the cigarette under the table. If visiting socially, you are generally expected to light up outside.

Bottled Water

Tap water is often harsh and loaded with minerals. Many people use bottled water.

Child and Infant Care, Day Care

For licensing California divides child-care facilities into these categories:

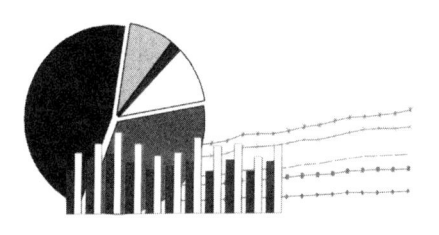

- Market Analysis
- Valid Statistics
- Quick Response

REAL/FACTS

Apartment Data for the Western Region

Critical Insights into Rents, Occupancies, Sales Trends, Individual Complexes and More

www.realfacts.com   (415) 884-2480

- Small family: up to 6 children in the providers's home.
- Large family: 7-12 children in the provider's home.
- Nursery schools or child-care centers.

Individual sitters are not licensed and neither are people with whom parents arrange informally to take care of their children but if a person is clearly in the business of child care from more than one family he or she should be licensed. Each of the three categories has restrictions. For example, the small-family provider with six children cannot have more than three under age 2. In everyday reality, many of the larger facilities will accept only children over age 2, and some have even higher age limits. The state and its local agencies maintain referral lists of local infant and day-care providers. A child is considered an infant from birth to age 2. For information and referrals, call a local agency near where you intend to live. The agencies are:

- Child and Family Services, L.A. (213) 427-2700
- Child Care Information Service, Pasadena-Arcadia (626) 449-8221
- Children's Home Society, Long Beach (562) 901-3145
- Connections for Children, Santa Monica (310) 452-3202
- Crystal Stairs, Los Angeles (323) 299-0199
- Equipoise, Compton (310) 605-1770
- Mexican-American Opportunity Foundation, Commerce (323) 890-9616
- Options, Baldwin Park (626) 856-5900
- Child Care Information Service, Pomona (909) 629-5011
- Child Care Resource Center, San Fernando Valley (818) 756-3360

Before you move... buy McCormack's GUIDES

The GUIDES have the information to make your move to a new location easier. Feel comfortable about the change because you have the facts about city profiles, school rankings, SAT scores, private school directories, medical care, commuting, recreation, crime ratings, area weather, and much more!

McCormack's Guides are published for these counties:

ALAMEDA • CONTRA COSTA-SOLANO
SANTA CLARA-SANTA CRUZ • SAN FRANCISCO-SAN MATEO
MARIN-NAPA-SONOMA
SAN DIEGO • LOS ANGELES • ORANGE COUNTY
GREATER SACRAMENTO-CENTRAL VALLEY
RIVERSIDE-SAN BERNARDINO • SANTA BARBARA-VENTURA

1-800-222-3602
www.mccormacks.com

$13.95 SINGLE COPY
VISA & MASTERCARD ACCEPTED
DISCOUNTS FOR BULK BUYERS. SEE LAST PAGE

Chapter 7

LOS ANGELES COUNTY
New Housing

SHOPPING FOR A new home? This chapter gives an overview of new housing underway in Los Angeles County. Smaller projects are generally ignored. If you know where you want to live, drive that town or ask the local planning department, what's new in housing.

Prices change. Incidentals such as landscaping fees may not be included. In the 1980s, to pay for services, cities increased fees on home construction. Usually, these fees are included in the home prices but in what is known as Mello-Roos districts, the fees are often assessed like tax payments (in addition to house payments).

Nothing secret. By law, developers are required to disclose all fees and, in fact, California has some of the toughest disclosure laws in the country. But the prices listed below may not include some fees.

After rocketing in the 1980s, home prices, new and resale, stabilized and in many instances dropped but in 1997, as the economy revived, so did home prices. Since then, prices in many towns have taken jumps.

This information covers what's available at time of publication. For latest information, call the developers for brochures.

If you have never shopped for a new home, you probably will enjoy the experience. In the larger developments, the builders will decorate models showing the housing styles and sizes offered. You enter through one home, pick up the sales literature, then move to the other homes or condos. Every room is usually tastefully and imaginatively decorated — and enticing.

An agent or agents will be on hand to answer questions or discuss financing or any other aspect you're interested in. Generally all this is done low-key. On Saturdays and Sundays thousands of people can be found visiting developments around Southern California.

Developers call attention to their models by flags. When you pass what appears to be a new development and flags are flying, it generally means that units are available for sale and inspection.

NEW HOUSING 305

MAGAZINE, MAP GUIDE AND ONLINE NETWORK
TO NEW HOME COMMUNITIES

Shopping For A New Home?

Start your home search with New Homes Magazine, the leading guide to new home communities throughout Northern California. With full color photos, easy-to-use maps, interesting articles, and up-to-date information on pricing and amenities, New Homes gives you all the information you need to find the perfect new home.

Call 1-800-400-2248
for your FREE copy!

www.newhomesmag.com

Copyright © 2001 McCormack's Guides. No reproduction without permission.

New Housing in Los Angeles County

(All developments are single-family detached unless otherwise noted.)

Agua Dulce
Cantilena, Trimark Pacific, 7168 Sale Ave, (818) 715-1130, single-family homes, 4BR, from low $400,000s.

Altadena
La Dina Estates, Compass Homes, 628 Coat Ct., (626) 797-9311, single-family homes, 3-5BR, from the low $600,000s.

Bellflower
Midway Park Estates, Pacific Homes, 10501 Midway St., (877) 232-7624, single-family homes, 3-4BR, from $394,000.

Burbank
Hallston, Lennar Homes, 3307 Castleman Ln, single-family homes, 3-5BR, from the $700,000s.

Calabasas
Mont Calabasas, Shea Homes, 26632 W. Alsace Dr., (866) 870-9718. single-family homes, 4-5BR, from the $800,000s.

Canyon Country (Santa Clarita)
Falcon Ridge, Ryland Group, 28088 White Canyon Rd., (661) 252-2099, single-family homes, 3-4BR, from the low $300,000s.
Heights at Stonecrest, Pacific Bay Homes, 14308 W. Platt Ct., (661) 250-0185., single-family homes, 3-5BR, from the high $200,000s to $350,000.

Castaic (near Santa Clarita)
Cedar Pointe, Centex Homes, 32224 N. Elk Ridge, (661) 295-0770, single-family homes, 4-6BR, from the low $300,000s.
Cimarron, Curtis Development., 32472 The Old Road, (661) 257-8384, single-family homes, 4BR, from low $300,000s.
Country Village, D. R. Horton, 30223 N. Briarwood, (661) 257-0526, single-family homes, 3-4BR, from the low $200,000s.
Highlands, MBK Homes, 30454 N. Barcelona, (661) 295-6600, single-family homes, 3BR, from the mid-$200,000s.
Ridgewood, Richmond American, 32141 N. Big Oak Ln., (661) 775-3911, single-family homes, 3-4BR, from the mid-$200,000s.
Wildwood, Centex Homes, 27617 W. Elk Ridge, (661) 295-1181, single-family homes, 3BR, from the mid-$200,000s.

Claremont
Bungalows, Walton Co., 2061 New Haven Ave., (877) 456-9083 single-family homes, 3BR, from the low $200,000s.
Chanteclair Estates, Premiere Homes, 4288 New Hampshire, Ave., (866) 419-6572, single-family homes, 4-6BR, from $550,000.
Courtyards, Pacific Crest Communities, 703 Charleston Dr., (909) 447-4603, single-family homes, 3BR, from low $500,000s.

Fair Oaks Ranch (near Santa Clarita)
Hunters Ridge, Pardee Homes, 26401 Misty Ridge Place, (661) 250-2610, single-family homes, 4BR, from the low $300,000s.

Oak Glen, Pardee Homes, 26537 Swan Ln., (661) 252-9931, single-family homes, 4-5BR, from low $300,000s.

Lancaster

Forecast/Lancaster, Forecast Homes, 45754 Knightsbridge, (661) 951-9779, single-family homes, 3-5BR, from low $100,000s.

Legends, Eliopulos Enterprises, 2808 Legends Way, (661) 942-1955, single-family homes, 3-5BR, from mid-$100,000s.

Rielly Homes, 1508 West Ave., (661) 951-7877, single-family homes, 2-5BR, from low $100,000s.

Willow Creek Village, Portrait Development., 44508 15th St. East, (661) 726-2828, 2BR condos from below $100,000.

Palmdale

Everspring, Everspring Homes, East Avenue, (408) 725-8282, single-family homes, 3-4BR, from low $100,000s.

Forecast Rancho Vista, Forecast Homes, 3823 Vitrina Ln, (661) 942-3327, single-family homes, 2-3 BR, from mid-$100,000s.

Granite Heights, Granite Homes, 36428 Rodeo Ave., (661) 285-4181, single-family homes, 6BR, from high $100,000s.

Harris At Ranch Vista, Harris Homes, 4125 Portola Dr., (661) 718-0608, single-family homes, 3-4BR, from mid-$100,000s.

Lyon Homes at Crown Ridge, Lyon Homes, 38348 Bonino Dr., (661) 274-7718, single-family homes, 3-5BR, from high $100,000s.

Mahogany, Diamond Crest, 5623 Cosita Ct., (949)955-2333, single-family homes, 3-5BR, from mid-$100,000s.

Mahogany Ridge, Overland Development, 312 Makin Ave., single-family homes, 3-4BR, from mid-$100,000s.

Meadow Crest, Forecast Homes, 3535 Parkridge Ln., (661) 224-2760, single-family homes, 3-5BR, from high $100,000s.

Pacific Collection, Pacific Communities, 38602 Cortina Way, (877) 865-7573, single-family homes, 2-4BR, from $130,000.

Rancho Vista, Beazer Homes, 4007 Portola Dr., (877) 456-9072, single-family homes, 3-5 BR, from mid-$100,000s.

Porter Ranch

Sorrento, Shapell, 20505 Bergamo Way, (818) 773-9110, single-family homes, 3-4BR, from mid-$300,000s.

Quartz Hill (Lancaster)

Estates, Spiegel Develpt., 40th Street West Avenue J, (661) 722-8437, single-family homes, 5BR, from high $200,000s.

Monterey Collection, Barrett American, 42235 Brittle Bush, (661) 722-1536, single-family homes, 3-6BR, from low $200,000s.

Somervale Estates, Greystone Homes, 42332 Ridge View Dr., (661) 718-2716, single-family homes, 4-5BR, from low $200,000s.

Rowland Heights

Rowland Heights Hilltop, K. Hovnanian Co., 2113 Whistler Ct., (909) 594-8862, single-family homes, 4-5BR, from low $800,000s.

San Dimas

The Estates, Boulevard Develpt., 116 Calle Colorado, (714) 632-7444, single-family homes, 5BR, from low $700,000s.

Santa Clarita

Canyon Heights, Davidon Homes, 21624 W. Canyon Heights, (661) 296-0044, single-family homes, 4BR, from mid-$300,000s.

Canyon View Estates, American Diversified, 20001 Canyon View Dr., (661) 252-0991, single-family homes, 2-4BR, from low $100,000s.

The Highlands, MBK Homes, 30454 N. Barcelona Rd., (877) 456-9097, single-family homes, 3BR, from $270,000.

Lantana Hills, Pardee Homes, 23830 Oakhurst Dr., (661) 799-2628, single-family homes, 4BR, from high $200,000s.

Miramonte, Davidon Homes, 28211 N. Gold Canyon Dr., (661) 263-0800, single-family homes, 4BR, from high $300,000s.

Monterey, Cornerstone Developers, 20305 Colina Dr., (661) 298-1400, single-family homes, 3-4BR, from high $200,000s.

Oak Lane, Beazer Homes, 22705 Sundance Creek, (877) 456-9130, single-family homes, 3-4BR, from $180,000.

Oak Ridge, Beazer Homes, 25322 Wooddale Ct., (877) 456-9114, single-family homes, 3-5BR, from high $200,000s.

Olympic Crest, Santa Clarita Homes, 27639 Atlas Ln., (661) 298-9396, single-family homes, 3-5BR, from low $200,000s.

Ridge Crest Country Estates, Griffin Industries, 26885 North Canyon End Rd., (877) 456-9085, single-family homes, 4-5BR, from $600,000.

Shadow Oaks, Jenna Group, 26502 Sheldon Ave., (661) 298-4500, single-family homes, 3BR, from mid-$300,000s.

Spring Lane at Pacific Hills, Pacific Bay Homes, 22905 W. Redwood Ct., (661)263-7260, single-family homes, 3BR, from high $200,000s.

Summer Moon at Pacific Hills, Pacific Bay Homes, 22915 W. Redwood Ct., (661) 23-2298, single-family homes, 3-5BR, from low $300,000s.

Saugus

Acacia, Western Pacific Housing, 28415 Silverking Tr., (661) 263-9289, single-family homes, 3BR, from the mid-$200,000s.

Crossroads, Pacific Bay Homes, 22270 Cyprus Pl., (661) 296-7966, single-family homes, 3-4BR, from the high $200,000s.

Sonata, Curtis Communities, Copper Hill and Canyon View, (661) 257-8380, single-family homes, 3-4BR, from the low $200,000s.

Timberline at Pacific Crest, Pacific Bay Homes, 28923 N. Pacific Ct., (661) 296-8832, single-family homes, 3-5BR, from the mid- $300,000s.

Whispering Oaks, Curtis Communities, Copper Hill and Deer Springs, (661)257-8380, single-family homes, 4BR, from the low $300,000s.

Wisteria, Western Pacific Housing, 28415 Silverking Tr., (661) 263-9289, single-family homes, 3-4BR, from the mid $200,000s.

Stevenson Ranch (near Santa Clarita)

Barrington at Stevenson Ranch, Richmond American, 25780 Thurbur Wy., (661) 260-1880, single-family homes, 3BR, from the low $300,000s.

Belcrest at Stevenson Ranch, Richmond American, 26808 Wyatt Ln., (661) 261-1925, single-family homes, 5-6BR, from the low $400,000s.

Breton at Stevenson Ranch, Greystone Homes, 25842 Forsythe Wy., (661) 799-8135, single-family homes, 5BR, from the mid-$300,000s.

Centex Heights at Stevenson Ranch, Centex Homes, 26654 Brooks Cir., (661) 260-1770, single-family homes, 4-5BR, from the mid-$300,000s.

Centex Ridge at Stevenson Ranch, Centex Homes, 26129 Beecher Ln., (661) 287-0188, single-family homes, 4BR, from the high $300,000s.

Mandeville at Stevenson Ranch, Richmond American, 25910 Voltaire Pl., (661) 288-2523, single-family homes, 4-5BR, from the mid $300,000s.
Netherwood, Jenna Group, 19304 Ackerman, (661) 298-4555, single-family homes, 2-3BR, from the mid-$200,000s.
Pacific Summit at Stevenson Ranch, Centex Homes, 26654 Brooks Cir., (661) 260-1770, gated single-family homes, 4-5BR, from the high $300,000s.
Southern Oaks Grove at Stevenson Ranch, Laing Homes, 25006 N. Southern Oaks Dr., (661) 287-1648, single-family homes, 3-5BR, from the low $500,000s.
Southern Oaks Manner at Stevenson Ranch, Laing Homes, 25643 W. Magnolia Ln., (661) 287-1648, single-family homes, 4BR, from the low $500,000s.
Skyview at Stevenson Ranch, D.R. Horton, 26341 W. Peacock Pl., (661) 254-4939, single-family homes, 4-5BR, from the high $300,000s.
Torcello at Stevenson Ranch, Greystone Homes, 26800 Grey Place, (661) 260-1387, gated single-family homes, 5BR, from the high $400,000s.
Twilight Vista, Shea Homes, 26024 N. Tennyson Ln., (877)456-9113 single-family homes, 3-4BR, from the low $400,000s.

Sylmar

Hubbard Gardens, K&S Construction, 13421 Hubbard St., (818) 833-3184, gated townhouses, 3BR, from the mid $100,000s.
Village Green, Braemar Homes, 14518 Village Wy., (818) 362-5308, single-family homes, 3-4BR, from the high $100,000s.

Tarzana

Braemer Estates, Braemar Group, 3991 Reseda Blvd., (818) 344-2300, gated single-family homes, 4-5BR, from the low $900,000s.
Mulholland Park, Capital Pacific Homes, 19001 Devonport Ln., (877) 456-9081, gated single-family homes, 4-6BR, from the low $1,000,000s.

Tujunga

Fontaine at Renaissance, Premier Homes, 11125 Provence Ln., (818) 951-9482, single-family homes, 3-4BR, from the mid $400,000s.
Rivemont at Renaissance, Premier Homes, 11137 Provence Ln., (866) 419-6577, single-family homes, 4BR, from the mid $400,000s.

Valencia (Santa Clarita)

Back Bay, Brookfield Homes, 24125 Back Bay Ct., (877) 807-1336, single-family homes, 4-5BR, call for prices.
Bridgeport at the Cove, Centex Homes, 27100 Breakers Cove, (661) 259-3529, single-family homes, 3BR, from the high $300,000s.
Cabot Bay at Bridgeport, 27005 Edgewater Ln., (661) 255-0767, single-family homes, 2-3BR, from the mid- $200,000s.
Carmelita at Woodlands, Taylor Woodrow Homes, 26883 Tourney Rd., (661) 799-8853, gated single-family homes, 3-4BR, from the high $200,000s.
Corner Stone at Copperhill, Shea Homes, 27902 North Cherry Blossom Pl., (877) 456-9086, single-family homes, 2-3BR, from the high $100,000s.
Garland at Woodlands, Taylor Woodrow Homes 26883 Turney Rd., (949) 206-2209, single-family homes, 3-4BR, from the low $500,000s.
Harvest Walk, Olson Company, 1235 N. Olive Grove Ln., (626) 934-7467, gated single-family homes, 2-4BR, from the low $200,000s.
Iron Wood at Woodland Waters, Taylor Woodrow Homes, 26883 Turney Rd., (661) 222-7914, gated single-family homes, 3-4BR, from the mid $300,000s.
The Island at Bridgeport, Standard Pacific Homes, 27066 West Island Rd., (661)254-0241, gated single-family homes, 3-4BR, from the low $500,000s.

The Landing at Maples, Richmond American, 23906 Windword Ln., (661) 799-7391, single-family homes, 3-4BR, from the low $400,000s.
Playa Village, Playa Village Inc., 29100 Anna Ct., (661) 263-1344, gated single-family homes, 5BR, from the high $400,000s.
Presidio at Woodlands, Taylor Woodrow Homes, 26833 Turney Rd., (661) 222-7925, gated single-family homes, 4-5BR, from the mid- $700,000s.
Promontory at Copper Hill, Shea Homes, 24224 West Edelweiss Ct., (661) 702-0100, single-family homes, 4-5BR, from the high $300,000s.
Silhouette at Copper Hill, Shea Homes, 24240 West Kirby Ct., (877) 456 9096, single-family homes, 3BR, from the high $200,000s.
Village Walk at North Park, D. R. Horton, 28246 N. Canterbury Ct., (661) 263-1073, single-family homes, 1-3BR, from the high $100,000s.
Waterford at Bridgeport, D.R. Horton, Newhall Ranch and Hillsborough Pkwy, (661) 513-0193, single-family homes, 3BR, from the high $200,000s.

West Covina

Claybourne Ridge, Rilley Homes, 2847 Panorama Ct., (626) 917-0739, single-family homes, 4-5BR, from the high $500,000s.

Whittier

Carmenita Walk, Olson Company, 13726 E. Marquita Ln., (562) 906-9862, gated single-family homes, 3-4BR, from the low $200,000s.

Winnetka

Versailles, Premier Homes, 20235 Arminta St., (866) 419-9575, single-family homes, 3-4BR, from the mid $300,000s.

Chapter 8

LOS ANGELES COUNTY
Hospitals and Health Care

GOOD HEALTH CARE. Where, how, do you get it? The question is particularly puzzling these days because so many changes are taking place in medicine and medical insurance.

The "operations" of a few years ago are the "procedures" of today, done in the office not the surgery, completed in minutes not hours, requiring home care not hospitalization. Large insurance companies, through their health maintenance plans, are setting limits on what doctors and hospitals can charge, and — critics contend — interfering with the ability of doctors to prescribe what they see fit. The companies strongly deny this, arguing they are bringing reforms to a profession long in need of reforming.

Many hospitals are now setting up their own insurance plans, structured according to the needs of local residents. Many hospitals are also merging or combining resources to bid on HMO contracts or working together in novel ways, the better to avoid unnecessary duplication and to save money by purchasing supplies and medicine in larger amounts.

Universal health insurance having failed to clear congress, over 40 million Americans are not covered by any medical plan. Unable to afford medical bills, many ignore ailments and illnesses.

The state legislature recently passed a law that makes it easier for patients to sue Health Maintenance Organizations and insurers. More changes are coming yet much of the old system remains in place.

This chapter will give you an overview of Southern California health care and although it won't answer all your questions — too complex a business for that — we hope that it will point you in the right directions.

For most people, health care is entwined with insurance, in systems that are called "managed care." But many individuals, for a variety of reasons, do not have insurance. This is a good place to start: with nothing, all options open. Let's use as our seeker for the best of all health care worlds — on a tight budget — a young woman, married, one child. Her choices:

No Insurance — Cash Care

The woman is self-employed or works at a small business that does not offer health benefits.

She comes down with the flu. When she goes into the doctor's office, she will be asked by the receptionist, how do you intend to pay? With no insurance, she pays cash (or credit card), usually right there. She takes her prescription, goes to the pharmacy and pays full cost.

If her child or husband gets sick and needs to see a doctor, the same procedure holds. Also the same for treatment of a serious illness, to secure X-rays or hospitalization. It's a cash system.

Medi-Cal

If an illness strikes that impoverishes the family or if the woman, through job loss or simply low wages, cannot afford cash care, the county-state health system will step in.

The woman fills out papers to qualify for Medi-Cal, the name of the system (it's known elsewhere as Medicaid), and tries to find a doctor that will treat Medi-Cal patients.

If unable to find an acceptable doctor, the woman could turn to a county hospital or clinic. There she will be treated free or at very low cost.

Drawbacks-Pluses of Medi-Cal

County hospitals and clinics, in the personal experience of one of the editors — who has relatives who work at or use county facilities — have competent doctors and medical personnel. If you keep appointments promptly, often you will be seen with little wait. If you want immediate treatment for, say, a cold, you register and you wait until an urgent-care doctor is free.

If you need a specialist, often the county facility will have one on staff, or will be able to find one at a teaching hospital or other facility. You don't choose the specialist; the county physician does.

County facilities are under-funded and, often, inconveniently located — a major drawback. Some counties, lacking clinics and hospitals, contract with adjoining counties that are equipped. You have to drive some distance for treatment.

County hospitals and clinics are not 100 percent free. If you have money or an adequate income, you will be billed for service. Some county hospitals run medical plans designed for people who can pay. These people can ask for a "family" doctor and receive a higher (usually more convenient) level of care.

Medicare— Veterans Hospital

If our woman were elderly, she would be eligible for Medicare, the federal insurance system, which covers 80 percent, with limitations, of medical costs or allowable charges. Many people purchase supplemental insurance to bring coverage up to 100 percent (long-term illnesses requiring hospitalization may exhaust some benefits.)

If the woman were a military veteran with a service-related illness, she could seek care at a Veteran's Administration clinic or hospital.

Indemnity Care

Usually the most expensive kind of insurance, this approach allows complete freedom of choice. The woman picks the doctor she wants. If her regular doctor recommends a specialist, she can decide which one, and if she needs hospital treatment, she can pick the institution. In reality, the choice of hospital and specialist will often be strongly influenced by her regular doctor but the patient retains control. Many indemnity plans have deductibles and some may limit how much they pay out in a year or lifetime. Paperwork may be annoying.

Managed Care

This divides into two systems, Preferred Provider Organizations (PPO) and Health Maintenance Organizations (HMO). Both are popular in California and if your employer provides health insurance, chances are almost 100 percent you will be pointed toward, or given a choice of, one or the other.

PPOs and HMOs differ among themselves. It is beyond the scope of this book to detail the differences but you should ask if coverage can be revoked or rates increased in the event of serious illness. Also, what is covered, what is not. Cosmetic surgery might not be covered. Psychiatric visits or care might be limited. If you have a chronic condition, the PPO might impose restrictions on care. Ask how emergency or immediate care is provided. If you must have a certain prescription drug (or drugs), find out how much the HMO charges for these medicines.

HMOs have a spinoff: called Point of Service (POS).

Preferred Provider

The insurance company approaches certain doctors, clinics, medical facilities and hospitals and tells them: we will send patients to you but you must agree to our prices — a method of controlling costs — and our rules. The young woman chooses her doctor from the list provided by the PPO.

The physician will have practicing privileges at certain local hospitals. The young woman's child contracts pneumonia and must be hospitalized. Dr. X is affiliated with XYZ hospital, which is also signed up with the PPO plan. The child is treated at XYZ hospital.

If the woman used an "outside" doctor or hospital, she would pay extra — the amount depending on the nature of the plan. It is important to know the doctor's affiliations because you may want your hospital care at a certain institution.

Hospitals differ. A children's hospital, for instance, will specialize in children's illnesses and load up on children's medical equipment. A general hospital will have a more rounded program. For convenience, you may want the hospital closest to your home.

If you need specialized treatment, you must, to avoid extra costs, use the PPO affiliated specialists. The doctor will often guide your choice.

Besides the basic cost for the policy, PPO insurance might charge fees, co-payments or deductibles. A fee might be $10 or $15 a visit. With co-payments, the bill, say, comes to $100. Insurance pays $80, the woman pays $20.

Deductible example: the woman pays the first $250 or the first $2,000 of any medical costs within a year, and the insurer pays bills above $250 or $2,000. With deductibles, the higher the deductible the lower the cost of the policy. The $2,000 deductible is really a form of catastrophic insurance.

Conversely, the higher the premium the more the policy covers. Some policies cover everything. (Dental care is usually provided through a separate insurer.) The same for prescription medicines. You may pay for all, part, or nothing, depending on the type plan.

The PPO doctor functions as your personal physician. Often the doctor will have his or her own practice and office, conveniently located. If you need to squeeze in an appointment, the doctor usually will try to be accommodating.

Drawback: PPOs restrict choice.

Health Maintenance Organization (HMO)

Very big in California because Kaiser Permanente, one of the most popular medical-hospital groups, is run as an HMO. The insurance company and medical provider are one and the same.

All or almost all medical care is given by the HMO. The woman catches the flu. She sees the HMO doctor at the HMO clinic or hospital. If she becomes pregnant, she sees an HMO obstetrician at the HMO hospital or clinic and delivers her baby there.

With HMOs you pay the complete bill if you go outside the system (with obvious exceptions; e.g., emergency care).

HMOs encourage you to pick a personal physician. The young woman wants a woman doctor; she picks one from the staff. She wants a pediatrician as her child's personal doctor; the HMO, usually, can provide one.

HMO clinics and hospitals bring many specialists and services together under one roof. You can get your eyes examined, your hearing tested, your prescriptions filled, your X-rays taken within a HMO facility (this varies), and much more.

If you need an operation or treatment beyond the capacity of your immediate HMO hospital, the surgery will be done at another HMO hospital within the system or at a hospital under contract with the HMO. Kaiser recently started contracting with other facilities to provide some of the services that it used to do in its own hospitals or clinics.

HMO payment plans vary but many HMO clients pay a monthly fee and a small ($10-$15) per visit fee. Often the plan includes low-cost or reduced-cost or free prescriptions.

Both HMOs and PPOs usually have very little paperwork. You present your card or identify your plan and that's about it.

Drawback: Freedom of choice limited. If HMO facility is not close, the woman will have to drive to another town.

Point of Service (POS)

Essentially, an HMO with the flexibility to use outside doctors and facilities for an extra fee or a higher deductible. POS systems seem to be popular with people who don't feel comfortable limiting themselves to an HMO.

They pay extra but possibly not as much as other alternatives.

Making Your Choice

If you are receiving medical insurance through your employer, you will be limited to the choices offered. In large groups, unions often have a say in what providers are chosen. Some individuals will base their choice on price, some on convenience of facilities, others on what's covered, and so on.

Once a year, typically the last quarter, many large businesses or government agencies with multiple plans allow you to switch plans during what is called "open enrollment."

Many private hospitals offer Physician Referral Services. You call the hospital, ask for the service and get a list of doctors to choose from. The doctors will be affiliated with the hospital providing the referral. Hospitals and doctors will also tell you what insurance plans they accept for payment and will send you brochures describing the services the hospital offers.

For Kaiser and other HMOs, call the local hospital or clinic.

A PPO will give you a list of its member doctors and facilities. Doctors will tell you what PPOs they are affiliated with.

Here's some advice from a pro on picking a health plan:

Make a chart with a list of prospective health plans in columns across the top. Down the left side of the chart, list the services or attributes that you think are important. Review the health plans and check off the "important" services in each plan. Choose or investigate further those plans that have the most check marks.

Common Questions

The young woman is injured in a car accident and is unconscious. Where will she be taken?

Generally, she will be taken to the closest emergency room or trauma center, where her condition will be stabilized. Her doctor will then have her admitted into a hospital. Or she will be transferred to her HMO hospital or, if indigent, to a county facility.

The young woman breaks her leg. Her personal doctor is an internist and does not set fractures. What happens?

The personal doctor refers the case to a specialist. Insurance pays the specialist's fee. In PPO, the woman would generally see a specialist affiliated with the PPO. In an HMO, the specialist would be employed by the HMO.

The young woman signs up for an HMO then contracts a rare disease or suffers an injury that requires treatment beyond the capability of the HMO. Will she be treated?

Often yes, but it pays to read the fine print. The HMO will contract treatment out to a facility that specializes in the needed treatment.

The young woman becomes despondent and takes to drink. Will insurance pay for her rehabilitation?

Depends on her insurance. And often her employer. Some may have drug and alcohol rehab plans. Some plans cover psychiatry.

The woman becomes pregnant. Her doctor, who has delivered many babies, wants her to deliver at X hospital. All the woman's friends say, Y Hospital is much better, nicer, etc. The doctor is not cleared to practice at Y Hospital. Is the woman out of luck?

With a PPO, the woman must deliver at a hospital affiliated with the PPO — or pay the extra cost. If her doctor is not affiliated with that hospital, sometimes a doctor may be given courtesy practicing privileges at a hospital where he or she does not have staff membership. Check with the doctor.

With HMOs, the woman must deliver within the HMO system.

The young woman goes in for minor surgery, which turns into major surgery when the doctor forgets to remove a sponge before sewing up. Upon reviving, she does what?

Some medical plans require clients to submit complaints to a panel of arbitrators, which decides damages, if any. The courts are starting to take a skeptical look at this requirement. Read the policy.

The woman wakes up at 3 a.m. with a sore throat and headache. She feels bad but not bad enough to drive to a hospital or emergency room. She should:

Many hospitals and medical plans offer 24-hour advice lines. This is something you should check on when you sign up for a plan.

While working in her kitchen, the woman slips, bangs her head against the stove, gets a nasty cut and becomes woozy. She should:

Call 9-1-1, which will send an ambulance. 9-1-1 is managed by police dispatch. It's the fastest way to get an ambulance.

Major Hospitals in Los Angeles County

Alhambra Medical Center, 100 S. Raymond Ave., Alhambra, (626) 570-1606.
Antelope Valley Hospital Medical Center, 1600 W. Ave. J, Lancaster, (661) 949-5000.
Avalon Municipal Hospital, 100 Falls Canyon Rd., Avalon, (310) 510-0700.
Behavioral Health Center - Alhambra Hospital, 4619 Rosemead Blvd., Rosemead, (626) 286-1191.
Bellflower Medical Center, 9542 E. Artesia Blvd., Bellflower, (562) 925-8355.
Bellwood General Hospital, 10250 E. Artesia Blvd., Bellflower, (562) 866-9028.
Beverly Hospital, 309 W. Beverly Blvd., Montebello, (323) 726-1222.
Brotman Medical Center, 3828 Delmas Ter., Culver City, (310) 836-7000.
California Medical Center, 1401 S. Grand Ave., Los Angeles, (213) 748-2411.
Casa Colina Hospital, 255 E Bonita Ave., Pomona, (909) 593-7521.
Cedars-Sinai Medical Center, 8700 Beverly Blvd., Los Angeles, (310) 855-5000.
Centinela Hospital, 555 E. Hardy St., Inglewood, (310) 673-4660.
Century City Hospital, 2070 Century Park East, Century City, (310) 553-6211.
Children's Community Mental Center 15220 Vanowen St., Van Nuys, (818) 787-0123.
Citrus Valley Inter-Community Medical Center, 210 W. San Bernardino Rd., Covina, (626) 331-7331.
City of Hope Medical Center, 1500 E. Duarte Rd., Duarte, (626) 359-8111.
Coast Plaza Doctors' Hospital, 13100 Studebaker Rd., Norwalk, (562) 868-3751.
College Hospital, 10802 College Pl., Cerritos, (562) 924-9581.
Columbia Las Encinas Hospital, 2900 E Del Mar Blvd., Pasadena, (626) 795-9901.
Community Hospital of Gardena, 1246 W. 155th St., Gardena, (310) 323-5330.
Community Hospital of Huntington Park, 2623 E. Slauson Ave., Huntington Park, (323) 583-1931.
Daniel Freeman Marina Hospital, 4650 Lincoln Blvd., Marina Del Ray, (310) 823-8911.
Daniel Freeman Memorial Hospital, 333 N. Prairie Ave., Inglewood, (310) 674-7050.
Del Amo Hospital, 23700 Camino Del Sol, Torrance, (310) 530-1151.
Doctors' Hospital of West Covina, 725 S. Orange Ave., West Covina, (626) 338-8481.
Downey Regional Medical Center, 11500 Brookshire Ave., Downey, (562) 904-5000.
East L.A. Doctors' Hospital, 4060 Whittier Blvd., Los Angeles, (323) 268-5514.
Encino-Tarzana Regional Medical Center, 16237 Ventura Blvd., Encino, (818) 995-5000.
Encino-Tarzana Regional Medical Center, 18321 Clark St., Tarzana, (818) 881-0800.
Foothill Presbyterian Hospital, 250 S. Grand Ave., Glendora, (909) 592-0198.

Copyright © 2001 McCormack's Guides. No reproduction without permission.

Air Pollution

It's about your health.

AMERICAN LUNG ASSOCIATION When You Can't Breathe, Nothing Else Matters®

1-800-LUNG-USA

HOSPITALS & HEALTH CARE

Garfield Medical Center, 525 N. Garfield Ave., Monterey Park, (626) 573-2222.
Gateways Hospital, 1891 Effie St., Los Angeles, (323) 644-2000.
Glendale Adventist Medical Center, 1509 Wilson Ter., Glendale, (818) 409-8000.
Glendale Memorial Hospital & Health Center, 1420 S. Central Ave., Glendale, (818) 502-1900.
Good Samaritan Hospital, 1225 Wilshire Blvd., Los Angeles, (213) 977-2121.
Granada Hills Community Hospital, 10445 Balboa Blvd., Granada Hills, (818) 360-1021.
Greater El Monte Community Hospital, 1701 Santa Anita Ave., South El Monte, (626) 579-7777.
Henry Mayo Newhall Hospital, 23845 W. McBean Pkwy., Santa Clarita, (661) 253-8000.
High Desert Hospital, 44900 N. 60th St. West, Lancaster, (661) 948-8581.
Hollywood Community Hospital, 6245 De Longpre Ave., Los Angeles, (323) 462-2271.
Huntington East Valley Hospital, 150 W. Alosta Ave., Glendora, (909) 599-0542.
Huntington Memorial Hospital, 100 W. California Blvd., Pasadena, (626) 397-5000.
Ingleside Hospital, 7500 Hellman Av., Rosemead, (626) 288-2371.
Kaiser Permanente Bellflower Medical Center, 9400 E. Rosecrans Ave., Bellflower, (562) 461-3000.
Kaiser Permanente Harbor City Medical Center, 25825 S. Vermont Ave., Harbor City, (310) 325-5111.
Kaiser Permanente Los Angeles Medical Center, 4867 Sunset Blvd., Los Feliz, (323) 783-4011.
Kaiser Permanente Panorama City Medical Center, 13652 Cantara, Panorama City, (818) 375-2000.
Kaiser Permanente Woodland Hills Medical Center, 5601 De Soto Ave., Woodland Hills, (818) 719-2000.
Kaiser Permanente West L.A. Medical Center, 6041 Cadillac Ave., Los Angeles, (323) 857-2000.

Lakewood Regional Medical Center, 3700 South St., Lakewood, (562) 531-2550.
Lancaster Community Hospital, 43830 10th St. West (661) 948-4781.
Lincoln Hospital, 443 S. Soto St., Boyle Hts., (323) 261-1181.
Little Company of Mary Hospital, 4101 Torrance Blvd., Torrance, (310) 540-7676.
Long Beach Community Medical Center, 1720 N. Termino Ave., Long Beach, (562) 498-1000.
Long Beach Memorial Medical Center, 2801 Atlantic Ave., Long Beach, (562) 933-2000.
Los Angeles Community Hospital, 4081 E. Olympic Blvd., L.A. (323) 267-0477.
Los Angeles Metropolitan Medical Center, 2231 S. Western Ave., Los Angeles, (323) 737-7372.
Mayflower Gardens Hospital, 6705 W Avenue M, Quartz Hill, (661) 943-3212.
Memorial Hospital of Gardena, 1145 W. Redondo Beach Blvd., Gardena, (310) 532-4200.
Methodist Hospital, 300 W. Huntington Dr., Arcadia, (626) 445-4441.
Metropolitan State Hospital, 11400 Norwalk Blvd., Norwalk, (562) 863-7011.
Midway Hospital Medical Center, 5925 San Vicente Blvd., Los Angeles, (323) 938–3161.
Mission Community Hospital, 14850 Roscoe Blvd., Panorama City, (818) 787-2222.
Mission Community Hospital, 700 Chatsworth Dr., San Fernando, (818) 361-7331.
Mission Hospital, 3111 E. Florence Ave., Huntington Park, (323) 582-8261.
Monrovia Community Hospital, 323 S. Heliotrope Ave., Monrovia, (626) 359-8341.
Monterey Park Hospital, 900 S. Atlantic Blvd., Monterey Park, (626) 570-9000.
Northridge Hospital Medical Center, 18300 Roscoe Blvd., Northridge, (818) 885-8500.

320 HOSPITALS & HEALTH CARE

Northridge Hospital Medical Center, 14500 Sherman Cir., Van Nuys, (818) 997-0101.
Norwalk Community Hospital, 13222 Bloomfield Ave., Norwalk, (562) 863-4763.
Olive View-UCLA Medical Center, 14445 Olive View Dr., Sylmar, (818) 364-1555.
Pacific Alliance Medical Center, 531 W. College St., Los Angeles, (213) 624-8411.
Pacific Hospital Long Beach, 2776 Pacific Ave., Long Beach, (562) 595-1911.
Pacifica Hospital of the Valley, 9449 San Fernando Rd., Sun Valley, (818) 767-3310.
Palmcrest Medallion Hospital, 3355 Pacific Pl., Long Beach, (562) 595-4336.
Pine Grove Hospital, 7011 Shoup Av., Canoga Park, (818) 348-0500.
Pomona Valley Hospital Medical Center, 1798 N. Garey Ave., Pomona, (909) 865-9500.
Presbyterian Inter-Community Hospital, 12401 E. Washington Blvd., Whittier, (562) 698-0811.
Providence Holy Cross Medical Center, 15031 Rinaldi St., Mission Hills, (818) 365-8051.
Providence-St. Joseph Medical Center, 501 S. Buena Vista St., Burbank, (818) 843-5111.
Queen of Angels Presbyterian Medical Center, 1300 N. Vermont Ave., Los Feliz, (213) 413-3000.
Queen of the Valley Hospital, 1115 Sunset Ave., West Covina, (626) 962-4011.
Robert. F. Kennedy Medical Center, 4500 W. 116th St., Hawthorne, (310) 973-1711.
St. Francis Medical Center, 3630 E. Imperial Hwy., Lynwood, (310) 900-8900.
St. John's Hospital & Health Center, 1328 22nd St., Santa Monica, (310) 446-6337.
St. Luke Medical Center, 2632 E. Washington Blvd., Pasadena, (626) 797-1141.
St. Mary's Medical Center, 1040 Linden Ave., Long Beach, (562) 491-9000.
St. Vincent Medical Center, 2131 W. 3rd St., Los Angeles, (213) 484-7111.
San Dimas Community Hospital, 1350 W. Covina Blvd., San Dimas, (909) 599-6811.
San Gabriel Valley Medical Center, 438 W. Las Tunas Dr., San Gabriel, (626) 289-5454.
San Pedro Peninsula Hospital, 1300 W. 7th St., San Pedro, (310) 832-3311.
Santa Marta Hospital, 319 N. Humphreys Ave., East L.A., (323) 266-6500.
Santa Monica UCLA Medical Center, 1250 16th St., Santa Monica, (310) 319-4000.
Santa Teresita Hospital, 819 Buena Vista St., Duarte, (626) 359-3243.
San Vicente Hospital, 6000 San Vicente Blvd., Los Angeles, (323) 937-2504.
Sherman Oaks Hospital & Health Center, 4929 Van Nuys Blvd., Sherman Oaks, (818) 981-7111.
Shriners Hospital for Crippled Children, 3160 Geneva St., L.A. (213) 388-3151.
Specialty Hospital, 845 N. Lark Ellen Ave., West Covina, (626) 339-5451.
Suburban Medical Center, 16543 S. Colorado Ave., Paramount, (562) 531-3110.
Temple Community Hospital, 235 N. Hoover St., Los Angeles, (213) 382-7252.
Torrance Memorial Medical Center, 3330 W. Lomita Blvd., Torrance, (310) 325-9110.
Tri-City Regional Medical Center, 21530 Pioneer Blvd., Hawaiian Gardens, (562) 860-0401.
UCLA Medical Center, 10833 Le Conte Ave., Los Angeles, (310) 825-8611.
USC University Hospital, 1500 San Pablo St., Los Angeles, (323) 442-8500.

Copyright © 2001 McCormack's Guides. No reproduction without permission.

HOSPITALS & HEALTH CARE

USC Woman and Child Hospital, 1240 N Mission Rd., Los Angeles, (323) 226-3054.

Valley Presbyterian Hospital, 15107 Vanowen St., Van Nuys, (818) 782-6600.

Vencor Hospital-L.A., 5525 W. Slauson Ave., Culver City, (310) 642-0325.

Verdugo Hills Hospital, 1812 Verdugo Blvd., Glendale, (818) 790-7100.

Vets. Affairs Long Beach Health Care System, 5901 E. 7th St., Long Beach, (562) 494-2611.

Vets. Affairs Greater L.A. Health Care System-West L.A., 1100 Wilshire Blvd., L. A., (310) 478-3711.

Washington Medical Center, 12101 Washington Blvd., Culver City, (310) 391-0601.

West Hills Hospital and Medical Center, 7300 Medical Center Dr., West Hills, (818) 676-4000.

White Memorial Medical Ctr, 1720 Cesar E. Chavez Ave., Los Angeles, (323) 268-5000.

Whittier Hospital Medical Center, 9080 Colima Rd., Whittier, (562) 945-3561.

Chapter 9

LOS ANGELES COUNTY
Crime

NO TOWN OR NEIGHBORHOOD IS CRIME FREE. Even communities surrounded by gates and patrolled by guards will on occasion see domestic violence or pilfering by visitors.

So the question to ask when shopping for a home or apartment is not: Is this neighborhood safe? But rather, how safe is it compared to other places?

In California, crime often follows demographics: High-income neighborhoods generally have low crime, middle-income places middling crime, and low-income towns and neighborhoods high crime.

The statistics are supplied by the California Department of Justice, the Los Angeles Police Department and the FBI.

Numbers Don't Tell All

In many instances, these figures mislead. You can take probably every high-crime city in the country and find within it low-crime neighborhoods. New York City seemingly is overrun with felons but the City includes Staten Island, generally suburban and low to middle in crime. The same for Sacramento, Oakland, San Francisco, San Diego and Los Angeles. These are not crime cities; they are cities with certain neighborhoods high in crime.

Sometimes the statistics give a false picture. Theft is the most common crime. A city with many stores or a regional shopping mall will often have a high number of thefts — and consequently, a higher crime rate. Number of homicides, in some instances, gives a clearer picture of local crime.

The demographic connection also can mislead. Many peaceful, law-abiding people live in the "worst" neighborhoods. But these neighborhoods also contain a disproportionate number of the criminally inclined.

Why does crime correlate with income and demographics? In many countries, it doesn't. Japan, devastated after World War II, did not sink into violence and thievery.

Many industrialized nations with lower standards of living than the U.S. have much less crime. In 1990, according to one study, handguns killed 10

Crime Statistics by City

City	Population	Rate	Homicides
Agoura Hills	22,143	13	0
Alhambra	92,809	22	4
Arcadia	54,013	26	0
Artesia	17,132	30	2
Avalon	3,608	68	0
Azusa	46,261	27	1
Baldwin Park	77,124	19	7
Bell	38,044	25	1
Bellflower	68,345	37	8
Bell Gardens	45,733	31	5
Beverly Hills	35,096	40	1
Bradbury	965	11	0
Burbank	106,480	26	2
Calabasas	20,455	12	0
Carson	93,196	37	9
Cerritos	58,063	45	0
Claremont	35,968	27	0
Commerce	13,370	96	3
Compton	97,966	50	54
Covina	47,988	41	4
Cudahy	25,857	21	1
Culver City	42,776	31	0
Diamond Bar	59,101	16	0
Downey	102,103	36	9
Duarte	23,000	24	1
El Monte	119,992	28	8
El Segundo	16,864	45	0
Gardena	59,557	44	4
Glendale	203,734	25	3
Glendora	53,761	20	0
Hawaiian Gardens	15,205	27	0
Hawthorne	80,459	44	8
Hermosa Beach	19,631	39	0
Hidden Hills	2,052	8	0
Huntington Park	63,626	38	6
Industry	689	*2,409	0
Inglewood	121,035	37	16
Irwindale	1,202	*196	2
La Cañada Flintridge	21,103	14	2
La Habra Heights	6,896	9	0
Lakewood	80,952	32	4
La Mirada	49,918	22	3
Lancaster	132,402	31	5
La Puente	42,189	25	4
La Verne	34,802	21	0
Lawndale	30,862	32	1
Lomita	20,951	24	1
Long Beach	457,608	40	46
Los Angeles	3,822,955	44	425
Lynwood	69,328	38	12

Copyright © 2001 McCormack's Guides. No reproduction without permission.

Crime Statistics by City

City	Population	Rate	Homicides
Malibu	13,324	25	0
Manhattan Beach	36,124	34	0
Maywood	30,408	19	0
Monrovia	41,027	25	0
Montebello	64,952	35	4
Monterey Park	67,409	21	4
Norwalk	104,473	31	10
Palmdale	122,392	32	6
Palos Verdes Estates	14,742	9	0
Paramount	56,596	45	11
Pasadena	143,874	35	2
Pico Rivera	65,202	25	9
Pomona	147,656	45	26
Rancho Palos Verdes	44,933	10	0
Redondo Beach	67,638	30	1
Rolling Hills	2,066	9	0
Rolling Hills Estates	8,787	17	0
Rosemead	57,328	26	8
San Dimas	37,357	20	0
San Fernando	24,722	33	1
San Gabriel	41,604	22	1
San Marino	14,006	8	0
Santa Clarita	151,260	18	2
Santa Fe Springs	16,463	83	3
Santa Monica	96,528	51	1
Sierra Madre	11,719	11	0
Signal Hill	9,247	78	0
South El Monte	22,717	27	2
South Gate	95,326	31	7
South Pasadena	25,997	23	0
Temple City	34,731	16	2
Torrance	147,414	31	3
Vernon	85	*6,870	2
Walnut	33,203	16	0
West Covina	107,631	40	3
West Hollywood	38,913	51	2
Westlake Village	8,593	18	0
Whittier	86,152	44	4
Los Angeles County	9,884,255	37	891

Source: Calif. Dept. of Justice using 1999 figures. Population estimates for California cities are 2000, from State Dept. of Finance. Rate is all reported willful homicide, forcible rape, aggravated assault, burglary, motor vehicle theft, larceny-theft and arson per 1,000 residents. Homicides include murders and non-negligent manslaughter. *Crime rates for industrial cities such as Industry, Irwindale and Vernon are statistical freaks. The low population of these towns pushes the rates up.

Crime in Other Cities Nationwide

City	Population	Rate	Homicides
Anchorage	254,250	52	19
Atlanta	414,262	140	149
Baltimore	662,253	109	312
Birmingham	259,453	87	85
Boise	159,050	53	3
Boston	559,631	63	34
Chicago	2,750,917	NA	703
Cleveland	495,516	70	81
Dallas	1,089,178	92	252
Denver	509,343	53	51
Des Moines	194,298	73	15
Honolulu	874,736	54	17
Jacksonville	703,251	78	74
Little Rock	176,377	105	25
Milwaukee	20,704	48	NA
Miami	372,949	120	86
New York	7,357,745	44	633
New Orleans	471,157	87	230
Oklahoma City	463,637	101	56
Pittsburgh, PA	360,374	60	36
Phoenix	1,225,692	85	185
Portland, OR	488,813	94	26
Reno	165,855	61	10
Salt Lake City	178,579	108	16
Seattle	538,105	98	49
Tucson	467,677	97	45
Washington, D.C.	523,000	88	260

Source: Annual 1999 FBI crime report, which uses 1998 data. Population estimates are based on updated estimates from 1990 census. **Key**: NA (not available).

people in Australia, 22 in Great Britain and 87 in Japan. The count for the U.S. was 10,567. (But in recent years Europeans have seen more burglaries and robberies, and in some categories, the U.S. is doing better than some European nations. The big exception: handgun deaths. Los Angeles County and the nation in recent years have seen sharp drops in crime.)

Spotting Trouble

Drive the neighborhood. The signs of trouble are often easily read: bars on windows, razor wire topping fences, men idling around liquor stores, excessive graffiti.

Security is a big concern in L.A. County. Many homes in the City of Los Angeles and other cities are protected by steel mesh doors. Whether this reflects concerns about crime or general unease is a matter of conjecture. But look for the other indicators.

Security services are used extensively in many movie-entertainment

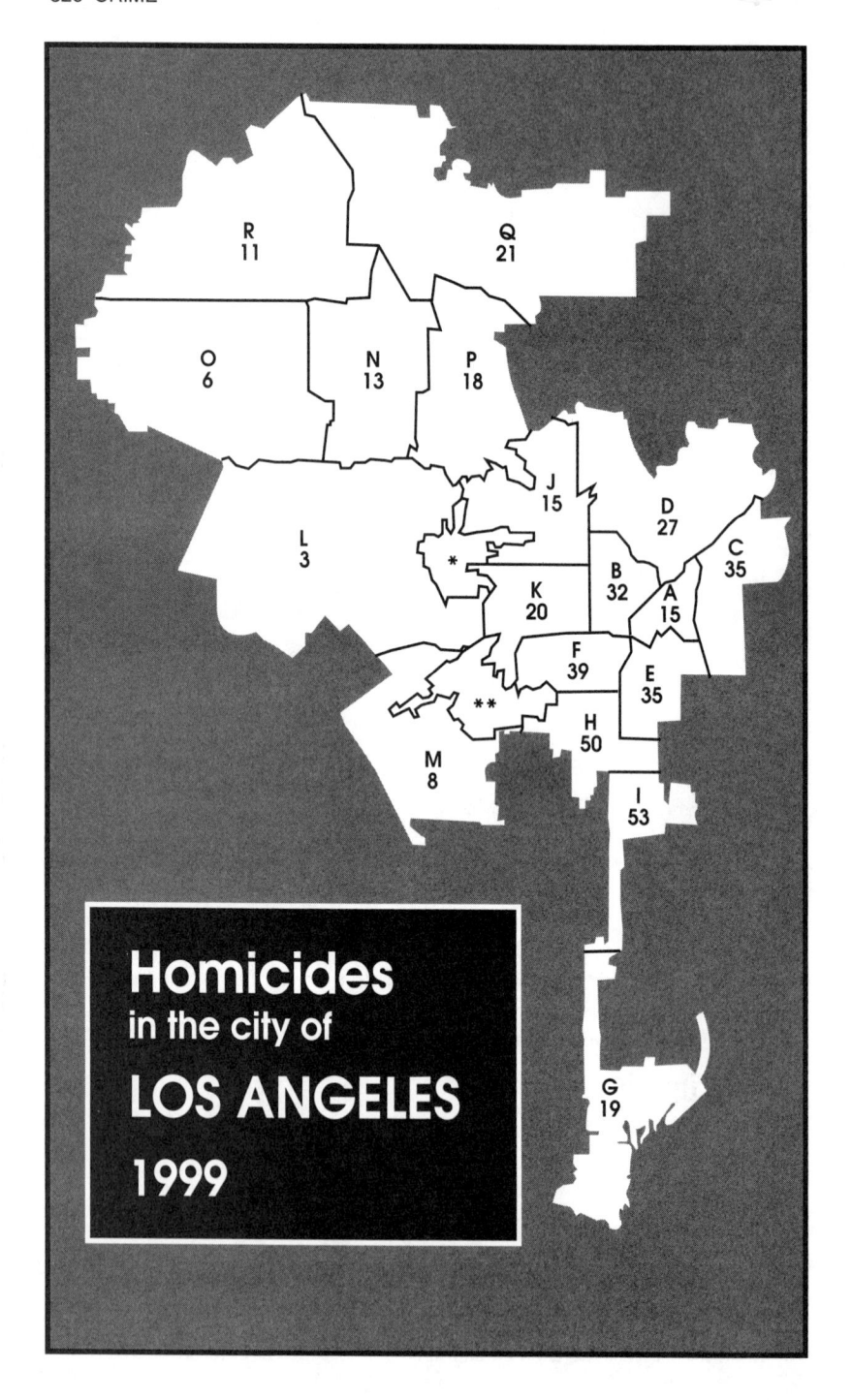

Homicides
in the city of
LOS ANGELES
1999

- R 11
- Q 21
- O 6
- N 13
- P 18
- J 15
- D 27
- L 3
- *
- K 20
- B 32
- A 15
- C 35
- F 39
- E 35
- **
- H 50
- M 8
- I 53
- G 19

Crime in City of L.A.

The chart on page 322 gives some idea of how Los Angeles crime breaks out. The chart can mislead because the police districts are so large. In some towns, most of the serious crime is confined to small areas. But always be wary.

City of Los Angeles Homicides 1999

Map Area	Neighborhood/Precinct	Homicides	Population
A	Central	15	41,597
B	Rampart	32	276,049
C	Hollenbeck	35	204,201
D	Northeast	27	257,141
E	Newton	35	147,478
F	Southwest	39	170,168
G	Harbor	19	177,731
H	77th Street	50	181,512
I	Southeast	53	132,352
J	Hollywood	15	200,419
K	Wilshire	20	242,016
L	West L.A.	3	223,108
M	Pacific	8	207,983
N	Van Nuys	13	264,705
O	West Valley	6	306,302
P	No. Hollywood	18	226,890
Q	Foothill	21	272,268
R	Devonshire	11	249,580
Total		420	3,781,500

Source: Los Angeles Police Department *Beverly Hills and West Hollywood, legal cities ** Inglewood and Culver City, legal cities. See chart on pages 323-324. Slight difference in total homicides between stats supplied by Calif. Dept. of Justice and L.A. Police Dept. This may reflect delays in reclassifying some crimes.

communities. In Beverly Hills, many homes hide behind gates. In the newer, upscale towns, the gated subdivision is popular. Developers acknowledge that they are selling safety but this does not mean the immediate community is unsafe. Rather it may indicate that people are more aware of crime than in the past. For some entertainment people, privacy is a big concern.

A Personal Decision

Should you avoid unsafe or marginal neighborhoods?

For some people, the answer depends on tradeoffs and personal circumstances. The troubled neighborhoods often carry low prices or rents and are located near job centers.

Many towns and sections are in transition; conditions could improve, the investment might be worthwhile. What's intolerable to a parent might be acceptable to a single person.

Crime in Other California Cities

City	Population	Rate	Homicides
Anaheim	310,654	33	16
Bakersfield	237,222	47	24
Fresno	420,594	70	26
Newport Beach	75,627	28	0
Oakland	402,104	78	60
Palm Springs	43,494	71	7
Riverside	259,738	46	30
Sacramento	405,963	67	54
San Bernardino	186,351	65	23
San Diego	1,277,168	39	57
San Francisco	801,377	54	64
San Jose	923,591	28	25
Santa Ana	317,685	35	15
Santa Barbara	92,826	24	1
Ventura	103,505	29	3

Source: California Crime Index from State Dept. of Justice, 1999 data, with population estimates from the California Dept. of Finance (Jan. 1, 2000). Rate is all reported willful homicide, forcible rape, aggravated assault, burglary, motor vehicle theft, larceny-theft and arson per 1,000 residents. Homicides include murders and non-negligent manslaughter.

If you don't have the bucks, often you can still buy safety but you may have to settle for a smaller house or yard.

Whatever your neighborhood, don't make it easy for predators. Lock your doors, install security devices, join the neighborhood watches, school your children in safety, take extra precautions when they are called for.

Miscellaneous:

- Number of homicides per year over the last 12 years for the City of Los Angeles: 425, 422, 736, 874, 983, 1,025, 1, 092, 1,077, 850, 838, 707, 569.

- Which are the worst months for homicides? Here are the 1998 monthly figures from the Los Angeles Police Department: January, 38; February, 31; March, 40; April, 23; May, 23; June, 36; July, 38; August, 50; September, 30; October, 34; November, 31; December, 45.

- In 1998, according to the latest FBI report, 14,088 people were murdered in the U.S. Of these, 9,143 or 65 percent were shot, 1,877 stabbed, 741 beaten with a blunt instrument and 949 assaulted with feet and fists. Of the 14,088 murdered, 10,606 were male, 3,419 female and 63 were unknown.

- Of the 14,088 murdered in 1988 in the U.S., 4,320 lost their lives in violence that stemmed from arguments. The next largest category was robbery victims, 1,232 homicides. Romantic triangles led to 184 homicides, narcotics 679, and gangland violence 70.

Crime in States

State	Population	Rate	Homicides
Alabama	4,352,000	46	354
Alaska	614,000	48	41
Arizona	4,669,000	66	376
Arkansas	2,538,000	43	201
California	32,667,000	43	2,171
Colorado	3,971,000	45	183
Connecticut	3,274,000	38	135
Delaware	744,000	54	21
Florida	14,916,000	69	967
Georgia	7,642,000	55	618
Hawaii	1,193,000	53	24
Idaho	1,229,000	37	36
Illinois	12,045,000	49	1,096
Indiana	5,899,000	42	454
Iowa	2,862,000	35	54
Kansas	2,629,000	49	154
Kentucky	3,936,000	29	182
Louisiana	4,369,000	61	560
Maine	1,244,000	30	25
Maryland	5,135,000	54	513
Massachusetts	6,147,000	34	124
Michigan	9,817,000	47	721
Minnesota	4,725,000	40	121
Mississippi	2,752,000	44	315
Missouri	5,439,000	48	499
Montana	880,000	41	36
Nebraska	1,663,000	44	51
Nevada	1,747,000	53	170
New Hampshire	1,185,000	24	18
New Jersey	8,115,000	37	322
New Mexico	1,737,000	67	190
New York	18,175,000	36	924
North Carolina	7,546,000	53	612
North Dakota	638,000	27	7
Ohio	11,209,000	43	443
Oklahoma	3,347,000	50	204
Oregon	3,282,000	56	126
Pennsylvania	12,001,000	33	333
Rhode Island	988,000	35	24
South Carolina	3,836,000	58	306
South Dakota	738,000	26	10
Tennessee	5,431,000	50	460
Texas	19,760,000	51	1,346
Utah	2,100,000	55	65
Vermont	591,000	31	13
Virginia	6,791,000	37	422
Washington	5,610,000	59	241
West Virginia	1,811,000	25	78
Wisconsin	5,224,000	35	190
Wyoming	481,000	38	23
Washington, D.C.	523,000	88	260

Source: FBI 1998 Figures.

Subject Index

—A-B—

ABC Unified Sch. Dist., 30-31
Acton/Agua Dulce Unified Sch. Dist., 31
Agoura Hills, 166
Alhambra City Elem. Sch. Dist., 31-32
Alhambra City High Sch. Dist., 32
Alhambra, 167
Altadena, 168
Antelope Valley Union High Sch. Dist., 32-33
Arcadia Unified Sch. Dist., 33
Arcadia, 169
Arleta, 245
Artesia, 170
Avalon, 266
Azusa Unified Sch. Dist., 33-34
Azusa, 171
Baby Names, 27
Baldwin Hills, 172
Baldwin Park Unified Sch. Dist., 34-35
Baldwin Park, 173
Bassett Unified Sch. Dist., 35
Bel Air Estates, 174
Bell, 174
Bellflower, 175
Bellflower Unified Sch. Dist., 35-36
Bell Gardens, 177
Beverly Glen, 174
Beverly Hills, 178
Beverly Hills Unified Sch. Dist., 36
Bonita Unified Sch. Dist., 36-37
Boyle Heights, 196
Bradbury, 179
Brentwood, 180
Burbank, 181
Burbank Unified Sch. Dist., 37

—C—

Calabasas, 182
Canoga Park, 183
Canyon Country, 267-268
Carson, 184
Castaic Union Sch. Dist., 38
Centinela Valley Union High Sch. Dist., 38
Century City, 290
Cerritos, 185
Charter Oak Unified Sch. Dist., 38
Chatsworth, 186
Cheviot Hills, 290
Chinatown, 196
Claremont, 187
Claremont Unified Sch. Dist., 38-39
College Admissions, 11-114, 115-118, 119-122, 143-144, 146-147
Commerce, City of, 188
Community Colleges, 127
Compton, 189
Compton Unified Sch. Dist., 39-40
Country Club Park, 292
Covina, 190
Covina Valley Unified Sch. Dist., 40-41
Crenshaw, 191
Crime Statistics, 322-329
Cudahy, 192
Culver City, 193
Culver City Unified Sch. Dist., 41
Cypress Park, 240

—D—

Day Care, 302
Diamond Bar, 194
Downey, 195
Downey Unified Sch. Dist., 41-42
Downtown L.A., 196
Drivers' License, 294-295
Duarte, 197
Duarte Unified Sch. Dist., 42

—E—

Eagle Rock, 240
Earthquakes, 13-14
East Los Angeles, 198
East Whittier City Elem. Sch. Dist., 42-43
Eastside Union Sch. Dist., 43
Echo Park, 199
El Monte, 200
El Monte City Elem. Sch. Dist., 43-44
El Monte Union High Sch. Dist., 44
El Rancho Unified Sch. Dist., 44-45
El Segundo, 201
El Segundo Unified Sch. Dist., 45
El Sereno, 240
Encino, 202

—F-G-H—

Florence, 274-275
Gardena, 203
Garvey Elem. Sch. Dist., 45-46
Glassell Park, 240
Glendale, 204
Glendale Unified Sch. Dist., 46-47
Glendora, 205
Glendora Unified Sch. Dist., 47-48
Gorman Elem. Sch. Dist., 48
Granada Hills, 206
Grocery Prices, 297-298
Hacienda Heights, 207
Hacienda La Puente Unified Sch. Dist., 48-49
Hancock Park, 292

INDEX 331

Hawaiian Gardens, 208
Hawthorne, 209
Hawthorne Elem. Sch. Dist., 49-50
Hermosa Beach, 210
Hermosa Beach City Elem. Sch. Dist., 50
Hidden Hills, 211
Highland Park, 240
Hollywood, 212
Hollywood Hills, 212
Home Prices, 24-26
Hospital Directory, 311-321
Housing (New), 304-310
Hughes-Elizabeth Lakes Union Elem. Sch. Dist., 50
Huntington Park, 213
—I-J-K-L—
Industry, City of, 214
Inglewood Unified Sch. Dist., 50-51
Inglewood, 215
Irwindale, 216
Jobless Rate, 26
Keppel Union Elem. Sch. Dist., 51
Knollwood, 206
La Cañada Flintridge, 217
La Cañada Unified Sch. Dist., 51
La Crescenta, 218
Ladera Heights, 172
La Habra Heights, 219
Lakeview Terrace, 245
Lakewood, 220
La Mirada, 221
Lancaster, 222
Lancaster Elem. Sch. Dist., 51-52
La Puente, 223
Las Virgenes Unified Sch. Dist., 52-53
La Verne, 224
Lawndale, 225
Lawndale Elem. Sch. Dist., 53
Leimart Park, 191

Lennox Elem. Sch. Dist., 53
Little Lake City Elem. Sch. Dist., 53-54
Lomita, 226
Long Beach, 227-228
Long Beach Unified Sch. Dist., 54-57
Los Angeles, 9, 229-230
Los Angeles County Office of Education, 57-58
Los Angeles Unified Sch. Dist., 58-84, 124, 126
Los Feliz, 199
Los Nietos Elem. Sch. Dist., 84
Lowell Joint Elem. Sch. Dist., 85
Lynwood, 231
Lynwood Unified Sch. Dist., 85
—M—
Malibu, 232
Manhattan Beach, 233
Manhattan Beach Unified Sch. Dist., 85-86
Maps, 7, 10, 11
Mar Vista, 234
Marina Del Rey, 234
Maywood, 235
Mission Hills, 236
Monrovia, 237
Monrovia Unified Sch. Dist., 86
Montebello, 238
Montebello Unified Sch. Dist., 86-87
Montecito Heights, 240
Monterey Park, 239
Mountain View Elem. Sch. Dist., 87-88
Mount Washington, 240
—N-O-P—
Newhall, 267-268

Newhall Elem. Sch. Dist., 88
Northeast L.A., 240
North Hills, 206
North Hollywood, 241
Northridge, 242
Norwalk, 243
Norwalk-LaMirada Unified Sch. Dist., 88-89
Pacific Highlands, 244
Pacific Palisades, 244
Pacoima, 245
Palmdale Elem. Sch. Dist., 89-90
Palmdale, 246
Palos Verdes Estates, 247
Palos Verdes Peninsula Unified Sch. Dist., 90-91
Panorama City, 236
Paramount, 248
Paramount Unified Sch. Dist., 91-92
Park La Brea, 292
Pasadena, 249-250
Pasadena Unified Sch. Dist., 92-94
Pico Rivera, 251
Playa Del Rey, 252
Pomona, 253
Pomona Unified Sch. Dist., 94-95
Population, 8, 9, 16-18
Porter Ranch, 254
Private Sch. Directory, 140-145
—Q-R—
Rainfall, 11-13
Rancho Palos Verdes, 255
Rancho Park, 290
Redondo Beach, 256
Redondo Beach Unified Sch. Dist., 95-96
Rents, 19-21, 27
Reseda, 257
Rolling Hills, 258

Rolling Hills Estates, 259
Rosemead, 260
Rosemead Elem. Sch. Dist., 96
Rowland Heights, 207
Rowland Unified Sch. Dist., 96-97

—S—

San Dimas, 261
San Fernando, 262
San Gabriel, 263
San Gabriel Unified Sch. Dist., 97
San Marino, 264
San Marino Unified Sch. Dist., 97-98
San Pedro, 265
Santa Catalina, 266
Santa Clarita, 267-268
Santa Fe Springs, 269
Santa Monica, 270
Santa Monica-Malibu Unified Sch. Dist., 98
SAT Scores, 107-110, 132, 135-136
Saugus, 267-268
Saugus Union Elem. Sch. Dist., 98-99
Sch. Dists, 133-134
Sch. Rankings, 28-105
Sch. Registration, 125
Sepulveda, 206
Sherman Oaks, 271
Sierra Madre, 272
Signal Hill, 273
Silver Lake, 199
South Central Los Angeles, 274-275
South El Monte, 276
South Gate, 277
South Pasadena, 278
South Pasadena Unified Sch. Dist., 99
South Whittier Elem. Sch. Dist., 99-100
Southeast Los Angeles, 274-275

Stevenson Ranch, 279
Studio City, 271
Sulphur Springs, 267-268
Sulphur Springs Union Elem. Sch. Dist., 100
Sun Valley, 241
Sunland, 280
Sylmar, 281

—T-U-V—

Tarzana, 202
Taxes, 295-296
Temperatures, 11-12, 14
Temple City, 282
Temple City Unified Sch. Dist., 100
Toluca Lake, 271
Torrance, 283
Torrance Unified Sch. Dist., 100-101
Tujunga, 280
Universal City, 271
Utilities, 295, 300-301
Valencia, 267-268
Valle Lindo Elem. Sch. Dist., 101-102
Valley Village, 241
Van Nuys, 284
Vehicle Registration, 294-295
Venice, 234
Vernon, 285
View Park, 172
Voter Registration, 22-23, 294

—W-X-Y-Z—

Walnut Park, 274-275
Walnut Valley Unified Sch. Dist., 102
Walnut, 286
Watts, 274-275
Weather, 11-13
West Adams, 191
West Covina, 287
West Covina Unified Sch. Dist., 102-103
West Hills, 183
West Hollywood, 288
Westchester, 252

Westlake, 196
Westlake Village, 289
Westside Union Elem. Sch. Dist., 103
Westwood, 290
Whittier, 291
Whittier City Elem. Sch. Dist., 103-104
Whittier Union High Sch. Dist., 104
William S. Hart Union High Sch. Dist., 104
Wilmington, 265
Wilshire Dist., 292
Wilsona Elem. Sch. Dist., 104-105
Windsor Hills, 172
Winnetka, 257
Wiseburn Elem. Sch. Dist., 105
Woodland Hills, 293

BUY 10 OR MORE & SAVE!

If your order adds up to 10 or more, the price drops to $5.95 per book. You also save on shipping. Fill out form and send with check to: McCormack's Guides, P.O. Box 1728, Martinez, CA 94553. Or fax to (925) 228-7223.

Visa and MasterCard accepted on phone orders. **VISA** **MasterCard** **1-800-222-3602**

Next to title, write in number of copies ordered and total below:

No.	McCormack's Guide Title	Single	Bulk
___	Alameda County 2001	$13.95	$5.95
___	Contra Costa & Solano 2001	$13.95	$5.95
___	Los Angeles County 2001	$13.95	$5.95
___	Marin, Napa & Sonoma 2001	$13.95	$5.95
___	Orange County 2001	$13.95	$5.95
___	Riverside, San Bernardino 2001	$13.95	$5.95
___	Sacramento & Central Valley 2001	$13.95	$5.95
___	San Diego County 2001	$13.95	$5.95
___	San Francisco & San Mateo 2001	$13.95	$5.95
___	Santa Barbara, Ventura 2001	$13.95	$5.95
___	Santa Clara/Silicon Valley 2001	$13.95	$5.95

_____ Books @ $_____ (Price) = $_____

CA sales tax (8.25%) _____

Shipping* _____

Total Amount of Order: $_____

* For orders of 10 or more, shipping is 45 cents per book. For orders of fewer than 10, shipping is $4.50 for first book, $1.50 per book thereafter.

Paid by (circle one) Check/MC/Visa or Bill Us

Name _____

Company _____

Address _____

City_____ State____ Zip_____

Phone: (____)_____ Fax: (____)_____

☐ **Check here to receive advertising information**

bookinfo@mccormacks.com • www.mccormacks.com

Before you move... buy McCormack's GUIDES

The GUIDES have the information to make your move to a new location easier. Feel comfortable about the change because you have the facts about city profiles, school rankings, SAT scores, private school directories, medical care, commuting, recreation, crime ratings, area weather, and much more!

McCormack's Guides are published for these counties:

ALAMEDA • CONTRA COSTA-SOLANO
SANTA CLARA-SANTA CRUZ • SAN FRANCISCO-SAN MATEO
MARIN-NAPA-SONOMA
SAN DIEGO • LOS ANGELES • ORANGE COUNTY
GREATER SACRAMENTO-CENTRAL VALLEY
RIVERSIDE-SAN BERNARDINO • SANTA BARBARA-VENTURA

1-800-222-3602
www.mccormacks.com

$13⁹⁵ SINGLE COPY
VISA & MASTERCARD ACCEPTED
DISCOUNTS FOR BULK BUYERS. SEE LAST PAGE

Advertisers' Index

Information Services

American Lung Association	318
DataQuick	139
New Homes Magazine	305
RealFacts	301

Realtors & Relocation Services

Barry Burnett Realty	3
ReMax, Lorraine Bird	29

School

Bishop Montgomery High School	141

To advertise in McCormack's Guides, call 1-800-222-3602

BUY 10 OR MORE & SAVE!

If your order adds up to 10 or more, the price drops to $5.95 per book. You also save on shipping. Fill out form and send with check to: McCormack's Guides, P.O. Box 1728, Martinez, CA 94553. Or fax to (925) 228-7223.

Visa and MasterCard accepted on phone orders.   VISA   MasterCard   **1-800-222-3602**

Next to title, write in number of copies ordered and total below:

No.	McCormack's Guide Title	Single	Bulk
___	Alameda County 2001	$13.95	$5.95
___	Contra Costa & Solano 2001	$13.95	$5.95
___	Los Angeles County 2001	$13.95	$5.95
___	Marin, Napa & Sonoma 2001	$13.95	$5.95
___	Orange County 2001	$13.95	$5.95
___	Riverside, San Bernardino 2001	$13.95	$5.95
___	Sacramento & Central Valley 2001	$13.95	$5.95
___	San Diego County 2001	$13.95	$5.95
___	San Francisco & San Mateo 2001	$13.95	$5.95
___	Santa Barbara, Ventura 2001	$13.95	$5.95
___	Santa Clara/Silicon Valley 2001	$13.95	$5.95

_____ Books @ $_____ (Price) = $_____

CA sales tax (8.25%) _____

Shipping* _____

Total Amount of Order: $_____

* For orders of 10 or more, shipping is 45 cents per book. For orders of fewer than 10, shipping is $4.50 for first book, $1.50 per book thereafter.

Paid by (circle one) Check/MC/Visa or Bill Us

Name _____

Company _____

Address _____

City _____ State ___ Zip _____

Phone: (___) _____   Fax: (___) _____

☐ **Check here to receive advertising information**

bookinfo@mccormacks.com • www.mccormacks.com